REAL ESTATE FINANCE:
A Practical Approach

TOM MORTON

C.R.A.

Scott, Foresman and Company

Glenview, Illinois

Dallas, Texas   Oakland, New Jersey   Palo Alto, California   Tucker, Georgia   London

For Annette, my wife, without whose help and reassurance this book would not have been possible.

123456-KPK-878685848382

Library of Congress Cataloging in Publication Data
Morton, Tom.
Real estate finance.

Includes index.
1. Housing—United States—Finance. 2. Mortgage loans—United States. 3. Real estate business—United States. I. Title.
HD7293.Z9M67 332.7'2'0973 82-20528
ISBN 0-673-16580-9

Preface

The purpose of this text is to give the student of real estate a practical look at real estate finance. This text can also be of great aid to licensees, both salespersons and brokers, as a ready reference. Because it is straightforward, this book should be helpful to anyone interested in the financing of his or her own home.

With a practical approach, this text reviews the mortgage instruments commonly used and the programs available for the financing of residential real estate through the federal government, primary lenders, and the secondary market. *Real Estate Finance* is an easy-to-follow guide to the procedures of loan application, processing, and underwriting.

The main difference between this text and others dealing with real estate finance is that it is a nuts-and-bolts approach that is simple, clear, and step-by-step. It is also an in-depth study of both conventional and federal mortgage programs.

As an integral part of this text, many of the standard forms are illustrated and explained. Understanding these forms is vital to the real estate practitioner.

This book is intended to convey general information about the field of real estate finance and is not a legal interpretation of any federal, state, or local rules, regulations, or statutes, or any rules of a lending institution or a secondary marketer. For any legal interpretation, you should contact an attorney of your choice.

Acknowledgments

I would like to express my deep appreciation to the following persons who have either given advice, answered many questions, or supplied valuable information that made this book possible.

Ms. Betty J. Armbrust, President, Real Estate Prep, Inc., Denver, Colorado
Mr. Tom Bacon, Retired, Public Information Office, Department of Housing and Urban Development, Washington, D.C.
Ms. Sharon C. Benson, Professor of Business and Real Estate, Shoreline Community College, Seattle, Washington
Mr. Tom Bond, Director, Information Services, State Board of Insurance, State of Texas, Austin, Texas
Mr. Jim Hodge, Mercantile Mortgage Corporation of Texas, Houston, Texas
Mr. Jim Breslin, Mortgage Guaranty Insurance Corporation, Milwaukee, Wisconsin
Ms. Nancy Harucki, Legislative Assistant, U.S. Congressman Manuel Lujan, New Mexico, Washington, D.C.
Mr. James E. Jacobs, The Mortgage Corporation, Washington, D.C.
Mr. John Keating, Assistant Professor, Business Administration, Tarrant County Junior College, Fort Worth, Texas
Ms. Annette Kolis, Attorney-Advisor, Federal Home Loan Bank Board, Office of Community Investment, Washington, D.C.
Mr. Karl P. Kuehn, El Paso Community College, El Paso, Texas
Mr. Thomas S. LaMalfa, Senior Analyst, Secondary Market, Mortgage Guaranty Insurance Corporation, Milwaukee, Wisconsin
Dr. Robert Lyon, Education Division, Texas Real Estate Research Center, Texas A & M University
Mr. D. B. McKinney, Executive Vice President, Mortgage Investment Company, El Paso, Texas
Ms. Elinor Maskell, Arizona Department of Real Estate, Phoenix, Arizona
Mr. George W. Ratterman, Vice President, Jones Real Estate Colleges, Denver, Colorado
Mr. R. D. Smith, Regional Economist, Department of Housing and Urban Development, Regional Office, Fort Worth, Texas
Mr. Robert L. Stanley, Robert L. Stanley and Associates, Appraisers, Houston, Texas
Mr. Dean Stout, Real Estate Instructor, Richland College of Dallas Community College District, Dallas, Texas
Ms. Beth Van Houten, Corporate Relations, Federal National Mortgage Association, Washington, D.C.
Mr. Jim Williams, Texas Department of Community Affairs, Austin, Texas
Mr. Timothy S. Wolf, Librarian, Mortgage Bankers Association of America, Washington, D.C.

Contents

CHAPTER 1 Money, the Monetary System, and the History of Real Estate

LEARNING OBJECTIVES

In this chapter we will briefly cover the history of real estate from the time of our earliest ancestors to the present. We will also cover the development of the monetary system in the United States.

Upon completion of the chapter you should be able to do the following:

- ★ **State how the ownership of real estate has developed.**
- ★ **Outline the Federal Reserve System and give a broad outline of how it works.**
- ★ **Explain how the management of the money supply can affect the financing of real estate.**
- ★ **Describe how interest rates are established and the effect of state usury laws on those interest rates.**

EUROPEAN BEGINNINGS

At first, men and women were nomadic and had no need to own or finance real estate. The concept of ownership did not start until we began to cultivate crops and develop the idea that we would want the exclusive right to use of the land.

This exclusive right, in earlier times, was usually not held by just one person, but by a group of persons or a tribe. The actual ownership or title to the land was held by the leader. This form of ownership gave birth to the feudal system.

Under the feudal system, the leader or ruler would allow persons to farm a parcel of land, and in return the persons would share a portion of the crop with the leader and would also help the leader defend any attack on the leader's dominion.

It was not until the late 1200s that there was a major change in this system. This change was that a landholder could pass title to an heir. Prior to this concept, upon the death of the landholder, ownership of the land would revert back to the ruler and all of the heirs of the landholder could be forced to vacate.

The concepts of property ownership as we know it today did not evolve until the Industrial Revolution, before which time people or workers did not have the ability to earn or accumulate money. Once this was possible, the workers wanted to provide their families with shelter on property that they had acquired title to through purchase, rather than be controlled by the whims of a leader or ruler.

COLONIAL TIMES

The Pilgrims were drawn to the New World not only by the pursuit of religious freedoms, but also by the desire for ownership of land. In the New World, the ability to acquire land was only limited by a person's ability to clear the land and defend it.

Along with ownership of land came the need for capital, or money, to purchase goods for the colonists' homes and businesses. This gave birth to the need for the saving of monies. The initial step was the formation of informal clubs or associations. Here the members could make regular payments into the treasury of the club or association. The funds that accumulated in the treasury were used to make lump sum payments to the survivors upon the death of a member. A member could also go to the treasury of the club and make a withdrawal or receive a loan.

These informal clubs or associations were the foundation for many modern institutions that are vital to the financing of real estate in the United States. One of the first of these institutions, the Presbyterian Ministers Fund, was formed in Pennsylvania in 1759. Its purpose was to insure the lives of the ministers and their wives. This is the oldest life insurance company in the United States, and it is still in existence today, now named the Presbyterian Annuity and Life Insurance Company. It was not until 1835 that New England Mutual, the first of the current type of life insurance company, was formed. As a source of funds for the financing of real estate, life insurance companies have been around a relatively short time.

Attempt at a Banking System

As the colonies grew and declared their independence from England, there was a need for a banking system. So in 1781, the Bank of North America was established. It was chartered by the Pennsylvania legislature and incorporated by the Continental Congress, thus making it the oldest commercial bank in North America.

The Bank of North America served its purpose, but as the United States grew there was a need for a banking system throughout the young nation. The first attempt at this system was the establishment of the First Bank of the United States, which operated from 1791 to 1811, when it was disbanded. The next attempt at a national banking system was in 1816, when the Second Bank of the United States was established. This bank continued in operation until 1836.

There was no federal regulation of the banking system from 1836 until 1913. During this time, each state issued its own currency and there was no single legal tender for the United States. Attempts to control the currency finally led to the establishment of the Federal Reserve System, which had its beginnings with the establishment of the Federal Bank in 1913.

FEDERAL RESERVE SYSTEM

There are two major purposes of the "Fed" or Federal Reserve System: to supply reserve funds when needed, and to control bank and consumer credit. The latter is the most important to the financing of real estate, as we will discuss later in this chapter.

The system is composed of twelve Federal Reserve Districts, each of the districts with a Federal Reserve Bank. With the Fed having not a central bank, but district banks located throughout the United States, it can better respond to the different economic needs of the various areas of the nation.

Many of the Federal Reserve Banks also operate Federal Reserve Branch Banks or offices. The purpose of the branch banks or offices is to further break down the districts in order to better serve the financial needs of the individual districts.

A map showing the boundaries of each Federal Reserve district and any branch office boundary is shown in Figure 1-1. The address of each of the Federal Reserve Banks and their branches, if any, is shown in Figure 1-2.

Board of Directors

The Federal Reserve Banks are not under the control of any governmental agency, but each Reserve Bank is under a Board of Directors. The board is composed of twelve members

Figure 1-1. The Federal Reserve System

Boundaries of Federal Reserve Districts and Their Branch Territories

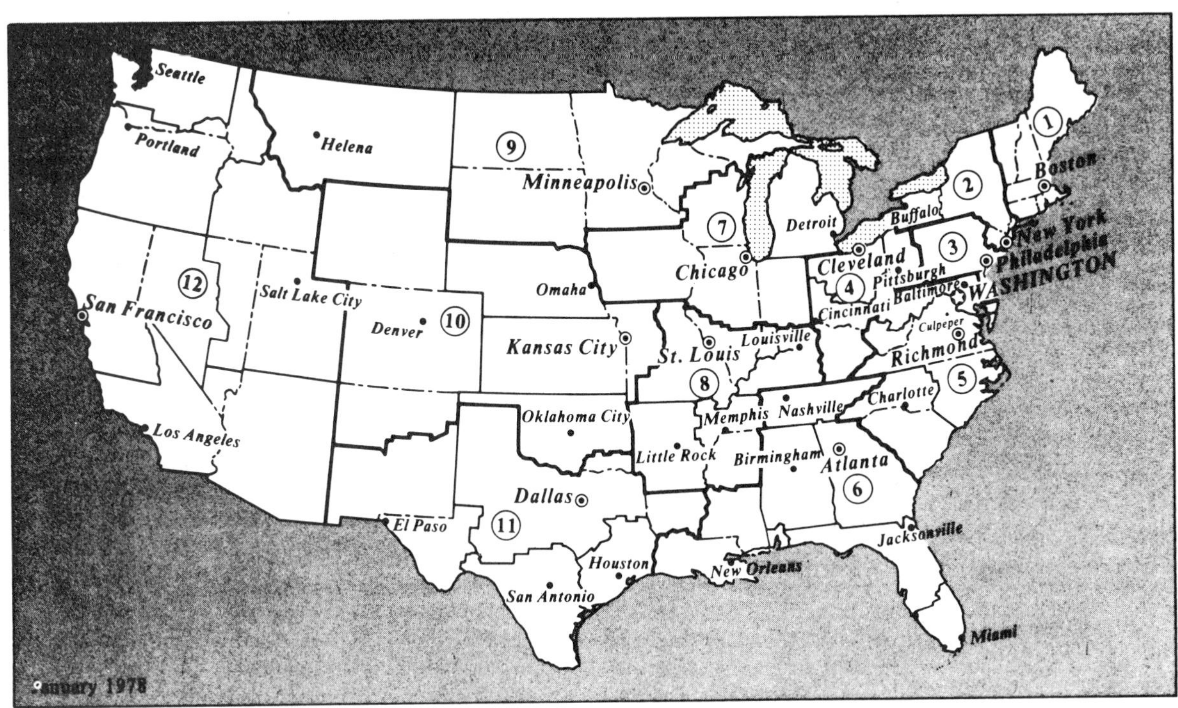

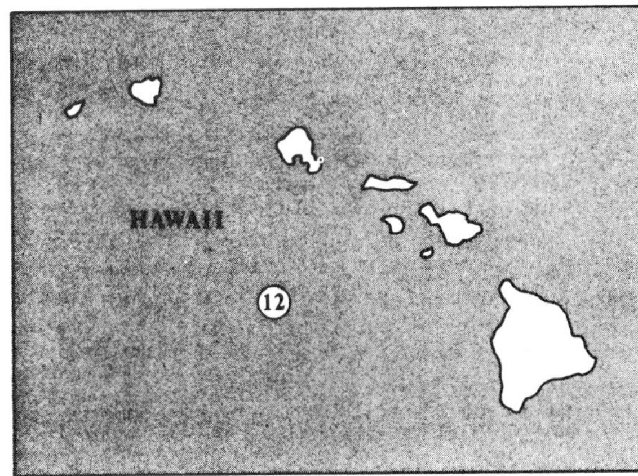

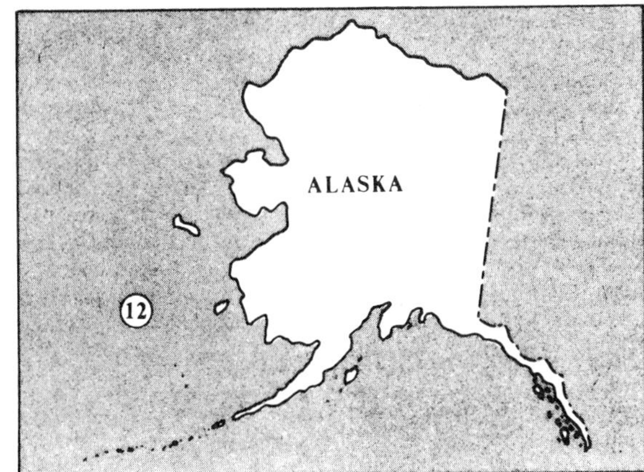

LEGEND

—— Boundaries of Federal Reserve Districts

—— Boundaries of Federal Reserve Branch Territories

✪ Board of Governors of the Federal Reserve System

◉ Federal Reserve Bank Cities

• Federal Reserve Branch Cities

· Federal Reserve Bank Facility

Source: U.S., Board of Governors of the Federal Reserve System, *Federal Reserve Bulletin—September, 1981*, vol. 67, no. 9, p. A78.

Figure 1-2. Federal Reserve Banks, Branches, and Offices

FEDERAL RESERVE BANK, branch, or facility	Zip	Chairman / Deputy Chairman	President / First Vice President	Vice President in charge of branch
BOSTON*	02106	Robert P. Henderson	Frank E. Morris	
		Thomas I. Atkins	James A. McIntosh	
NEW YORK*	10045	Robert H. Knight, Esq.	Anthony M. Solomon	
		Boris Yavitz	Thomas M. Timlen	
Buffalo	14240	Frederick D. Berkeley, III		John T. Keane
PHILADELPHIA	19105	John W. Eckman	Edward G. Boehne	
		Jean A. Crockett	Richard L. Smoot	
CLEVELAND*	44101	J. L. Jackson	Willis J. Winn	
		William H. Knoell	Walter H. MacDonald	
Cincinnati	45201	Martin B. Friedman		Robert E. Showalter
Pittsburgh	15230	Milton G. Hulme, Jr.		Harold J. Swart
RICHMOND*	23219	Maceo A. Sloan	Robert P. Black	
		Steven Muller	Jimmie R. Monhollon	
Baltimore	21203	Edward H. Covell		Robert D. McTeer, Jr.
Charlotte	28230	Naomi G. Albanese		Stuart P. Fishburne
Culpeper Communications and Records Center	*22701*			Albert D. Tinkelenberg
ATLANTA	30301	William A. Fickling, Jr.	William F. Ford	
		John H. Weitnauer, Jr.	Robert P. Forrestal	
Birmingham	35202	Louis J. Willie		Hiram J. Honea
Jacksonville	32231	Jerome P. Keuper		Charles D. East
Miami	33152	Roy W. Vandegrift, Jr.		F. J. Craven, Jr.
Nashville	37203	John C. Bolinger, Jr.		Jeffrey J. Wells
New Orleans	70161	Horatio C. Thompson		James D. Hawkins
CHICAGO*	60690	John Sagan	Silas Keehn	
		Stanton R. Cook	Daniel M. Doyle	
Detroit	48231	Herbert H. Dow		William C. Conrad
ST. LOUIS	63166	Armand C. Stalnaker	Lawrence K. Roos	
		William B. Walton	Donald W. Moriarty, Jr.	
Little Rock	72203	E. Ray Kemp, Jr.		John F. Breen
Louisville	40232	Sister Eileen M. Egan		Donald L. Henry
Memphis	38101	Patricia W. Shaw		Robert E. Matthews
MINNEAPOLIS	55480	Stephen F. Keating	E. Gerald Corrigan	
		William G. Phillips	Thomas E. Gainor	
Helena	59601	Norris E. Hanford		Betty J. Lindstrom
KANSAS CITY	64198	Paul H. Henson	Roger Guffey	
		Doris M. Drury	Henry R. Czerwinski	
Denver	80217	Caleb B. Hurtt		Wayne W. Martin
Oklahoma City	73125	Christine H. Anthony		William G. Evans
Omaha	68102	Robert G. Leuder		Robert D. Hamilton
DALLAS	75222	Gerald D. Hines	Robert H. Boykin	
		John V. James	William H. Wallace	
El Paso	79999	Josefina A. Salas-Porras		Joel L. Koonce, Jr.
Houston	77001	Jerome L. Howard		J. Z. Rowe
San Antonio	78295	Lawrence L. Crum		Thomas H. Robertson
SAN FRANCISCO	94120	Cornell C. Maier	John J. Balles	
		Caroline L. Ahmanson	John B. Williams	
Los Angeles	90051	Harvey A. Proctor		Richard C. Dunn
Portland	97208	John C. Hampton		Angelo S. Carella
Salt Lake City	84130	Wendell J. Ashton		A. Grant Holman
Seattle	98124	George H. Weyerhaeuser		Gerald R. Kelly

*Additional offices of these Banks are located at Lewiston, Maine 04240; Windsor Locks, Connecticut 06096; Cranford, New Jersey 07016; Jericho, New York 11753; Utica at Oriskany, New York 13424; Columbus, Ohio 43216; Columbia, South Carolina 29210; Charleston, West Virginia 25311; Des Moines, Iowa 50306; Indianapolis, Indiana 46204; and Milwaukee, Wisconsin 53202.

Source: U.S., Federal Reserve System, Board of Governors, *Federal Reserve Bulletin—September, 1981,* vol. 67 no. 9, p. A73.

who represent business, the banking industry, and the general public in their Federal Reserve District. The directors are classified as A-, B-, or C-Class Directors. Class A members can come from the banking community of the district, Class B members can represent the borrowers of the district, and Class C Directors will represent the general public. Both Class B and Class C Directors cannot in any way be connected to the banking industry, including the owning of bank stocks.

The members of the board are primarily chosen by the banking community in the district. The Class A and Class B Directors are elected by the member banks, and the selection process sees that all sizes of banks are represented. The Class C members are selected by the Board of Governors of the Federal Reserve.

As in any other corporation, the Board of Directors selects the president and the vice-president, and the board of the Reserve Bank will choose the members of boards of any branch bank established in their district. This process, therefore, insures that the branch banks reflect the needs of the area that the branch serves.

Board of Governors

The Board of Governors has supervisory control over all of the Reserve Banks throughout the system. The members are appointed by the President of the United States with the advice and consent of the Senate. The board is composed of seven individuals who each serve for a term of fourteen years. These appointments are staggered so that only one term expires each year. In order for the board to be truly representative of the whole system, the President tries to appoint only one member from each district.

The board has as one of its duties to publish the *Federal Reserve Bulletin*. This monthly publication gives information on the state of the economy in the nation and the world. The board also publishes reports on studies or research done for or under the authority of the Fed. One of the important groups of figures released each week by the Fed is "Federal Reserve Data." These figures reflect the changes in the weekly averages of member banks' reserves and other related items. These weekly figures also report the change in the basic money supply in the United States.

In addition to reporting weekly changes, the board can set the interest rate that member banks will have to pay when borrowing monies from the Fed. This rate is very important to the real estate industry, because banks use this rate to establish the *prime rate* (the rate their most credit-worthy corporate customer would pay). The prime rate is usually the basis for the cost of builders' interim funds and for the rate that you and I will pay for our car loans and loans for business operations. Besides the above, the board may raise or lower the reserve requirements of the member banks. This requirement will affect the amount of money the banks will have available to loan: the lower the requirement, the more money the banks will have for loans; the higher the requirement, the less money the banks will have for loans.

Member Banks

How does a bank become a member of the Federal Reserve System? Any national bank must belong, and any state bank that wishes may join. For a bank to join, it must buy stock in the Federal Reserve Bank System and agree to abide by the rules and rulings of the Federal Reserve. It must also meet the reserve requirements established from time to time to meet the fiscal policy of the Fed.

About 38 percent or 5471 of the 14,443 banks in the United States now belong to the Federal Reserve System. Even though this percentage may seem small, most of the larger banks are members, and member banks control approximately 82 percent of all bank deposits.

For the past several years membership in the Federal Reserve has been on the decline. This decline has been of concern to many economists because the Fed will not be able to control the supply of money or the rate of inflation as effectively as it might if the majority of the depository institutions were members. Realizing this problem, Congress passed the Depository Institutions Deregulation and Monetary Control Act of 1980, which was signed by the President and became law on March 31, 1980. This act comprises ten titles affecting many areas of operations of the depository institutions. One of the most important titles is Title I, which greatly strengthens the Fed's control over nonmember banks by requiring them to meet the reserve requirements set by the Fed. This requirement will be phased in over eight years. It has been estimated that this will bring approximately 8900 nonmember banks under control of the Fed.

Open Market Committee

The implementation of the change of the money supply is the responsibility of the Open Market Committee. The Federal Reserve Open Market Committee is presently composed of twelve members; five of the members are chosen by the Board of Governors and the remainder come from the twelve Federal Reserve Districts. With only seven members left to be chosen, you can see that not all of the banks get to choose a member singly. In fact, only the Reserve Bank of New York gets to choose a member by itself.

The committee members meet on a regular basis, usually the third Tuesday of the month, in an unannounced location to establish what action they should take to carry out the fiscal policy of the board. The decision they reach is not announced to the general public, but the decisions of the Open Market Committee are published on a delayed basis in the *Federal Reserve Bulletin*. The reason for this is to hinder speculation on government securities and the U.S. dollar. The decision is carried out through a small staff that operates within the Federal Reserve Bank in New York. If the decision of the committee is to increase the supply of money, a member of the staff contacts a dealer who is licensed to deal in government securities, and the dealer is given a check, drawn on the U.S. Treasury, to buy government securities. The check is then deposited into a member bank, thus increasing the supply of money available to the banking system in general. If the decision is to reduce the money supply, the committee makes recommendations to the Board of Governors to increase the reserve requirements or take any other action they may deem necessary.

Measurement of the Money Supply

One of the more important functions of the Federal Reserve is to control the supply of money in the hands of the public, as well as the amount held in bank accounts, both demand-type accounts and thrift deposits. The Fed must know the amount in bank accounts in order to manage the money supply. This measurement will tell if they must either increase or decrease the amount of money in circulation.

To measure the money supply, the Fed relies on information supplied by the member banks. From these figures, the Fed arrives with the following measurements of the money supply:

M1-A—Consists of private checking-account deposits at commercial banks plus cash in the public hands. This is similar to the old M1 measurement, which was once the primary guideline for the Fed. This figure is averaging approximately $370 billion.

M1-B—Consists of M1-A plus all NOW (negotiated order of withdrawal) accounts, ATS (automatic transfer service), credit union share accounts, and demand deposits at thrift institutions.

There are two additional measurements that should be mentioned:

M2—Consists of M1-B plus money market mutual fund shares, savings deposits at all depository institutions, and all small time deposits at all depository institutions. (For the purpose of this measuring device, a small time deposit is one of less than $100,000.) This measurement also contains overnight Eurodollar deposits held by U.S. nonbank residents at Caribbean branches of U.S. banks.

M3—Consists of M2 plus large time deposits at all depository institutions. These are deposits of $100,000 or more.

The measurements are reported each week by the member banks and the resulting figures are released each week and are published usually on each Friday. These figures are compared with the previous week and either an increase or decrease is noted. If there is an increase in either M1-A or M1-B that exceeds the guidelines set by the Fed, the Fed can take measures to slow or halt the growth in these two areas.

How Does the Fed Control the Supply of Money?

Many experts disagree on the Fed's attempts to control the supply of available money. Some feel that the economy should be allowed to operate by the law of supply and demand, and others feel that the economy or the supply of money should be strictly regulated. The system that is used, in this author's opinion, is probably the best of both worlds. The economy is allowed to grow within certain guidelines through the law of supply and demand, and if the growth rate exceeds these limits the Fed then steps in to slow things down by using one or more tools available to them. The major tools or combination of tools they may use are as follows:

1. Change the reserve requirements
2. Change the discount rate
3. Change the Fed fund rate

Each member bank must set aside a certain percentage of its deposits in a reserve account. These reserves have a twofold purpose: (1) to have monies in reserve in case the bank finds itself short of funds to meet the demand of depositors, and (2) to control the amount of monies available to the bank for the purpose of making loans.

For example, if the discount rate is 5 percent and the bank opens a new account in the amount of $1000, it will have to put 5 percent, or $50, into the reserve account, thus leaving it $950 to use for loans and the operation of the bank.

How does the Fed use this tool? Let's assume the Fed feels that at the present time the economy is growing too fast and is feeding inflation and it wants to shrink the supply of money available to the banks. All it has to do is raise the reserve rate requirement, and the banks must then make deposits to their reserve accounts to meet the new requirement. For example, a small bank has deposits of $2 million and the reserve requirement is 5 percent. That means the bank has to have $100,000 on account with the Fed. Now the Fed feels that there is too much money to loan, so it doubles the reserve requirement to 10 percent. The bank must immediately double the amount of money on account at the Fed. This takes another $100,000 out of the hands of the bank and leaves it less money available to loan. This would not only be true for this small bank, but for all of the banks in the system, thus reducing the money available rapidly and in large amounts. We then go back to the law of supply and demand. With the supply reduced, the interest rate should increase and, it is hoped, the demand will slow.

Another tool available to the Fed is to change the discount rate. The discount rate is the rate the Fed charges its member banks to borrow money. Why would a bank need to borrow? Whenever a bank has more commitments due than it has in cash available, it can use monies in its reserve account with the Fed. If in doing this the balance in a bank's reserve account drops below that required by the Fed, the bank must borrow to bring it into compliance. It's not surprising that some experts refer to the Fed as the ''Bankers' Bank''!

The third tool used by the Fed to control the supply of money is to increase or decrease the Fed fund rate. This is the rate charged by banks to other banks when reserves are traded among banks for overnight use. The amounts traded are usually very large, ordinarily in excess of $1 million.

How can the discount rate and/or the Fed fund rate be used to control the economy? That's simple. If it costs the banks more to borrow money, this cost will be passed along to the consumer in the form of higher interest rates, or if the rate is lowered, the consumer *should* get the benefit of lower interest rates.

There is a good example of how the use of increasing the reserve requirements and an increase in the discount rate can affect the economy. In the fall of 1979, the economy was in runaway inflation. Inflation was at an annual rate of 13 to 14 percent and the Fed felt that it had to do something quickly. So it raised the discount rate a full 1 percent, thus causing the interest rate to shoot up and cut the amount of money available. The real estate industry saw the interest rate on single-family loans go to 13 to 13.5 percent, if you could find a lender with funds to loan.

Effects of Money Supply Management

These major tools of money supply management can be used by the Fed to cause either *tight money* or *easy money*. Tight money is the policy of the Fed that makes money expensive (high interest rates). This is usually a restrictive policy, with high discount rates and increased reserve requirements. Thus, the money supply is reduced and, usually, the demand remains about the same: business still needs money to operate and to buy raw materials for production; the demand for housing goes on, but usually at a reduced rate. With about the same number of people pursuing a smaller number of dollars, the interest rate increases until the demand starts to fall.

A good example of this policy happened during the third quarter of 1979 and continued into 1982, when the Fed instituted a strong tight-money policy to try to stop inflation and stabilize the dollar. During this time of tight money we also saw the mood of the world change toward the Fed. Most of the world felt that the Fed would not keep with the tight-money policy due to the unpopularity of this policy and political pressures. They therefore thought inflation in the United States would continue to run wild. So the world turned to precious metals, and the price of gold and silver shot to all-time records. Gold sold for over $800 per ounce.

Even though the Fed came under attack, it continued its policy of tight money into 1982 and the inflation rate in the United States was reduced. Gold was less in demand, thus the price fell and gold was traded in the fourth quarter of 1981 in the $350- to $450-per-ounce range.

With the price of gold falling and interest rates staying relatively high due to the Fed's tight-money policy, the demand by foreign investors for the American dollar increased. Thus, the value of the dollar increased against many foreign currencies.

Easy money is just the opposite of tight money. The Fed's easy-money policy is to reduce the reserve requirements and lower the discount rate. This is usually implemented in a time of recession; the Fed uses this policy to stimulate the economy. It increases the supply of money, thus making it easier for business and individuals to get credit. As credit becomes available, companies can expand, hire more people, and increase salaries. As these monies go into the banks and thrift institutions, it tends to make more money available, and thus the cycle begins again.

How can these policies affect the real estate industry? In the second half of 1979, when the Fed started a tight-money policy, we saw the interest rates start to shoot up on builders' interim loans (those loans made to builders to construct homes), making the builders' costs go up, and thus the cost of the houses went up. In some cases, the rates got so high that builders were forced out of business. Mortgage rates were forced up as the cost of funds to mortgage lenders increased. As the rates increased, many states were forced out of the mortgage market as rates reached or exceeded state usury laws. (We will discuss usury laws later in the chapter.) These are only a few of the problems that can be brought about by a tight-money policy.

HUD, THE VA, AND OTHER AGENCIES

The Fed is not the only federal body that can have an effect on the monetary system or on the movement of money to the real estate industry.

Probably the federal agencies most familiar to us in the real estate industry are the Department of Housing and Urban Development (HUD) and the Veterans Administration, (VA). HUD—through the Federal Housing Administration (FHA)—and the VA have the most direct effect of any governmental agencies by the establishment of interest rates that affect either government-insured or VA-guaranteed loans. In addition to the setting of the interest rates, the FHA, through its loan insurance programs, can have a major effect on the real estate market. We will review these programs in depth later in this text. Some of the other agencies that can have a direct or indirect effect on real estate are listed below:

Small Business Administration This agency through its involvement in the community reinvestment program and its ability to make disaster loans to home owners, can have an effect on the real estate market.

Government Services Agency This agency has the responsibility of overseeing the real estate and buildings of the federal government. It can affect the value of real estate in a given market by acquiring or disposing of land or buildings.

The Federal Land Bank and the Farmers Home Administration These are both active in the financing of farms, farmland, and rural housing.

The Federal National Mortgage Association and the Government National Mortgage Association These two agencies have a strong influence over the very important secondary market. They will be discussed in depth in Chapters 9 and 10.

The Congress of the United States This one body, in one vote, can undo all of the work that any other agency has done to either stabilize the economy or to institute programs that will aid a segment of the real estate industry. An example would be if HUD, through the FHA, wanted to institute a program that would aid a lagging housing market, and it went to Congress for funding: if Congress does not feel the program is good, it does not vote the funds, and the program is dead no matter how badly needed.

Most of these agencies will be discussed in depth in later chapters.

INTEREST RATES

One of the most important factors affecting the financing of real estate is the amount of yield that an investor can receive. This yield is translated into the interest rate a mortgage will bear or the rate of return guaranteed. The higher the rate, the more likely the investor will make the loan. The factor of risk must also be considered.

Most investors seek the highest rate of return with the least amount of risk. The real estate mortgage is an investment that has a low-risk level, for it is usually secured by real property that can be sold and the investor is relatively sure of getting the monies back.

Taking the previous paragraph into consideration, it would seem that investors would be standing in line to make first-lien mortgages on real property. But this is not necessarily true, for we are working in a free market economy where industry, government, and many others are trying to convince the investors that they also are a good investment. Competition for funds brings into play the most important factor that affects the interest rates in the United States—the law of supply and demand.

The Law of Supply and Demand

If the supply of money remains basically the same and the demand stays about the same, interest rates do not vary substantially. That was the case for many years in real estate financing.

But in the last decade we have seen the federal government need monies. This need has come about because the federal government has not been able to finance its operation through the monies derived from the federal income tax. So where does the government get the money to operate? From the same source that all other persons look to when seeking financial help: the public.

With this increase in demand for lendable funds, only one thing can happen to the interest rates: they will go up. If this demand decreases, the interest rates should go down. This is a very simple explanation of the law of supply and demand.

Interest Rate Indicators

A real estate professional must have an idea of the present trend in mortgage rates. Some of the indicators are explained below.

$100,000 certificate of deposit rate As we learned earlier in this chapter, certificates of deposit, or CDs, are included in the measurement of the money supply and are very important. The certificate of deposit rate is the rate that banks and thrift institutions will pay a person who will deposit at least $100,000 in a CD for a minimum of three months and a maximum of one year.

This is the most volatile of all the rate indicators, for the rate can change every day, if not every hour. Why is such a rate of any concern to the real estate professional? Because this rate will tell what has to be paid for the use of the money for a given time. The lending institutions can use this rate as a basis for calculating the rate they will charge the general public. For example, if the institution has to pay 11 percent to use $100,000 for twelve months, it will not lend the money to you or me for any less than 11 percent. It usually will seek a rate of at least 2 percent over the costs of funds or, in this example, 13 percent. These rates are published daily in such papers as *The Wall Street Journal*. It is wise to review this rate regularly, for if the trend is up, you can expect that banks and savings and loan associations will soon start to raise rates. If the trend is down, the institutions should in the near future lower rates.

Fed fund rate As mentioned earlier, the Fed fund rate is the rate that one commercial bank charges another bank for the short-term use of reserves. This term may be as short as overnight. The minimum loan is $1 million. Banks have need for such funds if for the previous day they have funded a large number of loan commitments and find themselves short of the needed reserves to meet their reserve requirement. This rate during the first part of 1980 was approximately 14 percent. The Fed fund rate is used by some banks to establish their prime rate: the higher the Fed fund rate, the higher the prime rate.

Prime rate The prime rate is defined as the rate a commercial bank will charge its most credit-worthy corporate customer. Each bank may set its own prime rate, but usually the major banks on the East and West Coasts set a rate and the rest of the nation follows. As mentioned above, some banks use the Fed fund rate to establish prime. For example, if the Fed fund rate is 13 percent and the banks like to receive 3 percent above the cost of funds, this would set a prime rate of 16 percent. How can a prime rate affect the financing of real estate? First of all, it will affect the cost of funds for the interim financing of construction of homes; second, it will affect the cost to mortgage companies of their warehouse lines of credit. We will discuss both of these later in the text.

USURY LAW

In the *Glossary of Mortgage Banking Terms* compiled by the Mortgage Bankers Association of America, *usury* is defined as

> *a maximum legal rate, established by state law, for interest, discounts or other fees that may be charged for the use of money. The ceiling may vary depending on the nature of the loan.*

The implementation of usury laws by many states has affected the flow of capital into the state. For example, if the current national lending rate on mortgages secured by real property was 13.5 percent and a state legislature had enacted a statute making it illegal to charge more than 12 percent on a mortgage, then there would be no real estate mortgages made in that state.

Many of the states have passed usury laws limiting the rate that may be charged on real estate mortgages. These laws either set a flat maximum interest rate (for example, a state law may declare that the maximum interest rate that may be charged on a mortgage secured by real property, with a mortgage amount of less than $200,000, is 13 percent) or the law passed by a state may have a floating interest rate based on a specific index. This index can be based on the cost of funds to the thrifts, published yields on certain types of government securities, the Federal Reserve's discount rate, or the latest Federal National Mortgage Association (FNMA) required yield.

Even though a state legislature passes a usury law, the effect and scope of the law is severely limited by the passage of the federal Depository Institutions Deregulation and Monetary Control Act of 1980. This is the same law that was mentioned earlier in this chapter. Title V of this law preempts any state law that limits the amount of interest, discount points, finance charges, or other charges that will apply to certain types of mortgages.

Most important to the real estate industry is that the law exempted from any state usury law any first-lien mortgage on residential real property, any first lien on stock in a residential cooperative housing corporation where the loan, mortgage, or advance is used to finance the acquisition of stock in the cooperative, or any first lien on residential manufactured housing made or executed after March 31, 1980.

It should be noted that a state can pass legislation or certify that its voters have voted in favor of any provision, constitutional or otherwise, which states expressly that the state does not wish the provision of the act to apply in that state.

There are about twelve states or U.S. possessions that have enacted laws overriding the federal law limiting the effect of state usury laws. The states or possessions which have enacted such laws are Colorado, Hawaii, Iowa, Kansas, Maine, Massachusetts, Minnesota, Nevada, Puerto Rico, South Carolina, South Dakota, and Wisconsin. If you reside in one of these locations, you will need to contact either an attorney or a mortgage lender in your state to find the effect of the law passed on the financing of real estate.

When the original act became effective on April 1, 1980, the term *lender* was defined to be any lender approved by the Secretary of Housing and Urban Development for participation in any mortgage insurance program under the National Housing Act. The Housing and Community Development Act of 1980 in Section 324 made several amendments to the Depository Institutions Deregulation and Monetary Control Act of 1980, but one of the most important of all of the amendments was that the definition of a lender was expanded to include the following:

> *. . . and any individual who finances the sale or exchange of residential real property which such individual owns and which such individual occupies or has occupied as his principal residence.*[1]

This means that if a person wishes to sell his or her principal residence with a first-lien mortgage, the transaction will be exempt from state usury.

The Depository Institutions Deregulation and Monetary Control Act was again amended with the passage of the Omnibus Budget Reconciliation Act of 1981 (Public Law 97-35). Title III, Banking, Housing, and Related Programs, Subtitle B, amends Section 501 and extends the provisions of the Deregulation and Monetary Control Act to cover the sale of a "residential manufactured home" by an individual. It should be noted that this usury exemption is limited to a transaction financed by a first-lien mortgage.

With these exemptions, many state usury laws have a limited effect on the residential real estate market, and primarily affect second mortgages, contracts for deed, and real estate contracts.

REVIEW QUESTIONS

1. Trace the development of financing of real estate in the United States.
2. Name and define the two basic money supply measurements used by the Federal Reserve.
3. What is the purpose of the Federal Reserve?
4. How does the Federal Reserve implement its policy concerning the money supply?
5. What are the tools the Fed uses to control the supply of money?
6. Explain the difference between a tight-money policy and an easy-money policy.
7. Name three other government agencies besides the Fed that may have a direct or indirect effect on the real estate market.
8. Name and explain the most important factor that affects interest rates in the United States.
9. Name and explain two interest rate indicators a real estate professional may use to predict future interest rates.
10. Define the term *usury* and give a brief explanation of the usury law in your state and how has it been affected by federal legislation.

NOTES

[1]Public Law 96-399, October 8, 1980, (Housing and Community Development Act of 1980), Usury Provisions, Section 324(e).

CHAPTER 2 Mortgages and Mortgage Instruments

LEARNING OBJECTIVES

In this chapter we will look in depth at the types of mortgages and standard instruments that are in common use. We will study the standard mortgage instruments of the Federal National Mortgage Association/Federal Home Loan Mortgage Corporation, the Veterans Administration, and the Federal Housing Administration.

Upon completion of the chapter you should be able to do the following:

- ★ **Define the term *mortgage*.**
- ★ **Outline the early history of mortgages.**
- ★ **Explain the theories of mortgages.**
- ★ **List the categories and types of mortgages.**
- ★ **Thoroughly describe the mortgage instruments in common use.**

DEFINITION

In *Webster's Seventh New Collegiate Dictionary*, mortgage is defined as "a conveyance of property . . . on condition that the conveyance becomes void on payment or performance according to stipulated terms."

In this chapter, we are going to see how this definition relates to mortgage instruments. The primary mortgage instruments are the note and the deed of trust and/or mortgage.

HISTORY

The word *mortgage* has its roots in Latin and means *dead pledge*. In English common law there were two forms of property transfer when the property was used to secure a debt. One was known as *mortuum vadium*, so named because under the law the lender was entitled to all of the fruits of the land such as rents, minerals, and profits, thus making the land "dead" to the borrower. The second form, called *vivum vadium*, was more desirable. Under this form, the fruits of the land were still dead to the borrower, but they applied to the repayment of the loan. Out of these forms came the modern mortgage instruments.

In any transfer of property where the property is used as security for the debt, there are two distinct instruments used: the *promissory note* and the *deed of trust* or *mortgage*. The note is the instrument that creates a personal indebtedness and defines the repayment terms of the debt, such as when payments are due, any late charges, and prepayment.

The mortgage or deed of trust is the procedural instrument of the transaction. The two instruments are similar in that they outline the requirements placed on the borrower and the lender. Some of the requirements or conditions that may be outlined in the mortgage or deed of trust are as follows:

1. How payments made by the borrower will be applied by the lender

2. The responsibility of the borrower for the maintenance of the property

3. Under what conditions the existing mortgage on the property may be assumed

4. The procedure that will be used to foreclose on the property if the borrower fails to make the required payments and the note goes into default

The major difference between a mortgage and a deed of trust is that the deed of trust introduces a third party—the trustee—into the transaction. The sole function of the trustee, not the lender, is to institute foreclosure proceedings if the note goes into default. These procedures involving a trustee are usually nonjudicial proceedings. With this power given to the trustee by the deed of trust, the trustee is said to have ''naked title'' to the property, but the true title rests in the hands of the borrower. The trustee is appointed, for the most part, by the lender and is usually the attorney who drew up the original note and deed of trust. There are exceptions to this rule. In Colorado, for example, there is only one trustee who may be used and this person is an elected county official, known as the Public Trustee.

It should be noted that the use of the deed of trust or mortgage as the procedural document is established by each state. A listing of the states and the procedural document used for one- to four-family transaction is shown in Figure 2-1.

THREE THEORIES OF MORTGAGES

There are three theories of mortgages used in the United States. In some states, more than one theory is used.

The Lien Theory

The lien theory is the most widely used theory in the United States—over 50 percent of the states use it. Under the lien theory, the title to the property remains with the borrower and the mortgage becomes an ''encumbrance'' or ''cloud'' on the title. Upon repayment of the debt, the encumbrance or cloud is removed from the property title.

The Title Theory

Under the title theory, the borrower passes title to the lender, subject to conditions. One of the conditions is usually the repayment of the debt. When the debt is paid, the title reverts to the owner. There are fourteen states that use this theory. These states are located along the East Coast and are primarily the original thirteen colonies.

The Intermediate Theory

The intermediate theory is a combination of the two theories mentioned above. In this theory, when the property is used as security, the mortgage becomes a lien on the property. If the borrower does not make the payments and the mortgage goes into default, the title passes to the lender, who then forecloses on the property. This theory is used in seven states.

CATEGORIES OF MORTGAGES

Now that we have discussed the theories of mortgages, let us identify the three broad categories of mortgages: conventional, VA, and FHA. Each of these categories will be covered in detail in later chapters.

The conventional mortgage—Conventional mortgage commonly refers to any mortgage that is neither insured nor guaranteed by the United States government.

The FHA mortgage—This mortgage is insured from loss by the FHA.

The Veterans Administration guaranteed mortgage A portion of this mortgage is guaranteed by the VA.

There are many types of mortgages. They can, however, be divided into two distinct groups: *alternative mortgages* and *standard mortgages*.

Figure 2-1. Procedural Documents

STATE	DOCUMENT USED	STATE	DOCUMENT USED
Alabama	Mortgage	Nebraska	Mortgage
Alaska	Mortgage	Nevada	Deed of Trust
Arizona	Mortgage and Deed of Trust	New Hampshire	Mortgage
Arkansas	Mortgage	New Jersey	Mortgage
		New Mexico	Mortgage
California	Deed of Trust	New York	Mortgage
Colorado	Deed of Trust	North Carolina	Mortgage
Connecticut	Mortgage	North Dakota	Mortgage
Delaware	Mortgage	Ohio	Mortgage
D.C.	Deed of Trust	Oklahoma	Mortgage
		Oregon	Deed of Trust and Mortgage
Florida	Mortgage		
		Pennsylvania	Mortgage
Georgia	Deed of Trust	Puerto Rico/ Virgin Islands	Mortgage
Hawaii	Mortgage		
		Rhode Island	Mortgage
Idaho	Deed of Trust		
Illinois	Mortgage	South Carolina	Mortgage
Indiana	Mortgage	South Dakota	Mortgage
Iowa	Mortgage		
		Tennessee	Deed of Trust
Kansas	Mortgage	Texas	Deed of Trust
Kentucky	Mortgage		
		Utah	Deed of Trust or Mortgage
Louisiana	Mortgage		
		Vermont	Deed of Trust and Mortgage
Maine	Mortgage	Virginia	Deed of Trust
Maryland	Mortgage		
Massachusetts	Mortgage	Washington	Deed of Trust/Mortgage
Michigan	Mortgage	West Virginia	Deed of Trust
Minnesota	Mortgage	Wisconsin	Mortgage
Mississippi	Deed of Trust	Wyoming	Mortgage
Missouri	Deed of Trust		
Montana	Deed of Trust and Mortgage		

Source: Milwaukee, Wis., MGIC Investment Corporation, *The MGIC Guide to Secondary Marketing—March 1981*, pp. VIII-6-VIII-7.

Alternative mortgages are mortgages in which at least one of the four basic characteristics of a mortgage, listed below, are varied:

1. Amount of the principal
2. Interest rate
3. Payments, varied by time or amount
4. Repayment term

With standard mortgages, none of the four basic characteristics is allowed to change.

ALTERNATIVE MORTGAGES

Alternative mortgages are normally referred to as AMIs (alternative mortgage instruments). The AMI type of mortgage is becoming more common in the real estate industry as interest rates continue to increase and funds for real estate financing become less available. The most important factor that makes this type of mortgage appeal to the lender is that it allows the lender's return from the mortgage to keep up with the prevailing interest rate. It appeals to the borrower because many of the AMIs allow the borrower to qualify for a larger mortgage amount, by making the initial monthly payments lower and increasing them over a specified time as the borrower's income increases. Some of the more common AMIs are as follows:

Graduated payment mortgage (GPM)

Variable-rate mortgage (VRM)

Renegotiable-rate mortgage (RRM)

Pledged account

These and many of the newest AMIs will be discussed in detail in Chapter 3.

STANDARD MORTGAGES

As a professional in the real estate industry, you should have a thorough understanding of each of the standard mortgages described below.

Budget Mortgage

Budget mortgage is just another name for the standard real estate mortgage. The name is derived from the fact that the payments are budgeted so that they remain the same for the life of the mortgage and the borrower starts to gain equity from the first payment. Usually, the amount that is credited to the principal and pays the interest does not vary. The only variable in the payment is the amount needed to pay the taxes, insurance, private mortgage insurance (if any), and any other fees that if not paid may affect the title of the land. The amount to be collected each month is the total of the aforementioned, divided by twelve.

Package Mortgage

A package type of self-amortizing mortgage takes the budget mortgage one step further. It is not only secured by the real property, but it includes some of the appliances and other items that are a part of the structure to be financed. The items that are often included in the package mortgage are stoves, ovens, dishwashers, carpet, heating, and air conditioning. One reason to include such easily removed items in a mortgage is that the lender is better able to protect the investment. The property is more sellable with these items in place. An important advantage for the borrower is that he or she can include the cost of these items in the mortgage and, therefore, be able to budget their cost.

The Blanket Mortgage (with release clause)

A blanket mortgage with release clause is normally used for financing the purchase and development of land or subdivisions. Under the blanket mortgage, the developer has the opportunity to include more than one piece of property, usually subdivision lots, with the ability to release a lot from the mortgage as it is sold. This means, for example, if a developer has a subdivision with 100 lots financed under a blanket mortgage with release clause, as the developer sells one of the lots, the developer pays off 1/100 of the total mortgage. The lender will release the parcel or lot from the mortgage, thus giving the person purchasing the lot clear title. Without the release clause capability, the developer would have to sell all 100 lots before clear title could be issued for any of the lots.

The Open-End Mortgage

As the name implies, there is no end to the open-end mortgage, for it has no due date. The balance is usually not paid off and can be as little as one dollar. Thus, the mortgage is still alive and the lender can lend funds without having to start the procedures of a new loan; the collateral for the original loan is still used for the new funds. This type of loan is primarily used to finance agriculture in rural areas, where the lenders are quite familiar with the borrowers and their financial capabilities. It has no real use in today's real estate market.

Wrap or Wraparound Mortgage

As the name implies, a wraparound mortgage is used to include an existing mortgage on a piece of real property, thus wrapping the new financing around, or including, the existing mortgage. The wrap is usually at a higher interest rate than the existing mortgage, but the interest rate is usually less than the rate charged on new mortgages. This type of mortgage will be discussed in detail in Chapter 16.

Purchase-Money Mortgage or Owner-Financed Mortgage

With a purchase-money or owner-financed type of first-lien mortgage, the seller will execute a first-lien mortgage (that is, the first recorded mortgage on real property) for the remainder of the purchase price, after the prospective buyer has made the required down payment. This type of mortgage will also be explained in further detail in Chapter 16.

Second Mortgages or Junior Mortgages

As the name implies, second or junior mortgages are inferior to the first lien. The priority of the mortgages is established by the recording date: the mortgage that is recorded first is the first lien, the mortgage that is recorded second is the second, and so on. This priority becomes very important if a property is to be foreclosed against, because the mortgages will be paid off in the order of recording.

These types of mortgages are frequently used when a piece of real property is sold on assumption. An assumption sale involves the purchaser assuming the loan of the seller and paying the seller his or her equity in the property. For example, the seller wishes to sell a piece of real property for $60,000. If the mortgage has a balance of $40,000, the owner has an equity of $20,000. The lender will allow the purchaser to assume the existing mortgage and the purchaser can execute a second mortgage with the seller in the amount of $10,000. The purchaser, then, is only required to give the seller $10,000 in cash.

Construction Mortgage

A construction mortgage is used for the initial construction of a home or building, and it is sometimes called an *interim loan* or *interim financing*. Unlike other types of mortgages, it is funded as the work is completed on the improvement or home. These fundings are sometimes called *draws*. The interim lender usually makes periodic inspection of the construction site to see that the construction is progressing as scheduled.

This is a high-risk loan, unless the builder has a purchaser for the home or building, and therefore the interest rates are usually high. The rate is usually based upon the prime rate. The lender will charge anywhere from 1 to 6 percent above prime. If the prime rate is 15¾ percent, as it was in the first quarter of 1982, builders would have to pay anywhere from 16¾ to 21¾ percent interest on the construction loan, thus adding to the cost of the house. The term of these loans is relatively short, from as little as ninety days for a simple project to as long as three years for a major office building.

Contract for Deed/Real Estate Contract

The contract for deed/real estate contract is not a true mortgage. It is mentioned in this section only because it is used in some types of transactions. As its name implies, it is a contract, and if the purchaser meets all of the provisions of the contract, he or she *may* sometime in the future get a deed to the property. A contract for deed has been used in the past to sell recreational land where the developer, due to previous financing, cannot give clear title to the property until the previous financing is paid and released. It is also used to sell low-quality rental property to the present tenant.

There are some severe drawbacks to this type of financing, including the following:

The contract for deed normally is not recorded, thus allowing a less-than-honest developer to sell a piece of property more than once.

A title policy may not be secured on the property.

Most severely, even though the purchaser makes all of the payments in good faith, he or she may not be able to receive clear title due to insanity of the seller or a death, divorce, or bankruptcy concerning the seller or a member of his or her family.

Recognizing all of the possible dangers to a purchase of recreational or resort-type lots, the federal government, through HUD, established the Office of Interstate Land Sales Registration with the passage of the Interstate Land Sales Full Disclosure Act in 1969. The purpose of the act was to police the sale of land by developers in subdivisions of fifty lots or more for lots less than five acres. Under the act, each developer must prepare and submit an Office of Interstate Land Sales Property Report Form.

This report requires the developer to answer certain questions and supply certain information. The developer must supply this report to the prospective purchaser before he or she signs any contract. If the purchaser does not receive a copy of the report prior to or at the time he or she enters into a contract with seller, the purchaser may terminate the contract by notice to the seller. The purchaser must sign a statement that he or she has received a copy of the property report.

Deed of Trust/Mortgage

The deed of trust mortgage is used to secure payment of a debt secured by real property. With the deed of trust, the title to the property securing the debt stays in the name of the borrower. But as the name implies, there is a third party to the transaction, the trustee, who is granted limited title. This is sometimes called "naked" or "dormant" title. The trustee is usually appointed by the lender, with the right of substitution.

With a deed of trust/mortgage, there are actually two instruments involved. One is the deed of trust, which is a procedural document that actually names the trustee. The second document is the promissory note.

As discussed earlier, the trustee is given a limited title to the property and that lies dormant until there is necessity to foreclose. The trustee is the only person who has the right to initiate the foreclosure procedures. The process of foreclosure is started by the lender notifying the trustee that the borrower has not met the payment obligations of the note or is not in compliance with the covenants of the deed of trust and, therefore, the note has gone into default. The trustee is asked to start foreclosure procedures as outlined in the deed of trust.

Why was the deed of trust selected for use in some states? Due to a state's community property law, both husband and wife own the property. For example, in Texas, until the equal rights movement, women did not have the same legal rights or accountability as men, thus creating a doubt as to the outcome of court-ordered sale. For lenders to be encouraged to make a first-lien mortgage on real property in Texas, the state adopted the use of the deed of trust mortgage, which allows the trustee to sell the property without court proceedings when the note goes into default.

HOMESTEAD AND COMMUNITY PROPERTY LAWS

There are several states that have either a homestead act or a community property law, and in some cases they have both. We will review briefly both the broad concepts of a homestead law or act and the broad provisions of a community property law.

Homestead Act or Law

A homestead can be defined in broad terms as the place of residence of either a family or single adult that is protected from forced sale by certain types of creditors, including general creditors. (In some states where there is no homestead law, a home may be foreclosed against for nonpayment of a department store debt.) In some of the homestead acts, the property can only be sold at auction for nonpayment of taxes, for default on a purchase money mortgage, and, finally, for the nonpayment of a material and mechanic's lien for repairs made to a homestead. The homestead is established by either a statute passed by a state legislature or a state's constitution.

Community Property Law

Another law that is unique to several southwestern states is the Community Property Law. Under this law the husband and wife are considered as one, and all of the property acquired during the marriage is owned equally by both the husband and wife. This applies to the purchase of real property. Therefore, when any property is purchased by either the husband or wife out of funds not held separately prior to the marriage, the property is owned jointly, even though the husband or wife negotiated individually for the property.

For this reason some conventional lenders include a divorce covenant in the deed of trust/mortgage. This covenant broadly states that upon divorce of the parties to the mortgage, the party receiving title to the property must meet the qualification requirements of the lender or the outstanding balance of the mortgage is due and payable. If the person receiving title to the property can pay the outstanding principal balance from other sources, the property will not have to be sold. Even if the deed of trust/mortgage secured by real property does not contain a specific divorce covenant, a lender could possibly enforce an existing covenant in the deed of trust/mortgage to declare the note due and payable in case of divorce. For example, if the standard FNMA/FHLMC Deed of Trust/Mortgage is used, the lender could enforce uniform covenant 7 to declare the note due and payable.

STANDARD MORTGAGE INSTRUMENTS

In this section we will discuss in depth the standard notes and deeds of trust/mortgages that are used for most real estate transactions.

FNMA/FHLMC Note and Deed of Trust/Mortgage

First we will discuss the standard form used for most conventional loans: the standard Federal National Mortgage Association/Federal Home Loan Mortgage Corporation Note and Deed of Trust/Mortgage.

The note The note is the instrument that states that the borrower promises to pay to the lender a certain sum by a specific date.

The Federal National Mortgage Association/Federal Home Loan Mortgage Corporation has developed notes for each state that meets the statutory requirements of the states. We will review the Note developed for Texas (see Figure 2-2) which will give the major categories or subjects covered by the note; but to be completely familiar with the note used in your state, you can contact any Federal National Mortgage Association approved lender or any savings and loan association for a copy of the note for your state.

In the first paragraph, the borrower promises to pay to a specific company or person a principal amount with interest on the unpaid balance at a specific rate. This section also outlines to whom the payments are to be made, the amount of the payments, when the payments are due, and the date of the first and last payment.

The second paragraph outlines what remedies the lender has when any monthly installment is not paid and remains unpaid after a specific date contained in a notice to the borrower.

The third paragraph states that the borrower will have to pay a late charge if the payment is not received by a certain date after the payment is due. The industry standard for the late charge is 4 percent of the monthly installment, and the grace period is usually fifteen days. Thus, if the payment is due on the first of the month, the borrower has until the fifteenth of the month before a late charge may be collected. Before a late charge can be assessed by a lender, it must be spelled out in either the note or deed of trust/mortgage. If there is no mention of a late charge in either document, one may not be charged by the lender.

The fourth paragraph of the note states whether the borrower may prepay the note and whether a prepayment penalty exists. In the standard form shown, dated August 1979, the borrower may prepay the loan with no penalty. This is true only for the standard FNMA/FHLMC Note dated August 1979. All previous standard note forms did have a

Figure 2-2. Standard FNMA/FHLMC Note

NOTE

US $............................ ...., Texas
City

............................, 19....

FOR VALUE RECEIVED, the undersigned ("Borrower") promise(s) to pay.......................... ...., or order, the principal sum of ....Dollars, with interest on the unpaid principal balance from the date of this Note, until paid, at the rate of...................... ....percent per annum. Principal and interest shall be payable at....................... ....in consecutive monthly installments of ....Dollars (US $.............................), on the............................day of each month beginning ...., 19..... Such monthly installments shall continue until the entire indebtedness evidenced by this Note is fully paid, except that any remaining indebtedness, if not sooner paid, shall be due and payable on..

If any monthly installment under this Note is not paid when due and remains unpaid after a date specified by a notice to Borrower, the entire principal amount outstanding and accrued interest thereon shall at once become due and payable at the option of the Note holder. The date specified shall not be less than thirty days from the date such notice is mailed. The Note holder may exercise this option to accelerate during any default by Borrower regardless of any prior forbearance. If suit is brought to collect this Note, the Note holder shall be entitled to collect all reasonable costs and expenses of suit, including, but not limited to, reasonable attorney's fees.

Borrower shall pay to the Note holder a late charge of..........................percent of any monthly installment not received by the Note holder within..........................days after the installment is due.

Borrower may prepay the principal amount outstanding in whole or in part. The Note holder may require that any partial prepayments (i) be made on the date monthly installments are due and (ii) be in the amount of that part of one or more monthly installments which would be applicable to principal. Any partial prepayment shall be applied against the principal amount outstanding and shall not postpone the due date of any subsequent monthly installments or change the amount of such installments, unless the Note holder shall otherwise agree in writing.

Presentment, notice of dishonor, and protest are hereby waived by all makers, sureties, guarantors and endorsers hereof. This Note shall be the joint and several obligation of all makers, sureties, guarantors and endorsers, and shall be binding upon them and their successors and assigns.

Any notice to Borrower provided for in this Note shall be given by mailing such notice by certified mail addressed to Borrower at the Property Address stated below, or to such other address as Borrower may designate by notice to the Note holder. Any notice to the Note holder shall be given by mailing such notice by certified mail, return receipt requested, to the Note holder at the address stated in the first paragraph of this Note, or at such other address as may have been designated by notice to Borrower.

The indebtedness evidenced by this Note is secured by a Deed of Trust, dated.......................... ...., and reference is made to the Deed of Trust for rights as to acceleration of the indebtedness evidenced by this Note.

....

....

....
Property Address *(Execute Original Only)*

TEXAS—1 to 4 Family—8/79—**FNMA/FHLMC UNIFORM INSTRUMENT**

prepayment penalty. As a real estate professional, when working on any listing, you should secure a copy of the note in order to establish whether there is a prepayment penalty.

The fifth paragraph of the note outlines the procedures that the lender must use to give notice to a borrower. As the note states, the lender must send all notices to the borrower by certified mail, return receipt requested. If the notice is not sent according to the provision in the note, it can be said that notice has not been given.

The last paragraph of the note states that the note is secured by a deed of trust, usually dated the same as the note.

Deed of Trust/Mortgage Let us now examine the deed of trust/mortgage that must accompany the note. The mortgage or deed of trust is referred to in the note.

The major difference between the mortgage and the deed of trust occurs on the first page of the instrument. The first page of the mortgage is illustrated in Figure 2-3 and the first page of the deed of trust is illustrated in Figure 2-4.

In comparing the two instruments, one can see that the major difference is that the deed of trust has the added feature of naming the trustee. This occurs in the first paragraph of the deed of trust.

The deed of trust/mortgage is the instrument that will outline the procedures to be followed during the life of the mortgage. The first page of the standard FNMA/FHLMC Deed of Trust/ Mortgage indicates the date of the instrument. It identifies the grantor or borrower, the trustee, and the beneficiary or the lender. This section, therefore, identifies all three parties to the deed.

In the first paragraph of the FNMA/FHLMC Mortgage the parties to the mortgage are identified. As mentioned earlier, the major difference between the mortgage and the deed of trust occurs in this paragraph: the mortgage makes no mention of a trustee.

In the second paragraph of the deed, the borrower grants and conveys to the trustee the power of sale of the property that is used to secure the debt. As stated early in this chapter, the trustee may not sell the property until he or she is notified that: (1) the borrower has not made the payment in accordance with the note, or (2) the note is in default.

The second paragraph of the mortgage states that the borrower is indebted to the lender, the amount of the debt as evidenced by the note, and that the note provides for monthly installments of principal and interest. If the indebtedness is not paid sooner, the final monthly installment is due and payable on a specific date.

In the last paragraph of the first page of the mortgage/deed, the borrower states or covenants that he or she has the capacity to grant and convey the property and will defend the title of the property against any claims and demands other than the exceptions that are listed in a title policy.

The remainder of the deed of trust/mortgage contains the covenants or the rules to be followed by all parties. These covenants are divided into two parts. The first is the uniform covenants. This means that these covenants are the same in all standard FNMA/FHLMC uniform instruments. Thus, if you sign a standard FNMA/FHLMC deed of trust in Virginia, or any other state, the uniform covenants are the same.

The second group of covenants is the nonuniform covenants. This section is added to the deed of trust/mortgage to make it conform to each state's laws covering real property. The most important of these covenants is covenant 18, which outlines the procedures for foreclosure.

First, let us review some of the more important uniform covenants (Figure 2-5). Since the wording in the FNMA/FHLMC Deed of Trust and Mortgage is basically the same for the uniform covenants, only those in the Deed of Trust will be reviewed.

Covenant 1 This is the payment covenant in which the borrower agrees to make the payments on time and to pay any late charges as outlined in the note accompanying the deed of trust.

Covenant 2 Paragraph one of covenant 2 allows the lender to set up an escrow account until the note is paid in full. The escrow payment is due on the same day the monthly principal and interest payment is due. The amount of the payment is equal to one twelfth of the taxes and assessments, which may affect the title or take priority over the deed of trust. In addition, the lender may collect one twelfth of the annual premium for hazard insurance. This assures the lender that there is insurance coverage for any loss due to the

Figure 2-3. Standard FNMA/FHLMC Mortgage

MORTGAGE

THIS MORTGAGE is made this............................day of............................, 19...., between the Mortgagor,..(herein "Borrower"), and the Mortgagee,.., a corporation organized and existing under the laws of.., whose address is...(herein "Lender").

WHEREAS, Borrower is indebted to Lender in the principal sum of...Dollars, which indebtedness is evidenced by Borrower's note dated..........................(herein "Note"), providing for monthly installments of principal and interest, with the balance of the indebtedness, if not sooner paid, due and payable on..;

TO SECURE to Lender (a) the repayment of the indebtedness evidenced by the Note, with interest thereon, the payment of all other sums, with interest thereon, advanced in accordance herewith to protect the security of this Mortgage, and the performance of the covenants and agreements of Borrower herein contained, and (b) the repayment of any future advances, with interest thereon, made to Borrower by Lender pursuant to paragraph 21 hereof (herein "Future Advances"), Borrower does hereby mortgage, grant and convey to Lender the following described property located in the County of......................................, State of New Mexico:

which has the address of.., ...,
[Street] [City]

............................(herein "Property Address");
[State and Zip Code]

TOGETHER with all the improvements now or hereafter erected on the property, and all easements, rights, appurtenances, rents, royalties, mineral, oil and gas rights and profits, water, water rights, and water stock, and all fixtures now or hereafter attached to the property, all of which, including replacements and additions thereto, shall be deemed to be and remain a part of the property covered by this Mortgage; and all of the foregoing, together with said property (or the leasehold estate if this Mortgage is on a leasehold) are herein referred to as the "Property".

Borrower covenants that Borrower is lawfully seised of the estate hereby conveyed and has the right to mortgage, grant and convey the Property, that the Property is unencumbered, and that Borrower will warrant and defend generally the title to the Property against all claims and demands, subject to any declarations, easements or restrictions listed in a schedule of exceptions to coverage in any title insurance policy insuring Lender's interest in the Property.

NEW MEXICO—1 to 4 Family—6/75*—**FNMA/FHLMC UNIFORM INSTRUMENT**

Figure 2-4. Standard FNMA/FHLMC Deed of Trust

DEED OF TRUST

THIS DEED OF TRUST is made this .... day of ...., 19...., among the Grantor, ... (herein "Borrower"), ... (herein "Trustee"), and the Beneficiary, ..., a corporation organized and existing under the laws of ...., whose address is .... (herein "Lender").

BORROWER, in consideration of the indebtedness herein recited and the trust herein created, irrevocably grants and conveys to Trustee, in trust, with power of sale, the following described property located in the County of ...., State of Texas:

which has the address of ...., ..., [Street] [City]

.... (herein "Property Address"); [State and Zip Code]

TOGETHER with all the improvements now or hereafter erected on the property, and all easements, rights, appurtenances, rents (subject however to the rights and authorities given herein to Lender to collect and apply such rents), royalties, mineral, oil and gas rights and profits, water, water rights, and water stock, and all fixtures now or hereafter attached to the property, all of which, including replacements and additions thereto, shall be deemed to be and remain a part of the property covered by this Deed of Trust; and all of the foregoing, together with said property (or the leasehold estate if this Deed of Trust is on a leasehold) are herein referred to as the "Property";

TO SECURE to Lender (a) the repayment of the indebtedness evidenced by Borrower's note dated .... (herein "Note"), in the principal sum of .... Dollars, with interest thereon, providing for monthly installments of principal and interest, with the balance of the indebtedness, if not sooner paid, due and payable on ....; the payment of all other sums, with interest thereon, advanced in accordance herewith to protect the security of this Deed of Trust; and the performance of the covenants and agreements of Borrower herein contained; and (b) the repayment of any future advances, with interest thereon, made to Borrower by Lender pursuant to paragraph 21 hereof (herein "Future Advances").

Borrower covenants that Borrower is lawfully seised of the estate hereby conveyed and has the right to grant and convey the Property, that the Property is unencumbered, and that Borrower will warrant and defend generally the title to the Property against all claims and demands, subject to any declarations, easements or restrictions listed in a schedule of exceptions to coverage in any title insurance policy insuring Lender's interest in the Property.

TEXAS—1 to 4 Family—1/76—**FNMA/FHLMC UNIFORM INSTRUMENT**

Figure 2-5. FNMA/FHLMC Deed of Trust, Uniform Covenants 1-6

UNIFORM COVENANTS. Borrower and Lender covenant and agree as follows:

1. Payment of Principal and Interest. Borrower shall promptly pay when due the principal of and interest on the indebtedness evidenced by the Note, prepayment and late charges as provided in the Note, and the principal of and interest on any Future Advances secured by this Deed of Trust.

2. Funds for Taxes and Insurance. Subject to applicable law or to a written waiver by Lender, Borrower shall pay to Lender on the day monthly installments of principal and interest are payable under the Note, until the Note is paid in full, a sum (herein "Funds") equal to one-twelfth of the yearly taxes and assessments which may attain priority over this Deed of Trust, and ground rents on the Property, if any, plus one-twelfth of yearly premium installments for hazard insurance, plus one-twelfth of yearly premium installments for mortgage insurance, if any, all as reasonably estimated initially and from time to time by Lender on the basis of assessments and bills and reasonable estimates thereof.

The Funds shall be held in an institution the deposits or accounts of which are insured or guaranteed by a Federal or state agency (including Lender if Lender is such an institution). Lender shall apply the Funds to pay said taxes, assessments, insurance premiums and ground rents. Lender may not charge for so holding and applying the Funds, analyzing said account or verifying and compiling said assessments and bills, unless Lender pays Borrower interest on the Funds and applicable law permits Lender to make such a charge. Borrower and Lender may agree in writing at the time of execution of this Deed of Trust that interest on the Funds shall be paid to Borrower, and unless such agreement is made or applicable law requires such interest to be paid, Lender shall not be required to pay Borrower any interest or earnings on the Funds. Lender shall give to Borrower, without charge, an annual accounting of the Funds showing credits and debits to the Funds and the purpose for which each debit to the Funds was made. The Funds are pledged as additional security for the sums secured by this Deed of Trust.

If the amount of the Funds held by Lender, together with the future monthly installments of Funds payable prior to the due dates of taxes, assessments, insurance premiums and ground rents, shall exceed the amount required to pay said taxes, assessments, insurance premiums and ground rents as they fall due, such excess shall be, at Borrower's option, either promptly repaid to Borrower or credited to Borrower on monthly installments of Funds. If the amount of the Funds held by Lender shall not be sufficient to pay taxes, assessments, insurance premiums and ground rents as they fall due, Borrower shall pay to Lender any amount necessary to make up the deficiency within 30 days from the date notice is mailed by Lender to Borrower requesting payment thereof.

Upon payment in full of all sums secured by this Deed of Trust, Lender shall promptly refund to Borrower any Funds held by Lender. If under paragraph 18 hereof the Property is sold or the Property is otherwise acquired by Lender, Lender shall apply, no later than immediately prior to the sale of the Property or its acquisition by Lender, any Funds held by Lender at the time of application as a credit against the sums secured by this Deed of Trust.

3. Application of Payments. Unless applicable law provides otherwise, all payments received by Lender under the Note and paragraphs 1 and 2 hereof shall be applied by Lender first in payment of amounts payable to Lender by Borrower under paragraph 2 hereof, then to interest payable on the Note, then to the principal of the Note, and then to interest and principal on any Future Advances.

4. Charges; Liens. Borrower shall pay all taxes, assessments and other charges, fines and impositions attributable to the Property which may attain a priority over this Deed of Trust, and leasehold payments or ground rents, if any, in the manner provided under paragraph 2 hereof or, if not paid in such manner, by Borrower making payment, when due, directly to the payee thereof. Borrower shall promptly furnish to Lender all notices of amounts due under this paragraph, and in the event Borrower shall make payment directly, Borrower shall promptly furnish to Lender receipts evidencing such payments. Borrower shall promptly discharge any lien which has priority over this Deed of Trust; provided, that Borrower shall not be required to discharge any such lien so long as Borrower shall agree in writing to the payment of the obligation secured by such lien in a manner acceptable to Lender, or shall in good faith contest such lien by, or defend enforcement of such lien in, legal proceedings which operate to prevent the enforcement of the lien or forfeiture of the Property or any part thereof.

5. Hazard Insurance. Borrower shall keep the improvements now existing or hereafter erected on the Property insured against loss by fire, hazards included within the term "extended coverage", and such other hazards as Lender may require and in such amounts and for such periods as Lender may require; provided, that Lender shall not require that the amount of such coverage exceed that amount of coverage required to pay the sums secured by this Deed of Trust.

The insurance carrier providing the insurance shall be chosen by Borrower subject to approval by Lender; provided, that such approval shall not be unreasonably withheld. All premiums on insurance policies shall be paid in the manner provided under paragraph 2 hereof or, if not paid in such manner, by Borrower making payment, when due, directly to the insurance carrier.

All insurance policies and renewals thereof shall be in form acceptable to Lender and shall include a standard mortgage clause in favor of and in form acceptable to Lender. Lender shall have the right to hold the policies and renewals thereof, and Borrower shall promptly furnish to Lender all renewal notices and all receipts of paid premiums. In the event of loss, Borrower shall give prompt notice to the insurance carrier and Lender. Lender may make proof of loss if not made promptly by Borrower.

Unless Lender and Borrower otherwise agree in writing, insurance proceeds shall be applied to restoration or repair of the Property damaged, provided such restoration or repair is economically feasible and the security of this Deed of Trust is not thereby impaired. If such restoration or repair is not economically feasible or if the security of this Deed of Trust would be impaired, the insurance proceeds shall be applied to the sums secured by this Deed of Trust, with the excess, if any, paid to Borrower. If the Property is abandoned by Borrower, or if Borrower fails to respond to Lender within 30 days from the date notice is mailed by Lender to Borrower that the insurance carrier offers to settle a claim for insurance benefits, Lender is authorized to collect and apply the insurance proceeds at Lender's option either to restoration or repair of the Property or to the sums secured by this Deed of Trust.

Unless Lender and Borrower otherwise agree in writing, any such application of proceeds to principal shall not extend or postpone the due date of the monthly installments referred to in paragraphs 1 and 2 hereof or change the amount of such installments. If under paragraph 18 hereof the Property is acquired by Lender, all right, title and interest of Borrower in and to any insurance policies and in and to the proceeds thereof resulting from damage to the Property prior to the sale or acquisition shall pass to Lender to the extent of the sums secured by this Deed of Trust immediately prior to such sale or acquisition.

6. Preservation and Maintenance of Property; Leaseholds; Condominiums; Planned Unit Developments. Borrower shall keep the Property in good repair and shall not commit waste or permit impairment or deterioration of the Property and shall comply with the provisions of any lease if this Deed of Trust is on a leasehold. If this Deed of Trust is on a unit in a condominium or a planned unit development, Borrower shall perform all of Borrower's obligations under the declaration or covenants creating or governing the condominium or planned unit development, the by-laws and regulations of the condominium or planned unit development, and constituent documents. If a condominium or planned unit development rider is executed by Borrower and recorded together with this Deed of Trust, the covenants and agreements of such rider shall be incorporated into and shall amend and supplement the covenants and agreements of this Deed of Trust as if the rider were a part hereof.

nonpayment of taxes or loss due to lack of insurance coverage of the structure. This has an advantage for the homeowner in that he or she does not have to make one large payment at the end of each year to cover both the taxes and insurance. This paragraph also allows the lender to collect one twelfth of the annual premium for mortgage insurance, if any is required.

Also in this covenant, the lender is required to keep the funds collected in an institution that is insured or guaranteed by an agency of a state government. It provides that the lender may not charge the borrower for holding the funds, applying the funds, or supplying the borrower with an accounting of the funds.

Paragraph three of this covenant outlines the procedures to be followed if there is an excess in the account after all of the taxes and so on have been paid. If there are insufficient funds in the account to meet the necessary payments, the mortgage/deed declares what the lender must do to notify the borrower that there is a deficiency. The paragraph further states that the borrower has thirty days to make the necessary payment to bring the account to the required amount.

The last paragraph of this covenant specifies procedures to be followed regarding the balance in the escrow account when the loan is paid in full.

Covenant 3 This covenant indicates how the payments made by the borrower must be applied by the lender, unless otherwise dictated by law or agreed to by all parties in the deed of trust/mortgage.

Covenant 4 Here the mortgage/deed outlines the responsibility of the borrower as to the payment of any taxes, assessments, and other charges, fines, and impositions on the property that may, as the covenant says, "attain priority over this Deed of Trust, and lease hold payments or ground rents, if any."

Covenant 5 This part deals with hazard insurance that the borrower must carry on the property securing the debt, as mentioned in the deed of trust/mortgage. This covenant also states that the borrower may choose the carrier, but the carrier or insurance company must be acceptable to the lender. The last section of the covenant outlines the procedures to be followed in case of loss to the property, and how any proceeds paid by the insurance shall be applied to the restoration or repair of the property. The final paragraph of the covenant states that "unless the lender and borrower otherwise agree in writing, and any such applications of proceeds to principal shall not extend or postpone the due date of the monthly installments referred to in covenants 1 and 2—or change the amount of such installments."

Covenant 6 Here the borrower is charged with the responsibility for maintenance of the property. This covenant also outlines the duties of the borrower if he or she has property in a planned unit development (PUD). It further states that any bylaws and restrictions of a condominium or planned unit development will become a part of the deed of trust/mortgage.

Covenant 7 Covenant 7 (Figure 2-6) states that if the "borrower fails to perform the covenants and agreements . . . or if any action or proceeding is commenced which materially affects the lender's interest in the property, including but not limited to, eminent domain, insolvency . . . ," action can be taken by the lender to protect the investment, including entry to the property to make any necessary repairs. As outlined in the last paragraph of this covenant, any monies, plus interest, disbursed by the lender shall become part of the indebtedness of the borrower unless some other arrangement is made in writing between the borrower and the lender.

Covenant 8 This covenant allows the lender, with proper notice and reason for an inspection, to enter onto the property.

Covenant 9 Here the deed outlines the action that will be taken if the property is taken by condemnation. The first sentence declares that any proceeds of any award or claim of damages having to do with condemnation are assigned to the lender.

The second paragraph of this covenant states that if the property is taken in total, all awards will be applied to the mortgage secured by the deed of trust, and if there is any excess, the excess will be paid to the borrower. The second part of this paragraph outlines the procedures to be followed if the property is only partially taken.

Covenant 14 Covenant 14 sets the procedures for notification (for example, foreclosure, acceleration, or inspection) and states how that notice must be given unless otherwise specified by law. The lender is to

Figure 2-6. FNMA/FHLMC Deed of Trust, Uniform Covenants 7-17

7. Protection of Lender's Security. If Borrower fails to perform the covenants and agreements contained in this Deed of Trust, or if any action or proceeding is commenced which materially affects Lender's interest in the Property, including, but not limited to, eminent domain, insolvency, code enforcement, or arrangements or proceedings involving a bankrupt or decedent, then Lender at Lender's option, upon notice to Borrower, may make such appearances, disburse such sums and take such action as is necessary to protect Lender's interest, including, but not limited to, disbursement of reasonable attorney's fees and entry upon the Property to make repairs. If Lender required mortgage insurance as a condition of making the loan secured by this Deed of Trust, Borrower shall pay the premiums required to maintain such insurance in effect until such time as the requirement for such insurance terminates in accordance with Borrower's and Lender's written agreement or applicable law. Borrower shall pay the amount of all mortgage insurance premiums in the manner provided under paragraph 2 hereof.

Any amounts disbursed by Lender pursuant to this paragraph 7, with interest thereon, shall become additional indebtedness of Borrower secured by this Deed of Trust. Unless Borrower and Lender agree to other terms of payment, such amounts shall be payable upon notice from Lender to Borrower requesting payment thereof, and shall bear interest from the date of disbursement at the rate payable from time to time on outstanding principal under the Note unless payment of interest at such rate would be contrary to applicable law, in which event such amounts shall bear interest at the highest rate permissible under applicable law. Nothing contained in this paragraph 7 shall require Lender to incur any expense or take any action hereunder.

8. Inspection. Lender may make or cause to be made reasonable entries upon and inspections of the Property, provided that Lender shall give Borrower notice prior to any such inspection specifying reasonable cause therefor related to Lender's interest in the Property.

9. Condemnation. The proceeds of any award or claim for damages, direct or consequential, in connection with any condemnation or other taking of the Property, or part thereof, or for conveyance in lieu of condemnation, are hereby assigned and shall be paid to Lender.

In the event of a total taking of the Property, the proceeds shall be applied to the sums secured by this Deed of Trust, with the excess, if any, paid to Borrower. In the event of a partial taking of the Property, unless Borrower and Lender otherwise agree in writing, there shall be applied to the sums secured by this Deed of Trust such proportion of the proceeds as is equal to that proportion which the amount of the sums secured by this Deed of Trust immediately prior to the date of taking bears to the fair market value of the Property immediately prior to the date of taking, with the balance of the proceeds paid to Borrower.

If the Property is abandoned by Borrower, or if, after notice by Lender to Borrower that the condemnor offers to make an award or settle a claim for damages, Borrower fails to respond to Lender within 30 days after the date such notice is mailed, Lender is authorized to collect and apply the proceeds, at Lender's option, either to restoration or repair of the Property or to the sums secured by this Deed of Trust.

Unless Lender and Borrower otherwise agree in writing, any such application of proceeds to principal shall not extend or postpone the due date of the monthly installments referred to in paragraphs 1 and 2 hereof or change the amount of such installments.

10. Borrower Not Released. Extension of the time for payment or modification of amortization of the sums secured by this Deed of Trust granted by Lender to any successor in interest of Borrower shall not operate to release, in any manner, the liability of the original Borrower and Borrower's successors in interest. Lender shall not be required to commence proceedings against such successor or refuse to extend time for payment or otherwise modify amortization of the sums secured by this Deed of Trust by reason of any demand made by the original Borrower and Borrower's successors in interest.

11. Forbearance by Lender Not a Waiver. Any forbearance by Lender in exercising any right or remedy hereunder, or otherwise afforded by applicable law, shall not be a waiver of or preclude the exercise of any such right or remedy. The procurement of insurance or the payment of taxes or other liens or charges by Lender shall not be a waiver of Lender's right to accelerate the maturity of the indebtedness secured by this Deed of Trust.

12. Remedies Cumulative. All remedies provided in this Deed of Trust are distinct and cumulative to any other right or remedy under this Deed of Trust or afforded by law or equity, and may be exercised concurrently, independently or successively.

13. Successors and Assigns Bound; Joint and Several Liability; Captions. The covenants and agreements herein contained shall bind, and the rights hereunder shall inure to, the respective successors and assigns of Lender and Borrower, subject to the provisions of paragraph 17 hereof. All covenants and agreements of Borrower shall be joint and several. The captions and headings of the paragraphs of this Deed of Trust are for convenience only and are not to be used to interpret or define the provisions hereof.

14. Notice. Except for any notice required under applicable law to be given in another manner, (a) any notice to Borrower provided for in this Deed of Trust shall be given by mailing such notice by certified mail addressed to Borrower at the Property Address or at such other address as Borrower may designate by notice to Lender as provided herein, and (b) any notice to Lender shall be given by certified mail, return receipt requested, to Lender's address stated herein or to such other address as Lender may designate by notice to Borrower as provided herein. Any notice provided for in this Deed of Trust shall be deemed to have been given to Borrower or Lender when given in the manner designated herein.

15. Uniform Deed of Trust; Governing Law; Severability. This form of deed of trust combines uniform covenants for national use and non-uniform covenants with limited variations by jurisdiction to constitute a uniform security instrument covering real property. This Deed of Trust shall be governed by the law of the jurisdiction in which the Property is located. In the event that any provision or clause of this Deed of Trust or the Note conflicts with applicable law, such conflict shall not affect other provisions of this Deed of Trust or the Note which can be given effect without the conflicting provision, and to this end the provisions of the Deed of Trust and the Note are declared to be severable.

16. Borrower's Copy. Borrower shall be furnished a conformed copy of the Note and of this Deed of Trust at the time of execution or after recordation hereof.

17. Transfer of the Property; Assumption. If all or any part of the Property or an interest therein is sold or transferred by Borrower without Lender's prior written consent, excluding (a) the creation of a lien or encumbrance subordinate to this Deed of Trust, (b) the creation of a purchase money security interest for household appliances, (c) a transfer by devise, descent or by operation of law upon the death of a joint tenant or (d) the grant of any leasehold interest of three years or less not containing an option to purchase, Lender may, at Lender's option, declare all the sums secured by this Deed of Trust to be immediately due and payable. Lender shall have waived such option to accelerate if, prior to the sale or transfer, Lender and the person to whom the Property is to be sold or transferred reach agreement in writing that the credit of such person is satisfactory to Lender and that the interest payable on the sums secured by this Deed of Trust shall be at such rate as Lender shall request. If Lender has waived the option to accelerate provided in this paragraph 17, and if Borrower's successor in interest has executed a written assumption agreement accepted in writing by Lender, Lender shall release Borrower from all obligations under this Deed of Trust and the Note.

If Lender exercises such option to accelerate, Lender shall mail Borrower notice of acceleration in accordance with paragraph 14 hereof. Such notice shall provide a period of not less than 30 days from the date the notice is mailed within which Borrower may pay the sums declared due. If Borrower fails to pay such sums prior to the expiration of such period, Lender may, without further notice or demand on Borrower, invoke any remedies permitted by paragraph 18 hereof.

notify by certified mail, return receipt requested, and mail the notice to the borrower, at the property address or to an address designated by the borrower (by notice to the lender). The borrower, in order to give notice to the lender, must also send such notice certified mail, return receipt requested, to the lender's address or to another address the lender may designate (by notice to the borrower). (It is a good idea that *all* correspondence to the lender by you or your clients be sent by this method.)

Covenant 17 This is one of the more important paragraphs to the real estate professional, because it outlines the procedures to be followed by the borrower if he or she wishes to sell, by assumption, the property secured by a standard FNMA/FHLMC Mortgage/Deed of Trust.

This covenant states that if the borrower sells or transfers, by assumption, the property without the lender's prior written consent, the lender may at the lender's option accelerate the note, that is, declare all sums secured by the mortgage/deed of trust to be immediately due and payable.

This covenant further states that the lender waives the option to accelerate under the following conditions: (1) prior to the sale or transfer, the lender and the person to whom the property is to be sold reach an agreement in writing that the person's credit is acceptable; or (2) that the interest rate on the note secured by the mortgage/deed of trust shall be at the rate the lender requested.

The paragraph further outlines the procedures to be followed if the lender elects to accelerate the sums due because the borrower did not follow the procedures for the sale of the property by assumption.

As mentioned earlier, the covenants are in two sections; in the second section are the nonuniform covenants. The purpose of these covenants is to bring the mortgage/deed of trust into compliance with state law.

Covenant 18 This covenant (Figure 2-7) is used to bring the power of sale clause in the mortgage/deed of trust into compliance with the state law of the state in which the property is located. Most laws regarding foreclosure or forced sale of property for the nonpayment of a note are rather specific and this text will not review all of the laws in detail; but Figure 2-8 shows a brief synopsis of the types of foreclosure for each state as well as the usual redemption period. If you would like information regarding the specific foreclosure laws in your state, contact an attorney in your area.

Covenant 21 This covenant allows the lender, prior to the release of the deed of trust, to make advances to the borrower. The advances will be made as long as the property is not the homestead of the borrower. If advances are made along with the interest, they will be secured by the deed of trust. These advances could be made for repairs on the property, for deficiencies in escrow account, or for any other reason the lender chooses.

Covenant 22 This covenant requires the lender to release the deed of trust upon the payment in full of the sums secured by the deed of trust. This release will be done at no charge to the borrower, but the borrower will be responsible for the filing of the release in the county where the property is located.

FHA Note and Mortgage/Deed of Trust

Another important uniform document that the real estate professional needs to be familiar with is the FHA Note and Mortgage/Deed of Trust. We will start with the FHA Note, Form HUD-99155, dated March 1979 (Figure 2-9). This form is entitled *Mortgage Note*. If the note is to be used with a deed of trust, the note would then be entitled *Deed of Trust Note*. Since most states use the mortgage instead of the deed of trust, as was illustrated in Figure 2-1, we will review the mortgage note. The only major difference between the mortgage note and the deed of trust note is that the deed of trust note makes reference to a deed of trust and the trustee. The basic information is the same for both notes.

The note The first section of this note is similar to the FNMA/FHLMC Note in that it identifies the lender and states that the borrower "promises to pay," thus making it a promissory note. The first paragraph also outlines the amount to be repaid, the interest rate, the monthly payment with interest, and on what date the first and last payments are due, and finally states that the payments, except for the last payment, will be due on the first of the month. It should be pointed out that this paragraph contains a very

Figure 2-7. FNMA/FHLMC Deed of Trust, Non-Uniform Covenants

NON-UNIFORM COVENANTS. Borrower and Lender further covenant and agree as follows:

18. Acceleration; Remedies. Except as provided in paragraph 17 hereof, upon Borrower's breach of any covenant or agreement of Borrower in this Mortgage, including the covenants to pay when due any sums secured by this Mortgage, Lender prior to acceleration shall mail notice to Borrower as provided in paragraph 14 hereof specifying: (1) the breach; (2) the action required to cure such breach; (3) a date, not less than 30 days from the date the notice is mailed to Borrower, by which such breach must be cured; and (4) that failure to cure such breach on or before the date specified in the notice may result in acceleration of the sums secured by this Mortgage, foreclosure by judicial proceeding and sale of the Property. The notice shall further inform Borrower of the right to reinstate after acceleration and the right to assert in the foreclosure proceeding the non-existence of a default or any other defense of Borrower to acceleration and foreclosure. If the breach is not cured on or before the date specified in the notice, Lender at Lender's option may declare all of the sums secured by this Mortgage to be immediately due and payable without further demand and may foreclose this Mortgage by judicial proceeding. Lender shall be entitled to collect in such proceeding all expenses of foreclosure, including, but not limited to, reasonable attorney's fees, and costs of documentary evidence, abstracts and title reports.

19. Borrower's Right to Reinstate. Notwithstanding Lender's acceleration of the sums secured by this Mortgage, Borrower shall have the right to have any proceedings begun by Lender to enforce this Mortgage discontinued at any time prior to entry of a judgment enforcing this Mortgage if: (a) Borrower pays Lender all sums which would be then due under this Mortgage, the Note and notes securing Future Advances, if any, had no acceleration occurred; (b) Borrower cures all breaches of any other covenants or agreements of Borrower contained in this Mortgage; (c) Borrower pays all reasonable expenses incurred by Lender in enforcing the covenants and agreements of Borrower contained in this Mortgage and in enforcing Lender's remedies as provided in paragraph 18 hereof, including, but not limited to, reasonable attorney's fees; and (d) Borrower takes such action as Lender may reasonably require to assure that the lien of this Mortgage, Lender's interest in the Property and Borrower's obligation to pay the sums secured by this Mortgage shall continue unimpaired. Upon such payment and cure by Borrower, this Mortgage and the obligations secured hereby shall remain in full force and effect as if no acceleration had occurred.

20. Assignment of Rents; Appointment of Receiver; Lender in Possession. As additional security hereunder, Borrower hereby assigns to Lender the rents of the Property, provided that Borrower shall, prior to acceleration under paragraph 18 hereof or abandonment of the Property, have the right to collect and retain such rents as they become due and payable.

Upon acceleration under paragraph 18 hereof or abandonment of the Property, Lender, in person, by agent or by judicially appointed receiver, shall be entitled to enter upon, take possession of and manage the Property and to collect the rents of the Property including those past due. All rents collected by Lender or the receiver shall be applied first to payment of the costs of management of the Property and collection of rents, including, but not limited to, receiver's fees, premiums on receiver's bonds and reasonable attorney's fees, and then to the sums secured by this Mortgage. Lender and the receiver shall be liable to account only for those rents actually received.

21. Future Advances. Upon request of Borrower, Lender, at Lender's option prior to release of this Mortgage, may make Future Advances to Borrower. Such Future Advances, with interest thereon, shall be secured by this Mortgage when evidenced by promissory notes stating that said notes are secured hereby.

22. Release. Upon payment of all sums secured by this Mortgage, Lender shall release this Mortgage without charge to Borrower. Borrower shall pay all costs of recordation, if any.

23. Redemption Period. If this Mortgage is foreclosed, the redemption period after judicial sale shall be one month in lieu of nine months.

IN WITNESS WHEREOF, Borrower has executed this Mortgage.

.... —Borrower

.... —Borrower

STATE OF NEW MEXICO, ... County ss:

The foregoing instrument was acknowledged before me this .... (date)

by .... (person acknowledging)

My Commission expires:

.... Notary Public

(Space Below This Line Reserved For Lender and Recorder)

Figure 2-8. Foreclosure/Redemption Summary

State	Foreclosure Remedies	Waiting Period After Default	Length of Time To Complete Foreclosure	Period of Redemption
Alabama	Power of Sale	None	4-6 weeks, plus redemption	1 year
Alaska	Power of Sale		4-6 weeks	None
Arizona	Judicial Sale Mtg. or Trustee Sale D.O.T.	None	3 months	None with Trust Deed; 6 months with Mortgage, 30 days if abandoned
Arkansas	Judicial Sale	None	3-4 months	Usually waived
California	Trustee Sale	None	4 months	None
Colorado	Trustee Sale	None	6 months	75 days
Connecticut	Judicial Sale	None	3-4 months	None
Delaware	Judicial Sale	None	3-7 months	None
D.C.	Trustee Sale	None	4 weeks	None
Florida	Judicial Sale		3-4 months	10-day confirmation after sale; 60 days appeal prior to sale
Georgia	Power of Sale	None	1 month	None
Hawaii	Individual Sale	None	5 months	1 month to confirm
Idaho	Power of Sale	None	4 months	None
Illinois	Judicial Sale	None	3 months plus redemption	6 months after Sheriff's sale; 6 months after summons, whichever is later
Indiana	Judicial Sale	None	Mortgage Originated Prior to 1958—14 months 1958-7/1/75—8 months After 7/1/75—5 months	 12 months 6 months 3 months
Iowa	Judicial Sale	None	4-6 weeks plus redemption	12 months; 6 months if deficiency is waived; 60 days if abandoned
Kansas	Judicial Sale	None	3 months plus redemption	6 months
Kentucky	Judicial Sale	None	4 months	None; 1 month to confirm
Louisiana	Judicial Sale	None	3-4 months	None
Maine	Judicial Sale	None	3 weeks	12 months after 1st Ad.; 90 days before sale. Sale date 30 days after end of redemption 11-75
Maryland	Power of Sale	None	3-4 months	30 days ratification
Massachusetts	Power of Sale	30 days	3-4 months	None
Michigan	Power of Sale	None	1 month	12 mos.; over 3 acres, 6 mos.; 90-day strict F/C; 30 days if abandoned
Minnesota	Power of Sale	None	2 months	6 months
Mississippi	Trustee Sale	None	1 month	None
Missouri	Trustee Sale	None	1 month	None; 12 months if contested

Figure 2-8. continued

State	Foreclosure Remedies	Waiting Period After Default	Length of Time To Complete Foreclosure	Period of Redemption
Montana	Judicial Sale	None	3 months, redemption	Trust Deed—4 months Mortgage—12 months
Nebraska	Judicial Sale	None	6 months	None
Nevada	Judicial Sale	None unless bankruptcy	4 months	None
New Hampshire	Power of Sale	None	4-6 weeks	None
New Jersey	Judicial Sale	None	8 months	None
New Mexico	Judicial Sale	None	4-6 months, plus redemption	1 month standard, but court may extend to 9 months
New York	Power of Sale	None	5 months at earliest	None
North Carolina	Trustee Sale	None	1 month	None
North Dakota	Judicial Sale	None	4-6 weeks	6 months if 10 acres or less
Ohio	Judicial Sale	None	3 months	None
Oklahoma	Judicial Sale	None	6-8 months, including redemption	6 months expiring prior to sale
Oregon	Judicial Sale Trustee Sale	None	3 months	Trust Deed—None Mortgage—1 year
Pennsylvania	Judicial Sale	35 days	3-4 months	None
Puerto Rico/ Virgin Islands	Judicial Sale	None	12 months for noncontested cases	PR—30 days VI—6 months
Rhode Island	Power of Sale	None	4 weeks	None
South Carolina	Judicial Sale	None	4-5 months	None
South Dakota	Power of Sale		6 months	6 months
Tennessee	Trustee Sale	None	1 month	None
Texas	Judicial Sale Trustee Sale	None	3 weeks	None
Utah	Trustee Sale		3 months plus 3 weeks	Mortgage—3 months Deed of Trust—None
Vermont	Judicial Sale Trustee Sale	None	3 months or 12 months	3 months after Notice of Default or 12 months before sale
Virginia	Trustee Sale	None	4 weeks	None
Washington	Judicial Sale Trustee Sale	None	3-4 weeks	Trust Deed—None Mortgage—1 year
West Virginia	Trustee Sale	None	8-10 weeks	None
Wisconsin	Judicial Sale	None	14 months, 8 months without deficiency	12 months, 6 months, before sale without deficiency
Wyoming	Power of Sale	None	8-11 months	3 months

Source: Milwaukee, Wis., MGIC Investment Corporation, *The MGIC Guide to Secondary Marketing—March 1981*, pp. VIII-6-VIII-7.

Figure 2-9. FHA Mortgage Note

This form is used in connection with mortgages insured under the one- to four-family provisions of the National Housing Act.

MORTGAGE NOTE

FHA CASE NO.

$, New Mexico.

FOR VALUE RECEIVED, the undersigned promise(s) to pay to the order of

the principal sum of Dollars ($),

with interest from date at the rate of per centum (%) per annum on the unpaid balance until paid. The said principal and interest shall be payable at the office of in , or at such other place as the holder hereof may designate in writing, in monthly installments of Dollars ($), commencing on the first day of , 19 , and on the first day of each month thereafter, until the principal and interest are fully paid, except that the final payment of the entire indebtedness evidenced hereby, if not sooner paid, shall be due and payable on the first day of , . ∴ can be prepaid

In the event of default in the payment of any installment under this note, and if the default is not made good prior to the due date of the next such installment, the entire principal sum with accrued interest shall at once become due and payable without notice at the option of the holder of this note. Failure to exercise this option shall not constitute a waiver of the right to exercise it any other time. If suit is brought on this note, or if any attorney is employed to collect it, the undersigned promise(s) to pay all costs of collection, including reasonable attorney's fees.

Presentment, protest and notice are hereby waived. The makers and endorsers of this note also waive the benefit of any homestead, exemption, valuation, or appraisement laws as to this debt.

Replaces FHA-9155, which is Obsolete.

HUD-99155 (3-79)

GPO 940 486

important phrase, "if not sooner paid." Without this phrase, this note or any other note may not be prepaid.

One major difference between this note and the FNMA/FHLMC one is that there is no mention of any late charges or any grace period for payment. This note says that the payments are due on the first of each month. If a payment that is missed is not made prior to the due date of the next payment, at the option of the lender the note may become immediately due and payable without notice. This section further states that if the note goes into default and foreclosure is instituted, the borrower will pay an additional amount for cost of collection, including reasonable attorney's fees.

If the FHA Mortgage is insured under Section 245(a) or 245(b), the payment schedule over the life of the mortgage is shown in the large blank area.

As one can see, the FHA Note, Form 99155, is less complicated than the FNMA/FHLMC Note. If you would like to have a copy of this instrument, they are available from any mortgage lender who originates FHA mortgages.

The mortgage Now let us review the HUD Mortgage (Figures 2-10, 2-11, and 2-12). The form that we are using is HUD Form 92155M. At the time of this writing, this was the approved form for mortgages insured under the one- to four-family provisions of the National Housing Act for the state of New Mexico. Usually each of the states will have a prescribed form for use in that state. The form is developed by HUD to meet the statutory requirements of the particular state. You can secure a copy of the approved mortgage or deed of trust for your state from any FHA-approved lender or from the nearest HUD-FHA office. For the purpose of this review, we will use this mortgage form because all of the basic information is the same for all of the mortgages. When one first looks at this form in comparison to the FNMA/FHLMC Deed of Trust (Figure 2-4), one can see that the HUD document is not as easy to read and is more legalistic in its wording.

The first section of the mortgage is similar to the FNMA/FHLMC documents in that this section identifies the parties to the transaction.

Section 2 of the mortgage makes reference to the promissory note of the same date as the mortgage and restates the amount borrowed, the interest rate, the monthly payment including interest, and the due date of the first and last payment.

Section 3 of the mortgage is where the borrower or mortgagor conveys the property as well as all estate, right, title and interest to the property to the lender until the mortgage is paid in full.

Section 4 of the mortgage is the covenant section. It is different from the FNMA/FHLMC Deed in that it is not divided into conforming and nonconforming covenants.

We will now review some of the more important covenants, starting with covenant 1.

Covenant 1 This is the repayment covenant. The borrower declares that he or she will repay the principal with interest. There is, however, a very important statement contained in this covenant, and that is, "Privilege is reserved to pay the debt in whole. . . ." This allows the borrower to prepay the loan at any time and, since there was no mention of a penalty for the prepayment in the note, the borrower will be charged no prepayment penalty.

Covenant 2 Covenant 2 sets up the escrow account. Subparagraphs a and b define what will be collected and paid on the first of each month. In addition to the taxes, insurance, ground rent, or any other assessments, the covenant mentions that the borrower must pay on a monthly basis a sum sufficient to accrue annually to pay for the federal mortgage insurance premium. Subparagraph c states how the monthly payment, made by the borrower, will be applied: first, the premium for the federal mortgage insurance will be paid; second, taxes, insurance, special assessments and ground rents, if any, will be paid; third, interest on the mortgage will be paid; and fourth, amortization of the principal will be paid. The final paragraph, paragraph 3, outlines what is to be done if there is an overage in the escrow account or a deficiency in the account.

Covenant 5 Covenant 5 charges the borrower to keep the property in good repair and not permit any waste, impairment, or deterioration of the property.

Covenant 6 Here, the HUD Mortgage deals with condemnation and how any awards will be applied by the lender. The covenant states such awards will be applied to the balance owed the lender. The credit of the funds in no way relieves the borrower from making the

Figure 2-10. HUD (FHA) Mortgage, page 1

MORTGAGE

This form is used in connection with mortgages insured under the one- to four-family provisions of the National Housing Act.

THIS INDENTURE, made this day of , 19 , between

of , hereinafter called
the Mortgagor, and 1

, a corporation organized and existing under the laws of
, hereinafter called the Mortgagee, Witnesseth:

WHEREAS, the Mortgagor has executed and delivered to the Mortgagee his certain promissory note of even date herewith in the principal sum of Dollars ($),

with interest at the rate of
per centum (%) per annum on the unpaid balance until paid, the said principal and interest being payable
at the office of
in or at such other place as the holder of the note may designate in writing, in 2
monthly installments of Dollars ($),

commencing on the first day of , 19 , and on the first day of each month thereafter until the principal and interest are fully paid, except that the final payment of principal and interest, if not sooner paid, shall be due and payable on the first day of All conditions and obligations of said note are hereby referred to and made a part of this instrument.

NOW, THEREFORE, the Mortgagor, in consideration of the premises and of the sum of One Dollar *($1.00)* to him in hand paid, the receipt whereof is hereby acknowledged, does hereby grant, bargain, sell, mortgage, remise, release and convey unto the Mortgagee, forever, the following-described real estate situated in the
of County of , and State of New Mexico, to wit:

3

together with all the estate, right, title and interest of the Mortgagor, either in law or in equity, in and to said premises; to have and to hold the same, together with all and singular the land, tenements, hereditaments, reversion and reversions, remainder and remainders, rents, issues, profits, privileges, water rights and appurtenances of every kind and nature thereunto belonging or in any way appertaining, to the Mortgagee, forever as security for the payment of the sum of money evidenced by the aforesaid promissory note for the proper performance of all the terms of this mortgage.

And the Mortgagor convenants that at the time of the ensealing and delivery of these presents, he is well seized of said premises in fee simple and has good right, full power and lawful authority to convey and mortgage the same in manner and form aforesaid; that the same are free and clear of all liens and encumbrances whatsoever, and that he shall and will warrant and forever defend the quiet and peaceable possession of the said premises by the Mortgagee against all and every person claiming the whole or any part thereof.

And the Mortgagor further convenants;

1. He will pay the indebtedness, as hereinbefore provided. Privilege is reserved to pay the debt in whole, or in an amount equal to one or more monthly payments on the principal that are next due on the note, on the first day of any month prior to maturity; provided, however, that written notice of an intention to exercise such privilege is given at least thirty *(30)* days prior to prepayment. 4

2. Together with, and in addition to, the monthly payments of principal and interest payable under the terms of the note secured hereby, he will pay to the Mortgagee, on the first day of each month until the said note is fully paid, the following sums:

Replaces FHA-2155M, which is Obsolete.

STATE OF NEW MEXICO
HUD-92155M (2-79)

Figure 2-11. HUD (FHA) Mortgage, page 2

(a) An amount sufficient to provide the holder hereof with funds to pay the next mortgage insurance premium if this instrument and the note secured hereby are insured, or a monthly charge *(in lieu of a mortgage insurance premium)* if they are held by the Secretary of Housing and Urban Development, as follows:

(I) If and so long as said note, of even date and this instrument are insured or are reinsured under the provisions of the National Housing Act, an amount sufficient to accumulate in the hands of the holder one *(1)* month prior to its due date the annual mortgage insurance premium, in order to provide such holder with funds to pay such premium to the Secretary of Housing and Urban Development pursuant to the National Housing Act, as amended, and applicable Regulations thereunder; or

(II) If and so long as said note of even date and this instrument are held by the Secretary of Housing and Urban Development, a monthly charge *(in lieu of a mortgage insurance premium)* which shall be in an amount equal to one-twelfth *(1/12)* of one-half *(½)* per centum of the average outstanding balance due on the note computed without taking into account delinquencies or prepayments;

(b) A sum equal to the ground rents, if any, next due, plus the premiums that will next become due and payable on policies of fire and other hazard insurance covering the mortgaged property, plus taxes and assessments next due on the mortgaged property *(all as estimated by the Mortgagee)* less all sums already paid therefor divided by the number of months to elapse before one month prior to the date when such ground rents, premiums, taxes and assessments will become delinquent, such sums to be held by Mortgagee in trust to pay said ground rents, premiums, taxes and special assessments; and

(c) All payments mentioned in the two preceding subsections of this paragraph and all payments to be made under the note secured hereby shall be added together and the aggregate amount thereof shall be paid by the Mortgagor each month in a single payment to be applied by the Mortgagee to the following items in the order set forth

(I) premium charges under the contract of insurance with the Secretary of Housing and Urban Development, or monthly charge *(in lieu of mortgage insurance premium)*, as the case may be;
(II) taxes, special assessments, fire and other hazard insurance premiums;
(III) interest on the note secured hereby; and
(IV) amortization of the principal of said note.

Any deficiency in the amount of any such aggregate monthly payments shall, unless made good by the Mortgagor prior to the due date of the next such payment, constitute an event of default under this mortgage. The Mortgagee may collect a "late charge" not to exceed four cents *(4¢)* for each dollar *($1)* of each payment more than fifteen *(15)* days in arrears to cover the extra expense involved in handling delinquent payments.

3. If the total of the payments made by the Mortgagor under (b) paragraph 2 preceding shall exceed the amount of payments actually made by the Mortgagee for taxes or assessments or insurance premiums, as the case may be, such excess, if the loan is current, at the option of the Mortgagor, shall be credited on subsequent payments to be made by the Mortgagor, or refunded to the Mortgagor. If, however, the monthly payments made by the Mortgagor under (b) of paragraph 2 preceding shall not be sufficient to pay taxes and assessments and insurance premiums, as the case may be, when the same shall become due and payable, then the Mortgagor shall pay to the Mortgagee any amount necessary to make up the deficiency on or before the date when payment of such taxes, assessments or insurance premiums shall be due. If at any time the Mortgagor shall tender to the Mortgagee, in accordance with the provisions of the note secured hereby, full payment of the entire indebtedness represented thereby, the Mortgagee shall, in computing the amount of such indebtedness, credit to the account of the Mortgagor all payments made under the provisions of (a) of paragraph 2 hereof which the Mortgagee has not become obligated to pay to the Secretary of Housing and Urban Development, and any balance remaining in the funds accumulated under the provisions of (b) of paragraph 2 hereof. If there shall be a default under any of the provisions of this mortgage resulting in a public sale of the premises covered hereby, of if the Mortgagee acquires the property otherwise after default, the Mortgagee shall apply, at the time of the commencement of such proceedings, or at the time the property is otherwise acquired, the balance then remaining in the funds accumulated under (b) of paragraph 2 preceding, as a credit against the amount of principal then remaining unpaid under said note, and shall properly adjust any payments which shall have been made under (a) of paragraph 2.

4. He will pay all taxes, assessments, water rates and other governmental or municipal charges, fines or impositions, for which provision has not been made hereinbefore and in default thereof the Mortgagee may pay the same, and that he will promptly deliver the official receipts therefor to the Mortgagee.

5. He will keep the premises in as good order and condition as they are now and will not permit any waste thereof, reasonable wear and tear excepted.

6. That if the premises, or any part thereof, be condemned under any power of eminent domain, or acquired for a public use, the damages, proceeds and the consideration for such acquisition, to the extent of the full amount of indebtedness upon this mortgage, and the note secured hereby remaining unpaid, are hereby assigned by the Mortgagor to the Mortgagee and shall be paid forthwith to the Mortgagee to be applied by it on account of the indebtedness secured hereby, whether due or not.

7. Mortgagor will keep the improvements now existing or hereinafter erected on the mortgaged property, insured as may be required from time to time by the Mortgagee against loss by fire and other hazards, casualties and contingencies including war damage in such amounts and for such periods as may be required by Mortgagee, and will pay promptly, when due, any premiums on such insurance for payment of which provision has not been made hereinbefore. All insurance shall be carried in companies approved by Mortgagee and the policies and renewals thereof shall be held by Mortgagee and have attached thereto loss payable clauses in favor of and in form acceptable to the Mortgagee. In event of loss Mortgagor will give immediate notice by mail to Mortgagee, and Mortgagee may make proof of loss if not made promptly by Mortgagor, and each insurance company concerned is hereby authorized and directed to make payment for such loss directly to Mortgagee instead of to Mortgagor and Mortgagee jointly, and the insurance proceeds, or any part thereof, may be applied by Mortgagee at its option either to the reduction of the indebtedness hereby secured or to the restoration or repair of the property damaged. In event of foreclosure of this mortgage or other transfer of title to the mortgaged property in extinguishment of the indebtedness secured hereby, all right, title and interest of the Mortgagor in and to any insurance policies then in force shall pass to the purchaser or grantee.

8. Upon his failure to keep the premises in good repair or to pay any sums herein provided to be paid, then the Mortgagee, at its option, may make such repairs or pay such sums and all sums so paid shall bear interest at the rate set forth in the note secured hereby shall be payable on demand and shall be fully secured by this instrument.

9. The Mortgagor further agrees that should this mortgage and the note secured hereby not be eligible for insurance under the National Housing Act within THIRTY DAYS from the date hereof *(written statement of any officer of the Department of Housing and Urban Development or authorized agent of the Secretary of Housing and Urban Development dated subsequent to the* THIRTY DAYS *time from the date of this mortgage, declining to insure said note and this mortgage, being deemed conclusive proof of such ineligibility)*, the Mortgagee or the holder of the note may, at its option, declare all sums secured hereby immediately due and payable.

HUD-92155M (2-79)

Figure 2-12. HUD (FHA) Mortgage, page 3

10. He hereby authorizes the Mortgagee, at any time there is a default under this mortgage or in the note secured hereby, to take possession of the premises and collect the rents and profits thereof, and the Mortgagee shall have the right to apply such moneys to the debt secured hereby, deducting from such rents all costs of collection. The Mortgagee shal also have the right, in the event that foreclosure proceedings are started, to have a receiver of the mortgaged premises appointed, without regard to the solvency or insolvency of the Mortgagor and without regard to the value of the premises, who shall have the usual rights and powers of a receiver in such circumstances; and the receiver, after deducting all charges and expenses, shall apply the residue of any and all rents and profits collected to the payment of the debt secured hereby.

If there is any default in the terms of this mortgage, or in the terms of the note secured hereby, all sums owing by the Mortgagor shall, at the option of the Mortgagee, become immediately due and payable. This mortgage shall then be subject to foreclosure, and the premises may be sold in the manner and form prescribed by law, and in the event of any sale hereunder, it is understood and agreed that the Mortgagee or its assigns, may become the purchaser of the premises hereinbefore described, or of any part thereof; and the proceeds arising from the sale of the mortgaged premises shall be applied, first to the payment of the costs and expenses of foreclosure, including a reasonable attorney's fee to be fixed by the court; second, to the payment of all taxes, assessments or other sums then owing under this mortgage; third, to the payment of all sums owing to the Mortgagee by virtue of this mortgage or the note secured hereby, and the balance, if any, shall be paid to the Mortgagor.

If this mortgage is foreclosed the redemption period after judicial sale shall be one month in lieu of nine months.

No sale of the premises hereby mortgaged and no forbearance on the part of the Mortgagee and no extension of the time for the payment of the debt hereby secured given by the Mortgagee shall operate to release, discharge, modify, change or affect the original liability of the Mortgagor herein either in whole or in part. No waiver of any of the terms of this mortgage, or of the note secured hereby, shall at any time thereafter be held to be a waiver of the terms hereof or of the note secured hereby. Notice of the exercise of any option granted herein, or in the note secured hereby, is not required to be given.

The covenants herein contained shall bind, and the benefits and advantages shall inure to, the respective heirs, executors, administrators, successors and assigns of the parties hereto. Whenever used, the singular number shall include the plural, the plural the singular, and the use of any gender shall be applicable to all genders.

IN WITNESS WHEREOF, the Mortgagor(s) hereunto set hand(s) and seal(s) the day and year above written.

_______________ [SEAL]

_______________ [SEAL]

_______________ [SEAL]

_______________ [SEAL]

STATE OF NEW MEXICO)
COUNTY OF) *ss:*

On this day of , 19 , before me, the undersigned Notary Public within and for said County, personally appeared

to me known to be the person(s) described in and who executed the foregoing instrument, and acknowledged to me that executed the same as free act and deed.

IN WITNESS WHEREOF I have hereunto set my hand and notarial seal the day and year last above written.

____

My commission expires *Notary Public.*

Received for record this day of 19 at o'clock M., and recorded in Mortgage Record at pages records of County, New Mexico.

____

Recorder of *County, New Mexico*

HUD-92155M (2-79)
GPO 940 411

regular monthly payment, unless the award is sufficient to pay off the mortgage.

Covenant 7 Another important covenant is covenant 7 (Figure 2-11). This covenant is similar to covenant 5 of the FNMA/FHLMC Deed, in that it requires the borrower to have insurance on all improvements now on the property and those added in the future. The insurance carrier must be approved by the lender. In case of loss, the covenant states that the borrower must notify the lender by mail immediately. The last part of this covenant outlines how payments, made by insurance carriers, may be applied by the lender. In normal practice, the insurance carrier will issue any payment for loss jointly to the borrower and the lender.

Covenant 9 If the note and mortgage are not eligible for insurance under the National Housing Act within a specific time limit, usually thirty days, the noteholder, at his or her option, may declare all sums secured to be immediately due and payable.

Covenant 10 This covenant (Figure 2-12) outlines the foreclosure procedure to be followed if the borrower does not uphold the covenants of the mortgage. In addition to the procedures being outlined, the mortgage states how the proceeds of a foreclosure sale will be applied.

VA Note and Mortgage

The final two instruments that will be dealt with in this chapter are the Veterans Administration Note and Mortgage. At the time of this writing, the only forms approved for use with a Veterans Administration Mortgage are those shown.

The note The VA Note (Figure 2-13) is very similar to the HUD Note. To avoid redundancy, we will review only the major difference between these two notes.

The first sentence of the second paragraph of the VA Note includes the following: "Privilege is reserved to prepay at any time, without premium or fee, the entire indebtedness or any part thereof. . . ." A similar wording is included not in the HUD Note, but in the HUD Mortgage. This paragraph of the VA Note deals exclusively with the payment of the mortgage and states how payment in full or partial payment will be credited.

The mortgage We will review the accompanying VA Mortgage (Figure 2-14) by comparing it to the HUD Mortgage. Even though the wording is sometimes not identical, the HUD Mortgage and the VA Mortgage are parallel in construction.

The first difference appears in covenant 1 in the HUD Mortgage. The borrower has to give a thirty-day notice to the lender before exercising prepayment. The notice must be in writing. The VA Mortgage has no provision for the thirty-day notice.

The second of the differences appears in covenant 2 (Figure 2-15). In the VA Mortgage all mention of the National Housing Act, Secretary of HUD, and mortgage insurance has been omitted. The rest of this covenant is similar to the HUD Mortgage. It covers the setting up of an escrow account, the items to be collected, and the application of the collected funds.

The next major difference occurs in covenant 6 of the VA Mortgage (Figure 2-16) which deals with the requirement of the borrower to maintain hazard insurance. Covenant 6 of the HUD Mortgage is a covenant dealing with eminent domain and covenant 7 of the HUD Mortgage specifies the insurance requirement.

Covenant 8 is the next major difference. Neither this covenant nor any similar wording is included in the HUD Mortgage. This covenant in the VA Mortgage states that for any funds advanced by the lender, the borrower shall execute and deliver to the lender a supplemental note or notes for the amount of the funds advanced by the lender. This covenant outlines some examples of when the lender could advance funds, and states the interest rate this note or notes will carry and the payment schedule. The covenant further states that if the parties are not able to agree on the maturity of the note or notes, the sums advanced shall be due and payable thirty days after demand by the lender. The covenant also states that the maturity of the note or notes for the advanced funds may not extend beyond the maturity of the original mortgage.

Covenant 9 of the VA Mortgage corresponds to covenant 10 of the HUD Mortgage. Both deal with foreclosure. The HUD Mortgage covenant 9 deals with the securing of mortgage insurance through FHA. Since FHA has nothing to do with the VA, all such

Figure 2-13. VA Note

VA Form 26-6329a (Home Loan) Rev. March 1974. Use Optional. Section 1810, Title 38, U.S.C. Acceptable to Federal National Mortgage Association.

NEW MEXICO

MORTGAGE NOTE

, New Mexico.

$, 19

FOR VALUE RECEIVED, the undersigned promise(s) to pay to the order of

the principal sum of Dollars ($), with interest from date at the rate of per centum (%) per annum on the unpaid balance until paid. Said principal and interest shall be payable at the office of in , or at such other place as the holder hereof may designate in writing delivered or mailed to the debtor, in monthly installments of Dollars ($), commencing on the first day of , 19 , and continuing on the first day of each month thereafter, until this note is fully paid, except that, if not sooner paid, the final payment of the entire indebtedness evidenced hereby shall be due and payable on the first day of

Privilege is reserved to prepay at any time, without premium or fee, the entire indebtedness or any part thereof not less than the amount of one installment, or one hundred dollars ($100.00), whichever is less. Prepayment in full shall be credited on the date received. Partial prepayment, other than on an installment due date, need not be credited until the next following installment due date or thirty days after such prepayment, whichever is earlier.

If any deficiency in the payment of any installment under this note is not made good prior to the due date of the next such installment, the entire principal sum with accrued interest shall at once become due and payable without notice at the option of the holder of this note. Failure to exercise this option shall not constitute a waiver of the right to exercise it in the event of any subsequent default. If suit is brought on this note, or if an attorney is employed to collect it, the undersigned promise(s) to pay all costs of collection, including reasonable attorney's fees.

This note is secured by Mortgage of even date executed by the undersigned on certain property described therein and represents money actually used for the acquisition of said property or the improvements thereon.

The undersigned waives presentment, protest, and notice, and the benefit of any homestead, exemption, valuation, or appraisement laws as to this debt.

....

....

....

....

I HEREBY CERTIFY that this is the note described in and secured by Mortgage of even date herewith in the same principal amount as herein stated and secured by real estate situated in the county of , State of New Mexico.

Dated this day of , 19 .

....
Notary Public.

527226

Figure 2-14. VA Mortgage

VA Form 26–6329 (Home Loan)
Rev. March 1974. Use Optional.
Section 1810, Title 38, U.S.C.
Acceptable to Federal National
Mortgage Association

NEW MEXICO

MORTGAGE

THIS INDENTURE, made this day of , 19 , between

of , hereinafter called the

Mortgagor, and

, a corporation organized and existing under the laws of , hereinafter call the Mortgagee, Witnesseth:

WHEREAS, the Mortgagor has executed and delivered to the Mortgagee his certain promissory note of even date herewith in the principal sum of Dollars ($), with interest at the rate of per centum (%) per annum on the unpaid balance until paid, the said principal and interest being payable at the office of in , or at such other place as the holder of the note may designate in writing delivered or mailed to the debtor, in monthly installments of Dollars ($), commencing on the first day of , 19 , and continuing on the first day of each month thereafter until the principal and interest are fully paid, except that if not sooner paid, the final payment of principal and interest shall be due and payable on the first day of . All conditions and obligations of said note are hereby referred to and made a part of this instrument.

NOW, THEREFORE, the Mortgagor, in consideration of the premises and of the sum of One Dollar ($1.00) to him in hand paid, the receipt whereof is hereby acknowledged, does hereby grant, bargain, sell, mortgage, assign, remise, release and convey unto the Mortgagee, forever, the following-described property situated in the of , County of and State of New Mexico, to wit:

Should the Veterans' Administration fail or refuse to issue its Guaranty of the loan secured by this Mortgage under the provisions of the Servicemen's Readjustment Act of 1944, as amended, in the amount of the note secured hereby within sixty days from the date the loan would normally become eligible for such Guaranty, the Beneficiary herein, at its option, declare all sums secured by this Mortgage immediately due and payable.

together with all tenements, hereditaments, reversion and reversions, remainder and remainders, privileges, water rights, and appurtenances of every kind and nature thereunto belonging or in anyway appertaining, **and the rents, issues and profits thereof, (provided, however, that the Mortgagor shall be entitled to collect and retain the said rents, issues and profits until default hereunder) and all fixtures now or hereafter attached to or used in connection with the premises herein described; and in addition thereto the following described household appliances, which are, and shall be deemed to be, fixtures and a part of the realty, and are a portion of the security of the indebtedness herein mentioned:**

--;

The mortgagor covenants and agrees that so long as this
mortgage and the note secured hereby are insured under the
provisions of the Servicemen's Readjustment Act, he will not
execute or file for record any instrument which imposes a
restriction upon the sale or occupancy of the mortgaged property on basis of race, color, or creed. Upon any violation of
this undertaking, the mortgagee may, at its option, declare
the unpaid balance of the debt secured hereby immediately
due and payable.

to have and to hold the same, to the Mortgagee, as security for the payment of the sum of money evidenced by the aforesaid promissory note and for the proper performance of all the terms and obligations of this mortgage.

Mortgagor covenants that at the time of the ensealing and delivery of these presents, he is well seized of said premises in fee simple (or such other estate as is stated herein) and has good right, full power and lawful authority to convey and mortgage the same in manner and form aforesaid; that the same are free and clear of all liens and encumbrances whatsoever, except as herein otherwise recited, and that he shall and will warrant and forever defend the quiet and peaceable possession of the said premises by the Mortgagee against all and every person claiming the whole or any part thereof.

Figure 2-15. VA Mortgage, Covenants 1-5

Mortgagor further covenants:

1. He will pay the indebtedness, as herein provided. Privilege is reserved to prepay at any time, without premium or fee, the entire indebtedness or any part thereof not less than the amount of one installment, or one hundred dollars ($100.00), whichever is less. Prepayment in full shall be credited on the date received. Partial prepayment, other than on an installment due date, need not be credited until the next following installment due date or thirty days after such prepayment, whichever is earlier.

2. Together with, and in addition to, monthly payments of principal and interest payable under the terms of the note secured hereby, he will pay to the Mortgagee, as trustee, (under the terms of this trust as hereinafter stated) on the first day of each month until the said note is fully paid:

(*a*) A sum equal to the ground rents, if any, next due, plus the premiums that will next become due and payable on policies of fire and other hazard insurance covering the mortgaged property, plus taxes and assessments next due on the mortgaged property (all as estimated by the Mortgagee, and of which the Mortgagor is notified), less all sums already paid therefor, divided by the number of months to elapse before one month prior to the date when such ground rents, premiums, taxes and assessments will become delinquent, such sums to be held by Mortgagee in trust to pay said ground rents, premiums, taxes and assessments.

(*b*) The aggregate of the amounts payable pursuant to subparagraph (*a*) and those payable on the note secured hereby, shall be paid in a single payment each month, to be applied to the following items in the order stated:

(I) taxes, special assessments, fire and other hazard insurance premiums;

(II) interest on the indebtedness secured hereby; and

(III) amortization of the principal of said indebtedness.

Any deficiency in the amount of any such aggregate monthly payments shall, unless made good by the Mortgagor prior to the due date of the next such payment, constitute an event of default under this mortgage. At Mortgagee's option, Mortgagor will pay a "late charge" not exceeding four per centum (4%) of any installment when paid more than fifteen (15) days after the due date thereof to cover the extra expense involved in handling delinquent payments, but such "late charge" shall not be payable out of the proceeds of any sale made to satisfy the indebtedness secured hereby, unless such proceeds are sufficient to discharge the entire indebtedness and all proper costs and expenses secured thereby.

3. If the total of the payments made by the Mortgagor under (*a*) of paragraph 2 preceding shall exceed the amount of payments actually made by the Mortgagee, as trustee, for taxes or assessments or insurance premiums, as the case may be, such excess shall be credited on subsequent payments to be made by the Mortgagor for such items or, at Mortgagee's option, as trustee, shall be refunded to Mortgagor. If, however, such monthly payments shall not be sufficient to pay such items when the same shall become due and payable, then the Mortgagor shall pay to the Mortgagee, as trustee, any amount necessary to make up the deficiency within thirty (30) days after written notice from the Mortgagee stating the amount of the deficiency, which notice may be given by mail. If at any time the Mortgagor shall tender to the Mortgagee, in accordance with the provisions of the note secured hereby, full payment of the entire indebtedness represented thereby, the Mortgagee, as trustee, shall, in computing the amount of such indebtedness, credit to the account of the Mortgagor any credit balance accumulated under the provisions of (*a*) of paragraph 2 hereof. If there shall be a default under any of the provisions of this mortgage resulting in a public sale of the premises covered hereby, or if the Mortgagee acquires the property otherwise after default, the Mortgagee, as trustee, shall apply, at the time of the commencement of such proceedings, or at the time the property is otherwise acquired, the credit balance accumulated under (*a*) of paragraph 2 preceding, as a credit on the interest accrued and unpaid and the balance to the principal then remaining unpaid on said note.

4. He will pay all ground rents, taxes, assessments, water rates, and other governmental or municipal charges, fines, or impositions, levied upon said premises except when payment for all such items has theretofore been made under (*a*) of paragraph 2 hereof, and he will promptly deliver the official receipts therefor to the Mortgagee.

5. He shall not commit or permit waste; and shall maintain the property in as good condition as at present, reasonable wear and tear excepted. Upon any failure to so maintain, Mortgagee, at its option, may cause reasonable maintenance work to be performed at the cost of Mortgagor.

Figure 2-16. *VA Mortgage, Covenants 6-9*

6. He will continuously maintain hazard insurance, of such type or types and amounts as the Mortgagee may from time to time require, on the improvements now or hereafter on said premises, and except when payment for all such premiums has theretofore been made under (*a*) of paragraph 2 hereof, will pay promptly when due any premiums therefor. All insurance shall be carried in companies approved by Mortgagee and the policies and renewals thereof shall be held by Mortgagee and have attached thereto loss payable clauses in favor of and in form acceptable to the Mortgagee. In event of loss Mortgagor will give immediate notice by mail to Mortgagee, and Mortgagee may make proof of loss if not made promptly by Mortgagor. Each insurance company concerned is hereby authorized and directed to make payment for such loss directly to Mortgagee instead of to Mortgagor and Mortgagee jointly. The insurance proceeds, or any part thereof, may be applied by Mortgagee at its option either to the reduction of the indebtedness hereby secured or to the restoration or repair of the property damaged. In event of foreclosure of this mortgage, or other transfer of title to the mortgaged property in extinguishment of the indebtedness secured hereby, all right, title and interest of the Mortgagor in and to any insurance policies then in force shall pass to the purchaser or grantee.

7. Mortgagee may perform any defaulted covenant or agreement of Mortgagor to such extent as Mortgagee shall determine, and any moneys advanced by Mortgagee for such purposes shall bear interest at the rate provided for in the principal indebtedness, shall thereupon become a part of the indebtedness secured by this instrument, ratably and on a parity with all other indebtedness secured hereby, and shall be payable thirty (30) days after demand.

8. Upon the request of the Mortgagee, the Mortgagor shall execute and deliver a supplemental note or notes for the sum or sums advanced by the Mortgagee for the alteration, modernization, improvement, maintenance, or repair of said premises, for taxes or assessments against the same and for any other purpose elsewhere authorized hereunder. Said note or notes shall be secured hereby on a parity with and as fully as if the advance evidenced thereby were included in the note first described above. Said supplemental note or notes shall bear interest at the rate provided for in the principal indebtedness and shall be payable in approximately equal monthly payments for such period as may be agreed upon by the Mortgagor and Mortgagee. Failing to agree on the maturity, the whole of the sum or sums so advanced shall be due and payable thirty (30) days after demand by the Mortgagee. In no event shall the maturity extend beyond the ultimate maturity of the note first described above.

9. He hereby authorizes the Mortgagee, at any time there is a default under this mortgage or in the note secured hereby, to take possession of the premises and collect the rents and profits thereof, apply such moneys to the debt secured hereby, deducting from such rents all costs of collection. The Mortgagee shall also have the right, in the event that foreclosure proceedings are started, to have a receiver of the mortgaged premises appointed, without regard to the solvency or insolvency of the Mortgagor and without regard to the value of the premises, who shall have the usual rights and powers of a receiver in such circumstances; and the receiver, after deducting all charges and expenses, shall apply the residue of any and all rents and profits collected to the payment of the debt secured hereby.

If there is any default in the terms of this mortgage, or in the terms of the note secured hereby, all sums owing by the Mortgagor shall, at the option of the Mortgagee, become immediately due and payable. This mortgage shall then be subject to foreclosure, and the premises may be sold in the manner and form prescribed by law. In the event of any sale hereunder, Mortgagee or its assigns, may become the purchaser of the premises hereinafter described, or of any part thereof. The proceeds arising from the sale of the mortgaged premises shall be applied, first to the payment of the costs and expenses of foreclosure, including a reasonable attorney's fee to be fixed by the court; second, to the payment of all taxes or assessments then owing; third, to the payment of all sums owing to the Mortgagee by virtue of this mortgage or the indebtedness secured hereby; fourth, to reimbursement of the Veterans Administration for any sums paid by it on account of the guaranty or insurance of the indebtedness secured hereby; and the balance, if any, shall be paid to the Mortgagor.

No sale of the premises hereby mortgaged, no forbearance on the part of the Mortgagee, and no postponement or extension of the time for the payment of the debt hereby secured shall operate to release, discharge, modify, change or affect the original liability of the Mortgagor herein either in whole or in part nor shall the full force and effect of the lien of this instrument be altered thereby. No waiver of any of the terms of this mortgage, or of the note secured hereby, shall at any time thereafter be held to be a waiver of the terms hereof or of the note secured hereby. Notice of the exercise of any option granted herein, or in the note secured hereby, is not required.

If the indebtedness secured hereby be guaranteed or insured under Title 38, United States Code, such Title and Regulations issued thereunder and in effect on the date hereof shall govern the rights, duties and liabilities of the parties hereto, and any provisions of this or other instruments executed in connection with said indebtedness which are inconsistent with said Title or Regulations are hereby amended to conform thereto.

The covenants herein contained shall bind, and the benefits and advantages shall inure to, the respective heirs, executors, administrators, successors and assigns of the parties hereto. Whenever used, the singular number shall include the plural, the plural the singular, the use of any gender shall be applicable to all genders, and the term "Mortgagee" shall include any payee of the indebtedness hereby secured or any transferee thereof whether by operation of law or otherwise.

IN WITNESS WHEREOF, the Mortgagor(s) ha hereunto set hand(s) and seal(s) the day and year above written.

references have been deleted from the VA Mortgage. The VA Mortgage does state in a supplemental statement, usually added by the lender, that if the VA fails or refuses to issue a VA guaranty of the loan within sixty days from the date of the mortgage, the outstanding balance with accrued interest will be due and payable.

There are now efforts underway for HUD and the Veterans Administration to agree on a common form for the note and mortgage and/or deed of trust for all states. The first of the common forms will be introduced in Maryland and the rest of the common forms are to be introduced on a state-by-state basis as soon as possible.

This completes our review of the three more important notes and mortgages/deeds of trust: the FNMA/FHLMC, the HUD, and finally, the VA Note and Mortgage. The reason for the review is to give you, the real estate professional or the homeowner, an idea of the rights and duties of a homeowner. A real estate professional also needs to have a broad concept of the mortgage/deed to know whether a piece of property may be sold on assumption and if so, the terms of such a sale if there is a prepayment penalty and, finally, whether the original borrower will be released from the obligation if the note is assumed.

REVIEW QUESTIONS

1. Explain the differences among the three theories of mortgages.

2. Define *alternative mortgage instrument* and give three examples.

3. Explain the difference between an open-end mortgage and a package mortgage.

4. Define *mortgage*.

5. Explain the difference between a note and a mortgage/deed of trust.

6. Explain the major differences between the FNMA/FHLMC Note, the VA Note, and the FHA Note.

7. Name and define the categories of mortgages.

8. Name and explain some of the major covenants found in the FNMA/FHLMC Deed of Trust.

9. List the possible exceptions to homestead protection.

10. Outline two covenants that are common to the FHA and VA Mortgages and the FNMA/FHLMC Deed of Trust.

CHAPTER 3 Alternative Mortgage Instruments

LEARNING OBJECTIVES

In this chapter we will review the major alternative mortgage instruments that are presently being used in the financing of the real estate transaction.

Upon completion of this chapter, you should be able to do the following:

- ★ **Define an alternative mortgage instrument.**
- ★ **Define many of the major alternative mortgages in use.**
- ★ **Define two variations of the graduated-payment mortgage.**
- ★ **List the major differences in the adjustable rate mortgage and the adjustable mortgage loan.**
- ★ **List the disclosure requirements for each of the alternative mortgage instruments.**

BACKGROUND

As mentioned in Chapter 2, the alternative mortgage instrument is one of the two basic types of mortgage instruments. (The other type is the standard mortgage instrument.) The alternative mortgage instrument is the type of mortgage in which at least one of the four basic mortgage characteristics varies. The importance of AMIs has grown in the last few years because the increase in interest rates means fewer persons can qualify for housing. In the past, AMIs were thought to be a creative method of financing the real estate transaction, but today they are becoming the standard.

In December 1978 the Federal Home Loan Bank Board had published a final rule that would allow federally chartered savings and loan associations to originate, participate in, or purchase certain types of alternative mortgage instruments. After the FHLBB received comments from the general public, it made the regulations effective January 1, 1979. These regulations then allowed savings and loans to originate, purchase, or participate in the variable-rate mortgage, graduated-payment mortgage, and reverse-annuity mortgage.

This regulation was amended several times to allow the savings and loans not only to make the mortgages listed previously, but also to make the renegotiable rate mortgage.

In late 1980, the FHLBB published proposed regulations that allowed federally chartered savings and loans to make the shared-appreciation mortgage and the graduated-payment adjustable mortgage.

But in the second quarter of 1981, both the FHLBB and the comptroller of the currency adopted regulations that drastically changed the types of alternative mortgages that federally chartered savings and loans and the federally chartered banks were allowed to originate, purchase, and/or participate in.

With the adoption of these regulations, the previously authorized renegotiable-rate mortgage (RRM) and the variable-rate mortgage (VRM) have been canceled. In the place of the RRM and the VRM, the comptroller of the currency allows national banks to originate, purchase, or participate in the adjustable-rate mortgage, and the FHLBB allows the savings associations to originate, purchase, or participate in the adjustable mortgage loan. However, RRMs and VRMs are of course still offered by other lenders.

A discussion of the old FHLBB rules governing the canceled RRM and the VRM is included in this chapter to give some insight into these RRMs and VRMs offered by other lenders.

In this chapter, we will examine all of the listed AMIs, as well as some of the variations of the graduated-payment mortgages presently being made by some of the mortgage lenders.

ADJUSTABLE-RATE MORTGAGE (ARM)

With the cost of funds increasing in 1980 and 1981, the comptroller of the currency proposed a type of mortgage instrument that would allow all national banks to design an adjustable-rate mortgage that would meet the needs of the banks and the needs of the banks' customers. So on September 29, 1980, the Office of the Comptroller of the Currency published in the *Federal Register* a proposed regulation that would allow adjustable-rate mortgage lending by all national banks.

The comment period on this regulation was to expire on November 28, 1980, but since the Federal Home Loan Bank Board was also interested in a similar type of mortgage instrument, the comment period was extended to December 30, 1980, allowing the Office of the Comptroller of the Currency and the Federal Home Loan Bank Board to hold joint hearings on the proposed regulation. Public hearings were held on December 2, 1980, in Washington, D.C.; December 3, 1980, in Chicago; and on December 9, 1980, in Los Angeles.

As a result of these hearings and other comments received by the comptroller of the currency, a regulation was adopted on March 27, 1981, allowing the national banks to make, purchase, or participate in the adjustable-rate mortgage. Then on June 2, 1982, the comptroller of the currency published a proposed rule that would amend the existing ARM regulation. According to the introductory information, the proposed rule was to make the ARM conform more to the Federal Home Loan Bank Board's Adjustable Mortgage Loan (AML) and the National Credit Union Administration's ARM. Both of these mortgages will be discussed later in this chapter.

We will examine this regulation and the proposed changes in some depth, for this type of mortgage will become one of the major types of mortgages that will be used to finance residential real estate in the near future. As a real estate practitioner, you must be as familiar as possible with the major provisions of the ARM.

Definition of the ARM

First we need to define the ARM. According to the regulation, an adjustable-rate mortgage is

> *any loan made to finance or refinance the purchase of and secured by a lien on a one-to-four-family dwelling, including a condominium unit, cooperative housing unit, or a mobile home, where such loan is made pursuant to an agreement intended to enable the lender to adjust the rate of interest from time to time.*[1]

Thus, the ARM may include mortgages that have the rate adjusted periodically. It will also include fixed-rate mortgages that have the feature of rate adjustment by the mortgage having a demand feature or by the maturity of the note at a time prior to the end of the total amortization period. For example, if a borrower secures a mortgage on a home with a term of thirty years, but the note has a "call option" at the end of each seven-year period and the national bank has agreed to refinance the note at a different interest rate, the loan would be governed by this regulation.

Major Provisions

Rate changes The regulation limits both the frequency and the amount that the rate may change. In regard to the frequency of the change, the regulation limits the rate change to a minimum of every six months, but the bank may extend the length of the first rate change period. Thus, the bank could set the first adjustment period at one year with all subsequent adjustments occurring every six months.

The regulation also states that the maximum amount the rate may increase in each adjustment period is 1 percent. If the adjustment period is more than six months, then the rate may increase 1 percent for every six-month period, with a maximum adjustment of 5 percent. For example, if an ARM is written with the initial rate adjustment period of thirty months and is adjusted subsequently every twelve months, the maximum rate adjustment for the first rate adjustment period would be 5 percent, and the maximum adjustment for each of the following periods would be 2 percent. The reason is that in the first adjustment period there are five six-month periods, and with a maximum of 1 percent per six-month period, 5 × 1 percent equals a 5 percent maximum adjustment. There is no limit on the amount of adjustment over the life of the mortgage.

It should be noted that any upward adjustment warranted by the selected index may be taken at the bank's option, but any decrease warranted by the index is mandatory. Furthermore, the reduction in the ARM's rate is subject to the same limitations outlined in the previous paragraph.

The proposed rule would amend this section and would affect both the frequency and amount the rate may be changed. The proposed amendment would remove the frequency limitation. Thus, the six-month minimum limitation would be removed, allowing the rate to be adjusted as often as every thirty days. The proposed amendment would delete the requirement that interest rate adjustments occur at regularly prescribed intervals and would state that interest rate adjustments would occur at the times specified in the loan documents.

The amount the interest rate may be adjusted will also change. The proposed rule eliminates the adjustment limit of 1 percent per six months, as well as the 5 percent limit for any one adjustment period. The proposed rule does not change the provision in the regulation that allows for no maximum rate change over the life of the mortgage.

Another major change affecting interest rate changes modifies the requirement of optional increase/mandatory decrease to the interest rate warranted by the index. The amendment would still allow the bank the option to make any increase warranted by the index, but the mandatory decrease portion of the present regulation would be amended. According to the comptroller of the currency, many of the banks offering ARMs have initial interest rates that are below the market rate. To compensate for this, the bank will, at the time of origination of the mortgage, establish an increasing interest rate over the first few years of the mortgage. During this period of graduation or increasing interest rate, decreases warranted by a decrease in the interest rate index are not taken.

Rate change index Any rate adjustment in the ARM must be linked to some specific index, and this index must be specified in the original loan documents. For example,

> *A 1 basis point (1 basis point = .01 percentage point) change in the index must be translated into a 1 basis point change of the same direction in the contract interest rate, . . .*[2]

The regulation limits also the specific index to one of the following:

1. The monthly average contract interest rate charged by all lenders on mortgage loans for previously occupied homes, as published by the Federal Home Loan Bank Board in its *Journal* and made available by the Federal Home Loan Bank Board in news releases on or about the twelfth day of each month.

2. The monthly average yield on United States Treasury securities adjusted to a constant maturity of 3 years, as published in the *Federal Reserve Bulletin* and made available by the Federal Reserve Board in Statistical Release G.13(415) during the first week of each month.

3. The monthly average of weekly average auction rates on United States Treasury Bills with a maturity of 6 months, as published in the *Federal*

> *Reserve Bulletin* and made available by the Federal Reserve Board in Statistical Release G.13(415) during the first week of each month.[3]

This statistical release is shown in Figure 3-1. The section entitled *U.S. Government Securities* is divided into three major subsections. The subsection that shows the values of the indexes in paragraph 3 of the previous section is entitled "Treasury Constant Maturities." These constant maturities are listed for maturities of one, two, three, five, seven, ten, twenty, and thirty years. With these figures, one can establish the interest rate index that will be used for mortgages closed for the month. Since this is published monthly, the release illustrated would set the index for the month of January 1982. If the ARM called for an index using the three-year constant maturity and the transaction was to be closed in January, the index would be 13.66.

Now let us relate these indexes to actual interest rates and compare the three indexes. In reviewing the three rates in Figure 3-2, it can be seen that the mortgage rates on previously occupied homes and the six-month treasury rate have been consistently lower than the third index. Therefore, when advising your clients these are the indexes that should be suggested.

Before leaving our discussion of the rate indexes and the amount of change, it should be noted that in the case of a change warranted by an index and not taken by the bank, the change may be postponed and taken by the bank at a later adjustment period.

The postponement of any increase or decrease in the interest rate due to the movement in the index is authorized by what is called "the carry-over rule." This rule is rather important, so we will review how the rule works. If, for example, the index increases by 1.75 percentage points during the first adjustment period, but the amount of change is limited by the original loan documents to a maximum of 1.00 percentage point per adjustment period, the remaining 0.75 percentage point would be carried over to the next adjustment period.

If the index in the next adjustment period had remained the same, the mortgage interest rate would still have increased by the amount of the carry-over or 0.75 of a percent. Now let us see how a decrease in the index would have affected the interest. In case one, let us say that the index had decreased by 0.30 of a percent. The interest rate on the mortgage would still have gone up. The amount of the increase would have been the difference between the carry-over amount of +0.75 and the −0.30, or an increase of 0.45 of a percent. For case two, if the index indicated a decrease of 1.00 percent, the actual rate of the mortgage would only have decreased by the difference between the 1.00 percent decrease and the 0.75 increase, or a decrease of only 0.25 of a percent.

How would an increase in the index be affected by the carry-over rule? Let us assume that the index indicated an upward movement of 0.40 of a percent. We would, then, combine the carry-over of 0.75 and the new change indicated by the index of 0.40 for a combined change of 1.15 percent. Since the mortgage limits the amount of change to only 1.00 percent, we now would have a new carry-over amount of 0.15 of a percent.

On April 1, 1982, the Comptroller of the Currency amended the ARM regulation allowing all federally chartered national banks not only to use the interest rate indexes listed in the previous section, but also to use the following indexes:

1. The weekly average yield of U.S. Treasury securities adjusted to a constant maturity of three years

2. The weekly average of auction rates on U.S. Treasury bills with a maturity of six months

These indexes are published in the *Federal Reserve Bulletin* and are also made available weekly by the Federal Reserve in its Statistical Release H.15(519).

The proposed amendments would also affect this section of the existing rule. As mentioned, the banks are currently limited to the use of only five indexes. The amendments would delete the naming of any specific index and would allow the banks to use any measure of interest rate as an index that is readily available and verifiable by the borrower and beyond the control of the bank. This is very similar to the wording of the AML regulations authorized by the Federal Home Loan Bank Board.

Figure 3-1. Federal Reserve Statistical Release

FEDERAL RESERVE statistical release

G.13 (415)

For immediate release
January 7, 1982

SELECTED INTEREST RATES
Yields in percent per annum

Instruments	Week ending DEC 4	DEC 11	DEC 18	DEC 25	JAN 1	DEC	1981 ANN.
FEDERAL FUNDS (EFFECTIVE) 1/	12.48	12.04	12.26	12.43	12.54	12.37	16.38
COMMERCIAL PAPER 2/ 3/							
1-MONTH	11.48	11.70	12.39	12.64	12.59	12.16	15.69
3-MONTH	11.38	11.61	12.33	12.65	12.66	12.12	15.32
6-MONTH	11.30	11.60	12.34	12.71	12.78	12.14	14.76
FINANCE PAPER PLACED DIRECTLY 2/							
1-MONTH	11.09	11.49	12.15	12.51	12.22	11.89	15.30
3-MONTH	10.86	10.80	11.29	11.76	12.00	11.31	14.08
6-MONTH	10.84	10.81	11.26	11.56	11.82	11.24	13.73
BANKERS ACCEPTANCES (TOP RATED) 2/							
3-MONTH	11.31	11.66	12.26	12.80	12.63	12.13	15.32
6-MONTH	11.47	11.78	12.30	12.91	12.90	12.27	14.66
CDS (SECONDARY MARKET)							
1-MONTH	11.55	11.82	12.49	12.80	12.64	12.27	15.91
3-MONTH	11.62	11.96	12.68	13.16	13.03	12.49	15.91
6-MONTH	12.13	12.46	13.15	13.83	13.80	13.07	15.77
BANK PRIME LOAN 1/ 4/	15.93	15.75	15.75	15.75	15.75	15.75	18.87
DISCOUNT WINDOW BORROWING 1/ 5/	13.00	12.14	12.00	12.00	12.00	12.10	13.41
U.S. GOVERNMENT SECURITIES							
TREASURY BILLS 2/							
AUCTION AVERAGE (ISSUE DATE)							
3-MONTH	10.400	10.404	11.101	11.037	11.690	10.926	14.077
6-MONTH	10.701	10.772	11.595	11.838	12.448	11.471	13.811
1-YEAR	10.506				12.501	11.504	13.348
SECONDARY MARKET							
3-MONTH	10.39	10.47	10.94	11.14	11.35	10.85	14.03
6-MONTH	10.83	11.06	11.51	12.03	12.25	11.52	13.80
1-YEAR	10.85	11.13	11.53	12.16	12.23	11.57	13.14
TREASURY CONSTANT MATURITIES 6/							
1-YEAR	12.00	12.32	12.79	13.56	13.68	12.85	14.78
2-YEAR	12.61	12.92	13.22	13.86	13.88	13.29	14.56
3-YEAR	13.06	13.46	13.56	14.15	14.09	13.66	14.44
5-YEAR	13.03	13.47	13.44	14.03	14.04	13.60	14.24
7-YEAR	13.10	13.51	13.47	13.99	14.04	13.62	14.06
10-YEAR	13.32	13.66	13.58	14.00	14.07	13.72	13.91
20-YEAR	13.32	13.66	13.58	14.00	14.11	13.73	13.72
30-YEAR	13.05	13.40	13.35	13.70	13.78	13.45	13.44
COMPOSITE							
OVER 10 YEARS (LONG-TERM) 7/	12.41	12.81	12.78	13.12	13.26	12.88	12.87
CORPORATE BONDS (MOODYS), SEASONED							
ALL INDUSTRIES	15.05	15.25	15.37	15.56	15.69	15.38	15.06
AAA	13.99	14.16	14.11	14.36	14.50	14.23	14.17
BAA	16.15	16.42	16.55	16.75	16.86	16.55	16.04
STATE & LOCAL BONDS (MOODYS), AAA	10.70	11.33	11.95	11.95	11.95	11.70	10.43
CONVENTIONAL MORTGAGES 8/	16.90	16.94	16.90	16.95	17.04	16.92	16.63

1. WEEKLY FIGURES ARE AVERAGES OF 7 CALENDAR DAYS ENDING ON WEDNESDAY OF THE CURRENT WEEK; MONTHLY FIGURES INCLUDE EACH CALENDAR DAY IN THE MONTH.
2. QUOTED ON BANK-DISCOUNT BASIS.
3. RATES ON COMMERCIAL PAPER PLACED FOR FIRMS WHOSE BOND RATING IS AA OR THE EQUIVALENT.
4. RATE CHARGED BY BANKS ON SHORT-TERM BUSINESS LOANS.
5. RATE FOR THE FEDERAL RESERVE BANK OF NEW YORK.
6. YIELDS ON ACTIVELY TRADED ISSUES ADJUSTED TO CONSTANT MATURITIES. SOURCE: U.S. TREASURY.
7. UNWEIGHTED AVERAGE OF ALL ISSUES OUTSTANDING OF BONDS NEITHER DUE NOR CALLABLE IN LESS THAN 10 YEARS, INCLUDING SEVERAL VERY LOW YIELDING "FLOWER" BONDS.
8. CONTRACT INTEREST RATES ON COMMITMENTS FOR FIRST MORTGAGES. SOURCE: FHLMC.

NOTE: WEEKLY AND MONTHLY FIGURES ARE AVERAGES OF DAILY RATES, EXCEPT FOR STATE & LOCAL BONDS AND CONVENTIONAL MORTGAGES, WHICH ARE BASED ON THURSDAY AND FRIDAY FIGURES RESPECTIVELY.

Source: U.S., Federal Reserve System, Board of Governors, *Federal Reserve Statistical Release—January 7, 1982.*

Figure 3-2. Adjustable-Rate Mortgage Indexes (Monthly Rate for June and December 1969–80)

	Mortgage Rates on Previously Occupied Homes	*3-Year Treasury Rates*	*6-Month Treasury Rates*		*Mortgage Rates on Previously Occupied Homes*	*3-Year Treasury Rates*	*6-Month Treasury Rates*
1969:				1975:			
June	7.64%	6.83%	6.725%	June	8.86%	7.17%	5.463%
December	8.08%	8.10%	7.788%	December	9.09%	7.43%	5.933%
1970:				1976:			
June	8.19%	7.84%	6.907%	June	8.82%	7.32%	5.784%
December	8.12%	5.75%	4.848%	December	8.90%	5.68%	4.513%
1971:				1977:			
June	7.38%	6.32%	4.890%	June	8.78%	6.39%	5.198%
December	7.51%	5.27%	4.199%	December	8.93%	7.30%	6.377%
1972:				1978:			
June	7.36%	5.64%	4.270%	June	9.27%	8.30%	7.200%
December	7.45%	6.01%	5.287%	December	9.85%	9.33%	9.397%
1973:				1979:			
June	7.64%	6.83%	7.234%	June	10.46%	8.95%	9.062%
December	8.46%	6.81%	7.444%	December	11.59%	10.71%	11.847%
1974:				1980:			
June	8.66%	8.15%	8.232%	June	12.88%	8.91%	7.218%
December	9.39%	7.24%	7.091%	December	13.15%	13.65%	14.770%

Source: "Rules and Regulations," *Federal Register*, March 27, 1981, vol. 46, no. 59, p. 18947.

Prepayment Any bank that offers or purchases an ARM mortgage must allow the borrower to prepay in whole or in part the mortgage at any time beginning thirty days prior to the first rate adjustment date, but the bank may impose a prepayment fee if the mortgage is paid off in full or in part prior to thirty days before the first rate adjustment date. The prepayment of ARMs is also affected by the proposed rule of June 2, 1982. According to Section 29.5 of the amendment, the mention of the ability of the borrower to pay off the mortgage beginning thirty days prior to the first rate adjustment date is deleted. The amendment states that the banks may impose penalties for the prepayment of any ARM, regardless of any state law that prohibits any such fees.

Assumption Any bank offering or purchasing the ARM is not required by the regulation to allow the ARM to be assumed by a new purchaser. The bank may include a due-on-sale or an acceleration-upon-sale clause allowing the rate on the mortgage to increase to market and the new purchaser to make application and qualify as did the present owner. It should be noted that this assumption provision is exempt from any limitations set by state law. In other words, the ARM is exempt from state law.

Disclosure As with any other alternative mortgage instrument, the bank is required to give full disclosure to the prospective borrower. The regulation requires the bank to give a disclosure when either written information about an ARM is given to a borrower or at the time of application. It would be advisable that a person interested in the ARM should secure a copy of the ARM disclosure before the time of application, in order to better understand the ramifications of the ARM.

In addition to the requirement as to the time the disclosure is to be given, the regulations require that the disclosure contain the following information:

1. The fact that the interest rate will change and a brief description of the ARM.

2. The index that will be used by the bank to calculate the rate adjustment and at least one publication that reports the index.

3. A chart showing the value of the index for the past ten years. This is to be shown on a semiannual basis. For example, the rate as of June and December of each of the years is shown in Figure 3-2.

4. The disclosure must indicate the rate adjustment frequency as well as an indication of any extension of the time period before the first adjustment date.

5. A description as to how a rate change is to be implemented. If the implementation is to include negative amortization, it is to be explained to the borrower.

6. A statement concerning the fees to be charged in connection with the ARM, including fees that will be due at closing.

7. Finally, the disclosure must contain a worst case example showing the effect on the P and I payment (principal and interest payment) on a $10,000 loan if the rate increased as rapidly as possible.

An example of the initial ARM disclosure is illustrated in Figure 3-3.

In addition to the initial disclosure, the bank must give a notice or disclosure to the borrower at least thirty days, and no more than forty-five days, prior to any rate change. The model notice contained in the regulation is illustrated in Figure 3-4.

Section 29.9 of the regulation requires that, prior to the institution of an ARM program by any bank, all loan documents and disclosures must be sent to the chief national bank examiner, Office of the Comptroller of the Currency, for review before the ARM may be offered to the public. There is one exception to this requirement: if the ARM offered by the bank has meaningful limitations on the amount of increases in the rate and payment, the documents and disclosures do not have to be reviewed before the offering of the ARM, but the Office of the Comptroller has the right at any time to require a bank to modify or terminate such a program that does not sufficiently protect the borrower.

The proposed rule changes add several additional items which may be included in the disclosure form. Three of these items are as follows:

1. The method used to calculate the initial monthly payment, if the initial monthly payment differs from the required monthly payment to pay the mortgage in full

2. Any rules relating to changes in the interest rate, installment payment amount, and/or increases in the outstanding loan balance

3. A statement, if appropriate, of the rules or conditions relating to refinancing of short-term and demand mortgage loans, prepayment, and assumption

ADJUSTABLE MORTGAGE LOAN (AML)

As was mentioned in the section on the adjustable-rate mortgages, the Federal Home Loan Bank Board was interested in a similar type of mortgage that would allow the federally chartered S and Ls (that is, savings and loan associations) to make loans that would reflect the associations' cost of funds and assure the associations a fair return on monies lent. So after soliciting comments from the general public, the savings and loan associations, the building industry, and any group that had an interest in this type of mortgage, the FHLBB published a regulation effective on April 30, 1981, allowing the federally chartered S and Ls to make, purchase, participate in, or otherwise deal in an adjustable mortgage loan instrument. It should be noted again that, with the issuance of this regulation, the FHLBB has replaced the regulation allowing federally chartered savings and loan associations to make the renegotiable-rate mortgage and the variable-rate mortgage. With the issuance of the regulation, the FHLBB has preempted all state laws that would directly or indirectly restrict a federally chartered association or a federally chartered savings bank from making an AML. This includes any state law that would limit the charging of interest upon interest.

As with the ARM, we will review this regulation in some detail, for the adjustable mortgage loan will be the type used by the savings associations to finance most real estate transactions in the United States.

Figure 3-3. Model Form for Initial Adjustable-Rate Mortgage Disclosure

Important Mortgage Loan Information—
Please Read Carefully

If you wish to apply for an Adjustable-Rate Mortgage (ARM) loan with ________________ National Bank, you should read the information below concerning the difference between this mortgage and other mortgages with which you may be familiar.

General Description of Adjustable-Rate Mortgage Loan

THE LOAN OFFERED BY ____________ NATIONAL BANK IS AN ADJUSTABLE-RATE MORTGAGE. ITS INTEREST RATE WILL CHANGE [fill in frequency] BASED ON MOVEMENTS OF AN INTEREST RATE INDEX. YOUR MONTHLY PAYMENTS WILL INCREASE IF THE INTEREST RATE RISES OR DECREASE IF THE INTEREST RATE FALLS. BECAUSE FUTURE MOVEMENTS OF THE INDEX ARE RELATED TO MARKET CONDITIONS THAT CANNOT BE PREDICTED, IT IS IMPOSSIBLE TO KNOW IN ADVANCE HOW MUCH YOU WILL HAVE TO PAY, EITHER EACH MONTH OR OVER THE LIFE OF THE LOAN. INTEREST RATE AND PAYMENT CHANGES WILL BE MADE ACCORDING TO CERTAIN RULES THAT ARE EXPLAINED BELOW.

Key Terms of ____________ National Bank's Adjustable Rate Mortgage

The following outline of the terms on ARM's offered by ____________ National Bank is intended for easy reference only. You will find other essential information in this disclosure statement and in the loan note itself.

Loan Term . . . .
Frequency of rate changes . . . .
*[Grace period before first rate change . . . .]
Interest rate index . . . .
Maximum rate change at one time . . . .
Maximum rate change over life of loan . . . .
*[Minimum rate change at one time . . . .]
*[Minimum increments of rate change . . . .]
*[Prepayment fee . . . .]
Assumability [assumable, not assumable *or* at lender's discretion] . . . .
Possibility of increasing loan balance [yes *or* no] . . . .

*Bracketed items and footnotes are instructions to national banks or contain optional language to be selected as appropriate.

How Your Adjustable-Rate Mortgage Would Work

Starting Interest Rate

The starting interest rate offered by ____________ National Bank on an ARM will be specified [at loan closing, when we make a loan commitment to you, other] based on market conditions at that time.

Frequency of Interest Rate Changes

Your interest rate will be reviewed every ________ beginning ________ after the date on which you take out your loan, and may increase or decrease at those times based on changes in the index.

Index for Measuring Interest Rate Changes

The index to which your interest rate will be tied is ________________________.
Information on this index is published monthly in ________________. The table below shows a ten-year history of movements of this index. This does not necessarily indicate how the index may perform in the future.

10-Year History of ________ Index

Date	*Index*	*Change from preceding rate*
1/1/x0	. . . .	. . . .
7/1/x0	. . . .	. . . .
1/1/x1	. . . .	. . . .
*	*	*
7/1/x9	. . . .	. . . .

Figure 3-3. continued

Size of Interest Rate Changes

The interest rate on your ARM will increase or decrease based on movements in the index. A change in the index of 1 percentage point will be translated into a 1 percentage point change of the same direction in your ARM interest rate. However, no single change in the interest rate will be more than ________ percentage points no matter how much the index may have moved. [Also, there will be no change in your interest rate if the index moves less than ______ percentage points.] All changes will be in increments of ______ percentage points.]

Mandatory and Optional Rate Changes

Decreases in your interest rate warranted by decreases in the index will always be automatic within the rules for maximum [and minimum] changes. However, increases warranted by increases in the index may be forgone at the bank's option. If the bank forgoes an interest rate increase, we may take it at a later interest rate change date, unless doing so would conflict with the carryover rule described below.

Carryover of Unused Index Changes

Changes in the index not passed on to you as changes in your ARM interest rate will be carried over to the next interest rate change date. This can happen when the index has moved more than the maximum permitted change (percentage points) [or less than a minimum permitted change (percentage points)] or when the bank has forgone an interest rate increase to which it is entitled. The carryover is the amount by which the net index change exceeds the net interest rate change since the loan was made. The net change is the difference between the interest rate (or index) on a given date and the interest rate (or index) on the date the loan was made. In addition to new index changes, index changes carried over may be passed on to you at the next rate adjustment date as a change in your ARM interest rate. However, we may not pass these carryovers on to you to the extent they have been offset by an opposite movement in the index as of that date. Also, if the total of the new index change and the carryover still exceeds the maximum permitted change (percentage points) [or is less than a minimum permitted change (percentage points)] the excess must be carried over again.

[The following example may be included at the bank's option:

An example shows how this carryover rule works. Suppose the index increases by 1.60 percentage points during the first period, but your rate change is limited by the rules to 1.00 percentage point. The remaining .60 percentage point would be carried over, so that at your next rate change date:

If the index in the new period had *stayed the same*, your mortgage rate would *still rise* by .60 percentage point.

If the index had decreased by .20 percentage point your mortgage rate would *still rise* by .40 percentage point (the difference between the increase that was carried over and the decline).

If the index had *decreased* by 1.0 percentage point your mortgage rate would *decrease by only* .40 percentage point (again, the difference between the new decrease and the carried over increase).

If the index had *increased* by .70 percentage point, your mortgage rate would increase by only 1.0 percentage point because of the 1.0 percentage point limit, *but* there would be a *new carryover* of .30 percentage point into the next rate change period (the difference between the 1.0 percentage point limit and the 1.30 percentage points justified by the old carryover plus the index change).]

Payment Changes

Changes in the interest rate on your mortgage will mean that your monthly payment will change to an amount sufficient to repay your loan over its life at the new interest rate.

Notice of Rate Changes

______________ National Bank will send you notice of any rate change at least 30 days before it becomes effective. The notice will tell you how the index has changed and how your interest rate and payment schedule will be affected. This notice will also be sent whenever the bank forgoes an interest rate increase it is permitted to take [and/but not] when the index has not changed at a rate adjustment date. All interest rate changes will be based on index information available at the time the notice is sent, rather than when the rate change goes into effect.

Prepayment Penalty

You may prepay an ARM in whole or in part without penalty at any time after the first notice of index movement has been sent to you [or, if the index has not changed, any time after the last date on which such a notice would have been sent]. This prepayment may be a lump sum payment of all or part of the remaining debt or may be in the form of larger monthly payments than required under the terms of the loan. ______________ National Bank imposes a penalty charge of ______ for prepayments prior to the first rate change notice date.

Assumption of Mortgage Loan

Your ARM may be assumed by a purchaser of your home who meets our credit standards. [We have the right to change the loan terms, including the interest rate, upon assumption, and we may also charge the purchaser assumption fees.]

Figure 3-3. continued

Fees

You will be charged fees by ________________ National Bank and by other persons in connection with the origination of an ARM. We will give you an estimate of these fees within 3 days after receiving your loan application. However, ________________ National Bank will not charge you any finance or processing fees at the time of any rate adjustment.

How Rapidly Rising Interest Rates Could Affect Your Adjustable-Rate Mortgage Loan

The following table shows the effect a 10 percentage point increase in the index rate, taken as rapidly as possible, would have on monthly payments on a $10,000 ARM made at a starting interest rate of ______ %. To figure the equivalent potential payment increases for your mortgage, simply multiply the payments in the table times 2 for a $20,000 loan, times 3 for a $30,000 loan, etc.

[The table that follows would apply to an ARM with interest rate adjustments occurring every six months, a one percentage point periodic interest rate limit, an aggregate interest rate cap in excess of 10 percentage points, and an initial contract interest rate of 10%. Lender should insert relevant example.

Payments No.	*Year No.*	*Interest rate (percent)*	*Amount of payments*
1 to 6	1	10.0	$ 87.76
7 to 12		11.0	95.18
13 to 18	2	12.0	102.71
19 to 24		13.0	110.34
25 to 30	3	14.0	118.04
31 to 36		15.0	125.81
37 to 42	4	16.0	133.63
43 to 48		17.0	141.49
49 to 54	5	18.0	149.39
55 to 60		19.0	157.32
61 to 360	6+	20.0	165.27

Source: "Rules and Regulations," *Federal Register*, March 27, 1981, vol. 46, no. 59, pp. 18945-946.

Figure 3-4. Periodic Notice Form

Important Notice of Intent To Change the Interest Rate on
Your Adjustable-Rate Mortgage Loan

Dear ________________ :

This is to inform you that on [date] ________________ National Bank intends to [increase, decrease] the interest rate on your ARM loan from ____% to ____%. Beginning with your [date] payment, please remit your payments at this new amount.

The index upon which interest rate changes on your loan are based was ____% when your loan was made and is currently ____%, an [increase, decrease] of ____ percentage points. The interest rate on your loan was ____% when your loan was made and will be changed to ____% at the upcoming rate adjustment date, an [increase, decrease] of ____ percentage points. [Because the net index change exceeds the net interest rate change on your ARM, an index change of ____% will be carried over to the next period.]

You may repay the entire loan or any part of it without penalty at any time.

Thank you for your attention to this matter.

Source: "Rules and Regulations," *Federal Register*, March 27, 1981, vol. 46, no. 49, p. 18946.

Definition

Just what is the AML? The adjustable mortgage loan can be defined as

> *a loan that permits adjustment of the interest rate. Adjustments to the interest rate may be implemented through changes in the payment amount and/or through adjustments to the outstanding principal loan balance or loan term, provided that the total loan term may not exceed 40 years, and shall reflect the movement of one of the indices authorized.*[4]

As with the ARM, the AML may include a mortgage whose rate is adjusted periodically, or a fixed-rate mortgage that has the feature of rate adjustment by means of a demand feature or clause. These types of mortgages would be equivalent to a variable-rate mortgage and, in the case of the latter, a renegotiable-rate mortgage.

Major Provisions

Rate or payment change The regulation adopted by the FHLBB contains no provision to limit the amount the interest rate and/or the payment may change. The regulation also does not limit the frequency of rate and/or payment adjustment, thus the adjustment could be as often as every thirty days if the selected rate index changes that often. This is a major difference from the ARM authorized by the comptroller of the currency, which contains such limitations.

According to the FHLBB, the associations need the flexibility to design the frequency and amount of increase to meet the demands of their particular market, and the FHLBB believes that, in order to build public confidence in the AML, lenders will adopt limitations on the amount and frequency due to the competition in the marketplace. It is also thought that those in the secondary market who will purchase the AML will require such limitations on the rate and frequency of rate and/or payment increases.

Rate change indexes The adopted regulation states the following:

> *For the purpose of adjusting the interest rate, an association may use any interest rate index that is readily verifiable by the borrower and is beyond the control of the association.*[5]

Since one specific index will not meet the needs of all of the associations, the regulation does name the following indexes for possible use:

> (i) The national average mortgage contract rate for major lenders on the purchase of previously-occupied homes, as computed monthly by the Board, published in the Board's *Journal*, and made available in news releases;
>
> (ii) The average cost of funds to FSLIC-insured savings and loan associations, either for all Federal Home Loan Bank Districts or for a particular District or Districts, as computed semi-annually by the Board, published in the Board's *Journal*, and made available in news releases;
>
> (iii) The monthly average of weekly auction rates on United States Treasury bills with a maturity of three months or six months, as published in the *Federal Reserve Bulletin* and made available by the Federal Reserve Board in Statistical Release G.13(415) during the first week of each month;
>
> (iv) The monthly average yield on United States Treasury securities adjusted to a constant maturity of one, two, three, or five years, as published in the *Federal Reserve Bulletin* and made available by the Federal Reserve Board in Statistical Release G.13(415) during the first week of each month; or
>
> (v) Any other interest-rate index that meets the requirements of this paragraph.[6]

Thus, prior to the rate being adjusted in either direction, the change must be reflected in the chosen interest-rate index named in the original loan documents and selected by the lender. Since all of the above indexes are either published in the *Federal Home Loan Bank Board Journal* or the *Federal Reserve Bulletin*, real estate practitioners should be familiar with each of the publications and have access to each in order to better advise their clients of the status of the indexes used by savings associations in their area.

In addition to the above publications that include the indexes, the Federal Home Loan Bank Board now publishes a regular News Release entitled *AML Index Rates* (Figure 3-5). This release gives the value of two of the suggested indexes. The indexes are: (1) the contract interest rate on conventional mortgage loans closed for purchasing previously occupied single-family homes; and (2) the national average cost of funds for associations insured by the Federal Savings and Loan Insurance Corporation (FSLIC). You can contact the FHLBB to be added to the list to receive this release.

Figure 3-5. AML Index Rates

NEWS

FEDERAL HOME LOAN BANK SYSTEM FEDERAL HOME LOAN MORTGAGE CORPORATION FEDERAL SAVINGS & LOAN INSURANCE CORPORATION

1700 G Street, N.W., Washington, D.C. 20552 Telephone (202) 377-6923

FOR RELEASE TO A.M. NEWSPAPERS
Monday, December 14, 1981

For further information, contact:
(202) 377-6923

AML INDEX RATES

The Federal Home Loan Bank Board reported today that the final average contract interest rate on conventional mortgage loans closed for purchasing previously occupied single-family homes by all major lenders during early November was 15.80 percent. A new final average covering early December will be announced on or about January 12, 1982.

On September 29, 1981, the Bank Board reported that the national average cost of funds for FSLIC-insured associations for the six months ending June 30, 1981, was 10.31 percent. An average covering the six months ending December 31, 1981, will be announced in March 1982.

These two indexes are among those authorized for use by Federally chartered savings and loan associations in changing rates on adjustable mortgage loans made in accordance with Federal Savings and Loan System Regulation 545.6-4a, as amended April 30, 1981. Information about other authorized indexes is available from other sources.

Interested parties may also receive up-to-date information with regard to these two indexes by calling (800) 424-5405 (or 377-6988 if in the Washington, D.C.-MD-VA metropolitan area). Both numbers provide a recorded message of the most recent available information with regard to these indexes.

(more)

Figure 3-5. continued

National Average Mortgage Contract Rate for Major Lenders on the Purchase of Previously-Occupied Homes

Announcement Date	Index Month	Index Rate (%)
April 3, 1980	January 1980	11.78
April 7, 1980	February 1980	12.30
May 7, 1980	March 1980	12.56
May 21, 1980	April 1980	13.21
June 11, 1980	May 1980	13.74
July 11, 1980	June 1980	12.88
August 11, 1980	July 1980	12.23
September 11, 1980	August 1980	11.89
October 10, 1980	September 1980	12.00
November 10, 1980	October 1980	12.31
December 11, 1980	November 1980	12.85
January 13, 1981	December 1980	13.15
February 11, 1981	January 1981	13.24
March 12, 1981	February 1981	13.73
April 10, 1981	March 1981	13.91
May 12, 1981	April 1981	13.99
June 10, 1981	May 1981	14.19
July 13, 1981	June 1981	14.40
August 12, 1981	July 1981	14.77
September 14, 1981	August 1981	15.03
October 13, 1981	September 1981	15.38
November 12, 1981	October 1981	15.47
December 14, 1981	November 1981	15.80

National Average Cost of Funds to FSLIC-Insured Savings and Loan Associations

Announcement Date	Semiannual Period	Index Rate (%)
July 1, 1979	July - December, 1978	6.79
September 21, 1979	January - June, 1979	7.23
March 11, 1980	July - December, 1979	7.71
September 15, 1980	January - June, 1980	8.77
March 18, 1981	July - December, 1980	9.11
September 29, 1981	January - June, 1981	10.31

The mortgage contract interest rate is a weighted average of rates reported for loan transactions during the first five working days of the index month by a sample of major mortgage lenders. It reflects rates on new transactions, not rates on outstanding loans.

Cost of funds is defined as interest (dividends) paid or accrued on deposits, on FHLB advances and on other borrowed money during a half-year period as a percent of average deposits and borrowings. (Average based on seven month-end figures; ratio is annualized by doubling.) It reflects rates on all funds, not on new funds.

Source: U.S., Federal Home Loan Bank Board, *News Release: AML Index Rates*, December 14, 1981, pp. 1-2.

Figure 3-6. Adjustable Mortgage Loan Disclosure

Important Information About the Adjustable Mortgage Loan—Please Read Carefully

You have received an application form for an adjustable mortgage loan ("AML"). The AML may differ from other mortgages with which you are familiar.

General Description of Adjustable Mortgage Loan

The adjustable mortgage loan is a flexible loan instrument. Its interest rate may be adjusted by the lender from time to time. Such adjustments will result in increases or decreases in your payment amount, in the outstanding principal loan balance, in the loan term, or in all three (see discussion below relating to these types of adjustments). Federal regulations place no limit on the amount by which the interest rate may be adjusted either at any one time or over the life of the loan, or on the frequency with which it may be adjusted. Adjustments to the interest rate must reflect the movement of a single, specified index (see discussion below). This does not mean that the particular loan agreement you sign must, by law, permit unlimited interest-rate changes. It merely means that, if you desire to have certain rate-adjustment limitations placed in your loan agreement, that is a matter you should negotiate with the lender. You may also want to make inquiries concerning the loan terms offered by other lenders on AMLs to compare the terms and conditions.

Another flexible feature of the AML is that the regular payment amount may be increased or decreased by the lender from time to time to reflect changes in the interest rate. Again, Federal regulations place no limitations on the amount by which the lender may adjust payments at any one time, or on the frequency of payment adjustments. If you wish to have particular provisions in your loan agreement regarding adjustments to the payment amount, you should negotiate such terms with the lender.

A third flexible feature of the AML is that the outstanding principal loan balance (the total amount you owe) may be increased or decreased from time to time when, because of adjustments to the interest rate, the payment amount is either too small to cover interest due on the loan, or larger than is necessary to pay off the loan over the remaining term of the loan.

The final flexible feature of the AML is that the loan term may be lengthened or shortened from time to time, corresponding to an increase or decrease in the interest rate. When the term is extended in connection with a rate increase, the payment amount does not have to be increased to the same extent as if the term had not been lengthened. In no case may the total term of the loan exceed 40 years.

The combination of these four basic features allow an association to offer a variety of mortgage loans. For example, one type of loan could permit rate adjustments with corresponding changes in the payment amount. Alternatively, a loan could permit rate adjustments to occur more frequently than payment adjustments, limit the amount by which the payment could be adjusted, and/or provide for corresponding adjustments to the principal loan balance.

Index

Adjustments to the interest rate of an AML must correspond directly to the movement of an index, subject to such rate-adjustment limitations as may be contained in the loan contract. If the index has moved down, the lender must reduce the interest rate by at least the decrease in the index. If the index has moved up, the lender has the right to increase the interest rate by that amount. Although taking such an increase is optional by the lender, you should be aware that the lender has this right and may become contractually obligated to exercise it.

[Name and description of index to be used for applicant's loan, initial index value (if known) or date of initial index value, a source or sources where the index may be readily obtained by the borrower, and the high and low index rates during the previous calendar year.]

Key Terms of Federal Savings and Loan Association's Adjustable Mortgage Loan

Following is a summary of the basic terms on the type of AML to be offered to you. This summary is intended for reference purposes only. Important information relating specifically to your loan will be contained in the loan agreement.

[Provide summary of basic terms of the loan, including the loan term, the frequency of rate changes, the frequency of payment changes, the maximum rate change, if any, at one time, the maximum rate change, if any, over the life of the loan, the maximum payment change, if any, at one time, minimum increments, if any, of rate changes, and whether there will be adjustments to the principal loan balance, in the following format:

Loan term . . . .
Frequency of rate changes . . . .
Frequency of payment changes . . . .]

How Your Adjustable Mortgage Loan Would Work

Initial Interest Rate

The initial interest rate offered by ______________ Federal Savings and Loan Association on your AML will be established and disclosed to you on [commitment date, etc.] based on market conditions at the time.

[Insert a short description of each of the key terms of the type of AML to be offered to the borrower, using headings where appropriate.]

Prepayment The regulation states that an AML may be prepaid in full or in part at any time without penalty.

Assumption Unlike the ARM authorized by the comptroller of the currency, the FHLBB regulation makes no mention of assumption, thus leaving the question of assumption up to the individual association. It is imperative, therefore, that the real estate professional be familiar with the policy for each association in his or her area.

Negative amortization Under the FHLBB's regulation, negative amortization is authorized. This can occur when, after a rate adjustment, the payment is not sufficient to pay the interest due. The amount of interest not paid by the monthly payment will be added to the loan balance.

To reduce the effect of negative amortization, the term of the mortgage can be extended up to forty years, and if this is not sufficient to assure the payment of the loan in the remaining term, the association must schedule a "catch-up" adjustment at least once every five years so that the regular payment using the present interest rate would be sufficient to repay the mortgage over the remaining term of the mortgage. Thus, at the end of any five-year period, the borrower could possibly be required to make a large cash payment to reduce the principal amount, in order for the payments to be sufficient to repay the mortgage in the remaining term of the mortgage.

Disclosure As with the ARM, there are two required disclosures for the AML. The first disclosure will be given at the time of receipt of an application or upon the request of a potential borrower. The disclosure form will contain specific information about the AML as shown in Figure 3-6, which should be read carefully.

The second required disclosure is one that is sent to the borrower at least thirty days, but no more than forty-five days, prior to an adjustment date. This notice will contain the following:

(1) The fact that the payment on the loan with the association, secured by a mortgage or deed of trust on property located at the appropriate address, is scheduled to be adjusted on a particular date;

(2) The outstanding balance of the loan on the adjustment date, assuming timely payment of the remaining payments due by that date;

(3) The interest rate on the loan as of the adjustment date, the index value on which that rate is based, the period of time for which that interest rate will be in effect, the next following payment

Figure 3-6. continued

Notice of Payment Adjustments

__________________ Federal Savings and Loan Association will send you notice of an adjustment to the payment amount at least 30 but not more than 45 days before it becomes effective. [Describe what information the notice will contain.]

Prepayment Penalty

You may prepay an AML in whole or in part *without penalty at any time* during the term of the loan.

Fees

You will be charged fees by __________________ Federal Savings and Loan Association and by other persons in connection with the origination of your AML. The association will give you an estimate of these fees after receiving your loan application. However, you will not be charged any costs or fees in connection with any regularly-scheduled adjustment to the interest rate, the payment, the outstanding principal loan balance, or the loan term initiated by the lender.

Example of Operation of Your Type of AML

[Set out an example of the operation of the type of AML to be offered to the borrower, including, where appropriate, the use of a table.]

Source: "Rules and Regulations," *Federal Register*, April 30, 1981, vol. 46, no. 83, p. 24153.

adjustment date, and the rate adjustment dates, if any, between the upcoming payment adjustment date and the next following payment adjustment date;

(4) The payment amount as of the payment adjustment date;

(5) The date(s), if any, on which the rate was adjusted since the last payment adjustment, the rates on each such rate adjustment date, and the index values corresponding to each such date;

(6) The dates, if any, on which the outstanding principal loan balance was adjusted since the last payment adjustment, and the net change in the outstanding principal loan balance since the last payment adjustment;

(7) The fact that the borrower may pay off the entire loan or a part of it without penalty at any time; and

(8) The title and telephone number of an association employee who can answer questions about the notice.[7]

Administrative fees The regulation forbids any association from charging any type of fee connected with any interest rate change. This includes, but is not limited to, processing fees, administrative fees, closing fees, and finance charges or fees.

Payment-capped mortgages The regulation allows the associations to offer payment-capped mortgages. Under this provision, the FHLBB allows two types of capped mortgages. The first is the *interest-rate-capped mortgage*. This capped mortgage limits the amount that the interest rate may change, thus limiting the amount the monthly payment can change. The second type is the *payment-capped mortgage*. With this type of mortgage, the interest rate on the loan is adjusted to reflect the changes in the interest rate index; but to avoid any sharp increases in the monthly payment, any increase in the monthly payment is limited.

This feature of the FHLBB regulation is different from the regulation of the comptroller of the currency for the ARM in that all capped mortgages must be approved prior to being offered by a bank.

NATIONAL CREDIT UNION ADMINISTRATION'S ARM

Before we leave the discussion of the ARM and the AML, we should review the ARM authorized by the National Credit Union Administration (NCUA). On July 22, 1981, the NCUA implemented a rule allowing all federally chartered credit unions to make an adjustable-rate mortgage. Even though this mortgage is called *ARM*, it more closely resembles the AML authorized by the Federal Home Loan Bank Board.

On June 11, 1981, the NCUA board invited public comment on a proposal to allow the federal credit unions to make the ARM. According to NCUA, the majority of the comments received were favorable, but there were several recommendations. These recommendations were incorporated into a proposed rule that was published for comment on December 1, 1981. Now let us review some of the major provisions of the final rule.

Definition

The final rule defines the adjustable-rate mortgage loan as

> *a mortgage loan which permits the periodic adjustment of the rate of interest on the loan in response to the movement of an index which was agreed upon in advance by the borrower and the Federal credit union.*[8]

One can see that, by this definition, the ARM loan authorized is similar to those authorized by the FHLBB and the Comptroller of the Currency.

Interest Rate Index

According to section (e) of the rule, the Federal credit union may use any index whose movement is beyond the control of the credit union and is readily verifiable by the borrower. One can see that this is similar to the wording contained in the FHLBB rule authorizing the Federal savings and loans to make the AML. As was mentioned in the definition, the index to be used must be agreed upon in advance by the union and the borrower. Thus, this indicates that the index to be used is a negotiable item, and must be shown in the original loan documents.

As with the ARM and the FHLBB's AML, any increase or decrease in the face interest rate of the mortgage must be reflected in a corresponding movement in the index. All decreases indicated by movement in the index are mandatory except for certain limitations:

1. The decrease is offset by an amount of a previously indicated increase not taken at that time and postponed or carried over.
2. The decrease exceeds any limitation or cap on the amount the interest rate may increase or decrease.
3. The indicated decrease is less than one eighth of a percent
4. If there is a decrease that would move the interest rate to a level that is lower than a minimum rate which was agreed upon between the union and the borrower in advance of the execution of the original loan documents

Frequency of Adjustments

According to the rule, the interest rate of the mortgage may be adjusted as often as every thirty days as long as the adjustment is based on the movement of the index.

Implementation of Adjustments

The final rule states that the adjustment in the interest rate may be implemented through the increasing of the monthly payment, negative amortization, extension of the loan term, maturity, or a combination of any of these methods. It should be noted that the rule does allow for an "adjustment cap." Thus, the amount of increase or decrease may be limited. This must be contained in the original loan documents and negotiated prior to the execution of the original loan documents.

If the option of extension of loan term or maturity is used, the rule states that no adjustment may cause the maturity to exceed forty years.

Disclosures

Initial or application disclosure The proposed rule issued for public comment had two suggestions for initial disclosure. One of the proposed methods of disclosure was that the disclosure be made in accordance with the provision of the Truth-in-Lending Act (Regulation Z). The second method proposed would require the unions to make the disclosures contained in the Truth-in-Lending Act, but within three days of the application, and in addition to the information required to be disclosed by the Truth-in-Lending Act, the union would have to disclose the following:

1. The index to be used
2. How often an increase or decrease may occur
3. How any increase or decrease may be calculated

After receiving comments and reviewing the regulations implementing the new Truth-in-Lending Simplification Act, NCUA felt that the initial disclosure should be made, in form and content, similar to that required for an adjustable-rate mortgage under Regulation Z. It should be noted that NCUA did state that, if the credit union does not use the form suggested by the Truth-in-Lending Act, the union may develop its own form, but it must be a "plain language" form.

Rate and payment adjustments There is no requirement that the borrower be notified of any payment or rate change, but NCUA feels that the union will, in its normal business activities, provide some type of notification to the borrower.

Costs or Fees

As with the other ARM and AML, the regulation states that the borrower may not be charged any fees or costs in conjunction with the regularly scheduled interest rate and/or payment adjustment.

SHARED-APPRECIATION MORTGAGE (SAM)[9]

A *shared-appreciation mortgage* (SAM) is a mortgage in which the borrower agrees to share in the appreciation of the property. In return for the equity position, the lender will give the borrower an interest rate that is below the rate charged for a standard mortgage.

The primary reason for the Federal Home Loan Bank Board to authorize federally chartered savings and loans to make the SAM is that the lower the interest rate, the lower the monthly payment, and thus the income of the borrower can be less to qualify for the mortgage. In addition to the lower interest rate, the SAM differs from the standard mortgage in two other ways. First, the payments are based on an amortization period for up to forty years, but the mortgage is due and payable no later than the tenth year with guaranteed refinancing. Second, the SAM has a contingent interest feature. *Contingent interest* can be defined as an interest charge, assessed by the lender making the mortgage, that is equal to a specified percentage of the property's net appreciation over the life of the mortgage.

In regard to the percentage of the appreciation that the lender may require to make the mortgage, the Federal Home Loan Bank Board has set a limit of 40 percent; most of the savings and loans charge 30 percent.

It should be noted that if the contingent interest is due and payable prior to the sale of the property, the borrower may pay the contingent interest in full, or the amount of the mortgage and the contingent interest can be refinanced by the lender at the prevailing market rates.

Net Appreciated Value

How do we calculate net appreciation or the net appreciated value? It may be figured by two methods, depending on whether the loan goes to maturity and is prepaid in full or the property is sold or transferred. If the property is sold or transferred, the savings and loan making the mortgage may choose to accept the net sales price as the determination of the market value. According to the proposed regulations of the FHLBB, the *net selling price* is the gross selling price of the property less certain selling expenses such as real estate commissions, advertising, transfer fees, legal fees, and escrow and recording fees.

If the savings and loan does not wish to accept the net sales price or if the loan matures or the borrower pays the loan in full prior to the maturity date, the market value would be established by an appraisal. The appraiser is agreed upon by both the borrower and the savings and loan from a list of appraisers who have made appraisals that have been accepted by the FHLBB. If the borrower and the savings and loan cannot agree on a single appraiser, then the borrower and the savings and loan will each select an appraiser and the market value will be the average of the two appraisals.

After the market value is established by the appraisal method, the net appreciated value will be established by subtracting from the market value the following:

1. The original cost of the property
2. The cost of any capital improvements made to the property
3. The cost of the appraisal or appraisals needed to establish the market value

The original cost of the property is calculated by adding to the cost of the property any of the following:

1. Commissions
2. Cost of title search or title insurance
3. Legal, appraisal, and inspection fees
4. Payments to clear prior liens

Loan Term

The term of the SAM has been proposed by the FHLBB to be a maximum of ten years. The reason for the relatively short term is twofold:

1. If the term of the SAM was thirty years and the borrower held the SAM to maturity, the net appreciation of the property could be so great that the borrower could not be able to afford the cost of refinancing and thus would have to sell his or her home to pay the contingent interest.
2. With the increasing cost of money to the associations, the holding of a below-market interest rate loan by a lender to the thirty-year maturity could have an adverse impact on the profits of the lender.

Refinancing

Because of the relatively short term of the SAM, the proposed rules of the FHLBB provide for guaranteed refinancing of the outstanding principal amount of the SAM plus the full amount of the contingent interest if the loan is not paid in full or the property is sold prior to the maturity of the mortgage. The borrower will be allowed to choose the type of mortgage for refinancing the SAM. The mortgage may be a fixed-rate or a flexible-payment mortgage other than a SAM.

The minimum term of the refinancing of the SAM is thirty years, and all of the fees associated with the refinancing of the property will be borne by the association, except the cost of the appraisal and that is to be paid by the borrower.

If the borrower should decide to refinance, unless the interest rates have fallen below those of the original SAM, the borrower's monthly payment may increase greatly.

Required Disclosures

The FHLBB-proposed rules require two disclosures. The first disclosure is at the time of application and the second disclosure will be sent to the borrower at least ninety days prior to the maturity of the mortgage. These disclosures are shown in Figures 3-7 and 3-8.

Figure 3-7. Required disclosure sent to borrower at time of application

Information About the Appreciation Mortgage

You have received an application form for an appreciation mortgage. The appreciation mortgage differs from other mortgages commonly in use in that there are two elements used in calculating interest with the appreciation mortgage. The first element of interest is fixed at the beginning of the loan and is paid over the term of the loan as part of the monthly installment. The second element of interest is contingent in nature, based upon the amount of the increased value of the residence securing the loan between the time of purchase and either the maturity or payment in full of the loan or the sale or transfer of the property. The amount of Contingent Interest which you will pay cannot be determined at this time.

The contingent interest on the shared appreciation mortgage is equal to a percentage of the appreciation of the property not to exceed 40%, as agreed to by the borrower and lender. Contingent interest is payable on the earlier of the maturity or payment in full of the loan or the sale or transfer of the property. The obligation to pay contingent interest will diminish the amount of appreciation realized by you on the property. The attached table shows examples of the total cost of a shared appreciation mortgage and comparison with conventional mortgages. Contingent interest is calculated as follows:

Market value of the property [The association may choose to use the amount realized on the sale or transfer of the property as a measure of market value.]

- (less) Cost of the property to you [This amount includes certain costs paid by you incident to the the purchase. In the event that the loan will be used to refinance the property the cost of the property will be determined by the market value as of the time that the loan is made.].

- (less) Cost of capital improvements made by you [You will be required to provide proof of such costs.].

- (less) Cost of appraisal [If used to determine market value.].

= (equals) Net appreciated value.

X (times) Percentage of net appreciated value to be paid by the borrower.

= (equals) Total Contingent Interest.

If the property is not sold prior to the maturity of the loan, the lender must offer to refinance the outstanding obligation on the loan, including any contingent interest. The lender must offer refinancing using any fully amortizing mortgage instrument with a term of at least 30 years. You may request a loan with a shorter term. Refinancing may be by use of any home mortgage loan being made by the association at the time of refinancing under terms and conditions, including interest rates, then prevailing for home mortgage loans. If the association offers more than one type of loan for refinancing, you may choose between them. The association may not look to the forecast of your income in offering to refinance. However, as a condition of refinancing, the association may require that you satisfy any claims against your property arising since making of the original loan. The interest rate and specific terms of any refinancing are subject to then-prevailing market conditions. The interest rate and monthly payment on renewal cannot be determined at this time.

Use of the appreciation mortgage may have income tax or estate planning consequences. For further information, consult your accountant, attorney or other financial advisor.

[A side-by-side comparison of a SAM and a comparable standard mortgage instrument (with a fixed interest rate, level payments and full amortization) must be made in the following format. The initial property value, loan amount, fixed interest rate and ratio for sharing appreciation do not have to be exactly the same as the loan for which the applicant is applying, but must be similar enough to permit a fair comparison.].

Figure 3-7. continued

Examples of Total Cost of a Shared Appreciation Mortgage
[Initial property value[1]]

Loan amount -percentage of appreciation to lender	A number not to exceed 40		
	Monthly[2] interest	*Contingent[3] interest*	*Total interest cost*
5-year life:			
Conventional mortgage at ____% interest			
Shared appreciation mortgage at:			
[x]% fixed interest[2] and 5% property appreciation			
[x]% fixed interest[2] and 10% property appreciation			
[x]% fixed interest[2] and 15% property appreciation			
10-year life:			
Conventional mortgage at ____% interest			
Shared appreciation mortgage at:			
[x]% fixed interest[2] and 5% property appreciation			
[x]% fixed interest[2] and 10% property appreciation			
[x]% fixed interest[2] and 15% property appreciation			

[1] This chart assumes that no improvements to the property are made by the borrower. The cost of such improvements would be deducted from appreciation prior to calculating contingent interest.

[2] A fixed rate of interest of [x]% is assumed. The fixed rate on your loan may not be the same.

[3] Contingent interest equal to [number not to exceed 40] percent of net appreciated value is assumed. The rate on your loan may not be the same. This chart assumes that there are no costs incident to sale. Such costs are deducted prior to calculating interest.

Date Received: ____________________

Borrower Signature: ____________________

Lending Officer: ____________________

Source: "Proposed Rules," *Federal Register*, October 8, 1980, vol. 45, no. 197, p. 66806.

SAM Appeal

The SAM will probably be more attractive to the first-time homebuyers who do not have sufficient funds for a large down payment, and who traditionally do not reside for a long time in their first house and thus will sell prior to the term of the original SAM. Often, the first-time homebuyer is looking for a reduced payment; the following example will illustrate how the SAM can meet this desire.

Let's assume that the prospective homebuyer is looking for a mortgage of $50,000 with a term of thirty years, using a standard fixed-rate mortgage. With an interest rate of 13 percent, the monthly principal and interest payment would be $553.10. If the prospective borrower would use the SAM and give the lender a contingent interest covenant that would be equal to 30 percent of the appreciation and the lender would in turn give the borrower an interest rate of 9.5 percent, the monthly P and I payment would be reduced to $420.43. Let's assume that the taxes and insurance on the subject property would be $1000 per year or $83.33 per month. The total payments would be $634.43 for the fixed-rate mortgage and $503.76 for the SAM. In the underwriting of the mortgage, if the standard 25 percent rule is used, the borrower would need an income of $30,549 to qualify for the fixed-rate mortgage; but using the SAM, the annual income is reduced to $24,181. Thus, more borrowers could qualify to purchase homes using the SAM.

VARIABLE-RATE MORTGAGE (VRM)

A *variable-rate mortgage* can be defined as a long-term mortgage whose interest rate is adjusted at set intervals using a prescribed reference, or index rate, to establish the rate. In other words, with this type of alternative financing, the term of the mortgage remains constant and with each payment the principal

Figure 3-8. Required disclosure sent to borrower at least ninety days before mortgage matures

NOTICE

Your loan with ______________ Federal Savings and Loan Association, secured by a [mortgage/deed of trust] on the property located at [address], is due and payable on [no earlier than 90 days from date of notice]. Unless you choose to refinance the loan as set forth below, the outstanding indebtedness on your loan shall be payable on [no earlier than 90 days from date of notice]. The outstanding indebtedness on your loan on that date shall consist of the principal balance of [actual principal balance] and contingent interest in the amount of [number not to exceed 40] percent of the amount of appreciation on the property since the beginning of the loan. The amount of appreciation is determined by subtracting from the value of the property as of the date the loan is due (i) the cost of the property to you, (ii) the cost of improvements made by you, and (iii) the cost of appraisal to determine the value of the property.

The appraisal shall be performed by an appraiser selected by you and the association from a list of appraisers who have made appraisals accepted by the Federal Home Loan Mortgage Corporation or the Federal National Mortgage Association. You may obtain a copy of this list from the association. In the event that you do not agree with the association on the selection of an appraiser, you and the association shall each select an appraiser from the list and the market value shall be determined by an average of the two appraisals. In the event that you do not select an appraiser within 30 days from receipt of this notice, the appraisal shall be performed by an appraiser selected by the association.

The association is required to provide you with the opportunity to refinance the entire amount due with a loan for a term of not less than 30 years. Refinancing may be by use of any home mortgage loan presently being made by the association, including [specify types of loans being made], under current terms and conditions, including interest rates. The association may not look to the forecast of your income in offering to refinance the loan. However, as a condition of refinancing, the association may require that you satisfy any claims against your property arising since the making of the original loan. You may contact the association regarding the terms and conditions of such refinancing.

For further information with regard to this notice, please contact [title and telephone number of association employee.]

Source: "Proposed Rules," *Federal Register,* October 8, 1980, vol. 45, no. 197, p. 66806.

balance declines. The only variable is the interest rate, which can either increase or decrease, based on the prescribed interest rate index.

Interest Rate Indexes[10]

There are two basic types of interest rate indexes:

1. *Cost of funds index,* based on the cost of funds, or what the savings and loan association has to pay to depositors on savings accounts
2. *Mortgage rate index,* based on the average of interest charged in the market place

There are three cost of funds indexes that could be used:

1. The savings and loan association's own cost of funds, as calculated by the institution. This index fails to meet one of the very desirable criteria, and that is that the index be calculated and published by a reputable source and not subject to the influence of the lender.
2. The average cost of funds of the insured institutions located in a city or state, as calculated by the Federal Home Loan Bank Board.
3. The average cost of funds of FSLIC-insured institutions in the United States, as calculated by the Federal Home Loan Bank Board twice each year.

Rate Adjustment[11]

Some VRMs written in the United States have a limit to the amount that the interest rate may be increased. The regulations covering the rate adjustments state that any increase in rate based on the rate index can be made at the option of the lender, but any decrease in interest rate based on the rate index is mandatory and must be made.

Some VRM loan documents allow the rate to be adjusted only once a year or less often with a maximum adjustment of 0.5 percent each year and a maximum increase of 2.5 percent over the life of the mortgage. The Federal Home Loan Bank Board, prior to the cancellation of the VRM, had proposed the following amendments to their original rate adjustment rules:

1. The rate may be adjusted every six months after the first regular monthly loan payment
2. Once the adjustment period has been established, its length may not be altered (for example, if a savings and loan establishes twelve months as the period between the first regular monthly payment and the first interest rate adjustment, the savings and loan may not in the future shorten the period between adjustments to, say, six months or lengthen the period to twenty-four months)
3. The maximum rate adjustment will also be changed to a maximum of 0.5 percent every six months, with a maximum increase or decrease of 5 percent over the life of the mortgage

It should be noted that some lenders may use these rate adjustment limitations.

Rate Change Notification[12]

Prior to the lender either increasing or decreasing the interest rate, the loan documents may require the lender to give the borrower notice. Some documents may state that the borrower must be notified thirty days prior to a change in the interest rate when the one year adjustment period is used. The instruments may also prohibit prepayment penalties for ninety days after receipt of the notice.

Prior to the cancellation of the VRM regulations, the FHLBB felt that the thirty-day notice of adjustment was insufficient. Therefore, the FHLBB had proposed an increase in the notice period to sixty days, with a maximum of ninety days notice prior to the change in interest rate. The FHLBB had also proposed dropping any prepayment penalty at any time after commencement of the notice period for the first interest rate adjustment period.

Extension of Loan Maturity[13]

A VRM may allow the borrower to extend the term of a VRM up to a maximum of one third of the original term in order to lessen or avoid any increase in payment due to the increase in interest rates.

The FHLBB had proposed a change to this regulation that would still allow the extension of the term, but would limit the extension to a maximum of ten years. The reduction, however, could not be to such an extent that it would have reduced the payments to an amount below the original monthly payment.

Offer of Fixed-Rate Payment Mortgage[14]

The canceled regulations covering the VRM required lenders to offer eligible prospective borrowers a standard mortgage. This regulation was adopted by the FHLBB originally due to the concern it had about the newness of the VRM. After the adoption of the regulations and the experience gained by S and Ls offering the VRM, particularly those located in California, the FHLBB was satisfied that the required disclosures were sufficient to protect the consumer, and therefore it had proposed to delete this requirement.

Disclosure Requirements[15]

As mentioned above, the FHLBB had proposed to drop the requirement to offer the fixed-rate mortgage to prospective borrowers applying for a VRM. Since the association would no longer have been required to offer a fixed-rate mortgage, the side-by-side comparison and full-term "worst case" schedule would no longer have been required. These would have been replaced by an example of the effects of a maximum increase allowed at the first adjustment and the maximum possible rate change, both up and down, over the life of the mortgage. An example of such a disclosure is shown in Figure 3-9.

RENEGOTIABLE-RATE MORTGAGE (RRM)

The *renegotiable-rate mortgage* (RRM), sometimes called the rollover mortgage, can be defined as a series of short-term loans issued for terms of three to five years each, secured by a long-term mortgage. The short-term loans are automatically renewable for the entire term of the long-term mortgage.

Background[17]

The RRM is a variation of the variable-rate mortage and had its origin in Canada as early as 1930. Most residential mortgages in Canada

Figure 3-9. Variable-Rate Mortgage Disclosure

Information About the Variable-Rate Mortgage

You have received an application form for a variable-rate mortgage ("VRM"). The VRM differs from the fixed-rate, fixed-payment mortgage with which you may be familiar. Instead of having an interest rate that is set at the beginning of the mortgage and remains the same, the VRM has an interest rate that may increase or decrease as frequently as once each six months. This means that the amount of your monthly payment may also increase or decrease.

The term of the VRM is ______ years. The interest rate may be adjusted every ______ months (the "adjustment period").

Adjustments to the interest rate are based on changes in an index rate. The index used is computed by the Federal Home Loan Bank Board, an agency of the Federal government. The index is based on the national average cost of funds to institutions the accounts of which are insured by the Federal Savings and Loan Insurance Corporation.

At the time of adjustment of the interest rate, if the index has moved to a level higher than it was at the beginning of the mortgage, the lender has the right, subject to the limitations described in the paragraph below, to adjust the interest rate to a rate equalling the original interest rate plus the increase in the index rate. Although taking such an increase is optional with the lender, you should be aware that the lender has this right and may become contractually obligated to exercise it.

If the index has moved down, the lender must at the time of adjustment reduce the original interest rate by the decrease in the index rate. No matter how much the index rate increases or decreases, THE LENDER, AT THE TIME OF ADJUSTMENT, MAY NOT INCREASE OR DECREASE THE INTEREST RATE ON YOUR VRM LOAN BY AN AMOUNT GREATER THAN ______ OF ONE PERCENTAGE POINT PER ADJUSTMENT PERIOD, AND THE TOTAL INCREASE OR DECREASE OVER THE LIFE OF THE MORTGAGE LOAN MAY NOT BE MORE THAN ______ PERCENTAGE POINTS.

If the interest rate increases, you have the right to extend the maturity of the loan by up to 10 years, although the loan may not be lengthened to such an extent that the monthly loan payments would be reduced below the original monthly payment amount. In addition, you have the right to prepay the loan in part or in full without penalty at any time after notification of the first interest rate increase or decrease. This notification, which also sets out the new interest rate, monthly payment amount, and remaining principal balance, must be sent to you at least 60 but not more than 90 days prior to adjustment of the interest rate.

Example of Operation of VRM

The maximum interest-rate increase at the end of the first adjustment period, which is ______ months long, is ______ percentage points. On a $50,000 VRM with a term of ______ years and an original interest rate of [*lender's current commitment rate*] percent, this rate change would increase the monthly payment (principal and interest) from $ ______ to $ ______ . Using the same example, the highest interest rate you might have to pay over the life of the mortgage would be ______ percent, and the lowest would be ______ percent.

Source: Proposed Amendments—Alternative Mortgage Instruments, 12 CFR, Part 545 (October 23, 1980), FHLBB.

are financed using this type of mortgage. It is commonly referred to as the five-year rollover, or the renegotiable-rate mortgage. In Canada prior to 1969, all government-guaranteed mortgages were written as fixed-term mortgages of not less than twenty-five years. But in 1969, the laws were changed to allow the government-guaranteed loans in Canada to be made as RRMs, or rollovers, for a term of five years, and secured by a long-term mortgage for a period of not less than twenty-five years. In the first full year the RRMs were authorized, 58 percent of the real estate mortgages guaranteed by the Canadian government were RRMs. This percentage continued to increase until, by 1976, nearly 98 percent of the real estate loans guaranteed by the Canadian government were RRMs.

The RRMs have not been used extensively in the United States, and if they were used, they were used to finance commercial property. In late 1979, the Federal Home Loan Bank Board proposed an amendment to its lending regulations authorizing federally chartered savings and loan associations to make the RRM mortgage. The reason for the proposed change was to allow the savings and loan associations to have the flexibility to make mortgages that meet the rise and fall of the interest rates in the 1980s. This rule became effective on April 3, 1980. In mid-1980, the FHLBB proposed amendments to the rules that would standardize the RRM and make it similar to the VRM. These amendments, however, were not implemented. Instead, the FHLBB instituted the AML.

Interest Rate Index

As with the VRM, the interest rate on the RRM may change during the term of the mortgage. As was noted earlier, there are several indexes that may be used to establish the interest rate on the RRM at the time of the first renewal. The Federal Home Loan Bank Board, when it allowed the RRM, authorized the use of the following index:

The index to be used for calculating the adjustment in the interest rate for a RRM is the national average mortgage rate for all major lenders for the purchase of previously occupied homes.

This index is published monthly in the *Federal Home Loan Bank Board Journal*. It is also released to certain publications on a regular basis. You will note that the index may be different for a RRM when compared to a VRM.

Rate Adjustment

As was noted, the rate on the RRM is to be adjusted at a specific time, every three to five years. As with the VRMs, the RRMs are written with a provision that limits the amount of rate adjustment. Also, as with the VRMs, the RRMs normally state that the increase in the interest rate is made at the option of the lender. If the index reflects a decrease in the interest rate, however, the lender is normally mandated to make the decrease.

In regard to the amount of the rate adjustment, many RRMs limit the rate increase or decrease to a maximum of 0.5 to 1.0 percent per year of the loan term with a maximum increase or decrease over the life of the mortgage of 5 percent.

Extension of Loan Maturity

Some RRMs contain no provision that permits the borrower to extend the term of the RRM to reduce the effect of a rate increase. But it should be noted that some lenders may allow the borrower to extend the term up to ten years. Normally, though, the extension cannot reduce the monthly payment to a level below the original monthly payments.

Rate Adjustment Notification

As with the VRM, the loan documents normally require the lender to give notice to the borrower. Some documents require that the notice be given sixty or ninety days prior to any change in the interest rate. This notice is to be given at any time the rate is changed, either up or down.

Disclosure Requirement for the RRM

As with the VRM, the lender is required to give the prospective borrower information about the RRM, normally at the time of receipt of an application. An example of such a form is illustrated in Figure 3-10.

GRADUATED-PAYMENT MORTGAGE (GPM)

The most common type of GPM is the FHA 245 insured mortgage. This FHA GPM will be explained in depth in Chapter 6. In this section, we will review the conventional GPM and in particular the GPM that is authorized by the Federal Home Loan Bank Board. The FHLBB defines a GPM in this manner:

A graduated payment mortgage loan is a fixed-rate loan on which the monthly payments begin at a level lower than that of a level-payment fixed-rate loan. During a period the length of which is fixed at loan origination (the graduation period), the monthly payment amount gradually rises to a level sufficient to amortize the remaining principal balance over the remaining term of the loan.[18]

Graduation Period—Rate and Frequency

The FHLBB has authorized federally chartered savings and loan associations to make the GPM. As with the GPM insured by FHA, the savings and loans can offer several plans of graduation with a maximum graduation period of ten years.

Prior to the Federal Home Loan Bank Board issuing a final rule on July 12, 1981, a section of which revised the graduated-payment mortgage, the federally chartered thrifts were limited to the types of GPM which they could originate, purchase, or participate in. This rule, then, canceled all such restrictions. According to Section 1 of the rule, the rate and frequency of payment adjustments will be at any rate or frequency that is contained in the initial loan documents. It should be noted

Figure 3-10. Renegotiable-Rate Mortgage Disclosure

Information About the Renegotiable-Rate Mortgage

You have received an application form for a renegotiable-rate mortgage ("RRM"). The RRM differs from the fixed-rate mortgage with which you may be familiar. In the fixed-rate mortgage the length of the loan and the length of the underlying mortgage are the same, but in the RRM the loan is short-term (3-5 years) and is automatically renewable for a period equal to the mortgage (up to 30 years). Therefore, instead of having an interest rate that is set at the beginning of the mortgage and remains the same, the RRM has an interest rate that may increase or decrease at each renewal of the short-term loan. This means that the amount of your monthly payment may also increase or decrease.

The term of the RRM loan is ______ years, and the length of the underlying mortgage is ______ years. The initial loan term may be up to six months longer than later terms.

The lender must offer to renew the loan, and the only loan provision that may be changed at renewal is the interest rate. The interest rate offered at renewal is based on changes in an index rate. The index used is computed monthly by the Federal Home Loan Bank Board, an agency of the Federal government. The index is based on the national average contract rate for all major lenders for the purchase of previously-occupied, single-family homes.

At renewal, if the index has moved higher than it was at the beginning of the mortgage, the lender has the right to offer a renewal of the loan at an interest rate equalling the original interest rate plus the increase in the index rate. This is the maximum increase permitted to the lender. Although taking such an increase is optional with the lender, you should be aware that the lender has this right and may become contractually obligated to exercise it.

If the index has moved down, the lender *must* at renewal reduce the original interest rate by the decrease in the index rate. No matter how much the index rate increases or decreases, THE LENDER, AT RENEWAL, MAY NOT INCREASE OR DECREASE THE INTEREST RATE ON YOUR RRM LOAN BY AN AMOUNT GREATER THAN ______ OF ONE PERCENTAGE POINT PER YEAR OF THE LOAN, AND THE TOTAL INCREASE OR DECREASE OVER THE LIFE OF THE MORTGAGE MAY NOT BE MORE THAN ______ PERCENTAGE POINTS.

As the borrower, you have the right to prepay the loan in part or in full without penalty at any time after the beginning of the notice period of the first interest rate adjustment. To give you enough time to make this decision, the lender, at least ninety (90) but not more than one-hundred twenty (120) days before interest rate adjustment, will send a notice stating the date of adjustment, the principal balance as of that date, the new interest rate and the monthly payment amount. If you elect not to pay the loan in full by the due date, the interest rate will be adjusted to the new rate. You will not have to pay any fees or charges at the time of interest rate adjustment.

The *maximum* interest-rate increase at the first renewal is ______ percentage points. On a $50,000 mortgage with an original term of ______ years and an original interest rate of [*lender's current commitment rate*] percent, this rate change would increase the monthly payment (principal and interest) from $______ to $______. Using the same example, the highest interest rate you might have to pay over the life of the mortgage would be ______ percent, and the lowest would be ______ percent.

Source: Draft Final Rule, 12 CFR, Chapter V, Subchapter C, Part 545–Operations, p. 11, FHLBB, Washington, D.C.

that the changes in the GPM rule canceled the requirement that payments could not change more than once a year. The new rule now allows the federally chartered thrifts to change the payments as often as every thirty days, but the GPM rule change does limit the maximum period for graduations of the monthly payment to a maximum of ten years.

Therefore, as a real estate professional, you must be very familiar with the conventional GPMs offered by the thrifts in your area. As with the AML, the types offered by each lender can vary widely.

Conversion Option

FHLBB regulations also give the borrower the option to convert to a standard mortgage instrument at any time chosen by the borrower, provided the borrower can qualify for the mortgage using the standard underwriting guidelines of the lender. The regulations prohibit the assessment of any fees or penalties to the borrower when the borrower chooses to convert to the standard mortgage.

Disclosures

As with many of the other AMIs authorized by the FHLBB, an applicant for a conventional GPM must also be given a disclosure notice at the time the savings and loan receives the application. The disclosure notice should be in a form and should contain the basic information of the GPM disclosure notice illustrated in Figure 3-11.

Underwriting

As with the FHA-insured GPM, the underwriting or loan approval is based on the first year's payment, thus allowing the

Figure 3-11. Graduated-Payment Mortgage Disclosure

Information About the Graduated-Payment Mortgage

You have received an application form for a graduated-payment mortgage (GPM). The GPM differs from a level-payment mortgage in the following respect: during the early years of the loan, monthly payments are lower than they would be on a level-payment mortgage and are not sufficient to cover the interest being charged on the loan. As a result, the outstanding principal balance on the GPM loan actually increases somewhat during these years.

To compensate for the initial, lower payments, monthly payments increase gradually each year during a period of up to 10 years (the "graduation period") until they reach a level sufficient to pay all interest and principal by the end of the loan term. The length of the graduation period and limitations on the rate of increase of monthly payments are fixed at loan origination.

Payment amounts may not be changed more than once a year, and the first change may not occur sooner than one year after the date of the first regular loan payment.

You have the right to convert this mortgage, at any time you choose, to a level-payment mortgage instrument, provided that you are then eligible for such mortgage under the association's normal underwriting standards. You may not be charged any fees or penalties if you convert to a level-payment mortgage bearing the same interest rate and outstanding maturity as the GPM. Such a mortgage has a fixed interest rate and level payments sufficient to pay all interest and principal by the end of the loan term.

Example of Operation of GPM

Consider a $50,000 GPM that has an interest rate of [*lender's current commitment rate*] percent, a graduation period of ______________ years, and a term of ______________ years. The monthly payments in the first ________ years of the mortgage (the graduation period) will be as shown in the following table, which reflects a ________ percent graduation. After the______year, the payment will remain constant; it will not be increased beyond the level paid in the______year.

Year	*Principal at year-end*	*Monthly Payment*

By comparison, a $50,000 level-payment mortgage with the same interest rate and for the same term would carry a monthly payment of $ ______________ , and the remaining principal balance at the end of the [*number corresponding to year in which graduation period on above GPM would end*] year would be $ ___________ .

borrower to qualify for a larger mortgage than if he or she had applied for a standard fixed-payment mortgage.

Graduated-Payment Mortgage Variations

The pledged savings account mortgage and the escrow advance mortgage are two additional types of conventional loans that are variations of the GPM and will also allow a lower initial monthly payment with the provision for periodic increase in the monthly payments at prescribed intervals.

Pledged savings account mortgage This is a type of mortgage where part of the borrower's down payment is used to fund a pledged savings account, which is used to reduce the monthly payments of the borrower for a specified number of years. The PSAM, in other words, is just another type of graduated-payment mortgage. The use of the pledge savings account can reduce the borrower's monthly payment up to 25 percent in the first year after origination. The PSAM is authorized by the FHLBB, thus allowing federally chartered savings and loan associations to make it. The most common PSAM is marketed by the FLIP Mortgage Corporation of Newtown, Pennsylvania. FLIP is an acronym for Flexible Loan Insurance Program.

The PSAM combines the lower initial payments of the GPM for the homebuyer with level or full payments for the lender, and the seller gets the full amount of the agreed sales price. With the borrower able to get the lower initial payments, he or she can have a lower annual income and qualify for a higher mortgage.

The PSAM requires the borrower to make a down payment equal to 10 percent of the sales price. Since the majority of the down payment is deposited in a pledged savings account, the loan-to-value ratio (LTV) may be as high as 99 percent. As noted earlier, federally chartered savings and loans are normally limited to making loans with a maximum loan-to-value ratio of 95 percent. The regulation has been amended to allow the federally chartered savings and loans to make loans with LTVs in excess of 95 percent if the excess percentage of 95 percent is secured by a pledged savings account and if the following are met:

1. The loan amount does not exceed the purchase price of the property or the appraised value, whichever is the lesser

2. The funds in the pledged account are those of the borrower

3. The savings and loan association makes certain disclosures to the borrower

Another type of the PSAM is the Action!® Mortgage offered by the Mortgage Guaranty Insurance Corporation. Under the Action!® Mortgage, once again the majority of the down payment is used to fund a pledged interest-bearing savings account that is used to supplement the borrower's monthly payment for a period of five years. Thus, the borrower's out-of-pocket payment for the first five years of the mortgage is less than the monthly payment of the fixed-payment mortgage. Also, the Action!® Mortgage assumes that the borrower's income will increase a sufficient amount each year to match the increase of the payment, and by the sixth year of the mortgage the borrower's income will be sufficient to match the payment beginning with the sixth year. An example of how the Action!® Mortgage works is given in Figure 3-12.

Escrow advance mortgage Under this type of mortgage, the initial monthly payments are lower because for the first few years the homebuyer is only paying a portion of the escrow payments for taxes. The reduction can be as much as 20 percent for the initial year. Since the borrower is only paying a portion of the tax escrow, the lender will make up the difference by making advances that equal the amount not paid by the borrower. The advances are added to the principal mortgage amount and are repaid by the borrower over the remaining years of the mortgage.

One type of the escrow advance mortgage is marketed by the Mortgage Guaranty Insurance Corporation and called the MAGIC® Payment Mortgage. Under this program, the borrower's monthly payments gradually increase over a five-year period, and beginning in the sixth year the payments increase to a level sufficient to pay off the mortgage in full, including the advances made by the lender.

Some of the other features of the MAGIC® Payment Mortgage Program are as follows:

1. Maximum term is thirty years

2. Initial loan-to-value ratio is between 80 and 90 percent

3. Advances made by the lender over the five-year graduation period may not raise the loan-to-value ratio above 95 percent

4. Mortgage insurance will be purchased for the portion of the mortgage above a loan-to-value ratio of 80 percent

GROWING EQUITY MORTGAGE (GEM)

As with the other AMIs, the growing equity mortgage (GEM) is another attempt to reduce the effects of the high interest rates of the 1980s. First, let us define the GEM. The GEM is a fixed-rate, first-lien mortgage in which the monthly payment increases at a specific rate for a specified number of years. The increase, instead of a specific rate, may be based on a specified index. The first year's payments are based on the face rate of the mortgage and all increases in payments will be credited to principal reduction. From this definition, we can see that the GEM is a type of GPM, but does not have the feature of negative amortization.

Advantages

First, let us review the advantages to the borrower. One advantage was mentioned above: there is no negative amortization. A second advantage to the borrower is that since the first year's payments are based on the face rate to amortize over thirty years, the initial monthly payment of principal and interest is contributing to principal reduction. Thus, any increase in the payment will be credited to principal reduction. Thus, the loan will be repaid in less than thirty years saving the borrower many dollars in interest expense.

A third advantage is that since the lender or investor will have funds tied up for fewer years, the face interest rate is usually below the prevailing market rate for a fixed-rate, fixed-term mortgage.

Figure 3-12. Action!® Mortgage example

The example below is based on these assumptions:

$54,000 selling price with 10% down payment

30 year mortgage at 10¼%

The down payment is to be applied so that the borrower's out-of-pocket P&I payment will increase 7.5% from year 1 to year 2.

$810 annual real estate tax estimate

$150 annual hazard insurance estimate

The Action!Mortgage will allocate the homebuyer's down payment as follows:

$5,400 down payment
-$1,150 applied to purchase
$4,250 savings account balance at start

The Action! Mortgage payment schedule (example)

Beginning Year	*Homebuyer's Out-of-Pocket Payment*	*Pledged Savings Account Withdrawal*	*Total Monthly Principal & Interest*
1st	$344.54*	$129.05	$473.59
2nd	$370.35	$103.24	$473.59
3rd	$396.16	$ 77.43	$473.59
4th	$421.97	$ 51.62	$473.59
5th	$447.78	$ 25.81	$473.59
6th and thereafter	$473.59	$ 0.00	$473.59

*Borrower's monthly payment of Principal and Interest will increase by $25.81 each of first 5 years.

The lender will also receive several advantages for the GEM. One is the loanable funds will be tied up for fewer years. A second advantage is that since the borrower's equity is rapidly increasing, there is less likelihood of default. Finally, many of the standard notes and mortgages/deeds of trust can be used for the conventional GEM with only slight modifications.

Graduation Period—Rate and Frequency

There is no set rate and frequency of graduation with the GEM as there is with the negative amortization GPM, but the normal range of rate of graduation is 3 to 5 percent per year for a period of five to ten years. For example, HUD-FHA will issue mortgage insurance on GEMs with a 2 or 3 percent increase for a period of ten years. This GEM will be discussed in detail in Chapter 6. VA will also guarantee certain types of GEMs, which will be discussed in Chapter 7. The rate and frequency of the graduation will be set at the time of origination and will be outlined in the original loan documents.

Underwriting

As with the GPM and many of the other AMIs, the underwriting is based on the initial or first year's payments. Since the GEM will normally have a rate below market, the borrower will be able to qualify for a larger loan amount.

GEM Example and Comparison to a Fixed-Rate, Fixed-Term Mortgage

For this example we will use a fixed-rate, fixed-term mortgage of $75,000 with an interest rate of 15.50 percent and a term of thirty years. The GEM will be structured identically, but the payment will be increased by 3.5 percent per year for a period of ten

Figure 3-13. Growing Equity Loan

Year	Monthly Payments	Interest Paid	Principal Paid	Remaining Balance
1	978.39	11,616.42	124.26	74,875.74
2	1,012.63	11,565.25	586.31	74,289.42
3	1,048.08	11,436.06	1,140.90	73,148.52
4	1,084.76	11,213.45	1,803.67	71,344.85
5	1,122.72	10,879.34	2,593.30	68,751.55
6	1,162.02	10,412.57	3,531.67	65,219.88
7	1,202.69	9,788.34	4,643.94	60,575.94
8	1,244.78	8,977.66	5,959.70	54,616.23
9	1,288.35	7,946.57	7,513.63	47,102.60
10	1,333.45	6,655.40	9,346.00	37,756.60
11	1,380.12	5,057.75	11,503.69	26.252.90
12	1,380.12	3,142.39	13,419.05	12,833.85
12+6	1,380.12	755.25	7,525.47	5,308.38
12+8	1,380.12	875.45	10,165.51	2,668.33
12+9	1,380.12	909.95	11,511.17	1,322.71
12+10	1,339.81	917.01	1,322.71	- 0 -

Total Principal Paid =	75,000.00
Total Payments	$184,618.67
Less Principal Reduction	- 75,000.00
TOTAL INTEREST	109,618.67

Figure 3-14. Conventional Loan

Year	Monthly Payments	Interest Paid	Principal Paid	% Principal Repaid	Remaining Balance
1	978.39	11,616.42	124.26	0.17	74,875.74
2	978.39	11,595.73	144.95	0.36	74,730.79
3	978.39	11,571.59	169.09	0.58	74,561.70
4	978.39	11,543.76	197.24	0.85	74,364.46
5	978.39	11,510.92	230.08	1.16	74,134.38
6	978.39	11,447.29	268.39	1.52	73,865.99
7	978.39	11,427.61	311.07	1.93	73,552.91
8	978.39	11,370.80	365.20	2.42	73,187.72
9	978.39	11,314.67	426.01	2.99	72,761.71
10	978.39	11,243.74	496.94	3.65	72,264.77
11	978.39	11,161.01	579.67	4.42	71,685.09
12	978.39	11,064.49	676.19	5.32	71,008.90
12+6	978.39	5,491.13	379.21	5.83	70,629.68
12+8	978.39	7,314.87	512.25	6.00	70,496.65
12+9	978.39	8,225.46	580.05	6.10	70,428.85
12+10	978.39	9,135.16	648.74	6.19	70,360.16

Total Principal Paid = 4,639.83

Total Payments (12 years and 10 months @ 978.39)	$150,672.06
Less Principal Reduction	- 4,639.83
TOTAL INTEREST	146,032.23

years. It should be noted that the ten-year period will not begin until the end of the first year, thus the graduation period will be year 2 through 11. The GEM is shown in Figure 3-13 and the conventional mortgage is shown in Figure 3-14.

Now let us do our comparison. We can see that the monthly payments for the GEM increase annually but for the conventional mortgage the payments remain constant. With the payments increasing and all of the increase being credited to principal reduction, we can see that the GEM is paid in full in twelve years and ten months. When this is compared to the conventional mortgage, the principal has only been reduced by $4,639.83.

Another interesting comparison is that over the twelve-year, ten-month period, the conventional borrower has paid some $146,032.23 in interest and with the GEM, the borrower will have paid $109,618.67 or 75 percent of the conventional amount with over 50 percent of the interest paid during the first five years.

GEM Appeal

This type of mortgage would appeal to the persons or family who have decided that this is the home of their choice and would like to live there for the rest of their lives. For example, a GEM might appeal to a person being transferred into a job where he or she will finish his or her career and hope to retire at that present location. In some cases, the GEM would appeal to the young homebuyer who owns his or her own business and the home meets all of the present and anticipated needs of his or her family.

GRADUATED-PAYMENT ADJUSTABLE MORTGAGE LOAN (GPAML)[20]

The graduated-payment adjustable mortgage loan (GPAML) is a hybrid mortgage that combines the rate adjustment features of the AML with the graduated-payment feature of the graduated-payment mortgage.

The FHLBB issued proposed rules for this type of mortgage on October 10, 1980, and, while studying the AML, has considered the possibility of incorporating the GPAML into the final rule authorizing the AML. But, the FHLBB decided that all of the ramifications of such an incorporation had not been explored. Thus, the GPAML was still under study and a final rule authorizing the GPAML was to be issued in the future.

Since the spring of 1976, the Federal Home Loan Bank Board has been studying the use of the alternative mortgage instrument in order to meet the needs of the homeowners during different financial phases of their lives. The study has resulted in the introduction of the graduated-payment mortgage, the variable-rate mortgage, and the last of the approved types, introduced on April 3, 1980, the renegotiable-rate mortgage.

A study done by the FHLBB staff, entitled *Improving the Ability of Thrifts to Write Variable Rate Mortgages*, had proposed that the natural extension of the GPM and the RRM would be the graduated-payment adjustment mortgage. Under the GPAML, the payments would start at a lower rate than a conventional mortgage and graduate up. In addition to the payments increasing, the interest rate can also increase. Thus, the GPAML would differ from a conventional mortgage in two respects. First, the payments in the early years of the GPAML would be lower than on a standard fixed-rate mortgage or even on a mortgage with an adjustable interest rate. Thus, these GPAML payments would not be sufficient to cover the interest charges on the loan. In other words, for the first few years of the GPAML, the loan would be in negative amortization (that is, the loan balance would actually increase). The second difference is that the interest rate could be adjusted either up or down at specific intervals. The monthly payments, then, could increase from not only the prescribed payment increase, but also from an increase in the interest rate.

On July 22, 1981, the Federal Home Loan Bank Board issued the Final Rule allowing the federally chartered savings and loan associations and federally chartered mutual savings banks to make, purchase, participate, or otherwise deal in GPAMLs. The following is a review of the major sections of the rule.

Interest Rate Index

The interest rate index to be used for the GPAML is the same index that is used for the AML. The only requirement as to the index used is that the value of the index must be readily verifiable by the borrower and not under the control of the institution.

Adjustments: Payment and Interest Rate

Payment The monthly payment for principal and interest could not increase during the period of graduation more than the percent agreed upon at the time of application. For example, if the payment graduation was agreed to be 3 percent per year for ten years, this amount could not be increased later in the mortgage.

Interest rate As with the AML, the GPAML monthly payment may be adjusted due to change in the interest rate, which may be as often as monthly. So, for the first ten years of the mortgage, the payment will be increased as per the graduation schedule outlined in the original loan documents and by the amount the interest rate index warrants a change. There is no limitation to the amount the monthly payment may either increase or decrease from one adjustment period to the next. As with the AML, the payment adjustment due to an index change may be as often as once a month.

Now let us examine how a GPAML can work and the effects of a graduation of the monthly payment and an interest rate index change. For this example, we will use a $50,000 mortgage with a 95 percent loan-to-value ratio and an initial interest rate of 13 percent. We will assume a payment graduation of 7.5 percent for the first five years of the mortgage and the interest rate will be adjusted every three years.

The effects of the graduation and interest rate adjustment is shown in Figure 3-15. From this illustration, we can see that the first year's monthly payments are not sufficient to pay all of the interest, as per a GPM, and the ending balance for year one is $51,447.13. Since the original loan documents call for an increase or graduation in the monthly payment of 7.5 percent, the monthly payment in the second year will increase to $460.20 and the payments will increase again in the third year by 7.5 percent to $494.72. Then, at the end of the fourth year, we not only must increase the payments by the amount of the graduation, but also change the interest rate that is scheduled for an adjustment. In this case, the index indicates an increase of 1.5 percent. The interest rate, therefore, will increase to 14.5 percent. Combining both the graduation and the interest rate, we can see that the payment will increase to $585.75 or an increase of 18.4 percent from the previous year. In addition, we can see that the outstanding principal balance has increased to $54,456.40. This negative amortization continues through the fifth year with the maximum outstanding loan balance of $54,819.95.

As with the AML, the FHLBB feels the mortgage will not exceed the original loan-to-value ratio even though the mortgage is in negative amortization for the first year. Thus, the borrower will not have to put any additional money down. This is the thinking of the FHLBB, but some lenders may require the borrower to make a larger down payment and use the highest balance as the amount to establish the down payment. For example, in Figure 3-15, the mortgage was in negative amortization for the first five years and the outstanding loan balance increased from the initial $50,000 to $54,819.95; thus, the lender may require the borrower to put down an initial amount equal to the amount of negative

Figure 3-15. ***Example of the GPAML for a $50,000 mortgage, 5 year/7.5 percent per year graduation, interest rate adjustment every 3 years.***

Year	Balance at End	Rate	Monthly Payment	Payment Increase
1	$51,447.13	13%	$428.09	-0-%
2	52,684.89	13	460.20	7.5
3	53,653.66	13	494.72	7.5
4	54,456.40	14.5	585.75	18.4
5	54,819.95	14.5	629.68	7.5
6	54,633.87	14.5	676.91	7.5
7	54,018.53	16	776.08	14.65
8	53,297.15	16	776.08	-0-
9	52,451.50	16	776.08	-0-
10	51,479.28	17.5	839.64	8.19

amortization, $4,819.95, and the initial down payment of approximately $2,631 for a total down payment of $7,450.95. If the lender would require that the negative amortization be included in the down payment, the initial loan-to-value ratio would be approximately 86 percent.

The FHLBB also requires that the borrower maintain private mortgage insurance during any period that the loan exceeds 90 percent of the value of the security property. It should be noted that this is a requirement of the FHLBB, but many lenders may require the private mortgage insurance during any period that the loan exceeds 80 percent of the value of the property used as security.

Catch-Up Payment

As with the AML, the GPAML rule requires that a "catch-up" payment is scheduled every five years. A catch-up payment is an increase in the monthly payment to a level sufficient to amortize the remaining principal balance over the remaining life of the mortgage. This payment will increase irrespective of any payment increase limitation contained in the original loan documents. Let us review what effect this catch-up payment will have on our example. At the end of the fifth year the outstanding principal balance is $54,819.95 and the payment beginning with the sixth year is $676.91. Since the original term of the mortgage was thirty years and payments have been made for five full years, the remaining original term is twenty-five years. The required monthly payment to amortize the remaining principal balance over the remaining term of twenty-five years is $680.95. Thus, the payment is not sufficient to amortize the remaining principal balance. Now, the lender has two choices: one is to increase the payment by some $4.04 per month or, as the GPAML rule allows, the lender can extend the term of the mortgage up to a maximum of forty years from the date of the closing of the loan. If the lender would extend the term of the mortgage, the $676.91 payment would be sufficient with no increase.

Adjustment Notification

The FHLBB requires savings and loan associations making the GPAML to give notice of a rate adjustment at least ninety days prior to the adjustment, but not more than one hundred twenty days prior to any change in the interest rate. In addition, the savings and loan associations are required to send a written notice to the borrower. The borrower would have the right to prepay the mortgage in full without penalty at any time after the savings and loan has notified the borrower of the first interest increase.

Disclosure Requirement

As with the RRM, VRM, and SAM, the FHLBB will require the lender to give the prospective borrower a sample disclosure notice, as illustrated in Figure 3-16.

REVERSE-ANNUITY MORTGAGE (RAM)

The reverse-annuity mortgage is not a true mortgage, but it is a method by which homeowners can obtain income based on the equity in their homes. The RAM is especially helpful to older families who have a home paid in full and wish to secure the value of the property in regular monthly income without having to sell the property and move.

The RAM was authorized by the Federal Home Loan Bank Board on January 1, 1979. Then on October 23, 1981, the FHLBB revised the original rule allowing the federally chartered thrifts to make the reverse-annuity mortgage. One of the changes was to the description or definition of a RAM. Section 545.6-4 Alternative Mortgage Instruments (c) defines the reverse annuity mortgage:

> *This instrument provides periodic payments to homeowners based on accumulated equity. The payments are made monthly directly by the lender, or are made through the purchase of an annuity from an insurance company. The loan becomes due on a specified date after disbursement of the entire principal amount of the loan or when a specified event occurs, such as sale of the property or death of the borrower. The interest rate on this instrument may be fixed, or may be adjusted periodically . . . . Interest-rate adjustments may be implemented through changes to the principal loan balance.*[21]

Figure 3-16. Graduated Payment Adjustable Mortgage Loan Disclosure

IMPORTANT INFORMATION ABOUT THE GRADUATED PAYMENT ADJUSTABLE MORTGAGE LOAN—PLEASE READ CAREFULLY

You have received an application form for a graduated payment adjustable mortgage loan ("GPAML"). The GPAML may differ from other mortgages with which you are familiar.

General Description of Graduated Payment Adjustable Mortgage Loan

The graduated payment adjustable mortgage loan is a flexible loan instrument on which the scheduled monthly payment amount at the beginning of the loan term is insufficient to fully amortize the loan. Within ten years of the date of the closing of the loan, and at least every five years after that, the payment amount must be adjusted to a level that will fully amortize the loan. The interest rate on a GPAML may be adjusted by the lender from time to time. Such adjustments will result in increases or decreases in your payment amount, in the outstanding principal loan balance, in the loan term, or in all three (see discussion below relating to these types of adjustments). Federal regulations place no limit on the amount by which the interest rate may be adjusted either at any one time or over the life of the loan, or on the frequency with which it may be adjusted. Adjustments to the interest rate must reflect the movement of a single, specified index (see discussion below). This does not mean that the particular loan agreement you sign must, by law, permit unlimited interest-rate changes. It merely means that, if you desire to have certain rate-adjustment limitations placed in your loan agreement, that is a matter you should negotiate with the lender. You may also want to make inquiries concerning the loan terms offered by other lenders on GPAMLs to compare the terms and conditions.

Another flexible feature of the GPAML is that the regular payment amount, in addition to being increased because it was too small to fully amortize the loan at the beginning of the loan term, may be increased or decreased by the lender from time to time to reflect changes in the interest rate. Again, Federal regulations place no limitations on the amount by which the lender may adjust payments at any one time, or on the frequency of payment adjustments. If you wish to have particular provisions in your loan agreement regarding adjustments to the payment amount, you should negotiate such terms with the lender prior to entering such an agreement.

A third flexible feature of the GPAML is that the outstanding principal loan balance (the total amount you owe) may be increased or decreased from time to time when, because of adjustments to the interest rate or because the payment amount was too small at the beginning of the loan term to fully amortize the loan, the payment amount is either too small to cover interest due on the loan, or larger than is necessary to pay off the loan over the remaining term of the loan.

The final flexible feature of the GPAML is that the loan term may be lengthened or shortened from time to time, corresponding to an increase or decrease in the interest rate. When the term is extended in connection with a rate increase, the payment amount does not have to be increased to the same extent as if the term had not been lengthened. In no case may the total term of the loan exceed 40 years.

Page 1 of 3

Figure 3-16. continued

Index

Adjustments to the interest rate of an GPAML must correspond directly to the movement of an index, subject to such rate-adjustment limitations as may be contained in the loan contract. If the index has moved down, the lender must reduce the interest rate by at least the decrease in the index. If the index has moved up, the lender has the right to increase the interest rate by that amount. Although taking such an increase is optional by the lender, you should be aware that the lender has this right and may become contractually obligated to exercise it.

[Name and description of index to be used for applicant's loan, initial index value (if known) or date of initial index value, a source or sources where the index may be readily obtained by the borrower, and the high and low index rates during the previous calendar year.]

Key terms of Federal Savings and Loan Association's graduated payment adjustable mortgage loan

Following is a summary of the key terms of the type of GPAML to be offered to you. This summary is intended for reference purposes only. Important information relating specifically to your loan will be contained in the loan agreement, which alone will establish your rights under the loan plan.

[Provide summary of key terms of the loan, including the loan term, over what period and by what amounts the payment will be adjusted to fully amortize the loan, the frequency of rate changes, the frequency of payment changes, the maximum rate change, if any, at one time, the maximum rate change, if any, over the life of the loan, the maximum payment change, if any, at one time, miminum increments, if any, of rate changes, and whether there will be adjustments to the principal loan balance, in the following format:

Loan term . . . .
Graduation period . . . .
Rate of payment increases during graduation period . . . .
Frequency of payment increases during graduation period . . . .
Frequency of rate changes . . . . (etc.)]

How Your Graduated Payment Adjustable Mortgage Loan Would Work

Initial Interest Rate

The initial interest rate offered by ________________ Federal Savings and Loan Association on your GPAML will be established and disclosed to you on [commitment date, etc.] based on market conditions at the time.

[Insert a short description of each of the key terms of the type of GPAML to be offered to the borrower, using headings where appropriate.]

Page 2 of 3

Figure 3-16. continued

Notice of payment adjustments

________________ Federal Savings and Loan Association will send you notice of an adjustment to the payment amount at least 30 but not more than 45 days before it becomes effective. [Describe what information the notice will contain.]

Prepayment penalty

You may prepay an GPAML in whole or in part *without penalty at any time* during the term of the loan.

Fees

You will be charged fees by ________________ Federal Savings and Loan Association and by other persons in connection with the origination of your GPAML. The association will give you an estimate of these fees after receiving your loan application. However, you will not be charged any costs or fees in connection with any regularly-scheduled adjustment to the interest rate, the payment, the outstanding principal loan balance, or the loan term initiated by the lender.

Example of operation of your type of GPAML

[Set out an example of the operation of all of the features of the type of GPAML to be offered to the borrower, including, where appropriate, the use of a table.]

Source: U.S., Federal Home Bank Board, 12 CFR, Part 545, "Graduated Payment Adjustable Mortgage Loan Instruments: Final Rule," July 22, 1981.

Page 3 of 3

These changes no longer require the lender to submit a RAM to the board for approval, but the FHLBB gives the following requirements that any RAM offered by the institution must meet:

> (i) Loan applicants shall not be bound for seven days after the loan commitment is made.
>
> (ii) Associations shall obtain a statement signed by the borrower acknowledging disclosure of all contractual contingencies which could force a sale of the home.
>
> (iii) If the loan instrument provides that the interest rate will be adjusted more frequently [than] the payment to the borrower will be adjusted, the payment to the borrower, then, in addition to the notification of payment adjustment required . . ., the association must also send the borrower a notification of each rate adjustment within the time period and with the disclosure required . . .
>
> (iv) The loan instrument shall provide for prepayment in whole or part without penalty at any time during the loan term.
>
> (v) If payments are to be made to the borrower through purchase of an annuity, the association shall use an insurance company authorized to engage in such business and supervised by the state in which it is incorporated.[22]

As with all of the AMIs authorized by the FHLBB, the rules require that the prospective borrower be given some disclosure information. The changes do not specify the time the disclosure is to be given, but only state that the disclosure must be in writing and specify the material or subjects to be covered by the disclosure. These items or subjects are as follows:

> (i) A general description of reverse-annuity mortgage;
>
> (ii) If refinancing is not guaranteed, a prominent notice indicating that a large payment (and the elements of which it is comprised) will be due at the end of the loan term;
>
> (iii) Schedule and explanation of payments to the borrower and whether property taxes and insurance are to be deducted;
>
> (iv) Schedule of outstanding debt over time;
>
> (v) Repayment date or event (such as sale of home or death of one or more mortgagors) which causes loan to become due;
>
> (vi) Method of repayment and schedule, if any;
>
> (vii) All contractual contingencies including lack of home maintenance and other default provisions, which may result in forced sale of the home;
>
> (viii) Interest rate, annual percentage rate, and total interest payable on the loan;
>
> (ix) Effective interest rate and interest earned or expected to be earned on purchased annuities, based on standard mortality tables;
>
> (x) Name and address of insurance company issuing a purchased annuity;
>
> (xi) Initial loan fees and charges;
>
> (xii) Description of prepayment features and refinancing features, if any;
>
> (xiii) Inclusion of a statement that such mortgages have tax and estate-planning consequences and may affect levels of, or eligibility for, certain government benefits, grants, or pensions, and that applicants are advised to explore these matters with appropriate authorities; and
>
> (xiv) An example of the operation of the type of reverse-annuity mortgage offered to the applicant.[23]

Basic Types of RAMs

The two basic types of RAMs are the *rising-debt RAM* and the *fixed-debt RAM*.

The rising-debt RAM is the most common. With this type of RAM, the lender agrees to pay the borrower an annuity on a regular basis, usually monthly. Thus, with each payment the debt of the homeowner increases. The total indebtedness of the borrower is usually payable upon a certain event such as the sale of the property, the death of the borrower, or the loan-to-value ratio reaching a certain percentage, or at some specific date.

The fixed-debt RAM is one in which the principal balance of the debt is established immediately and does not change over either the life of the debt or the life of the borrower.

There are many variations of either of these two basic types of RAMs and they can be tailored to the needs of a prospective borrower.

PRICE-LEVEL ADJUSTED MORTGAGE (PLAM)

The *price-level adjusted mortgage* (PLAM) type of AMI has been used in South America and Israel since the early 1970s, but has seen only limited use in the United States.

The PLAM can be defined as a mortgage that has a periodic adjustment in the principal as well as in the interest rate. Both may be adjusted monthly or annually. The PLAM, as opposed to the other AMIs, is affected by the actual rate of inflation rather than by an expected rate of inflation; the interest rate and the principal balance are adjusted by the actual rate of inflation. The interest rate for the PLAM is established by the investor's or lender's real rate of return, plus the actual rate of inflation as measured by a specific inflation rate index. This rate is sometimes referred to as the *nominal interest rate*. For example, if the investor seeks a real rate of return of 3 percent, and the inflation rate is running at the rate of 10 percent by the referenced index, the rate of the PLAM would be 13 percent, but if the inflation rate was at only 4 percent, the rate on the PLAM would only be 7 percent.

In addition to the adjustment to the interest rate on the PLAM, the outstanding principal balance is also increased by the indexed rate of inflation. For example, if a person borrows an initial $30,000 using the PLAM and the inflation rate was 10 percent for the first year, the principal balance would increase by $3000, thus making the outstanding balance approximately $33,000 at the end of the first year. The rationale behind this increase is that the value of the property used to secure the mortgage is also increasing at the same rate, as is the income of the borrower.

One can see that the advantage to the borrower under a PLAM is that under the standard type of mortgage the lender or investor will hedge against inflation by charging a higher interest rate. For example, if the lender expects that inflation will continue at a rate of 12 percent for the next several years, the lender will charge an interest that will be at least equal and probably more than the inflation rate. The PLAM will take into consideration the variation in the inflation rate.

The major disadvantage to the borrower under a PLAM is that, if the borrower's income or the appreciation of the home price does not keep up with inflation, the borrower could possibly not make the increased monthly payments and the value of the property would not be sufficient, if sold, to pay off the outstanding balance of the mortgage.

Unlike the other AMIs we have examined, the PLAM is neither approved nor proposed by the Federal Home Loan Bank Board.

REVIEW QUESTIONS

1. Define the term *alternative mortgage instrument.*

2. Define the interest indexes that may be used to establish the rate on the variable-rate mortgage.

3. Define the term *net appreciation* as related to the shared appreciation mortgage.

4. With which of the AMIs is the lender required to offer the prospective borrower a fixed-rate, fixed-payment mortgage?

5. What is another name for the renegotiable-rate mortgage, and what country pioneered this type of mortgage?

6. What are the two variations to the graduated-payment mortgage that will also allow for a reduced initial monthly payment?

7. Outline the development of the AMIs by the Federal Home Loan Bank Board.

8. Name and explain the major differences between the ARM and the AML.

9. Explain the *carry-over rule* and give an example.

10. Name at least three sources for many of the approved or suggested interest rate indexes.

11. Define the term *net appreciated value*.

12. Name two types of AMIs that no longer are authorized to be made by federally chartered savings and loan associations.

NOTES

[1]12 CFR Part 29—Adjustable-Rate Mortgages, Section 29.2, "Rules and Regulations," *Federal Register*, March 27, 1981, vol. 46, no. 59, p. 18943.

[2]12 CFR Part 29—Adjustable-Rate Mortgages, Section 29.4, "Rules and Regulations," *Federal Register*, March 27, 1981, vol. 46, no. 59, p. 18943.

[3]ibid.

[4]12 CFR, Subchapter C—Federal Savings and Loan System, Part 545, Operations, Section 545.6-4a, Adjustable mortgage loan instruments, (b) Description, "Rules and Regulations," *Federal Register*, April 30, 1981, vol 46, no. 83, p. 24152.

[5]12 CFR, Subchapter C—Federal Savings and Loan System, Part 545, Operations, Section 545.6-4a, Adjustable mortgage loan instruments, (c) (2), "Rules and Regulations," *Federal Register*, April 30, 1981, vol. 46, no. 83, p. 24152.

[6]ibid.

[7]12 CFR, Subchapter C—Federal Savings and Loan System, Part 545, Operations, Section 545.6-4a, Adjustable mortgage loan instruments, (e), "Rules and Regulations," *Federal Register*, April 30, 1981, vol. 46, no. 83, p. 24152.

[8]U.S., National Credit Union Administration, *Advance Copy—Final Rules and Regulations*, July 31, 1981, p. 22.

[9]Most of this section is based upon material from U.S., Federal Home Loan Bank Board, *The Federal Home Loan Bank Board Journal*, November 1980, vol. 13, no. 11, pp. 11–15.

[10]Most of this section is based upon material from U.S., Federal Home Loan Bank Board, *The Federal Home Loan Bank Board Journal*, August 1980, vol, 13, no. 8, pp. 4–5.

[11]Most of this section is based upon material from U.S., Federal Home Loan Bank Board, "Proposed Amendments, Alternative Mortgage Instruments," Code of Federal Regulations, October 23, 1980, Part 545, no. 80-653.

[12]ibid.

[13]ibid.

[14]ibid.

[15]ibid.

[16]ibid.

[17]U.S., Federal Home Loan Bank Board, Michael L. Unger, "Abstract VII, The Canadian Mortgage Market and the Renegotiable Term Mortgages," *Alternative Mortgage Instruments Research Study, Volume 1.*

[18]U.S., Federal Home Loan Bank Board, "Proposed Amendments, Alternative Mortgage Instruments," Code of Federal Regulations, October 23, 1980, Part 545, no. 80-653.

[19]Milwaukee, Wis., Mortgage Guaranty Insurance Corporation, *Action!® Mortgage: A Simple GPM Program That Works,* rev. 1, p.4.

[20]Most of this section is based on material from *Federal Register*, October 8, 1980, vol. 45, no. 197, pp. 66789–801.

[21]U.S., "Rules and Regulations," *Federal Register*, October 23, 1981, vol. 46, no. 205, p. 51897.

[22]ibid.

[23]ibid.

CHAPTER 4 Mortgage Lenders—Institutional (Primary) Lenders

LEARNING OBJECTIVES

In this chapter we will discuss the institutional, or primary, lenders in the United States. We will also examine the four basic institutional lenders: savings and loan associations, commercial banks, mutual savings banks, and life insurance companies. Upon completion of the chapter you should be able to do the following:

- ★ **Define *institutional lender.***
- ★ **Outline the amount of mortgage debt and distribution of the debt by type of lender.**
- ★ **Select the proper institutional lender to use in a particular lending situation.**
- ★ **Explain the lending policies of the various institutional lenders.**

DEFINITION

An *institutional lender* is a lender that meets the following two criteria: (1) the lender is highly regulated by either federal or state agencies and, in some cases, by both agencies; and (2) it is an institution or depository that pools funds from individuals and/or companies and reinvests these funds in some type of securities, such as real estate loans. In other words, an institutional lender uses its deposits, or income, to make real estate loans.

INTERMEDIATION AND DISINTERMEDIATION

Whenever institutional lenders, or any lenders who accumulate funds from outside sources, are discussed, two important terms must be understood. One is *intermediation*. This is the term used for the gathering of funds by a lender and then the lending or supplying of the funds to a borrower. Thus, the lender is serving as an intermediary, or go-between, between persons with funds and the person who needs funds. As we shall see in this chapter, this process is very important to the real estate industry.

The opposite of intermediation is *disintermediation*. This is the taking out or the withdrawal of funds from the institutional lender and the reinvesting in some other savings instrument with a higher yield. Disintermediation was a very important action that happened during the recession of 1979-1981. Depositors were withdrawing their savings from the savings associations in record amounts in order to try to keep up with inflation. The term became frequently used during the recession, and it has a great impact on the real estate market. The more disintermediation, the less funds there are available to lenders to make real estate loans.

Now that we have some idea of what an institutional lender is, let us see how mortgage loans are distributed among the institutional lenders.

AMOUNT OF MORTGAGE DEBT[1]

The residential mortgage debt, or the amount of residential credit, since 1950 has been growing faster than any other form of credit. The total amount of the credit debt has risen from $427 billion in 1950 to $4,663.1 billion at the end of 1980. This is over a tenfold increase. Accordingly, the residential debt rose during the same period, but at an even faster pace. In 1950, the total outstanding residential debt was $54.5 billion. By the end of 1980, the preliminary figures show this debt to have risen more than twenty times to $1,094.3 billion, or over 23 percent of the total outstanding credit in the United States. The only other debt of similar magnitude is the national debt. At the end of 1980, the federal debt was $1,043.5 billion. When we compare this to the national debt in 1950 of $218.4 billion, one can see that the national debt is not growing nearly as fast as the residential debt.

How does the residential debt break down according to types of loans? The one- to four-family homes make up a major portion of the debt. They account for $956.5 billion of the total debt of $1,094.3 billion. The remainder of the debt is to finance the construction or the purchase of multifamily units. Using Figure 4-1, we can compare the residential mortgage loans not only to the national debt, but also to the credit of consumers, state and local governments, and mortgages on commercial properties. This comparison shows that not only is residential credit the largest, it is also the fastest growing. This rapid growth points out the Great American Dream of everyone owning a home of their own.

The volatility of residential credit is quite evident when a year-to-year comparison is made as is illustrated by Figure 4-2. One can see that in 1970 the annual increase of residential credit declined to only 6.7 percent due to the credit crunch in that year. In the late sixties and early seventies, the annual increase continued to rise until the recession of 1974 and 1975. The annual increase was only 7.9 percent in 1974 and decreased even further in 1975 to 7.6 percent. In the following year, the rate of increase jumped to 11.8 percent. The decreases in the annual increase reflect the decrease or distinermediation of the loanable funds from the *thrift institutions*. Thrift institutions are savings and loan associations, mutual savings banks, and credit unions.

Figure 4-1. Growth In Selected Types of Credit (in billions of dollars)

Type of Credit	1960	1980*	Increase
Total Credit Outstanding	$777.7	$4,663.1	$3,885.4
Residential Mortgage Loans:			
One- to Four-family Homes	141.9	956.5	814.6
Apartments	20.8	137.9	117.1
Total	162.7	1,094.3	931.6
Corporate and Foreign Bonds	90.0	491.3	401.3
State and Local Government Obligations	70.8	334.9	264.1
Consumer Credit	56.1	385.4	329.3
Mortgages on Commercial Properties	33.4	258.8	225.4
Federal Debt	243.1	1,043.5	800.4

Note: Components may not add to totals due to rounding.
*Preliminary.

Source: Federal Reserve Board; United States League of Savings Associations. Reprinted with permission from United States League of Savings Associations, *'81 Savings and Loan Sourcebook*, p. 24.

Figure 4-2. Total Residential Mortgage Loans Outstanding (in billions of dollars)

Year	Total Residential Debt	Annual Increase†	Percentage Increase†	Year	Total Residential Debt	Annual Increase†	Percentage Increase†	Year	Total Residential Debt	Annual Increase†	Percentage Increase†
1960	$ 162.7	$ 12.2	9.8%	1971	$ 397.6	$ 39.8	11.1%	1976	$ 661.0	$ 69.6	11.8%
1965	258.7	19.2	9.7	1972	454.1	56.5	14.2	1977	768.4	107.4	16.2
1970	357.8	19.8	6.7	1973	509.3	55.2	12.2	1978	885.5	117.1	15.2
				1974	549.4	40.1	7.9	1979	1,005.1	119.6	13.5
				1975	591.4	42.0	7.6	1980*	1,094.3	89.2	8.9

*Preliminary.
†1960, 1965 and 1970 increases are five-year annual averages.

Source: Federal Reserve Board. Reprinted with permission from United States League of Savings Associations, *'81 Savings and Loan Sourcebook*, p. 24.

DISTRIBUTION OF DEBT BY LENDERS

Now that we have examined the amount of the mortgage debt and how it is divided among various types of real estate loans, let us look at how this debt is divided among the various types of lenders.

As of the end of 1980, the major source of mortgage credit was the savings and loan associations. The savings and loans accounted for 43.6 percent of all of the one- to four-family loans made in the United States. The savings and loan associations also are the single largest holders of mortgages on multifamily dwellings, accounting for 28.2 percent of all mortgages.

The importance of the savings and loan associations can be seen in Figure 4-3. One can see that for residential loans, the nearest competitor to the S and Ls are the commercial banks, who at the end of 1980 had outstanding $160.7 billion in first-lien mortgages on one- to four-family dwellings. When comparing this to the amount of loans outstanding by the S and Ls, one can see that the S and Ls had almost three times the dollar amount outstanding at the end of 1980.

Looking further at the distribution of the residential mortgages outstanding, one can see that even when combined, mutual savings banks with $65.3 billion in one- to four-family loans, the life insurance companies with $18.4 billion in loans outstanding, and all other lenders with $294.3 billion, still do not equal the loans outstanding or made by the S and Ls by the end of 1980.

In Figure 4-4, one can see that since 1960 the S and Ls have been the leader, but there are some interesting trends that have been developing in the past few years. One is that

Figure 4-3. Mortgage Loans Outstanding, by Type of Property and Lender, Year-End 1980* (in billions of dollars)

	RESIDENTIAL PROPERTIES					
Lender	*One- to Four-family*	*Multi family*	*Total*	*Commercial Properties*	*Farm Properties*	*Total Mortgage Loans*
Savings Associations	$417.8	$ 39.0	$ 456.8	$ 45.9	†	$ 502.8
Commercial Banks	160.7	12.3	173.0	82.7	$ 8.9	264.6
Mutual Savings Banks	65.3	17.3	82.6	17.1	0.1	99.8
Life Insurance Companies	18.4	19.8	38.2	79.8	12.8	130.9
All Others	294.3	49.5	343.7	33.3	74.6	451.5
Total	$956.5	$137.9	$1,094.3	$258.8	$96.5	$1,449.6

Note: Components may not add to totals due to rounding.
*Preliminary.
†Less than $50 million.

Sources: Federal Home Loan Bank Board; Federal Reserve Board. Reprinted with permission from United States League Savings Associations, *'81 Savings and Loan Sourcebook*, p. 25.

Figure 4-4. ***One- To Four-Family Mortgage Loans Outstanding, by Lender (Billions of Dollars)***

Year-end	Savings Associations	Mutual Savings Banks	Commercial Banks	Life Insurance Companies	Federally Supported Agencies†	All Others	Total
1960	$ 55.4	$20.6	$ 19.2	$24.9	$ 7.1	$ 14.7	$141.9
1965	94.2	33.8	30.4	29.6	6.6	25.9	220.5
1970	124.5	42.1	42.3	26.8	24.7	37.3	297.7
1971	141.0	43.4	48.0	24.6	30.5	40.1	327.6
1972	165.6	46.2	57.0	22.3	36.1	44.2	371.4
1973	187.1	48.8	68.0	20.4	41.9	50.0	416.2
1974	201.0	49.2	74.8	19.0	53.5	51.9	449.4
1975	223.9	50.0	77.0	17.6	67.9	54.4	490.8
1976	260.8	53.1	86.2	16.1	80.0	60.3	556.5
1977	310.7	57.6	105.1	14.7	99.2	69.3	656.6
1978	356.1	62.3	129.2	14.4	123.0	79.2	764.2
1979	394.4	64.7	149.5	16.2	157.3	93.8	875.9
1980*	417.8	65.3	160.7	18.4	186.6	107.7	956.5

*Preliminary.
†Includes mortgage pools.

Source: Federal Reserve Board. Reprinted with permission from United States League of Savings Associations, *'81 Savings and Loan Sourcebook*, p. 26.

the commercial banks are starting to make more of these types of loans. This is seen if we compare the percentage held by these banks in 1965 to the percentage in 1980, as illustrated in Figure 4-5: the commercial banks have increased their percentage from 13.8 to 16.8. The most dramatic change, however, has come in the percentage of the outstanding loans held by the insurance companies, which has dropped from 13.4 percent in 1965 to 1.9 percent in 1980. Another major change is the role of federally supported agencies—the Federal National Mortgage Association, the Government National Mortgage Association, and the Federal Home Loan Bank System. In Figure 4-5, one can see that these agencies have increased their percentage of outstanding loans over six times since 1965 and this trend will probably continue for the next few years. The reason is that these agencies do not have to rely on the money from depositors. They can sell bonds in the open market secured by first-lien mortgages to raise money for mortgages.

When studying the outstanding mortgages on multifamily properties, one can see that the S and Ls still are the leader with $38.5 billion outstanding at the end of 1979, as shown in Figure 4-3. Looking further at this figure, one can see that for commercial property loans

Figure 4-5. ***Mortgage Loans Outstanding on One- To Four-Family Homes by Type of Lender, Year-End 1965 and 1980***

Lender	Percent of Debt	
	*1965**	*1980†*
Savings Associations	42.7%	43.7%
Mutual Savings Banks	15.3%	6.8%
Commercial Banks	13.8%	16.8%
Life Insurance Companies	13.4%	1.9%
Federally Supported Agencies	3.0%	19.3%

*Source: Federal Home Loan Bank Board; Federal Reserve. Reprinted with permission from United States League of Savings Associations, *1979 Savings and Loan Fact Book*, p. 32.

†Source: U.S., Federal Reserve, *Federal Reserve Bulletin*, October 1981, p. A41.

outstanding, the commercial banks and the insurance companies are the leaders.

Now that we have looked at the amount of the mortgage credit outstanding and how it is distributed among the major lenders in the United States, let us examine the major institutional lenders. We will cover the development and the number of each in the United States.

SAVINGS AND LOAN ASSOCIATIONS

As we learned in Chapter 1, the savings and loan associations had their roots in colonial times with the formation of informal clubs or associations. The members of these groups would pool their funds in a central treasury, and the money was lent to the members for various needs. These clubs, or pools of funds, had no regulation, and therefore most went bankrupt, usually due to the borrowers not repaying the loans. It is not until 1831 that we find the beginnings of the modern-day savings and loan associations, then called building associations. These associations were formed for the specific purpose of accumulating funds from the general public in order to supply funds for the construction of homes. The first loan made by a building association was the amount of $375, and it was to be repaid at the rate of $4.90 per month. All of the early savings and loan associations were regulated by the states in which they were located.

Federal regulation was nonexistent before the Depression. In 1932, with the passage of the Federal Home Loan Bank Act, the Federal Home Loan Bank Board was established to oversee the operations of the savings and loan associations. The activity of the FHLBB is similar to that of the Federal Reserve. As with the banks and the Federal Reserve, all federally chartered savings and loan associations must belong to the FHLBB. All state-chartered associations may join if they wish.

The Federal Home Loan Bank Board organization is similar to that of the Federal Reserve in that the United States is divided into twelve districts with each district having a district bank. The districts are shown in Figure 4-6, with the address and the area served listed in Figure 4-7.

As with the Federal Reserve, the Federal Home Loan Bank Board has a board, but the board for the FHLBB is somewhat smaller in that it has only three members. In addition to being smaller, the President of the United States appoints all three persons with the advice and consent of the Senate. The term for each member is four years. Since these positions are political appointments, the law requires that no more than two of the board members be from the same political party.

The Federal Home Loan Bank Board office is in Washington, D.C., and has the responsibility of chartering and regulating all federal savings associations and overseeing the operation of the Federal Savings and Loan Insurance Corporation (FSLIC) and the Federal Home Loan Mortgage Corporation (FHLMC).

Another important piece of legislation implemented as a result of the Depression was the National Housing Act of 1934. In addition to this act establishing the Federal Housing Administration, it established the Federal Savings and Loan Insurance Corporation. The purpose of this corporation was to insure the savings accounts in savings and loan associations. As with the Federal Home Loan Bank Board, the federally chartered savings and loan associations must belong to this corporation, but the state-chartered associations may join if they wish. As illustrated in Figure 4-8, as of the end of 1980 only 611 of the 4613 total savings associations were not insured by the FSLIC. As of 1980, the FSLIC insured any account in a participating S and L up to a limit of $100,000.

In reviewing the history of the S and Ls, we should examine the types of charters and forms of ownership. All of the savings and loan associations were originally founded as mutual associations. With this type of ownership, the depositors are the owners of the association. The associations did not sell stock, therefore they did not have stockholders. This form of ownership has undergone some change in the last few years as some of the federally chartered savings and loan associations have been allowed to sell stock to the general public and have become public-held corporations.

The distribution by state of all of the federally chartered S and Ls and their assets as of December 31, 1980, is given in Figure 4-9.

Now that we have briefly covered the history of the savings and loan associations in the United States, let us review their lending policies.

Figure 4-6. Federal Home Loan Bank Districts

Source: U.S., Federal Financial Institutions Examination Council, *A Citizen's Guide to CRA*, January 1981, p. 31.

Figure 4-7. Federal Home Loan Bank Districts

Federal Home Loan Bank of Boston One Federal Street, 30th Floor P.O. Box 2196 Boston, Massachusetts 02106	(617) 223-5300 Connecticut, Maine, Massachusetts, New Hampshire, Rhode Island, Vermont
Federal Home Loan Bank of New York One World Trade Center, Floor 103 New York, New York 10048	(212) 432-2000 New Jersey, New York Puerto Rico
Federal Home Loan Bank of Pittsburgh Eleven Stanwix Street, Fourth Floor Gateway Center Pittsburgh, Pennsylvania 15222	(412) 288-3400 Delaware, Pennsylvania, West Virginia
Federal Home Loan Bank of Atlanta Coastal States Building P.O. Box 56527 260 Peachtree Street, N. W. Peachtree Center Station Atlanta, Georgia 30343	(404) 522-2450 Alabama, District of Columbia, Florida, Georgia, Maryland, North Carolina, South Carolina, Virginia
Federal Home Loan Bank of Cincinnati 2500 DuBois Tower P.O. Box 598 Cincinnati, Ohio 45201	(513) 852-7500 Kentucky, Ohio, Tennessee
Federal Home Loan Bank of Indianapolis 1350 Merchants Plaza, South Tower 115 West Washington Street P.O. Box 60 Indianapolis, Indiana 46204	(317) 269-5200 Indiana, Michigan
Federal Home Loan Bank of Chicago 111 East Wacker Drive, Suite 800 Chicago, Illinois 60601	(312) 565-5700 Illinois, Wisconsin
Federal Home Loan Bank of Des Moines 907 Walnut Street Des Moines, Iowa 50309	(515) 243-4211 Iowa, Minnesota, Missouri, North Dakota, South Dakota
Federal Home Loan Bank of Little Rock 1400 Tower Building Little Rock, Arkansas 72201	(501) 372-7141 Arkansas, Louisiana Mississippi, New Mexico, Texas
Federal Home Loan Bank of Topeka 3 Townsite Plaza 120 East 6th Street P.O. Box 176 Topeka, Kansas 66601	(913) 233-0507 Colorado, Kansas, Nebraska, Oklahoma
Federal Home Loan Bank of San Francisco 600 California Street P.O. Box 7948 San Francisco, California 94120	(415) 393-1000 Arizona, California, Nevada
Federal Home Loan Bank of Seattle 600 Stewart Street Seattle, Washington 98101	(206) 624-3980 Alaska, Hawaii, Guam, Idaho, Montana, Oregon, Utah, Washington, Wyoming

Source: U.S., Federal Financial Institutions Examination Council, *A Citizen's Guide to CRA*, January 1981, pp. 33-34.

Figure 4-8. Number and Assets of Savings Associations, by Charter

Year-end	Federally Chartered†	STATE-CHARTERED Total	FSLIC-insured	Noninsured‡	Grand Total
1960	1,873	4,447	2,225	2,222	6,320
1965	2,011	4,174	2,497	1,677	6,185
1970	2,067	3,602	2,298	1,304	5,669
1971	2,049	3,425	2,222	1,203	5,474
1972	2,044	3,254	2,147	1,107	5,298
1973	2,040	3,130	2,123	1,007	5,170
1974	2,060	2,963	2,081	882	5,023
1975	2,048	2,883	2,030	853	4,931
1976	2,019	2,802	2,025	777	4,821
1977	2,012	2,749	2,053	696	4,761
1978	2,000	2,725	2,053	672	4,725
1979	1,989	2,695	2,050	645	4,684
1980*	1,985	2,628	2,017	611	4,613
		MILLIONS OF DOLLARS			
1960	$ 38,511	$ 32,965	$ 28,919	$ 4,046	$ 71,476
1965	66,715	62,865	57,861	5,004	129,580
1970	96,259	79,924	74,386	5,538	176,183
1971	114,229	91,794	85,755	6,039	206,023
1972	135,925	107,202	100,424	6,778	243,127
1973	152,240	119,665	112,557	7,108	271,905
1974	167,671	127,874	120,552	7,322	295,545
1975	195,410	142,823	134,849	7,974	338,233
1976	225,763	166,144	157,409	8,735	391,907
1977	261,920	197,321	188,078	9,243	459,241
1978	298,195	225,347	215,115	10,232	523,542
1979	323,058	255,904	245,049	10,855	578,962
1980*	348,461	281,368	270,004	11,364	629,829

*Preliminary.
†All federally chartered associations are insured by the Federal Savings and Loan Insurance Corporation.
‡Includes the assets of institutions insured by the Co-operative Central Bank of Massachusetts, the Maryland Savings-Share Insurance Corporation, the North Carolina Savings Guaranty Corporation, the Ohio Deposit Guarantee Fund and the Pennsylvania Savings Association Insurance Corporation.

Sources: Federal Home Loan Bank Board; United States League of Savings Associations. Reprinted with permission from the United States League of Savings Associations, *'81 Savings and Loan Sourcebook*, p. 37.

Lending Policy

Savings and loan associations keep most of their assets in mortgages secured by real estate. At the end of 1979, 83 percent of the mortgages held by insured associations were on one- to four-family homes. In addition to the loans secured by one- to four-family homes, 7.8 percent of the associations' outstanding loans were on multifamily homes. This means that the loans on dwellings represent 90.8 percent of the total loan portfolio of these insured associations. These figures show that the S and Ls are an important factor in the financing of housing in the United States.

These associations usually make loans in an area of influence. This area can vary with each association. An association located in a major metropolitan market may make loans within so many miles of its office or branch offices. This can be as little as two miles and as much as thirty miles. Associations do not like to make loans in areas where they do not have experience or to builders that they have not made loans to in the past.

What type of loans do savings and loan associations make? As stated earlier, the associations make the majority of their loans as real estate loans on homes. These loans are usually held to 90 percent of the appraised value of the home except for those loans insured by the government or by private mortgage insurance or guaranteed by the Veterans Administration. The terms of the loans made by these associations are normally thirty years. In some cases, this term has been extended to forty years. In addition to the standard mortgage, savings and loan associations are allowed to use the alternative mortgage instruments. The authorized alternative mortgage instruments were discussed in Chapter 3.

Federally chartered S and Ls Prior to the implementation of Title IV of the Depository Institutions Deregulation and Monetary Control Act of 1980, the federally chartered savings and loan associations were somewhat limited, but on November 10, 1980, the lending restrictions were significantly liberalized. Some of the major changes are as follows:

1. All statutory dollar limits on home loans secured by real estate, including loans on apartments, have been removed. In addition, the Federal Home Loan Bank Board eliminated the maximum dollar amounts for home improvement loans.

2. In implementing a provision of the act, the Federal Home Loan Bank Board revised the loan-to-value ratio for real estate mortgages. Under the previous regulations, the Federal Home Loan Bank Board required that the residential loan not exceed 80 percent of the value of the property unless the mortgage was insured by the FHA, guaranteed by the Veterans Administration, or insured by an approved private mortgage insurance company. This percentage has been increased to 90 percent of the value, thus making the 90 percent loan the basic home mortgage. The board has increased the multifamily loan limit from 80 percent to 90 percent.

Figure 4-9. Number and Assets of Savings Associations, by State, December 31, 1980*

State	Number of Associations	Total Assets (Millions)	Per Capita Assets	State	Number of Associations	Total Assets (Millions)	Per Capita Assets
Alabama	58	$ 5,012	$1,288	Montana	15	$ 1,128	$1,433
Alaska	5	411	1,027	Nebraska	39	5,457	3,476
Arizona	18	6,570	2,417	Nevada	8	2,444	3,059
Arkansas	75	4,502	1,970	New Hampshire	17	1,151	1,250
California	195	120,532	5,092	New Jersey	207	25,209	3,423
Colorado	46	10,007	3,464	New Mexico	34	2,616	2,013
Connecticut	39	4,417	1,421	New York	115	27,719	1,579
Delaware	18	270	455	North Carolina	194	12,315	2,097
District of Columbia	14	5,050	7,916	North Dakota	11	2,426	3,715
Florida	130	53,372	5,480	Ohio	384	40,602	3,760
Georgia	97	11,147	2,040	Oklahoma	55	5,854	1,935
Guam	2	70	592	Oregon	33	7,129	2,708
Hawaii	8	4,263	4,418	Pennsylvania	358	24,941	2,102
Idaho	12	1,042	1,104	Puerto Rico	12	2,302	640
Illinois	370	46,159	4,043	Rhode Island	5	770	813
Indiana	161	10,421	1,898	South Carolina	75	6,473	2,075
Iowa	73	7,235	2,484	South Dakota	19	1,135	1,645
Kansas	79	7,332	3,103	Tennessee	99	7,425	1,617
Kentucky	102	5,986	1,635	Texas	320	35,303	2,481
Louisiana	131	8,528	2,029	Utah	15	4,263	2,918
Maine	19	693	616	Vermont	7	246	481
Maryland	188	10,707	2,540	Virginia	84	9,701	1,815
Massachusetts	154	8,385	1,461	Washington	48	9,709	2,351
Michigan	63	18,426	1,990	West Virginia	32	1,621	831
Minnesota	56	10,637	2,609	Wisconsin	108	12,689	2,697
Mississippi	59	2,975	1,180	Wyoming	12	1,029	2,185
Missouri	110	16,149	3,284				
				Entire U.S.	4,613	$629,829	$2,759

Note: Components do not add to totals because of differences in reporting dates and accounting systems.
*Preliminary.

Sources: Bureau of the Census; Federal Home Loan Bank Board; United States League of Savings Associations. Reprinted with permission from United States League of Savings Associations, *'81 Savings and Loan Sourcebook*, p. 38.

3. The board has authorized all federally chartered saving and loans to make home loans of up to forty years instead of the previous thirty-year term.

4. The act also eliminated requiring all federally chartered savings and loans to make only real estate mortgages that were secured by first-lien mortgages. This permits federally chartered S and Ls to make junior or second mortgages. The only restriction on the S and Ls making the junior mortgage is that they maintain sufficient documentation to indicate that the prior liens on the property do not exceed the prescribed loan-to-value ratios.

In addition to making loans on homes, savings and loans make construction loans. These are loans for the construction of one- to four-family homes. This type of loan had accounted for more than 30 percent of all of the associations lending in the 1950s, but it has been declining and now represents approximately 18 percent.

In addition to construction loans, S and Ls make home improvement loans and mobile home loans.

State-chartered S and Ls In addition to federally chartered savings and loan associations, the states have the authority to charter S and Ls for operation in the individual states. The lending policies for these state-chartered S and Ls are set by the individual state legislatures and/or the state commission charged with overseeing and regulating these associations.

Since this policy will vary widely from state to state, the individual lending policies for every state will not be reviewed in this text. To secure the lending information for state-chartered S and Ls, contact the appropriate commission or agency in your state.

LIFE INSURANCE COMPANIES[2]

As do the other institutional lenders, the life insurance companies have their roots in colonial times. At the end of 1980, there were 1,948 legal reserve life insurance companies in operation in the United States. The most rapid growth of the life insurance companies came after World War II. In 1900, there were only 84 companies in operation. By 1905, the number had increased to 126. The trend for growth continued at the same pace, and by 1930 there were 438 companies in existence. By 1940, the number had grown to 444. Then in the 1950s, the rapid growth started. The number of companies had grown to 649 in 1950 and in just five years, this number had almost doubled to 1,107. During the 1960s, the industry grew from 1,441 in 1960 to 1,773 by 1969. The 1970s saw a slowing of the growth pattern with only the addition of 16 new companies by 1977, for a total of 1,789.

Life insurance companies can be organized as either mutuals or stock companies. The mutual life insurance company is a company that is owned by the policyholders and the policyholders share in the profits of the company through the reduction of premiums. If the life insurance company is a stock company, like any other corporation it is operated for the benefit and profit of the stockholders. No matter what the type of life insurance company, all life insurance companies are regulated by the state in which they do business. This means, for example, that if a life insurance company has its main office in Maine and wishes to do business in Texas, it must seek a license or the authority from the State Board of Insurance in Texas before it may do business in Texas.

If you would like more information on life insurance companies, the American Council of Life Insurance prepares a *Life Insurance Fact Book* each year that reviews the industry in depth.

Mortgage Lending in the United States

Life insurance company holdings in mortgages at the end of 1980 amounted to $131.1 billion, or 27.4 percent of their total assets. Real estate mortgages have always been a very attractive investment for life insurance companies because of the safety (secured by real property), good yields or returns to the company, and favorable maturities. Insurance companies are looking for a longer maturity of their investments because they can, through the use of mortality tables, predict very accurately the deaths of their policyholders; thus they can predict the need for cash. With the regular payments of mortgage loans, they can predict the income from their mortgage loan portfolios. For these reasons, life insurance companies rank third among the major institutional lenders.

During the 1950s, life insurance companies were heavily involved with residential loans, but they have reduced this type of loan dramatically in the past twenty years. In 1958, the residential mortgage represented approximately 60 percent of the mortgages they held. By 1968 this percentage had dropped to 41 percent, and by the end of 1980 this type of loan was a mere 13.5 percent of the total mortgages outstanding. This dramatic reduction in the one- to four-family loans reflected a change in the investment policy of the life insurance companies from one- to four-family loans to the nonresidential loan. These nonresidential loans are loans secured by commercial, industrial, and institutional types of properties. This type of loan has risen from only 23 percent of the total outstanding loans in 1958 to 61.5 percent in 1980.

Mortgage Lending

Since a life insurance company is controlled by the state in which it operates, the type of real estate loans that can be made is set either by the state agency that oversees the operation of the life insurance companies or by the state legislature by the enactment of laws.

Normally the life insurance company will be rather conservative in its real estate lending policy. The reason for this attitude is that the life insurance companies are required by law to protect the funds of its policyholders. Therefore, the regulations implemented by the states allowing the insurance companies to make real estate loans are more restrictive.

Usually the loan-to-value ratio on any mortgage made by a life insurance company is held to a maximum of 75 percent of the value of the real property. In some cases, several of the states will allow the loan-to-value ratio to go as high as 90 percent as long as the portion of the mortgage above 75 to 80 percent loan-to-value ratio is insured by a mortgage insurance company licensed to operate in the state where the property is located. Some states also have passed laws or implemented regulations stating that prescribed loan-to-value ratios do not apply to mortgages either insured or guaranteed by an agency of the federal government.

One additional feature of the lending policy of the life insurance companies should be pointed out. Since the insurance companies are more interested in the long-term income generated by the thirty-year mortgage, these mortgages normally will have a prepayment penalty which is usually expressed as a percentage of the remaining principal balance.

For the lending policy allowed in your state, you will need to contact the state agency which has the responsibility for the regulation of life insurance companies. A listing of the state insurance officials as listed in the *1981 Life Insurance Fact Book* is shown in Figure 4-10.

COMMERCIAL BANKS

As we learned in Chapter 1, the development of commercial banks can also be traced to colonial times, with the first being founded in 1781. Commercial banks were for the most part chartered by the states, with very little federal regulation. The first attempt at federal regulation of commercial banks came with the passage of the National Bank Act in 1863. It continued in 1913 with the establishment of the Federal Reserve Bank, whose purpose it was to administer and regulate federally chartered banks.

There were no major changes in the national banking system until the Great Depression, when nearly one half of the commercial banks in the United States failed. As a result of these failures, Congress passed the Banking Act of 1933 which, as one of its provisions, established the Federal Deposit Insurance Corporation. The purpose of the Corporation was to insure the accounts held by commercial banks. As with membership in the Federal Reserve, membership in FDIC is mandatory for all national banks, but any state-chartered bank may be insured by FDIC if it will adhere to the banking practices outlined in the act. Over 95 percent of all commercial banks are insured by FDIC.

As with any other thrift institution, a commercial bank serves as a depository of funds and as an institution where money may be borrowed. The commercial bank has two sources of funds: *demand deposits* and *time deposits*. Demand deposits are deposits that are held in accounts that the customer, or depositor, may withdraw without notice. An example of such an account is a checking account. A time deposit can be defined as an

Figure 4-10. State Insurance Officials

State, Capital	Official	Title
Alabama, Montgomery	Tharpe Forrester	*Commissioner of Insurance*
Alaska, Juneau	Kenneth C. Moore	*Director of Insurance*
Arizona, Phoenix	J. Michael Low	*Director of Insurance*
Arkansas, Little Rock	William H. L. Woodyard, III	*Insurance Commissioner*
California, Los Angeles	Robert C. Quinn	*Insurance Commissioner*
Colorado, Denver	J. Richard Barnes	*Commissioner of Insurance*
Connecticut, Hartford	Joseph C. Mike	*Insurance Commissioner*
Delaware, Dover	David H. Elliot	*Insurance Commissioner*
D.C., Washington	James R. Montgomery, III, Acting	*Superintendent of Insurance*
Florida, Tallahassee	Bill Gunter	*Insurance Commissioner*
Georgia, Atlanta	Johnnie L. Caldwell	*Insurance Commissioner*
Hawaii, Honolulu	Mary G. F. Bitterman, Ph.D.	*Insurance Commissioner*
Idaho, Boise	Trent M. Woods	*Director of Insurance*
Illinois, Chicago	Phillip R. O'Connor	*Director of Insurance*
Indiana, Indianapolis	Don H. Miller	*Commissioner of Insurance*
Iowa, Des Moines	Bruce Foudree	*Commissioner of Insurance*
Kansas, Topeka	Fletcher Bell	*Commissioner of Insurance*
Kentucky, Frankfort	Daniel D. Briscoe	*Commissioner of Insurance*
Louisiana, Baton Rouge	Sherman A. Bernard	*Commissioner of Insurance*
Maine, Augusta	Theodore T. Briggs	*Superintendent of Insurance*
Maryland, Baltimore	Edward J. Birrane, Jr.	*Insurance Commissioner*
Massachusetts, Boston	Michael J. Sabbagh	*Commissioner of Insurance*
Michigan, Lansing	Nancy A. Baerwaldt	*Commissioner of Insurance*
Minnesota, St. Paul	Michael D. Markman	*Commissioner of Insurance*
Mississippi, Jackson	George Dale	*Commissioner of Insurance*
Missouri, Jefferson City	C. Donald Ainsworth	*Director of Insurance*
Montana, Helena	E.V. "Sonny" Omholt	*Commissioner of Insurance*
Nebraska, Lincoln	Walter D. Weaver	*Director of Insurance*
Nevada, Carson City	Patsy Redmond	*Commissioner of Insurance*
New Hampshire, Concord	Frank E. Whaland	*Insurance Commissioner*
New Jersey, Trenton	James J. Sheeran	*Commissioner of Insurance*
New Mexico, Santa Fe	Manuel A. Garcia, Jr.	*Superintendent of Insurance*
New York, New York	Albert B. Lewis	*Superintendent of Insurance*
North Carolina, Raleigh	John R. Ingram	*Commissioner of Insurance*
North Dakota, Bismarck	J.O. "Bud" Wigen	*Commissioner of Insurance*
Ohio, Columbus	Robert L. Ratchford, Jr.	*Superintendent of Insurance*
Oklahoma, Oklahoma City	Gerald Grimes	*Insurance Commissioner*
Oregon, Salem	Wilfred W. Fritz	*Commissioner of Insurance*
Pennsylvania, Harrisburg	Michael L. Browne	*Commissioner of Insurance*
Rhode Island, Providence	Thomas J. Caldarone, Jr.	*Insurance Commissioner*
South Carolina, Columbia	John W. Lindsay	*Insurance Commissioner*
South Dakota, Pierre	Henry J. Lussem, Jr.	*Director of Insurance*
Tennessee, Nashville	John C. Neff	*Commissioner of Insurance*
Texas, Austin	E.J. Voorhis	*Commissioner of Insurance*
Utah, Salt Lake City	Roger C. Day	*Commissioner of Insurance*
Vermont, Montpelier	George A. Chaffee	*Commissioner of Insurance*
Virginia, Richmond	James W. Newman, Jr.	*Commissioner of Insurance*
Washington, Olympia	Dick Marquardt	*Insurance Commissioner*
West Virginia, Charleston	Richard G. Shaw	*Insurance Commissioner*
Wisconsin, Madison	Susan M. Mitchell	*Commissioner of Insurance*
Wyoming, Cheyenne	John T. Langdon	*Insurance Commissioner*

Source: American Council of Life Insurance, *1981 Life Insurance Fact Book*, p. 107.

account or certificate of deposit that cannot be drawn against before a specific notice is given or before a specific date. If these funds are withdrawn, there will be a penalty imposed.

Most commercial banks are operated as corporations and are owned by stockholders. They are operated for the benefit of the stockholders of the corporation. Commercial banks operate under either a federal charter or a state charter. If the bank operates under a federal charter, it is known as a national bank and it must be a member of the Federal Reserve and FDIC. If the bank is operating under a state charter, the bank will be a state bank and it will operate under the control of a state agency. At the end of 1978, there were 14,729 commercial banks in the United States.

Real Estate Loan Policy

Since the majority of the deposits in these banks are demand-type deposits and can be withdrawn quickly, most commercial banks are not interested in making long-term commitments. Thus, most banks are not a good source of long-term real estate loans. They are more interested in the short-term, high-yield type of loan, such as automobile and other consumer loans.

Banks are an excellent source of funds for the interim or construction loan, especially if the builder or borrower has arranged for permanent financing prior to making application for the interim loan.

There have been some recent changes, however, in the thinking of the larger banks. Some have started to make long-term first-lien mortgages. This is not due to the change in the type of deposits the banks are receiving, but to the growth of the secondary markets. (We will discuss the secondary market in Chapters 9 and 10.) With the growth of these markets, the banks can make the long-term mortgage and sell it in the secondary market. Thus, the bank can derive income from the loan origination fee, from the servicing of the loan and, finally, from selling a loan with *participation*. In a participation sale of a mortgage, only a portion of the principal is sold to another lender and the bank can receive interest income on the portion of the principal not sold.

With the preceding in mind, one can see that commercial banks are a good source for the interim loan or short-term financing. In the near future, they may play a more important role in the long-term financing of real estate.

MUTUAL SAVINGS BANKS

Mutual savings banks are a unique type of thrift institution. They operate much like savings and loan associations, but in some areas offer the services of commercial banks. The mutuals were established along the same lines as the savings institutions of Europe. Prior to the early 1800s, most of the commercial banks would not accept deposits from individuals, and workers had no place to deposit small sums of money. So the mutuals were established. As the name implies, mutuals are owned by the depositors.

A mutual savings bank is chartered by the state in which it operates and is subject to the banking rules of that state. In some cases, mutual savings banks will join the Federal Deposit Insurance Corporation and/or the Federal Home Loan Bank Board. Then, in addition to the state authority, they are subject to federal regulations.

The majority of the approximately five hundred mutual savings banks are located on the East Coast, primarily in Massachusetts, New York, Connecticut, Maine, New Hampshire, New Jersey, Pennsylvania, Rhode Island, Vermont, Maryland, and Delaware. There are a few mutual savings banks in Wisconsin, Washington, Indiana, Oregon, and Alaska. Mutual savings banks are important because of their investment policy and their location. As we noted, most of the associations are located along the East Coast, where the building of single-family homes has slowed. The amount of deposits in these institutions, however, is still strong. The mutuals, therefore, are looking to make secure investments, and one of the most secure investments is in first-lien mortgages secured by real estate. So the mutuals, through correspondents, are looking at the rapid growth areas to invest in mortgages. Since the investment policy of the mutuals is quite conservative, they normally will not make loans on real estate at more than 80 percent of the value or sales price, whichever is lower. In some states, the mutuals may not make loans of more than 50 percent of the value, unless the loan is insured or has some type of guarantee. Thus, with the advent of the FHA-insured loan and VA-guaranteed loan, the mutuals were able to expand the number of loans they were able to originate or purchase through their correspondents. With this correspondent relationship in mind, we can see why these mutuals are important to the United States. These institutions have large pools of funds to loan, but the activity or need for loans in their area of operation has been slowing due to the movement of people from the East Coast to the Sunbelt. So the mutuals have been either purchasing loans from other thrift institutions or through their correspondents have been originating FHA and VA loans throughout the United States.

If you would like more information about mutual savings banks, a good source is the annual *Mutual Savings Bank Fact Book.*

REVIEW QUESTIONS

1. Define the terms *intermediation* and *disintermediation.*

2. Briefly describe the lending policies of savings and loan associations, life insurance companies, and commercial banks in your state.

3. What are the sources of the loanable funds in the United States?

4. In your opinion, how will real estate be financed in the future?

5. Why are mutual savings banks important?

6. Why have commercial banks just started to enter into the financing of real estate?

7. Which of the institutional lenders would be a source of funds to finance a single-family dwelling, a hospital, and an office building, and to provide a building loan?

NOTES

[1]Most of this section is based on material from United States League of Savings Associations, *'81 Savings and Loan Sourcebook.*

[2]Most of this section is based on material from American Council of Life Insurance, *1981 Life Insurance Fact Book.*

CHAPTER 5 Noninstitutional Lenders

LEARNING OBJECTIVES

In this chapter, we will discuss the noninstitutional lenders. A noninstitutional lender is not as strictly regulated as the institutional lender, or may have no regulation at all by either the federal or state governments. For our purposes, we will examine mortgage bankers, mortgage brokers, credit unions, and pension and retirement funds as noninstitutional lenders.

When you have completed your study of this chapter, you should be able to do the following:

- ★ **Explain the difference between a mortgage banker and a mortgage broker.**
- ★ **Outline the lending policy of credit unions in the United States.**
- ★ **Briefly explain each of the areas of operation of a mortgage banker.**
- ★ **Identify the sources of income for a mortgage banker.**

MORTGAGE COMPANIES

The common name for a mortgage company is *mortgage banker*. The term *mortgage banker* would imply that this type of lender is like the institutional one because the banker would accumulate funds through deposits and then loan these accumulated funds to the general public, but this is not the case. The modern mortgage banker is an intermediary and can be defined as "a firm or individual active in the field of Mortgage Banking. Mortgage Bankers, as local representatives of regional or national institutional lenders, act as correspondents between lenders and borrowers."[1]

History[2]

As with all of the other lenders in the United States, the origins of the mortgage banker, sometimes referred to as a mortgage company, can be traced back to a European counterpart. The modern mortgage banker, however, was nonexistent before the Civil War and those that began after the Civil War were primarily involved with the financing of farms. The majority of the operation of the lenders was in the Midwest, the Ohio Valley. The loans were of low loan-to-value ratio, usually 40 to 50 percent. The loans were not amortized over the term of the loan, but had a balloon payment, meaning the entire principal was due at the end of the term. Interest on these loans was payable either quarterly or semiannually. Like the mortgage bankers of today, these lenders were not making loans to keep in their portfolios. They were made for sale to institutional lenders or wealthy individuals.

The industry grew rapidly until the Great Depression. The reason for the bankruptcy of many mortgage bankers during the Depression was that they guaranteed the loans sold to the investors. This guarantee was not a true guarantee, but was more the custom of the industry. On a loan that went into default, the investor could choose between two plans: either the mortgage banker would substitute a new loan, or the mortgage banker would buy back the loan. As this practice grew, the companies were called, simply, *mortgage guarantee companies*. As with all of the other major financial operations, these were located primarily in New York City. As the economy in the late twenties and early thirties started to decline, many of the mortgages held by these guarantee companies went into default. More and more investors asked the companies to buy back the loans rather than substitute new loans. Many of the companies did not have the cash to do so and thus had to declare bankruptcy.

Why were there so many defaults during the Depression? Even though the borrower could keep a job, the problem came about at the end of the term, when the loan was to be refinanced. The term of a home loan at that time was normally five years, with no guarantee of refinancing. The Depression brought a severe lack of funds, and therefore the borrower could not refinance, nor did the borrower have the funds to repay the loan in total. The loan, therefore, went into default.

To help such persons keep their homes and to stop foreclosure, the federal government established the Homeowners' Loan Corporation in 1933. The purpose of this federal agency was to purchase the home that had been foreclosed, refinance the loan, and then have the homeowner repay the loan on a monthly basis. This was the beginning of the amortized mortgage.

The industry did not grow much until after World War II. Because of all of the people returning from the war, and because the thrift institutions had a large amount of savings on deposit, the housing industry and therefore the mortgage bankers grew overnight. Another reason for the rapid growth of the mortgage banking industry was the advent of the Federal Housing Administration. The FHA mortgages provided three very important elements that helped develop a national mortgage market: dependability, transferability, and minimal risk. This brings us to current mortgage banking. The industry as we know it today owes its growth to the decision of the insurance companies to engage in national lending because of the mortgage insurance provided by the FHA. With this growth of the mortgage market and the continued demand for housing, the mortgage banking industry has grown from small family operations to large corporations operating in several states. How important the mortgage bankers are to the financing of housing, particularly in the areas of the FHA and the VA, was illustrated in 1979 when mortgage bankers originated over 75 percent of all FHA and VA loans in the United States.

Regulation

There is no direct regulation of the mortgage banking industry. This means that neither the state nor the federal government has the ability to regulate this group of lenders in the same fashion as a bank, a savings and loan association, or a mutual savings bank. The only state laws that may affect a mortgage banker are laws governing the formation of corporations and/or partnerships. The only way that a mortgage banker is subject to federal review is if the lender is an approved FHA lender or FNMA seller/servicer. Then, the lender is subject to periodic audits. To strengthen its hold on the mortgage bankers, the Department of Housing and Urban Development has issued guidelines on how lenders are to handle problems with the borrower. Furthermore, the passage of federal laws involving equal credit and other antidiscrimination has affected the mortgage banker as well as other lenders. But, for the most part, they have remained relatively free of governmental control.

Lending Policy

Mortgage bankers conduct their lending operations rather differently from other lenders in that they normally lend not their own money, but the money of others through the use of commitments. These commitments are issued by the source of funds, such as savings and loans, insurance companies, FNMA, or FHLMC, the latter two being the largest source of these commitments. So, the mortgage company only implements the underwriting, or lending policies, of the institution issuing the commitment. For example, if a Georgia-based mortgage company serves as a correspondent for a life insurance company that is licensed to operate or has its home office in Georgia, the mortgage banker must make the real estate loans in accordance with Georgia laws governing the operation of life insurance companies.

Mortgage Banker Operations

The operation of the mortgage banker is similar to the operation of any other lender, except that the mortgage banker has no savings accounts or other sources of funds, as do institutional lenders. Rather, the mortgage banker originates the loans and sells them in the secondary market, or has previously arranged for an investor to purchase the loans. When making these loans, the mortgage banker executes seven steps:

1. Loan origination
2. Loan processing
3. Loan underwriting
4. Loan closing
5. Loan warehousing
6. Packaging and shipping
7. Loan servicing

Loan origination The process of loan origination is the solicitation of mortgages from realtors, builders, and so forth. The persons who actively seek to make loans on real property are sometimes called *loan solicitors* or *loan officers*, and these persons call on the real estate firms or builders. The loan officers seek clients or sources of loans, in order to fill commitments or to replace the loans that are paid off. These are the salespersons for the mortgage banking industry. As a real estate salesperson, you will become familiar with these persons as they come to your office and ask for the mortgages of the firm or from the individual salespersons. In the mortgage banking field, these loans are called *spot loans*. In most states, there is no license required for a person to become a loan solicitor.

Loan processing Loan processing is the actual gathering of the information that will enable the mortgage banker either to approve or reject the loan, based on the applicant or the property. This process is divided into two parts. First, the application is taken on a standard application form. Second, along with the application, additional forms are completed to allow the mortgage banker to verify the credit, employment, and financial condition of the applicant. (The application form and verification forms will be discussed in Chapter 13). The processing of a loan can take as little as a week or as long as six months. Loan processing has been complicated by the passage of several laws such as the Equal Credit Opportunity Act, the Real Estate Settlement Procedure Act, and the Fair Credit Reporting Act. These will be reviewed later in this text.

Loan underwriting Loan underwriting is defined as the "analysis of risk and the matching of it to an appropriate rate of return."[3] In other words, the process of underwriting is to see if the applicant, as well as the property, meets the requirements of the lender or investor. Since the mortgage banker deals with several investors, it is the underwriter's task to match the loan application to the proper investor. For example, a mortgage banker may have an investor that will make only 80 percent loan-to-value ratio loans on frame houses that are less than three years old. It would be foolish to submit to this investor a 90 percent loan of this type because it would be rejected.

With the growth of the conventional secondary market, primarily through the Federal National Mortgage Association and the Federal Home Loan Mortgage Corporation, the mortgage banking industry has adopted the two income ratios of these organizations for underwriting many conventional mortgages. These ratios are the income-to-total-house-payment ratio and the income-to-long-term-debt (including the total house payment) ratio. In addition to the ratios of FNMA and FHLMC, many mortgage bankers will only make mortgages that conform to the mortgage amounts acceptable to FNMA and FHLMC. With the adoption of these standards, it is easier for the mortgage banker to sell a package of conventional loans if all of the mortgages conform to the underwriting guidelines set forth by FNMA and FHLMC. The underwriting guidelines for FNMA and FHLMC will be discussed in Chapter 12.

Loan closing After all of the documents relating to the borrower and the property have been received, they will be checked to see that they conform to the lender's underwriting guidelines. If so, a letter is then issued to the borrower stating that the loan has been approved. The mortgage banker will then set a closing date for the transaction. It is hoped that the date set by the mortgage banker is on or before the date specified in the contract. Prior to the closing or the conclusion of the transaction, the mortgage banker will prepare or have prepared the necessary documents required by the investor or the person purchasing the loan, to be signed by the parties to the transaction. In addition to these documents, the mortgage banker will send to the closing agent a set of instructions to be followed at the time of closing. These instructions will be discussed in detail in Chapter 14.

Loan warehousing Loan warehousing is the borrowing of funds by the mortgage banker for a short term in order to fund the loan prior to the investor or lender actually purchasing or funding the loan. The warehousing loan is usually made at a commercial bank, using the closed mortgage or mortgages as collateral. Some banks require a copy of the commitment agreement from the investor. Without this ability, the mortgage banker could not fund the loan at closing or within twenty-four hours. The reason for this is that the investors do not buy loans one at a time, but in a package usually amounting to $1 million. This could be weeks later.

In using this warehouse line of credit, the mortgage banker hopes that the bank will charge an interest rate that is less than the rate on the mortgage and thus allow the mortgage banker a slight margin of profit. But in some cases, the rate on the warehouse loan is more than that charged on the mortgage. The mortgage banker then will lose money on the mortgage while it is in the warehouse. If, for example, the face interest rate on the mortgage is 12 percent and the warehouse loan rate is 14 percent, it is costing the mortgage banker 2 percent until the loan is delivered to the investor. Normally, the mortgage banker will absorb the loss, but in some cases the mortgage banker will pass this charge along, usually to the borrower, as a warehouse fee. During the high short-term interest rates of late 1979 through 1980, this was being done by many lenders.

Packaging and shipping As stated above, loans are shipped in a group, and this group is usually called a *package*. This package of loans will always conform to the requirements of the investor who is buying the loans. Normally, the package, when sold to the investor, will state the average loan-to-value ratio and the average term. Prior to the loans being packaged for shipment, a person in the mortgage company will, upon receipt of the closing papers from the closing agent, check to see whether all of the lender's instructions have been followed and all of the documents have been signed. If all things are in order, he or she will place the closed loans in a package for shipment to the investor.

Loan servicing After the loan is packaged and shipped to the investor, the mortgage banker still can perform one more function for the investor, and that is to service the loan. This servicing of the loan is the most profitable of all of the operations. Since many of the investors, including FNMA, do not have a servicing function in their operation, they will pay the originator of the loan to service the loan. What is involved in servicing the loan? It may include any or all of the following:

1. The collection of the monthly payment, the application of principal and interest, and the establishment of the escrow account where the proper amount is credited each month for taxes, insurance, and any other required fees.

2. Making the necessary payments on time for the taxes and insurance, including hazard insurance and private mortgage insurance, if any.

3. Acting for the investor in the event of loss due to fire or storm damage. In the case of condemnation procedures, the servicer will receive all awards to be applied to the loan balance and pay all fees and taxes.

4. Providing the borrower, as per the deed of trust or mortgage, with an annual statement of all collections and disbursements from

the escrow account, including all taxes and interest paid. This information is to be used by the borrower for federal and state income tax returns.

5. In case of default of the borrower, the mortgage banker or the trustee will handle all of the steps to foreclose against the borrower and secure the property for the investor.

For all of these services, the mortgage banker is paid a fee, usually no less than three-eighths of 1 percent of the loan balance. This amount may seem small, but it represents a major source of income to the mortgage banker.

Mortgage Bankers' Income

The major source of the mortgage banker's income is the servicing of loans. The mortgage banker can also earn income from other sources.

Origination fee This is a fee charged for taking the application, processing, closing, and any other operation that is necessary to get the loan on the books of the mortgage banker and into the servicing portfolio. This origination fee is also the source of payment of the loan officer who is in the field generating loans. The origination fee is usually 1 percent of the loan amount, but when dealing with a mortgage lender for the first time, it is good to ask the loan officer what his or her company charges for origination, prior to your sending a client.

Insurance sales Some of the mortgage bankers, in addition to making loans, are licensed by a state insurance commission either to sell insurance or accept a commmission from an insurance company. If the mortgage company is licensed to sell insurance, it will usually have a separate insurance company established. The mortgage banker will ask applicants if they have an insurance company they wish to use. If not, the mortgage company will place the required insurance with the insurance company that is owned by the mortgage company. If the mortgage company does not have an insurance company, it will recommend that the applicant use a company that has agreed to pay the mortgage banker a fee or commission for all clients referred to the insurance company.

Real estate sales Some of the larger mortgage bankers have set up, in addition to insurance companies, real estate firms. These firms usually will sell new homes in subdivisions that are financed by the mortgage banker, but they may also engage in the resale market. One such mortgage banker with a large real estate sale operation is First Mortgage of Texas, located in Houston.

Real estate development This, for the larger mortgage bankers, is a major source of income. Here, the mortgage banker buys large tracts of land, subdivides, and develops the land for sale to builders. A good example of this is Clear Lake City, near Houston, a development of First Mortgage of Texas. The development and sales of such subdivisions is usually done through the real estate or development company of the mortgage banker.

Gains made from the sales of mortgages This income is derived when a mortgage banker can sell to an investor mortgages that have a higher yield than is required. For example, an investor issues a commitment to a mortgage banker requiring a yield of 10.50 percent. The interest rate that is in the market place goes to 11.50 percent. The mortgage banker makes the loans at the prevailing rate and then sells them to the investor at the required yield of 10.50 percent. The mortgage banker, then, will be able to keep the dollars generated by the spread, or the difference, between the 10.50 required yield and the 11.50 yield on the mortgages. This spread will be in addition to the servicing fee paid by the investor.

THE MORTGAGE BROKER

A term sometimes used incorrectly to describe a mortgage banker is *mortgage broker*. The mortgage broker is much like a stockbroker, in that he or she is a specialist in matching persons with money to loan with persons who need to borrow money. His or her services are normally used for the unusual or large loans; for example, the loan on a large office building. For these services, the mortgage broker is paid a fee ranging from one-fourth of 1 percent to 1 percent of the loan amount.

Mortgage brokers differ from mortgage bankers in that the broker does not usually originate the loan or have anything to do with processing the loan, closing the loan, or servicing the loan. Nor does the broker have the financial ability to actually fund the loan. A mortgage banker may sometimes act as a mortgage broker, but the true mortgage broker will never act as a mortgage banker. The mortgage broker is in no way involved in the mortgage after the commitment is issued by the lender.

THE FUTURE OF MORTGAGE LENDING

The future of the mortgage banking industry is limitless. As the need for housing continues to grow, the need for mortgage money will also continue to grow. The only limitation on the growth of the industry will be the leadership in the industry. Since the savings and loan associations are the major source of mortgage funds and are now seeking the higher yields of short-term lending, the mortgage bankers will be called on more and more to seek investors that will make the thirty-year straight amortization mortgage.

Another factor that will work in the favor of the mortgage banker in the future is the vast number of contacts that have been made by them in the financial field. It is easy for them to move capital from areas of the country with an excess of funds to those areas that are in need of loanable funds.

One of the major problems facing the mortgage banking industry is the lack of trained or knowledgeable personnel. (This need is not unique to the mortgage banking industry.) A person in real estate sales may find that mortgage banking is a good alternate career. The future for the industry as a whole is very bright.

CREDIT UNIONS

The credit union is a mutual type of financial institution where all of the depositors are stockholders in the credit union. Usually, the credit union is founded by a group of individuals who have a common interest. For example, one of the largest credit unions organized to serve the employees involved in education is the Houston Area Teachers Credit Union. This credit union is open to any full-time or part-time employee of a public school, college, or university. In some cases, students attending a college or university are eligible for membership. A credit union can be chartered by either the federal government or the government of the state in which it operates.

The credit unions that are federally chartered are under the control of the Federal Credit Union Act of 1934. This act set forth operating standards and also set the maximum interest rates a credit union could charge. The rate was set at 12 percent and remained at that maximum until the act was amended in July 1981 to allow credit unions to charge up to 21 percent on all loans.

The provisions of the Federal Credit Union Act are administered through the National Credit Union Administration (NCUA). NCUA has its headquarters in Washington, D.C., but, like the Federal Reserve and the Federal Home Loan Bank Board, NCUA has several regional offices that serve various sections of the United States. A map showing the regional structure and the addresses of the regional offices is shown in Figure 5-1. If you are interested, you may secure a list of the federally chartered credit unions in your state by contacting the regional office serving your state.

In addition to the federally chartered credit unions, the states will also charter credit unions. These will be under the supervision of an agency of the state in which the credit union is located and will operate in accordance with the laws of that state.

Real Estate Lending

The following review will be for the federally chartered credit unions since the lending policy in each of the fifty states for state-chartered credit unions will vary. For the lending policy for the credit unions in your state, contact the agency with supervisory responsibility for credit unions.

The regulation covering the real estate lending policy of federally chartered credit unions is contained in the Code of Federal Regulations Title 12, Chapter 7, National Credit Union Administration, beginning with section 701.21-6.

Figure 5-1. National Credit Union Administration

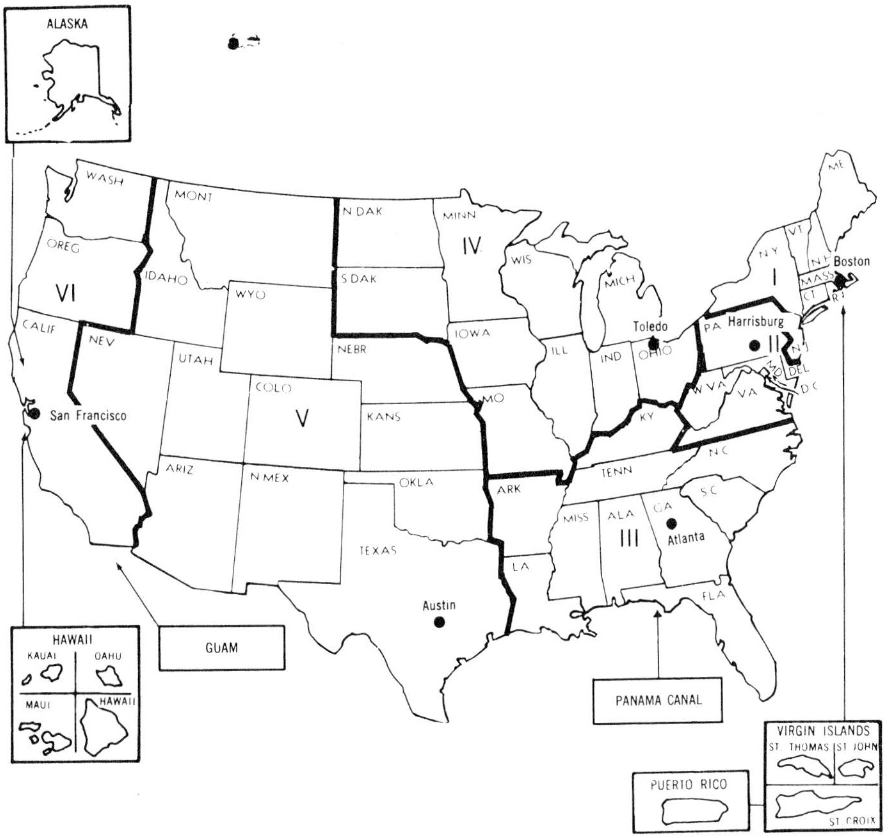

National Credit Union Administration

Region, director, address, and phone

Region I:

Bernard Ganzfried
441 Stuart St.
Boston, MA 02116
617-223-6807

Region II:

Carl Zysk
228 Walnut St.
Harrisburg, PA 17108
717-782-4595

Region III:

Stephen Raver
1365 Peachtree St., NE
Atlanta, GA 30309
404-881-3127

Region IV:

Robert E. Boon
234 N. Summit St.
Toledo, OH 43604
419-259-7511

Region V:

Ray Motsenbocker
515 Congress Ave.
Austin, TX 78701
512-397-5131

Region VI:

Earl Bradley
2 Embarcadero Center
San Francisco, CA 94111
415-556-6277

Source: U.S., Office of the Federal Register, National Archives and Records Service, General Services Administration, *United States Directory of Federal Regional Structures 1980-1981*, May 1, 1980, p. 125.

Maximum loan-to-value ratio Any federally chartered credit union with assets of $2 million or more, and other smaller credit unions with prior written consent, may make real estate loans secured by a first lien on residential property with a maximum loan-to-value ratio of 95 percent as long as the portion of the loan above 90 percent is covered by private mortgage insurance. The exceptions to this rule are loans insured or guaranteed by any agency of a state or the federal government.

Maximum term The maximum term for a loan secured by real property is thirty years. The regulations further state that these mortgages should have a term of at least twelve years.

Type of properties The regulation states that the mortgage shall be made to finance or refinance a one- to four-family dwelling and that the dwelling shall be used as the principal residence of a member of the federal credit union making the loan.

Sales price limitation Under the regulation, the sales price of the real estate and improvements shall not exceed 150 percent of the median sales price of residential property in the area in which the property to be used as security for a loan is located.

Interest rate As stated earlier, the maximum interest rate allowed is 21 percent. It is important to remember that this is the maximum and the actual rate charged by an individual credit union may be less.

Other requirements All conventional mortgages made by the federally chartered credit unions will be executed on the latest FNMA/FHLMC approved instruments for the state in which the property is located and will *not* contain any prepayment penalty. Insured or guaranteed mortgages originated by the unions will be on the approved instruments of the agency issuing the insurance or guarantee. All fixed-rate, fixed-term mortgages are required to contain a due-on-sale clause. An appraisal on an approved form must be prepared and signed prior to the making of any conventional mortgage. In the case of an insured or guaranteed mortgage, the appraisal must be on a form approved by the insuring or guaranteeing agency.

Interest rate adjustment mortgages All of the federally chartered credit unions have been given the ability to make, purchase, or participate in mortgages that have the feature of interest-rate adjustment. These were reviewed in Chapter 3.

PENSION FUNDS

Pension and retirement funds are not a major source of financing real estate, but they are included in this section to make the real estate professional aware of another available source of funds. The money that is accumulated in these types of funds is for the future use of the participants in the fund. The overriding investment philosophy of the funds, then, is security.

It was not until the passage of the Employee Retiree Income Security Act of 1974 that those persons responsible for the operation of these funds were mandated to exercise care in the selection of their investments. They must ensure that the investments are widespread, in order to keep the funds' assets from being placed into one area or type and increasing the chance of loss. The funds have traditionally been invested in stocks and bonds, but with the recent poor showing of these investments, pension funds have been looking for other areas in which to invest. One is the financing of real estate. One of the major forms of real estate financing by these funds is the purchase of GNMA mortgage-backed securities. Some of the major funds are now exploring the possibilities of financing commercial properties and are trying to acquire experienced people for this purpose.

REVIEW QUESTIONS

1. Explain the difference between a mortgage banker and a mortgage broker.
2. In your opinion, what are the three major sources of income for a mortgage banker? Explain.
3. Define the term *mortgage servicing*, and briefly outline three functions that would be included in the servicing of a loan.

4. Contact several credit unions in your area to see if they are federally or state-chartered. Do they make real estate loans, and, if they do, what is their lending policy?

5. Explain why pension and retirement funds may turn to the financing of real estate.

NOTES

[1]Mortgage Bankers Association of America, *Mortgage Banking Terms—A Working Glossary*, 3rd ed., Washington, D.C.: January 1978, p. 68.

[2]Most of this section is based on material from Mortgage Bankers Association of America, *Evolution of an Industry*, Washington, D.C.: 1973.

[3]Mortgage Bankers Association of America, *Mortgage Banking Terms—A Working Glossary*, 3rd ed., Washington, D.C.: January 1978, p. 108.

CHAPTER 6 Programs of HUD-FHA

LEARNING OBJECTIVES

In this chapter we will examine the mortgage insurance programs of the Federal Housing Administration.

Upon the completion of this chapter you should be able to do the following:

- ★ **Define the basic programs of FHA.**
- ★ **Define the major loan reforms established by FHA.**
- ★ **Calculate the maximum loan amount available through several FHA programs.**
- ★ **List and define the advantages of FHA insured loans.**
- ★ **Define *FHA acquisition cost.***

HOMEOWNERS LOAN CORPORATION (HOLC)

Before the Depression, there were very few governmental programs available for the financing of real estate. For the person who wished to purchase a single-family dwelling, there was no government help. As with many other types of investment, the Depression saw the housing industry collapse and millions of people lose their homes due to foreclosure. Realizing the problem of foreclosures, the administration of Franklin D. Roosevelt set up several agencies that would help the homeowner.

The Homeowners Loan Corporation (HOLC) was one of the programs that was established in 1933. The HOLC was to help the homeowner out of the crisis by either refinancing mortgages that were delinquent or purchasing those loans that had gone into default. HOLC put the homeowners back into their homes and set up monthly payments that could be afforded. This agency was later phased out and in its place was created the Federal Housing Administration (FHA).

HISTORY OF FHA

The Federal Housing Administration was created by the passage of the National Housing Act of 1934. With the passage of the Department of Housing and Urban Development Act, Public Law 89-174, all of the functions, powers, and duties of FHA were transferred to the control of the secretary of HUD. FHA was initially established as an experimental agency to help the national housing industry through the creation of a mutual fund for insuring mortgages made by private lenders. Many of the agencies that were created during the post-Depression era have disappeared—but not the FHA. It has become a self-sustaining and standards-setting agency for the federal government.

The purpose of FHA is threefold: (1) to upgrade the nation's housing standards; (2) to promote wider homeownership; and (3) to provide continuing and sound methods of financing home mortgages. But the majority of the financial community that was active in the financing of real estate looked upon FHA as governmental intrusion into the private financing of real estate, and it was not accepted as an answer to the housing problems.

The federal government was determined to make FHA a strong force in the financing of real estate. In 1938, the federal government set up an agency to sell bonds in the open market. The funds raised would be used to purchase mortgages insured by FHA from private lenders. The agency created for this purchase was the Federal National Mortgage Association (FNMA). This, then, made the federal insurance of mortgages even more attractive and was the birth of the secondary market as we know it today. The advent of FNMA allowed lenders to sell mortgages that met the insurance requirements of FHA.

It must be remembered that FHA is not a lender. It does not make loans. FHA issues an insurance policy on loans that meet the underwriting requirements of the National Housing Act. This insurance policy ensures the lender that if the loan goes into default, FHA will make the loan good by taking the property and paying off the lender either in cash or with debentures guaranteed by the United States government.

FHA does appraise the property, and if the property is under construction, it inspects the property throughout construction. In addition to the appraisal and approval of the property, FHA will approve the borrower. If the property and the borrower meet the underwriting requirements, FHA will insure the loan.

The insurance issued by FHA is called mutual mortgage insurance, and FHA now charges one-half of 1 percent per annum on the unpaid balance. This charge is referred to as MIP, or the mortgage insurance premium. The premium is collected as part of the monthly payment and is forwarded to FHA each month. The premium for this insurance is collected for the life of the mortgage. This insurance should not be confused with any other type of insurance, such as mortgage payment insurance carried on the borrower. The FHA insurance protects the lender from loss.

Since HUD-FHA was founded to serve all of the United States, the headquarters is in Washington, D.C. The United States has been divided into ten regions and these regions have further been divided with the establishment of area offices to make FHA more responsive to the needs of the different areas of the country. In Figure 6-1, all of the regional offices are listed with service offices. The address for each of the area and service offices is listed in Appendix A.

MAJOR LOAN REFORMS

In addition to the introduction of mortgage insurance, FHA also introduced major loan reforms.

Fully amortized mortgages Before the formation of FHA, most mortgages were like balloon mortgages, with all of the principal due at the term of the mortgage. In some cases, the mortgages were interest only with the interest payment due annually, and the full amount of principal due at the end of the term. The life of the mortgage prior to FHA was as little as three years, but FHA extended the term of the mortgages to as long as twenty years, with the payments due on a monthly basis. These payments were level payments. Each monthly payment was the same; only the amount applied to principal and interest changed.

Higher loan-to-value ratios Prior to FHA, the loans on property were usually based on 50 to 60 percent of the sales price. FHA raised the loan-to-value ratio to 80 percent of value, a very high ratio for that time. Many lenders also had objections to the high loan-to-value ratio, saying that the investment was not covered by sufficient value even though the loan was insured for 100 percent.

Lower down payments The advent of the higher loan-to-value ratio meant a lower down payment to the homebuyer and thus made housing available to more of the general public.

Figure 6-1. HUD Regional Offices

Region I John F. Kennedy Federal Building Boston, Massachusetts 02203	*Area Offices:* Boston, Mass.; Hartford, Conn. *Service Offices:* Manchester, N.H.; Providence, R.I.
Region II 26 Federal Plaza New York, New York 10007	*Area Offices:* New York, N.Y.; Newark, N.J.; Buffalo, N.Y.; Caribbean *Service Offices:* Albany, N.Y.; Camden, N.J.
Region III Curtis Building 6th and Walnut Streets Philadelphia, Pennsylvania 19106	*Area Offices:* Pittsburgh, Pa.; Philadelphia, Pa.; District of Columbia; Baltimore, Md.; Richmond, Va. *Service Office:* Charleston, W. Va.
Region IV Richard B. Russell Federal Bldg. 75 Spring St., S.W. Atlanta, Georgia 30303	*Area Offices:* Birmingham, Ala.; Jacksonville, Fla.; Atlanta, Ga.; Louisville, Ky.; Jackson, Miss.; Greensboro, N.C.; Columbia, S.C.; Knoxville, Tenn. *Service Offices:* Coral Gables, Fla.; Tampa, Fla.; Orlando, Fla.; Memphis, Tenn.; Nashville, Tenn.
Region V 300 South Wacker Drive Chicago, Illinois 60606	*Area Offices:* Detroit, Mich.; Chicago, Ill.; Indianapolis, Ind.; Minneapolis, Minn.; Columbus, Ohio; Milwaukee, Wisc. *Service Offices:* Cincinnati, Ohio; Cleveland, Ohio; Grand Rapids, Mich.; Flint, Mich.
Region VI 221 W. Lancaster Ave. P.O. Box 2905 Fort Worth, Texas 76113	*Area Offices:* Dallas, Tex.; Oklahoma City, Okla.; San Antonio, Tex.; New Orleans, La.; Little Rock, Ark. *Service Offices:* Ft. Worth, Tex.; Houston, Tex.; Lubbock, Tex.; Albuquerque, N. Mex.; El Paso, Tex.; Shreveport, La.; Tulsa, Okla.
Region VII Professional Bldg. 1103 Grand Ave. [Kansas City, Missouri 64106]	*Area Offices:* Kansas City, Mo.; St. Louis, Mo.; Omaha, Nebr. *Service Office:* Des Moines, Iowa
Region VIII Executive Tower 1405 Curtis Street Denver, Colorado 80202	*Area Office:* Denver, Colo. *Service Offices:* Helena, Mont.; Salt Lake City, Utah
Region IX 450 Golden Gate Avenue P.O. Box 36003 San Francisco, California 94102	*Area Offices:* San Francisco, Calif.; Los Angeles, Calif.; Honolulu, Hawaii *Service Offices:* Santa Ana, Calif.; San Diego, Calif.; Phoenix, Ariz.; Tucson, Ariz.; Fresno, Calif.; Sacramento, Calif.; Reno, Nev.; Las Vegas, Nev.
Region X Arcade Plaza Building 1321 Second Avenue Seattle, Washington 98101	*Area Offices:* Seattle, Wash.; Portland, Oreg.; Anchorage, Alaska *Service Offices:* Boise, Idaho; Spokane, Wash.

Source: U.S., Department of Housing and Urban Development, *Departmental Programs—August 1980*, pp. 90-91.

Lower interest rates In keeping with the investment policy that the lower the risk the lower the return, the FHA loan usually has a lower interest rate than the conventional loan. The reason is that the lender is protected from loss by the FHA insurance.

Escrow accounts Prior to the FHA-insured loan, the person receiving the loan was responsible for seeing that all taxes were paid on time and that there was insurance on the property. As with most people, they did not make allowances for the once-a-year payments, and in many cases the property was lost due to a tax lien. Often the property was damaged by fire and the owner did not have insurance to cover the loss. FHA, with the advent of the escrow account, made sure that the lender was less likely to lose the property due to a tax lien and made sure that there was insurance coverage on the property. This was also an advantage for the property owner in that he or she did not have to make one lump sum payment for taxes and insurance, but would set aside one-twelfth of the cost each month.

Minimum property standards FHA was the first lender or insurer of mortgages to set minimum standards for the property. These standards have constantly been upgraded to make sure that the property securing the mortgage is safe, sanitary, and livable. The standards now cover such things as the amount of insulation, the arrangement of rooms, the number of baths, and the type of wiring used in a house. Some have referred to these standards as a *national housing code*. The requirements of FHA are basically the same no matter where in the United States the property is located.

Standard borrower qualifications Lenders, prior to the advent of FHA, had no firm guidelines for the qualifying of the borrower, thus allowing the lender to set the rule for each person or applicant. They could have refused the applicant for any reason. Sometimes a loan was refused due to the type of work, marital status, race, or religion of the applicant. The standards for qualifying the borrower will be discussed in depth in Chapter 12.

ADVANTAGES OF FHA

There are several advantages of FHA for the borrower. With the increase of the loan-to-value ratio, the borrower is required to make a lower down payment. The down payment now required is 3 percent of the first $25,000 of the loan and 5 percent on the amount in excess of $25,000 to the maximum loan available through FHA.

The 3 and 5 percent method of calculating the required down payment applies to properties that have been constructed for one year or more or were constructed under FHA inspection. For those homes that are less than one year old or were not inspected during construction by FHA and/or VA, the required down payment is 10 percent of the value. Even though there is a difference in the down payment, the maximum loan amount is the same.

The usual down payment is 3 and 5 percent, but it may vary with some of the programs available through FHA. As stated earlier, the easing of the down payments from approximately 50 percent allowed more people to purchase homes. Since the loans of FHA are relatively safe and possible loss to the lender is reduced, these loans usually have an interest rate that is below that charged on conventional mortgages or those loans with no governmental backing. With a lower interest rate, the monthly payments are lower, thus allowing a person to qualify for a greater loan amount with no increase in income. The effect that interest rates can have on the amount of the loan was dramatically illustrated in the high interest rates of late 1979 and into 1981. During this period, rates shot up from approximately 9.5 percent to over 18 percent. It was estimated that, with residential mortgage interest rates at 18 percent, only 5 percent of the population could afford housing.

FHA also pioneered allowing a person to assume an existing mortgage without a penalty or escalation of the interest rate. This escalation of interest and a penalty for the assumption of a mortgage still exists today for some types of conventional mortgages. FHA felt that with America being a mobile society, the transfer of property should be made as easy as possible and one way was to allow those mortgages meeting the standards of FHA to be assumable.

Probably one of the most important mortgage reforms instituted by FHA to help the borrower was to allow the borrower to pay off the mortgage prior to the due date of the mortgage without any prepayment penalty or prepayment premium. This lack of prepayment penalty is now a standard feature of all mortgages insured by FHA, but the penalty still can be found in many conventional mortgages. As a real estate professional, you need to know which conventional lenders in your area have prepayment penalties.

As mentioned in the previous section, one of the reforms instituted by FHA was minimum property standards. This is important to a purchaser of a new home in that they assure that the property has been inspected on a periodic basis by FHA and has been certified to conform to a minimum set of standards set by FHA for safe and sanitary housing.

DISADVANTAGES OF FHA

Like all programs, the FHA loan has advantages as well as disadvantages. This section will discuss the major disadvantages.

The first disadvantage is that the seller in some cases will have to pay a discount or points to have a property financed through FHA. Since the interest rate on an FHA loan is usually below the market rate for conventional mortgages, sometimes the interest on FHA is too much below the conventional market and thus lenders are not interested in making FHA loans even though the risk is less. In order for the lender to be interested, he will require the seller to pay additional money up front. This money is usually expressed as a percentage of the loan, called *points*. Each point is equal to 1 percent of the loan amount. These points are to be paid by the seller. The National Housing Act states that no buyer will pay any discount points. These discount points can range from 1 to as many as 15. Thus, if a person wishes to sell a house and the FHA loan is $51,000, each point of discount that is charged by the lender will cost the seller $510, or 1 percent of the loan amount.

Another disadvantage of a FHA loan is that the amount of time for FHA loan approval may be long. For conventional loans, a lender in some cases can give what is called "in-house approval," thus cutting the time required for approval. But FHA requires that upon completion of the application and after all of the supporting data has been received, these materials must be sent to the nearest underwriting office. After the materials are received, checked, and found to have no major errors, FHA will issue a conditional commitment or conditional approval. It can take as long as six months in rare cases and usually takes about six weeks from the time of application to approval by FHA.

The final major disadvantage to the FHA program is that if the property does not meet the minimum standards, prior to the final approval of the loan, the property must be brought to the minimum. This cost can range from a few dollars to several thousand. The cost of repairs is usually borne by the seller, thus making this a disadvantage to the seller. In some instances, sellers will not sell their property FHA-insured because they know that it will not meet the minimum standards. From the purchaser's point of view, however, it is an advantage.

HUD-FHA PROGRAMS

The National Housing Act of 1934 that created the Federal Housing Administration and its programs divided these programs into major categories called *titles* and these were further subdivided into sections. The section numbers are the identifying numbers that the real estate professional uses when referring to FHA programs. Before we review some of the more commonly used sections of the National Housing Act, let us review some of the general rules that apply to most programs.

1. FHA will approve loans on one- to four-family dwellings, in subdivisions, planned unit development condominiums, and in rural areas.

2. The maximum term of most loans is thirty years.

3. There is no maximum sales price, but the buyer can pay no more than the FHA appraisal. If the appraised price is lower than the sales price, this will affect the maximum amount of loan FHA will authorize. The only maximum under any of the FHA programs is the loan amount. This amount is set by the U.S. Congress and the secretary of HUD.

4. The maximum interest rate that can be charged on any FHA loan is either set by the secretary of HUD or is negotiated between the borrower and the lender. The negotiated rate can only apply to loans that are insured under Section 203 (b). No lender may exceed either the rate set or the negotiated rate at the time of funding. For example, you or your client make loan application when the FHA rate is 10.5 percent, and three days before closing the secretary raises the rate to 11 percent. The lender must close the loan at 11 percent. This also will work in reverse. If the interest rate at the time of application is 11 percent and the rate drops to 10 percent before the loan closes, the lender must charge the lower rate. This is not a rule of the lenders but one that FHA has implemented. This rule in some cases has caused hardships, for if the rate is increased, the application must be resubmitted to the FHA underwriting section to see if the person can still qualify. This resubmission in the past has not only seen buyers not able to qualify, but in some cases has held up closing for several weeks.

5. Normally, the borrower must occupy the property, but there are a few sections of the National Housing Act that will allow loans on nonowner occupied property. If you have a question about one of these programs, you should contact the HUD-FHA office nearest you or a lender that is familiar with the programs of HUD-FHA.

6. FHA does not allow any secondary financing on the property when making a new loan.

7. FHA requires that an escrow account be established and that the taxes, insurance on the property, mutual mortgage insurance, principal and interest, and any other fees or assessments that can affect the title to the property be collected monthly.

This chapter will examine the major programs of Titles I and II. We will cover the major programs that you as a real estate professional will use on a regular basis. Appendix H outlines many of the other programs available through HUD-FHA.

Section 203(b) Home Mortgage Insurance

This section of the National Housing Act is the oldest and the most commonly used of all of the HUD-FHA programs. For insurance under this section, the properties must meet the minimum property standards of HUD-FHA, but there are no special qualifications for the borrowers. Any individual who has a good credit record and can demonstrate the ability to make the required down payment and the payments on the mortgage can be approved.

This program, as well as the other HUD-FHA single-family insurance programs, is available for use in all areas, both rural and urban, provided that the market exists for the property. Full mortgage insurance is available for properties that are approved prior to the beginning of construction or are completed for more than one year. Those properties that are under construction or that have been completed less than one year, if not covered by a homeowner warranty, can be approved for insurance, but only to a maximum of 90 percent of the value and closing cost up to the maximum loan available.

The following maximum loan amounts were established by Congress in December 1979:

One-family	$ 67,500
Two-family	$ 76,000
Three-family	$ 92,000
Four-family	$107,000

Since 1980, with the passage of the Housing and Community Development Act, Public Law 96-399 allows the secretary of HUD to increase these maximum mortgage amounts on an area-by-area basis annually. This authority to increase mortgage amounts on mortgages insured under Section 203(b) was implemented for the first time on November 20, 1980, by then Secretary Moon Landrieu. This adjustment in the maximum mortgage for areas of the United States is shown in Appendix B.

If the area in which you live is not listed, the maximum mortgage amount that will be insured is the amount that was authorized by the Congress in 1979. These amounts may change annually. To find the present maximum mortgage amount for your area, contact any FHA-approved lender or the nearest office of HUD.

The down payment for Section 203(b) is calculated in the following manner:

1. 3 percent of the first $25,000 of value and closing costs, plus

2. 5 percent of the value and closing costs in excess of $25,000 to the maximum loan available.

You will notice that in calculating the down payment, the closing costs are included. When the closing costs are included, HUD-FHA refers to this as the *acquisition cost* of the property. The closing costs that are to be used when figuring the acquisition cost are the average for your area. In some cases, the HUD-FHA office will furnish you with a schedule of closing costs used in your area, or you can call a mortgage lender that originates HUD-FHA loans and they will be glad to furnish you with the estimated closing costs.

An example of the information that will be furnished by your local HUD office is illustrated in Figure 6-2. For example, if you are selling real estate in Phoenix and your client would like to purchase a home valued

Figure 6-2. Closing Costs

TYPICAL CLOSING COSTS OF PURCHASER ONLY

FHA VALUE	1 FAM	2 FAM	3 FAM	4 FAM
7,000 - 9,999	550	550	550	550
10,000 - 14,999	600	600	600	600
15,000 - 20,999	650	650	650	650
21,000 - 25,999	700	700	700	700
26,000 - 30,999	750	750	750	750
31,000 - 35,999	800	800	800	800
36,000 - 40,999	850	850	850	850
41,000 - 46,999	900	900	900	900
47,000 - 51,999	950	950	950	950
52,000 - 56,999	1,000	1,000	1,000	1,000
57,000 - 62,999	1,050	1,050	1,050	1,050
63,000 - 67,999	1,100	1,100	1,100	1,100
68,000 - 72,999	1,150	1,150	1,150	1,150
73,000 - 77,999	1,150	1,200	1,200	1,200
78,000 - 83,999	1,150	1,200	1,250	1,250
84,000 - 88,999	1,150	1,200	1,300	1,300
89,000 - 93,999	1,150	1,200	1,350	1,350
94,000 - 98,999	1,150	1,200	1,350	1,400
99,000 - 104,999	1,150	1,200	1,350	1,450
105,000 - 109,999	1,150	1,200	1,350	1,500
110,000 - 114,999	1,150	1,200	1,350	1,550
115,000 - 119,999	1,150	1,200	1,350	1,550

NOTE: Add $50.00 for 203(k).

These typical Closing Costs include the following:

Site Survey, Credit Report, FHA Appraisal Fee, One Percent Origination Fee, Drawing of Note and Deed of Trust, Recording Fees, Escrow Fees, Mortgagees Title Policy, Messenger Fee, Photographs, Copy of Restrictions and Amortization Schedule.

Source: U.S., Department of Housing and Urban Development, Southeast Texas District, Houston, Texas, Office of the Supervisor, *Circular Letter No. 80-6—August 4, 1981*, p. 1

at $54,700, the acquisition cost of this home would be the sales price of $54,700 plus the estimated FHA closing costs of $1000, or $55,700. It is quite important that when dealing with HUD-FHA you know the difference between the value of the house and the acquisition costs of the property.

As outlined earlier in this chapter, the maximum term for a loan insured under this section is thirty years. Prior to the passage of the Housing and Community Development Act of 1980, the term of the FHA 203(b) mortgage was either thirty years or three-quarters of the remaining economic life, whichever was less. Section 333 of the act deleted all references to remaining economic life as one of the criteria for determining the maximum term for an insurable FHA mortgage. This deletion was made in several programs, including any mortgage insured under Section 203(b) of the National Housing Act.

The interest rate on all loans insured under this section in the past has been set by the Secretary of Housing and Urban Development, and has been as low as 4.25 percent and as high as 17.5 percent in 1981. The Housing and Community Development Act of 1980 allows for a negotiated interest rate on mortgages insured under Section 203(b). The act, in Section 332, states that the interest negotiated between the lender and borrower is subject to the following limitations:

1. The lender discloses to the borrower, prior to the commitment, information on the applicable maximum FHA rate and a good faith estimate of the prevailing number of discount points associated with that rate.

2. The agreement contains a commitment with respect to any discount points to be charged in connection with the negotiated rate.

3. The agreement commits the lender to the specified rate and discount points for at least thirty days after the date on which it is entered into.

The number of mortgages that may be insured under this negotiated interest program each fiscal year may not exceed 10 percent of all mortgages insured under Section 203, or 50,000 mortgages, whichever is greater.

To implement Section 332, the negotiated interest-rate program, the Office of the Assistant Secretary of Housing-Federal Housing Commissioner (HUD) published a proposed rule in the Federal Register, which was implemented in July 1982. The rule amends Chapter 24 of the Code of Federal Regulations by adding a new section numbered 203.51 which allows the negotiated interest-rate mortgage to be insured by FHA. The major provisions of the rule are as follows:

1. The borrower and the lender will enter into a commitment agreement that will be in a form acceptable to the Commissioner. A proposed form that would be acceptable is shown in Figure 6-3.

2. The negotiated interest-rate mortgage may be insured only under Sections 203(b) and 244 of the National Housing Act.

3. The lender may not charge a commitment fee as compensation for the entering into an agreement stating the negotiated interest rate.

4. Failure of the lender to honor the commitment to close a loan according to any agreement entered into under the new section shall be grounds for withdrawal of the lender's FHA approval.

This new program can be of importance to the real estate professional in the time of high discount points, where the seller will have to pay cash based on the loan amount to sell his or her house. The buyer may be able to qualify for a higher interest rate on a mortgage and thus reduce the number of points the seller will have to pay. For example, say the current FHA interest rate is 14.5 percent. For lenders to make FHA-insured loans at this rate they charge 8 points. The borrower could enter into an agreement with a lender stating that he or she will be willing to pay 15.5 percent. The seller, then, would not have to pay any discount points. The reason is that 1 point of discount relates to one-eighth of 1 percent of interest rate, thus 8 points will equal one full percent of interest.

203(b) Veteran This is a special program for veterans through FHA. This program should not be confused with the Veterans Administration guaranteed home loan that will be discussed in the next chapter. This program is sometimes called 203(b) Vet mortgage insurance. For a veteran to qualify under this program, it is best for the veteran to have used up all of his or her entitlement under the program authorized by the Veterans Administration. Furthermore, the veteran must have served for ninety consecutive days on active duty, or in some cases the veteran who served less than ninety days may be allowed to use the plan if the Secretary of Defense will certify that the veteran served on hazardous duty. In addition to the service requirements, the veteran must have received a discharge other than dishonorable.

This insurance program is only available for single-family dwellings and the veteran must reside in the dwelling. The insurance will not cover mortgages on duplexes, triplexes, or fourplexes. The mortgage term for this program is thirty years. The maximum loan amount for the 203(b) Vet mortgage insurance is $67,500, or the same as the limit for a single-family dwelling under the regular 203(b).

The major difference in this program and the standard 203(b) program is the amount of down payment. Under the FHA Vet insurance program, the veteran pays no down payment of either the first $25,000 of value and closing costs, or $25,000 plus prepaid expenses less $200, whichever is less. It should be noted that the $200 is the minimum closing cost for 203(b) Vet. The veteran will pay 5 percent of the value and closing costs on the excess above $25,000 to the maximum of $67,500.

One additional advantage of FHA Vet insurance is that a veteran can use the program more than once.

With the FHA Vet program, a veteran can actually afford the same house as under

Figure 6-3. Negotiated Interest Rate Form

COMMITMENT TO MAKE A FHA INSURED MORTGAGE LOAN
AT A NEGOTIATED INTEREST RATE

This agreement, made on ______________________ between ________________________________ located at ____________________ (Lender) and ____________________________ located at ___________ _____________________ (Borrower) commits the Lender to make a mortgage loan to the Borrower in the amount of $________________ payable in ________ months at an interest rate of _______ % per annum, for the purpose of financing the purchase of, or refinancing the existing debt on, property located at _________________ ________________ (property) under the following terms and conditions:

1. The loan shall be closed not later than ______ days from the date on which the application for an FHA firm commitment has been received by the HUD field office.

2. The mortgage shall be eligible for FHA insurance under its negotiated interest rate program.

3. In addition to a loan origination fee not to exceed one percent, the Lender will be paid ________ discount points by the Borrower and ________ discount points by the seller.

The Lender has advised the Borrower that under the regular FHA Section 203(b) program, the maximum interest rate permitted is ________ percent and that ________ discount points are generally quoted in this market area to close such a loan. Most FHA mortgages are insured under the regular program.

The Borrower has read and understands the above and has elected to finance the property under the negotiated interest rate program rather than the regular program.

Lender:
(Name of officer)____
(Title)____

Borrower:
(Name)____
Co-Borrower:
(Name)____

Page 1 of 2

Figure 6-3. continued

By mutual agreement the above commitment is extended for another ________ days, with no additional fees to be paid by the borrower.

Lender:
(Name of officer)____
(Title)____

Borrower:
(Name)____
Co-Borrower:
(Name)____

Date of Receipt by HUD Field Office
Serial Number

Page 2 of 2

Source: 24 CFR Part 203, Mutual Mortgage Insurance and Insured Home Improvement Loans, Section 203.51; Federal Register; Vol. 46, No. 138; Monday, July 20, 1981; Proposed Rules; page 37281.

203(b), but the amount of front money, or the money needed for the down payment, is less. Using the same example as in the previous section, a veteran would like to purchase a house valued at $54,700 with an estimated closing cost of $1000, equaling an acquisition cost of $55,700. The veteran would be required to make a down payment calculated as follows:

No down on the first $25,000	0
5% of the excess of $25,000, or $55,700 minus $25,000 = $30,700 × 5%	$1535
Total down payment	$1535

The amount of money that would be needed for the down payment under 203(b) would be calculated as follows:

3% of first $25,000	$750
5% of the excess of $25,000, or $30,700	$1535
Total down payment	$2285

From this comparison, one can see that a veteran can save $750 in down payment, but the $750 will be added to the mortgage balance. The dollar savings may not seem significant, but the loan-to-value ratio changes significantly. Under 203(b), the loan-to-value ratio is approximately 96 percent, whereas under the 203(b) Vet, this ratio is increased to 97 percent.

In regard to the loan amount, FHA will only insure loans that are rounded down to the nearest $50. The maximum loan that FHA would insure on the previous two examples would be:

203(b)

Acquisition costs	$55,700
Less down payment	$ 2,285
Loan amount	$53,415

The actual loan amount when rounded down to the nearest $50 would be $53,400. The $15 dropped from the loan amount would have to be added to the down payment, making it $2300.

203(b) Vet

Acquisition costs	$55,700
Less down payment	$ 1,535
Loan Amount	$54,165

Using the same criteria, rounding down to the nearest $50, the actual loan amount would be $54,150. Once again, the amount that the loan is reduced will be added to the down payment, thus making it $1550.

203 buy down Under this program HUD will allow the seller/builder to set up an escrow account to be used to reduce the monthly payment of the buyer/borrower.

This represents a change in HUD's policy regarding any gift or contribution of monies to the buyer of a property. Prior to the issuance of HUD's Mortgagee Letter 81-23, in June 1981, HUD held that any such gift and/or contribution was an inducement to the buyer to purchase a property. HUD felt that the loan-to-value ratio was also reduced.

With the issuance of the Mortgagee Letter, HUD revised its policy to allow the institution of the buydown program. Under this program, the interest rate is reduced in the early years of the mortgage with the establishment of an escrow account to supplement the monthly payment made by the buyer.

According to HUD, this program will allow more people to become eligible for mortgages, particularly first-time homebuyers.

The program will use the reduced initial payment as the basis for underwriting the mortgage and is only available under Section 203 of the National Housing Act.

The program authorized is subject to the following rules:

1. The mortgage loan must be a level payment, unsubsidized mortgage. Both new and existing homes are eligible for this procedure.

2. The payments to reduce the interest chargeable to the buyer shall run for a minimum of three years.

3. The assistance payments will not diminish the normally required Monthly P.&I. payments by more than the payment which would be calculated on a mortgage with an interest rate which is three percentage points less than the interest rate on the mortgage. For example, on a 15½ percent mortgage, the assistance payment could not reduce the amount the mortgagor would pay below the monthly

payment on a 12½ percent mortgage. Any scheduled reductions of the assistance payments during this period must be uniform and must occur on the annual anniversary date of the mortgage payment.

4. Payments will be made by the escrow agent. The escrow agreement must require the escrow agent to make the payments to the mortgagee which is the holder of the mortgage, or its servicing agent.

5. The agreement may provide for reversion of undistributed escrow funds to builder/seller if the property is sold by the borrower or the mortgage is prepaid in full. At the option of the builder/seller, the agreement may also provide that assistance payments will be made for the benefit of buyers who assume the mortgage.

6. Repayment of escrow funds may not be required.

7. In order that the buyer may be fully protected, the funds must be held in an escrow account with a financial institution which is not the originating or servicing mortgagee and is supervised by a federal or state agency. (All banks and savings associations are supervised financial institutions.) This will insure the availability of the funds and preclude any possibility that the buyer will be forced to make the payments called for in the note prior to the scheduled termination of the escrow. However, if, for some unforeseen reason the escrow payments are not forthcoming, it is the mortgagor's responsibility to make the total payment set forth in the mortgage note.

8. In the event of foreclosure, the claim for mortgage insurance benefits will be reduced by the amount of the remaining escrow only if the mortgagee has received the balance of the escrow at the time of the claim. The escrow agreement must provide that, should the mortgage be foreclosed, the balance remaining in the escrow account must be immediately paid to the mortgagee which acquired title to the property.

9. Applications will be processed on the basis of the reduced mortgage payment for the first year.

10. Firm commitments involving applications in which underwriting has been based on the reduced monthly payment must contain a condition which requires assurance that the funds described in the approved plan have been placed in escrow prior to or at closing and meet the requirements set forth herein.

In these particular situations the acquisition cost shall not be reduced to reflect the amount of cash placed in escrow for the benefit of the buyer. The mortgage will be computed on our estimate of value plus closing costs or acquisition cost, whichever is the lesser.

Applications involving escrow arrangements which do not meet *all* of the above criteria are to be processed with the monthly assistance payments considered as a strong compensating factor. In these instances, there will be no commitment requirement for evidence that the funds have been placed in escrow.[1]

Section 221(d)(2) Homeowner Assistance for Low- and Moderate-Income Families

Section 221(d)(2) of the National Housing Act provides mortgage insurance for the purchase of homes by low- and moderate-income families and by families displaced by government action or by major disaster declared by the President of the United States. HUD-FHA has not set an income maximum. As long as the applicant meets one of the other qualifications, the income can be any amount. This is particularly true for those people displaced by governmental action or by natural disaster. The program can also be used to finance the rehabilitation of substandard properties, but, in regard to this type of property, HUD-FHA will have to be supplied with a certificate showing that the property meets the minimum housing standards after rehabilitation.

The terms of the loans insured by this section are divided into three categories. The first category is for displaced families. The normal term is thirty years, but terms of thirty-five or forty years are authorized if the person or family cannot qualify for a thirty-year term. This means that if the applicant's income is insufficient to meet the thirty-year payment, it may be extended to thirty-five or forty years to help the applicant qualify. For other than displaced families, the normal term is thirty years, but if the applicant is unacceptable under the thirty-year term, it may be extended to thirty-five or forty years. Also, the house must have been built under HUD-FHA or VA inspections. The last category is for other than HUD-FHA existing construction. For this type, the maximum term is thirty years.

The maximum loan amounts that can be insured under this section are divided into two categories. One is for normal or average cost areas and the second is for properties located in areas designated by HUD-FHA as areas of high cost. These costs refer to the cost of construction. The current maximum loan amounts for a normal cost area are as follows:

One-family unit	$31,000
Two-family unit	$35,000
Three-family unit	$48,600
Four-family unit	$59,400

The maximum of $31,000 for a one-family unit is increased to $36,000 if the property is occupied by a family of five or more and the property has four or more bedrooms. In areas where the costs so require, the above limits can be increased up to the following:

One-family unit	$36,000
Two-family unit	$45,000
Three-family unit	$57,600
Four-family unit	$68,400

As before, if the one-family unit is occupied by a family of five or more and the property has four or more bedrooms, the maximum loan amount is increased to $42,000.

Each of the HUD-FHA offices is responsible for the designations of areas of high costs. To find the maximum loan allowed in your area, you will need to contact a HUD-FHA lender in your area or the nearest HUD-FHA office.

Loan-to-value ratios The loan-to-value ratios under this section are calculated as follows:

1. Displaced families
   - A. For properties approved by HUD-FHA prior to construction or completed one year or more, the loan-to-value ratio is 100 percent of either the sum of the FHA estimate of value and closing costs, or the sum of the FHA estimate of value, closing costs, and prepaids, less $200 per unit, whichever is less.
   - B. For construction completed less than one year, the maximum loan-to-value ratio is 90 percent of the sum of the HUD-FHA estimate of value and closing costs.
   - C. For the rehabilitation of property, the loan-to-value ratio is 100 percent of either the HUD-FHA estimate of value before rehabilitation, plus closing costs, plus the estimated costs of rehabilitation, or, the HUD—FHA estimate of value, plus the prepaid expenses, plus the closing costs minus $200 per unit, whichever is less.

2. Low- to moderate-income families
   - A. One unit
     1. For properties approved by HUD-FHA prior to construction or completed more than one year, HUD-FHA uses the following method to calculate the loan-to-value ratio. The loan-to-value ratio is either 100 percent of the sum of the HUD-FHA estimate of value and closing costs, or 97 percent of the sum of the HUD-FHA estimate of value and closing costs, plus prepaids, whichever is less.
     2. For construction completed less than one year, the ratio is 90 percent of the sum of the HUD-FHA estimate of value and closing costs.
   - B. Two- to four-family units
     1. For construction completed more than one year, or approved by HUD-FHA prior to construction, the ratio is figured identically to the method used for 203(b). It is 97 percent of the first $25,000 of estimated value and closing costs and 95 percent of the excess of $25,000 in estimated value and closing costs to the maximum loan amount.
     2. For construction completed less than one year, the maximum loan is calculated in the same manner as Section 203(b), or 90 percent of the estimated value and closing costs.

3. For rehabilitiation, the maximum loan-to-value ratio is figured using the same method as outlined for the displaced family.

Even though Section 221(d)(2) indicates that the loan-to-value ratio can be 100 percent in some cases, the prospective homeowner is required to make a minimum cash investment in the property. This cash investment may not be less than 3 percent of the total cost of acquisition and may include items of prepaid expenses.

Section 221(d)(2) was designed to aid the homeowner displaced by urban renewal. In the past three years, this program has become less important to the real estate professional.

Section 235(i)(Revised): Homeownership Assistance for Low- and Moderate-Income Families

Section 235(i) provides for insurance and interest subsidies to low- and moderate-income families to enable these families to afford safe and sanitary housing that meets HUD-FHA standards.

The use of this section was reduced with the passage of the Omnibus Budget Reconciliation Act of 1981. This act in Title III Subtitle A, The Housing and Community Development Amendments of 1981, limited the authority of the secretary of Housing and Urban Development to enter into commitments. According to a section of the act, the secretary of HUD cannot enter into any new contracts under Section 235 after March 31, 1982. Keep in mind though that Congress could in future years give the secretary the authority once again to enter into contracts under Section 235.

This housing can either be new construction or substantially rehabilitated single-family units, with the construction or rehabilitation approved by HUD-FHA on or after October 17, 1975.

For the purpose of this section, *substantially rehabilitated* is defined as the improvement of a unit in deteriorating or substandard condition to a decent, safe, and sanitary level meeting HUD-FHA standards for mortgage insurance. One other measure of substantial rehabilitation is that the cost of the rehabilitation must be at least 25 percent of the value of the property after the completion of the rehabilitation.

The latest amendments to the National Housing Act allow insurance to be issued on an existing dwelling or a family unit in an existing condominium project which meets HUD-FHA standards.

Under this program, HUD-FHA can make supplemental payments for eligible families directly to the mortgage lender in an amount that will reduce the payment for the homeowner to a level that would equal an interest rate of 4 percent. For example, if the prevailing interest rate on all HUD-FHA insured loans is 11 percent, then HUD-FHA can make payments for the homeowner that would reduce the payment equal to a principal and interest payment on a 4 percent mortgage. What does this mean in real dollars? Say an applicant wishes to get a loan in the amount of $35,000 and the interest rate is 11.5 percent. The payment for principal and interest would be $297.09. If the applicant, however, qualifies for the 235 subsidy, the payment would be reduced to a 4 percent level, or $167.30 per month. It must be pointed out that the 4 percent interest rate is the maximum subsidy that is allowed under this section.

As with other sections, HUD-FHA has maximum loan amounts for which it can issue insurance. As with Section 221(d)(2), the loan amounts are divided into two categories: one for the normal-cost areas and another for high-cost areas. The maximum will vary if the house has three or four bedrooms. The loan amounts authorized in the 1980 Housing and Community Development Act are as follows:

	Normal Cost	*High Cost*
Three-bedroom	$40,000	$47,500
Four-bedroom house with five or more people	$47,500	$55,000
Two-family dwellings	$55,000	$61,250

In many areas of the United States, the HUD-FHA maximum loan limit is set at the maximum (high cost). To find the maximum loan available in an area, contact an approved HUD-FHA lender or the nearest HUD-FHA office.

The maximum loan amount in your area will also establish the maximum sales price. The guidelines state that the sales price may be up to, but not exceed, 120 percent of the maximum mortgage amount. In some cases, this will require a greater cash investment by the buyer to reduce the purchase price down to the maximum. Another stipulation regarding sales price is that no property may be purchased under Section 235 at a price, excluding closing costs, which exceeds the FHA estimate of value.

This section also requires a buyer to make a minimum cash investment. This amount shall be 3 percent of the acquisition cost and is to be paid in cash by the buyer. As explained in the previous paragraph, the buyer can put down any amount of money he or she wishes, but 3 percent is the minimum.

In addition to the minimum investment and the type of property, this section also limits the amount of income a person or family may be making in order to qualify for the subsidies. These incomes will vary with each area and the size of the family. Contact any approved FHA lender for the income limits in your area.

There is one additional requirement placed on the applicant by Section 811 of the Housing and Community Development Act of 1974. It requires that HUD-FHA provide counseling and advice to Section 235 homeowners. This counseling and advice will deal with such subjects as home maintenance, financial management, and any other subjects to assist the homeowner in improving housing conditions and meeting the responsibilities of homeownership.

To keep any area from becoming too concentrated with Section 235 homeowners, as occurred under the program prior to the present revision, the revised Section 235 states that no subdivision, neighborhood, or single residential area shall have over 40 percent of the homes assisted by Section 235. This 40 percent rule is applicable to the sum of vacant lots plus built-upon lots within a tract under centralized control.

Furthermore, the 235 mortgage is assumable. The person who is planning to assume such a loan must qualify under the same requirements as the original borrower. One fact should be noted regarding the assumption: even though the person assuming the mortgage is anticipating no subsidy payments and will make the regular principal and interest payments, there will be no reduction in the premium charges for the mortgage insurance. This factor will increase the regular payment slightly, for the insurance premium on Section 235 is set at 0.7 percent instead of the 0.5 percent as charged on other HUD-FHA insured loans.

Section 245(a): Federal Mortgage Insurance for Graduated Mortgages

The graduated-payment mortgage was authorized under Section 245 of the National Housing Act and was implemented in November 1976 under provision of the Housing and Community Development Act of 1974. It was not until the passage of the Housing and Community Development Act of 1977, however, that we found the present form of the Graduated Payment Mortgage (GPM). HUD's objective with the GPM was to develop and promote new methods of mortgage financing that would allow early homeownership for families with stable incomes and a potential to grow in the future. The GPM allows these homeowners to make lower payments in the initial years of the mortgage and for the payments to increase gradually over a specified time.

The GPM is likely to appeal to the first-time homebuyer, but is not limited to the first-time buyer in the middle-income range because it allows homebuyers to tailor their monthly installments to present income and the future growth potential of that income. As with any of the other mortgage insurance programs of HUD, the program is open to all persons or families that have good credit and show the ability to make the necessary initial investment and the potential to make the monthly payments. They must also show that they have, or expect to have, enough steady and increasing income to make the future mortgage payments.

How does the GPM work? Simply stated, the GPM is a mortgage where the early payments are low and rise over a period of time. It should be noted that the early payments of a GPM are not sufficient to cover the amount needed to amortize the loan fully, so the homeowner is borrowing additional monies that are added to the principal balance to be paid back in the future. To state this another way, it is said that the GPM for the first few years is in negative amortization.

Persons applying for the GPM must be aware that the monthly payments to principal and interest will increase each year for the next five to ten years depending upon which of the GPM plans is selected. Applicants should also be aware that over the life of the mortgage, they will pay more interest than if they had secured a level-payment loan. Finally, any persons that will use the GPM must be made aware that they will have to make a larger down payment than those required under Section 203(b) or a level-term mortgage.

As stated earlier in this section, there are several GPM plans available to the prospective homebuyer. The GPM offers five separate plans. The five basic GPM plans vary the rate of the annual monthly payment increase from 2 percent per year to 7.5 percent per year and vary the number of years over which the payments will increase from five to ten years.

The following will give the percent of increase and the number of years of increase for each plan:

Plan I—The payment will increase at the rate of 2.5 percent per year for five years.

Plan II—The payment will increase at the rate of 5 percent per year for five years.

Plan III—The payment will increase at the rate of 7.5 percent per year for five years.

Plan IV—The payment will increase 2 percent per year for ten years.

Plan V—The payment will increase 3 percent per year for ten years.

It is important to note that the monthly payments only increase yearly, not monthly, and that at the end of either the fifth or tenth year the payments are level and are higher than those of a level or straight amortized mortgage. The reason for the higher payment, as stated previously, is that the homeowner has been in negative amortization and is now starting to repay the funds borrowed.

Of all the plans listed, Plan III has become the most popular, for it allows the lowest initial monthly payment. This can be easily illustrated when comparing the monthly payments on a mortgage of $50,000 with an interest rate of 9 percent for a term of thirty years (see Figure 6-4). Since the homebuyers are qualified based on the first year's monthly payment and other housing expenses, one can see that under Plan III the prospective homebuyer would need a lesser income to qualify.

The GPM has the same term as mortgages insured under Section 203(b), that is, up to a maximum of thirty years. The interest on these loans is set by the Secretary of Housing and Urban Development. The premium for the mortgage insurance is similar to Section 203(b) or 0.5 percent.

The maximum loan amount under Section 245(a) is $67,500, but the loan must be calculated for each sales price, according to Section 203.45 of HUD regulations. The maximum mortgage amount shall not exceed the lesser of the following:

1. 97 percent of the first $25,000 of value and closing costs, plus 95 percent of the remaining value and closing costs
2. "An amount which, when added to all deferred interest pursuant to the financing plan selected, shall not exceed 97 percent of the appraised value of the property

Figure 6-4. Monthly Payment (P & I)—Section 245(a)

Year	203(b)	I	II	III	IV	V
1	$402.50	$366.22	$333.53	$303.94	$355.97	$334.47
2	$402.50	$375.38	$350.21	$326.74	$363.09	$344.51
3	$402.50	$384.76	$367.72	$351.24	$370.35	$354.84
4	$402.50	$394.38	$386.11	$377.59	$377.76	$365.49
5	$402.50	$404.24	$405.41	$405.91	$385.32	$376.45
6	$402.50	$414.35	$425.68	$436.35	$393.02	$387.75
7	$402.50	$414.35	$425.68	$436.35	$400.88	$399.38
8	$402.50	$414.35	$425.68	$436.35	$408.90	$411.36
9	$402.50	$414.35	$425.68	$436.35	$417.07	$423.70
10	$402.50	$414.35	$425.68	$436.35	$425.42	$436.41
11-30	$402.50	$414.35	$425.68	$436.35	$433.92	$449.50

covered by the mortgage as of the date the mortgage is accepted for insurance. However, if the mortgagor is a veteran, the mortgage amount, when added to all deferred interest pursuant to the financing plan selected, shall not exceed the applicable limits prescribed for veterans under Section 203(b). It is necessary, therefore, to compute the allowable loan amount both on the basis of the method applicable to Section 203(b) as well as on the basis of 97 percent of the value including deferred interest."[2]

To better understand the meaning of these methods, let us work through an example. We assume the following:

HUD Value	$53,000
Closing Costs	$ 800
Acquisition Cost	$53,800

As per the regulation, the maximum loan amount will be the lesser of the two methods, or:

Criterion I

97 percent of $25,000	$24,250
95% of the remaining ($28,800)	$27,360
Calculated maximum loan	$51,610

Since HUD-FHA will only insure loans rounded down to the nearest $50, the actual maximum loan is $51,600.

Now let us review Criterion II. The initial calculation is different from Criterion I in that we take 97 percent of the total cost plus the closing costs, or 97 percent of $53,800, resulting in $52,186. Then this value is divided by the highest outstanding balance loan factor. This factor is used to calculate the highest loan balance that will occur. These factors will change each time the interest rate either increases or decreases or a different plan is selected. For this example, we will use the factor for 9 percent interest and Plan III. That value is 1043.5603. Therefore, $52,186 divided by 1043.5603 is $50,000. In this case, the lesser of the two criteria is Criterion II, thus establishing the maximum loan as $50,000.

Now let us review how an increase in the interest rate will affect the maximum loan for this same piece of property. In this case, the interest rate will be 11.5 percent. The calculation for Criterion I will remain the same as in the example above. Under Criterion II, however, the calculation will change because of the change in the interest rate. We still begin with 97 percent of $53,800, or $52,186. Then we divide $52,186 by the highest outstanding loan balance factor for Plan III with an interest rate of 11.5 percent, or 1072,8307. This results in a maximum loan of $48,643.27. In this case, we can see that Criterion II is the lesser and the maximum loan amount is reduced to $48,600, by some $1400, when the interest rate is increased to 11.5 percent.

The highest outstanding loan balance factors for Plan III, the most commonly used plan, are shown in Appendix C. The appendix lists these factors for interest rates from 7.75 to 17.50 and is broken down in one-quarter percent steps. To find a factor using these tables, first locate the appropriate interest rate at the top of the column, then find the underlined factor listed below it. This is the highest outstanding balance factor. For example, if the present interest rate is 13.75 percent and the client is interested in Plan III, first find the pages in Appendix C for interest rates from 12.75 to 15.00 percent. Then, look for the 13.75 interest rate below which you will find the underlined factor appears as the sixtieth payment and is 1097.6900. This factor would be used to calculate the maximum loan amount.

You will note that this table not only gives the maximum outstanding balance factor, but also the factors to be used to calculate the outstanding principal balance of the mortgage at any time over the life of the mortgage. For example, if you as a real estate professional have listed a home financed by a GPM Section 245 with an interest rate of 10.00 percent using Plan III and the present owner has just made the fortieth payment, the factor for that payment is 1051.3538. This factor would then be multiplied by the original loan amount (in thousands) to get the present outstanding principal balance. For example, if the original loan amount was $50,000, the balance would be 50 × 1051.3538 = $52,567.69.

Now that we have figured the maximum loan that is available on this property, let us calculate the required down payment. Using the maximum loan for 9 percent interest, the prospective homeowner would have the following required down payment:

Acquisition price	$53,800
Maximum loan amount as calculated earlier	$50,000
Required down payment	$ 3,800

How does this down payment compare with the required down payment under Section 203(b)?

97% of the first $25,000	$24,250
95% of remaining $28,800	$27,360
Maximum loan	$51,610 or $51,600

In order to get the required down payment, we will subtract the maximum loan amount from the acquisition cost:

Acquisition cost	$53,800
Maximum loan amount	$51,600
Required down payment	$ 2,200

From this example, one can see that under Section 245, the required down payment is substantially increased—from $2200 under Section 203(b) to $3800 under Section 245(a). It also must be remembered that the down payment is not all of the initial investment the prospective homebuyer may be required to make. The additional cost will include the required prepaids, and if the seller does not wish to pay the closing costs, the buyer will also have these expenses.

Now that we have figured the maximum loan amount and the required down payment, we need to learn how to calculate the first year's monthly payment, for this will be the payment that will be used to qualify the client. The monthly payment is divided into three basic portions: (1) the amount of the payment to be applied to interest charges and principal reduction, (2) the amount needed to pay for the FHA mortgage insurance, and (3) the amount to be escrowed to pay the taxes, insurance, and any other fees that may affect the title to the property. In the following we will discuss how to calculate the first two items. Once again using Plan III, this time with an interest rate of 10.75, the monthly payment is calculated by multiplying the original loan amount by a factor. These factors are shown in Appendix D. Turning to this appendix and looking for the proper interest rate under Plan III, we find that the factor for the first year is 7.1277. Multiply this factor by the original loan amount (expressed in thousands) and obtain a monthly payment for principal and interest of:

$7.1277 \times 50.00 = \$356.385$ or $356.39

The second item of the monthly payment, the insurance premium, is also calculated by the use of a factor. This factor can be found in Appendix E. Once again using the interest rate of 10.75 and an original principal balance of $50,000, we turn to the proper table and find that the factor for a Plan III mortgage with an interest rate of 10.75 is 0.4210. Thus, we multiply the original loan balance (in thousands) by this factor as follows:

$0.4210 \times 50.000 = \$21.05$

Next, we add the amount for principal and interest and the amount needed to pay the insurance premium to get the first year's payment less the necessary amount for escrows. This amount would equal:

$356.39
21.05
$377.44

With these tables one can calculate the monthly payment (excluding escrows) for a Plan III mortgage at any time during the term of the mortgage.

Section 245(b)

In addition to the standard Section 245, Congress has authorized an additional 245 program. This program in no way alters the existing Section 245(a), but it creates an all-new mortgage insurance program. This section is presently known as Section 245(b). This section will permit the principal obligation of the mortgage to rise during the mortgage to an amount higher than the initial appraised value of the property.

This program of insurance will have the following limitations. First, insurance under this section will only be issued on the properties approved by HUD-FHA prior to the start of construction or substantial rehabilitation, or on properties under construction involving Section 203(b) that are covered by an approved insured-homeowner warranty plan.

The program is limited to 50,000 mortgages or 10 percent of the original principal balance of all mortgages on one- to four-family dwellings insured by HUD in the previous fiscal year, whichever is greater.

This program is available only to prospective homebuyers who have not held title to property within the three-year period preceding their application for a Section 245(b) GPM. The homebuyer must sign a statement to this effect.

Also, this program is limited to applicants for mortgage insurance who could not reasonably afford to purchase their home under the original Section 245 or other FHA insurance programs.

This program is limited to two plans, in contrast to the five plans offered under the original 245 program. The two programs are as follows:

1. The payments will increase at the rate of 4.9 percent per year for a period of ten years.

2. The payments will increase at the rate of 7.5 percent per year for a period of five years.

Maximum mortgage amounts will be established locally. This established limit may not exceed the maximum mortgage amount for Section 203(b).

The FHA field offices have been given formulas that will be used to calculate the maximum loan amounts for both plans. The formulas are based on the face interest rate of the mortgage. Some of the formulas are illustrated in Figure 6-5. In regard to the amount of down payment or investment required, there are formulas to calculate these amounts. According to Mortgagee Letter 80-33 from the Office of the Assistant Secretary for Housing—Federal Housing Commissioner, formulas shown in Figure 6-5 will be used to calculate the minimum down payments for the two plans authorized. In other words, you will have to figure the amount of the down payment under Section 203(b) for the amount of the loan for which your client is making application and also multiply the acquisition cost by the proper percentage to see which is larger.

This section has certain limits as to the amount the mortgage balance may increase. There are two limitations, but the one that will have the greatest effect is that the mortgage amount may increase to an amount which, when all of the deferred interest is added, can never exceed 113 percent of the original appraised value of the home, or 97 percent of the projected value of the property. The projected value is determined by increasing the value of the property at a rate not to exceed 2.5 percent per year during the period when the payments of the mortgage are increasing.

Growing Equity Mortgage (GEM)

On June 4, 1982 the Department of Housing and Urban Development issued a memorandum announcing the growing equity mortgage. According to the memo, Section 245(a) of the National Housing Act authorizes the insuring of mortgages with varying rates of amortization, both negative and positive. In the previous section, we reviewed the graduated payment mortgage with negative amortization. In this section, we review the GEM, also insured under Section 245(a). One major difference is that the GEM allows for accelerated amortization.

First, we should define *growing equity mortgage*. This mortgage is very similar to the GEM discussed in Chapter 2 and the definition is very similar. A GEM can be defined as a first-lien mortgage secured by real property, with a fixed interest rate, where the first-year payment is based on a thirty-year amortization of the mortgage amount and the fixed-interest rate. The remaining monthly payments increase at a specified amount for a specified number of years, with all increase credited to principal balance. What is the difference then? For example, with this GEM the number of available plans for payment increase is limited.

According to the HUD memo, with the scheduled increase in monthly payments credited to principal reduction the term of the mortgage is shortened. Even though the first-year payment is based on a thirty-year

Figure 6-5. Loan-to-value Ratio Tables and Cash Investment for Section 245(b)

7½ Percent for 5 Years

	11½%*	**12%**	**13%**	**14%**
Maximum insurable loan non-veteran as well as veteran	Lesser of 203(b) limits or 96.98% of value	Lesser of 203(b) limits or 96.86% of value	Lesser of 203(b) limits or 96.63% of value	Lesser of 203(b) limits or 96.29% of value
Minimum investment requirements non-veteran loans only	Greater of 203(b) requirement or 3.02% acquisition cost	Greater of 203(b) requirement or 3.14% of acquisition cost	Greater of 203(b) requirement or 3.37% of acquisition cost	Greater of 203(b) requirement or 3.71% of acquisition cost

*At rates less than 11½ percent, the maximum insurable mortgage will be limited by the 203(b) loan-to-value and cash investment ratios. At rates falling between those listed above, use the loan-to-values for the next higher rate. For example, if the rate is 11⅞ percent, use the loan-to-value ratio at 12 percent.

4.9 Percent for 10 Years

	12%*	**13%**	**14%**
Maximum insurable loan non-veteran as well as veteran	Lesser of 203(b) limits or 96.76% of value**	Lesser of 203(b) limits or 96.08% of value	Lesser of 203(b) limits or 94.43% of value
Minimum investment requirements non-veteran loans only	Greater of 203(b) requirement or 3.24% of acquisition cost	Greater of 203(b) requirement or 3.92% of acquisition cost	Greater of 203(b) requirement or 5.57% of acquisition cost

*At rates less than 12 percent, the maximum insurable mortgage will be limited by the 203(b) loan-to-value and cash investment ratios. If the interest rate falls between the amounts shown, the loan-to-value ratio will be the same as the next highest rate. For example, if the rate is shown as 12½ percent, use the loan-to-value ratios at 13 percent.

**Value means the HUD estimate of value including closing cost.

Source: U.S., Department of Housing and Urban Development, Office of the Assistant Secretary for Housing—Federal Housing Commissioner, *Mortgagee Letter 80-33—August 7, 1980*, p. 3.

amortization, the term of the mortgage is dramatically shortened. The actual term of the mortgage will be determined by the amount of the annual payment increase and the interest rate. Since the term of the mortgage is greatly shortened and the lender's funds are tied up for a shorter period, normally the interest rate on the GEM is below the current rate on thirty-year fixed-rate mortgages.

Authorized plans According to HUD-FHA, the only plans authorized under Section 245(a) that may be focused for a GEM are Plans IV and V. Thus, the payments will increase at a rate of either 2 percent per year for ten years or 3 percent per year for ten years.

Term The term of the GEM is limited to the term shown in Appendix F. For example, if the GEM is increasing at the rate of 2.00 percent per year and the interest rate is 15.50, the term in months listed at the bottom of the column is 197 months or 16 years and 5 months. Therefore, even though the initial monthly payment is calculated for a term of 30 years, the actual term is only 16 years and 5 months. If you review each of the interest rates for each of the plans, you can see that the term for the GEM varies for each of the interest rates.

Down payment According to the HUD memo, since there is no negative amortization the down payment will be calculated in the same manner as for Section 203(b).

Monthly payments As with the GPM, HUD-FHA has prepared tables for the calculation of the GEM monthly payments as well as the monthly mortgage insurance premiums. Appendix F shows both the monthly payment factors and the insurance factors for both authorized programs. It should be noted that the monthly payment factors are only for the P and I portion of the payment. You will have to add the utilities, maintenance, and mortgage insurance cost to get the total housing expenses.

For example, if you are working with a client and he or she is interested in a $64,500 insured mortgage and the GEM interest rate is 14.75, you would calculate the first year's principal and interest and mortgage insurance payments as follows: For the 2.00 percent increase GEM principal and interest payment, turn to the proper table in Appendix F (with increasing payments for ten years at 2.00 percent each year) and read across the column headings until you find the interest rate 14.75. Look down that column on the line opposite year 1: the factor listed is 12.444757. The factor is then multiplied by the loan amount in thousands or 64.50. This gives 802.686 or $802.69. For mortgage insurance payments, use the proper 2.00 percent Monthly Mortgage Insurance Factor Table for the first year and the 14.75 interest rate as you did above. The factor for this is .4163, which is then multiplied by the loan amount in thousands or 64.50, giving 26.851 or $26.85.

The entire procedure above would then be repeated for the 3.00 percent increase plan. It could then be decided which of the plans would best suit your client.

Application and underwriting When making application for the GEM, the standard HUD-FHA application will be used; but the applicant will be required to sign a *GEM Certification*, shown in Figure 6-6.

All underwriting of the GEM will be based on the first year's payment. The actual process of underwriting the loan will be discussed in Chapter 13.

Note and mortgage/deed of trust As with the negative amortization mortgages insured under Section 245(a), the standard HUD-FHA note and mortgage/deed of trust must be altered. One of the major modifications is the inclusion of the subtitle "With Increasing Monthly Installments" on both the note and the mortgage/deed of trust. The note will also show the schedule of payments. These modifications are shown in Figures 6-7 and 6-8.

Temporary Mortgage Assistance Payments Program (TMAP)

The Housing and Community Development Act of 1980 revised Section 230 of the National Housing Act to authorize the Secretary of Housing and Urban Development to make all or part of the mortgage payments on such a mortgage directly to the lender on behalf of the homeowner.

Homeowner eligibility Before a homeowner can be eligible for the program, the secretary must determine that the temporary mortgage

Figure 6-6. GEM Certification

GEM Certification

I/We certify that I/we fully understand the obligation I/we am/are undertaking, that my/our mortgage payment to principal and interest will start at $ ______ and will increase by __% each year for 10 years to a maximum payment of $ ______ at the end of the 10th year. I/we understand that the __% increase for the first 10 years of my/our mortgage is being used to reduce my/our outstanding principal balance.

Principal Interest	Mortgage Insurance Premium
$ ______ During the 1st note year	$ ______ During the 1st note year
$ ______ During the 2nd note year	$ ______ During the 2nd note year
$ ______ During the 3rd note year	$ ______ During the 3rd note year
$ ______ During the 4th note year	$ ______ During the 4th note year
$ ______ During the 5th note year	$ ______ During the 5th note year
$ ______ During the 6th note year	$ ______ During the 6th note year
$ ______ During the 7th note year	$ ______ During the 7th note year
$ ______ During the 8th note year	$ ______ During the 8th note year
$ ______ During the 9th note year	$ ______ During the 9th note year
$ ______ During the 10th note year	$ ______ During the 10th note year
$ ______ During the 11th note year and thereafter	$ ______ During the 11th note year and thereafter

In addition I/we will be required to make payment toward taxes, hazard insurance and other costs of homeownership.

Also, I/we certify that I/We have been advised of the present maximum FHA interest rate for 30-year level payment mortgages, which is __%.

Signed

____
Mortgagor

____
Mortgagor

Source: U.S., Department of Housing and Urban Development, Seattle Area Office, Seattle, Washington, *Circular Letter No. 82-08—June 18, 1982.*

Figure 6-7. GEM Note

This form is used in connection with mortgages insured under the one-to four-family provisions of the National Housing Act.

NOTE

FHA CASE NO.

SECTION 245
APPROVED FORM

(To be used with Deed or Trust or Mortgage)
WITH INCREASING MONTHLY INSTALLMENTS

Rev. 6-80

$

, Washington.
, 19

FOR VALUE RECEIVED, the undersigned promise(s) to pay to the order of

the principal sum of
Dollars
($), with interest from date at the rate of
per centum (%) per annum on the balance remaining from time to time unpaid. The said principal and interest shall be payable at the office of
in
, or at such other place as the holder may designate, in writing, in monthly installments of

$	during the 1st Note Year	$	during the 7th Note Year
$	during the 2nd Note Year	$	during the 8th Note Year
$	during the 3rd Note Year	$	during the 9th Note Year
$	during the 4th Note Year	$	during the 10th Note Year
$	during the 5th Note Year	$	during the 11th Note Year
$	during the 6th Note Year		and thereafter,

commencing on the first day of , 19 , and on the first day of each month thereafter, until the principal and interest are fully paid, except that the final payment of the entire indebtedness evidenced hereby, if not sooner paid, shall be due and payable on the first day of

If default be made in the payment of any installment under this note, and if such default is not made good prior to the due date of the next such installment, the entire principal sum and accrued interest shall at once become due and payable at the option of the holder of this note. Failure to exercise this option shall not constitute a waiver of the right to exercise the same in the event of any subsequent default. If any suit or action is instituted to collect this note or any part thereof the undersigned promise(s) and agree(s) to pay, in addition to the costs and disbursements provided by statute, a reasonable sum as attorney's fees in such suit or action.

The undersigned, whether principal, surety, guarantor, endorser, or other party hereto, agrees to be jointly and severally bound, severally hereby waive demand, protest and notice of demand, protest and nonpayment, and expressly agree that this note or any payment thereunder may be extended from time to time and consent to the acceptance of further security, including other types of security, all without in any way affecting the liability of such parties.

Source: U.S., Department of Housing and Urban Development, Seattle Area Office, Seattle, Washington, *Circular Letter No. 82-08—June 18, 1982.*

Figure 6-8. GEM Deed of Trust

STATE OF WASHINGTON

DEED OF TRUST

This form is used in connection with deeds of trust insured under the one- to four-family provisions of the National Housing Act.

WITH INCREASING MONTHLY INSTALLMENTS

THIS DEED OF TRUST, is made this ______________ **day of** ______________, **19** ___,

BETWEEN ______________________________, **as Grantor,**

whose address is ______________________________;

and ______________________________, **as Trustee,**

whose address is ______________________________;

and ______________________________

______________________________, **as Beneficiary,**

whose address is ______________________________

Grantor hereby irrevocably grants, bargains, sells and conveys to Trustee in trust, with power of sale, the following described property in ______________________________ County, Washington:

TOGETHER WITH all the tenements, hereditaments, and appurtenances now or hereafter thereunto belonging or in anywise appertaining, and the rents, issues and profits thereof.

THIS DEED IS FOR THE PURPOSE OF SECURING PERFORMANCE of each agreement of Grantor herein contained and payment of the sum of Dollars ($),

with interest thereon according to the terms of a promissory note of even date herewith, payable to Beneficiary or order and made by Grantor, and also such further sums as may be advanced or loaned by Beneficiary to Grantor, or any of their successors or assigns, together with interest thereon at such rate as shall be agreed upon.

The Grantor covenants and agrees as follows:

1. That he will pay the indebtedness secured hereby, Privilege is reserved to pay the debt in whole, or in an amount equal to one or more monthly payments on the principal that are next due on the note, on the first day of any month prior to maturity: *Provided, however,* That written notice of an intention to exercise such privilege is given at least thirty (30) days prior to prepayment.

2. Grantor agrees to pay to Beneficiary together with and in addition to the monthly payments of principal and interest payable under the terms of the note secured hereby, on the first day of each month until said note is fully paid, the following sums:

(a) An amount sufficient to provide the Beneficiary with funds to pay the next mortgage insurance premium if this instrument and the note secured hereby are insured, or a monthly charge (in lieu of a mortgage insurance premium) if they are held by the Secretary of Housing and Urban Development, as follows:

(I) If and so long as said note and this instrument are insured or are reinsured under the provisions of the National Housing Act, an amount sufficient to accumulate in the hands of the Beneficiary one (1) month prior to its due date the annual mortgage insurance premium, in order to provide the Beneficiary with funds to pay such premium to the Secretary of Housing and Urban Development pursuant to the National Housing Act, as amended, and applicable regulations thereunder; or

(II) If and so long as said note and this instrument are held by the Secretary of Housing and Urban Development, a monthly charge (in lieu of a mortgage insurance premium) which shall be in an amount equal to one-twelfth (1/12) of one-half (1/2) per centum of the average outstanding balance due on said note computed without taking into account delinquencies or prepayments:

(b) A sum, as estimated by the Beneficiary, equal to the ground rents, if any, and the taxes and special assessments next due on the premises covered by this Deed of Trust, plus the premiums that will next become due and payable on such insurance policies as may be required under paragraph 9 hereof, satisfactory to Beneficiary, Grantor agreeing to deliver promptly to Beneficiary all bills and notices therefor, less all sums already paid therefor divided by the number of months to elapse before one (1) month prior to the date when such ground rents, premiums, taxes and assessments will become delinquent, such sums to be held by the Beneficiary in trust to pay said ground rents, premiums, taxes and special assessments; and

(c) All payments mentioned in the two preceding subsections of this paragraph and all payments to be made under the note secured hereby shall be added together and the aggregate amount thereof shall be paid by the Grantor each month in a single payment to be applied by Beneficiary to the following items in the order set forth:

(I) premium charges under the contract of insurance with the Secretary of Housing and Urban Development, or monthly charge (in lieu of mortage insurance premium), as the case may be:

(II) ground rents, if any, taxes, special assessments, fire and other hazard insurance premiums;

(III) interest on the note secured hereby; and

(IV) amortization of the principal of said note.

Any deficiency in the amount of any such aggregate monthly payment shall, unless made good by the Grantor prior to the due date of the next such payment, constitute an event of default under this Deed of Trust. The arrangement provided for in paragraph 2 is solely for the added protection of the Beneficiary and entails no responsibility on the Beneficiary's part beyond the allowing of due credit, without interest, for the sums actually received by it. Upon assignment of this Deed of Trust by the Beneficiary, any funds on hand shall be turned over to the assignee and any responsibility of the assignor with respect thereto shall terminate. Each transfer of the property that is the subject of this Deed of Trust shall automatically transfer to the Grantee all rights of the Grantor with respect to any funds accumulated hereunder.

Replaces FHA-2189T, which may be used. HUD-92189T (3-79)

Source: U.S., Department of Housing and Urban Development, Seattle Area Office, Seattle, Washington, *Circular Letter No. 82-08—June 18, 1982.*

assistance payments, or TMAPs, are necessary to avoid foreclosure, and that the homeowner will be able to meet the following:

1. Resume full mortgage payments within thirty-six months after the beginning of the TMAP or upon the termination of the TMAP

2. In addition to making the regular monthly payment on the mortgage, be able to start the repayment of all funds advanced under the TMAP at the time designated by the Secretary of Housing and Urban Dvelopment

3. Be able to repay the mortgage by its maturity date or by a later date established by the secretary

Amount of payments TMAPs can be made in an amount that is equal to the total monthly mortgage payment. The initial payment under the TMAP may include an amount that will bring the mortgage current. It should be noted that this payment may not exceed the amount established by the secretary deemed necessary to supplement the amount the homeowner can contribute toward the total monthly mortgage payment.

Payment period TMAPs can be made for an initial period of eighteen months and any period of default. The period can be extended by the secretary for a period not to exceed an additional eighteen months. The primary reason for the extension is to keep the mortgage from going into foreclosure. There must be a reasonable expectation that, with the extension, the homeowner will be able to repay the mortgage as well as all of the funds advanced under the TMAP.

Repayment of the TMAP The funds advanced under the TMAP are regarded as a loan and are required to be repaid by the homeowner receiving the TMAP. The term of the repayment will be set by the secretary and may include any monies paid by the secretary to the lender for expenses incurred in conjunction with the delinquency of the mortgage. The secretary may require that interest be charged on the amount advanced under the TMAP, but the interest rate shall not exceed the interest rate established for mortgages insured under Section 203(b) at the time the TMAP assistance is approved. It should also be noted that these interest charges are exempt from any state or local usury law.

Section 234(c): Mortgage Insurance for Condominium Units

Section 234(c) was originally designed to insure only mortgages on condominiums in HUD-approved projects. This authority, however, has been expanded. With the passage of the Housing and Community Development Amendments of 1979, HUD, through FHA, was allowed to insure mortgages on individual units in a condominium project that were built without HUD-FHA project approval and inspection during construction. The purpose of this authority is to provide FHA insurance on the resale of the units that were conventionally financed, in order to help in the resale of these units.

For the project to qualify for this program it must meet the following requirements:

1. All units were built for conventional financing

2. The project has been under construction for at least one year

3. Seventy percent of the units are sold or have intent or contracts to be sold to owner occupants

4. The developer or declarant has no remaining interest (there is one exception to this: if the construction or conversion has not reached a level where the developer or declarant no longer has an interest, but the documents of the development or conversion contains a provision for such a phasing out of the developer, the project may qualify)

To make application under this program of mortgage insurance, the person will make application on the standard FHA application form, and supply some additional exhibits which must accompany the application. (This information is only required to accompany the first application in a project.)

Figure 6-9. Required Exhibits for Existing Condominiums

REQUIRED EXHIBITS FOR EXISTING CONDOMINIUMS

I. CONVENTIONAL or FNMA APPROVED	***Existing Not HUD Approved***	***Existing Resale in HUD Approved Project***
1. PROJECT APPROVAL		
a. Master Deed or Declaration of Condominium with recording date, include any amendments	X	
b. By-Laws of the Condominium Association	X	
c. Recorded project plat, map and/or air lot survey	X	
d. Management Agreement	AA	
e. Articles of Incorporation of the Condominium Association	X	
f. Attorney's certification that legal documents meet HUD objectives or evidence FNMA has approved the Project	X	
g. Mortgagee Certification that the project construction is over one year old	X	
h. Certification the Declarant's rights have expired or have been waived	X	
i. Certification that at least 70% of the units are owner-occupied	X	
j. Current financial statement (or budget) of the condominium project (including reserves for replacement expected life of Assets)	X	
k. Statement signed by Office of Board of Directors of Council of Co-owners specifying any existing or pending special assessments and any pending litigation affecting the condominium	X	
l. Minutes of last two Council of Co-owners meetings	X	
2. UNIT APPRAISAL		
a. HUD 92800	X	X
b. Mortgagees certification that there have been no changes to the legal or organizational documents since HUD approved letter		X

II. VA APPROVED	
No project exhibits required for preapproval.	After Project Acceptances by VA
UNIT APPRAISAL	
a. HUD 92800 Application	X
b. Copy of VA Approval Letter or Loan Guaranty Letter indicating approval by VA	X

FOOTNOTE:
1. Submit a single set of documents which will not be returned.
2. Legend: X Required AA if Applicable
3. Section 1: Organizational documents one-time submission for the project, drafts are not acceptable.
4. Section 2: Exhibits will accompany the first appraisal requests. Once project approved, only Section 2 items need be submitted.

Source: U.S., Department of Housing and Urban Development, Seattle Area Office, Seattle, Washington, *Circular Letter No. 81-26—October 29, 1981,* Attachment I.

The number of required exhibits depends on whether the project was approved by FNMA or VA. Approval by FHLMC will not be recognized by FHA. For projects which have only FHLMC approval, you will need to contact your local FHA office for approval requirements.

HUD has prepared a listing (Figure 6-9) of the documents that must accompany the first application for mortgage insurance in such a condominium project. You will notice that under the portion of the figure dealing with conventional or FNMA approval, it lists the information for project approval and unit appraisal.

Under the section dealing with VA-approved projects, HUD-FHA will require no information or documents; but for the individual unit appraisal HUD-FHA will require certain information. Figure 6-9 also shows what is needed when making application for mortgage insurance for a resale in a HUD-approved project.

The maximum loan amount under Section 234(c) is identical to that of Section 203(b) and that is $67,500, unless the secretary of HUD has designated an area to be a high-cost area and has increased the maximum mortgage amount. Those areas so designated by the secretary are in Appendix G.

Under this program, mortgages on both owner-occupied and nonowner-occupied units are eligible for mortgage insurance. In regard to the nonowner-occupied units, HUD has some additional rules. The most important rule is that nonowner-occupied units may not be insured unless the borrower is an owner occupant of a unit in the complex. If the borrower is a resident of the complex, HUD will allow the borrower to purchase up to three units as a nonowner occupant.

It should be noted that many lenders will not usually offer to help either the applicant or the Homeowners Association in getting HUD's approval for a condominium project because the lender could expend a large amount of time and will not be given an exclusive approval (that is, other HUD/FHA approved lenders will be able to make loans in the project). As a real estate professional you may be helped in making condominium sales if you work with a project to secure HUD-FHA approval.

Mobile Home or Manufactured Housing Loans

As the demand and cost of housing constantly increases, many prospective homebuyers are looking for alternatives. One that has been selected by many is mobile homes or manufactured housing. The real estate professional must have some knowledge of the methods for financing manufactured housing. Probably one of the best finance methods is through HUD-FHA.

Under Title I, Section 2, of the National Housing Act, HUD-FHA is authorized to offer mortgage insurance on mobile homes or manufactured housing that meet HUD-FHA standards.

This mortgage insurance is available to anyone who demonstrates the ability to make the cash investment and the mortgage payment and has good credit. One of the major restrictions placed on this program is that the mobile home must be the primary residence of the applicant. HUD has defined the primary residence as one in which the applicant lives at least nine months of the year.

Under this program, HUD-FHA will insure loans to the maximums shown in Figure 6-10.

In addition to the limits shown in Figure 6-10, the Housing and Community Development Amendments of 1981 will allow insurance on a maximum loan of up to $12,500 for a "suitably developed" manufactured home lot. The amendments also allow the basic maximum loan amounts for manufactured homes on improved lots to be increased by an additional $7500 in areas that can show there is such a need to meet the higher cost of land acquisition, site development, and construction of a permanent foundation. Another important change authorized by the 1981 amendments allows the inclusion of garages, patios, carports, and comparable appurtenances as part of manufactured home loans and combination loans as long as the loan is secured by a first lien. A final important provision of the manufactured home section of the 1981 amendments is to allow the refinancing of presently owned manufactured home lots through the combination program. The combination program allows for the financing of both a manufactured home and the lot on which it will be placed.

Figure 6-10. HUD-FHA Maximum Loans

	Loan Amount	*Term*
Singular modular	$22,500	20 years, 32 days
Double modular	$35,000	20 years, 32 days
Single homes on lot	$35,000	20 years, 32 days
Double wide or larger on lot	$47,500	25 years, 32 days

In addition to the mortgage insurance issued under Title I, HUD will also issue mortgage insurance on manufactured housing under Title II, Section 203(b). The mortgage insurance under Section 203(b) will be issued for both proposed and existing construction as long as the unit meets certain requirements. Some of the requirements for proposed construction are as follows:

1. The unit must be of double-wide construction (that is, two single units joined)

2. The unit must be owner occupied and the title to the land, or the leasehold, shall be vested to the owner occupant

3. The unit must be classified and taxed as real property by the state in which the unit is located

4. The unit must bear a seal or identification that the unit complies with HUD's mobile home construction and safety standards

5. Only units built after June 15, 1976, may be used as security for a mortgage to be insured under Title II Section 203(b)

6. The unit must be permanently affixed to a foundation

7. The wheels, axles, and hitch or tongue must be removed

8. The unit must have the required crawl space, between the bottom of the unit and the ground (According to HUD, the minimum crawl space is eighteen inches; will require access to the crawl space and the space will be ventilated)

9. As with the other types of construction, HUD will require the proposed construction to be inspected (HUD now requires a minimum of two inspections: a foundation inspection and a final inspection)

The following are some of the requirements for mortgage insurance if the unit is to be insured as existing construction:

1. The unit must be of double-wide construction

2. The unit must be owner occupied similar to the requirements under proposed construction

3. The unit must be permanently affixed to a foundation with the wheels, axles, and hitch or tongue removed

4. The unit must be connected to permanently installed utilities that are protected from freezing.

5. HUD will require the unit to be constructed prior to June 15, 1976, and bear the proper identification as to the construction meeting the HUD mobile home requirements

6. The unit must have the proper crawl space similar to the requirements for proposed construction

7. HUD will not insure units that have a basement if the unit is located in a federally designated flood area

These are only some of the requirements. Before working with a client seeking a double-wide unit financed with a mortgage insured

Figure 6-11. Deed of Trust, Example 1

4240.2 REV CHG

APPENDIX 4

STATE OF ARIZONA
FHA Form No. 2101 DT
Revised October 1975

EXAMPLE 1

This form is used in connection with deeds of trust insured under the one- to four-family provisions of the National Housing Act.

DEED OF TRUST

WITH DEFERRED INTEREST AND INCREASING MONTHLY INSTALLMENTS
With Assignment of Rents

THIS DEED OF TRUST, made this ____________ day of ______________________, 19____,

BETWEEN ______________________________

______________________________, as TRUSTOR,

______________ (Street and number) ______________ (City) ______________ (State)

____

______________________________, as TRUSTEE, and

____

______________________________, as BENEFICIARY,

... WITH POWER OF SALE,

... described as:

TOGETHER WITH the rents, issues, and profits thereof, SUBJECT, HOWEVER, to the right, power, and authority hereinafter given to and conferred upon Beneficiary to collect and apply such rents, issues, and profits;

FOR THE PURPOSE OF SECURING Performance of each agreement of Trustor herein contained and payment of the sum of $____________ with interest thereon according to the terms of a promissory note of even date herewith, payable to Beneficiary or order and made by Trustor. DEFERRAL OF INTEREST MAY INCREASE THE PRINCIPAL BALANCE TO $ __________.

1. Privilege is reserved to pay the debt secured hereby in whole or in an amount equal to one or more principal payments next due on the note, on the first day of any month prior to maturity, provided written notice of intention so to do is given at least thirty days prior to prepayment.

2. Trustor agrees to pay to Beneficiary in addition to the monthly payments of principal and interest payable under the terms of said note, on the first day of each month until said note is fully paid, the following sums:

a. An amount sufficient to provide the holder hereof with funds to pay the next mortgage insurance premium if this instrument and the note secured hereby are insured, or a monthly charge (in lieu of a mortgage insurance premium) if they are held by the Secretary, Department of Housing and Urban Development, as follows:

(I) If and so long as said note of even date and this instrument are insured or are reinsured under the provisions of the National Housing Act, an amount sufficient to accumulate in the hands of the holder one (1) month prior to its due date the annual mortgage insurance premium, in order to provide such holder with funds to pay such premium to the Secretary, Department of Housing and Urban Development pursuant to the National Housing Act, as amended, and applicable Regulations thereunder; or

(II) If and so long as said note of even date and this instrument are held by the Secretary, Department of Housing and Urban Development, a monthly charge (in lieu of a mortgage insurance premium) which shall be in an amount equal to one-twelfth (1/12) of one-half (1/2) per centum of the average outstanding balance due on the note computed without taking into account delinquencies or prepayments;

b. An installment of the ground rents, if any, and of the taxes and special assessments levied or to be levied against the premises covered by this Deed of Trust; and an installment of the premium or premiums that will become due and payable to renew the insurance on the premises covered hereby against loss by fire or such other hazard as may be required by Beneficiary in amounts and in a company or companies satisfactory to Beneficiary; trustor agreeing to deliver promptly to Beneficiary all bills and notices therefor. Such installments shall be equal respectively to one-twelfth (1/12) of the annual ground rent, if any, plus the estimated premium or premiums for such insurance, and taxes and assessments next due (as estimated by Beneficiary) less all installments already paid therefor, divided by the number of months that are to elapse before one month prior to the date when such premium or premiums and taxes and assessments will become delinquent. Beneficiary shall hold such payments in trust to pay such ground rents, premium or premiums and taxes and special assessments before the same become delinquent; and

c. All payments mentioned in the two preceding subsections of this paragraph and all payments to be made under the note secured hereby shall be added together and the aggregate amount thereof shall be paid each month in a single payment to be applied by Beneficiary to the following items in the order set forth:

(I) premium charges under the contract of insurance with the Secretary, Department of Housing and Urban Development, or monthly charge (in lieu of mortgage insurance premium), as the case may be;
(II) grounds rents, taxes, special assessments, fire and other hazard insurance premiums;
(III) interest on the note secured hereby; and
(IV) amortization of the principal of said note.

Any deficiency in the amount of any such aggregate monthly payment shall, unless made good prior to the due date of the next such payment, constitute an event of default under this Deed of Trust.

8/78

HUD-Wash., D.C.

Page 4

Source: U.S., Department of Housing and Urban Development, *The Graduated Payment Mortgage Program—A HUD Handbook*, June 1978, Appendix 4, p. 4.

by HUD under Title II, Section 203(b), you should contact any HUD-approved lender or your nearest HUD office.

Since this mortgage is insured under Section 203(b), the maximum loan amounts are the same as shown earlier in this chapter. The term for these mortgages is also the same as that listed for Section 203(b).

This completes our discussion of the more important programs of mortgage insurance available through HUD-FHA. A synopsis of other HUD-FHA mortgage insurance programs is found in Appendix H. If you have any questions regarding any of these programs listed in Appendix H, contact an aproved HUD-FHA lender or the HUD-FHA office nearest you.

MORTGAGE INSTRUMENTS FOR SECTION 245

The standard HUD Note and Mortgage/Deed of Trust was reviewed in Chapter 2. These standard documents can be used with many of the programs of HUD-FHA, but some of the programs will require these documents to be modified. Any mortgage insured under Section 245(a) and (b) will require modified standard instruments.

Both the note and the mortgage/deed of trust will have to be modified. First let us review the modification to the mortgage instrument. In all states under the document caption or title, the following must be added in all caps: ''WITH DEFERRED INTEREST AND INCREASING MONTHLY INSTALL-MENTS.'' The second modification to the mortgage instrument in all states is the addition of the following: ''DEFERRAL OF INTEREST MAY INCREASE THE PRINCIPAL BALANCE TO $______ .'' The location of this additional statement will depend on available space in the mortgage, but it should be as close as possible to the section identifying the amount of the mortgage. These modifications are illustrated in Figure 6-11. In some states there will not be room in this section of the mortgage instrument and the addition of the ''DEFERRAL OF INTEREST'' will be placed in the margin of the document and asterisks will be placed in the proper area of the mortgage. This is illustrated in Figure 6-12.

The modifications to the note are more detailed. The first modification to the note is similar to the first modification to the mortgage/deed of trust. A similar statement is added below the caption or title. The statement to be added in all caps is ''WITH DEFERRED INTEREST AND INCREASING MONTHLY PAYMENTS.''

The second modification to the note occurs in the space where the monthly payment is given. Instead of a dollar amount, the following statement will be added: ''ACCORDING TO SCHEDULE A.'' The final change or modification to the note is the following addition: ''DEFERRED INTEREST SHALL BE ADDED TO THE PRINCIPAL BALANCE MONTHLY AND SHALL INCREASE THE PRINCIPAL BALANCE TO NOT MORE THAN $ ______ .'' This statement should be added as shown in Figure 6-13, but if there is not sufficient room for this statement, it may be added as an attachment.

The monthly payments as shown in Schedule A will be added to the front of the note in the large space provided (illustrated in Chapter 2). HUD-FHA has specified the form that will be used for Schedule A for Plans I, II, and III as well as Plans IV and V. This form is illustrated in Figure 6-14.

It should be noted that the maximum principal balance to be shown on both the note and mortgage/deed of trust is calculated by using the highest outstanding balance factor. These factors of Plan III are shown in Appendix C. To find the dollar amount that will be placed in the blank in the statement ''MAY INCREASE THE PRINCIPAL BALANCE TO $ ______ ,'' you would turn to Appendix C, locate the proper interest rate, look for the underlined factor, and multiply the original principal balance (in thousands) by the factor. This will give the highest outstanding balance.

REVIEW QUESTIONS

1. Identify by section number and explain the basic mortgage insurance programs of HUD-FHA.

2. Define the term acquisition cost and give an example.

3. Name and explain at least three advantages of mortgages insured by HUD-FHA.

Figure 6-12. Deed of Trust, Example 2

4240.2 REV CHG

APPENDIX 4

FHA FORM NO. 9122
Revised July 1970

EXAMPLE 3

This form is used in connection with mortgages insured under the one- to four-family provisions of the National Housing Act.

MORTGAGE NOTE

FHA CASE NO.

WITH DEFERRED INTEREST AND INCREASING MONTHLY INSTALLMENTS

$, Kentucky.
, 19 .

FOR VALUE RECEIVED, the undersigned promise(s) to pay to the order of

the principal sum of Dollars
($), with interest from date at the rate of
per centum (%) per annum on the unpaid balance until paid. Principal and interest shall be payable at the office of
in
or at such other place as the holder hereof may designate in writing, in monthly installments ACCORDING TO SCHEDULE A ATTACHED Dollars ($), commencing on the first day of , 19 , and on the first day of each month thereafter, until the principal and interest are fully paid, except that the final payment of the entire indebtedness evidenced hereby, if not sooner paid, shall be due and payable on the first day of ,
DEFERRED INTEREST SHALL BE ADDED TO THE PRINCIPAL BALANCE MONTHLY AND SHALL INCREASE THE PRINCIPAL BALANCE TO NOT MORE THAN $ ________.

If default be made in the payment of any installment under this note, and if such default is not made good prior to the due date of the next such installment, the entire principal sum and accrued interest shall at once become due and payable without notice at the option of the holder of this note. Failure to exercise this option shall not constitute a waiver of the right to exercise the same in the event of any subsequent default.

The undersigned, whether principal, surety, guarantor, endorser, or other party hereto, agree(s) to be jointly and severally bound, and severally hereby waive demand, protest, and notice of demand, protest, and nonpayment.

SCHEDULE A

$_______ during the 1st note year
_______ during the 2nd note year
_______ during the 3rd note year
_______ during the 4th note year
_______ during the 5th note year
_______ during the 6th note year and thereafter

8/78

HUD-Wash., D.C.
Page 6

Source: U.S., Department of Housing and Urban Development, *The Graduated Payment Mortgage Program—A HUD Handbook*, June 1978, Appendix 4, p. 5.

Figure 6-13. Mortgage Note

4240.2 REV CHG

APPENDIX 4

STATE OF MARYLAND
FHA FORM NO. 2127M
Rev. June 1975

EXAMPLE 2

This form is used in connection with deeds of trust insured under the one- to four-family provisions of the National Housing Act.

DEED OF TRUST

WITH DEFERRED INTEREST AND INCREASING MONTHLY INSTALLMENTS

THIS DEED, made this day of , 19 , by and between

party of the first part and , Trustee, as hereinafter set forth, party of the second part:

WHEREAS, the party of the first part is justly indebted unto

, a corporation organized and existing under the laws of , in the principal sum of Dollars ($), with interest from date at the rate of per centum (%) per annum on the unpaid balance until paid, for which amount the said party has signed and delivered a certain promissory note bearing even date herewith and payable in monthly installments ~~of~~ ACCORDING TO THE SCHEDULE ATTACHED TO SAID NOTE ~~Dollars ($~~ ~~)~~, commencing on the first day of , 19 , and on the first day of each month thereafter until the principal and interest are fully paid, except that the final payment of principal and interest, if not sooner paid, shall be due and payable on the first day of , **

AND WHEREAS, the party of the first part desires to secure the prompt payment of said debt, and interest thereon, ... the same shall become due and payable, and all costs and expenses incurred in respect thereto, including ... incurred or paid by the said party of the second part or substituted Trustee, or by any person hereby ... litigation at law or in equity which may arise in respect to this trust or the property hereinafter ... may be advanced as provided herein, with interest on all such costs and advances from

... WITNESSETH, that the party of the first part, in consideration of the ... States of America, to in hand paid by the party of the second part, the ... hereby acknowledged, has granted and conveyed, and ... successors and assigns, the following-described ... Maryland, known and distinguished as

** DEFERRAL OF INTEREST MAY INCREASE THE PRINCIPAL BALANCE TO $

together with all the improvements in anywise appertaining, and all the estate, right, title, interest, and claim, either at law or in equity, or otherwise however, of the party of the first part, of, in, to, or out of the said land and premises.

By the execution of this instrument, Mortgagors, Grantors or parties of the first part (whichever applies) certify and acknowledge that prior thereto they have received both a fully executed agreement as to the contractural rate of interest and a loan disclosure statement in connection with the loan secured hereby both as required by Article 49 of the Annotated Code of Maryland.

TO HAVE AND TO HOLD the said property and improvements unto the party of the second part, its successors and assigns

IN AND UPON THE TRUSTS, NEVERTHELESS, hereinafter declared; that is to say: IN TRUST to permit said party of the first part, or assigns, to use and occupy the said described land and premises, and the rents, issues, and profits thereof, to take, have, and apply to and for sole use and benefit, until default be made in the payment of any manner of indebtedness hereby secured or in the performance of any of the covenants as hereinafter provided.

AND upon the full payment of all of said note and the interest thereon, and all moneys advanced or expended as herein provided, and all other proper costs, charges, commissions, half-commissions, and expenses, at any time before the sale hereinafter provided for to release and reconvey the said described premises unto the said party of the first part or assigns, at cost. Prior to the execution and delivery of any partial or complete release, each trustee shall be entitled to charge and receive a fee of $5.00, plus 50 cents for Notary's fee, for each release. The right to charge and receive said fee shall be limited to two Trustees.

HUD-Wash., D.C. 8/78

Page 5

Source: U.S., Department of Housing and Urban Development, *The Graduated Payment Mortgage Program—A HUD Handbook*, June 1978, Appendix 4, p. 6.

Figure 6-14. Schedule A

PAYMENT SCHEDULE

(for Plans I, II, III)		*(for Plans IV, V)*	
	SCHEDULE A		*SCHEDULE A*
$ ________	during the 1st note year	$ ________	during the 1st note year
$ ________	during the 2nd note year	$ ________	during the 2nd note year
$ ________	during the 3rd note year	$ ________	during the 3rd note year
$ ________	during the 4th note year	$ ________	during the 4th note year
$ ________	during the 5th note year	$ ________	during the 5th note year
$ ________	during the 6th note year	$ ________	during the 6th note year
	and thereafter	$ ________	during the 7th note year
		$ ________	during the 8th note year
		$ ________	during the 9th note year
		$ ________	during the 10th note year
		$ ________	during the 11th note year
			and thereafter

Source: U.S., Department of Housing and Urban Development, *The Graduated Payment Mortgage Program—A HUD Handbook, June 1978,* Appendix 4, p.2.

4. Calculate the maximum loan under Section 203(b) for the following situation: the sales price of the property is $51,250 and the estimated closing costs are $1200.

5. What is the only fee that the borrower may pay when the mortgage is insured by HUD-FHA?

6. What is the current rate for mortgages insured by HUD-FHA?

7. What are the current discount points charged for mortgages insured under Section 203(b) and Section 245(a) and (b)? If there is a difference in the discount points charged, give your reasons for the difference.

8. For the purposes of Section 221(d)(2), is your city located in a high-cost area? If so, what is the maximum mortgage that can be insured on a single-family dwelling?

9. Explain the Graduated Payment Mortgage (GPM). Is there more than one plan available under Section 245(a) and 245(b)?

NOTES

[1]U.S., Department of Housing and Urban Development, Fort Worth Service Office, *Circular Letter No. 81-6*, June 19, 1981, p. 2.

[2]U.S., Department of Housing and Urban Development/FHA, HUD-H-318(3), *Lending and Selling with a Graduated Payment Mortgage*, December 1978, p. 8.

CHAPTER 7 Other Governmental Programs

LEARNING OBJECTIVES

Besides HUD-FHA, there are other agencies of the federal and state governments that either guarantee or make mortgages on family dwellings in urban and/or rural areas. The agencies we will examine here are the Veterans Administration, the Farmers Home Administration, the Federal Land Bank, and state housing agencies.

Upon completion of this chapter you should be able to do the following:

- ★ **Define and explain the loan guaranty benefits of the Veterans Administration.**
- ★ **Explain the advantages and disadvantages of loans guaranteed by the Veterans Administration**
- ★ **Explain the basic program available through the Farmers Home Administration for rural housing.**

VETERANS ADMINISTRATION

The Veterans Administration is similar to FHA in that VA does not usually make loans, but VA does have the ability to make direct loans in some rural or small communities where VA has determined that private mortgage financing is not available. Whereas FHA insures 100 percent of the loan, VA only guarantees a portion of the loan. This ability to guarantee a portion of an eligible veteran's loan was made possible when Congress passed the Serviceman's Readjustment Act of 1942. This act has been amended several times, but the loan guaranty section of the act has basically remained the same. Under the provision of the act, the VA can presently guarantee up to 60 percent of the loan, or $27,500, whichever is less. Later in this chapter we will discuss the guaranty and the maximum loan, but first let us examine the advantages and disadvantages of a Veterans Administration guaranteed loan.

Advantages

The advantages of the VA loan guaranty are very similar to the advantages of an FHA-insured loan.

Low interest rates As with the FHA-insured mortgage, the VA-guaranteed loan interest rate is usually less than the interest rate on conventional loans. The reason for the lower interest rate is that the lender is protected from loss by a guaranty from the Veterans Administration. If there is a difference between the VA rate and the conventional rate, many lenders will charge discount points to the seller.

No down payment One of the major differences between the FHA and VA is that with the VA loan, the eligible veteran normally does not have to make any down payment. The seller is allowed to pay all of the closing costs as well as all of the prepaids. In other words, a veteran can move into a home with no cash investment.

Borrower qualification Under the VA guaranty program, the borrower qualifications are less strenuous and less formal than under the FHA-insured loan. These qualifications will be discussed in detail in Chapter 12.

No prepayment penalty As with the FHA-insured mortgage, the borrower may pay off the loan on or before the due date and the VA does not allow the lender to charge a penalty.

Loans are assumable As with the FHA loans, loans guaranteed by the VA are usually assumable. There is, however, a drawback or penalty to the veteran regarding assumption: the veteran in some cases may not be released from the liability for the mortgage and may not be able to qualify for another VA guaranty mortgage.

No charge for the VA guaranty There is no charge for the VA guaranty, thus making the monthly payment to the veteran somewhat lower.

Disadvantages

We have discussed the major advantages for the veteran in using the VA guaranty, but as with any program there are disadvantages. Like the advantages, the disadvantages are very similar for FHA- and VA-guaranteed loans.

Discount points As with the FHA loans, points are usually charged by the lenders who make the VA-guaranteed loan. The reason for these points is the same as for the FHA loan. They are used to bring the yield on the VA-guaranteed mortgage in line with other mortgages. As with the FHA-insured loan, the points may not be paid by the veteran. The law allows the veteran to pay only for the origination of the loan and this fee may not exceed 1 percent of the loan amount. So the only person to whom the discount points are a disadvantage is the seller. For this reason, when the discount points are at a high level, many sellers are reluctant to sell to a veteran wishing to use his "GI loan."

Processing time Since the VA is a government agency, the time for the application to be approved is sometimes longer than for conventional loans. This is only true if the lender making the loan is not a *supervised lender*. According to Section 500(b) of the Servicemen's Readjustment Act, the Veterans Administration classifies any lender that is subject to examination and supervision by an agency of the United States or any state government including the District of Columbia as a supervised lender. These lenders have the authority to make a VA home loan which the Veterans Administration must automatically guarantee. Examples of such supervised lenders are savings and loan associations, commercial banks, and life insurance companies. Therefore, the disadvantage of processing time applies to the nonsupervised lenders, such as mortgage companies, for they must submit the completed application and all of the supporting information to the nearest VA office for approval.

One can see that these disadvantages of a VA loan are not major and in most cases are not disadvantages to the veteran, but are to the person selling the property.

Elgibile Veterans

Not all veterans are eligible to take advantage of the VA's loan guaranty program, and as a real estate professional you must know the eligibility requirements for a VA loan guaranty. Only those veterans who served on active duty during one of the following periods may be eligible. (One additional fact to be remembered is that only active duty counts—not active duty for training.)

World War II To qualify, a veteran must have served on active duty for at least ninety days and must have a discharge under conditions other than dishonorable or have been released with less than ninety days of service due to a service-connected disability. This service must have been not before September 16, 1940, and no later than July 25, 1947.

Cold War Era The Veterans Housing Amendments Act of 1976 extended the home loan guaranty to those who served during the period that is sometimes referred to as the Cold War Era. For a veteran to qualify under these amendments, he or she must either have served for at least 181 days and received a discharge or have been released under conditions other than dishonorable, or have been released with less than 181 days due to a service-connected disability. This service must have occurred after July 25, 1947, and prior to June 27, 1950.

Korean Conflict To be eligible under the Korean Conflict, a veteran must have served on active duty for ninety days or more and have been either discharged or released from active duty under conditions other than dishonorable. If any portion of the ninety days of service was during the period of June 27, 1950, to January 31, 1955, or if a veteran was released from service due to a service-connected disability with less than ninety days, the veteran is still eligible.

Noncombat To be eligible under this category, a veteran must have served for a period of continuous active duty for a period of 181 days or more, and the active duty must have been after January 31, 1955, and prior to August 5, 1964. In addition, a veteran must have been discharged or released from active duty under conditions other than dishonorable or have been released or discharged due to a service-connected disability.

Vietnam Era For veterans to be eligible under the Vietnam Era benefits, they must have served on active duty between August 5, 1964, and May 7, 1975, for a period of ninety days or more and have been discharged or released under conditions other than dishonorable, or have been released or discharged with less service due to a service-connected disability.

Current active duty Under the present law a person on active duty for 180 or more days, even though not discharged or released from service, is eligible while his or her service continues without breaks.

In addition to the veterans being eligible, an unmarried surviving spouse of a veteran who served during any of the above periods is eligible if the veteran died while on active duty or as a result of a service-connected disability. Spouses of service personnel who have been missing in action, captured in the line of duty by a hostile force, or forcibly detained or interned by a foreign government or power for a period of more than ninety days are also eligible for a VA loan guaranty.

Certificate of Eligibility

When dealing with a veteran in the purchase of a home or mobile home, the only true way to establish the eligibility and the amount of entitlement available is for the veteran to secure a Certificate of Eligibility from the Veterans Administration. A sample certificate is shown in Figure 7-1.

If the veteran was released from active service after August 1973, he or she should have received a certificate showing the amount of entitlement available. If the veteran has not used any of his or her entitlement and the amount of entitlement shown on the back of the certificate is less than $27,500, the veteran should have the certificate updated. This can be done by the veteran by sending the Certificate of Eligibility along with a completed VA Form 26-1880 (Figure 7-2) to the nearest VA office.

If the veteran was released prior to August 1973, the following procedure should be followed to secure a Certificate of Eligibility. If the veteran has never been issued a certificate in the past, he or she can go to any VA office with a copy of his or her separation papers (Defense Department Form 214, sometimes referred to as a DD-214) or discharge papers and meet with the guaranty section. Usually the certificate will be issued at that time.

If the veteran has had a previous certificate issued and it has been lost, he or she should complete VA Form 26-1880 and bring or mail it with the separation papers to the guaranty section of the nearest VA office. The veteran must fill out sections 7A through 8C of the form.

One other problem may arise: the veteran may have lost his or her separation papers. Without the separation papers, the VA will not issue a certificate. If this is the case, prior

Figure 7-1. VA Certificate of Eligibility (both sides)

DUPLICATE

Veterans Administration
7739765

Certificate of Eligibility

FOR LOAN GUARANTY BENEFITS

NAME OF VETERAN (First, Middle, Last)		SERVICE SERIAL NUMBER/SOCIAL SECURITY NUMBER
Thomas Jackson MORTON		05-412-667
ENTITLEMENT CODE	**BRANCH OF SERVICE**	**DATE OF BIRTH**
Code 3 10/63	Army	10/29/37

IS ELIGIBLE FOR THE BENEFITS OF CHAPTER 37, TITLE 38, U.S. CODE, AND HAS THE AMOUNT OF ENTITLEMENT SHOWN AS AVAILABLE ON THE REVERSE, SUBJECT TO THE STATEMENT BELOW, IF CHECKED.

☐ Valid unless discharged or released subsequent to date of this certificate. A certification of continuous active duty as of date of note required.

ADMINISTRATOR OF VETERANS AFFAIRS

J Bawley
(Signature of Authorized Agent)

July 16, 1981
(Date Issued)

Regional Office
Albuquerque, N.M.
(Issuing Office)

"THIS IS A DUPLICATE CERTIFICATE OF ELIGIBILITY ISSUED UPON THE REQUEST OF THE VETERAN"

DO NOT WRITE ON THIS SIDE—FOR VA USE ONLY

LOAN NUMBER (Include amount if direct loan)	ENTITLEMENT USED 1810	ENTITLEMENT USED OTHER	ENTITLEMENT AVAILABLE	DATE AND INITIALS OF VA AGENT
			27,500	
LH 93897 NM 12/79	$25,000	-----	$2,500	7/16/81 JB

NOTE: The figure shown as available entitlement represents the portion of a loan which may be guaranteed or insured by VA to a lender. For information about maximum loan amounts, see VA Pamphlets 26-4 and 26-71-1, or contact the nearest VA office for further information.

Available entitlement is subject to reduction if VA incurs actual liability or loss on the loan(s), if any, listed below, obtained by the veteran with the assistance of loan benefits derived from military service in WW II or the Korean conflict.

OUTSTANDING LOAN NUMBER(S)	DATE	INITIALS OF VA AGENT

REDUCED

ITEM	DATE	INITIALS OF VA AGENT

VA FORM DEC 1980 **26-8320**

SUPERSEDES VA FORM 26-8320, FEB 1979, WHICH WILL NOT BE USED.

Figure 7-2. VA Form 26-1880

Form Approved
OMB No. 76-RO371

VETERANS ADMINISTRATION **REQUEST FOR DETERMINATION OF ELIGIBILITY AND AVAILABLE LOAN GUARANTY ENTITLEMENT**	TO	**VETERANS ADMINISTRATION** ATTN: Loan Guaranty Division

NOTE: Please read instructions on reverse before completing this form. If additional space is required, attach separate sheet.

1. FIRST-MIDDLE-LAST NAME OF VETERAN	2. ADDRESS OF VETERAN *(No., street or rural route, city or P.O., State and ZIP code)*
3. DATE OF BIRTH	

4. MILITARY SERVICE DATA–I request the Veterans Administration to determine my eligibility and the amount of entitlement based on the following period(s) of active military duty: (Start with latest period of service and list all periods of active duty since September 16, 1940.)

PERIOD OF ACTIVE SERVICE		NAME *(Show your name exactly as it appears on your separation papers (DD Form 214) or statement of service)*	SERVICE NUMBER	BRANCH OF SERVICE
DATE FROM	DATE TO			
4A.				
4B.				
4C.				
4D.				

5A. WERE YOU DISCHARGED, RETIRED, OR SEPARATED FROM SERVICE BECAUSE OF DISABILITY, OR DO YOU NOW HAVE ANY SERVICE-CONNECTED DISABILITIES? ☐ YES ☐ NO *(If "Yes," complete Item 5B)*	5B. VA FILE NUMBER C-	6. IS THERE A CERTIFICATE OF ELIGIBILITY FOR LOAN GUARANTY OR DIRECT LOAN PURPOSES ENCLOSED? ☐ YES ☐ NO *(If "No," complete Items 7A and 7B)*

7A. HAVE YOU PREVIOUSLY APPLIED FOR A CERTIFICATE OF ELIGIBILITY FOR LOAN GUARANTY OR DIRECT LOAN PURPOSES? ☐ YES ☐ NO *(If "Yes," give location of VA office(s) involved)*	7B. HAVE YOU PREVIOUSLY RECEIVED SUCH A CERTIFICATE OF ELIGIBILITY? ☐ YES ☐ NO *(If "Yes," give location of VA office(s) involved)*

8A. HAVE YOU PREVIOUSLY SECURED A VA DIRECT HOME LOAN? ☐ YES ☐ NO *(If "Yes," give location of VA office(s) involved and complete Items 9 through 18)*	8B. HAVE YOU PREVIOUSLY OBTAINED HOME, FARM, CONDOMINIUM OR BUSINESS LOAN(S) WHICH WERE GUARANTEED OR INSURED BY VA? ☐ YES ☐ NO *(If "Yes," give location of VA office(s) involved and complete Items 9 through 18)*	8C. HAVE YOU PREVIOUSLY OBTAINED A VA MOBILE HOME AND/OR LOT LOAN(S)? ☐ YES ☐ NO *(If "Yes," give location of VA office(s) involved)*

NOTE: Complete Items 9 through 18 only if you have previously acquired property with the assistance of a GI Loan.	9. ADDRESS OF PROPERTY PREVIOUSLY PURCHASED WITH GUARANTY ENTITLEMENT	10. DATE YOU PURCHASED PROPERTY 11. DO YOU NOW OWN THE REAL PROPERTY DESCRIBED IN ITEM 9? ☐ YES ☐ NO *(If "Yes," do not complete Items 12 through 18)*

12. CHECK WHETHER YOU ☐ ENTERED INTO AN INSTALLMENT SALE CONTRACT WITH THE PURCHASER, OR ☐ EXECUTED AND DELIVERED A DEED TO THE PURCHASER CONVEYING ALL YOUR RIGHTS, TITLE, AND INTEREST IN THE PROPERTY	13. NAMES OF PERSONS TO WHOM YOU SOLD THE PROPERTY	14. DATE THE DEED, IF ANY, WAS DELIVERED TO PURCHASER 15. IS THERE ANY UNDERSTANDING OR AGREEMENT WRITTEN OR ORAL BETWEEN YOU AND THE PURCHASERS THAT THEY WILL RECONVEY THE PROPERTY TO YOU? ☐ YES ☐ NO

NOTE: It will speed processing if you can furnish the information in Items 16, 17, and 18.	16. NAME AND ADDRESS OF LENDER TO WHOM LOAN PAYMENTS WERE MADE	17. LENDER'S LOAN OR ACCOUNT NO. 18. VA LOAN NO. (LH)

19. Check only if this is a request for a DUPLICATE Certificate of Eligibility ▶	☐ PLEASE ISSUE A DUPLICATE CERTIFICATE OF ELIGIBILITY IN MY NAME. THE CERTIFICATE PREVIOUSLY ISSUED TO ME IS NOT AVAILABLE BECAUSE IT HAS BEEN LOST, DESTROYED OR STOLEN. IF IT IS RECOVERED, IT WILL BE RETURNED TO THE VA FOR CANCELLATION.	
I certify that the statements herein are true to the best of my knowledge and belief.	20. SIGNATURE OF VETERAN	21. DATE

FEDERAL STATUTES PROVIDE SEVERE PENALTIES FOR FRAUD, INTENTIONAL MISREPRESENTATION, CRIMINAL CONNIVANCE, OR CONSPIRACY PURPOSED TO INFLUENCE THE ISSUANCE OF ANY GUARANTY OR INSURANCE BY THE ADMINISTRATOR.

THIS SECTION FOR VA USE ONLY

DATE CERTIFICATE ISSUED AND DISCHARGE OR SEPARATION PAPERS AND VA PAMPHLETS GIVEN TO VETERAN OR MAILED TO ADDRESS SHOWN BELOW	TYPE OF DISCHARGE OR SEPARATION PAPERS RETURNED	SIGNATURE AND TITLE OF APPROPRIATE OFFICIAL *(If applicable)*	STATION NUMBER CERTIFICATE NUMBER

VA FORM 26-1880, JAN 1977 DO NOT DETACH

to October 19, 1981, the veteran had only one option—to fill out a Request Pertaining to Military Records (Figure 7-3) and mail it to the proper agency as listed on the reverse side of the form. After the military records were received, the veteran would fill out VA Form 26-1880, attach a copy of the separation papers, and either mail it or take it to the nearest VA office. The VA cut this lengthy process on October 19, 1981, when it published a final regulation in the Federal Register that again allows the VA to accept a copy of a veteran's discharge papers as long as the copy was certified by a public custodian of records as a true and exact copy.

According to the VA, this regulation was implemented as a means to cut the time required to establish a veteran's eligibility if his or her DD-214 had been lost.

Service personnel presently on active duty for 180 days or more may also apply for a Certificate of Eligibility by submitting a Statement of Service with any supporting material to the nearest VA office. The VA will process the request and either mail the certificate to the service person or he or she may go by the office and pick it up.

The importance of the Certificate of Eligibility cannot be over-emphasized. Without a certificate the VA will not guarantee a veterans loan. In most cases a lender will not even start the processing of a VA loan application without the veteran having the Certificate of Eligibility.

If you have any questions regarding a veteran's eligibility, you should contact any VA-approved lender or the nearest VA office. Offices are listed in Appendix I.

The Loan Guaranty or Veterans Entitlement

Standard home loan The Veterans Administration loan guaranty is the amount of the loan expressed as either a dollar amount or a percent of the loan. This amount is referred to as the *veterans entitlement*. This entitlement or loan guaranty for home loans is now $27,500 or 60 percent of the loan, whichever is less.

As we stated earlier, the amount of entitlement available to the veteran will establish the maximum loan the veteran can get with no money down. The Veterans Administration has set no maximum loan, only the maximum guaranty. The lending industry has set the maximum loan with no money down as roughly four times the veterans entitlement. This means that a veteran with the full entitlement of $27,500 or 60 percent can usually get a maximum loan of four times $27,500, or $110,000 with no money down.

This does not say the veteran will automatically get the $110,000 loan. The veteran must meet the underwriting requirements of the VA. From this formula of four times the veterans entitlement, the lenders are making a 75 percent loan-to-value ratio loan. If the VA is guaranteeing $27,500 of a $110,000 loan, the lender's exposure to loss is $82,500, or 75 percent. If a veteran wishes to secure a VA-guaranteed loan in excess of four times the entitlement, most mortgage lenders require the veteran to put down 25 percent of the excess, thus keeping the loan-to-value ratio at 75 percent. For example, a veteran wishes to purchase a home for $125,000 and has his full entitlement of $27,500. Using the industry standard of four times the entitlement, the maximum loan with no money down would be $110,000. With a loan amount of $110,000 and purchase price of $125,000 we see the veteran must make up the difference with a down payment of $15,000 (although some lenders will only require a down payment of 25 percent of the excess $15,000, or $3750). Even with a down payment, the veteran has a small cash investment in relation to the total value of the house.

As stated earlier, the present entitlement is 60 percent of the loan amount up to a maximum of $27,500, but the entitlements have increased over the years as the value of houses have increased. The increases in the entitlements will be outlined later in this chapter.

In addition to the purchase of new homes, the loan guaranty may be used for the following:

1. To refinance existing mortgages or other liens of record on homes owned and occupied by the eligible veteran
2. To finance the alterations, repairs, or improvements on homes already owned and occupied by an eligible veteran
3. To purchase individual residence units in certain condominium projects

Figure 7-3. Request Pertaining to Military Records

REQUEST PERTAINING TO MILITARY RECORDS

Please read Privacy Act Statement and instructions on reverse. If more space needed, attach additional sheets.

DATE OF REQUEST

SECTION I—INFORMATION NEEDED TO LOCATE RECORDS *(Furnish as much information as possible)*

1. NAME USED DURING SERVICE *(Last, first, middle)* | 2. SOCIAL SECURITY NO. | 3. DATE OF BIRTH | 4. PLACE OF BIRTH

For an effective records search, it is important that ALL periods of service be shown below.

ACTIVE SERVICE—PAST AND PRESENT

5. BRANCH OF SERVICE *(Show also last organization, if known)* | 6. DATES OF ACTIVE DUTY: Date Entered, Date Released | 7. Check One: Officer, Enlisted | 8. SERVICE NUMBER DURING THIS PERIOD

RESERVE SERVICE—PAST AND PRESENT IF NONE, CHECK ☐ NONE

9. BRANCH OF SERVICE | 10. DATES OF MEMBERSHIP: Beginning Date, Ending Date | 11. Check One: Officer, Enlisted | 12. SERVICE NUMBER DURING THIS PERIOD

NATIONAL GUARD MEMBERSHIP IF NONE, CHECK ☐ NONE

13. ARMY | 14. AIR | 15. State | 16. ORGANIZATION | 17. DATES OF MEMBERSHIP: Beginning Date, Ending Date | 18. Check One: Officer, Enlisted | 19. SERVICE NUMBER DURING THIS PERIOD

20. IS SERVICE PERSON DECEASED? ☐ NO ☐ YES *(If "Yes" enter date:)* DATE OF DEATH

21. IS (Was) INDIVIDUAL A MILITARY RETIREE OR FLEET RESERVIST? ☐ NO ☐ YES

SECTION II—REQUEST

1. EXPLAIN WHAT INFORMATION OR DOCUMENTS YOU NEED OR CHECK ITEMS 2 OR 3 BELOW

2. ☐ CHECK THIS BOX IF YOU NEED A STATEMENT OF SERVICE ONLY

3. LOST SEPARATION DOCUMENT REPLACEMENT REQUESTED *(Check One)*

☐ REPORT OF SEPARATION (DD Form 214 or equivalent) ISSUED IN ______ *(Yr.)* *(This contains information normally needed to determine eligibility for benefits. It may be furnished only to the veteran, his surviving next of kin, or to his representative with veteran's signed release authorization—item 6.)*

☐ DISCHARGE CERTIFICATE ISSUED IN ______ *(Yr.)* *(This shows only date and character of discharge and is of little value in determining eligibility for benefits. It may be issued only to veterans discharged honorably or under honorable conditions, or, if deceased, to the surviving spouse.)*

3A. HOW WAS SEPARATION DOCUMENT LOST?

4. PURPOSE FOR WHICH INFORMATION OR DOCUMENTS ARE NEEDED *(Explain)*

5. REQUESTER IS *(Check proper box)*
☐ PERSON IDENTIFIED IN SECTION 1
☐ SURVIVING SPOUSE
☐ NEXT OF KIN *(Show relationship)*
☐ OTHER *(Specify)*

5A. SIGNATURE OF REQUESTER

6. RELEASE AUTHORIZATION, IF REQUIRED *(Read instruction 3 on reverse)*
I hereby authorize release of the requested information/documents to the addressee shown at right.

7. REQUESTER *(Please type or print complete return address. Include ZIP code)*

6A. SIGNATURE OF VETERAN *(If signed by other than veteran, complete 6B)*

6B. RELATIONSHIP TO VETERAN

180–104

STANDARD FORM 180 (REV. 1–76)
Prescribed by GSA
FPMR 101–11.410–7

Graduated-Payment Mortgage Loan On October 17, 1981, the President of the United States signed Public Law 97-66 that permitted the Veterans Administration to guarantee loans with a graduated-payment feature. The VA-GPM is limited to the purchase of single-family dwellings and does include the purchase of new and existing, not previously occupied, homes and condominiums in VA-approved projects. It should be noted that the VA-GPM may not be used for refinancing an existing debt, alterations, repair or improvements. The GPM also may not be used for the purchase of manufactured housing or a lot or both.

Only one method of graduated-payment amortization is now authorized. The plan is based on Plan III Section 245 of the Department of Housing and Urban Development.

A major difference between this loan and the standard VA loan is a required down payment. The amount of this payment will be reviewed later in this section.

The features and requirements of the VA-GPM, as follows, are based on the information contained in DVB Circular 26-81-36 dated November 12, 1981. The veteran's down payment must be paid in cash from the veteran's own resources. The property must have a remaining economic life of at least thirty years to be eligible to be used as security for the VA-GPM. As with the FHA underwriting, the first year's payments will be used as the basis for underwriting. The DVB circular states that in the cases where the veteran's present income is marginal and some doubt exists as to whether his or her income will increase to keep pace with the increased payments, the VA will disapprove the application. The actual underwriting guidelines for the Veterans Administration will be reviewed in Chapter 11. The maximum entitlement under the VA-GPM is the same as under the standard VA home loan: $27,500 or 60 percent of the loan amount, whichever is smaller.

Now that we have reviewed some of the provisions of the VA-GPM, let us see how the VA will compute the maximum loan amount, monthly payment, and the required down payment.

Since the VA-GPM is similar to the FHA 245 GPM, the tables shown in Appendix C will be used to calculate the *maximum loan amount*. Using an interest rate of 14.50 percent, we turn to Appendix C and find the interest rate of 14.50 percent and find the highest outstanding loan-balance factor. This underlined value is 1105.1441. If the value of the property has been established by the CRV as $65,000, we would then divide the CRV value of the property by this factor:

$$\frac{65{,}000}{1105.1441} = 58.815859$$

Next, this is multiplied by $1000 to get the maximum loan amount of $58,815.86. Accordingly, the $58,815.86 will be rounded down to the nearest dollar. Thus, the maximum loan amount would be $58,815.00.

To calculate the required down payment, one would subtract the maximum loan amount from the CRV value of the property. In this example, the down payment would be calculated as:

CRV	$65,000
Less maximum loan amount	58,815
Required down payment	6,185

From this, one can see that, to qualify for this program, a veteran must have a substantial down payment. This program would appeal to the veteran who has saved a rather large amount for a down payment and has not reached his or her potential highest income.

Since this program is similar to the 245, the monthly payments are calculated as they are for the FHA 245. To calculate the monthly payment, we would turn to Appendix D and locate the proper interest rate, in this case 14.50, and locate the proper factor for the first year's payment. We find the factor is 9.5621. Calculate the first year's payment (principal and interest only) by multiplying the original principal balance (in thousands) by this factor:

$$58.815 \times 9.5621 = \$562.39$$

To calculate the monthly payments for the second, third, fourth, fifth, and each year thereafter, multiply the original principal balance by the proper factor given in the table.

There is one additional requirement: the veteran must sign a statement which must accompany the application or the automatic loan report from a supervised lender. This statement is as follows:

I fully understand that because of the graduated-payment loan obligation I am undertaking, my mortgage payment excluding taxes and insurance will start at $ _______ and will increase by 7.5 percent each year for 5 years to a maximum payment of $ _______ and the mortgage balance will increase to no more than $ _______at the end of the _______ year. The maximum total amount by which the deferred interest will increase the principal is $ Monthly installments will be due according to the following schedule:

$ _______ during the 1st year of the loan
$ _______ during the 2nd year of the loan
$ _______ during the 3rd year of the loan
$ _______ during the 4th year of the loan
$ _______ during the 5th year of the loan
$ _______ during the 6th year of the loan and every year therafter.[1]

Buydown mortgages On April 16, 1982, the Administrator of Veterans Affairs authorized the VA to guarantee mortgages that have a temporary mortgage interest rate buydown. It should be noted that this buydown feature may only be used with the standard fixed-rate, fixed-payment mortgage. Thus, the interest rate buydown may not be combined with the graduated payment mortgage. In the past, the VA has reduced the value of properties when the seller or builder/developer would offer an "inducement" to the veteran to purchase a home. According to the VA, the buydown rate mortgage has, due to market conditions and the acceptance of the secondary market, become a useful tool for the financing of homes. The VA, therefore, will not reduce the reasonable value of a property if financed by a buydown mortgage that meets certain requirements. Some of the major requirements are as follows:

1. The assistance or buydown payments will run for a minimum of three years and a maximum of five years
2. The buydown payments must remain constant for twelve months
3. The annual increase in the monthly payments must be equal or approximately equal
4. The buydown funds will be held by a third party escrow agent and must be beyond the reach of the seller or builder/developer and lender, unless the mortgage is purchased by FNMA who will take custody of the funds
5. The buydown funds may not revert to the seller or builder/developer
6. If the property is sold on an assumption, the buydown will continue

Growing equity mortgage (GEM) At approximately the same time as HUD-FHA announced the growing equity mortgage, the Veterans Administration also announced that they would guarantee a GEM. The VA stated that the GEMs are being guaranteed under the authority of DVB Circular 26-82-17, but the VA GEM is not in all respects identical to the GEM of HUD-FHA.

The GEM has previously been defined in Chapters 3 and 6. Please see these chapters if you need to review the definition.

VA has authorized two basic types of GEMs. In one, the payment increases at the rate of 3 percent per year for the first ten years of the mortgage; the second type is a GEM where the annual payment increase is based on a percentage of the Department of Commerce index that measures per capita, after-tax disposable personal income. VA has stated that if the GEM is based on the Department of Commerce index, the loan documents must be written in such a manner to limit the annual payment increase to a maximum of 4 percent. Here, we can see one of the major differences. First, the VA does not offer the 2 percent per year increase GEM and HUD, at the present time, does not offer the "Indexed GEM."

The term for the VA GEM is similar to the HUD-FHA GEM in that the interest rate and the amount of annual increase will determine the term of the mortgage. Underwriting for the VA GEM is similar to the HUD-FHA GEM in that it is generally based on the first-year payments. An interesting statement in the VA literature on the GEM is that it hopes the lenders will "cooperate" with veteran-borrowers who may have difficulty with the increased payments in the later years of the mortgage. In order to reinforce this hope, VA has sited VA Regulation 4314. This regulation provides for the extension or reamortization of a VA-guaranteed loan to prevent or cure a default. Another major difference between the HUD-FHA and the VA GEM is that VA requires all lenders wishing to offer the GEM to submit the proposed GEM to VA for approval. The lenders must submit a detailed description of the GEM, a proposed loan disclosure statement, loan documents, and the acknowledgment statement to be signed by the veteran-borrower. This acknowledgment must explain the effect of the GEM on the borrower's future monthly payments.

There is one additional fact that should be mentioned. VA will not allow the GEM to be used in conjunction with the graduated payment mortgage. If you want more information on the VA GEM or a list of lenders in your area making the VA-guaranteed GEM, you should contact the nearest VA Loan Guarantee Office.

Mobile home loan guaranty The Veterans Administration also has a loan guaranty program for the purchase of mobile homes by an eligible veteran. The present entitlement or guaranty on a loan secured by a mobile home and/or mobile home lot is up to 50 percent of the value or $20,000, whichever is less. In regard to the maximum loan possible with no money down, there is no standard for mobile homes as there is for single-family dwellings. In order to secure the maximum in your area, call several lenders, particularly savings and loans or the larger mobile home dealers in your area.

Partial Use of Entitlement

Home loan Even though a veteran has previously purchased a home and has used his entitlement, he or she may still be able to purchase a second home using the VA while still owning the previous home. Even if the first home was sold on assumption where the veteran is still liable, he or she may possibly be able to secure another home using VA. In order for you as the real estate professional to see if the veteran can purchase the second home, you must establish the following:

1. When the first home was purchased
2. The VA entitlement or guaranty at the time of purchase

The maximum guaranty has been increased steadily since 1944, in the following amounts:

Date	*Maximum Entitlement*
Before 1945	$2,000
December 28, 1945	50% of the loan or $4,000
July 12, 1950	60% of the loan or $7,500
May 7, 1968	60% of the loan or $12,500
December 31, 1974	60% of the loan or $17,500
October 1, 1978	60% of the loan or $25,000
October 1, 1980	60% of the loan or $27,500

After establishing the date of the original loan and the amount of entitlement at that time, we then subtract the veterans entitlement at the time of the loan from the amount of entitlement at the present time. For example, a veteran purchased a home in 1967 for $30,000. First we must establish the veteran's entitlement in 1967. It was 60 percent of the loan amount to a maximum $7500. Now let us figure the amount of entitlement used by the veteran at the time the home was purchased:

$30,000 × 60% = $18,000 or $7500, whichever is lower

So we can see that the veteran had used all of the original entitlement at the time he or she purchased the first home.

Can the veteran now purchase a second home without being released from the liability of the first home? The answer is yes. How much loan can the veteran expect with no money down? First, we will subtract the entitlement at the time of the original loan from the entitlement in effect today:

Entitlement in effect today	$27,500
Entitlement in effect at time of original loan	−$ 7,500
Remaining entitlement	$20,000

The amount of the maximum loan with no money down is calculated by multiplying the amount of the remaining entitlement by a factor of 4:

$20,000 × 4 = $80,000 maximum loan with no money down

Let us take the same veteran as in the previous example. Instead of purchasing an $80,000 home, however, the veteran wishes to purchase an $82,000 home. What would be the veteran's down payment?

We figured that the maximum loan with no money down was $80,000. Using the rules that most lenders follow, we would calculate the down payment as 75 percent of the sales price plus the remaining entitlement or:

Sales price	$82,000
	×75%
	$61,500
Remaining entitlement	$20,000
Maximum loan	$81,500

This, then, requires a down payment of $1500. This is one method used by lenders to figure the down payment required.

Some lenders use the method outlined earlier in the chapter for new loans to calculate the down payment required on a partial use of entitlement. If this were the case, the calculation would be as follows:

Sales price	$82,000
Maximum loan with no money down, $20,000 × 4	$80,000
Difference	$ 2,000

Lenders require the veteran to put down 25 percent of the excess, or

$2000 × 25% = $500.

Mobile homes If the veteran wishes to purchase a second mobile home, the VA rules are different. If a veteran has obtained a prior VA loan for the purchase of a mobile home, any remaining entitlement may not be used to purchase a second mobile home unless the veteran has disposed of the previously purchased mobile home.

Release of Liability and Reinstatement of Entitlement

Even though the veteran can apply for a second VA guaranteed loan using the remainder of the entitlement, there is only one way for a veteran to get the full entitlement after once purchasing a home using the VA guaranty, and that is through the release of liability and the requesting of reinstatement of entitlement.

Release of liability First, let us discuss the process of release of liability. Release of liability can be accomplished in one of three ways.

First, a veteran who is selling his or her home that is financed with a VA guaranty may be released from the liability to the government provided the loan is current, the buyer is obligated contractually to purchase the property and to assume the veteran's liability, and the VA is satisfied that the purchaser is a good credit risk.

Second, the veteran can be released from the liability of a VA-guaranteed loan if the purchaser of the veteran's property is also a veteran who is qualified and will substitute his or her own entitlement to assume the loan.

The third method of release of liability is for the home to be sold, and the purchaser to secure a new loan, and the veteran to pay off the VA-guaranteed loan. Upon payment of the loan, the veteran will secure evidence that the loan is paid off and submit this evidence to the VA with a request for release of liability. Normally the VA will release the veteran from the liability.

Restoration of entitlement Prior to the passage of the Veterans Housing Act of 1974, even though a veteran had been released from the liability of a VA-guaranteed loan, he or she could never again apply for another VA loan. Now, a veteran may qualify for the restoration of full entitlement if the property has been disposed of, the prior loan has been paid in full, and the government has been released from the guaranty. It should be noted that even though the veteran has been released from liability to the government on a loan, the government is still liable to the lender for the guaranty until the loan is paid off.

There is one additional method for the veteran to be restored to full entitlement, as mentioned earlier: if the property is sold by assumption and the person assuming the property is a veteran who is willing and qualified to substitute his or her entitlement, the veteran may be restored to full entitlement.

The restoration of entitlement is not automatic, and the veteran must make application to the nearest VA office and request the restoration. For the exact process for the restoration of entitlement, have the veteran contact a local lender or the nearest VA office.

Maximum Loan and Term

Under the VA home loan guaranty and mobile home loan guaranty, there is no maximum loan. Most lenders use the rough rule of four times the veterans entitlement as the maximum loan with no money down.

One should note that the VA will not issue a guaranty on a loan that exceeds the value established by the Certificate of Reasonable Value (CRV). The CRV is the VA appraisal and will be discussed in depth later in this text.

The maximum term for a VA loan is as follows:

1. Home loan: 30 years and 32 days.
2. Mobile home loans:
    a. New single-wide unit with or without lot—20 years and 32 days
    b. Lot only—20 years and 32 days
    c. New double-wide unit with or without lot—20 years and 32 days
    d. Used mobile home—the term may not exceed those listed above or the remaining physical life of the mobile home as established by the VA, whichever is less

FARMERS HOME ADMINISTRATION (FmHA)

The Farmers Home Administration (FmHA) serves as a rural credit agency for the Department of Agriculture and was established during the administration of Franklin D. Roosevelt to aid the farmers devastated by the depression. The agency has had several names since its beginning in 1935, but it was not until Congress passed the Farmers Home Administration Act of 1946 that the agency received its name and purpose as we know them today. The purpose of FmHA is to serve eligible families and residents of rural communities of the United States with credit and technical help. FmHA has many loan programs available, but this section will deal with only one of the major programs for the financing of rural homes. Some of the other programs available through FmHA are outlined in Appendix J.

The agency, as are many other government agencies, is headquartered in Washington, D.C., with each state having a state office. The state office has the responsibility of coordinating the FmHA's programs in that state.

Section 502—Rural Housing Mortgages

The objective of Section 502 loans is to enable eligible individuals or families who live in rural areas to obtain adequate, modest, decent, safe, and sanitary homes and related facilities.

The 502 loan may be for the following purposes:

1. To purchase, construct, or relocate a dwelling and related facilities if the dwelling is to be used as his or her permanent home
2. To purchase a suitable building site for a home if the applicant does not own a suitable site
3. To purchase essential equipment for use in the home such as a range, refrigerator, or clothes washer or dryer
4. To install heaters or approved solar systems, and storm cellars and similar protective structures

For the 502 program, FmHA has established income limits for a family for each of the states. The income figures used are referred to as adjusted incomes. The adjusted income for this program is calculated as follows: the total gross income of the family or individual, less a 5 percent deduction, less $300 per child member of the household. For example, let us figure the annual adjusted income for a family of four with a total gross income of $19,000 living in District 1 of Oregon. The calculation for two adults and two minor children would be as follows:

Total gross income	$19,000
less 5 percent	−$ 950
less $300 per child	−$ 600
Annual adjusted income	$17,450

For the state of Oregon, the low income maximum is $18,000; thus, this family could possibly qualify for a 502 loan.

The 502 loans are limited to rural areas of the United States. According to FmHA, a rural area is defined as:

1. Open country that is not associated or part of an urban area

2. Any town, city, or village which has the following population:

   a. 10,000 or less if the town, city, or village is rural in character

   b. A population in the excess of 10,000, but less than 20,000, that is not part of a Standard Metropolitan Statistical Area or has a serious lack of mortgage funds for low- and moderate-income households.

For areas in your state that possibly will meet this criteria, you should contact the office of your state director.

In addition to income limitations, there are limitations to the size of the home that can be financed under this program. According to the regulations, new dwellings should be designed to fit the needs of the applicant and may have three bedrooms and one and a half baths. All new dwellings will contain no more than 1200 square feet of living area. Existing dwellings must be structurally sound, functionally adequate, and in good repair or able to be placed in good repair with the funds loaned. The footage requirement for the existing dwelling is flexible in order to adjust to the size of the housing available.

Under this program, the interest rate on these loans is based on the family's ability to repay the loan. For the interest rate range, you will need to contact the nearest FmHA office. Under this program, FmHA will loan up to 100 percent of the FmHA appraised value of the site and the improvements if the new home was built with inspections made by HUD-FHA, FmHA, or the VA. The FmHA will also make loans up to 100 percent of the appraised value of homes and improvements made to a home that is over one year old. The maximum term of the loan under this program is forty years.

STATE HOUSING AGENCIES

The first state housing agency was established in the state of New York when the state legislature authorized the creation of the New York Housing Finance Agency in 1960. The authority sold its first tax-exempt bonds in 1961.

The other forty-nine states have formed state housing agencies for the purpose of generating funds through the sale of tax-exempt bonds secured by first lien mortgages to provide mortgages to low- and moderate-income families.

The goal of a state's mortgage finance authority may be one or all of the following:

1. To increase the supply of safe and sanitary housing for low- to moderate-income families

2. To provide short- and long-term financing for single-family and multifamily housing

3. To support and encourage private industry to provide housing units for eligible families

The type of housing financed by the agencies is single-family, but many of the agencies have also issued bonds backed by mortgages on multifamily dwellings and manufactured housing.

The underwriting requirements for mortgages funded through a state finance agency are not standard across the nation and are set by each housing agency. Many of the agencies will set an income limit as well as a maximum mortgage amount and required down payment. It should be noted that the maximum income can vary according to the size of the family that will occupy the dwelling. To learn about the particular programs available through the state housing agency in your state, you will need to contact the agency and secure the requirements for its programs or contact the Council of State Housing Agencies, 1133 15th Street Northwest, Suite 514, Washington, D.C., 20005.

Most of the agencies do not originate the mortgages under this program, but they do issue commitments to lenders to purchase mortgages that meet all of the requirements set forth by the agency in the commitments it issues. This program is known as a *forward commitment program*. In this type of program, the agency issues a commitment to the participating lender to purchase mortgages in a specific amount that meets the guidelines of the agency.

Another type of mortgage program that may be used is the loan-to-lenders program. Under this program, the housing agency would loan funds to the lenders who wish to participate in the program, with the stipulation that the funds would be used to make mortgages on housing that meet the guidelines set by the housing agency.

Federal Regulation

Prior to the passage of the Omnibus Reconciliation Act of 1980, there had been no federal regulations governing either a state housing agency or any governmental body in the issuances of tax-exempt bonds secured by mortgages on single-family dwellings.

When this legislation became law on December 31, 1980, it placed several limitations on the issuance of such bonds. One of the limitations was that the maximum amount of bonds that could be issued per year in a state was set at either $200 million or 9 percent (whichever is higher) of the average of all mortgages originated in the state for the past three years.

Some of the other major restrictions are listed below:

1. *Principal residency requirement.* The law requires that any residence purchased with funds from a sale of bonds be used as the primary residence of the borrower.

2. *Three-year requirement.* The act further requires that the borrower must not have been a homeowner within the last three years.

3. *Purchase price limitations.* The law has set the maximum purchase price for homes as 90 percent of the average purchase price in the preceding year in the Standard Metropolitan Statistical Area (SMSA) in which the mortgage is placed.

4. *New mortgage requirement.* The law states that a mortgage funded by tax-exempt bond funds may only be used for a new mortgage and may not be used to acquire or replace an existing mortgage unless it is a construction loan, bridge loan, or similar temporary initial financing.

5. *Assumption of mortgages.* Individuals assuming a mortgage originally financed with tax-exempt bonds must meet the residency requirement, the three-year requirement, and the purchase price requirement.

6. *Terminations of tax-free status of bonds.* In one of its more important provisions, the law allows for the issuance of single-family, owner-occupied bonds as tax-free bonds for a period of two years, and any interest paid on such bonds after that date will be taxable. This date is generally considered to be January 31, 1983.

One major change that has been brought about by the passage of this legislation is that the VA and FHA have had to modify their note and mortgage/deed of trust documents to comply with restriction 5 listed above. As our review of the standard HUD and VA note and mortgage/deed of trust revealed, neither of these sets of documents contained any assumption or due-on-sale clause. Restriction 5 states that any person or persons assuming a mortgage financed through the sale of tax-exempt bonds must meet certain requirements. HUD and VA have issued instructions allowing for the inclusion of a

Figure 7-4. Veteran's Consent Form—Due-on-Sale

Your home purchase is being financed with a mortgage made available with the assistance of ________ Housing Authority. This mortgage is made at an interest rate below what is usually being charged. Because of this you cannot sell your home to a person ineligible for assistance from the Housing Authority, unless you pay your loan in full. If you sell your home to a party ineligible for the Housing Authority's assistance and allow the buyer to make your payments for you (assume your loan), the Housing Authority may refuse to allow the sale and demand immediate full repayment of the loan. This could result in foreclosure or repossession of the property. If the lender takes your home through a foreclosure of the mortgage because of this, VA will not be able to help you. In addition, VA may have to pay a claim to the Housing Authority for any loss incurred on your loan. You may then be obligated to the VA for any claim paid by the VA to the Housing Authority.

You may avoid such actions by paying your loan in full when you sell your home or by making certain that any person who purchases your home and takes over your payments meets the necessary qualifications established by the Housing Authority. Those requirements are: (Complete as appropriate for the particular housing assistance program).

________ Date

________ Veteran's signature

Source: Veterans Administration, Department of Veterans Benefits, DVB Circular 26-81-34, Due-on-Sale Provisions—October 23, 1981, pp. 1-2.

Figure 7-5. HUD Mortgage Addendum for Due-on-Sale

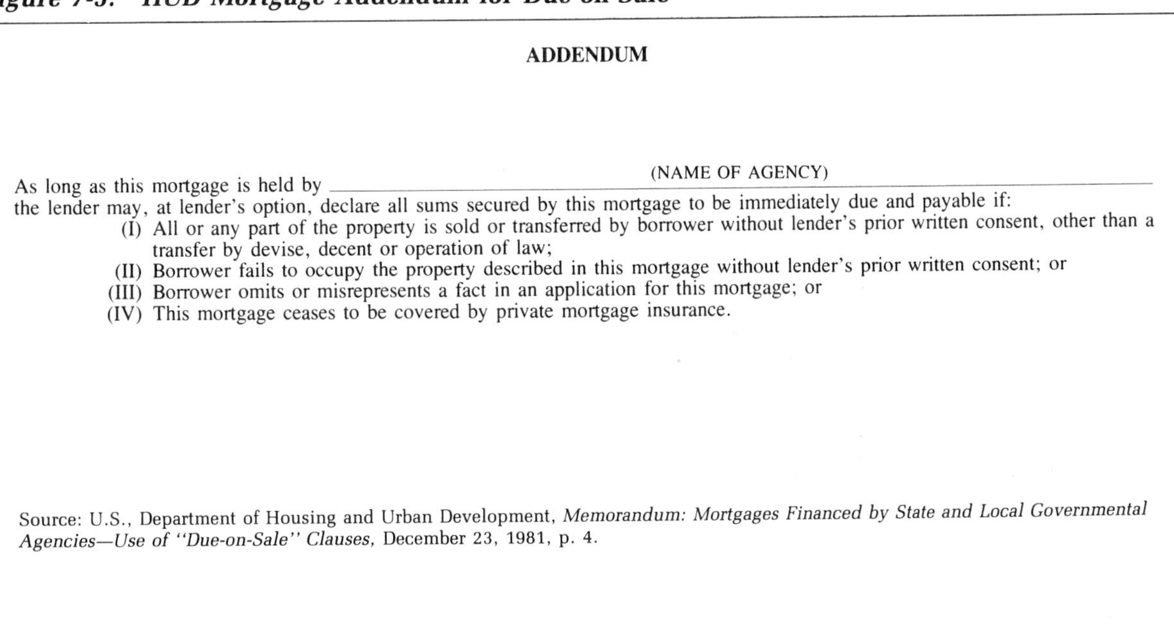

ADDENDUM

As long as this mortgage is held by ________ (NAME OF AGENCY)
the lender may, at lender's option, declare all sums secured by this mortgage to be immediately due and payable if:

(I) All or any part of the property is sold or transferred by borrower without lender's prior written consent, other than a transfer by devise, decent or operation of law;
(II) Borrower fails to occupy the property described in this mortgage without lender's prior written consent; or
(III) Borrower omits or misrepresents a fact in an application for this mortgage; or
(IV) This mortgage ceases to be covered by private mortgage insurance.

Source: U.S., Department of Housing and Urban Development, *Memorandum: Mortgages Financed by State and Local Governmental Agencies—Use of "Due-on-Sale" Clauses,* December 23, 1981, p. 4.

due-on-sale clause in mortgages financed by tax-exempt bonds. On October 23, 1981, the Veterans Administration issued its regulation allowing for the inclusion of due-on-sale in mortgages guaranteed by the VA and funded through the sale of tax-exempt bonds. According to the regulation, the veteran must be fully informed by the lender or the state housing agency that the veteran's ability to sell his or her property by assumption is restricted. The veteran must sign a statement indicating that he or she is aware of the restriction. The Veterans Administration has suggested the format in Figure 7-4.

On April 29, 1981, the Department of Housing and Urban Development issued to all of its offices instructions that were later updated on December 23, 1981. These instructions permit the inclusion of a due-on-sale clause, allowing the acceleration of a mortgage financed through the sale of tax-exempt bonds (1) if the property is sold to an unqualified buyer, (2) if the property is not occupied by the borrowers because it is being rented or has been purchased by others, or (3) because of fraud by the borrowers or misrepresentation by the borrowers. The instructions state that the borrower must be given thirty days to correct that situation before the due-on-sale is implemented. The mortgage must contain an addendum for due-on-sale, and reference to this addendum must be made in the mortgage. The suggested format for the addendum is shown in Figure 7-5.

FEDERAL LAND BANKS

The Federal Land Banks were established by the passage of the Federal Farm Loan Act of 1916. The present activities of the banks and associations are authorized by the Farm Credit Act of 1971. This act supersedes all previous laws governing the operation of the banks. There is not one central bank; the United States is divided into twelve districts, each with its own bank.

The primary purpose of the Federal Land Banks is to provide a dependable and permanent source of loanable funds—at reasonable rates—to the agricultural community. The banks were originally funded by the federal government, but the original legislation contained a provision allowing the banks to be owned by its borrowers through the Federal Land Bank Association. All of the initial money advanced to the banks was repaid by 1947. Today the banks are owned completely by the borrowers or customers of the banks.

The banks make primarily agricultural loans to farmers, ranchers, and legal entities as defined by the banks. The banks will make loans for the purpose of purchasing, remodeling, building, refinancing, and improving a home. The amount of the loan or mortgage will be based on the agricultural holdings or assets of the borrower.

The term of the mortgages will range from five to forty years, with payments made annually, semiannually, quarterly, or monthly. Any loan from a bank may be repaid at any time without penalty. The interest rate on a loan from a Federal Land Bank will be a variable rate based on the bank's cost of funds. As was noted earlier, the banks receive no funds from the federal government, thus they must secure their funds from the open market. The variable-rate feature of the bank's loans allows them to react quickly to the changes in the nation's money markets. According to the banks, it allows them to provide the funds at the lowest possible rate. In regard to the loan-to-value ratio of Federal Land Bank loans, they are authorized to make loans that do not exceed 85 percent of the appraised value of the real estate used as security. For more information, contact the nearest Federal Land Bank and they will supply you with data on the present loan programs available and current interest rates.

REVIEW QUESTIONS

1. List and explain three advantages of a VA guaranteed loan.
2. Which veterans are eligible for VA loan benefits?
3. Explain how a veteran can secure a Certificate of Eligibility.
4. Define the term *entitlement* and the amount of a veteran's entitlement as it refers to VA home loans and VA mobile home loans.
5. Explain how a veteran can secure a release of liability and the reinstatement of his or her entitlement.
6. Name and explain the two basic home loan programs of the Farmers Home Administration.
7. State the purposes of a housing agency.
8. Explain how federal legislation has affected state housing agencies.
9. Explain how a veteran may be able to secure more than one VA-guaranteed home loan.

NOTES

[1]U.S., Veterans Administration, *Graduated Payment Mortgage Loans,* DVB Circular 26-81-36, November 12, 1981, p. 20420.

CHAPTER 8 Conventional Loans and Private Mortgage Insurance

LEARNING OBJECTIVES

In this chapter we will discuss the conventional loan and lenders, as well as private mortgage insurance. Upon completion of this chapter you should be able to do the following:

- ★ **Define *conventional mortgage*.**
- ★ **Choose the best type of mortgage, either government-backed or conventional.**
- ★ **Explain private mortgage insurance and why it is important to the conventional lender.**

CONVENTIONAL LOANS

A *conventional loan* may be defined as a loan that is neither insured nor guaranteed by any agency of a state or the federal government.

Until the advent of FHA, the Farmers Home Administration, the Veterans Administration, and state housing agencies, conventional loans were the only type of real estate loans made. These loans were made by commercial banks, savings and loan associations, and in some sections of the nation by mutual savings banks. Prior to the advent of the mortgage banker, most conventional loans were made by savings and loan associations. Life insurance companies were also a source of real estate loans. As was stated earlier in the text, most of these loans had low loan-to-value ratios, in some cases as low as 50 percent of the value. The term was short, usually three to five years, with no escrow for taxes, insurance, or other fees or assessments that could affect the title to the property. With the advent of the FHA-insured loan with its long amortization, level monthly payments, and other reforms, the conventional lenders did adopt many of the reforms of FHA. One of the major reforms that was not adopted by the conventional lenders was the higher loan-to-value ratio. The reason for this was that many of the institutional lenders by law could not make a loan that had a loan-to-value ratio above 75 percent. This was true until the advent of private mortgage insurance. Private mortgage insurance (PMI) allows the lender to make loans up to a loan-to-value ratio of 95 percent, which will be discussed in depth later in this chapter.

COMPARISON OF CONVENTIONAL vs. GOVERNMENTAL LOANS

In the previous two chapters the advantages and disadvantages were listed for FHA and VA loans. This will not be done for the conventional loan. Rather, the conventional loan will be compared to the VA- and FHA-insured mortgages. As a real estate professional, you must be able to help your client select the best financing possible. To do this, you must be able to compare the financing available and advise your client. The following comparisons will be made: loan limits, processing time, interest rates, down payments or loan-to-value ratios, assumption procedures, prepayment penalties, loan fees, and underwriting guidelines.

Loan Limits

Unlike governmental loans the conventional loans or lenders have no set loan limits. This limit is usually set by the investor. For example, if the company originating the loan is a lender using the funds of an investor, the investor will set the loan limit. If the investor that has issued the commitment is the Federal National Mortgage Association (FNMA) or the Federal Home Loan Mortgage Corporation (FHLMC), the limit on the mortgage is set by the U.S. Congress, (which will be outlined in Chapters 9 and 10).

If the investor is an insurance company, the loan limits will be different from that of FNMA and FHLMC. The insurance companies usually only make loans with a low loan-to-value ratio in amounts in the excess of the FNMA and FHLMC limits. For example, the present limit on FNMA/FHLMC loans is $107,000. Normally the insurance companies will make loans at approximately $107,000+. For a conventional loan, the best method to determine the current loan limits is to contact lenders in your area.

Processing Time

The processing time on a conventional loan is usually less than for a government-insured or government-guaranteed loan. Usually, the originator of the loan has been given the underwriting guidelines of the investor and is allowed to approve any loan that, in the opinion of the originator, meets the guidelines. This is even true for conventional loans that are to be sold to FNMA. This allows a lender to give in-house approval on FNMA loans.

The actual processing time for a conventional loan can take as little as a week if all of the information to be verified is from local sources. This faster processing time is one of the major factors that will make the conventional mortgage more attractive to your clients.

Interest Rates

The interest rate on conventional loans is set in the marketplace and is affected greatly by supply and demand, unlike the interest rate on either FHA or VA loans. The FHA and VA rates are set by the government and reflect only slightly the interest rates in the marketplace. Interest rates on conventional loans can be different for the amount of the loan and the loan-to-value ratio. In some cases, the lower the ratio—that is, 80 percent or less—the lower the interest rate.

One of the major factors that will affect the interest rate on a conventional loan is the source of the funds. For example, a Chicago mortgage company is using a commitment from a savings and loan located in California that has a cost of funds of 9.5 percent. This savings and loan will not allow a mortgage lender to make a loan at the same rate as the savings and loan is paying to its depositors. The S and L will usually like to receive a yield at least 2 to 3 percent above the cost of funds or a rate of 11.5 to 12.5 percent. Usually the conventional loans made by insurance companies or by mortgage bankers using a commitment from an insurance company will have a lower interest rate because the cost of funds to the insurance company is less.

When comparing the interest rates on conventional mortgages to government-insured or guaranteed mortgages, one must also compare one additional item: the amount of discount points being charged. As stated earlier, one point is equal to 1 percent of the loan amount. Each point increases the yield (effective interest rate) to the investor one-eighth of 1 percent. For example, if a government-insured loan has a face interest rate of 11.5 percent, but the investor wishes a return of 12.5 percent, the lender would have to charge eight points (1/8 × 8 = 8/8 or 1%).

Usually the interest rate on the government-insured loan is lower, but the discount or points is higher. For example, when the rate on FHA/VA loans was 11.5 percent and the rate on the conventional loans was between 12 and 12.75 percent, the points charged by some lenders on FHA/VA loans ranged between four and six points, as compared to one to three points on the conventional loan. One thing that should be noted is that unlike the FHA/VA loan, the buyer can pay any or all of the points being charged. So if you are the agent for the seller, possibly the conventional loan would be an advantage.

Down Payments

When comparing the down payment required on the conventional loan to that required on either the FHA or VA loan, the conventional down payment is more. For example, the minimum down payment required by most of the conventional lenders is 5 percent, as compared to the FHA, which only requires a down payment of 3 percent on the first $25,000 and 5 percent on the remaining amount up to the maximum loan amount. For VA, most lenders require no money down on loans up to four times the veteran's entitlement.

Let us work through an example of the down payment required on a property with a sales price of $70,000. For this example, let us assume that the closing costs for the borrower are zero and the maximum FHA loan amount for the area is $67,500.

First, the conventional loan, using a lender that will make a 95 percent loan, requires a down payment of 5 percent:

Sales price	$70,000
Down payment 5% of sales price	−$ 3,500
Loan amount	$66,500

Second, let us calculate the FHA down payment with the acquisition cost of $70,000:

Acquisition cost (sales price + closing costs)	$70,000
Down payment 3% of first $25,000 = $750 5% of the remaining, or 5% of ($70,000 − $25,000) =5% of $45,000 =$2,250	
Total down payment	$ 3,000
Loan amount	$67,000

This would be possible since the present maximum FHA loan on a single-family dwelling is $67,500.

Finally, what is the down payment required for the VA-guaranteed loan? We will assume the veteran has all of his or her entitlement of $27,500 available. Using the factor of four times the entitlement for the maximum loan with no money down, let us calculate as follows:

Entitlement	$27,500
Loan factor	× 4
Maximum loan with no money down	$110,000

Thus for the home in question, the veteran would have no down payment requirement.

From this comparison of the minimum conventional down payment to FHA and VA, one can see that the FHA and VA down payments are less. One must remember that the loan limit on the FHA is lower than most of the conventional loans including those loans purchased by FNMA and FHLMC. The VA loan program is not open to all buyers.

Assumptions

As we noted earlier, the FHA and VA loans are assumable and the procedure is rather easy. The conventional loan is not always assumable. As a real estate professional, when dealing with a conventional lender, you should ask if the loan can be assumed and what the procedure will be. There is no standard procedure, but since the advent of FNMA and FHLMC and the standard note and deed of trust, those lenders that use the forms and have adopted their procedures will allow the mortgage to be assumed and the original borrower to be released from liability. The conventional lender will usually charge an assumption fee that will range from a few dollars to a certain percentage of the remaining loan balance. In some cases, the lender may try to increase the yield on the mortgage at the time of assumption under the due-on-sale clause of the mortgage.

It should be noted that FNMA began enforcing the due-on-sale provision on all conventional loans originated after November 10, 1980, that are owned by FNMA. This includes when the ownership of property is transferred using a wraparound or second mortgage by an institutional lender. This provision requires on mortgages that are assumed that the assumptor make application and his or her credit will be checked, and that the interest rate will be adjusted to the market interest rate. FNMA defines this market interest rate to be a rate based on the FHLBB's rate entitled Contract Interest Rates on Loans Closed for Purchase of Previously Occupied Homes. FNMA publishes this rate monthly. The due-on-sale provision will be enforced unless there is a state law or a court decision that makes this practice illegal. Many states have passed laws or their courts have made rulings that have halted or amended this practice.

In these states where FNMA cannot fully enforce the due-on-sale, or acceleration-upon-sale provision of the mortgage or deed of trust, FNMA requires that the note be modified and a call option rider executed by the borrower be attached to either the mortgage or deed of trust.

This call option rider in effect makes the note have a term of seven years, and the mortgage or deed of trust a term of thirty years. The required call option rider is shown in Figure 8-1. One can see that the provision of the call option rider allows the lender, at the lender's option, to declare the total outstanding sum of the mortgage due and payable in full. If the borrower is unable to pay the amount due, the lender can then notify the trustee to start foreclosure proceedings, or the lender on his own may institute the remedies permitted in the state where the property is located. It should be noted that in addition to the mortgage or deed of trust, the note must also be altered to include additional wording similar to that added to either the mortgage or deed of trust. This additional information is shown in Figures 8-2 and 8-3.

Those states in which FNMA is presently requiring the call option rider are divided into two groups. In the first group of eleven states FNMA requires the rider on mortgages dated November 10, 1980, or after. These states are Arizona, California, Colorado, Georgia, Illinois, Iowa, Michigan, Minnesota, New Mexico, South Carolina, and Washington. For the second group of six states, FNMA requires the call option rider to be included in all mortgages secured by real property dated on or after January 19, 1981. These states are Arkansas, Florida, Mississippi, New York, Ohio, and Oklahoma.

FNMA has further amended its assumption procedure by requiring both parties to the assumption to execute the FNMA form entitled, "Modification and Assumption Agreement With Release." A copy of the form that must be used in Texas is shown in Figures 8-4, 8-5, and 8-6. This change in procedure became effective in March 1981.

Once again, when dealing with a conventional lender, be sure to have a thorough knowledge of the lender's assumption policies and procedures so that you may be able to advise your client properly.

Prepayment Penalties

In comparing the conventional to the FHA or VA mortgages, neither the FHA nor VA mortgage has any mention of a prepayment penalty. The conventional mortgage, however, may have such a penalty. If the conventional lender is using the FNMA/FHLMC standard note and mortgage/deed of trust, there is a mention of a prepayment penalty, but many of the lenders using these forms do not implement the penalty. If the mortgage is sold to FNMA or FHLMC, even though the note makes reference to a penalty, after September 1979 the penalties will not be charged. In addition to not charging the penalty, all lenders selling mortgages to FNMA and FHLMC after January 1, 1980, will be required to use the revised note and mortgage/deed of trust that deletes the penalty completely.

Usually, if the loan is originated by or sold to an insurance company, there will be a prepayment penalty. Normally these penalties are graduated. That means the penalty is more in the first years of the mortgage and is reduced over the life of the mortgage. For

Figure 8-1. FNMA Call Option Rider

CALL OPTION RIDER

THIS RIDER is made this . . . . .day of . . . . ,
19 . . . . . ., and is incorporated into and shall be deemed to amend and supplement the Mortgage, Deed of Trust, or Deed to Secure Debt (the "Security Instrument") of the same date given by the undersigned (the "Borrower") to secure Borrower's Note to . . . . (the "Lender") of the same date (the "Note") and covering the property described in the Security Instrument and located at:

. . . .
(Property Address)

ADDITIONAL COVENANT. In addition to the covenants and agreements made in the Security Instrument, Borrower and Lender further covenant and agree as follows:

A. Lender's Call Option. During the thirty day period beginning on a date seven years from the date of the Note, Lender shall have the option to require payment in full of the sums secured by the Security Instrument. If Lender elects to exercise this call option, notice of such election shall be given to Borrower who shall pay all such sums to Lender on the payment date specified in the notice, which date shall be at least 60 days from the date of mailing. If Borrower fails to pay such sums when due, Lender may invoke any remedies permitted by the Security Instrument.

IN WITNESS WHEREOF, Borrower has executed this Call Option Rider.

______________________________ – Borrower

______________________________ – Borrower

9/80

Figure 8-2. FNMA Note (front)

NOTE

US $............................ ...., Arizona
City
............................, 19....

FOR VALUE RECEIVED, the undersigned ("Borrower") promise(s) to pay.......................... ...., or order, the principal sum of .... Dollars, with interest on the unpaid principal balance from the date of this Note, until paid, at the rate of..................... .... percent per annum. Principal and interest shall be payable at...................... ...., or such other place as the Note holder may designate, in consecutive monthly installments of... .... Dollars (US $...........................), on the.................. .... day of each month beginning..........................., 19..... Such monthly installments shall continue until the entire indebtedness evidenced by this Note is fully paid, except that any remaining indebtedness, if not sooner paid, shall be due and payable on...

If any monthly installment under this Note is not paid when due and remains unpaid after a date specified by a notice to Borrower, the entire principal amount outstanding and accrued interest thereon shall at once become due and payable at the option of the Note holder. The date specified shall not be less than thirty days from the date such notice is mailed. The Note holder may exercise this option to accelerate during any default by Borrower regardless of any prior forbearance. If suit is brought to collect this Note, the Note holder shall be entitled to collect all reasonable costs and expenses of suit, including, but not limited to, reasonable attorney's fees.

Borrower shall pay to the Note holder a late charge of.......................... percent of any monthly installment not received by the Note holder within........................... days after the installment is due.

Borrower may prepay the principal amount outstanding in whole or in part. The Note holder may require that any partial prepayments (i) be made on the date monthly installments are due and (ii) be in the amount of that part of one or more monthly installments which would be applicable to principal. Any partial prepayment shall be applied against the principal amount outstanding and shall not postpone the due date of any subsequent monthly installments or change the amount of such installments, unless the Note holder shall otherwise agree in writing.

Presentment, notice of dishonor, and protest are hereby waived by all makers, sureties, guarantors and endorsers hereof. This Note shall be the joint and several obligation of all makers, sureties, guarantors and endorsers, and shall be binding upon them and their successors and assigns.

Any notice to Borrower provided for in this Note shall be given by mailing such notice by certified mail addressed to Borrower at the Property Address stated below, or to such other address as Borrower may designate by notice to the Note holder. Any notice to the Note holder shall be given by mailing such notice by certified mail, return receipt requested, to the Note holder at the address stated in the first paragraph of this Note, or at such other address as may have been designated by notice to Borrower.

The indebtedness evidenced by this Note is secured by a Deed of Trust, dated.......................... ...., and reference is made to the Deed of Trust for rights as to acceleration of the indebtedness evidenced by this Note.

See reverse side of this Note for provision concerning option to call.

....

....

....
Property Address

(Execute Original Only)

–1 to 4 Family—8/79—**FNMA/FHLMC UNIFORM INSTRUMENT**

Figure 8-3. FNMA Note (back)

During the thirty day period beginning on a date seven years from the date of this Note, the Note holder shall have the option to require payment in full of the entire principal amount outstanding and any accrued interest thereon. If the Note holder elects to exercise this call option, notice of such election shall be given to Borrower who shall pay such principal and interest in full to the Note holder on the payment date specified in the notice, which date shall be at least 60 days from the date of mailing.

Date: ____________________ ____________________

____

____

Figure 8-4. ***FNMA Modification and Assumption Agreement with Release, page 1***

MODIFICATION AND ASSUMPTION AGREEMENT
WITH RELEASE

THIS AGREEMENT is made this ______ day of ______________, 19____, between

____
(here "BORROWER"),

____
(here "ASSUMER"), and

FEDERAL NATIONAL MORTGAGE ASSOCIATION, a corporation organized and existing under the laws of the United States, whose address is 2001 Bryan Tower, Suite 1200, Dallas, Texas, (here "LENDER"),

for a modification, assumption, and release with respect to that promissory note dated ____________________, in the original amount of $______________, bearing interest at the rate of _________ percent per annum, secured by a mortgage or deed of trust (here "security instrument"), dated ____________, made by BORROWER to

____
recorded in ______________________________ secured by the property described in Exhibit "A" hereto, located in the County of ____________, State of __________, which has the address of ____
(here "PROPERTY ADDRESS"); (street) (city) (state and zip code)

WHEREAS, LENDER acquired the note and security instrument described above by an assignment dated ____________________ and recorded in ____________________ ____________________;

WHEREAS, BORROWER is indebted to LENDER under the note and security instrument described above, payable in ________ monthly installments of $______________ due on the _________ day of each month; and

WHEREAS, BORROWER desires to sell and ASSUMER desires to purchase such property subject to such indebtedness and to assume the unpaid principal owing to LENDER, but such security instrument requires the written consent of LENDER prior to any sale or transfer of all or any part of such property, and a sale or transfer without consent of LENDER would constitute a default under such security instrument, and BORROWER and ASSUMER wish to obtain the consent of LENDER to such sale or transfer.

NOW, THEREFORE, for and in consideration of the granting of such consent by LENDER and of the benefits flowing to each of the parties hereto, BORROWER and ASSUMER do agree as follows:

1. As of the date of the transfer of the property on ____________________, or as a result of such transfer, payments of principal and interest on the indebtedness are current, and the unpaid principal balance of the indebtedness to LENDER is $__________________ as of such date, subject to payment of all checks in process of collection.

2. The terms of the note evidencing such indebtedness are hereby modified by increasing the rate of interest payable thereunder to _________ percent per annum, effective on ____________________. Such indebtedness shall, beginning on __________________ and continuing thereafter, be payable in monthly installments of $________________ per month together with any amounts required for escrow deposits. The dates on which payments are due shall remain unchanged.

FNMA Conv. M&A
TEXAS - 12/1/80 (R)

1 of 3

Figure 8-5. FNMA Modification and Assumption Agreement with Release, page 2

3. ASSUMER hereby assumes such indebtedness as modified in paragraph 2 above, and shall hereafter make all monthly payments as called for therein. If this Agreement is entered into after the date of the transfer of the property, ASSUMER agrees and tenders herewith an amount necessary to make the loan current as modified in paragraph 2. Further, ASSUMER agrees to abide by all provisions of such note and of the security instrument securing such indebtedness as described above, excepting as specifically modified by this agreement. In the event of any default by ASSUMER under the terms of such note or such security instrument, LENDER may exercise all remedies available to it under the terms of such note or security instrument, including an action at law against ASSUMER to collect any monies due under the note, and exercise of the remedies contained in NON-UNIFORM COVENANT 18 of the security instrument. ASSUMER hereby acknowledges that LENDER has made all disclosures to ASSUMER as may be required under the Consumer Credit Protection Act of 1968 and Regulation Z (Title 12, part 226, Code of Federal Regulations).

4. BORROWER hereby relinquishes and transfers to ASSUMER all BORROWER'S interest in any monies which may be held by LENDER as escrow deposits for the purposes of application to taxes, assessments, fire or other insurance premiums, or any other purposes for which deposits are being required by LENDER. ASSUMER assumes the liability for payment of any unpaid taxes, assessments, fire, or other insurance and agrees to continue making monthly deposits for such purposes if required by LENDER.

5. LENDER hereby consents to the sale and transfer of such property to ASSUMER by BORROWER, hereby accepts ASSUMER as its obligor, and shall amend its records to indicate the transfer of such indebtedness from the name of BORROWER to the name of ASSUMER, and LENDER shall henceforth in all respects treat ASSUMER as its borrower. LENDER hereby releases BORROWER from all obligations or liabilities under such note or security instrument. All other terms of this agreement to the contrary notwithstanding, the remedies contained in NON-UNIFORM COVENANT 18 of the security instrument shall remain in full force and effect in accordance with their terms.

6. ASSUMER agrees that the granting of consent by LENDER to this transfer shall not constitute a waiver of the restrictions on transfer contained in such security instrument, and such restrictions shall continue in full force and any future transfer or sale by ASSUMER without the written consent of LENDER shall constitute a default of the terms of such security instrument, and LENDER, at its option, may exercise all remedies available to it under the terms of such note and security instrument.

7. Wherever the words "BORROWER" or "ASSUMER" are used in this agreement, they shall represent the plural as well as the singular, the feminine and neuter genders as well as the masculine, and shall include heirs, successors or assigns.

IN WITNESS WHEREOF, the parties have executed this agreement on the day and year first above written.

BORROWER(S):	ASSUMER(S):
______________________	______________________
______________________	______________________

FEDERAL NATIONAL MORTGAGE ASSOCIATION

Attest: ______________________	By ______________________
Assistant Secretary	Assistant Vice President

FNMA Conv. M&A
TEXAS - 12/1/80

2 of 3

Figure 8-6. FNMA Modification and Assumption Agreement with Release, page 3

ACKNOWLEDGMENT - BORROWER(S)

STATE OF §
COUNTY OF §

BEFORE ME, the undersigned authority, on this day personally appeared __________ ____________________________ known to me to be the person(s) whose name(s) _______ subscribed to the foregoing instrument, and acknowledged to me that ___he___ executed the same for the purposes and consideration therein expressed.

GIVEN UNDER MY HAND AND SEAL OF OFFICE, this _____ day of __________, 19_____.

Notary Public

My commission expires:____________

ACKNOWLEDGMENT - ASSUMER(S)

STATE OF §
COUNTY OF §

BEFORE ME, the undersigned authority, on this day personally appeared __________ ____________________________ known to me to be the person(s) whose name(s) _______ subscribed to the foregoing instrument, and acknowledged to me that ___he___ executed the same for the purposes and consideration therein expressed.

GIVEN UNDER MY HAND AND SEAL OF OFFICE, this _____ day of __________, 19_____.

Notary Public

My commission expires:____________

ACKNOWLEDGMENT - FNMA

STATE OF TEXAS §
COUNTY OF DALLAS §

BEFORE ME, the undersigned authority, on this day personally appeared __________ ____________________________ known to me to be the person whose name is subscribed to the foregoing instrument as Assistant Vice President of the Federal National Mortgage Association, a party thereto, and acknowledged to me that he executed the same as Assistant Vice President for the said Federal National Mortgage Association, and as the act and deed of Federal National Mortgage Association, a corporation, for the purposes and consideration therein expressed and in the capacity therein stated.

GIVEN UNDER MY HAND AND SEAL OF OFFICE, this _____ day of __________, 19_____.

Notary Public in and for Dallas County, Texas

My commission expires:____________

FNMA Conv. M&A
TEXAS - 12/1/80

3 of 3

example, the penalty may be 3 percent of the loan balance if the loan is paid off in the first five years; then the penalty may be reduced to 2 percent of the balance if the mortgage is paid off in the next five years; and finally, it may be reduced to 1 percent of the loan balance if the loan is paid off prior to the thirtieth year or the term of the loan. This is only an example and is not the only form of penalty. So, as a real estate professional, when you are suggesting a conventional lender to your client, you should know whether the lender has a penalty and, if so, what the penalty is.

Loan Fee or Origination Fee

First, we should define the term *loan fee* or *origination fee*. This is the fee charged by the lender for taking the loan application, processing the application, and all of the other operations required to close the loan. This fee should not be confused with the other fees that are connected with the processing of the loan application, such as appraisal fee, credit report fee, attorney fees, and so forth. Only the origination fee is paid directly to the lender for services. The FHA and the VA limit this fee to 1 percent of the loan amount, but there is no such limitation on most conventional loans. The lenders can charge any amount for this fee. The charge is usually expressed as a percentage of the loan amount. On the normal single-family dwelling, the loan fee will be 1 percent, but the fee may be increased for two- to four-family dwellings. This is done by some conventional lenders if they feel loan application and processing will be involved and will require additional persons and/or time. This fee, as with any of the fees charged on a conventional loan, may be paid by either party to the transaction, but the origination fee is usually paid by the purchaser. When dealing with conventional lenders, you should find out what the lender is charging for a loan origination fee and who may pay the fee.

Loan Programs Available

As outlined in the previous chapter, FHA in particular has many loan programs available, but many of the conventional lenders do not have such a wide selection. As a real estate professional, you should have knowledge of the conventional lenders and the types of loans that each makes. For example, some of the conventional lenders will only make loans on property that is built by a builder who has received his interim financing from the lender. Some savings and loan associations will only make loans within the city in which they have offices and in some cases will limit their loan operation to within a specific radius of the offices of the association. This limiting of the area of operation is a rule of the S and L and not of the Federal Home Loan Bank Board.

Underwriting Guidelines

In comparing the underwriting guidelines of the conventional loan to those of the FHA or VA, the FHA or VA guidelines are rather specific and are set by regulation of the FHA or VA, whereas there are no set guidelines for the conventional loan. Each conventional lender sets the guidelines it wishes to use. Some lenders are more lenient than others. Some lenders rely more on the income and the potential increase of the income, some are more interested in the past credit history of the applicant, and others are more interested in the property that will serve as security for the mortgage.

The above is true for all mortgages that will not be sold to FNMA and/or FHLMC. Mortgages that will be sold to either of these corporations must meet their strict underwriting guidelines. There is a growing trend among the conventional lenders to use the income and other guidelines of FNMA and FHLMC for the qualification of the conventional borrower.

The informed real estate professional will be familiar with the underwriting guidelines of the conventional lenders in his or her area. This will allow the salesperson to better match the borrower to the proper lender.

Selection of a Conventional Lender

From the previous paragraphs, one can see that the selection of the proper conventional lender for a client is an involved process and should be done with great care. A real estate salesperson should look at all of the conventional lenders and not just at the interest rate. The salesperson who selects a lender based only on the interest rate may be doing a disservice to his or her client.

Also, the policies of a conventional lender can change from time to time. One reason for this change may be that the lender has a commitment from a different investor and the underwriting guidelines of that investor are different, thus the lender must change its policies. So it is important, then, for you to check the conventional market on a continuing basis, for what was true last week may not be true this week.

When dealing with the conventional mortgage, one thing must be kept in mind: because a client is rejected by one conventional lender does not mean that the client will be rejected by all of the conventional lenders. Each lender has its own set of rules for accepting or rejecting a loan application. This is not true for VA or FHA loans. If either the VA or the FHA rejects the application, there is usually little hope of getting the application approved by the other.

PRIVATE MORTGAGE INSURANCE

Private mortgage insurance may be defined as an insurance policy issued from a licensed company to an approved lender, protecting that lender from financial loss due to the default of a borrower. This insurance is issued only on first-lien mortgages that are secured by improved residential property. Usually the insurance is only issued on mortgages that exceed 80 percent of the appraised value of the property.

History

Private mortgage insurance (PMI) is not a new idea. It can be traced to companies that issued such policies since the late 1800s. Most of these companies were located in New York City and normally issued their insurance not on single-family dwellings, but on commercial buildings. Prior to the Depression, the industry was made up of only private companies. There was little regulation of these insurance companies, and as with many companies, they either went into bankruptcy or stopped operation as a result of the Depression.

Out of the reform instituted during the Roosevelt era, the federal government entered the mortgage insurance business with the formulation of the FHA. The FHA was the only source of mortgage insurance until 1957, when the Wisconsin Insurance Commission issued a license to the Mortgage Guaranty Insurance Corporation. This was the beginning of the PMI industry as we know it today. Currently there are several companies licensed to issue PMI in the United States. Even though there are many companies licensed to issue PMI, the giant of the industry is still Mortgage Guaranty Insurance Corporation (MGIC).

Two events that happened in the early 1970s greatly enhanced the PMI industry. The first was in 1970, when Congress passed the Emergency Home Finance Act of 1970. One of the provisions of this act, which went into effect in 1971, allowed FNMA to purchase conventional loans in excess of the 75 percent loan-to-value ratio where either the seller kept a 10 percent participation or the loan was insured by a PMI company that was approved by FNMA. This LTV (loan-to-value) has been amended to 80 percent.

The second event that was of significance to the PMI industry occurred in 1972 when the Federal Home Loan Bank Board allowed savings and loan associations to make 95 percent loan-to-value loans on single-family dwellings as long as the amount of the loan above 75 percent was insured by a PMI company. Thus 75 percent as the basic loan for S and Ls was modified to 80 percent, and as of August 1980 the basic loan for S and Ls has been increased to 90 percent by the Federal Home Loan Bank Board. The PMI companies approved by FHLMC are listed in Appendix K.

It should be noted that the passage and/or enactment of the above-mentioned laws and regulations was the basis that made PMI a viable alternative to FHA insurance.

This ends our discussion of the history of the PMI industry. If you have any questions, contact the nearest office of one of the PMI companies listed in the appendix or any PMI-approved lender in your area.

PMI Coverage

Types of properties As a real estate professional, you should have knowledge of the types of properties and the amount of insurance that is available. All PMI companies will normally issue policies on first lien mortgages on a one- to- four-family dwelling that is used as a primary residence where the loan does not exceed 95 percent of the appraised value. Some PMI companies will issue mortgage insurance on a mortgage for a second home or a leisure home. In this case, the loan may not exceed 90 percent of the appraised value. Some PMI companies will issue insurance on mortgages of one- to four-family dwellings that are not the primary residence, but are held as investment property. For the investment property, the loan-to-value ratio generally should not exceed 80 percent. Not only will PMI companies issue insurance on single-family dwellings, but some of the companies will issue mortgage insurance on manufactured housing. To get the details on this coverage, you will have to contact the various PMI companies to see if they issue this type of insurance.

Insurance issued Many references have been made to the issuance of insurance by the company on mortgages, but what is the coverage of the insurance? First, it should be made very clear that PMI insurance is not the same as the insurance issued by FHA. PMI does not insure 100 percent of the mortgage, but only a portion of the mortgage. What portion of the mortgage is insured? The PMI companies are limited by law to the maximum percent of the loan they can insure. In New Mexico, for example, this maximum is 25 percent. This protection is available on a high loan-to-value ratio loan of 80 percent or more and issued almost exclusively on 90 and 95 percent loans. With this type of coverage available, institutions that are limited to maximum loan-to-value ratio loans of 75 percent are able to make 95 percent loans. With the 25 percent coverage on a 95 percent loan on a home selling for $70,000, the lender would have the following amount of risk:

Sales price	$70,000
Loan amount—95%	$66,500
Borrower's down payment	$ 3,500
Loan amount	$66,500
PMI coverage	×25%
Total PMI coverage	$16,625

Thus, the lender's exposure on the property would be the sales price, less the down payment, less the insurance coverage, or:

$70,000 − $3500 − $16,625 = $49,875

When the items are subtracted from the sales price and the lender's exposure of $50,000 is divided by the sales price, the lender is actually making a 71.25 percent loan.

$$\frac{\$49{,}875}{\$70{,}000} = 71.25\%$$

In addition to the 25 percent coverage on loans above 80 percent, there is also a 20 percent coverage available on loans above 80 percent. The other standard coverage offered is 10 percent coverage on loans of 80 percent or less.

These are the standard coverages that most lenders require; but if the mortgage is to be sold to either FNMA or FHLMC, the required coverages are less. These coverages are as follows:

95% loans	22% coverage
90% loans	17% coverage
85% loans	12% coverage
80% loans	No coverage

One can see, then, that FNMA and FHLMC require less coverage, thus increasing the lender's exposure slightly. Let us use the same example as before and calculate the lender's exposure to loss through FNMA or FHLMC.

Sales price	$70,000
95% loan	$66,500
Required down payment	$ 3,500
Loan amount	$66,500
PMI coverage	22%
Total PMI coverage	$14,630

Once again, the lender's exposure to loss would be the sales price, less the down payment, less the PMI coverage, or:

$70,000 − $3,500 − $14,630 = $51,870

This would have the lender actually making a 74.1 percent loan, increasing the lender's exposure by less than 3 percent.

The coverages discussed above are only the basic coverages and many are available. You as a real estate professional, however, will normally deal only with the coverages outlined above.

PMI Premiums

As the PMI companies' operations are regulated, so too are the rates they can charge. The following discussion of rates is based on the rates charged in New Mexico. There are several premium payment plans, but the most common is as follows.

For a 90 to 95 percent loan with 25 percent coverage, the initial premium is 1 percent of the loan amount collected at closing, usually paid by the buyer. To pay for the annual renewal of the coverage, a fee of 0.240 of a percent of the original loan balance is collected for years 2 through 10, and 0.125 of a percent of the original loan balance is collected for years 11 through 30. If the lender only requires 20 percent coverage, the initial premium collected at closing is 0.65 of a percent of the original loan balance. The amount for the annual renewal is the same.

If the loan has a loan-to-value ratio between 85 to 90 percent, the annual renewal is the same. The initial premiums, however, are as follows:

25% coverage—the initial cost is 0.50 of one percent of the loan amount

20% coverage—the initial cost is 0.35 of one percent of the loan amount

In addition to the annual plan, most of the PMI companies offer several other payment plans. The single payment plan allows the purchase of a policy for terms of from four years up to fifteen years. For the plans available, contact any lender or PMI company in your area.

There are major differences in the coverage and premiums of PMI and the mortgage insurance issued by FHA. One of the major differences is that PMI insurance is not for the life of the loan, as is FHA mortgage insurance. Once the loan balance reaches the 80 percent loan-to-value ratio based on the original sales or appraised price, the PMI insurance coverage is dropped and the premium is discontinued. This usually takes ten years.

It should be noted that even though the lender is ordering or requesting the insurance coverage, the borrower will pay the cost of the PMI insurance.

Application for PMI

Each of the PMI companies has its own procedures for the application of coverage. Usually the lender will submit a completed loan package to the PMI company. Using the form of the investor or those supplied by the PMI company, the PMI company will review the materials and approve or disapprove the borrower based on the materials.

Normally the PMI companies will have standard underwriting guidelines concerning the relationship of the total monthly income to the total mortgage payment, including all escrows and any fees that may affect the title to the property. In addition to the ratio of the total monthly income to mortgage payment, the PMI companies will review the ratio of the total monthly income to the total long-term obligations of the borrower, including the total mortgage payment. In most cases, the PMI companies define *long-term obligation* as any obligation that will take ten or more months to pay off.

The PMI company will review the credit history of the borrower, his and/or her work record, and any other factor that may affect the borrower's ability or willingness to repay the obligations. Some of these factors are court judgments, pending lawsuits, and bankruptcy.

The PMI company will also review the property that will serve as the security for the mortgage. The economic life of the property will be checked to see if it is sufficient to support the term of the loan. Also considered is whether the property can be sold rapidly if it is taken back, and whether it is an existing construction or proposed construction. These are only a few of the guidelines that are used by the PMI companies. If you would like further information, you may contact a PMI company and they will be able to supply you with the in-depth underwriting guidelines they use.

If all of the underwriting guidelines are met and the PMI company will issue the requested coverage, the originating lender will be notified by phone, and later a written confirmation of the approval will be furnished. This underwriting procedure will normally take only one or two days. One can see that the underwriting by the PMI companies is a great deal faster than that of FHA, which can take weeks.

Claims Payment

When a lender has notified the PMI company that an insured loan is in default as per the procedures of the PMI company, the insuring company has two ways of handling the claim. First, the company can pay the lender the full amount of the remaining loan balance. If this is done, the PMI company will take title to the property and then dispose of the property. Second, the PMI company can pay the lender as per the coverage purchased (20, 25, or 10 percent of the loan balance) plus other expenses in the policy of the PMI company, and the lender will then dispose of the property.

Claims under insurance issued by a PMI company are handled differently from claims filed against FHA mortgage insurance. The FHA will pay the lender the outstanding loan balance either in cash or debentures secured by the United States Treasury and FHA will take the property.

Benefits of PMI Coverage

One can see that there are many benefits for both the borrower and the lender with the purchase of PMI coverage. Some of the benefits to the *lender* are listed below:

1. The PMI insurance allows the lender to make 90 and 95 percent loans and to sell these loans in the secondary market
2. With the ability to make higher loan-to-value ratio loans, the amount of possible loans is expanded
3. The lender can secure an additional amount of security for the loan at no extra cost
4. The processing time and the issuance of the insurance commitment is usually faster from a PMI company than the FHA.

Advantages for the *borrower* include the following:

1. The borrower has the ability to purchase a home with a conventional loan with as little as 5 percent down payment
2. With the need for less money down, the borrower can buy a home sooner and sometimes larger than expected
3. The processing time for the insurance commitment is usually faster than with the FHA
4. The payment of the insurance premiums is for a shorter period than FHA

Other Services Offered by PMI Companies

In addition to the insurance of conventional loans, some of the PMI companies offer other services to the lender and the real estate industry. The most important of these services is operation of a secondary market department or facility. This department of a PMI company helps lenders locate sources of either funds to loan or commitments to purchase loans. In effect, this will bring together those with funds to loan and those who need funds to loan.

Some PMI companies have branched out and offer a wide range of financial services. For example, the parent company of Mortgage Guaranty Insurance Corporation offers commercial mortgage insurance, municipal bond insurance, and officer's and director's insurance.

REVIEW QUESTIONS

1. Define the term *conventional loan*.
2. Compare the loan limits, processing time, and down payments for a conventional loan to those of VA and FHA insured loans.
3. Contact a lender in your area and inquire as to the assumption procedures and cost charged by a conventional lender.
4. If you presently own a home and have a mortgage on that home, outline the prepayment penalties in your note and mortgage/deed of trust.

5. Define the term *origination fee*. What is the usual fee charged by lenders in your area?

6. Name and define the items that you feel are important in the selection of a conventional lender.

7. What is private mortgage insurance?

8. Explain the insurance coverage issued by a PMI company and give an example.

9. What are the premiums charged by PMI companies in your area?

10. How may a PMI company pay claims filed by an insured lender?

CHAPTER 9 The Secondary Market, Part 1

LEARNING OBJECTIVES

In this chapter we will discuss the secondary market in general, and in particular the conventional mortgage purchase programs of the Federal National Mortgage Association.

Upon completion of this chapter you should be able to do the following:

- ★ **Define the term *secondary market* as it relates to mortgage lending.**
- ★ **Identify the primary secondary markets.**
- ★ **Outline some of the major mortgage purchase programs of the Federal National Mortgage Association.**
- ★ **Outline the methods used by the Federal National Mortgage Association to generate funds for the purchase of mortgages**

A FEW DEFINITIONS

First, we should define the term *secondary market*. The secondary market is the market in which closed real estate loans are bought and sold.

When discussing the secondary market, one must understand that there is also a *primary market*. The primary market can be defined as those lenders that originate the loan and process the loan. These lenders are referred to as *primary lenders*. Many of the primary lenders do not wish to keep the closed loans in their portfolios and keep their funds tied up. They, therefore, will sell the loan in the secondary market. It should be noted that the secondary market is not like the stock market. It is not organized, regulated, or structured. As a primary lender, normally you cannot call up a mortgage broker as you can a stockbroker and sell a mortgage. How mortgages are sold in the secondary market will be discussed later in this chapter.

Among those investors that are purchasing real estate loans in the secondary market are insurance companies, savings and loan associations, commercial banks, title companies, other private companies and individuals, and agencies of the federal government. It should be noted that some of the companies that purchase loans in the secondary market also operate in the primary market as originating lenders.

PURPOSE OF THE SECONDARY MARKET

The primary purpose of the secondary market is to move funds from an area of the country with a surplus of capital for real estate loans to an area of the country that has a deficiency of capital for real estate loans. Since the supply of money is never static or in balance in all sections of the nation, the need for money and the supply of money is always changing. The secondary market tries to keep things in balance. For example, a mortgage banker in Portland has a large demand for loans due to a rapid influx of families to that area. Since mortgage companies normally do not lend their own funds, they will turn to the secondary market for help. The mortgage banker will call financial institutions in sections of the country that have a large supply of loanable funds, but do not have a great demand for real estate loans; or, the mortgage banker can secure a commitment from one of the government or quasi-government agencies that purchase loans.

How does a mortgage banker or any other lender keep up with the area of the country that has a surplus of funds? This is done by either a person or several people in the company who keep in contact with other lenders throughout the United States. Usually, there is a surplus of funds in savings institutions in Florida and the Midwest. The wise primary lender tries to keep up with the institutions in those areas in order to secure funds.

MAJOR SECONDARY MARKETS

There are three organizations that are the heart of the secondary market and purchase most of the real estate loans in the secondary market. These are the Federal National Mortgage Association (FNMA), the Government National Mortgage Association (GNMA), and the Federal Home Loan Mortgage Corporation (FHLMC). These organizations, particularly FNMA, gave birth to a national secondary market. GNMA and FHLMC will be reviewed in depth in the next chapter.

FEDERAL NATIONAL MORTGAGE ASSOCIATION (FNMA)[1]

Prior to the Great Depression, there was no secondary market as we know it today. The first attempt at a secondary market was the creation of the Home Owners Loan Corporation (HOLC) with the enactment of the Home Owners' Loan Act of 1933. The purpose of this corporation was to help home owners refinance an existing loan that was in danger of going into foreclosure or being taken due to back taxes. This agency is no longer in existence.

As we learned earlier, the Federal Housing Administration was created with the passage of the National Housing Act of 1934. In addition to the creation of FHA, Title III, Section 301 allowed the establishment of secondary market facilities for home mortgages and also provided that the operations of this secondary market would be financed with private capital, to the maximum extent possible. This was the authority under which FNMA was subsequently created, thus beginning the modern secondary market.

The actual creation of the corporation was not until February 10, 1938, upon the request of the President under the authority of Title III of the National Housing Act. When the secondary marketing corporation was founded it was not known as the Federal National Mortgage Association, but was named the National Mortgage Association of Washington. The name was changed on April 5, 1938, to the Federal National Mortgage Association. At this time, the operations of FNMA were controlled by the Reconstruction Finance Corporation. The control of FNMA remained under this federal agency until September 1950, when the control of the operations was shifted to the Housing and Home Finance Agency. This agency was the forerunner to the Department of Housing and Urban Development. Then in 1965, when the Department of Housing and Urban Development was created, the control of FNMA was transferred to HUD.

The final and most major change to the operations of FNMA came about in 1968 with the passage of the 1968 amendments to the National Housing Act. Under Section 801 of these amendments, FNMA was partitioned into two separate and distinct corporations. One of these corporations was to be known as the Federal National Mortgage Association and was to be a government-chartered, shareholder-owned, for-profit corporation. FNMA would continue to operate in the secondary market as authorized by the National Housing Act. The other corporation was to be known as the Government National Mortgage Association, and the ownership and control of this corporation was to remain with the government. Today, GNMA is under the control of the Department of Housing and Urban Development.

In the amendments of 1968, FNMA was to be responsible for its own operations and management after a period of transition. This transition was to be completed on or after May 1, 1970. According to Section 801, FNMA could not be classified as a separate corporation responsible for its own operations until at least one-third of the common stock was owned by persons or institutions in the mortgage lending business, home construction industry, real estate industry, or other related industries. This one-third ownership of the stock was to be established by the Board of Directors of FNMA in concurrence with the Secretary of Housing and Urban Development. The board found that the necessary stock was being held by the specified industries in February 1970, and the Secretary of HUD concurred with such findings on May 21, 1970, thus establishing FNMA as a privately owned and controlled corporation with a public purpose.

The Purpose of FNMA

The purposes, or functions, of FNMA were established by the enactment of the FNMA Charter Act of 1954 and became effective in August 1954. These purposes are listed below:

1. To establish a secondary market operation for the purpose of buying and selling real estate mortgages

2. To help in the financing of special housing programs and to help ease the effect of adverse economic conditions on the housing market

3. To manage and liquidate the FNMA mortgage portfolio with the least adverse effect on the mortgage market and the federal government

In 1968, the second and third purposes were transferred to GNMA.

Governmental Interaction[2]

Even though FNMA is a private corporation and is listed on the New York Stock Exchange, it still has a close relationship to the federal government—in particular to HUD. Since FNMA has been given some advantages by the federal government with the passage of the FNMA Charter Act and other laws, it is also subject to some governmental supervision and control.

Let's discuss some of the advantages accorded to FNMA. First, the Secretary of the Treasury has the authority to purchase up to $2.25 billion of FNMA outstanding debts. This authority has become known as a *treasury backstop authority*, although it has never been used. It should be noted that the debt of FNMA is not an obligation of the federal government, nor is it guaranteed by the federal government. The debt is solely an obligation of FNMA. Even though FNMA is a private corporation, its obligations, along with the obligations of federally owned corporations, are known as *federal agency securities*.

The second advantage accorded to FNMA is that its stock is exempt from the federal registration requirements and other laws enforced by the Securities and Exchange Commission.

Another advantage is that although FNMA is required to pay federal corporate income tax, it is exempt from all state and local taxes except for real estate taxes.

Finally, all issues of notes and debentures or other obligations of FNMA are issued through and payable by the Federal Reserve Banks. Any service that is rendered by a Reserve Bank is paid for by FNMA. All of the obligations sold by FNMA are legal investments for federally supervised institutions, as well as for many state-supervised institutions.

Along with these advantages, FNMA has accepted some forms of federal supervision and regulation. Five of the fifteen members of the FNMA Board of Directors are appointed by the President of the United States. Three of the five must be selected as follows: one from the home building industry, one from the mortgage lending industry, and one from the real estate industry. The remaining ten directors are elected by the FNMA stockholders.

The Secretary of HUD has the authority to see that a reasonable portion of FNMA's mortgage purchases is related to the national goal of providing adequate housing for low- and moderate-income families. It should be noted that these loans are to provide FNMA a reasonable economic return.

The Secretary of Housing and Urban Development has certain regulatory powers over FNMA. This means that the secretary has the power to make and enforce regulations to see that FNMA accomplishes the purposes of the Federal National Mortgage Association Charter Act.

All issuance of debt by FNMA must be approved by the Secretary of the Treasury. It should be noted that the largest borrower of funds is the United States Treasury, and in some years FNMA is the second largest borrower of funds. The activities of the two need to be coordinated, thus the issuance of debt obligations of FNMA are approved by the Secretary of the Treasury, who reviews the debt obligations as to the maturities and rates of interest.

The Secretary of HUD may examine and audit the FNMA books and require FNMA to make reports as the Secretary of HUD deems necessary.

These are a few of the direct forms of federal supervision or control of FNMA. In addition to direct federal supervision, the Secretary of HUD has the power to issue regulations that have a direct effect on FNMA and its operation. These regulations were revised in 1978; three of the revisions were as follows:

1. To establish standards and goals for the secondary marketing operations of FNMA

2. To set forth regulations that would insure that FNMA is complying with the nondiscrimination statutes

3. To provide for annual audits of the books and financial transactions of FNMA

The first revision is one of the more significant changes, for it establishes goals for FNMA regarding the purchase of mortgages on properties in the inner-city areas of standard metropolitan statistical areas, as well as the purchase of conventional mortgages on housing of low- and moderate-income families.

FNMA Corporate Offices

The National Housing Act in Title III requires that FNMA maintain its principal office in the Washington, D.C. area. It is located at 3900 Wisconsin Avenue NW, Washington, D.C., 20016. In addition to that home office, FNMA operates five regional offices. The location of the five regional offices and the area served by each are listed below:

FNMA Midwestern Region
150 South Wacker Drive
Chicago, IL 60606

Area Served: Illinois, Indiana, Iowa, Michigan, Minnesota, Nebraska, North Dakota, Ohio, South Dakota, and Wisconsin

FNMA Northeastern Region
510 Walnut Street, 16th Floor
Philadelphia, PA 19106

Area Served: Connecticut, Delaware, District of Columbia, Maine, Maryland, Massachusetts, New Hampshire, New Jersey, New York, Pennsylvania, Puerto Rico, Rhode Island, Vermont, Virgin Islands, Virginia, and West Virginia

FNMA Southeastern Region
100 Peachtree Street, NW
Atlanta, GA 30303

Area Served: Alabama, Florida, Kentucky, Mississippi, North Carolina, South Carolina, and Tennessee

FNMA Southwestern Region
2001 Bryan Tower, Suite 1200
Dallas, TX 75201

Area Served: Arkansas, Colorado, Kansas, Louisiana, Missouri, New Mexico, Oklahoma, and Texas

FNMA Western Region
10920 Wilshire Boulevard, Suite 1800
Los Angeles, CA 90024

Area Served: Alaska, Arizona, California, Guam, Hawaii, Idaho, Montana, Nevada, Oregon, Utah, Washington, and Wyoming

FNMA Source of Funds

Since FNMA is in the business of purchasing loans, it must have funds to accomplish this function, and it derives these funds from the capital market.

The major source of FNMA funds is the sale of debt instruments. These instruments are either short- or long-term. The long-term

Figure 9-1. ***FNMA Debenture Offering***

Federal National Mortgage Association
3900 WISCONSIN AVENUE, N.W., WASHINGTON, D.C. 20016

News Release

For further information contact: Paul Paquin (202) 537-7115

FOR IMMEDIATE RELEASE   WEDNESDAY, SEPTEMBER 3, 1980   #4264

DEBENTURE OFFERING

Date of Release: WEDNESDAY, SEPTEMBER 3, 1980

Date of Offering: THURSDAY, SEPTEMBER 4, 1980

Price: Par

Issue Date	Term	Interest Rate	Amount (in millions)	Maturity Date	Date of First Interest Payment (then-semiannually)
9/10/80	1 year 4 mos.	10.90%	$400	1/11/82	1/11/81

Uses to Which Proceeds will be Put: The net proceeds of this offering will be used to partially redeem the $400,000,000 7.50% and the $650,000,000 8.75% debentures that mature on September 10, 1980.

Debentures will be issued in book-entry form only. The minimum purchase is $10,000 and multiples of $5,000 thereafter. The offering is being made through FNMA's Vice President and Fiscal Agent, John J. Meehan, 100 Wall Street, New York, assisted by a nationwide selling group of recognized security dealers.

The issues which are offered tomorrow will be free to trade at 12:00 NOON Eastern Daylight Time.

instruments usually take the form of a debenture and the short-term instruments are in the form of short-term discount notes. The debenture is a debt obligation that, when issued, is not secured by any tangible asset, but by the soundness or financial strength of FNMA. An example of such a debenture offering is shown in Figure 9-1. As we learned earlier in the chapter, all of the obligations of FNMA are viewed by the market as federal agency securities and have for many years been looked upon favorably by the financial community. Since most assets of FNMA are in the form of secured real estate loans, most members of the financial community feel there is little chance of default by FNMA. In addition to all of the assets being secured real estate loans, FNMA also has the ability to call on the Treasury of the United States for the purchase of a portion of its debt.

In regard to the term of the debt instruments of FNMA, the short-term notes are issued for a term of from 30 days to 360 days. The debentures are issued for a term of one year to twenty-five years.

In addition to the borrowing of funds, FNMA also has portfolio income. This portfolio income is not only derived from interest on mortgages, but also from discounts on mortgages.

One other method that may be used by FNMA to raise capital is the selling of stock in the corporation. Even though FNMA has close ties with the federal government, it is still a private corporation and has the right to issue stock, as any other corporation would.

A new method used by FNMA to provide funds to the mortgage market is through the issuance and guaranty of Conventional Mortgage Pass-Through Securities. The purpose of this program is to tap the long-term investor market, including pension funds, which have traditionally invested little or nothing in mortgages. In other words, this is an additional means that FNMA can use to support the mortgage market without itself purchasing loans.

Under this program, FNMA will issue guaranteed securities representing an undivided fractional interest in a pool of conventional first lien mortgages. These securities will be similar to those guaranteed by the Government National Mortgage Association. The GNMA securities program will be explained in Chapter 10. There is one major difference between the "certificates" issued by GNMA and the "securities" of FNMA. Since GNMA is a federal agency, their "certificates" are guaranteed by the federal government, whereas the "securities" issued by FNMA carry no such guarantee, but only the guarantee of FNMA. The guarantee issued by FNMA is for the full and timely payment of principal and interest on the 25th of each month.

The mortgages that will be used as the collateral for these securities are grouped or packaged into what is referred to as a pool. The mortgages that are grouped or pooled must meet or conform to certain specifications, which are essentially the same as those pertaining to loans purchased for FNMA's own portfolio:

1. The property used to secure the mortgage must be a single-family or two- to four-family dwelling
2. Each mortgage in the pool must have an original term of no more than thirty years and when sold to FNMA must have a remaining term of at least twenty years
3. All mortgages in the pool that have a loan-to-value ratio in excess of 80 percent must be insured by private mortgage insurance issued by a private mortgage insurance company approved by FNMA and authorized by the state in which the property is located to issue such mortgage insurance

These are the major specifications that each of the mortgages must meet prior to being included in a pool of mortgages. For *all* of the requirements, you should contact a FNMA-approved lender.

There are now two types of pools authorized to be packaged. One type of pool is called a *single-user pool*. With this type of pool, the lender packages a number of mortgages that meet all of the specifications and that equal $1 million or more. The second type of pool is a *multiple-issuer pool* in which loan packages—minimum $1 million each, from more than one lender—are combined to back a single security offering.

The minimum face amount for a certificate of ownership of an undivided fractional interest in one of these pools is $25,000, with additional interests sold in multiples of $5000, thus making these "securities" available to the general public, corporations, pension funds and financial institutions.

FNMA Loan Approval

Prior to the purchase of a mortgage by FNMA, the mortgage must meet certain criteria. For most FHA/VA mortgages, if the mortgage has been insured by FHA or has been issued a guaranty by the Veterans Administration, FNMA will purchase it without reviewing its credit and property underwriting.

For conventional mortgages, before December 1, 1981, when FNMA instituted a major change in the approval process, there were two methods for conventional approval. This change was that FNMA would no longer require, or even offer, the option of "prior approval," prior to the purchase of a mortgage from an approved lender. It should be noted that FNMA refers to its approved lenders as approved seller/servicers. This was a major change in the approval procedures of FNMA. Before this change, all lenders without a "FNMA Delegated Underwriter" had to submit all mortgage applications with all of the documents to FNMA for approval either before the closing of the mortgage or when the loans were submitted for purchase. For example, if a mortgage company located in South Dakota originated a mortgage to be sold to FNMA, the mortgage company would have to mail the application along with all of the supporting data to the FNMA regional office in Chicago for prior approval. The mailing and approval process at the regional office could take as long as two weeks. If this time is added to the normal processing time, one can see that the prior approval method could be rather time consuming.

With the implementation of the change allowing the lenders to give *in-house* approval, the processing and approval time can be cut significantly. As with any other delegation of authority, FNMA has placed some requirements on the seller/servicer. One of the major requirements is that the lender must establish internal procedures to monitor credit, appraisals of property, underwriting requirements, and the accuracy of appraisals and all supporting documents that will accompany any application used in the underwriting of a mortgage loan.

As with any other program, there are certain limitations. FNMA may require newly approved lenders to submit to FNMA credit and property documents for an underwriting review prior to the purchase of mortgages for a limited period of time. The purpose of this is for FNMA to see if the lender is following the underwriting guidelines of FNMA. The only other exception to the program are those lenders that are "under sanction" by FNMA.

The importance of this change in the FNMA procedures cannot be overemphasized for it has streamlined the processing and approval of loans to be sold to FNMA. This streamlining will be of great value to the real estate professional due to the ability for closer coordination with the lender on necessary information for the underwriting of the mortgage and thus for faster approval.

Mortgage Purchase Programs

FNMA, since its beginning, has had the ability to purchase mortgages on one- to four-family dwellings. It never mattered whether the property was new or existing construction, but there once was the requirement that the mortgage had to be either insured or guaranteed by an agency of the federal government. This meant that FNMA was limited to the purchase of only FHA or VA mortgages. This limitation was lifted by the passage of an amendment to the Charter Act in July 1970. It was not until February 1972, however, that FNMA purchased its first conventional mortgage. The purchase of conventional loans has increased at a rapid rate and today represents approximately one-half of the mortgages purchased by FNMA. In relation to the total portfolio of FNMA, conventional mortgages represent approximately one-third. In regard to the size and importance of the purchase of mortgages by FNMA, its portfolio of purchased mortgages had grown to over $60 billion by the end of 1981.

Let us now examine the major conventional mortgage purchase programs available through FNMA.

Single Family Home FNMA will purchase conventional mortgages on single-family homes or units on a spot basis located in subdivisions, de minimus PUD projects, and in FNMA-approved condominiums or PUDS. (A de minimis PUD may be defined as a Planned Unit Development in which the common areas, if removed from the PUD, would have little or no effect on the value of the individual units or reduce the enjoyment of the homeowners.) In addition to the homes listed previously, FNMA will purchase mortgages on detached, semi-detached, row, or townhouse structures.

FNMA has set no minimum term for the mortgages it purchases, but has set the maximum term as thirty years. FNMA accepts conventional mortgages with loan-to-value ratios as high as 95 percent. On a loan of 80 percent or less, FNMA does not require any PMI coverage. Such coverage, down to 75 percent of value, is required on higher loan-to-value ratio loans. The maximum loan amount, irrespective of loan-to-value ratio, for a single-family dwelling is $107,000.

With the passage of the Housing and Community Development Act of 1980, the maximum single-family loan amount is to be adjusted as of January 1 of each year. This practice began January 1, 1981. The act states that the maximum limitation will be increased by an amount equal to the percentage of increase in prices for new and existing homes based upon a survey conducted by the Federal Home Loan Bank Board for the previous twelve months, as measured October to October.

FNMA allows second liens on the property used as security for the first lien mortgage to be purchased provided that the following conditions are met:

1. The second must be junior to the mortgage that FNMA is purchasing.

2. The terms of the second mortgage must be fully disclosed to FNMA.

3. When the amount of the first and second liens are combined, they may not exceed 95 percent of the value of the property in the case of owner-occupied properties. For nonowner-occupied property, the combined loan-to-value ratio may not exceed 90 percent and the first lien cannot exceed 80 percent.

4. The monthly payments required to repay a subordinate lien must remain constant for a period of twelve months. If the monthly payment will change from one twelve-month period to the next, the increase may not exceed 7.5 percent of the previous monthly payment.

5. If the subordinate lien does not require a monthly payment, the lien may not have a term, maturity, or call option date of less than five years.

This use of secondary financing is not allowed by all conventional lenders and can be important to a client.

Prior to June 22, 1981, FNMA would only purchase mortgages on single-family dwellings that would serve as the primary residence of the applicant. This policy was revised allowing FNMA to purchase conventional mortgages secured by nonowner-occupied single-family dwellings under any commitments issued on or after June 22, 1981. The maximum loan-to-value ratio authorized is 80 percent and the maximum term is thirty years. FNMA will, at the time of purchase of a nonowner-occupied mortgage, charge an additional commitment fee of 1.5 percent and will require an additional yield of one half of one percent above the yield on the commitment. This means that if the lender will sell the mortgage to FNMA under a commitment that requires a yield of 13.50, FNMA will add a 0.50 percent making the yield 14.0.

In addition to purchasing conventional mortgages on nonowner-occupied single-family dwellings, FNMA will now purchase conventional mortgages secured by single-family dwellings in resort areas. Before FNMA will purchase such a mortgage, there are certain criteria that must be met, including the following:

1. The property is suitable for year-round occupancy.

2. The property is occupied by the borrower or the borrower intends to rent the property for long-term use. According to FNMA, if the property is to be rented, it will have to be demonstrated that there is a rental market for year-round occupancy.

According to FNMA Program Announcement Number 1, October 14, 1981, mortgages secured by residential properties that will be used or rented on a seasonal basis may be eligible for purchase under a negotiated transaction. For more information on this type of transaction, you will need to contact a FNMA-approved lender.

Buydown interest rate mortgage In May 1981, FNMA offered for the first time a conventional mortgage purchase program other than the traditional fixed-rate, fixed-payment, fixed-term mortgage. This new mortgage is a conventional mortgage that will allow the interest rate to be bought down with the payment of a lump sum when the mortgage is closed.

This buydown mortgage is a type of graduated-payment mortgage in that the initial monthly payments made by the borrower are lower than a fixed-payment mortgage of the same amount. The buyer is qualified on the basis of the lower bought-down payment. The difference in the monthly payments is made up from the monies furnished by the borrower, seller, homebuilder, borrowers' parents, or anyone else at the time of origination. This feature of the buydown mortgage is similar to the pledged account mortgage, which was discussed in Chapter 3.

FNMA will purchase conventional mortgages secured by a home or unit on new or existing property that is subject to interest rate buydown (fixed rate or Plans 2, 4, and 6 of the Adjustable Rate Mortgage Purchase Program), provided the buydown plan meets the following characteristics:

1. The buydown period is limited to a minimum term of one year and a maximum of ten years.

2. The payments for a buydown period must be constant over each twelve-month period of the buydown. Thus, the payments may not increase, for example, every three months.

3. The payment increase should not be more than 7.5 percent a year or 15 percent from one year to the next. For example, if the payments were level for three years, they could not increase by more than 15 percent in year four.

4. The maximum interest rate buydown from a seller or builder is 3 percent below the face rate of the note, or a total of ten discount points (six discount points for loans over 90 percent loan-to-value).

5. Buydowns from any source other than the seller, or builder, are unlimited. These may be used alone or in combination with a builder or seller buydown.

6. Within the payment increase limits, the buydown may be level (3 percent each year for three years) or graduated (3 percent of the first year, 2 percent the second, and 1 percent the third).

7. Special arrangements are available for corporate relocation plans.

8. FNMA requires that there be a written agreement between the borrower and the lender outlining the terms of the buydown.

For conventional buydown mortgages, FNMA will require the enforcement of the acceleration-upon-sale (that is, due-on-sale) provision of the mortgage/deed of trust, unless prohibited or limited by law, regulation, or court decision. In regard to the approval of buyer by assumption, if the term of the buydown has twelve or more months, FNMA will use the reduced interest rate allowed by the remaining buydown funds as the rate to be used for loan approval. If the term of the buydown has less than twelve months to run, FNMA will use the face interest rate of the mortgage as the rate for loan approval. These are some of the major rules that a buydown plan must meet prior to FNMA's approval of the plan.

Borrower approval will be based on the lower first-year payment, thus allowing a lower annual income for the borrower. This will allow more borrowers or families to qualify for housing.

FNMA will also allow subordinate financing, a second mortgage, with certain limitations, as follows:

1. The combination of the first and second lien may not exceed a loan-to-value ratio of 95 percent based on the initial value of the property used as security.

Figure 9.2 Part 1: Examples of Buydown Plans Which Are Satisfactory to FNMA

1. A builder wishes to offer a buydown plan to assist prospective purchasers to meet the mortgage payments on a 15.50% mortgage. The builder proposes a three-year graduated mortgage payment plan, that will effectively give the home purchaser a 12.50% interest rate payment for the first year; 13.50% for the second year and 14.50% for the third year. Starting with the mortgage's 37th payment the mortgage instrument's stated mortgage payments, based upon a 15.50% rate, will become the complete responsibility of the mortgagor.

EXAMPLE:

Loan Amount	$50,000	
Interest Rate	15.50%	
Mortgage Term	30 years	
Level Monthly Payment	$652.26	
Cost first year	= $1423.56	(at $118.63 per month)
Cost second year	= $ 954.60	(at $79.55 per month)
Cost third year	= $ 479.76	(at $39.98 per month)
Total cost to builder	$2857.92	

The Mortgage Payment Schedule:

Monthly Pmts. Nos.	*Borrower's Pmt.*	*Buydown Pmt.*	*Total Mtg. Pmt.*
1-12	$533.63	$118.63	$652.26
13-24	$572.71	$ 79.55	$652.26
25-36	$612.28	$ 39.98	$652.26
37-360	$652.26	—0—	$652.26

Note: In this example the borrower's first twelve monthly payments under the buydown plan change to $572.71 in the second twelve-month phase. This is an increase of $39.08 which represents a 7.3% increase. The change from the second to the third twelve-month phase represents a 6.9% increase and from the third to the fourth represents a 6.5% increase. The amount of these increases does not exceed the FNMA 7½% guideline, so the plan is acceptable.

2. Using the same facts described above, a home seller wishes to offer a level or straight buydown of 2% per year for the first three years.

The Mortgage Payment Schedule:

Monthly Pmts. Nos.	*Borrower's Pmt.*	*Buydown Pmt.*	*Total Mtg. Pmt.*
1-36	$572.71	$ 79.55	$652.26
37-360	$652.26	—0—	$652.26

Note: In this example, the payment increase ($652.26 - $572.71) is $79.55 or 13.9%. Since the year-to-year increase from year 2 to year 3 does not exceed 15%, this plan also would be acceptable to FNMA.

Total Cost to home seller
($79.55 × 36 Months) = $2,863.80

Source: Federal National Mortgage Association, memo, May 26, 1981.

Figure 9-2. Part 2: Example of Subordinate Financing to Secure Buydown

Assuming that the value of a property is $56,000, the following is an example of a plan which would be acceptable to FNMA:

FNMA First Mortgage		*Second Mortgage*	
Loan Amount	$50,000	Loan Amount	$3,000
Interest Rate	15.50%	Interest Rate	12%
Mortgage Term	30 years	Mortgage Term	5 years
Monthly Pmt.	$652.26	Level Mortgage Pmt. (interest only)	$30.00
Total Builder Buydown	$2,857.92	Balloon - $3,000, due and payable after 5 years.	

In the buydown example shown on Exhibit I, the developer and purchaser agreed that the lump sum of $2,857.92 (say $3,000) would be in the form of a second mortgage that provided for regular monthly interest payments of $30.00 per month (12.00% per annum) with the total principal due (balloon payment) at the end of five years. This second mortgage ($3,000) when added to the first mortgage ($50,000) resulted in a combined loan-to-value percent of 94.64% based upon the sale price of $56,000. This example of a second mortgage used to secure a buydown would be acceptable to FNMA because:

1. The sum of the first and the second mortgages equals no more than 95% of value.
2. Monthly payments remain constant.
3. In this case, there is no change in second mortgage payments.
4. The maturity date of this non-amortizing plan is the minimum 5 years.

Source: Federal National Mortgage Association, memo, May 26, 1981.

2. Any monthly payments on the second mortgages must remain constant for twelve months and may not increase by more than 7.5 percent from any year to the next.
3. If the mortgage is not a level payment mortgage that will be repaid in full at the end of the term, it may not have a call option or maturity of less than five years.

Now that we have reviewed the major provisions of the FNMA buydown mortgage, let us see how such a mortgage may work. A sample buydown plan is shown in Figure 9-2.

Two- to Four-Family Homes Under this mortgage purchase program, FNMA will purchase mortgages secured by duplexes, triplexes, and fourplexes. It should be emphasized that the property does not have to be occupied by the borrower, thus making this program ideal for the small investor who is interested in these types of properties. FNMA is one of the few secondary marketers that will purchase mortgages on these types of properties.

As with the single-family purchase program, FNMA will purchase mortgages on two- to four-family dwellings that are under construction, existing, or proposed for construction. The structures can be detached, semi-detached, row or townhomes, in a subdivision or Planned Unit Development, or in a de minimis PUD. This program is not available to units located in condominiums. This program is excellent for use in the rehabilitation of properties in the inner cities and declining areas of a city.

The maximum mortgage amounts for this FNMA program underwent a major revision with the passage of the Housing and Community Development Act of 1980. Prior to the passage of the legislation, the maximum loan amount was keyed to the number of bedrooms in each of the units. The current multifamily maximum mortgage amounts are as follows:

Two-family dwelling	$136,800
Three-family dwelling	$165,100
Four-family dwelling	$205,300

As with the mortgage limits for the single-family loan maximum, the limits for the two- to four-family program are to be adjusted on January 1 each year using the results of the survey of major lenders conducted by the Federal Home Loan Bank Board for a twelve-month period.

As stated earlier, this program is available to the investor wishing to buy this type of property for rehabilitation and resale or for rental. The maximum loan and terms for the nonowner-occupant is 80 percent loan-to-value ratio and the maximum term is twenty years if the property is held for resale. If the property is held for investment, a term of thirty years is available. The maximum term and loan available for the owner-occupant is somewhat different from that of the nonowner-occupant. The maximum term of the owner-occupant loan is thirty years and the maximum loan-to-value ratio is 95 percent.

This program of FNMA, as with the single family program, allows for both subordinate financing and refinancing. The subordinate or second financing allowed on the two- to four-family mortgage purchase program is the same as that allowed under the single-family mortgage purchase program.

In addition to the increases in the mortgage amounts, there are some other differences that should be noted with this program. The first is that, in addition to the applicant's regular income, FNMA will recognize and count the operating income derived from the property toward the income used to qualify the applicant. FNMA will not use the total income produced by the property, but will use an amount referred to as *operating income*. Operating income is calculated as the economic rent of the property or the total amount of rent possible from the property, less certain expenses. The expenses to be deducted are expenses for vacancy/credit loss and expenses for the operation of the property, which will include replacement reserves and mortgage payments. FNMA has prepared Form 216 for the calculation of these expenses, shown in Figure 9-3. FNMA also requires an additional 1.5 percent commitment fee at the time of loan delivery and a 0.50 percent additional yield on two- to four-family loans for nonowner occupants.

The second major difference is the appraisal report that is required for the two- to four-family dwelling. FNMA requires the appraisal on its Form 1025, entitled Appraisal Report, Two- to Four-Family Residential Property. Also required to accompany the appraisal is the appraiser's comments on the information contained in the operating statement prepared by the applicant.

One final difference is that FNMA will require a statement from the appropriate agency that the structure meets the minimum standards of the area. For example, if the property is located in Houston, FNMA must be supplied with a certificate from the Housing Code Enforcement Department of the City of Houston, indicating that the property meets Houston's minimum property standards.

A word of caution in regard to the two- to four-family program: some of the Regional Offices of FNMA are receiving an increasing number of submissions for newly established or proposed subdivisions devoted primarily to this type of property. If you are working with a developer or investor who wishes to rehabilitate larger housing in the inner-city, it may also be important to contact an FNMA-approved seller/servicer in your area to see if a subdivision approval will be necessary.

Condominium and PUD Unit Mortgage Purchase Program As with many other FNMA mortgage purchase programs, this program has undergone a major revision and streamlining. Prior to FNMA Program Announcement Number 6 on November 16, 1981, there had been two purchase programs for these types of mortgages. One was for mortgages secured by condominium or PUD units located in projects that had been approved by FNMA prior to the start of construction, and the other was a program for the purchase of mortgages located in existing projects. Now there is basically one program.

The new program states that FNMA may substantially reduce the submission and approval requirements for a condominium or PUD project. The requirements will be based on FNMA's knowledge of the property and the developer and/or the market area. In addition to these factors, FNMA will rely a great deal on the lender who will be making the request for approval of either a new or existing project. Thus, it will be important for you as a real estate professional to become familiar with the lenders in your area and find those

Figure 9-3. FNMA Operating Income Statement for Two- to Four-Family Property

FEDERAL NATIONAL MORTGAGE ASSOCIATION

OPERATING INCOME STATEMENT — 2-4 Family Property

DATE: ________________

PROPERTY ADDRESS ______________________________ (Street) ______________________ (City, State, Zip)

RENT SCHEDULE :

UNIT No. 1 _____ ROOMS _____ BEDRMS _____ BATHS @ $ _____ PER MONTH
UNIT No. 2 _____ ROOMS _____ BEDRMS _____ BATHS @ $ _____ PER MONTH
UNIT No. 3 _____ ROOMS _____ BEDRMS _____ BATHS @ $ _____ PER MONTH
UNIT No. 4 _____ ROOMS _____ BEDRMS _____ BATHS @ $ _____ PER MONTH
TOTAL _____ ROOMS _____ BEDRMS _____ BATHS $ _____ PER MONTH

UTILITY EXPENSE :

	ON OWNER	ON TENANT
ELECTRICITY	☐	☐
HEATING	☐	☐
COOKING	☐	☐
HOT WATER	☐	☐
WATER	☐	☐
SEWER	☐	☐

ANNUAL INCOME AND EXPENSE PROJECTION FOR NEXT 12 MONTHS	BY APPLICANT	INITIAL ADJUSTMENTS BY SELLER'S UNDERWRITER	FINAL ADJUSTMENTS BY SELLER'S UNDERWRITER
INCOME			
ANNUAL RENTAL @ 100% OCCUPANCY	$	$	$
OTHER INCOME	+		
TOTAL	$		
LESS OWNER-OCCUPANT UNIT (UNIT No. ____)	−		
TOTAL	$		
LESS VACANCY/RENT LOSS	− (%)	(%)	(%)
EFFECTIVE GROSS INCOME	$	$	$
EXPENSES (OMIT OWNER-OCCUPANT EXPENSES)			
HEATING ( )	$	$	$
COOKING ( )			
HOT WATER ( )			
ELECTRICITY			
WATER/SEWER			
CASUAL LABOR			
INTERIOR PAINT / DECORATING			
GENERAL REPAIRS / MAINTENANCE			
MANAGEMENT EXPENSE	(%)	(%)	(%)
SUPPLIES			
EQUIPMENT REPLACEMENT-SEE SCHEDULE			
CARPETING REPLACEMENT-SEE SCHEDULE			
MISCELLANEOUS			
TOTAL OPERATING EXPENSES	$	$	$

PAGE 1 OF 2

FNMA Form 216
Oct. 79

Figure 9-3. continued

OPERATING INCOME RECONCILIATION

\$________ – \$________ = \$________ ÷ 12 = \$________ OPERATING INCOME PER MONTH
(EFFECT. GROSS INC.) – (OPERATING EXPENSES) = (OPERATING INCOME)   (ENTER ON LINE 34 of FNMA FORM 1008)

REPLACEMENT RESERVE SCHEDULE

EQUIPMENT:		BY APPLICANT	INITIAL ADJUSTMENTS	FINAL ADJUSTMENTS
STOVES / RANGES	@ \$____ ea. ÷ ____ YRS X ____ UNITS =	\$____	\$____	\$____
REFRIGS.	@ \$____ ea. ÷ ____ YRS X ____ UNITS =	\$____	\$____	\$____
D. WASHER	@ \$____ ea. ÷ ____ YRS X ____ UNITS =	\$____	\$____	\$____
A/C UNITS	@ \$____ ea. ÷ ____ YRS X ____ UNITS =	\$____	\$____	\$____
C.WASHER/DRYER	@ \$____ ea. ÷ ____ YRS X ____ UNITS =	\$____	\$____	\$____
HW HEATER	@ \$____ ea. ÷ ____ YRS X ____ UNITS =	\$____	\$____	\$____
(OTHER)	@ \$____ ea. ÷ ____ YRS X ____ UNITS =	\$____	\$____	\$____
(OTHER)	@ \$____ ea. ÷ ____ YRS X ____ UNITS =	\$____	\$____	\$____
TOTAL		\$____	\$____	\$____
CARPETING:				
(UNITS) ____	TOTAL SQ. YDS. @ \$____ PER SQ. YD. ÷ ____ YRS. =	\$____	\$____	\$____
(PUBLIC AREAS) ____	TOTAL SQ. YDS. @ \$____ PER SQ. YD. ÷ ____ YRS. =	\$____	\$____	\$____
TOTAL		\$____	\$____	\$____

APPRAISER INSTRUCTIONS

The subject 2-4 family property is being considered for a mortgage application. Operating income is defined as a property's gross monthly rent less allowances for rental income of an owner-occupant's unit (if applicable), for vacancy/rent loss and operating expenses (including replacements and management expenses and excluding the pro-rata expenses attributable to an owner-occupant's unit) but before deductions for taxes, hazard insurance, mortgage insurance and the mortgage's monthly principal and interest charges. Operating income as used in this analysis does not meet the characteristics of net operating income as the term is commonly used and is intended for credit underwriting purposes only. As part of your appraisal instructions you are requested to comment upon the reasonableness of the projected operating income. If applicable, the property's past two year-end operating statements are attached to assist you in your analysis.

UNDERWRITER NAME ________ UNDERWRITER SIGNATURE ________ DATE ________

APPRAISER'S COMMENTS

APPRAISER ________ DATE ________

PAGE 2 OF 2

that have experience in working with FNMA for the approval of condominium or PUD projects.

One other major change that was authorized by this program announcement was that for the first time FNMA may, in certain cases, purchase *spot loans* or individual mortgages in condominium projects and PUDs without requiring prior approval of the entire project. According to FNMA, this will be generally done for resale mortgages secured by units in older projects or projects where most of the units have been sold and financed by other lenders. It should be noted that the purchase of spot loans in condominium projects or Planned Unit Developments is a significant change for FNMA. Before this announcement, FNMA would not purchase *any* spot loans in a condominium or PUD project. If you feel that you have a project which may qualify for this mortgage purchase program, you should contact a FNMA-approved lender in your area. If none of the lenders you contact is willing to work with you, contact your area FNMA office and they will assist you in finding a lender who will be willing to work with you.

Refinance/Resale Program On March 30, 1981, FNMA offered for the first time the Refinance/Resale Program to all FNMA-approved seller/servicers. First let us review the refinance portion of the program.

Under this portion of the program, any credit-worthy homeowner, whose current mortgage is owned by FNMA, may refinance the mortgage to include any equity in the property. This is true for all types of mortgages: VA-guaranteed, FHA-insured, or conventional. Usually a homeowner, to tap the cash reserve in his or her home, will have to negotiate a second mortgage. This type of mortgage will normally have a rather short term and the interest rate will be substantially above interest rates charged on first-lien mortgages. Under this program, FNMA will allow the homeowner to execute a new conventional first lien on his or her home up to 90 percent of the current value and the interest rate will generally be below the prevailing market rate. (The rate is a function of the balance, rate, and remaining term of the old loan, and the amount and term of the new loan.) In other words, this is a type of blended-yield mortgage (BYM). It should be noted that this program is not limited to owner-occupied properties. If you should have a client who has property that he or she no longer occupies, but FNMA owns the mortgage, this type of property can still be refinanced under this program, but the maximum loan is reduced to 80 percent of the appraised value. It should be noted that the major limitation to this program is any state law that may limit the refinancing of one's primary domicile. This is true in a few of the states which have a homestead law. You will need to contact an approved FNMA lender in your area to see if there are any restrictions on the program in your state.

The second portion of the program is the resale program. Under this program, a person wishing to purchase property using a wraparound or a second mortgage can, if the existing first lien mortgage is owned by FNMA, combine both the existing mortgage and the second or wraparound into a new first lien mortgage from FNMA with an interest rate that normally will be below the present market level. The program does require a minimum interest rate on the new mortgage of 11 percent.

Let us work through an example of how the Refinance Program may work, as illustrated in Figure 9-4.

The actual interest rate or yield on the refinance mortgage will be established by FNMA, but FNMA has published a "FNMA Refinance/Resale Mortgage Yield Estimating Table" as a guide. An excerpt of this table, shown in Figure 9-5, allows a lender or real estate salesperson to estimate the yield that will be required on a refinance mortgage.

This table is to be used for estimating purposes only. For the actual yield on resale mortgages, you will have to contact an approved FNMA seller/servicer, who in turn will contact FNMA for the actual yield.

One very important fact should be emphasized. FNMA will not enforce the acceleration-upon-sale (due-on-sale) provision on conventional mortgages originated under this program—either to refinance or upon the resale of a home where FNMA owns the mortgage—if the transfer of ownership occurs within one year from the date of the resale/refinance mortgage. It should be noted that the nonenforcement of the acceleration-upon-sale provisions is limited to increase in note rate, but the provision of credit

Figure 9-4. FNMA Resale Finance Program Example

The Thorntons plan to buy a house that is selling for $94,750, and they've checked different ways of financing its purchase. When they asked about getting a new, 30-year loan, the lender quoted them a rate of 16%; their monthly principal and interest payments, after putting 5% or $4,750 down, would be $1,210.28. Since the existing $41,592.01 VA-guaranteed loan on the house is assumable, they looked into taking over the payments on that mortgage and getting a $48,407.99 second mortgage at 18% for 10 years. The payments on the existing loan are $338.36 a month and payments on the new second mortgage would be $872.24, for a total of $1,210.60. Since the existing loan is owned by FNMA, they had one other option: a FNMA Resale Finance mortgage. They could get a $90,000 resale loan at 13.4 percent, with monthly payments of $1023.79, $186.49 a month less than a new first mortgage and $186.81 a month less than assuming the old loan and getting a new second mortgage.

	Existing Mortgage	*Resale Mortgage*	*New Mortgage*	*Old First And New Second Mortgage*	
Amount	$41,592.01	$90,000	$90,000	$41,592.01	(First)
				+48,407.99	(Second)
Rate	8.5%	13.4%	16%	8.5%	(First)
				18.00%	(Second)
Monthly Payment	$338.36	$1,023.79	$1,210.28	$338.36	(First)
				+872.24	(Second)
				$1,210.60	

Source: Federal National Mortgage Association news release, "FNMA's Refinance/Resale Finance Program."

Figure 9-5. FNMA Refinance/Resale Mortgage Yield Estimating Table

Old Note Rate and	*Loan Amounts*	*New Mortgage Amount ($,000)* 20	30	40	50	60	70	80	90	98.5
	10,000	12.600	14.250	15.100	15.600	15.875	16.125	16.300	16.500	16.600
7%	15,000	10.100*	12.600	13.875	14.600	15.100	15.500	15.700	15.875	16.100
	25,000	—	9.200*	11.375	12.600	13.500	14.000	14.500	14.800	15.100
	10,000	12.875	14.500	15.200	15.700	16.000	16.200	16.375	16.500	16.600
7½%	15,000	10.500*	12.875	14.100	14.750	15.200	15.600	15.800	16.000	16.100
	25,000	—	9.625*	11.700	12.875	13.625	14.200	14.625	15.000	15.200
	20,000	—	11.200	12.800	13.750	14.375	14.875	15.200	15.500	15.625
8%	30,000	—	—	10.375*	11.875	12.800	13.500	14.000	14.375	14.700
	40,000	—	—	—	9.875*	11.200	12.125	12.800	13.375	13.700
	20,000	—	11.600	13.100	14.000	14.600	15.000	15.300	15.600	15.750
8½%	30,000	—	—	10.800*	12.200	13.100	13.700	14.200	14.600	14.875
	40,000	—	—	—	10.375*	11.600	12.500	13.100	13.600	13.900
	20,000	—	11.800	13.250	14.100	14.700	15.100	15.375	15.625	15.800
9%	30,000	—	—	11.100	12.375	13.250	13.875	14.375	14.700	15.000
	40,000	—	—	—	10.600*	11.800	12.625	13.250	13.750	14.100
	30,000	—	—	11.375	12.600	13.500	14.100	14.500	14.800	15.100
9½%	40,000	—	—	—	11.000	12.100	12.875	13.500	13.900	14.200
	50,000	—	—	—	—	10.700*	11.700	12.400	13.000	13.375
	30,000	—	—	11.700	12.875	13.700	14.250	14.625	15.000	15.200
10%	40,000	—	—	—	11.300	12.375	13.100	13.700	14.100	14.400
	50,000	—	—	—	—	11.100	12.000	12.700	13.250	13.600

To estimate FNMA's minimum required yield on a new Refinance/Resale Mortgage, find the note rate and mortgage amount in the left column which most nearly approximate a mortgagor's old loan characteristics and read across to the yield under the new mortgage amount nearest that requested by the mortgagor.

*Minimum yield 11%.

Source: Federal National Mortgage Association, memo, *Resale and refinance program*, May 12, 1981.

Figure 9-6. FNMA/FHLMC Home Improvement Note, page 1

NOTE

...., 19......... ...., Colorado
City

....
Property Address City State Zip Code

1. BORROWER'S PROMISE TO PAY

In return for a loan that I have received, I promise to pay U.S. $.. (this amount will be called "principal"), plus interest, to the order of the Lender. The Lender is .... I understand that the Lender may transfer this Note. The Lender or anyone who takes this Note by transfer and who is entitled to receive payments under this Note will be called the "Note Holder."

2. INTEREST

I will pay interest at a yearly rate of ....%.

Interest will be charged on that part of principal which has not been paid. Interest will be charged beginning on the date of this Note and continuing until the full amount of principal has been paid.

3. PAYMENTS

I will pay principal and interest by making payments each month of U.S. $ ....

I will make my payments on the .... day of each month beginning on ...., 19 .... I will make these payments every month until I have paid all of the principal and interest and any other charges, described below, that I may owe under this Note. If, on ...., ..., I still owe amounts under this Note, I will pay all those amounts, in full, on that date.

I will make my monthly payments at .... or at a different place if required by the Note Holder.

4. BORROWER'S FAILURE TO PAY AS REQUIRED

(A) Late Charge for Overdue Payments

If the Note Holder has not received the full amount of any of my monthly payments by the end of .... calendar days after the date it is due, I will pay a late charge to the Note Holder. The amount of the charge will be ....% of my overdue payment, but not less than U.S. $ ....and not more than U.S. $ .... I will pay this late charge only once on any late payment.

(B) Default

If I do not pay the full amount of each monthly payment by the date stated in Section 3 above, I will be in default. Even if, at a time when I am in default, the Note Holder does not require me to pay immediately in full as described below, the Note Holder will still have the right to do so if I am in default at a later time.

(C) Notice From Note Holder

If I am in default for 10 days , the Note Holder may send me a written notice telling me that if I do not pay the overdue amount by a certain date the Note Holder may require me to pay immediately the full amount of principal which has not been paid and all the interest that I owe on that amount. That date must be at least 20 days after the date on which the notice is mailed to me or, if it is not mailed, 20 days after the date on which it is delivered to me.

(D) Payment of Note Holder's Costs and Expenses

If the Note Holder has required me to pay immediately in full as described above, the Note Holder will have the right tobe paid back for all of its reasonable costs and expenses to the extent not prohibited by applicable law. Those expenses include, for example, reasonable attorneys' fees.

5. THIS NOTE SECURED BY A DEED OF TRUST

In addition to the protections given to the Note Holder under this Note, a Deed of Trust, dated .... , 19..........., protects the Note Holder from possible losses which might result if I do not keep the promises which I make in this Note. That Deed of Trust describes how and under what conditions I may be required to make immediate payment in full of all amounts that I owe under this Note.

6. BORROWER'S PAYMENTS BEFORE THEY ARE DUE

I have the right to make payments of principal at any time before they are due. A payment of principal only is known as a "prepayment." When I make a prepayment, I will tell the Note Holder in a letter that I am doing so. A prepayment of all of the unpaid principal is known as a "full prepayment." A prepayment of only part of the unpaid principal is known as a "partial prepayment."

I may make a full prepayment or a partial prepayment without paying any penalty. The Note Holder will use all of my prepayments to reduce the amount of principal that I owe under this Note. If I make a partial prepayment, there will

COLORADO—HOME IMPROVEMENT—1/80—**FNMA/FHLMC UNIFORM INSTRUMENT**

Figure 9-7. FNMA/FHLMC Home Improvement Note, page 2

be no delays in the due dates or changes in the amounts of my monthly payments unless the Note Holder agrees in writing to those delays or changes. I may make a full prepayment at any time. If I choose to make a partial prepayment, the Note Holder may require me to make the prepayment on the same day that one of my monthly payments is due. The Note Holder may also require that the amount of my partial prepayment be equal to the amount of principal that would have been part of my next one or more monthly payments.

7. BORROWER'S WAIVERS

I waive my rights to require the Note Holder to do certain things. Those things are: (A) to demand payment of amounts due (known as "presentment"); (B) to give notice that amounts due have not been paid (known as "notice of dishonor"); (C) to obtain an official certification of nonpayment (known as a "protest"). Anyone else who agrees to keep the promises made in this Note, or who agrees to make payments to the Note Holder if I fail to keep my promises under this Note, or who signs this Note to transfer it to someone else also waives these rights. These persons are known as "guarantors, sureties and endorsers."

8. GIVING OF NOTICES

Any notice that must be given to me under this Note will be given by delivering it or by mailing it by certified mail addressed to me at the Property Address above. A notice will be delivered or mailed to me at a different address if I give the Note Holder a notice of my different address.

Any notice that must be given to the Note Holder under this Note will be given by mailing it by certified mail to the Note Holder at the address stated in Section 3 above. A notice will be mailed to the Note holder at a different address if I am given a notice of that different address.

9. RESPONSIBILITY OF PERSONS UNDER THIS NOTE

If more than one person signs this Note, each of us is fully and personally obligated to pay the full amount owed and to keep all of the promises made in this Note. Any guarantor, surety, or endorser of this Note (as described in Section 7 above) is also obligated to do these things. The Note Holder may enforce its rights under this Note against each of us individually or against all of us together. This means that any one of us may be required to pay all of the amounts owed under this Note. Any person who takes over my rights or obligations under this Note will have all of my rights and must keep all of my promises made in this Note. Any person who takes over the rights or obligations of a guarantor, surety, or endorser of this Note (as described in Section 7 above) is also obligated to keep all of the promises made in this Note.

....

Borrower

....

Borrower

....

Borrower

(Sign Original Only)

Figure 9-8. FNMA/FHLMC Home Improvement Deed of Trust

DEED OF TRUST

THIS DEED OF TRUST is made this . . . . day of . . . . ,
19. . . . , among the Grantor, ...
. . . . (herein "Borrower"), the Public Trustee of
. . . . County (herein "Trustee"),
and the Beneficiary, ... , a corporation
organized and existing under the laws of . . . . ,
whose address is . . . .
. . . . (herein "Lender").

BORROWER, in consideration of the indebtedness herein recited and the trust herein created, irrevocably grants and conveys to Trustee, in trust, with power of sale, the following described property located in the County of . . . . , State of Colorado:

which has the address of . . . . , ... ,
[Street] [City]
Colorado . . . . (herein "Property Address");
[Zip Code]

TOGETHER with all the improvements now or hereafter erected on the property, and all easements, rights, appurtenances and rents (subject however to the rights and authorities given herein to Lender to collect and apply such rents), all of which shall be deemed to be and remain a part of the property covered by this Deed of Trust; and all of the foregoing, together with said property (or the leasehold estate if this Deed of Trust is on a leasehold) are hereinafter referred to as the "Property";

TO SECURE to Lender the repayment of the indebtedness evidenced by Borrower's note dated . . . . and extensions and renewals thereof (herein "Note"), in the principal sum of U.S. $ . . . . , with interest thereon, providing for monthly installments of principal and interest, with the balance of the indebtedness, if not sooner paid, due and payable on . . . . ; the payment of all other sums, with interest thereon, advanced in accordance herewith to protect the security of this Deed of Trust; and the performance of the covenants and agreements of Borrower herein contained.

Borrower covenants that Borrower is lawfully seised of the estate hereby conveyed and has the right to grant and convey the Property, and that the Property is unencumbered, except for encumbrances of record. Borrower covenants that Borrower warrants and will defend generally the title to the Property against all claims and demands, subject to encumbrances of record.

UNIFORM COVENANTS. Borrower and Lender covenant and agree as follows:

1. Payment of Principal and Interest. Borrower shall promptly pay when due the principal and interest indebtedness evidenced by the Note and late charges as provided in the Note.

COLORADO—HOME IMPROVEMENT—1/80—**FNMA/FHLMC UNIFORM INSTRUMENT**

Figure 9-9. FNMA/FHLMC Home Improvement Deed of Trust, Covenants 2-10

2. Funds for Taxes and Insurance. Subject to applicable law or a written waiver by Lender, Borrower shall pay to Lender on the day monthly payments of principal and interest are payable under the Note, until the Note is paid in full, a sum (herein "Funds") equal to one-twelfth of the yearly taxes and assessments (including condominium and planned unit development assessments, if any), which may attain priority over this Deed of Trust, and ground rents on the Property, if any, plus one-twelfth of yearly premium installments for hazard insurance, plus one-twelfth of yearly premium installments for mortgage insurance, if any, all as reasonably estimated initially and from time to time by Lender on the basis of assessments and bills and reasonable estimates thereof. Borrower shall not be obligated to make such payments of Funds to Lender to the extent that Borrower makes such payments to the holder of a prior mortgage or deed of trust if such holder is an institutional lender.

If Borrower pays Funds to Lender, the Funds shall be held in an institution the deposits or accounts of which are insured or guaranteed by a Federal or state agency (including Lender if Lender is such an institution). Lender shall apply the Funds to pay said taxes, assessments, insurance premiums and ground rents. Lender may not charge for so holding and applying the Funds, analyzing said account or verifying and compiling said assessments and bills, unless Lender pays Borrower interest on the Funds and applicable law permits Lender to make such a charge. Borrower and Lender may agree in writing at the time of execution of this Deed of Trust that interest on the Funds shall be paid to Borrower, and unless such agreement is made or applicable law requires such interest to be paid, Lender shall not be required to pay Borrower any interest or earnings on the Funds. Lender shall give to Borrower, without charge, an annual accounting of the Funds showing credits and debits to the Funds and the purpose for which each debit to the Funds was made. The Funds are pledged as additional security for the sums secured by this Deed of Trust.

If the amount of the Funds held by Lender, together with the future monthly installments of Funds payable prior to the due dates of taxes, assessments, insurance premiums and ground rents, shall exceed the amount required to pay said taxes, assessments, insurance premiums and ground rents as they fall due, such excess shall be, at Borrower's option, either promptly repaid to Borrower or credited to Borrower on monthly installments of Funds. If the amount of the Funds held by Lender shall not be sufficient to pay taxes, assessments, insurance premiums and ground rents as they fall due, Borrower shall pay to Lender any amount necessary to make up the deficiency in one or more payments as Lender may require.

Upon payment in full of all sums secured by this Deed of Trust, Lender shall promptly refund to Borrower any Funds held by Lender. If under paragraph 17 hereof the Property is sold or the Property is otherwise acquired by Lender, Lender shall apply, no later than immediately prior to the sale of the Property or its acquisition by Lender, any Funds held by Lender at the time of application as a credit against the sums secured by this Deed of Trust.

3. Application of Payments. Unless applicable law provides otherwise, all payments received by Lender under the Note and paragraphs 1 and 2 hereof shall be applied by Lender first in payment of amounts payable to Lender by Borrower under paragraph 2 hereof, then to interest payable on the Note, and then to the principal of the Note.

4. Prior Mortgages and Deeds of Trust; Charges; Liens. Borrower shall perform all of Borrower's obligations under any mortgage, deed of trust or other security agreement with a lien which has priority over this Deed of Trust, including Borrower's covenants to make payments when due. Borrower shall pay or cause to be paid all taxes, assessments and other charges, fines and impositions attributable to the Property which may attain a priority over this Deed of Trust, and leasehold payments or ground rents, if any.

5. Hazard Insurance. Borrower shall keep the improvements now existing or hereafter erected on the Property insured against loss by fire, hazards included within the term "extended coverage", and such other hazards as Lender may require and in such amounts and for such periods as Lender may require.

The insurance carrier providing the insurance shall be chosen by Borrower subject to approval by Lender; provided, that such approval shall not be unreasonably withheld. All insurance policies and renewals thereof shall be in a form acceptable to Lender and shall include a standard mortgage clause in favor of and in a form acceptable to Lender. Lender shall have the right to hold the policies and renewals thereof, subject to the terms of any mortgage, deed of trust or other security agreement with a lien which has priority over this Deed of Trust.

In the event of loss, Borrower shall give prompt notice to the insurance carrier and Lender. Lender may make proof of loss if not made promptly by Borrower.

If the Property is abandoned by Borrower, or if Borrower fails to respond to Lender within 30 days from the date notice is mailed by Lender to Borrower that the insurance carrier offers to settle a claim for insurance benefits, Lender is authorized to collect and apply the insurance proceeds at Lender's option either to restoration or repair of the Property or to the sums secured by this Deed of Trust.

6. Preservation and Maintenance of Property; Leaseholds; Condominiums; Planned Unit Developments. Borrower shall keep the Property in good repair and shall not commit waste or permit impairment or deterioration of the Property and shall comply with the provisions of any lease if this Deed of Trust is on a leasehold. If this Deed of Trust is on a unit in a condominium or a planned unit development, Borrower shall perform all of Borrower's obligations under the declaration or covenants creating or governing the condominium or planned unit development, the by-laws and regulations of the condominium or planned unit development, and constituent documents.

7. Protection of Lender's Security. If Borrower fails to perform the covenants and agreements contained in this Deed of Trust, or if any action or proceeding is commenced which materially affects Lender's interest in the Property, then Lender, at Lender's option, upon notice to Borrower, may make such appearances, disburse such sums, including reasonable attorneys' fees, and take such action as is necessary to protect Lender's interest. If Lender required mortgage insurance as a condition of making the loan secured by this Deed of Trust, Borrower shall pay the premiums required to maintain such insurance in effect until such time as the requirement for such insurance terminates in accordance with Borrower's and Lender's written agreement or applicable law.

Any amounts disbursed by Lender pursuant to this paragraph 7, with interest thereon, at the Note rate, shall become additional indebtedness of Borrower secured by this Deed of Trust. Unless Borrower and Lender agree to other terms of payment, such amounts shall be payable upon notice from Lender to Borrower requesting payment thereof. Nothing contained in this paragraph 7 shall require Lender to incur any expense or take any action hereunder.

8. Inspection. Lender may make or cause to be made reasonable entries upon and inspections of the Property, provided that Lender shall give Borrower notice prior to any such inspection specifying reasonable cause therefor related to Lender's interest in the Property.

9. Condemnation. The proceeds of any award or claim for damages, direct or consequential, in connection with any condemnation or other taking of the Property, or part thereof, or for conveyance in lieu of condemnation, are hereby assigned and shall be paid to Lender, subject to the terms of any mortgage, deed of trust or other security agreement with a lien which has priority over this Deed of Trust.

10. Borrower Not Released; Forbearance By Lender Not a Waiver. Extension of the time for payment or modification of amortization of the sums secured by this Deed of Trust granted by Lender to any successor in interest of Borrower shall not operate to release, in any manner, the liability of the original Borrower and Borrower's successors

Figure 9-10. FNMA/FHLMC Home Improvement Deed of Trust, Covenants 11-17

in interest. Lender shall not be required to commence proceedings against such successor or refuse to extend time for payment or otherwise modify amortization of the sums secured by this Deed of Trust by reason of any demand made by the original Borrower and Borrower's successors in interest. Any forbearance by Lender in exercising any right or remedy hereunder, or otherwise afforded by applicable law, shall not be a waiver of or preclude the exercise of any such right or remedy.

11. Successors and Assigns Bound; Joint and Several Liability; Co-signers. The covenants and agreements herein contained shall bind, and the rights hereunder shall inure to, the respective successors and assigns of Lender and Borrower, subject to the provisions of paragraph 16 hereof. All covenants and agreements of Borrower shall be joint and several. Any Borrower who co-signs this Deed of Trust, but does not execute the Note, (a) is co-signing this Deed of Trust only to grant and convey that Borrower's interest in the Property to Trustee under the terms of this Deed of Trust, (b) is not personally liable on the Note or under this Deed of Trust, and (c) agrees that Lender and any other Borrower hereunder may agree to extend, modify, forbear, or make any other accommodations with regard to the terms of this Deed of Trust or the Note, without that Borrower's consent and without releasing that Borrower or modifying this Deed of Trust as to that Borrower's interest in the Property.

12. Notice. Except for any notice required under applicable law to be given in another manner, (a) any notice to Borrower provided for in this Deed of Trust shall be given by delivering it or by mailing such notice by certified mail addressed to Borrower at the Property Address or at such other address as Borrower may designate by notice to Lender as provided herein, and (b) any notice to Lender shall be given by certified mail to Lender's address stated herein or to such other address as Lender may designate by notice to Borrower as provided herein. Any notice provided for in this Deed of Trust shall be deemed to have been given to Borrower or Lender when given in the manner designated herein.

13. Governing Law; Severability. The state and local laws applicable to this Deed of Trust shall be the laws of the jurisdiction in which the Property is located. The foregoing sentence shall not limit the applicability of Federal law to this Deed of Trust. In the event that any provision or clause of this Deed of Trust or the Note conflicts with applicable law, such conflict shall not affect other provisions of this Deed of Trust or the Note which can be given effect without the conflicting provision, and to this end the provisions of this Deed of Trust and the Note are declared to be severable. As used herein, "costs", "expenses" and "attorneys' fees" include all sums to the extent not prohibited by applicable law or limited herein.

14. Borrower's Copy. Borrower shall be furnished a conformed copy of the Note and of this Deed of Trust at the time of execution or after recordation hereof.

15. Rehabilitation Loan Agreement. Borrower shall fulfill all of Borrower's obligations under any home rehabilitation, improvement, repair, or other loan agreement which Borrower enters into with Lender. Lender, at Lender's option, may require Borrower to execute and deliver to Lender, in a form acceptable to Lender, an assignment of any rights, claims or defenses which Borrower may have against parties who supply labor, materials or services in connection with improvements made to the Property.

16. Transfer of the Property. If Borrower sells or transfers all or any part of the Property or an interest therein, excluding (a) the creation of a lien or encumbrance subordinate to this Deed of Trust, (b) a transfer by devise, descent, or by operation of law upon the death of a joint tenant, or (c) the grant of any leasehold interest of three years or less not containing an option to purchase, Borrower shall cause to be submitted information required by Lender to evaluate the transferee as if a new loan were being made to the transferee. Borrower will continue to be obligated under the Note and this Deed of Trust unless Lender releases Borrower in writing.

If Lender, on the basis of any information obtained regarding the transferee, reasonably determines that Lender's security may be impaired, or that there is an unacceptable likelihood of a breach of any covenant or agreement in this Deed of Trust, or if the required information is not submitted, Lender may declare all of the sums secured by this Deed of Trust to be immediately due and payable. If Lender exercises such option to accelerate, Lender shall mail Borrower notice of acceleration in accordance with paragraph 12 hereof. Such notice shall provide a period of not less than 30 days from the date the notice is mailed or delivered within which Borrower may pay the sums declared due. If Borrower fails to pay such sums prior to the expiration of such period, Lender may, without further notice or demand on Borrower, invoke any remedies permitted by paragraph 17 hereof.

NON-UNIFORM COVENANTS. Borrower and Lender further covenant and agree as follows:

17. Acceleration; Remedies. Except as provided in paragraph 16 hereof, upon Borrower's breach of any covenant or agreement of Borrower in this Deed of Trust, including the covenants to pay when due any sums secured by this Deed of Trust, Lender prior to acceleration shall give notice to Borrower as provided in paragraph 12 hereof specifying: (1) the breach; (2) the action required to cure such breach; (3) a date, not less than 20 days from the date the notice is mailed to Borrower, by which such breach must be cured; and (4) that failure to cure such breach on or before the date specified in the notice may result in acceleration of the sums secured by this Deed of Trust and sale of the Property. The notice shall further inform Borrower of the right to reinstate after acceleration and the right to bring a court action to assert the nonexistence of a default or any other defense of Borrower to acceleration and sale. If the breach is not cured on or before the date specified in the notice, Lender, at Lender's option, may declare all of the sums secured by this Deed of Trust to be immediately due and payable without further demand and may invoke the power of sale and any other remedies permitted by applicable law. Lender shall be entitled to collect all reasonable costs and expenses incurred in pursuing the remedies provided in this paragraph 17, including, but not limited to, reasonable attorneys' fees.

If Lender invokes the power of sale, Lender shall give written notice to Trustee of the occurrence of an event of default and of Lender's election to cause the Property to be sold. Lender shall mail a copy of such notice to Borrower as provided in paragraph 12 hereof. Trustee shall record a copy of such notice in the county in which the Property is located. Trustee shall publish a notice of sale for the time and in the manner provided by applicable law and shall mail copies of such notice of sale in the manner prescribed by applicable law to Borrower and to the other persons prescribed by applicable law. After the lapse of such time as may be required by applicable law, Trustee, without demand on Borrower, shall sell the Property at public auction to the highest bidder for cash at the time and place and under the terms designated in the notice of sale in one or more parcels and in such order as Trustee may determine. Trustee may postpone sale of all or any parcel of the Property by public announcement at the time and place of any previously scheduled sale. Lender or Lender's designee may purchase the Property at any sale.

Trustee shall deliver to the purchaser Trustee's certificate describing the Property and the time when the purchaser will be entitled to Trustee's deed thereto. The recitals in Trustee's deed shall be prima facie evidence of the truth of the statements made therein. Trustee shall apply the proceeds of the sale in the following order: (a) to all reasonable costs and expenses of the sale, including, but not limited to, reasonable Trustee's and attorneys' fees and costs of title evidence; (b) to all sums secured by this Deed of Trust; and (c) the excess, if any, to the person or persons legally entitled thereto.

18. Borrower's Right to Reinstate. Notwithstanding Lender's acceleration of the sums secured by this Deed of

Figure 9-11. FNMA/FHLMC Home Improvement Deed of Trust, Covenants 18-21

Trust due to Borrower's breach, Borrower shall have the right to have any proceedings begun by Lender to enforce this Deed of Trust discontinued at any time prior to the earlier to occur of (i) the fifth day before sale of the Property pursuant to the power of sale contained in this Deed of Trust or (ii) entry of a judgment enforcing this Deed of Trust if: (a) Borrower pays Lender all sums which would be then due under this Deed of Trust and the Note had no acceleration occurred; (b) Borrower cures all breaches of any other covenants or agreements of Borrower contained in this Deed of Trust; (c) Borrower pays all reasonable expenses incurred by Lender and Trustee in enforcing the covenants and agreements of Borrower contained in this Deed of Trust, and in enforcing Lender's and Trustee's remedies as provided in paragraph 17 hereof, including, but not limited to, reasonable attorneys' fees and Trustee's expenses and withdrawal fee; and (d) Borrower takes such action as Lender may reasonably require to assure that the lien of this Deed of Trust, Lender's interest in the Property and Borrower's obligation to pay the sums secured by this Deed of Trust shall continue unimpaired. Upon such payment and cure by Borrower, this Deed of Trust and the obligations secured hereby shall remain in full force and effect as if no acceleration had occurred.

19. Assignment of Rents; Appointment of Receiver; Lender in Possession. As additional security hereunder, Borrower hereby assigns to Lender the rents of the Property, provided that Borrower shall, prior to acceleration under paragraph 17 hereof or abandonment of the Property, have the right to collect and retain such rents as they become due and payable.

Upon acceleration under paragraph 17 hereof or abandonment of the Property, Lender, in person, by agent or by judicially appointed receiver shall be entitled to enter upon, take possession of and manage the Property and to collect the rents of the Property including those past due. All rents collected by Lender or the receiver shall be applied first to payment of the costs of management of the Property and collection of rents, including, but not limited to, receiver's fees, premiums on receiver's bonds and reasonable attorneys' fees, and then to the sums secured by this Deed of Trust. Lender and the receiver shall be liable to account only for those rents actually received.

20. Release. Upon payment of all sums secured by this Deed of Trust, Lender shall request Trustee to release this Deed of Trust and shall produce for Trustee duly cancelled all notes evidencing indebtedness secured by this Deed of Trust. Trustee shall release this Deed of Trust without further inquiry or liability. Borrower shall pay all costs of recordation, if any, and shall pay the statutory Trustee's fees.

21. Waiver of Homestead. Borrower hereby waives all right of homestead exemption in the Property.

**REQUEST FOR NOTICE OF DEFAULT
AND FORECLOSURE UNDER SUPERIOR
MORTGAGES OR DEEDS OF TRUST**

Borrower and Lender request the holder of any mortgage, deed of trust or other encumbrance with a lien which has priority over this Deed of Trust to give Notice to Lender, at Lender's address set forth on page one of this Deed of Trust, of any default under the superior encumbrance and of any sale or other foreclosure action.

IN WITNESS WHEREOF, Borrower has executed this Deed of Trust.

.... —Borrower

.... —Borrower

STATE OF COLORADO, ... County ss:

The foregoing instrument was acknowledged before me this .... day of ...., 19...., by ....

WITNESS my hand and official seal.

My Commission expires:

....
Notary Public

Figure 9-12. FNMA/FHLMC Home Improvement Due-on-Transfer Rider

DUE-ON-TRANSFER RIDER

Notice: This rider adds a provision to the Security Instrument allowing the Lender to require repayment of the Note in full upon transfer of the property.

This Due-On-Transfer Rider is made this .... day of ...., 19........., and is incorporated into and shall be deemed to amend and supplement the Mortgage, Deed of Trust, or Deed to Secure Debt (the "Security Instrument") of the same date given by the undersigned (the "Borrower") to secure Borrower's Note to .... (the "Lender") of the same date (the "Note") and covering the property described in the Security Instrument and located at:

....
(Property Address)

AMENDED COVENANT. In addition to the covenants and agreements made in the Security Instrument, Borrower and Lender further covenant and agree as follows:

A. TRANSFER OF THE PROPERTY OR A BENEFICIAL INTEREST IN BORROWER

Uniform Covenant 16 of the Security Instrument is amended to read as follows:

16. Transfer of the Property or a Beneficial Interest in Borrower. If all or any part of the Property or an interest therein is sold or transferred by Borrower (or if a beneficial interest in Borrower is sold or transferred and Borrower is not a natural person or persons but is a corporation, partnership, trust or other legal entity) without Lender's prior written consent, excluding (a) the creation of a lien or encumbrance subordinate to this Security Instrument which does not relate to a transfer of rights of occupancy in the property, (b) the creation of a purchase money security interest for household appliances, (c) a transfer by devise, descent or by operation of law upon the death of a joint tenant or (d) the grant of any leasehold interest of three years or less not containing an option to purchase, Lender may, at Lender's option, declare all the sums secured by this Security Instrument to be immediately due and payable.

If Lender exercises such option to accelerate, Lender shall mail Borrower notice of acceleration in accordance with paragraph 12 hereof. Such notice shall provide a period of not less than 30 days from the date the notice is mailed within which Borrower may pay the sums declared due. If Borrower fails to pay such sums prior to the expiration of such period, Lender may, without further notice or demand on Borrower, invoke any remedies permitted by paragraph 17 hereof.

Lender may consent to a sale or transfer if: (1) Borrower causes to be submitted to Lender information required by Lender to evaluate the transferee as if a new loan were being made to the transferee; (2) Lender reasonably determines that Lender's security will not be impaired and that the risk of a breach of any covenant or agreement in this Security Instrument is acceptable; (3) interest will be payable on the sums secured by this Security Instrument at a rate acceptable to Lender; (4) changes in the terms of the Note and this Security Instrument required by Lender are made, including, for example, periodic adjustment in the interest rate, a different final payment date for the loan, and addition of unpaid interest to principal; and (5) the transferee signs an assumption agreement that is acceptable to Lender and that obligates the transferee to keep all the promises and agreements made in the Note and in this Security Instrument, as modified if required by Lender. To the extent permitted by applicable law, Lender also may charge a reasonable fee as a condition to Lender's consent to any sale or transfer.

Borrower will continue to be obligated under the Note and this Security Instrument unless Lender releases Borrower in writing.

IN WITNESS WHEREOF, Borrower has executed this Due-On-Transfer Rider.

....(Seal)
-Borrower

....(Seal)
-Borrower

DUE-ON-TRANSFER RIDER-Second Mortgage—4/82-**FNMA UNIFORM INSTRUMENT**

underwriting of the person or persons acquiring title to the property will still be enforced.

Second Mortgage Purchase Program On November 30, 1981, FNMA initiated a program of purchasing second mortgages in several states. With this program, FNMA will purchase an interest in pools of second mortgages originated by primary lenders that have experience in the origination of second mortgages. The interest or participation by FNMA in a pool of second mortgages can range from 50 percent to a maximum of 95 percent of the value of the loans. Due to the passage of usury laws (or other laws that may affect second mortgages) by several states, this program will not be available to all of the states. For availability in your state, you will need to contact any FNMA approved seller/servicer in your area.

FNMA has issued, jointly with the Federal Home Loan Mortgage Corporation, a note and mortgage/deed of trust. These FNMA/FHLMC forms are identified by a title appearing at the bottom of the page of the note and the first page of the mortgage/deed of trust. The identification information will be: "Name of the State—Home Improvement—Date of the form—FNMA/FHLMC Uniform Instrument." A sample of the note and deed of trust authorized for use with the second mortgage purchase program is illustrated in Figures 9-6 through 9-11.

In addition to the creation of a uniform note and mortgage/deed of trust, FNMA has created a "Due on Transfer." This document, Figure 9-12, has the legend or title: "Due-On-Transfer—Home Improvement—Date of the form—FNMA Uniform Instrument." This Due-on-Transfer Rider must accompany any second mortgage sold to FNMA.

FNMA will purchase conventional second mortgages on one- to four-family homes including units in a condominium project and/or a planned unit development. Accordingly, the underlying first lien can be either a conventional, VA-guaranteed, or FHA-insured mortgage.

The maximum loan-to-value ratio authorized under this program is as follows:

1. If the property is owner-occupied, the first and second lien combined outstanding principal balance may not exceed 80 percent of the property's value.
2. If the property is nonowner-occupied, the first and second liens' combined outstanding principal balance may not exceed 70 percent of the property's value.

In addition to the maximum loan-to-value ratio, FNMA has set the following maximum terms:

1. If the mortgage is fully amortizing over the term of the mortgage, the term may be from three to fifteen years.
2. If the mortgage is not fully amortizing, the term of the mortgage may be from five to fifteen years, but the payments may be calculated as if the mortgage were to be repaid in thirty years. It should be noted that with this type of amortization schedule, the borrower will have a lump sum payment due at the end of the five- to fifteen-year term.

The maximum loan amount under this program is calculated in two ways: (1) if FNMA owns both the first and second mortgage, and (2) if FNMA owns only the second mortgage. If FNMA owns both, the combined outstanding principal balance of the first and second may not exceed FNMA's conventional mortgage maximum. If FNMA does not own the first, the limits apply to the second only.

One-family	$107,000
Two-family	$136,800
Three-family	$165,100
Four-family	$205,300

The maximum amounts are increased by 50 percent for the states of Alaska and Hawaii.

One very important fact should be noted at this time: in addition to second mortgages originated by approved lenders, purchase-money second mortgages that are taken back by a home seller may also be eligible for purchase under this program. To be eligible, the second mortgage must be originated by a FNMA-approved second lender according to FNMA's second mortgage guidelines and executed on the FNMA-approved forms, including the due-on-transfer rider.

Adjustable-Rate Mortgage Purchase Program On June 25, 1981, FNMA announced its program to purchase adjustable-rate mortgages beginning August 7, 1981. In this initial program FNMA purchases eight different types of ARMs based upon five different indexes.

According to the rules of the program, any standard ARM or plan must be based on one of the five approved indexes listed below:

1. Six-month U.S. Treasury bills
2. One-year U.S. Treasury securities
3. Three-year U.S. Treasury securities
4. Five-year U.S. Treasury securities
5. Federal Home Loan Bank Board series of closed loans (which translates to the monthly average contract interest rate charged by all lenders on mortgage loans for previously occupied homes)

The indexes based on the U.S. securities are published weekly in the Federal Reserve Board Statistical Release H.15(519). The Federal Home Loan Bank Board publishes the monthly average contract interest rate in the *Federal Home Loan Bank Board Journal* monthly.

FNMA may consider purchasing other ARMs not based on their standard indexes, but based on some other indexes, including the following:

1. Federal Home Bank Board individual districts costs of funds
2. Federal Home Loan Bank Board system cost of funds
3. Three-month U.S. Treasury bills
4. Two-year U.S. Treasury securities

Adjustment Intervals In addition to specifying the indexes to be used, FNMA has established the interval between interest rate adjustment for each standard plan. The intervals range from six months to five years.

Interest rate adjustment Unless the plan has an interest rate change cap, the interest rate will be adjusted at any one adjustment period by the amount of change in the index, based on the latest published value of the index. Thus, the new mortgage rate at the date of adjustment would be the new index value plus the margin or spread over the index built into the mortgage rate at the time of origination. This margin or spread reflects the lenders' cost of funds over the index plus a return on investment.

For example, if at the time of origination the weekly average for the six-month U.S. Treasury bills is 12.65 and is the basis or index on the mortgage and the lender is seeking a margin or spread of 4 percent, the face interest rate at the time of origination would be 12.65 plus 4 percent, or 16.65 percent. What happens if at an adjustment period the index falls to 10.65? In this case, the new interest rate would be the current index, 10.65, plus the spread or margin of 4 percent, or 14.65 percent. It should be noted that the margin or spread is set at origination and may not be changed. As a real estate professional, you should "shop" your lenders to see which have the lowest margin or spread.

FNMA has limited the amount of interest rate adjustment either up or down on two of the standard plans (plans 5 and 8). Each of these plans limits the adjustment to 2 percent per year. Thus, on plan 5 where the interest is adjusted every two and a half years, the maximum adjustment at any one time would be 5 percent. It should be noted that this is a limit for each adjustment period with no limit over the life of the mortgage. In fact, none of the plans has any lifetime limit on interest rate adjustment, either up or down.

Principal and interest payment adjustment Three of the standard plans (plans 1, 3, and 4) that FNMA will purchase may have principal and interest payment caps that will limit the increases in the monthly payment to 7.5 percent per year for an ARM that is based on the one-year treasury securities or 7.5 percent every six months for those ARMs based on the six-month treasury bills. It should be noted that if the index indicates an increase in the excess of 7.5 percent, the borrower must be given the option of either increasing the payments by more than the 7.5 percent, or invoking the cap. If the cap is used, the mortgage will either go into negative amortization or reduced amortization of the outstanding principal balance. Reduced amortization means that the amount of the payment credited to the reduction of principal will be less than the original amount calculated at the time of origination. If negative amortization occurs, it is limited by FNMA. The limitation is that the amount of negative amortization may not increase the outstanding loan balance to more than 125 percent of the original principal balance. These types of ARMs contain a provision that will require the payment to be reset every five years, without regard to the 7.5 percent cap, to a level that will allow the mortgage to be paid off over its remaining life.

According to FNMA, the five-year adjustment will prevent a large buildup in the borrower's debt, thus not making a large balloon payment due upon the sale of the house.

Interestingly, all but one of the plans call for an adjustment in the interest rate to be reflected in a change in the payment at the time of each interest rate change. Plan 2 calls for a rate adjustment every six months, but the payment is only adjusted every three years. If the index has been constantly going up over the three-year period, the mortgage will go into negative amortization. Since there is no cap on the amount the monthly payment may increase, the payment will be increased to a level sufficient to amortize the mortgage, including the amount of negative amortization at each three-year adjustment based on the new payment rate. This is quite different from the three plans already discussed.

Summary of standard plans We have reviewed the basic provisions of the eight standard ARM plans of FNMA, but to better understand the plans, Figure 9-13 lists all of the programs, showing the interest rate index, the interest rate adjustment period, the payment adjustment period, the maximum interest rate adjustment, if any, and the maximum payment adjustment.

For three of its ARM plans (2, 4, and 6), FNMA offers a graduated payment feature as an option. With this feature, the mortgage is then called a Graduated-Payment Adjustable Rate Mortgage

Underwriting The ARM purchased by FNMA will be underwritten using the initial interest rate and the standard FNMA guidelines for income ratios and property standards. According to FNMA, for any mortgage with a loan-to-value ratio in excess of 90 percent and which provides for negative amortization, the 25 to 28 percent income-to-payment ratio will be strictly enforced.

Due-on-sale or acceleration-on-sale A due- or an acceleration-on-sale clause is mandatory for all eight ARM plans and will be enforced where allowed.

Figure 9-13. Summary of FNMA's Standard Adjustable-Rate Mortgage Plans

Plan	*Interest Rate Index*	*Interest Rate Adjustment Period*	*Payment Adjustment Period*	*Maximum Interest Rate Adjustment*	*Maximum Payment Adjustment*
1	6 month T-Bills	6 months	6 months	—	7.5% each 6 months
2	6 month T-Bills	6 months	3 years	—	—
3	1-year Treasury Security	1 year	1 year	—	7.5% each year
4	3-year Treasury Security	2.5 years	2.5 years	—	18.75% each 2.5 years
5	3-year Treasury Security	2.5 years	2.5 years	5% each 2.5 years	—
6	5-year Treasury Security	5 years	5 years	—	—
7	FHLBB Series of Closed Loans	1 year	1 year	—	—
8	FHLBB Series of Closed Loans	1 year	1 year	2% each year	—

Source: Federal National Mortgage Association, memo, *Adjustable-Rate Mortgages*, July 21, 1981, p. 4

Graduated-payment adjustable rate mortgage On February 25, 1982, FNMA announced its intention to purchase these types of mortgages. These GPARMs that will be purchased by FNMA are primarily using variations of Plans 2, 4, and 6 of the ARM mentioned in the previous section. According to FNMA's Program Announcements 18 and 21, the graduated payment period for Plans 2 and 4 is three years and the graduated payment period for Plan 6 is five years.

The initial monthly payment will be calculated to be an amount that when the 7.5 percent annual increase is taken over the life of the graduation period—three years for Plans 2 and 4 and five years for Plan 6—the monthly payment at the end of the authorized graduation period will be sufficient to pay off the outstanding principal balance over the remaining life of the mortgage at the initial interest rate. In other words, if the initial interest rate is 14 percent, the monthly payment at the end of the graduation will be sufficient to pay the remaining principal balance using the 14 percent rate. To simplify the calculations, FNMA has prepared "Monthly Payment Factor Tables" for both Plans 4 and 6. These tables are available from any FNMA-approved lender.

In regard to the adjustment in the interest rates for the GPARMs that FNMA will purchase, they are authorized for Plans 2 and 4 every three years and for Plan 6 every five years. Thus, during the graduation period of these mortgages, there would only be an increase in the monthly payment based on the authorized payment graduation and only after the end of the graduation period may the interest rate be adjusted.

It should be noted that the GPARM purchase plan of FNMA does have the provision that will allow the borrower to select a payment cap of 7.5 percent payment increase per year per adjustment period for the life of the mortgage. The reason for this option is to soften the effect of a change in the interest rate at each of the interest rate adjustment dates. If you have a question about

Figure 9-14. Authorized Notes and Riders for FNMA Adjustable-Rate Mortgage Program

FNMA ADJUSTABLE RATE MORTGAGE PROGRAM

Plan Number	*Note Form*	*Rider Form*
1	*Adjustable Rate Note (With Deferred Payment Provisions)*	*Adjustable Rate Rider (Deferred Payment Provisions)*
2	*Not Available at this time*	*Not Available at this time*
3	*Adjustable Rate Note (With Deferred Payment Provisions)*	*Adjustable Rate Rider (Deferred Payment Provisions)*
4	*Adjustable Rate Note (With Deferred Payment Provisions)*	*Adjustable Rate Rider (Deferred Payment Provisions)*
5	*Adjustable Rate Note (With Interest Rate Limit)*	*Adjustable Rate Rider (Limit on Interest Rate Changes)*
6	*Adjustable Rate Note*	*Adjustable Rate Rider*
7	*Adjustable Rate Note*	*Adjustable Rate Rider*
8	*Adjustable Rate Note (With Interest Rate Limit)*	*Adjustable Rate Rider (Limit on Interest Rate Changes)*

Source: Federal National Mortgage Association, Dallas, Texas, memo, *Adjustable-Rate Mortgage Forms—August 14, 1981,* p. 2.

this purchase program or any other FNMA mortgage purchase program, you should contact any FNMA-approved lender.

ARM and GPARM Notes and Mortgage/Deed of Trust Riders As with many of the other mortgage purchase programs, FNMA has developed standard instruments for use with the ARM and the GPARM purchase programs. Figure 9-14 shows the note form and the rider to be used with each of the ARM plans. Copies of these note and riders can be secured by contacting any FNMA-approved lender. In reviewing the figure, we can see that FNMA has developed three uniform notes and adjustable riders.

FNMA has also developed uniform instruments to be used by approved lenders selling mortgages to FNMA using the GPARM purchase program. Since, according to FNMA, the GPARM mortgage is the most popular, you as a real estate professional will most likely come in contact with this type of mortgage. We will review the notes and rider used in conjunction with the Plan 4 GPARM and Plan 6 GPARM.

First, see the Plan 4 Graduated Payment Note, Figures 9-15, 9-16, and 9-17. The first page of the note, Figure 9-15, indicates the the interest rate of the note will change every three years. At the top of the note in bold type, the borrower is advised that the monthly payment will increase at the rate of 7.5 percent per year for the first three years of the note. Also in this section, the borrower is advised that he or she may be able to limit the amount the payment may increase for the second three years of this note. The borrower is further advised that the payments may increase or decrease, depending on the change in the interest rate. Finally, the borrower is told that the amount he or she repays may be more than he or she borrowed, but the amount is limited to 125 percent of the original amount. This mortgage, then, has the feature of negative amortization.

Now for the main body of page one. Paragraph 1 is similar to the standard note illustrated in Chapter 2. Paragraph 2, INTEREST, is divided into three subsections. The first subsection states the "initial rate of interest" of the note and that this rate will change every thirty-six months. The second subsection indicates the interest rate index that will be used and where the interest rate index is published. The final subsection identifies the interest rate that will be paid before and after default.

Paragraph 3 of the note gives the date of the first and last payment of the note, as well as the address. The borrower will be required to make each monthly payment unless this address is changed and the borrower is notified of such a change.

Paragraph 5, Figure 9-16, indicates the amount of the first twelve payments and gives the factor that the borrower may use to multiply the previous monthly payment in order to calculate the payment for the next year. For example, if the initial payment of P and I was $879.53, the borrower would multiply the payment by the factor of 1.075 ($879.53 × 1.075) to calculate the payment for the second year of $945.49. To calculate the monthly payment for the third year, the borrower would then multiply the second year's P and I payment by the same factor. To determine the total monthly payment, the borrower would have to add the amount of the required escrows.

Paragraph 6, BORROWER'S RIGHT TO LIMIT AMOUNT OF MONTHLY PAYMENTS 37-72, is rather self-explanatory in that it does allow the borrower to limit the payments for the second three years of the note with certain limitations that are outlined in subparagraphs (B) and (C). The borrower is given information on how to calculate the monthly payments for each of the second three years, as long as they are not affected by subsection (B) and (C) of this paragraph.

Paragraph 7 is self-explanatory.

The next paragraph, INCREASE IN THE PRINCIPAL AMOUNT TO BE PAID, explains how the negative amortization will be figured and states that interest will be charged on the amount of negative amortization. Subsection (B) of this paragraph limits the amount of negative amortization to an amount that would equal 125 percent of the original amount borrowed. This means that if $100,000 was the original amount borrowed, the maximum amount of negative amortization is $25,000. Thus, the maximum outstanding loan amount would be $125,000.

Paragraph 9, NOTICE, is similar to that contained in the standard note and is self-explanatory.

The following paragraph, BORROWER'S RIGHT TO REPAY, is rather important in that

Figure 9-15. ***FNMA Graduated Payment Note—Plan 4, page 1***

GRADUATED PAYMENT NOTE
(With Interest Rate Changes Every 3 Years)

This Note contains provisions allowing for changes in my interest rate and monthly payments.

My monthly payment will increase by 7½% each year during the first three years of this Note. If the provisions of this Note permit me to do so, I will be able to limit my monthly payment increases to 7½% each year during the second three years of this Note. My remaining monthly payments also could increase or decrease, depending on changes in my interest rate.

The principal amount I must repay will be larger than the amount I originally borrowed, but not more than 125% of the original amount.

...., ...
[City] [State]

...., 19.......

....
(Property Address)

1. BORROWER'S PROMISE TO PAY

In return for a loan that I have received, I promise to pay U.S. $... plus any amounts added in accordance with Section 8 (A) of this Note (the total amount is called "principal"), plus interest, to the order of the Lender. The Lender is .... I understand that the Lender may transfer this Note. The Lender or anyone who takes this Note by transfer and who is entitled to receive payments under this Note is called the "Note Holder."

2. INTEREST

(A) Interest Owed

Interest will be charged on that part of principal which has not been paid. Interest will be charged beginning on the date of this Note and continuing until the full amount of principal has been paid.

Beginning on the date of this Note, I will owe interest at a yearly rate of .... %. This rate is called the "Initial Rate of Interest." The rate of interest I will pay will change in accordance with Section 4 (A) of this Note on the first day of ...., 19......... and on that day every 36th month thereafter. Each date on which my rate of interest could change is called an "Interest Change Date."

(B) The Index

Any changes in my rate of interest will be based on changes in the Index. The "Index" is the weekly average yield on United States Treasury securities adjusted to a constant maturity of 3 years, as made available by the Federal Reserve Board. The most recently available Index figure as of the date 45 days before each Interest Change Date is called the "Current Index."

If the Index is no longer available, the Note Holder will choose a new index which is based upon comparable information. The Note Holder will give me notice of this choice.

(C) Interest After Default

The rate of interest required by this Section 2 and Section 4 (A) below is the rate I will pay both before and after any default described in Section 12 (B) below.

3. TIME AND PLACE OF PAYMENTS

I will pay principal and interest by making payments every month. My monthly payments will be applied to interest before principal.

I will make my monthly payments on the first day of each month beginning on ...., 19.......... I will make these payments every month until I have paid all the principal and interest and any other charges described below that I may owe under this Note. If, on ...., 20........., I still owe amounts under this Note, I will pay those amounts in full on that date, which is called the "maturity date."

I will make my monthly payments at .... or at a different place if required by the Note Holder.

4. FULL PAYMENT AMOUNT

(A) Calculation of Full Payment Amount

Each of my first 72 monthly payments could be less than a Full Payment Amount. A "Full Payment Amount" is the monthly amount sufficient to repay the amount I originally borrowed, or the unpaid principal balance of my loan as of an Interest Change Date, in full on the maturity date at the rate of interest I am required to pay by Section 2 above or this Section 4 (A) in substantially equal payments. Beginning on the date of this Note, my first Full Payment Amount will be U.S. $... until the first Interest Change Date. My first Full Payment Amount will be larger than each of my first 36 monthly payments.

Before each Interest Change Date, the Note Holder will determine a new Full Payment Amount for my loan. The Note Holder will first calculate my new rate of interest by adding .... percentage points (..................%) to the Current Index. The Note Holder will then round the result of this addition to the nearest one-eighth of one percentage point (0.125%). This rounded amount will be my new rate of interest until the next Interest Change Date. The Note Holder will then calculate the new amount of a monthly payment that would be sufficient to repay my unpaid principal balance as of the Interest Change Date in full on the maturity date at my new rate of interest in substantially equal payments. The result of this calculation is my new Full Payment Amount.

Figure 9-16. FNMA Graduated Payment Note—Plan 4, page 2

Each new rate of interest will become effective on each Interest Change Date, and each new Full Payment Amount will become effective on the first monthly payment date after the Interest Change Date.

(B) Required Full Payment Amount

I will pay the Full Payment Amount as my monthly payment beginning with my 37th monthly payment if my new rate of interest is equal to or less than the Initial Rate of Interest or if I do not choose to limit the amount of my monthly payment as permitted by Section 6 (A) below. Even if I choose to limit my monthly payment, I will pay the Full Payment Amount beginning with my 73rd monthly payment.

5. GRADUATED MONTHLY PAYMENTS 1–36

My first 12 monthly payments will each be in the amount of U.S. $.. On each of the first two anniversaries of the date my first monthly payment is due, I will begin paying a new monthly payment which will be equal to the amount I have been paying multiplied by the number 1.075. I will pay the new amount of my monthly payment until it changes in accordance with this Section 5 or Sections 6 or 7 below.

6. BORROWER'S RIGHT TO LIMIT AMOUNT OF MONTHLY PAYMENTS 37–72

(A) Calculation of Graduated Monthly Payment Amount

If my new rate of interest at the first Interest Change Date is greater than the Initial Rate of Interest, I may choose to limit the amount of my new monthly payment. If I do so, on each of the 3rd, 4th and 5th anniversaries of the date my first monthly payment is due, I will begin paying a new monthly payment which will be equal to the amount I have been paying multiplied by the number 1.075. Even if I have chosen to limit my monthly payment, Sections 6 (B) or 6 (C) below may require me to pay a different amount. I will give the Note Holder notice that I have chosen to limit my monthly payments at least 15 days before my 37th monthly payment is due.

(B) Reduced Monthly Payment Amount

My 49th or 61st graduated monthly payment calculated under Section 6 (A) above could be greater than the amount of a monthly payment which then would be sufficient to repay my unpaid principal balance in full on the maturity date at my current rate of interest in substantially equal payments. If so, I will instead then begin paying a new monthly payment, which will be equal to the lower amount, until my 73rd monthly payment when I will begin paying my new Full Payment Amount.

(C) Increased Monthly Payment Amount

My paying a monthly payment calculated under Section 6 (A) above could cause my unpaid principal balance to exceed the limit stated in Section 8 (B) below. If so, on the date that my paying a monthly payment would cause me to exceed that limit, I will instead begin paying a new monthly payment. This new monthly payment will be in an amount which would be sufficient to repay my then unpaid principal balance in full on the maturity date at my current rate of interest in substantially equal payments, until my 73rd monthly payment when I will begin paying my new Full Payment Amount.

7. MONTHLY PAYMENT 73 AND REMAINING PAYMENTS

Beginning with my 73rd monthly payment, I will pay the Full Payment Amount as my monthly payment.

8. INCREASES IN THE PRINCIPAL AMOUNT TO BE PAID

(A) Additions to My Unpaid Principal Balance

Each of my first 72 monthly payments could be less than the amount of the interest portion of a monthly payment which then would be sufficient to repay my unpaid principal balance in full on the maturity date at my current rate of interest in substantially equal payments. If so, each month that the amount of my monthly payment is less than the interest portion, the Note Holder will subtract the amount of my monthly payment from the amount of the interest portion and will add the difference to my unpaid principal balance. The Note Holder will also add interest on the amount of this difference to my unpaid principal balance each month. The rate of interest on the interest added to principal will be the rate required by Sections 2 or 4 (A) above.

(B) Limit on Unpaid Principal Balance

My unpaid principal balance can never exceed a maximum amount equal to one hundred twenty-five percent (125%) of the principal amount I originally borrowed.

9. NOTICE OF CHANGES

The Note Holder will mail or deliver to me a notice of any changes in the amount of my monthly payment before the effective date of any change. The notice will include information required by law to be given me and also the title and telephone number of a person who will answer any question I may have regarding the notice.

10. BORROWER'S RIGHT TO PREPAY

I have the right to make payments of principal at any time before they are due. A payment of principal only is known as a "prepayment." When I make a prepayment, I will tell the Note Holder in a letter that I am doing so.

I may make a full prepayment or a partial prepayment without paying any penalty. The Note Holder will use all of my prepayments to reduce the amount of principal that I owe under this Note. If I make a partial prepayment, there will be no delays in the due dates of my monthly payments unless the Note Holder agrees in writing to those delays. My partial prepayment will affect the amount of my monthly payment only after the first Interest Change Date following my partial prepayment, unless my monthly payment is reduced in accordance with Section 6 (B) above.

11. LOAN CHARGES

If a law, which applies to this loan and which sets maximum loan charges, is finally interpreted so that the interest or other loan charges collected or to be collected in connection with this loan exceed the permitted limits, then: (i) any such loan charge shall be reduced by the amount necessary to reduce the charge to the permitted limit; and (ii) any sums already collected from me which exceeded permitted limits will be refunded to me. The Note Holder may choose to make this refund by reducing the principal I owe under this Note or by making a direct payment to me. If a refund reduces principal, the reduction will be treated as a partial prepayment.

12. BORROWER'S FAILURE TO PAY AS REQUIRED

(A) Late Charge for Overdue Payments

If the Note Holder has not received the full amount of any of my monthly payments by the end of .... calendar days after the date it is due, I will pay a late charge to the Note Holder. The amount of the charge will be ....% of my overdue payment. I will pay this late charge only once on any late payment.

(B) Default

If I do not pay the full amount of each monthly payment on the date it is due, I will be in default.

Figure 9-17. FNMA Graduated Payment Note—Plan 4, page 3

(C) Notice of Default

If I am in default, the Note Holder may send me a written notice telling me that if I do not pay the overdue amount by a certain date, the Note Holder may require me to pay immediately the full amount of principal which has not been paid and all the interest that I owe on that amount. That date must be at least 30 days after the date on which the notice is mailed to me or if it is not mailed, 30 days after the date on which it is delivered to me.

(D) No Waiver By Note Holder

Even if, at a time when I am in default, the Note Holder does not require me to pay immediately in full as described above, the Note Holder will still have the right to do so if, at a later time, I am in default again.

(E) Payment of Note Holder's Costs and Expenses

If the Note Holder has required me to pay immediately in full as described above, the Note Holder will have the right to be paid back for all of its costs and expenses in enforcing this Note to the extent not prohibited by applicable law. Those expenses include, for example, reasonable attorneys' fees.

13. GIVING OF NOTICES

Unless applicable law requires a different method of giving notice, any notice that must be given to me under this Note will be given by delivering it or by mailing it by first class mail addressed to me at the Property Address above or at a different address if I give the Note Holder a notice of my different address.

Any notice that must be given to the Note Holder under this Note will be given by mailing it by first class mail to the Note Holder at the address stated in Section 3 above or at a different address if I am given a notice of that different address.

14. OBLIGATIONS OF PERSONS UNDER THIS NOTE

If more than one person signs this Note, each person is fully and personally obligated to keep all of the promises made in this Note, including the promise to pay the full amount owed. Any person who is a guarantor, surety, or endorser of this Note is also obligated to do these things. Any person who takes over the obligations under this Note or any person who takes over the obligations of a guarantor, surety, or endorser of this Note is also obligated to keep all of the promises made in this Note. The Note Holder may enforce its rights under this Note against each person individually or against all of us together. This means that any one of us may be required to pay all of the amounts owed under this Note.

15. WAIVERS

I and any other person who has obligations under this Note waive the rights of presentment and notice of dishonor. "Presentment" means the right to require the Note Holder to demand payment of amounts due. "Notice of dishonor" means the right to require the Note Holder to give notice that amounts due have not been paid.

16. THIS NOTE SECURED BY A SECURITY INSTRUMENT

In addition to the protections given to the Note Holder under this Note, a Mortgage, Deed of Trust, or Deed to Secure Debt (the "Security Instrument") with a Graduated Payment Rider, dated the same day as this Note, protects the Note Holder from possible losses which might result if I do not keep the promises which I make in this Note. That Security Instrument and Rider describe how and under what conditions I may be required to make immediate payment in full of all amounts I owe under this Note. Some of those conditions are described as follows:

> "**Transfer of the Property or a Beneficial Interest in Borrower.** If all or any part of the Property or an interest therein is sold or transferred by Borrower (or if a beneficial interest in Borrower is sold or transferred and Borrower is not a natural person or persons but is a corporation, partnership, trust or other legal entity) without Lender's prior written consent, excluding (a) the creation of a lien or encumbrance subordinate to this Security Instrument which does not relate to a transfer of rights of occupancy in the property, (b) the creation of a purchase money security interest for household appliances, (c) a transfer by devise, descent or by operation of law upon the death of a joint tenant or (d) the grant of any leasehold interest of three years or less not containing an option to purchase, Lender may, at Lender's option, declare all the sums secured by this Security Instrument to be immediately due and payable.
>
> If Lender exercises such option to accelerate, Lender shall mail Borrower notice of acceleration in accordance with paragraph 14 hereof. Such notice shall provide a period of not less than 30 days from the date the notice is mailed within which Borrower may pay the sums declared due. If Borrower fails to pay such sums prior to the expiration of such period, Lender may, without further notice or demand on Borrower, invoke any remedies permitted by paragraph 18 hereof.
>
> Lender may consent to a sale or transfer if: (1) Borrower causes to be submitted to Lender information required by Lender to evaluate the transferee as if a new loan were being made to the transferee; (2) Lender reasonably determines that Lender's security will not be impaired and that the risk of a breach of any covenant or agreement in this Security Instrument is acceptable; (3) interest is payable on the sums secured by this Security Instrument at a rate acceptable to Lender; (4) changes in the terms of the Note and this Security Instrument required by Lender are made, including, for example, periodic adjustment in the interest rate, a different final payment date for the loan, and addition of unpaid interest to principal; and (5) the transferee signs an assumption agreement that is acceptable to Lender and that obligates the transferee to keep all the promises and agreements made in the Note and in this Security Instrument, as modified if required by Lender. To the extent permitted by applicable law, Lender also may charge a reasonable fee as a condition to Lender's consent to any sale or transfer.
>
> Borrower will continue to be obligated under the Note and this Security Instrument unless Lender releases Borrower in writing."

Witness the hand(s) and seal(s) of the undersigned.

....(Seal)
-Borrower

....(Seal)
-Borrower

....(Seal)
-Borrower

(Sign Original Only)

it allows the borrower to make principal payments before they are due. If the borrower does make such payments, he/she must tell the lender that he/she is making the payment prior to the due date of such payment. In addition, the paragraph states that the borrower can make the advanced principal payments or repay the loan in full without any penalty.

Paragraph 12, BORROWER'S FAILURE TO PAY AS REQUIRED, allows the lender to charge a late payment. Subparagraph (B) states that if the borrower fails to pay the full amount of the monthly payment, he or she will be in default. Subparagraph (C), Figure 9-17, states the method that will be used by the lender to give notice to the borrower that, if the overdue amount is not paid by a specific date, the lender may declare the total remaining principal balance due and payable which may include any interest owed. Subparagraph (E) states that in addition to the amount outstanding, the lender has the right to charge the borrower for expenses in conjunction with the enforcement of provisions of the note, unless there is a limitation by state law.

The paragraph entitled THIS NOTE SECURED BY A SECURITY INSTRUMENT states that the note is secured by either a mortgage or deed of trust. The section entitled "Transfer of the Property or a Beneficial Interest in Borrower" states that if any part of the property or interest in the property is transferred by the borrower, the lender may declare the remaining outstanding principal due and payable. This section outlines that if the lender is *not* notified of the change, excluding certain items, only then can the lender declare the outstanding principal balance due and payable.

Accompanying the Note is a Graduated Payment Rider (With Interest Rate Changes Every 3 Years). The purpose of this document is to amend the FNMA/FHLMC Uniform Mortgage/Deed of Trust, as reviewed in Chapter 2. This fact is stated in the first paragraph of the document, Figure 9-18.

Section A, INTEREST RATE AND MONTHLY PAYMENT CHANGES, basically restates paragraphs 2 through 9 of the note reviewed in the previous section (Figure 9-18 and 9-19).

Section C, NOTICE, amends Uniform Covenant 14 of the standard mortgage/deed of trust to make it conform to the notice provisions of the note. The major change is that the notice does not have to be sent certified mail with return receipt requested. Under this change, then, notice is given upon placing the notice in the mail.

Section E, TRANSFER OF THE PROPERTY OR A BENEFICIAL INTEREST IN BORROWER, amends Uniform Covenant 17 of the standard mortgage/deed of trust, Figure 9-20. In fact, this section basically rewrites Covenant 17. Note that in the first paragraph a transfer of interest in the property to a corporation, partnership, or other legal entity is now covered and is subject to the requirements listed in the second paragraph.

Sections G and H are self-explanatory.

A different set of documents is used for the GPARM purchased by FNMA under Plan 6. First, let us review the Note, Figures 9-21 through 9-23.

The first major difference from the previous note (GPARM Plan 4) is in the subtitle. We see that the interest rate is adjusted every five years instead of every three years and the graduation period is also five years instead of three years.

In comparing the two notes, we see that paragraph 1 is identical. The first major difference occurs in paragraph 2, INTEREST. With this note, the index to be used is "the weekly average yield on United States Treasury securities adjusted to a constant maturity of 5 years," instead of a constant maturity of 3 years as in the previous note. From the index used, therefore, we can see why the interest rate is adjusted every five years in this note.

The next major difference occurs in paragraph 4, FULL PAYMENT AMOUNT. In this note, the first 120 payments, instead of 72 as in the previous note, *could be* less than full payment. Since the graduation period is five years, the first 60 payments will be less than full payments. If the borrower options to limit the increase of the next five years of payments, the second 60 payments may be less than full payments.

The paragraph entitled GRADUATED MONTHLY PAYMENTS 1-60, Figure 9-22, is similar to paragraph 5 of the previous note except the payments will graduate for five years. Thus, the first 60 payments, instead of the first 36 payments, will increase at 7.5 percent per year.

Figure 9-18. FNMA Graduated Payment Rider—Plan 4, page 1

GRADUATED PAYMENT RIDER

(With Interest Rate Changes Every 3 Years)

THIS GRADUATED PAYMENT RIDER is made this .... day of ...., 19........., and is incorporated into and shall be deemed to amend and supplement the Mortgage, Deed of Trust, or Deed to Secure Debt (the "Security Instrument") of the same date given by the undersigned (the "Borrower") to secure Borrower's Graduated Payment Note to .... (the "Lender") of the same date (the "Note") and covering the property described in the Security Instrument and located at:

....

(Property Address)

The Note contains provisions allowing for changes in the interest rate and monthly payments.

The Borrower's monthly payment will increase by 7½% each year during the first three years of the Note. The Borrower also may be able to limit monthly payment increases to 7½% each year during the second three years of the Note. The remaining monthly payments also could increase or decrease, depending on changes in the interest rate.

The principal amount the Borrower must repay will be larger than the amount originally borrowed, but not more than 125% of the original amount.

ADDITIONAL COVENANTS. In addition to the covenants and agreements made in the Security Instrument, Borrower and Lender further covenant and agree as follows:

A. INTEREST RATE AND MONTHLY PAYMENT CHANGES

The Note provides for an Initial Rate of Interest of ....%. Sections 2 through 9 of the Note provide for changes in the interest rate and the monthly payments, as follows:

"2. INTEREST

(A) Interest Owed

Interest will be charged on that part of principal which has not been paid. Interest will be charged beginning on the date of this Note and continuing until the full amount of principal has been paid.

Beginning on the date of this Note, I will owe interest at a yearly rate of .... %. This rate is called the "Initial Rate of Interest." The rate of interest I will pay will change in accordance with Section 4 (A) of this Note on the first day of ...., 19......... and on that day every 36th month thereafter. Each date on which my rate of interest could change is called an "Interest Change Date."

(B) The Index

Any changes in my rate of interest will be based on changes in the Index. The "Index" is the weekly average yield on United States Treasury securities adjusted to a constant maturity of 3 years, as made available by the Federal Reserve Board. The most recently available Index figure as of the date 45 days before each Interest Change Date is called the "Current Index."

If the Index is no longer available, the Note Holder will choose a new index which is based upon comparable information. The Note Holder will give me notice of this choice.

(C) Interest After Default

The rate of interest required by this Section 2 and Section 4 (A) below is the rate I will pay both before and after any default described in Section 12 (B) below.

3. TIME AND PLACE OF PAYMENTS

I will pay principal and interest by making payments every month. My monthly payments will be applied to interest before principal.

I will make my monthly payments on the first day of each month beginning on ...., 19.......... I will make these payments every month until I have paid all the principal and interest and any other charges described below that I may owe under this Note. If, on ...., 20........., I still owe amounts under this Note, I will pay those amounts in full on that date, which is called the "maturity date."

I will make my monthly payments at ....
....
or at a different place if required by the Note Holder.

4. FULL PAYMENT AMOUNT

(A) Calculation of Full Payment Amount

Each of my first 72 monthly payments could be less than a Full Payment Amount. A "Full Payment Amount" is the monthly amount sufficient to repay the amount I originally borrowed, or the unpaid principal balance of my loan as of an Interest Change Date, in full on the maturity date at the rate of interest I am required to pay by Section 2 above or this Section 4 (A) in substantially equal payments. Beginning on the date of this Note, my first Full Payment Amount will be U.S. $... until the first Interest Change Date. My first Full Payment Amount will be larger than each of my first 36 monthly payments.

Before each Interest Change Date, the Note Holder will determine a new Full Payment Amount for my loan. The Note Holder will first calculate my new rate of interest by adding .... percentage points (..................%) to the Current Index. The Note Holder will then round the result of this addition to the nearest one-eighth of one percentage point (0.125%). This rounded amount will be my new rate of interest until the next Interest Change Date. The Note Holder will then calculate the new amount of a monthly payment that would be sufficient to repay my unpaid principal

GRADUATED PAYMENT RIDER - Plan 4 GPARM—Single Family-4/82—**FNMA Uniform Instrument**

Figure 9-19. FNMA Graduated Payment Rider—Plan 4, page 2

balance as of the Interest Change Date in full on the maturity date at my new rate of interest in substantially equal payments. The result of this calculation is my new Full Payment Amount.

Each new rate of interest will become effective on each Interest Change Date, and each new Full Payment Amount will become effective on the first monthly payment date after the Interest Change Date.

(B) Required Full Payment Amount

I will pay the Full Payment Amount as my monthly payment beginning with my 37th monthly payment if my new rate of interest is equal to or less than the Initial Rate of Interest or if I do not choose to limit the amount of my monthly payment as permitted by Section 6 (A) below. Even if I choose to limit my monthly payment, I will pay the Full Payment Amount beginning with my 73rd monthly payment.

5. GRADUATED MONTHLY PAYMENTS 1–36

My first 12 monthly payments will each be in the amount of U.S. $.. On each of the first two anniversaries of the date my first monthly payment is due, I will begin paying a new monthly payment which will be equal to the amount I have been paying multiplied by the number 1.075. I will pay the new amount of my monthly payment until it changes in accordance with this Section 5 or Sections 6 or 7 below.

6. BORROWER'S RIGHT TO LIMIT AMOUNT OF MONTHLY PAYMENTS 37–72

(A) Calculation of Graduated Monthly Payment Amount

If my new rate of interest at the first Interest Change Date is greater than the Initial Rate of Interest, I may choose to limit the amount of my new monthly payment. If I do so, on each of the 3rd, 4th and 5th anniversaries of the date my first monthly payment is due, I will begin paying a new monthly payment which will be equal to the amount I have been paying multiplied by the number 1.075. Even if I have chosen to limit my monthly payment, Sections 6 (B) or 6 (C) below may require me to pay a different amount. I will give the Note Holder notice that I have chosen to limit my monthly payments at least 15 days before my 37th monthly payment is due.

(B) Reduced Monthly Payment Amount

My 49th or 61st graduated monthly payment calculated under Section 6 (A) above could be greater than the amount of a monthly payment which then would be sufficient to repay my unpaid principal balance in full on the maturity date at my current rate of interest in substantially equal payments. If so, I will instead then begin paying a new monthly payment, which will be equal to the lower amount, until my 73rd monthly payment when I will begin paying my new Full Payment Amount.

(C) Increased Monthly Payment Amount

My paying a monthly payment calculated under Section 6 (A) above could cause my unpaid principal balance to exceed the limit stated in Section 8 (B) below. If so, on the date that my paying a monthly payment would cause me to exceed that limit, I will instead begin paying a new monthly payment. This new monthly payment will be in an amount which would be sufficient to repay my then unpaid principal balance in full on the maturity date at my current rate of interest in substantially equal payments, until my 73rd monthly payment when I will begin paying my new Full Payment Amount.

7. MONTHLY PAYMENT 73 AND REMAINING PAYMENTS

Beginning with my 73rd monthly payment, I will pay the Full Payment Amount as my monthly payment.

8. INCREASES IN THE PRINCIPAL AMOUNT TO BE PAID

(A) Additions to My Unpaid Principal Balance

Each of my first 72 monthly payments could be less than the amount of the interest portion of a monthly payment which then would be sufficient to repay my unpaid principal balance in full on the maturity date at my current rate of interest in substantially equal payments. If so, each month that the amount of my monthly payment is less than the interest portion, the Note Holder will subtract the amount of my monthly payment from the amount of the interest portion and will add the difference to my unpaid principal balance. The Note Holder will also add interest on the amount of this difference to my unpaid principal balance each month. The rate of interest on the interest added to principal will be the rate required by Sections 2 or 4 (A) above.

(B) Limit on Unpaid Principal Balance

My unpaid principal balance can never exceed a maximum amount equal to one hundred twenty-five percent (125%) of the principal amount I originally borrowed.

9. NOTICE OF CHANGES

The Note Holder will mail or deliver to me a notice of any changes in the amount of my monthly payment before the effective date of any change. The notice will include information required by law to be given me and also the title and telephone number of a person who will answer any question I may have regarding the notice."

B. CHARGES; LIENS

Uniform Covenant 4 of the Security Instrument is amended to read as follows:

4. Charges; Liens. Borrower shall pay all taxes, assessments, and other charges, fines and impositions attributable to the Property which may attain a priority over this Security Instrument, and leasehold payments or ground rents, if any, in the manner provided under paragraph 2 hereof or, if not paid in such manner, by Borrower making payment, when due, directly to the payee thereof. Borrower shall promptly furnish to Lender all notices of amounts due under this paragraph, and in the event Borrower shall make payment directly, Borrower shall promptly furnish to Lender receipts evidencing such payments. Borrower shall promptly discharge any lien which has priority over this Security Instrument; provided, that Borrower shall not be required to discharge any such lien so long as Borrower: (a) shall agree in writing to the payment of the obligation secured by such lien in a manner acceptable to Lender; (b) shall in good faith contest such lien by, or defend against enforcement of such lien in, legal proceedings which in the opinion of Lender operate to prevent the enforcement of the lien or forfeiture of the Property or any part thereof; or (c) shall secure from the holder of such lien an agreement in a form satisfactory to Lender subordinating such lien to this Security Instrument.

If Lender determines that all or any part of the Property is subject to a lien which may attain a priority over this Security Instrument, Lender shall send Borrower notice identifying such lien. Borrower shall satisfy such lien or take one or more of the actions set forth above within ten days of the giving of notice.

C. NOTICE

Uniform Covenant 14 of the Security Instrument is amended to read as follows:

Figure 9-20. FNMA Graduated Payment Rider—Plan 4, page 3

14. Notice. Except for any notice required under applicable law to be given in another manner, (a) any notice to Borrower provided for in this Security Instrument shall be given by delivering it or by mailing it by first class mail addressed to Borrower at the Property Address or at such other address as Borrower may designate by notice to Lender as provided herein, and (b) any notice to Lender shall be given by first class mail to Lender's address stated herein or to such other address as Lender may designate by notice to Borrower as provided herein. Any notice provided for in this Security Instrument shall be deemed to have been given to Borrower or Lender when given in the manner designated herein.

D. UNIFORM SECURITY INSTRUMENT; GOVERNING LAW; SEVERABILITY

Uniform Covenant 15 of the Security Instrument is amended to read as follows:

15. Uniform Security Instrument; Governing Law; Severability. This form of Security Instrument combines uniform covenants for national use and non-uniform covenants with limited variations by jurisdiction to constitute a uniform security instrument covering real property. This Security Instrument shall be governed by federal law and the law of the jurisdiction in which the Property is located. In the event that any provision or clause of this Security Instrument or the Note conflicts with applicable law, such conflict shall not affect other provisions of this Security Instrument or the Note which can be given effect without the conflicting provision, and to this end the provisions of this Security Instrument and the Note are declared to be severable.

E. TRANSFER OF THE PROPERTY OR A BENEFICIAL INTEREST IN BORROWER

Uniform Covenant 17 of the Security Instrument is amended to read as follows:

17. Transfer of the Property or a Beneficial Interest in Borrower. If all or any part of the Property or an interest therein is sold or transferred by Borrower (or if a beneficial interest in Borrower is sold or transferred and Borrower is not a natural person or persons but is a corporation, partnership, trust or other legal entity) without Lender's prior written consent, excluding (a) the creation of a lien or encumbrance subordinate to this Security Instrument which does not relate to a transfer of rights of occupancy in the property, (b) the creation of a purchase money security interest for household appliances, (c) a transfer by devise, descent or by operation of law upon the death of a joint tenant or (d) the grant of any leasehold interest of three years or less not containing an option to purchase, Lender may, at Lender's option, declare all the sums secured by this Security Instrument to be immediately due and payable.

If Lender exercises such option to accelerate, Lender shall mail Borrower notice of acceleration in accordance with paragraph 14 hereof. Such notice shall provide a period of not less than 30 days from the date the notice is mailed within which Borrower may pay the sums declared due. If Borrower fails to pay such sums prior to the expiration of such period, Lender may, without further notice or demand on Borrower, invoke any remedies permitted by paragraph 18 hereof.

Lender may consent to a sale or transfer if: (1) Borrower causes to be submitted to Lender information required by Lender to evaluate the transferee as if a new loan were being made to the transferee; (2) Lender reasonably determines that Lender's security will not be impaired and that the risk of a breach of any covenant or agreement in this Security Instrument is acceptable; (3) interest is payable on the sums secured by this Security Instrument at a rate acceptable to Lender; (4) changes in the terms of the Note and this Security Instrument required by Lender are made, including, for example, periodic adjustment in the interest rate, a different final payment date for the loan, and addition of unpaid interest to principal; and (5) the transferee signs an assumption agreement that is acceptable to Lender and that obligates the transferee to keep all the promises and agreements made in the Note and in this Security Instrument, as modified if required by Lender. To the extent permitted by applicable law, Lender also may charge a reasonable fee as a condition to Lender's consent to any sale or transfer.

Borrower will continue to be obligated under the Note and this Security Instrument unless Lender releases Borrower in writing.

F. COVENANT DELETED

Non-Uniform Covenant 21 of the Security Instrument ("Future Advances") is deleted.

G. LOAN CHARGES

If the loan secured by the Security Instrument is subject to a law which sets maximum loan charges, and that law is finally interpreted so that the interest or other loan charges collected or to be collected in connection with the loan exceed permitted limits, then: (1) any such loan charge shall be reduced by the amount necessary to reduce the charge to the permitted limits; and (2) any sums already collected from Borrower which exceeded permitted limits will be refunded to Borrower. Lender may choose to make this refund by reducing the principal owed under the Note or by making a direct payment to Borrower. If a refund reduces principal, the reduction will be treated as a partial prepayment under the Note.

H. LEGISLATION

If, after the date hereof, enactment or expiration of applicable laws have the effect either of rendering the provisions of the Note, the Security Instrument or this Graduated Payment Rider (other than this paragraph H) unenforceable according to their terms, or all or any part of the sums secured hereby uncollectable, as otherwise provided in the Security Instrument and this Graduated Payment Rider, or of diminishing the value of Lender's security, then Lender, at Lender's option, may declare all sums secured by the Security Instrument to be immediately due and payable.

IN WITNESS WHEREOF, Borrower has executed this Graduated Payment Rider.

....(Seal)
-Borrower

....(Seal)
-Borrower

....(Seal)
-Borrower
(Sign Original Only)

Figure 9-21. FNMA Graduated Payment Note—Plan 6, page 1

GRADUATED PAYMENT NOTE
(With Interest Rate Changes Every 5 Years)

This Note contains provisions allowing for changes in my interest rate and monthly payments.

My monthly payment will increase by 7½% each year during the first five years of this Note. If the provisions of this Note permit me to do so, I will be able to limit my monthly payment increases to 7½% each year during the second five years of this Note. My remaining monthly payments also could increase or decrease, depending on changes in my interest rate.

The principal amount I must repay will be larger than the amount I originally borrowed, but not more than 125% of the original amount.

...., ...
[City] [State]

...., 19.......

....
(Property Address)

1. BORROWER'S PROMISE TO PAY

In return for a loan that I have received, I promise to pay U.S. $... plus any amounts added in accordance with Section 8 (A) of this Note (the total amount is called "principal"), plus interest, to the order of the Lender. The Lender is .... I understand that the Lender may transfer this Note. The Lender or anyone who takes this Note by transfer and who is entitled to receive payments under this Note is called the "Note Holder."

2. INTEREST

(A) Interest Owed

Interest will be charged on that part of principal which has not been paid. Interest will be charged beginning on the date of this Note and continuing until the full amount of principal has been paid.

Beginning on the date of this Note, I will owe interest at a yearly rate of .... %. This rate is called the "Initial Rate of Interest." The rate of interest I will pay will change in accordance with Section 4 (A) of this Note on the first day of ...., 19......... and on that day every 60th month thereafter. Each date on which my rate of interest could change is called an "Interest Change Date."

(B) The Index

Any changes in my rate of interest will be based on changes in the Index. The "Index" is the weekly average yield on United States Treasury securities adjusted to a constant maturity of 5 years, as made available by the Federal Reserve Board. The most recently available Index figure as of the date 45 days before each Interest Change Date is called the "Current Index."

If the Index is no longer available, the Note Holder will choose a new index which is based upon comparable information. The Note Holder will give me notice of this choice.

(C) Interest After Default

The rate of interest required by this Section 2 and Section 4 (A) below is the rate I will pay both before and after any default described in Section 12 (B) below.

3. TIME AND PLACE OF PAYMENTS

I will pay principal and interest by making payments every month. My monthly payments will be applied to interest before principal.

I will make my monthly payments on the first day of each month beginning on ...., 19.......... I will make these payments every month until I have paid all the principal and interest and any other charges described below that I may owe under this Note. If, on ...., 20........., I still owe amounts under this Note, I will pay those amounts in full on that date, which is called the "maturity date."

I will make my monthly payments at .... or at a different place if required by the Note Holder.

4. FULL PAYMENT AMOUNT

(A) Calculation of Full Payment Amount

Each of my first 120 monthly payments could be less than a Full Payment Amount. A "Full Payment Amount" is the monthly amount sufficient to repay the amount I originally borrowed, or the unpaid principal balance of my loan as of an Interest Change Date, in full on the maturity date at the rate of interest I am required to pay by Section 2 above or this Section 4 (A) in substantially equal payments. Beginning on the date of this Note, my first Full Payment Amount will be U.S. $.. until the first Interest Change Date. My first Full Payment Amount will be larger than each of my first 60 payments.

Before each Interest Change Date, the Note Holder will determine a new Full Payment Amount for my loan. The Note Holder will first calculate my new rate of interest by adding .... percentage points (..................%) to the Current Index. The Note Holder will then round the result of this addition to the nearest one-eighth of one percentage point (0.125%). This rounded amount will be my new rate of interest until the next Interest Change Date. The Note Holder will then calculate the new amount of a monthly payment that would be sufficient to repay my unpaid principal balance as of the Interest Change Date in full on the maturity date at my new rate of interest in substantially equal payments. The result of this calculation is my new Full Payment Amount.

Figure 9-22. FNMA Graduated Payment Note—Plan 6, page 2

Each new rate of interest will become effective on each Interest Change Date, and each new Full Payment Amount will become effective on the first monthly payment date after the Interest Change Date.

(B) Required Full Payment Amount

I will pay the Full Payment Amount as my monthly payment beginning with my 61st monthly payment if my new rate of interest is equal to or less than the Initial Rate of Interest or if I do not choose to limit the amount of my monthly payment as permitted by Section 6 (A) below. Even if I choose to limit my monthly payment, I will pay the Full Payment Amount beginning with my 121st monthly payment.

5. GRADUATED MONTHLY PAYMENTS 1–60

My first 12 monthly payments will each be in the amount of U.S. $.. On each of the first four anniversaries of the date my first monthly payment is due, I will begin paying a new monthly payment which will be equal to the amount I have been paying multiplied by the number 1.075. I will pay the new amount of my monthly payment until it changes in accordance with this Section 5 or Sections 6 or 7 below.

6. BORROWER'S RIGHT TO LIMIT AMOUNT OF MONTHLY PAYMENTS 61–120

(A) Calculation of Graduated Monthly Payment Amount

If my new rate of interest at the first Interest Change Date is greater than the Initial Rate of Interest, I may choose to limit the amount of my new monthly payment. If I do so, on each of the 5th through 9th anniversaries of the date my first monthly payment is due, I will begin paying a new monthly payment which will be equal to the amount I have been paying multiplied by the number 1.075. Even if I have chosen to limit my monthly payment, Sections 6 (B) or 6 (C) below may require me to pay a different amount. I will give the Note Holder notice that I have chosen to limit my monthly payments at least 15 days before my 61st monthly payment is due.

(B) Reduced Monthly Payment Amount

My 73rd, 85th, 97th or 109th graduated monthly payment calculated under Section 6 (A) above could be greater than the amount of a monthly payment which then would be sufficient to repay my unpaid principal balance in full on the maturity date at my current rate of interest in substantially equal payments. If so, I will instead then begin paying a new monthly payment, which will be equal to the lower amount, until my 121st monthly payment when I will begin paying my new Full Payment Amount.

(C) Increased Monthly Payment Amount

My paying a monthly payment calculated under Section 6 (A) above could cause my unpaid principal balance to exceed the limit stated in Section 8 (B) below. If so, on the date that my paying a monthly payment would cause me to exceed that limit, I will instead begin paying a new monthly payment. This new monthly payment will be in an amount which would be sufficient to repay my then unpaid principal balance in full on the maturity date at my current rate of interest in substantially equal payments, until my 121st monthly payment when I will begin paying my new Full Payment Amount.

7. MONTHLY PAYMENT 121 AND REMAINING PAYMENTS

Beginning with my 121st monthly payment, I will pay the Full Payment Amount as my monthly payment.

8. INCREASES IN THE PRINCIPAL AMOUNT TO BE PAID

(A) Additions to My Unpaid Principal Balance

Each of my first 120 monthly payments could be less than the amount of the interest portion of a monthly payment which then would be sufficient to repay my unpaid principal balance in full on the maturity date at my current rate of interest in substantially equal payments. If so, each month that the amount of my monthly payment is less than the interest portion, the Note Holder will subtract the amount of my monthly payment from the amount of the interest portion and will add the difference to my unpaid principal balance. The Note Holder will also add interest on the amount of this difference to my unpaid principal balance each month. The rate of interest on the interest added to principal will be the rate required by Sections 2 or 4 (A) above.

(B) Limit on Unpaid Principal Balance

My unpaid principal balance can never exceed a maximum amount equal to one hundred twenty-five percent (125%) of the principal amount I originally borrowed.

9. NOTICE OF CHANGES

The Note Holder will mail or deliver to me a notice of any changes in the amount of my monthly payment before the effective date of any change. The notice will include information required by law to be given me and also the title and telephone number of a person who will answer any question I may have regarding the notice.

10. BORROWER'S RIGHT TO PREPAY

I have the right to make payments of principal at any time before they are due. A payment of principal only is known as a "prepayment." When I make a prepayment, I will tell the Note Holder in a letter that I am doing so.

I may make a full prepayment or a partial prepayment without paying any penalty. The Note Holder will use all of my prepayments to reduce the amount of principal that I owe under this Note. If I make a partial prepayment, there will be no delays in the due dates of my monthly payments unless the Note Holder agrees in writing to those delays. My partial prepayment will affect the amount of my monthly payment only after the first Interest Change Date following my partial prepayment, unless my monthly payment is reduced in accordance with Section 6 (B) above.

11. LOAN CHARGES

If a law, which applies to this loan and which sets maximum loan charges, is finally interpreted so that the interest or other loan charges collected or to be collected in connection with this loan exceed the permitted limits, then: (i) any such loan charge shall be reduced by the amount necessary to reduce the charge to the permitted limit; and (ii) any sums already collected from me which exceeded permitted limits will be refunded to me. The Note Holder may choose to make this refund by reducing the principal I owe under this Note or by making a direct payment to me. If a refund reduces principal, the reduction will be treated as a partial prepayment.

12. BORROWER'S FAILURE TO PAY AS REQUIRED

(A) Late Charge for Overdue Payments

If the Note Holder has not received the full amount of any of my monthly payments by the end of .... calendar days after the date it is due, I will pay a late charge to the Note Holder. The amount of the charge will be ....% of my overdue payment. I will pay this late charge only once on any late payment.

(B) Default

If I do not pay the full amount of each monthly payment on the date it is due, I will be in default.

Figure 9-23. FNMA Graduated Payment Note—Plan 6, page 3

(C) Notice of Default

If I am in default, the Note Holder may send me a written notice telling me that if I do not pay the overdue amount by a certain date, the Note Holder may require me to pay immediately the full amount of principal which has not been paid and all the interest that I owe on that amount. That date must be at least 30 days after the date on which the notice is mailed to me or if it is not mailed, 30 days after the date on which it is delivered to me.

(D) No Waiver By Note Holder

Even if, at a time when I am in default, the Note Holder does not require me to pay immediately in full as described above, the Note Holder will still have the right to do so if, at a later time, I am in default again.

(E) Payment of Note Holder's Costs and Expenses

If the Note Holder has required me to pay immediately in full as described above, the Note Holder will have the right to be paid back for all of its costs and expenses in enforcing this Note to the extent not prohibited by applicable law. Those expenses include, for example, reasonable attorneys' fees.

13. GIVING OF NOTICES

Unless applicable law requires a different method of giving notice, any notice that must be given to me under this Note will be given by delivering it or by mailing it by first class mail addressed to me at the Property Address above or at a different address if I give the Note Holder a notice of my different address.

Any notice that must be given to the Note Holder under this Note will be given by mailing it by first class mail to the Note Holder at the address stated in Section 3 above or at a different address if I am given a notice of that different address.

14. OBLIGATIONS OF PERSONS UNDER THIS NOTE

If more than one person signs this Note, each person is fully and personally obligated to keep all of the promises made in this Note, including the promise to pay the full amount owed. Any person who is a guarantor, surety, or endorser of this Note is also obligated to do these things. Any person who takes over the obligations under this Note or any person who takes over the obligations of a guarantor, surety, or endorser of this Note is also obligated to keep all of the promises made in this Note. The Note Holder may enforce its rights under this Note against each person individually or against all of us together. This means that any one of us may be required to pay all of the amounts owed under this Note.

15. WAIVERS

I and any other person who has obligations under this Note waive the rights of presentment and notice of dishonor. "Presentment" means the right to require the Note Holder to demand payment of amounts due. "Notice of dishonor" means the right to require the Note Holder to give notice that amounts due have not been paid.

16. THIS NOTE SECURED BY A SECURITY INSTRUMENT

In addition to the protections given to the Note Holder under this Note, a Mortgage, Deed of Trust, or Deed to Secure Debt (the "Security Instrument") with a Graduated Payment Rider, dated the same day as this Note, protects the Note Holder from possible losses which might result if I do not keep the promises which I make in this Note. That Security Instrument and Rider describe how and under what conditions I may be required to make immediate payment in full of all amounts I owe under this Note. Some of those conditions are described as follows:

> "**Transfer of the Property or a Beneficial Interest in Borrower.** If all or any part of the Property or an interest therein is sold or transferred by Borrower (or if a beneficial interest in Borrower is sold or transferred and Borrower is not a natural person or persons but is a corporation, partnership, trust or other legal entity) without Lender's prior written consent, excluding (a) the creation of a lien or encumbrance subordinate to this Security Instrument which does not relate to a transfer of rights of occupancy in the property, (b) the creation of a purchase money security interest for household appliances, (c) a transfer by devise, descent or by operation of law upon the death of a joint tenant or (d) the grant of any leasehold interest of three years or less not containing an option to purchase, Lender may, at Lender's option, declare all the sums secured by this Security Instrument to be immediately due and payable.
>
> If Lender exercises such option to accelerate, Lender shall mail Borrower notice of acceleration in accordance with paragraph 14 hereof. Such notice shall provide a period of not less than 30 days from the date the notice is mailed within which Borrower may pay the sums declared due. If Borrower fails to pay such sums prior to the expiration of such period, Lender may, without further notice or demand on Borrower, invoke any remedies permitted by paragraph 18 hereof.
>
> Lender may consent to a sale or transfer if: (1) Borrower causes to be submitted to Lender information required by Lender to evaluate the transferee as if a new loan were being made to the transferee; (2) Lender reasonably determines that Lender's security will not be impaired and that the risk of a breach of any covenant or agreement in this Security Instrument is acceptable; (3) interest is payable on the sums secured by this Security Instrument at a rate acceptable to Lender; (4) changes in the terms of the Note and this Security Instrument required by Lender are made, including, for example, periodic adjustment in the interest rate, a different final payment date for the loan, and addition of unpaid interest to principal; and (5) the transferee signs an assumption agreement that is acceptable to Lender and that obligates the transferee to keep all the promises and agreements made in the Note and in this Security Instrument, as modified if required by Lender. To the extent permitted by applicable law, Lender also may charge a reasonable fee as a condition to Lender's consent to any sale or transfer.
>
> Borrower will continue to be obligated under the Note and this Security Instrument unless Lender releases Borrower in writing."

Witness the hand(s) and seal(s) of the undersigned.

....(Seal)
-Borrower

....(Seal)
-Borrower

....(Seal)
-Borrower

(Sign Original Only)

Paragraph 6, BORROWER'S RIGHT TO LIMIT MONTHLY PAYMENTS 61-120, is similar to the Plan 4 note in that it allows the borrower to limit the payments for an additional period equal to the initial adjustment period. In this case, it will be an additional five-year period.

The final document that will be reviewed is the Graduated Payment Rider (With Interest Rate Changes Every 5 Years), Figures 9-24, 9-25, and 9-26. If one compares the two riders, it is obvious that the documents are identical in construction. The two main differences are the graduation period and the index used. The percent of graduation, however, remains the same: 7.5 percent per year.

FNMA prepayment penalty FNMA does not require a provision for a prepayment charge to be included in any mortgage sold to FNMA. If a mortgage that is sold to FNMA does include such a provision, it will be strictly enforced and any proceeds derived from the provision will go to FNMA.

Plan origination by lenders According to FNMA the following lenders may originate the following plans:

1. *National banks:* Plans 5 and 8
2. *Federal savings and loans*: All of FNMA's ARM plans
3. *Lenders not exempt from interest-on-interest statutes* may use FNMA plans 5, 6, 7, and 8, if their laws otherwise authorize ARMs as planned by FNMA

Manufactured Housing Mortgage Purchase Program On August 20, 1981, FNMA instituted a program for the purchase of mortgages secured by manufactured housing units that are legally classified as real property. These mortgages can be sold to FNMA through any of its mortgage purchase programs. According to FNMA, the mortgages can be either VA guaranteed, FHA insured, or conventional. Any mortgage secured by manufactured housing must meet the following requirements:

A. The manufactured housing unit must be permanently affixed to a foundation and assume the characteristics of residential property.

B. If manufactured as a mobile unit, the wheels and axles must be removed when the unit is permanently sited.

C. The purchase of the land and home must represent a single real estate transaction under state law and must be evidenced by a recorded mortgage or deed of trust. (The combination of a chattel and real estate mortgage is not eligible.) The appropriate one- to four-family FNMA/FHLMC Uniform Instruments, or other documents acceptable to the FNMA regional office, must be used for conventional loans, and the mortgage or deed of trust must include an identification of the unit by manufacturer, model, and serial number.

D. The required title insurance policy must identify the unit as part of the real property and must insure against any loss sustained should the manufactured home be determined not to be part of the real property and that the insured mortgage is prior and superior to all other recorded real property or personal property liens or claims.

E. The mortgage amount must not include the financing of furniture (except for kitchen/laundry appliances and carpeting) credit life insurance, property damage insurance or any other form of insurance.

F. The unit and land package must be taxed as real property except that, in those jurisdictions where real estate taxation is prohibited by law, FNMA will consider submissions where the unit is taxed as personal property.

G. The Seller must obtain from the borrower, and retain in the loan file, a written "acknowledgement of intent" specifying that it is the borrower's intent that the unit be a fixture and part of the real property securing the mortgage. The form and content of this acknowledgement may be drafted by the Seller.[3]

There is no limitation regarding whether the home is a single-section or multi-section located on an individually owned lot, a leasehold estate that is acceptable to FNMA, or in the case of a conventional mortgage, a lot in a subdivision, in an approved

Figure 9-24. FNMA Graduated Payment Rider—Plan 6, page 1

GRADUATED PAYMENT RIDER

(With Interest Rate Changes Every 5 Years)

THIS GRADUATED PAYMENT RIDER is made this .... day of ...., 19........., and is incorporated into and shall be deemed to amend and supplement the Mortgage, Deed of Trust, or Deed to Secure Debt (the "Security Instrument") of the same date given by the undersigned (the "Borrower") to secure Borrower's Graduated Payment Note to .... (the "Lender") of the same date (the "Note") and covering the property described in the Security Instrument and located at:

....

(Property Address)

The Note contains provisions allowing for changes in the interest rate and monthly payments.

The Borrower's monthly payment will increase by 7½% each year during the first five years of the Note. The Borrower also may be able to limit monthly payment increases to 7½% each year during the second five years of the Note. The remaining monthly payments also could increase or decrease, depending on changes in the interest rate.

The principal amount the Borrower must repay will be larger than the amount originally borrowed, but not more than 125% of the original amount.

ADDITIONAL COVENANTS. In addition to the covenants and agreements made in the Security Instrument, Borrower and Lender further covenant and agree as follows:

A. INTEREST RATE AND MONTHLY PAYMENT CHANGES

The Note provides for an Initial Rate of Interest of ....%. Sections 2 through 9 of the Note provide for changes in the interest rate and the monthly payments, as follows:

"2. INTEREST

(A) Interest Owed

Interest will be charged on that part of principal which has not been paid. Interest will be charged beginning on the date of this Note and continuing until the full amount of principal has been paid.

Beginning on the date of this Note, I will owe interest at a yearly rate of .... %. This rate is called the "Initial Rate of Interest." The rate of interest I will pay will change in accordance with Section 4 (A) of this Note on the first day of ...., 19........ and on that day every 60th month thereafter. Each date on which my rate of interest could change is called an "Interest Change Date."

(B) The Index

Any changes in my rate of interest will be based on changes in the Index. The "Index" is the weekly average yield on United States Treasury securities adjusted to a constant maturity of 5 years, as made available by the Federal Reserve Board. The most recently available Index figure as of the date 45 days before each Interest Change Date is called the "Current Index."

If the Index is no longer available, the Note Holder will choose a new index which is based upon comparable information. The Note Holder will give me notice of this choice.

(C) Interest After Default

The rate of interest required by this Section 2 and Section 4 (A) below is the rate I will pay both before and after any default described in Section 12 (B) below.

3. TIME AND PLACE OF PAYMENTS

I will pay principal and interest by making payments every month. My monthly payments will be applied to interest before principal.

I will make my monthly payments on the first day of each month beginning on ...., 19......... I will make these payments every month until I have paid all the principal and interest and any other charges described below that I may owe under this Note. If, on ...., 20........., I still owe amounts under this Note, I will pay those amounts in full on that date, which is called the "maturity date."

I will make my monthly payments at .... or at a different place if required by the Note Holder.

4. FULL PAYMENT AMOUNT

(A) Calculation of Full Payment Amount

Each of my first 120 monthly payments could be less than a Full Payment Amount. A "Full Payment Amount" is the monthly amount sufficient to repay the amount I originally borrowed, or the unpaid principal balance of my loan as of an Interest Change Date, in full on the maturity date at the rate of interest I am required to pay by Section 2 above or this Section 4 (A) in substantially equal payments. Beginning on the date of this Note, my first Full Payment Amount will be U.S. $.. until the first Interest Change Date. My first Full Payment Amount will be larger than each of my first 60 monthly payments.

Before each Interest Change Date, the Note Holder will determine a new Full Payment Amount for my loan. The Note Holder will first calculate my new rate of interest by adding .... percentage points (..................%) to the Current Index. The Note Holder will then round the result of this addition to the nearest one-eighth of one percentage point (0.125%). This rounded amount will be my new rate of interest until the next Interest Change Date. The Note Holder will then calculate the new amount of a monthly payment that would be sufficient to repay my unpaid principal

Figure 9-25. FNMA Graduated Payment Rider—Plan 6, page 2

balance as of the Interest Change Date in full on the maturity date at my new rate of interest in substantially equal payments. The result of this calculation is my new Full Payment Amount.

Each new rate of interest will become effective on each Interest Change Date, and each new Full Payment Amount will become effective on the first monthly payment date after the Interest Change Date.

(B) Required Full Payment Amount

I will pay the Full Payment Amount as my monthly payment beginning with my 61st monthly payment if my new rate of interest is equal to or less than the Initial Rate of Interest or if I do not choose to limit the amount of my monthly payment as permitted by Section 6 (A) below. Even if I choose to limit my monthly payment, I will pay the Full Payment Amount beginning with my 121st monthly payment.

5. GRADUATED MONTHLY PAYMENTS 1–60

My first 12 monthly payments will each be in the amount of U.S. $.. On each of the first four anniversaries of the date my first monthly payment is due, I will begin paying a new monthly payment which will be equal to the amount I have been paying multiplied by the number 1.075. I will pay the new amount of my monthly payment until it changes in accordance with this Section 5 or Sections 6 or 7 below.

6. BORROWER'S RIGHT TO LIMIT AMOUNT OF MONTHLY PAYMENTS 61–120

(A) Calculation of Graduated Monthly Payment Amount

If my new rate of interest at the first Interest Change Date is greater than the Initial Rate of Interest, I may choose to limit the amount of my new monthly payment. If I do so, on each of the 5th through 9th anniversaries of the date my first monthly payment is due, I will begin paying a new monthly payment which will be equal to the amount I have been paying multiplied by the number 1.075. Even if I have chosen to limit my monthly payment, Sections 6 (B) or 6 (C) below may require me to pay a different amount. I will give the Note Holder notice that I have chosen to limit my monthly payments at least 15 days before my 61st monthly payment is due.

(B) Reduced Monthly Payment Amount

My 73rd, 85th, 97th or 109th graduated monthly payment calculated under Section 6 (A) above could be greater than the amount of a monthly payment which then would be sufficient to repay my unpaid principal balance in full on the maturity date at my current rate of interest in substantially equal payments. If so, I will instead then begin paying a new monthly payment, which will be equal to the lower amount, until my 121st monthly payment when I will begin paying my new Full Payment Amount.

(C) Increased Monthly Payment Amount

My paying a monthly payment calculated under Section 6 (A) above could cause my unpaid principal balance to exceed the limit stated in Section 8 (B) below. If so, on the date that my paying a monthly payment would cause me to exceed that limit, I will instead begin paying a new monthly payment. This new monthly payment will be in an amount which would be sufficient to repay my then unpaid principal balance in full on the maturity date at my current rate of interest in substantially equal payments, until my 121st monthly payment when I will begin paying my new Full Payment Amount.

7. MONTHLY PAYMENT 121 AND REMAINING PAYMENTS

Beginning with my 121st monthly payment, I will pay the Full Payment Amount as my monthly payment.

8. INCREASES IN THE PRINCIPAL AMOUNT TO BE PAID

(A) Additions to My Unpaid Principal Balance

Each of my first 120 monthly payments could be less than the amount of the interest portion of a monthly payment which then would be sufficient to repay my unpaid principal balance in full on the maturity date at my current rate of interest in substantially equal payments. If so, each month that the amount of my monthly payment is less than the interest portion, the Note Holder will subtract the amount of my monthly payment from the amount of the interest portion and will add the difference to my unpaid principal balance. The Note Holder will also add interest on the amount of this difference to my unpaid principal balance each month. The rate of interest on the interest added to principal will be the rate required by Sections 2 or 4 (A) above.

(B) Limit on Unpaid Principal Balance

My unpaid principal balance can never exceed a maximum amount equal to one hundred twenty-five percent (125%) of the principal amount I originally borrowed.

9. NOTICE OF CHANGES

The Note Holder will mail or deliver to me a notice of any changes in the amount of my monthly payment before the effective date of any change. The notice will include information required by law to be given me and also the title and telephone number of a person who will answer any question I may have regarding the notice."

B. CHARGES; LIENS

Uniform Covenant 4 of the Security Instrument is amended to read as follows:

4. Charges; Liens. Borrower shall pay all taxes, assessments, and other charges, fines and impositions attributable to the Property which may attain a priority over this Security Instrument, and leasehold payments or ground rents, if any, in the manner provided under paragraph 2 hereof or, if not paid in such manner, by Borrower making payment, when due, directly to the payee thereof. Borrower shall promptly furnish to Lender all notices of amounts due under this paragraph, and in the event Borrower shall make payment directly, Borrower shall promptly furnish to Lender receipts evidencing such payments. Borrower shall promptly discharge any lien which has priority over this Security Instrument; provided, that Borrower shall not be required to discharge any such lien so long as Borrower: (a) shall agree in writing to the payment of the obligation secured by such lien in a manner acceptable to Lender; (b) shall in good faith contest such lien by, or defend against enforcement of such lien in, legal proceedings which in the opinion of Lender operate to prevent the enforcement of the lien or forfeiture of the Property or any part thereof; or (c) shall secure from the holder of such lien an agreement in a form satisfactory to Lender subordinating such lien to this Security Instrument.

If Lender determines that all or any part of the Property is subject to a lien which may attain a priority over this Security Instrument, Lender shall send Borrower notice identifying such lien. Borrower shall satisfy such lien or take one or more of the actions set forth above within ten days of the giving of notice.

C. NOTICE

Uniform Covenant 14 of the Security Instrument is amended to read as follows:

Figure 9-26. FNMA Graduated Payment Rider—Plan 6, page 3

14. Notice. Except for any notice required under applicable law to be given in another manner, (a) any notice to Borrower provided for in this Security Instrument shall be given by delivering it or by mailing it by first class mail addressed to Borrower at the Property Address or at such other address as Borrower may designate by notice to Lender as provided herein, and (b) any notice to Lender shall be given by first class mail to Lender's address stated herein or to such other address as Lender may designate by notice to Borrower as provided herein. Any notice provided for in this Security Instrument shall be deemed to have been given to Borrower or Lender when given in the manner designated herein.

D. UNIFORM SECURITY INSTRUMENT; GOVERNING LAW; SEVERABILITY

Uniform Covenant 15 of the Security Instrument is amended to read as follows:

15. Uniform Security Instrument; Governing Law; Severability. This form of Security Instrument combines uniform covenants for national use and non-uniform covenants with limited variations by jurisdiction to constitute a uniform security instrument covering real property. This Security Instrument shall be governed by federal law and the law of the jurisdiction in which the Property is located. In the event that any provision or clause of this Security Instrument or the Note conflicts with applicable law, such conflict shall not affect other provisions of this Security Instrument or the Note which can be given effect without the conflicting provision, and to this end the provisions of this Security Instrument and the Note are declared to be severable.

E. TRANSFER OF THE PROPERTY OR A BENEFICIAL INTEREST IN BORROWER

Uniform Covenant 17 of the Security Instrument is amended to read as follows:

17. Transfer of the Property or a Beneficial Interest in Borrower. If all or any part of the Property or an interest therein is sold or transferred by Borrower (or if a beneficial interest in Borrower is sold or transferred and Borrower is not a natural person or persons but is a corporation, partnership, trust or other legal entity) without Lender's prior written consent, excluding (a) the creation of a lien or encumbrance subordinate to this Security Instrument which does not relate to a transfer of rights of occupancy in the property, (b) the creation of a purchase money security interest for household appliances, (c) a transfer by devise, descent or by operation of law upon the death of a joint tenant or (d) the grant of any leasehold interest of three years or less not containing an option to purchase, Lender may, at Lender's option, declare all the sums secured by this Security Instrument to be immediately due and payable.

If Lender exercises such option to accelerate, Lender shall mail Borrower notice of acceleration in accordance with paragraph 14 hereof. Such notice shall provide a period of not less than 30 days from the date the notice is mailed within which Borrower may pay the sums declared due. If Borrower fails to pay such sums prior to the expiration of such period, Lender may, without further notice or demand on Borrower, invoke any remedies permitted by paragraph 18 hereof.

Lender may consent to a sale or transfer if: (1) Borrower causes to be submitted to Lender information required by Lender to evaluate the transferee as if a new loan were being made to the transferee; (2) Lender reasonably determines that Lender's security will not be impaired and that the risk of a breach of any covenant or agreement in this Security Instrument is acceptable; (3) interest is payable on the sums secured by this Security Instrument at a rate acceptable to Lender; (4) changes in the terms of the Note and this Security Instrument required by Lender are made, including, for example, periodic adjustment in the interest rate, a different final payment date for the loan, and addition of unpaid interest to principal; and (5) the transferee signs an assumption agreement that is acceptable to Lender and that obligates the transferee to keep all the promises and agreements made in the Note and in this Security Instrument, as modified if required by Lender. To the extent permitted by applicable law, Lender also may charge a reasonable fee as a condition to Lender's consent to any sale or transfer.

Borrower will continue to be obligated under the Note and this Security Instrument unless Lender releases Borrower in writing.

F. COVENANT DELETED

Non-Uniform Covenant 21 of the Security Instrument ("Future Advances") is deleted.

G. LOAN CHARGES

If the loan secured by the Security Instrument is subject to a law which sets maximum loan charges, and that law is finally interpreted so that the interest or other loan charges collected or to be collected in connection with the loan exceed permitted limits, then: (1) any such loan charge shall be reduced by the amount necessary to reduce the charge to the permitted limits; and (2) any sums already collected from Borrower which exceeded permitted limits will be refunded to Borrower. Lender may choose to make this refund by reducing the principal owed under the Note or by making a direct payment to Borrower. If a refund reduces principal, the reduction will be treated as a partial prepayment under the Note.

H. LEGISLATION

If, after the date hereof, enactment or expiration of applicable laws have the effect either of rendering the provisions of the Note, the Security Instrument or this Graduated Payment Rider (other than this paragraph H) unenforceable according to their terms, or all or any part of the sums secured hereby uncollectable, as otherwise provided in the Security Instrument and this Graduated Payment Rider, or of diminishing the value of Lender's security, then Lender, at Lender's option, may declare all sums secured by the Security Instrument to be immediately due and payable.

IN WITNESS WHEREOF, Borrower has executed this Graduated Payment Rider.

....(Seal)
-Borrower

....(Seal)
-Borrower

....(Seal)
-Borrower
(Sign Original Only)

condominium project, PUD, or de minimus PUD. There are some limitations if the home is financed through VA or FHA: if the home is financed by FHA under Title I or guaranteed under the VA Mobile Home Program, the mortgage is not eligible for purchase.

On February 17, 1982, the FNMA regional office in Dallas issued Circular Letter No. 82-1. This letter listed some additional program requirements. The major additional requirements concerned property guidelines. Some of the more important requirements are listed below:

1. The manufactured unit may be either a single-wide or double-wide, but a single-wide unit must be at least 12 feet wide and contain 700 square feet of living area.

2. FNMA stated that only units built after June 15, 1976, will qualify as security for a mortgage to be sold to FNMA.

3. In regard to the foundation for the unit, FNMA has established the following guidelines:

   a. The foundation must be designed to the soil characteristics and sufficient to withstand wind loads of the individual site.

   b. Any foundation made from materials other than concrete or cement block must be approved by FNMA.

4. FNMA further requires that the manufactured property must be comparable to a house built on a standard lot in the local market place. According to FNMA, this means that the units should have pitched roofs, covered front and rear entrances, in-place built steps and porches, and the exterior finish is to be either real or standard wood siding, stucco, brick, or combination.

Even though these requirements were issued by a regional office of FNMA, they may apply to your area. Prior to working with a client in your area, you should contact a FNMA approved lender.

Loan Participation Program In order to simplify many of the FNMA programs, FNMA announced the Loan Participation Program on June 1, 1981. This program is a consolidation of two existing FNMA programs: Urban Loan Participation, implemented on February 1, 1978, and the Rural Loan Participation program implemented on July 1, 1980. The reason for the consolidation is to simplify the procedures for both of these previous programs and allow for FNMA's purchase of a participation in a pool of mortgages regardless of the location of the property.

Under this program FNMA will purchase a participation, or an interest, in a pool of mortgages. The amount of the participation can range from as little as 50 percent to a maximum of 95 percent of the pool. All of the mortgages in the pool must be secured by one- to four-family properties. In addition to the minimum percentage of participation, FNMA has established a $250,000 minimum for the dollar amount FNMA will purchase in any pool of mortgages.

The underwriting requirements for mortgages in the pool are generally the same as for the conventional loan purchase program mentioned earlier in the chapter. One unique feature of the program is that the use of the standard FNMA/FHLMC Uniform Note and Mortgage/Deed of Trust is suggested, but is not required. Also, many of the other procedures for the program have been streamlined. For example, FNMA will purchase and fund a participation in a pool of mortgages upon receipt of a participation certificate, including a loan schedule, and will not review the loans prior to funding.

The program is available to any FNMA-approved conventional lender or any institution that is either insured and supervised by an agency of the federal government or any state government.

Mandatory Delivery Commitment Program
The last of the commitments offered by FNMA is the Mandatory Delivery Commitment Program. This program was instituted by FNMA on May 28, 1981. Under this program, the lender must deliver mortgages by a specific date and at a specific yield, which is different from the mortgage purchase program described in the Free Market System section. If a lender wishes to sell a mortgage to FNMA under this program, the lender will contact FNMA for a required yield for the mortgages to be delivered. It should be noted that the yield on the

mandatory commitment program may change without notice and the lender must always contact FNMA to find the actual yield for any specific commitment. It is, however, generally lower than that for optional delivery. The fees are also lower.

The term of the mandatory commitment is much shorter than the FMS commitments, only thirty or sixty days.

Free Market System Auction FNMA has several methods for the purchase of mortgages from approved lenders. Traditionally the most common, but expected to account for less activity as more alternatives have been introduced, is the free market auction. This free market system, more commonly known as FMS, was started in 1968 and is a method of issuing commitments for the purchase of mortgages on one- to four-family dwellings for delivery in four months. Prior to the institution of the FMS, FNMA would post or state the price at which they would purchase mortgages for immediate delivery. The price or yield at which FNMA would purchase these loans would vary by geographical area of the country and was determined by the sampling of mortgage yields in those areas.

There were three basic disadvantages with this system of establishing prices, or yields, for mortgages. First, this method tended to be discriminatory in that it was difficult for FNMA to secure a realistic evaluation of the yields in all localities. Furthermore, it did not reflect the difference in demand in localities throughout the United States, for it was impossible to contact every lender in every city and town. In effect, this method did not distribute or allocate the funds available for the purchase of mortgages equitably to all areas.

The second disadvantage was that with an immediate purchase program, lenders and builders were not able to plan ahead, nor were they able to make loans with the confidence that there was a willing buyer for the closed loan—and if there was, what interest rate would be charged by the purchaser of the mortgages?

The last disadvantage was that the yields were changed frequently, and it was difficult for the lenders to keep up with the changes.

All of these disadvantages were overcome with the institution of the free market system auction. The first auction was held June 1969.

Under FMS, there are three auctions held every other Monday, unless the Monday is a holiday, and then the FMS is held on Tuesday. The three separate but simultaneous auctions are held to sell commitments for the purchase of conventional mortgages, FHA/VA mortgages, and FHA 245 graduated payment mortgages. The first of the auctions to sell FHA 245 commitments was held on July 7, 1980, and some $53.8 million in commitments was issued. The FMS commitments today are for four-month optional delivery.

This auction system, as its name implies, is a true auction. Lenders who wish to sell mortgages to FNMA submit bids. These bids state the yield FNMA would receive on mortgages sold to it under the commitment. The auction is open to all FNMA-approved lenders throughout the United States, thus it truly reflects the demand for mortgage funds. These lenders submit offers via telephone to the Washington, D.C., FNMA office between 9 A.M. and 3 P.M. EST on the bid day. This verbal bid is confirmed in writing by the submission of FNMA Form 550.

The lender can submit two types of bids: the competitive bid or the noncompetitive bid. A lender cannot submit both types of bids in the same auction. Under the competitive bid, the lender specifies the yield FNMA would receive on loans bought under the commitment. This yield will include the three-eighths of 1 percent servicing fee paid to the lender by FNMA. It is important that the servicing fee is included. If it were not, the lender would later include the fee, thus increasing the face interest rate on the mortgage. When a yield is quoted without the servicing fee, the yield is said to be a net yield. In the competitive auction, a lender can submit up to five bids in each of the three auctions, or fifteen bids. There are some additional rules regarding bids currently in effect. These rules are of interest to the mortage lender, but will have no direct effect on you as a real estate professional. When making bids under the competitive auction, the lenders are charged the following nonrefundable fees:

1. An offer or bid fee of one-fiftieth of 1 percent is charged on the first through the fifth bid.

2. If any or all of the bids are accepted, an additional commitment fee of 2 percent of the commitment amount will be charged.

The second type of bid that a lender can submit is the noncompetitive bid. Under this type of bid, the lender is stating that it will accept the commitment at the weighted average yield of the competitive offers accepted by FNMA in that auction. You might ask why all of the lenders do not submit noncompetitive bids. FNMA, seeing this as a possibility, has placed the following limitations on the noncompetitive bids. First, a lender can submit only one per auction. The maximum amount for the single noncompetitive bid is $500,000 for conventional FHA/VA or FHA/VA-GPMs auctions. When one of these offers is submitted, the lender does not have to specify the yield, as is the case with the competitive offer. As with the competitive bid, FNMA charges a lender certain fees for the commitment. Under the noncompetitive bid, a bid or offer fee of one-fiftieth of 1 percent is charged.

In order to calculate the weighted average yield to accept, FNMA takes all of the competitive bids placed prior to 3 P.M. on bid day and also reviews the mortgage and credit market conditions, as well as its cost of borrowing.

The amount of money available in the secondary market can be determined by the bidding patterns of the lenders. For example, if there is sufficient money to meet the demands from other sources in the Northeast section of the nation, these lenders will not seek large commitments from FNMA. If, however, there is a great demand for mortgage money in the Southwest, the lenders in this area would submit bids for commitments in large amounts at yields that might be above market. This would be done to insure the issuance of a commitment.

Once the minimum is established, all of the lenders who submitted bids in the auction are notified as to whether their bids were accepted or rejected. It should be noted that if a lender's bids are accepted, the lender does not have to deliver mortgages to FNMA under the issued commitment if the lender should find another investor that will purchase the mortgages under better terms. This type of commitment, where the lender is not required to deliver the mortgages, is called *optional, or nonmandatory*. Thus, if interest rates rise during the commitment term, the lender will probably use it to sell loans to FNMA; if rates fall, the lender will sell to another investor on an immediate-purchase basis. The commitments, therefore, provide a certain interest-rate protection. But as outlined earlier in this section, all of the fees, both the bid or offer fee and the commitment fee, are nonrefundable, and thus the fees would be a loss to the lender who regards them somewhat like insurance payments. The yields on FMS commitments remain fixed for four months.

The importance of these bid results cannot be underestimated, for the results and the minimum yield established by FNMA through this nationwide auction give a strong indication as to the rates in the future, and to you selling real estate they can serve as a good market indicator of what may happen in the future. For example, if the bid range in the auctions is increasing and the minimum yield is increasing, it is a good indication that rates will be on the increase in the near future. If the bid range and minimum are declining, the rates should be declining in the near future.

In addition to notifying the lenders as to the results of the most recent auction, FNMA also notifies major papers and wire services throughout the United States, and the results are published in such papers as the *Wall Street Journal*. If you would like to receive information on the results of the auctions, you may request it from the FNMA headquarters in Washington, D.C.

A sample of the information that you may receive is shown in Figure 9-27. In addition to the results of the latest bid, you will be furnished with information on past auctions, thus allowing you to establish a possible trend. This information includes the bid range for each of the auctions. In addition to the bid range in the FHA/VA and the FHA 245 auctions, FNMA gives the price that each of the high and low bids would be in relationship to the present FHA/VA rates. This price is another way of stating points. The price for the minimum yield acceptable to FNMA on FHA/VA mortgages is given in the Average Yield Price column under the Standard FHA/VA Auction heading. For example, in the latest auction shown in Figure 9-27, the price for the FHA/VA was 89.33. This means that for FNMA to purchase a

Figure 9-27. ***FMS Auction Results***

Federal National Mortgage Association
3900 WISCONSIN AVENUE, N.W., WASHINGTON, D.C. 20016

News Release

#4310 - 1980

FOR IMMEDIATE RELEASE

WASHINGTON, D.C., December 9 -- Yields were mixed in yesterday's Federal National Mortgage Association biweekly auctions of four-month commitments to purchase home mortgages from lenders. The corporation today issued $98.0 million in four-month commitments to purchase both government-backed and conventional loans.

FNMA issued $51.9 million in commitments for standard FHA-insured and VA-guaranteed mortgages. The weighted average yield of accepted bids for commitments on standard FHA and VA mortgages was 15.496 percent, which converts to an average price of 89.33 for 13 1/2 percent loans. (The average in the previous auction was 15.493 percent.) The range of these bids was from 15.389 percent to 15.618 percent. FNMA received 134 such bids totaling $96.7 million and accepted 88 bids, including 64 noncompetitive offers.

The corporation accepted $12.0 million in bids for FHA graduated payment (Section 245) mortgages at an average yield of 16.020 percent, which converts to an average price of 89.42 for 14 percent loans. (The average in the previous auction was 16.070 percent.) The corporation received 53 bids, for $24.5 million, and accepted 35 bids, including 29 noncompetitive, at yields ranging from 15.932 percent to 16.109 percent.

For conventionally financed mortgages, FNMA issued $34.1 million in commitments at a weighted average yield of 15.650 percent, compared with 15.349 percent in the last auction. Accepted bids ranged from 15.440 percent to 15.700 percent. The 80 offers totaled $56.1 million. FNMA accepted 61 bids, including 53 noncompetitive.

The next auction will be December 22, 1980.

(All yields quoted are gross: 3/8 percent servicing fees are not deducted.)

# # #

Figure 9-27. continued

Details of Recent FHA/VA, FHA Graduated Payment and Conventional Auctions
(Dollars in Millions)

	STANDARD FHA/VA			FHA GRADUATED PAYMENT			CONVENTIONAL		
Date	Offers Rec'd/Accept	Avg. Yield Price	Yield/ Price Range	Offers Rec'd/Accept	Avg. Yield Price	Yield/ Price Range	Offers Rec'd/Accept	Avg. Yield	Yield- Range
FHA/VA	rate at 11 1/2%			FHA-GPM	rate at 11 1/2%				
7/7	$629.0-$256.3	12.527 (93.81)	12.971-12.463 (91.31) (94.18)	$120.3-$ 44.7	12.948 (91.43)	13.009-12.902 (91.10) (91.69)	$107.4-$ 58.4	12.763	12.877-12.662
7/21	$426.6-$174.0	12.781 (92.37)	12.900-12.727 (91.70) (92.67)	$ 79.4-$ 31.0	13.223 (89.93)	13.286-13.177 (89.59) (90.18)	$120.8-$ 82.0	12.838	13.100-12.750
8/4	$643.1-$354.6	13.578 (88.04)	13.793-13.506 (86.93) (88.42)	$158.3-$ 94.8	14.017 (85.79)	14.444-13.899 (83.68) (86.39)	$204.9-$106.7	13.309	13.750-13.250
8/18	$420.2-$273.5	14.257 (84.60)	14.573-14.149 (83.06) (85.13)	$126.2-$ 51.7	14.837 (81.81)	15.146-14.723 (80.38) (82.35)	$225.5-$112.1	14.001	14.350-13.879
FHA/VA	rate at 12%			FHA-GPM	rate at 12 1/2%				
9/2	$324.4-$183.0	14.413 (86.58)	14.734-14.309 (85.00) (87.10)	$103.1-$ 42.5	14.991 (86.45)	15.105-14.930 (85.90) (86.75)	$120.5-$ 71.0	14.193	14.627-14.007
9/15	$224.5-$136.4	14.596 (85.67)	14.738-14.534 (84.98) (85.98)	$121.6-$ 73.6	15.180 (85.54)	15.303-15.118 (84.95) (85.84)	$103.9-$ 67.9	14.290	14.510-14.156
FHA/VA	rate at 13%			FHA-GPM	rate at 13 1/2%				
9/29	$358.1-$218.5	15.299 (87.63)	15.451-15.239 (86.90) (87.93)	$135.9-$ 86.9	15.866 (87.55)	15.968-15.782 (87.07) (87.95)	$123.3-$ 70.9	14.862	15.125-14.750
10/13	$196.3-$118.3	14.566 (91.31)	15.006-14.409 (89.08) (92.13)	$ 83.7-$ 50.2	15.220 (90.70)	15.548-15.003 (89.08) (91.80)	$ 28.9-$ 17.9	14.469	15.250-14.391
10/27	$231.5-$139.4	15.304 (87.61)	15.537-15.186 (86.49) (88.19)	$ 72.2-$ 36.2	16.023 (86.81)	16.200-15.909 (85.99) (87.35)	$ 78.7-$ 46.4	14.915	15.097-14.800
11/10	$126.3-$ 63.6	15.572 (86.32)	15.726-15.525 (85.60) (86.55)	$ 49.3-$ 24.6	16.196 (86.01)	16.252-16.144 (85.75) (86.25)	$ 51.8-$ 47.5	15.249	15.376-15.128
FHA/VA	rate at 13 1/2%			FHA-GPM	rate at 14%				
11/24	$125.7-$ 72.0	15.493 (89.35)	15.732-15.412 (88.19) (89.75)	$ 29.5-$ 15.0	16.070 (89.18)	16.161-16.012 (88.75) (89.46)	$ 29.8-$ 21.3	15.349	15.500-15.252
12/8	$ 96.7-$ 51.9	15.496 (89.33)	15.618-15.389 (88.74) (89.86)	$ 24.5-$ 12.0	16.020 (89.42)	16.109-15.932 (89.00) (89.85)	$ 56.1-$ 34.1	15.650	15.700-15.440

mortgage under a commitment issued at this auction's weighted average yield, and with the interest rate set by FHA/VA, FNMA would purchase the mortgage at 89.33 percent of the dollar amount of the mortgage. This would establish the points for a mortgage sold under this commitment at 10.67 or 100 percent minus 89.33 percent. This information is also provided for the FHA graduated payment mortgages. With this information, one can see that if the price is dropping, the number of points that will have to be charged by the lenders will increase.

From this brief discussion of the FMS auctions, one can see the importance of their results.

Other Commitments Offered In addition to the commitments offered through the FMS auction, FNMA also has several other commitments that it will issue. One of these commitments is the *standby commitment*. This commitment is not issued through the FMS auction. Under this commitment FNMA issues an optional delivery commitment to purchase either FHA/VA, FHA-GPM, or conventional mortgages on one- to four-family dwellings that are either proposed, under construction, or existing. These commitments are issued for nine or twelve months in specified dollar amounts. Any time after the day of issuance, the lender may convert the commitment to a thirty- or sixty-day mandatory commitment at the prevailing yield on such commitments. Why is this type of commitment important to you as a person working in the field of real estate? For example, you are working with a client who wishes to build a house that will take at least four months to complete. To be sure that there will be mortgage money available at the time of completion, you and your client may secure FNMA standby commitment, thus assuring the money for the permanent financing.

REVIEW QUESTIONS

1. Define the term *secondary market.*
2. Name the major secondary marketers.
3. Outline the development of the Federal National Mortgage Association.
4. Define the term *governmental interaction*, as it applies to FNMA.
5. Outline the conventional single-family and two- to four-family mortgage purchase programs of FNMA.
6. Outline the operation of the free market system auction.
7. Explain the meaning of the competitive and noncompetitive bids.
8. Name and explain at least four of the general characteristics of the FNMA buydown interest rate mortgage purchase program.
9. Outline the general limitations for subordinate financing when used in conjunction with the financing of a single-family dwelling or a two- to four-family dwelling.
10. Define the term *operating income* as it applies to two- to four-family properties.
11. List the approved interest rate indexes and adjustment interval for the Adjustable Rate Mortgage Purchase Program.
12. List four requirements that must be met by a mortgage to be purchased under the Manufactured Housing Mortgage Purchase Program.

NOTES

[1]Most of this section is based on material from U.S. House of Representatives, 90th Congress, First Session, Committee on Banking and Urban Affairs, *Basic Laws and Authorities on Housing and Community Development*, revised through January 3, 1979, part 1, pp. 645-80.

[2]Most of this section is based on material from Federal National Mortgage Association, *A Guide to Fannie Mae, 1979*, pp. 60-65.

[3]Federal National Mortgage Association, Dallas, Texas, memo, *Manufactured Housing—August 20, 1981*, pp. 1-2.

CHAPTER 10 The Secondary Market, Part 2

LEARNING OBJECTIVES

In this chapter we will discuss the two remaining major secondary marketers, the Federal Home Loan Mortgage Corporation (FHLMC) and the Government National Mortgage Association (GNMA).

Upon completion of this chapter you should be able to do the following:

- **Outline the development of GNMA and FHLMC.**
- **Outline the operations of the two governmental agencies.**
- **Outline the programs of the two agencies.**

THE FEDERAL HOME LOAN MORTGAGE CORPORATION (FHLMC)

The Federal Home Loan Mortgage Corporation was created in 1970 with the passage of the Emergency Home Finance Act of 1970. Under Section 305 of the act, FHLMC was authorized to purchase and make commitments to purchase residential mortgages from any federal home loan bank, the Federal Savings and Loan Insurance Corporation, or any financial institution where the deposits or accounts are insured by any agency of the federal government or an agency of any state government.

The Federal Home Loan Mortgage Corporation, sometimes called Freddie Mac and since the late 1970s called the Mortgage Corporation, is under the control of the Federal Home Loan Bank Board. The Mortgage Corporation is authorized to purchase or commit to purchase both conventional and FHA/VA mortgages. In recent years, however, it has reduced its holding of FHA/VA mortgages and discontinued all purchases of FHA/VA mortgages on March 1, 1981. The conventional mortgages purchased by the Mortgage Corporation can be secured by either single-family or two to four-family units. These units can be located in any FHLMC-approved planned unit development or condominium.

Under Section 303 of Title III of the legislation, the Mortgage Corporation was authorized to be incorporated and to be under the direction of a board of directors, with its principal office in Washington, D.C. It was also authorized to establish branch offices as needed. The Mortgage Corporation now operates five regional offices. A map illustrating the five regions is shown in Figure 10-1, and the addresses of the regional offices and the states that each office serves is shown in Figure 10-2.

Figure 10-1. Mortgage Corporation Offices Throughout the U.S.

	States and Territories
NORTHEAST **Regional Office** (703) 685-2400 Federal Home Loan Mortgage Corporation 2001 Jefferson Davis Highway, Suite 901 Arlington, Virginia 22202	Connecticut, Delaware, District of Columbia, Maine, Maryland, Massachusetts, New Hampshire, New Jersey, New York, Pennsylvania, Puerto Rico, Rhode Island, Vermont, Virginia, Virgin Islands, West Virginia
SOUTHEAST **Regional Office** (404) 659-3377 Federal Home Loan Mortgage Corporation Peachtree Center, Cain Tower Building Post Office Box 56566 Atlanta, Georgia 30343	Alabama, Florida, Georgia, Kentucky, Mississippi, North Carolina, South Carolina, Tennessee
NORTH CENTRAL **Regional Office** (312) 861-8400 Federal Home Loan Mortgage Corporation 111 East Wacker Drive, Suite 1515 Chicago, Illinois 60601	Illinois, Indiana, Iowa, Michigan, Minnesota, North Dakota, Ohio, South Dakota, Wisconsin
SOUTHWEST **Regional Office** (214) 387-0600 Federal Home Loan Mortgage Corporation 12700 Park Central Place, Suite 1800 Dallas, Texas 75251	Arkansas, Louisiana, Missouri, New Mexico, Oklahoma, Texas
Denver Underwriting Office (303) 770-1435 Federal Home Loan Mortgage Corporation Denver Technological Center Building B-7 8000 East Prentice Avenue Englewood, Colorado 80111	*Colorado, Kansas, Nebraska, Wyoming
WESTERN **Regional Office** (213) 738-8200 Federal Home Loan Mortgage Corporation 3435 Wilshire Boulevard, Suite 1000 Los Angeles, California 90010	Arizona, California, Guam, Hawaii, Nevada, Utah
Seattle Underwriting Office (206) 622-9904 Federal Home Loan Mortgage Corporation 600 Stewart Street, Suite 1315 Seattle, Washington 98101	*Alaska, Idaho, Montana, Oregon, Washington
San Francisco Underwriting Office (415) 433-1822 Federal Home Loan Mortgage Corporation 600 California Street, Suite 311 San Francisco, California 94108	*Designated Sellers, as assigned by the Western Regional Office
Newport Beach Underwriting Office (714) 955-0322 Federal Home Loan Mortgage Corporation 4000 MacArthur Boulevard, Suite 4700 Newport Beach, California 92660	*Designated Sellers, as assigned by the Western Regional Office

Source: Federal Home Loan Mortgage Corporation, *Announcement of a New Program from the Mortgage Corporation: ARM Invitation—Adjustable Rate Mortgage Pilot Purchase Program*, July 1, 1981, p. 4.

Figure 10-2. Mortgage Corporation Areas Served

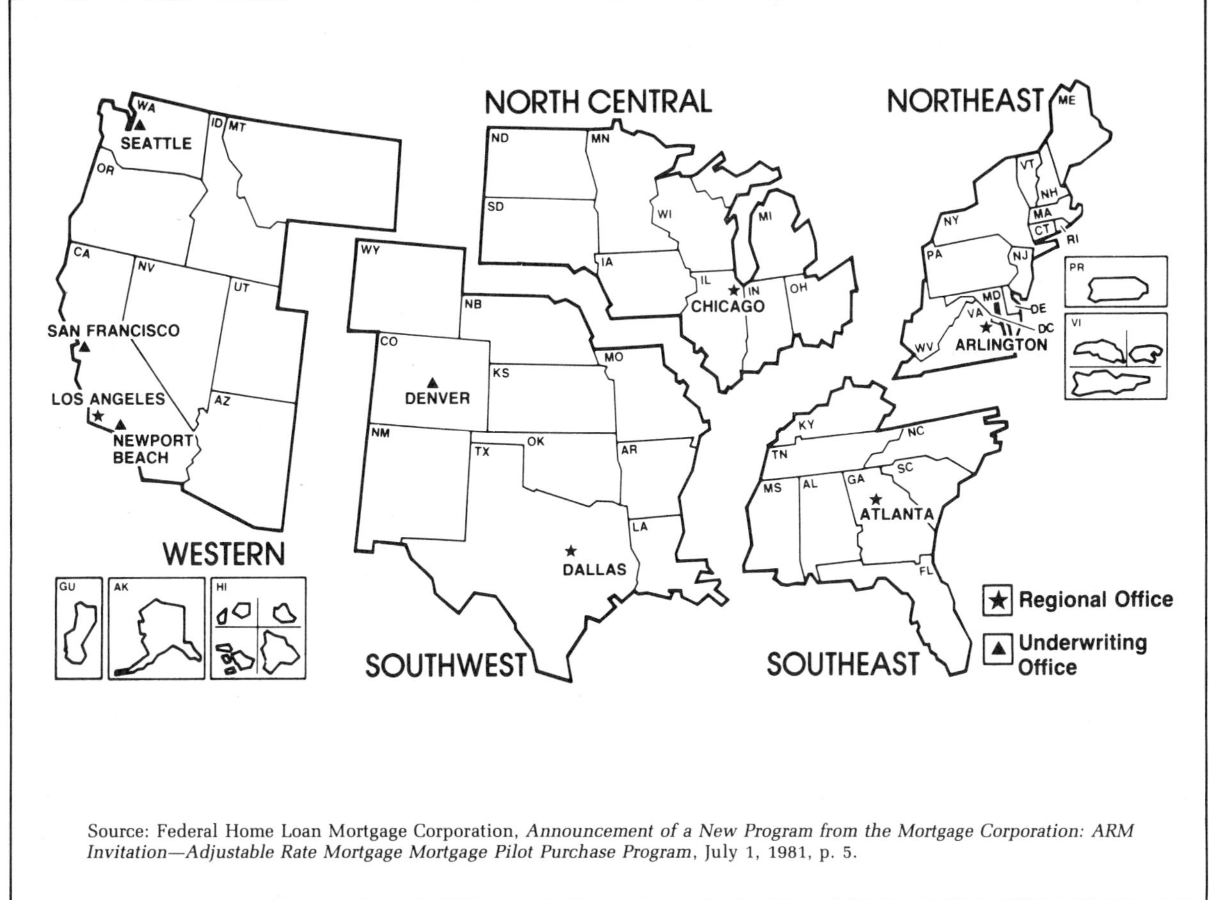

Source: Federal Home Loan Mortgage Corporation, *Announcement of a New Program from the Mortgage Corporation: ARM Invitation—Adjustable Rate Mortgage Mortgage Pilot Purchase Program*, July 1, 1981, p. 5.

Conventional Mortgage Purchase Programs

As stated earlier, the Mortgage Corporation was authorized to purchase mortgages from certain types of financial institutions. These mortgages can be purchased by the corporation under three types of programs: the immediate delivery program, the eight-month forward commitment program, and the adjustable rate mortgage purchase program. The immediate delivery program and the eight-month forward commitment program are each divided into a whole loan program and a participation program.

Immediate Delivery Program The immediate delivery program is made up of the whole loan program and the participation program. Under the whole loan program, the Mortgage Corporation will issue commitments to purchase 100 percent of conventional loans for delivery within sixty days at a specified yield. This yield is established by a bid pricing system operated by the Federal Home Loan Mortgage Corporation. (This system will be discussed later in this chapter.) The Mortgage Corporation will purchase mortgages under this program that are secured by either single-family or two- to four-family dwellings. The single-family dwelling mortgages are limited to a maximum loan-to-value ratio of 95 percent and to a maximum loan amount of $107,000. For the two- to four-family mortgages, the mortgages are limited to a 95 percent loan-to-value ratio and the following maximum loan amounts:

Two-family dwelling	$136,800
Three-family dwelling	$165,100
Four-family dwelling	$205,300

These limits may be increased by 50 percent in Alaska and Hawaii.

The Housing and Community Development Act of 1980 requires that single-family mortgage limits be adjusted annually beginning January 1, 1981. The adjustment will be equal to the percentage of increase in single-family housing prices during a twelve-month period from October to October. For multifamily property, the limits may not be increased to exceed 125 percent of the limits established under Section 207(c)(3).

Approved institutions can also deliver mortgages that refinance existing mortgages, but these types of mortgages may not exceed an 80 percent loan-to-value ratio.

Since this is an immediate delivery program, mortgages under this program must be delivered within sixty days of the issuance of a commitment by FHLMC.

Under the loan participation program, the Mortgage Corporation will purchase an interest in a mortgage from any approved institution. That interest will range from a 95 percent maximum to a 50 percent minimum of the balance of the mortgage. The types of loans that may be sold under this program are similar to those that are eligible for sale under the whole loan program.

Since this is also an immediate delivery program, the approved lender must deliver to FHLMC within sixty days of commitment conventional mortgages that will meet the amount of the commitment issued by the Federal Home Loan Mortgage Corporation.

Eight-Month Forward Commitment Purchase Program This is the second program through which approved lenders may sell mortgages to FHLMC. Under this program, lenders may sell conventional mortgages within eight months after FHLMC accepts the lender's bid as to yield on the mortgages to be sold. The maximum mortgage amounts are identical for this program as those of the immediate whole loan and participation program described above. The types of property that may be used as security and the loan-to-value ratios are also identical.

Adjustable-Rate Mortgage Purchase Program The Federal Home Loan Mortgage Corporation initiated a pilot program to purchase the adjustable-rate mortgage in late May 1981. This pilot program was the first in a series of programs instituted by a major secondary marketer to purchase the adjustable-rate mortgage.

This program is very similar to other purchase programs offered by FHLMC. FHLMC made an effort to change only those items in the Whole Loan Program to allow for the purchase of the adjustable-rate mortgage. The major characteristics of the pilot program are shown in Figure 10-3.

As with FNMA, FHLMC has developed a standard adjustable-rate note and security instrument rider. The adjustable-rate note is shown in Figures 10-4, 10-5, 10-6 and 10-7. In reviewing the note, one can see that the instrument is a "plain language" instrument with the important sections, such as the Borrower's Promise to Pay, Interest Rate, and Interest Rate Changes, in bold face type.

Many of the sections are similar to the standard FNMA/FHLMC Note that was reviewed in Chapter 2. One of the major differences is, of course, the section dealing with interest rate changes. This section, Figure 10-5, is divided into four subsections. Subsection (A) states that any change in the interest rate will be based on the movement of any index and has two boxes (one of the boxes will be checked). If the mortgage is to be sold to FHLMC, box 1 will be checked. Subsection (B) states how the new interest rate will be set or calculated. This section also indicates whether the mortgage will have a cap or a maximum amount that the interest rate will increase. If neither box is checked, however, what is indicated is that there is no maximum on the amount the interest rate may increase or decrease. Subsections (C) and (D) are self-explanatory.

The uniform Adjustable-Rate Loan Rider, Figure 10-8, is, as its name implies, a rider or attachment to the uniform FNMA/FHLMC Mortgage/Deed of Trust that was also reviewed in Chapter 2. In the first paragraph of the rider, reference is made to the mortgage/deed of trust that the rider is amending, as well as the property used as security. Section (A) of the rider restates that the interest rate on the note may either increase or decrease, and again gives the index which will be used to determine whether the rate does increase or decrease. This section also has the provision for a limitation to the amount the interest rate may increase or decrease.

Bid-pricing system As with FNMA, the Mortgage Corporation sells, or offers to buy, mortgages in the whole loan program based on a weighted average yield. This average yield is established through both a weekly and a monthly bid pricing program. The weekly

Figure 10-3. FHLMC Adjustable-Rate Mortgage Pilot Purchase Program Characteristics

PURCHASE AMOUNT — Section 3.101 and 3.102.

Whole Loans — 100% of loan balance or lower percent to equate lower Note Interest Rate (Coupon Rate) to Minimum Gross Yield.

Participations — 95% maximum and 50% minimum of unpaid principal balance of each loan when the Note Interest Rate (Coupon Rate) is equal to or exceeds the FHLMC net yield requirement.

FHLMC will not purchase adjustable rate mortgage loans on a participation basis if the Note Interest Rate (Coupon Rate) is less than the FHLMC net yield requirement.

MAXIMUM ORIGINAL LOAN-TO-VALUE RATIO AND LOAN AMOUNTS — Section 3.201a.

LTV is based on the lower of the purchase price or appraised value at time of loan closing.

Number of Dwelling Units	*Maximum LTV Ratio*	*Maximum Mortgage Loan Amount*
1	95%	$107,000
2	95%	136,800
3	90%	165,100
4	90%	205,300

Properties located in Alaska, Guam, and Hawaii have maximum amounts of up to fifty percent higher.

For refinanced mortgage loans, the maximum LTV is 80% based on appraised value at time of loan closing, except LTV may be increased to 90% for 1-2 family dwellings if proceeds of refinance were exclusively for improvement to property.

TYPE OF LIEN — A long-term note, secured by a mortgage of equal term.

MINIMUM CASH DOWN PAYMENT OR EQUITY — Section 3.201b.

Purchase — 5% of purchase price must be cash or other equity.

Refinance — Difference between appraised value and mortgage amount must be equity.

MORTGAGE INSURANCE — Section 3.201c.

LTV less than/equal to 80% — Not required.

LTV in excess of 80% — Required on mortgage amount in excess of 75% LTV.

INDEX — FHLBB Mortgage Contract Rate is published in the FHLBB *Journal*, Table S.5.1. The contract interest rate on conventional home mortgage loans made for purchase of previously occupied homes: national averages for all major types of lenders.

INITIAL ADJUSTMENT PERIOD — The initial interest rate/payment adjustment period of an ARM loan must be for a minimum of twelve (12) months and correspond to a uniform schedule. Loans closed during the months of March through August must be scheduled to adjust on the first of September of the following year; and loans closed during the months of September through February must be scheduled to adjust on the first of March of the following year. For example, loans closed during a period from September 1, 1981 to February 28, 1982 would be scheduled for adjustment on March 1, 1983.

ADJUSTMENT PERIOD — After the initial adjustment, ARM loans shall adjust both the interest rate and payment in accordance with the movement of the required index every twelve (12) months. The change date shall be on the first day of the adjustment month.

INTEREST RATE/PAYMENT ADJUSTMENT — ARM loans shall provide for an interest rate/payment adjustment in accordance with the movement of the required index and shall provide that any adjustment have either no limit per adjustment period, or have a limit of ±2.00 percent per adjustment period.

[continued]

Figure 10-3. continued

BASE INDEX VALUE	The base index value (initial index value) shall be the most recently available value of the required index at, or within six months prior to, the date of the closing of the loan.
NOTICE PERIOD	ARM loans shall provide that notice of interest rate/payment adjustment be sent to the borrower thirty (30) to forty-five (45) days prior to the date of adjustment and in accordance with FHLMC Adjustable Rate Note and applicable law/regulation.
ADJUSTMENT	ARM loans shall adjust using the most recently available value of the required index as of the date of adjustment notice and in accordance with FHLMC Adjustable Rate Note.
MINIMUM ADJUSTMENT AMOUNT	ARM loans shall provide for a minimum adjustment per period of 1/8 of one (1) percent.
ADJUSTMENT ROUNDING	ARM loans shall provide for rounding of the interest rate after adjustment to the nearest 1/8 of one (1) percent.

Source: Federal Home Loan Mortgage Corporation, *Seller/Servicer Letter*, May 29, 1981.

bid pricing program establishes the weighted average for the immediate purchase program, where the mortgages are delivered in sixty days. The monthly bid-pricing program establishes the weighted average yield for the forward commitments. Until mid-1980, the Mortgage Corporation issued two forward commitments—one for six months and one for eight months—but now they issue only one forward commitment for an eight-month period.

In addition to the single-family and multifamily bid-pricing, the Mortgage Corporation on January 7, 1981, initiated a program to accept offers to sell to the Mortgage Corporation Home Improvement Loans (HILs). Under this first acceptance of offers, the required yield was 15.5 percent and each of the sellers was limited to a maximum amount of $500,000. The purchases will be the first in a series of purchases scheduled by the Mortgage Corporation. This program is a pilot program in order to establish if there is a need for a secondary market for HILs as a permanent part of the Mortgage Corporation mortgage purchase program.

The process used for this bid pricing system is very similar to that of the FNMA FMS Auction in that for the weekly auction the approved financial institutions submit bids via the telephone to the Washington, D.C., office of the Mortgage Corporation stating the amount of the bid and the yield the institution is willing to pay. As with the FMS Auction, there are maximum and minimum bids. The maximum bid is changed without notice, but the minimum bid is set at the present time at $100,000. Also, the bids may be submitted as either competitive or noncompetitive.

The results of these auctions are usually released on the day following the auction and are available to the general public. A sample of the weekly bid pricing results is shown in Figure 10-9. You will notice that the results are not as detailed as those for the FNMA auctions.

The results of the auction show not only the net yield required for fixed-rate mortgages, but also the required net yield for two types of adjustable-rate mortgages: the adjustable-rate mortgages with a 2 percent cap on the amount that the interest rate may increase, and the adjustable-rate mortgages with no limit on the amount that the interest rate may increase.

Figure 10-10 shows the results for a monthly forward commitment program. It should be noted that all yields are shown as net. Thus, the rates are less the 0.375 percent servicing fee that is to be added by the institution for servicing the loans. In order to determine the interest rate an institution would charge a person seeking a loan, you would take either the minimum or weighted average yield and add 0.375 percent. This

Figure 10-4. FHLMC Adjustable-Rate Note, page 1

ADJUSTABLE RATE NOTE

NOTICE TO BORROWER: THIS NOTE CONTAINS A PROVISION ALLOWING FOR CHANGES IN THE INTEREST RATE. INCREASES IN THE INTEREST RATE WILL RESULT IN HIGHER PAYMENTS. DECREASES IN THE INTEREST RATE WILL RESULT IN LOWER PAYMENTS.

............................, 19..... ...., ...
City *State*

....
Property Address *City* *State* *Zip Code*

1. BORROWER'S PROMISE TO PAY

In return for a loan that I have received, I promise to pay U.S. $................... (this amount will be called "principal"), plus interest, to the order of the Lender. The Lender is ....
....

I understand that the Lender may transfer this Note. The Lender or anyone who takes this Note by transfer and who is entitled to receive payments under this Note will be called the "Note Holder".

2. INTEREST

Interest will be charged on that part of outstanding principal which has not been paid. Interest will be charged beginning on the date I receive principal and continuing until the full amount of principal I receive has been paid.

Beginning on the date of this Note, I will pay interest at a yearly rate of ....% (the "Initial Interest Rate"). The interest rate that I will pay will change in accordance with Section 4 of this Note until my loan is paid. Interest rate changes may occur on the ..... day of the month beginning on ...., 19..... and on that day of the month every .... months thereafter. Each date on which the rate of interest may change will be called a "Change Date".

3. PAYMENTS

(A) Time and Place of Payments

I will pay principal and interest by making payments every month. I will make my monthly payments on the ..... day of each month beginning on ....,19...... I will make these payments until I have paid all of the principal and interest and any other charges, described below, that I may owe under this Note. I will pay all sums that I owe under this Note no later than ...., ... (the "final payment date").

I will make my monthly payments at ....
.... or at a different place if required by the Note Holder.

(B) Borrower's Payments Before They Are Due

I have the right to make payments of principal at any time before they are due. A payment of principal only is known as a "prepayment". When I make a prepayment, I will tell the Note Holder in writing that I am doing so. I may make a full prepayment or a partial prepayment without paying any penalty. The Note Holder will use all of my prepayments to reduce the amount of principal that I owe under this Note. If I make a partial prepayment, there will be no delays in the due dates of my monthly payments unless the Note Holder agrees in writing to those delays. My partial prepayment will reduce the amount of my monthly payments after the first Change Date following my partial prepayment. However, any reduction due to my partial prepayment may be offset by an interest rate increase.

(C) Amount of Monthly Payments

My initial monthly payments will be in the amount of U.S. $..................... If the interest rate that I pay changes, the amount of my monthly payments will change. Increases in the interest rate will result in higher payments (unless my prepayments since the last Change Date offset the increases in my monthly payments). Decreases in the interest rate will result in lower payments. The amount of my monthly payments will always be sufficient to repay my loan in full in substantially equal payments by the final payment date. In setting the monthly payment amount on each Change Date, the Note Holder will assume that the Note interest rate will not change again prior to the final payment date.

NEW MEXICO—ADJUSTABLE RATE LOAN NOTE—6/81—FHLMC UNIFORM INSTRUMENT

Figure 10-5. FHLMC Adjustable-Rate Note, page 2

4. INTEREST RATE CHANGES

(A) The Index

Any changes in the interest rate will be based on changes in an interest rate index which will be called the "Index". The Index is the: *[Check one box to indicate Index.]*

(1) ☐* "Contract Interest Rate, Purchase of Previously Occupied Homes, National Average for all Major Types of Lenders" published by the Federal Home Loan Bank Board.

(2) ☐* ....

If the Index ceases to be made available by the publisher, or by any successor to the publisher, the Note Holder will set the Note interest rate by using a comparable index.

(B) Setting the New Interest Rate

To set the new interest rate, the Note Holder will determine the change between the Base Index figure and the Current Index figure. The Base Index figure is .... The Current Index figure is the most recent Index figure available .... days prior to each Change Date. If the amount of the change is less than one-eighth of one percentage point, the change will be rounded to zero. If the amount of the change is one-eighth of one percentage point or more, the Note Holder will round the amount of the change to the nearest one-eighth of one percentage point.

If the Current Index figure is larger than the Base Index figure, the Note Holder will add the rounded amount of the change to the Initial Interest Rate. If the Current Index figure is smaller than the Base Index figure, the Note Holder will subtract the rounded amount of the change from the Initial Interest Rate. The result of this addition or subtraction will be the preliminary rate. If there is no change between the Base Index figure and the Current Index figure after rounding, the Initial Interest Rate will be the preliminary rate.

[Check one box to indicate whether there is any maximum limit on interest rate changes; if no box is checked, there will be no maximum limit on changes.]

(1) ☐ If this box is checked, there will be no maximum limit on changes in the interest rate up or down. The preliminary rate will be the new interest rate.

(2) ☐ If this box is checked, the interest rate will not be changed by more than .... percentage points on any Change Date. The Note Holder will adjust the preliminary rate so that the change in the interest rate will not be more than that limit. The new interest rate will equal the figure that results from this adjustment of the preliminary rate.

(C) Effective Date of Changes

Each new interest rate will become effective on the next Change Date. If my monthly payment changes as a result of a change in the interest rate, my monthly payment will change as of the first monthly payment date after the Change Date.

(D) Notice to Borrower

The Note Holder will mail me a notice by first class mail at least thirty and no more than forty-five days before each Change Date if the interest rate is to change. The notice will advise me of:

(i) the new interest rate on my loan;
(ii) the amount of my new monthly payment; and
(iii) any additional matters which the Note Holder is required to disclose.

5. BORROWER'S FAILURE TO PAY AS REQUIRED

(A) Late Charge for Overdue Payments

If the Note Holder has not received the full amount of any of my monthly payments by the end of .... calendar days after the date it is due, I will pay a late charge to the Note Holder. The amount of the charge will be .... % of my overdue payment of principal and interest. I will pay this late charge only once on any late payment.

(B) Notice from Note Holder

If I do not pay the full amount of each monthly payment on time, the Note Holder may send me a written notice telling me that if I do not pay the overdue amount by a certain date I will be in default. That date must be at least 30 days after the date on which the notice is mailed to me.

(C) Default

If I do not pay the overdue amount by the date stated in the notice described in (B) above, I will be in default. If I am in default, the Note Holder may require me to pay immediately the full amount of principal which has not been paid and all the interest that I owe on that amount.

Even if, at a time when I am in default, the Note Holder does not require me to pay immediately in full as described above, the Note Holder will still have the right to do so if I am in default at a later time.

* *If more than one box is checked or if no box is checked, and Lender and Borrower do not otherwise agree in writing, the first Index named will apply.*

Figure 10-6. FHLMC Adjustable-Rate Note, page 3

(D) Payment of Note Holder's Costs and Expenses

If the Note Holder has required me to pay immediately in full as described above, the Note Holder will have the right to be paid back by me for all its reasonable costs and expenses to the extent not prohibited by applicable law. Those expenses may include, for example, reasonable attorneys' fees.

6. WAIVERS

Anyone who signs this Note to transfer it to someone else (known as an "endorser") waives certain rights. Those rights are (A) the right to require the Note Holder to demand payment of amounts due (known as "presentment") and (B) the right to require the Note Holder to give notice that amounts due have not been paid (known as "notice of dishonor").

7. GIVING OF NOTICES

Except for the notice provided in Section 4(D), any notice that must be given to me under this Note will be given by mailing it by certified mail. All notices will be addressed to me at the Property Address above. Notices will be mailed to me at a different address if I give the Note Holder a notice of my different address.

Any notice that must be given to the Note Holder under this Note will be given by mailing it by certified mail to the Note Holder at the address stated in Section 3(A) above. Notices will be mailed to the Note Holder at a different address if I am given a notice of that different address.

8. RESPONSIBILITY OF PERSONS UNDER THIS NOTE

If more than one person signs this Note, each of us is fully and personally obligated to pay the full amount owed and to keep all of the promises made in this Note. Any guarantor, surety, or endorser of this Note is also obligated to do these things. The Note Holder may enforce its rights under this Note against each of us individually or against all of us together. This means that any one of us may be required to pay all of the amounts owed under this Note.

Any person who takes over my rights or obligations under this Note will have all of my rights and must keep all of my promises made in this Note. Any person who takes over the rights or obligations of a guarantor, surety, or endorser of this Note is also obligated to keep all of the promises made in this Note.

9. LOAN CHARGES

It could be that this loan is subject to a law which sets maximum loan charges and that law is interpreted so that the interest or other loan charges collected or to be collected in connection with this loan would exceed permitted limits. If this is the case, then: (A) any such loan charge shall be reduced by the amount necessary to reduce the charge to the permitted limit; and (B) any sums already collected from me which exceeded permitted limits will be refunded to me. The Note Holder may choose to make this refund by reducing the principal I owe under this Note or by making a direct payment to me. If a refund reduces principal, the reduction will be treated as a partial prepayment.

10. THIS NOTE SECURED BY A MORTGAGE

In addition to the protections given to the Note Holder under this Note, a Mortgage, dated ...., 19..... protects the Note Holder from possible losses which might result if I do not keep the promises which I make in this Note. That Mortgage describes how and under what conditions I may be required to make immediate payment in full of all amounts that I owe under this Note. One of those conditions relates to any transfer of the property covered by the Mortgage. In that regard, the Mortgage provides in paragraph 17:

17. Transfer of the Property; Assumption. If all or any part of the Property or an interest therein is sold or transferred by Borrower without Lender's prior written consent, excluding (a) the creation of a lien or encumbrance subordinate to this Mortgage, (b) the creation of a purchase money security interest for household appliances, (c) a transfer by devise, descent or by operation of law upon the death of a joint tenant or (d) the grant of any leasehold interest of three years or less not containing an option to purchase, Lender may, at Lender's option, declare all the sums secured by this Mortgage to be immediately due and payable. Lender shall have waived such option to accelerate if, prior to the sale or transfer, Lender and the person to whom the Property is to be sold or transferred reach agreement in writing that the credit of such person is satisfactory to Lender and that the interest payable on the sums secured by this Mortgage shall be at such rate as Lender shall request. If Lender has waived the option to accelerate provided in this paragraph 17, and if Borrower's successor in interest has executed a written assumption agreement accepted in writing by Lender, Lender shall release Borrower from all obligations under this Mortgage and the Note.

If Lender exercises such option to accelerate, Lender shall mail Borrower notice of acceleration in accordance with paragraph 14 hereof. Such notice shall provide a period of not less than 30 days from the date the notice is mailed within which Borrower may pay the sums declared due. If Borrower fails to pay such sums prior to the expiration of such period, Lender may, without further notice or demand on Borrower, invoke any remedies permitted by paragraph 18 hereof.

Figure 10-7. FHLMC Adjustable-Rate Note, page 4

An Adjustable Rate Loan Rider supplements the Mortgage and provides:

If there is a transfer of the Property subject to paragraph 17 of the Security Instrument, Lender may require (1) an increase in the current Note interest rate, or (2) an increase in (or removal of) the limit on the amount of any one interest rate change (if there is a limit), or (3) a change in the Base Index figure, or all of these, as a condition of Lender's waiving the option to accelerate provided in paragraph 17.

.... (Seal)
Borrower

.... (Seal)
Borrower

.... (Seal)
Borrower
(Sign Original Only)

Figure 10-8. FHLMC Adjustable-Rate Note Loan Rider

ADJUSTABLE RATE LOAN RIDER

NOTICE: THE SECURITY INSTRUMENT SECURES A NOTE WHICH CONTAINS A PROVISION ALLOWING FOR CHANGES IN THE INTEREST RATE. INCREASES IN THE INTEREST RATE WILL RESULT IN HIGHER PAYMENTS. DECREASES IN THE INTEREST RATE WILL RESULT IN LOWER PAYMENTS.

This Rider is made this .... day of ...., 19....., and is incorporated into and shall be deemed to amend and supplement the Mortgage, Deed of Trust, or Deed to Secure Debt (the "Security Instrument") of the same date given by the undersigned (the "Borrower") to secure Borrower's Note to ....
....
(the "Lender") of the same date (the "Note") and covering the property described in the Security Instrument and located at ....

Property Address

Modifications. In addition to the covenants and agreements made in the Security Instrument, Borrower and Lender further covenant and agree as follows:

A. INTEREST RATE AND MONTHLY PAYMENT CHANGES

The Note has an "Initial Interest Rate" of ..... %. The Note interest rate may be increased or decreased on the ..... day of the month beginning on ...., 19..... and on that day of the month every ..... months thereafter.

Changes in the interest rate are governed by changes in an interest rate index called the "Index". The Index is the:

[Check one box to indicate Index.]

(1) ☐* "Contract Interest Rate, Purchase of Previously Occupied Homes, National Average for all Major Types of Lenders" published by the Federal Home Loan Bank Board.

(2) ☐* ....
....

[Check one box to indicate whether there is any maximum limit on changes in the interest rate on each Change Date; if no box is checked there will be no maximum limit on changes.]

(1) ☐ There is no maximum limit on changes in the interest rate at any Change Date.

(2) ☐ The interest rate cannot be changed by more than ..... percentage points at any Change Date.

If the interest rate changes, the amount of Borrower's monthly payments will change as provided in the Note. Increases in the interest rate will result in higher payments. Decreases in the interest rate will result in lower payments.

B. LOAN CHARGES

It could be that the loan secured by the Security Instrument is subject to a law which sets maximum loan charges and that law is interpreted so that the interest or other loan charges collected or to be collected in connection with the loan would exceed permitted limits. If this is the case, then: (A) any such loan charge shall be reduced by the amount necessary to reduce the charge to the permitted limit; and (B) any sums already collected from Borrower which exceeded permitted limits will be refunded to Borrower. Lender may choose to make this refund by reducing the principal owed under the Note or by making a direct payment to Borrower.

C. PRIOR LIENS

If Lender determines that all or any part of the sums secured by this Security Instrument are subject to a lien which has priority over this Security Instrument, Lender may send Borrower a notice identifying that lien. Borrower shall promptly act with regard to that lien as provided in paragraph 4 of the Security Instrument or shall promptly secure an agreement in a form satisfactory to Lender subordinating that lien to this Security Instrument.

D. TRANSFER OF THE PROPERTY

If there is a transfer of the Property subject to paragraph 17 of the Security Instrument, Lender may require (1) an increase in the current Note interest rate, or (2) an increase in (or removal of) the limit on the amount of any one interest rate change (if there is a limit), or (3) a change in the Base Index figure, or all of these, as a condition of Lender's waiving the option to accelerate provided in paragraph 17.

By signing this, Borrower agrees to all of the above.

....(Seal)
—Borrower

....(Seal)
—Borrower

* *If more than one box is checked or if no box is checked, and Lender and Borrower do not otherwise agree in writing, the first Index named will apply.*

ADJUSTABLE RATE LOAN RIDER—6/81—FHLMC UNIFORM INSTRUMENT

Figure 10-9. Weekly Offers Under Immediate Delivery Programs for Fixed-Rate and Adjustable-Rate Mortgages

	1/7/82	CURRENT WEEK 12/31/81	12/24/81	12/17/81
FIXED-RATE MORTGAGES				
Offers Submitted:				
Amount	$ 9,998,000	$ 5,028,000	$ 9,241,000	$ 9,967,000
Number	17	18	30	30
Range of Yields*	17.500-17.512	17.150-17.250	16.90-16.95	16.750-16.876
Offers Accepted:				
Amount	$ 9,998,000	$ 5,028,000	$ 9,241,000	$ 9,967,000
Number	17	18	30	30
Minimum Net Yield*	17.500	17.150	16.90	16.750
Weighted Average Yield*	17.504	17.170	16.915	16.765
ADJUSTABLE-RATE MORTGAGES— Two Percent Interest-Rate Cap				
Offers Submitted:				
Amount	$ 110,000	$ 429,000	$ 1,143,000	$ 517,000
Number	1	2	3	3
Range of Yields*	N/A	N/A	15.57-16.66	16.200-16.250
Offers Accepted:				
Amount	$ 110,000	$ 429,000	$ 1,143,000	$ 517,000
Number	1	2	3	3
Minimum Net Yield*	17.050	16.700	16.55	16.200
Weighted Average Yield*	17.050	16.700	16.648	16.227
ADJUSTABLE-RATE MORTGAGES— No Interest-Rate Cap				
Offers Submitted:				
Amount	$ 873,000	$ 1,600,000	$ 1,312,000	$ 816,000
Number	3	5	5	5
Range of Yields*	N/A	16.450-16.550	16.30-16.30	15.950-15.960
Offers Accepted:				
Amount	$ 873,000	$ 1,600,000	$ 1,312,000	$ 816,000
Number	3	5	5	5
Minimum Net Yield*	16.800	16.450	16.30	15.950
Weighted Average Yield*	16.800	16.470	16.30	15.952
Total Adjustable-Rate Mortgages Accepted:				
Amount	$ 983,000	$ 2,029,000	$ 2,455,000	$ 1,333,000
TOTAL ACCEPTED				
Amount	$10,981,000	$ 7,057,000	$11,696,000	$11,300,000

*Yields are quoted at a net yield exclusive of the .375 percent servicing fee applicable for whole loans.

Source: The Mortgage Corporation, *News*; Federal Home Loan Mortgage Corporation, *Auction Results*, Washington, D.C.

Figure 10-10. Monthly Offers Under Forward Commitment Program

Table I -- Monthly Offers Under Forward Commitment Program

	8 Month Program			
	August 12 1980	July 8 1980	June 10 1980	May 13 1980
Offers Submitted:				
Number:	221	223	137	280
Amount:	$229,930,000	$212,282,000	$127,210,000	$258,365,000
Range of Yields*	11.001-14.250	10.000-13.025	10.000-13.102	10.500-13.750
Offers Accepted				
Number:	42	32	40	35
Amount:	$ 25,200,000	$ 25,600,000	$ 30,760,000	$ 30,100,000
Minimum Net Yield*	14.000	12.800	12.759	13.301
Weighted Average Yield*	14.087	12.894	12.852	13.470

*Yields are quoted at a net yield exclusive of the .375 percent servicing fee applicable for whole loans.

Source: The Mortgage Corporation, *News*; Federal Home Loan Mortgage Corporation, *Eight-Month Forward Commitment Activity*, Washington, D.C.

would give you the range of interest the loan would carry. Once again, if you follow the results of the bidding, you can have an idea as to the movement of interest rates. For example, if one looks at the trend of the weighted average yield, one can see that the trend is up. If you would like to get the results of the bid pricing systems, you may contact the Washington, D.C., office of the Mortgage Corporation and ask to be put on the mailing list to receive the results:

The Mortgage Corporation
1776 G. Street, NW
Washington, D.C. 20013

The Mortgage Corporation Source of Funds

As with FNMA, the Mortgage Corporation has the ability to sell bonds in the open market to derive cash for its operation. The Mortgage Corporation, however, can also sell mortgages and interest in mortgages to the general public. These sales are done through the issuing of two types of certificates: the Mortgage Participation Certificate, or PC, and the Guaranteed Mortgage Certificate, or GMC.

The PC represents an undivided interest in geographically disbursed first lien mortgages held by the Mortgage Corporation and is sold every business day through a group of securities dealers. PCs are sold only in fully registered form in denominations of $25,000, $100,000, $200,000, $500,000, $1 million, or $5 million. On a monthly basis, the Mortgage Corporation will pass through the payments of principal and interest to the purchaser of the PC.

The other certificate offered by the Mortgage Corporation, the GMC, differs from the PC in two major ways. First, the interest payments are made semiannually and principal reduction payments are made annually. Second, the Mortgage Corporation unconditionally guarantees the payment of interest and principal reduction. The Mortgage Corporation warrants that until the GMC is paid in full, payments or principal reduction will be sufficient to return to the holder of the GMC a minimum annual principal reduction as specified in the offering. For example, an investor purchases a GMC in the amount of $100,000 with a term of ten years and an interest rate of 10 percent. Therefore, the investor is guaranteed that the principal will be reduced at the rate of 10 percent per year. Thus, in the first year, the investor will receive the following:

Principal payment (annually)	$10,000
Interest payment of $5,000 (semiannually)	$10,000
First-year total	$20,000

Remember that 10 percent interest is charged on the remaining balance of $90,000 for the following year. These GMCs are sold in denominations of $100,000, $500,000 and $1 million, with all certificates fully registered.

This completes our discussion of the Mortgage Corporation. One can see that a person engaged in the sale of real estate is not likely to come in contact directly with the Mortgage Corporation, but it is a major secondary marketer to the savings and loan associations.

THE GOVERNMENT NATIONAL MORTGAGE ASSOCIATION (GNMA)

The Government National Mortgage Association, sometimes known as "Ginnie Mae," was created September 1, 1968, with the passage of an amendment to Title III of the National Housing Act. In the amendment in Section 302 of Title III, FNMA was rechartered into two separate corporations: the Federal National Mortgage Association (FNMA) and a governmental corporation to be known as the Government National Mortgage Association (GNMA). GNMA is under the control of the Department of Housing and Urban Development. HUD is responsible for the establishment of all of the policies of, as well as responsible for all of the operations of GNMA. The Secretary of HUD was given the power to adopt, amend, or repeal any bylaws of the corporation governing the performance of the duties imposed by the enacting law.

Also included in the amendment was the authority to establish the position of President of the Government National Mortgage Association, in the Department of Housing and Urban Development. Section 308 of Title III, as amended in 1976, states that the President of the GNMA will be appointed by the President of the United States with the advice and consent of the Senate, and that the remaining executive officers of GNMA will be appointed by the Secretary of Housing and Urban Development.

The Functions of GNMA

The functions or purposes of GNMA are in three specific areas. One of the three functions of GNMA is the special assistance function. Under this function, GNMA will purchase whole loans, or participations in certain types of loans, in order to meet two statutory requirements: (1) the purchase of residential loans, originated under special housing programs for which the financing is not presently available through the normal sources in the open market; and (2) the purchase of, or the participation in, residential mortgages in order to stop or counter declines in mortgage lending or home construction. This function will be discussed in detail later in this chapter.

The second function is the management and liquidation function. Under this function, GNMA is authorized to be responsible for the orderly management and liquidation of mortgages acquired by FNMA prior to the close of business on October 31, 1954. The dollar amount of these mortgages transferred to GNMA was $3,012,905,653. As well as the mortgages from FNMA,

> GNMA was responsible for the management and liquidation of other mortgages, loans, and other obligations acquired and to be acquired, in an orderly manner, with a minimum of adverse effect upon the home mortgage market and minimum loss to the Federal Government.[1]

Under this function, GNMA is also authorized to purchase mortgages on residential properties from any federal agency and also to purchase any obligation offered by the Department of Housing and Urban Development. One other operation authorized under this function by the corporate charter is to guarantee the timely payment of principal and interest on securities that are backed by a pool of mortgages.

The ability to insure the timely payment of principal and interest allows GNMA to carry out its third major function: the mortgage backed securities program. This program will be covered later in this chapter.

Corporate Offices

As they require of FNMA, the amendments to the National Housing Act require that the corporate headquarters of GNMA be located in Washington, D.C. The act also allows GNMA to maintain branch or regional offices, but at the present time GNMA now operates through the five regional offices of FNMA. If you should have any questions about any of the programs of GNMA, contact the regional office nearest you.

Source of Funds

The major source of funds for the operation of GNMA is the U.S. Treasury, but GNMA also generates income from the following sources: sales of mortgages, commitment fees, fees charged for the processing of commitments, and discount fees charged in some of the special assistance programs. These fees are sometimes referred to as income from operations.

Special Assistance Programs

History When FNMA was divided in 1968 into the two corporations, FNMA was to continue its activities in the support of the secondary market in general, whereas GNMA was chartered to conduct or support specialized programs in the secondary market. This function of GNMA has come to be called the Special Assistance Function (SAF). The SAF is to support certain types of mortgages and the housing market in times of tight money, as well as to stimulate home construction when the industry is declining.

The original SAF was limited to the purchase of government-underwritten mortgages, but with the enactment of the Emergency Home Purchase Act of 1974, the function was expanded to include conventional mortgages. The President of the United States was given the authority, under Section 305 of the title, to institute a Special Assistance Program. The President,

> after taking into account (1) the conditions in the building industry and the national economy and (2) conditions affecting the home mortgage investment market, generally, or affecting various types or classifications of home mortgages, or both, and after determining that such action is in the public interest, may under this section authorize the Association, for such period of time and to such extent as he shall prescribe, to exercise its powers to make commitments to purchase such types, classes, or categories of home mortgages (including participations therein) as he shall determine.

This authority was later delegated to the Secretary of Housing and Urban Development by Executive Order No. 11732, approved July 30, 1973.

Eligible sellers or participants For a lender to be eligible to sell to GNMA, the lender must meet certain requirements and execute a GNMA Seller Agreement, known as GNMA Form 301. In addition to the agreement, the GNMA will require the lender to have the ability to service the loans sold to GNMA either through a service agreement with a company specializing in the servicing of mortgage loans or through an in-house ability.

If the lender wishes to sell a HUD/FHA-insured loan or VA-guaranteed mortgage to GNMA through one of the special assistance programs, the lender must be an approved FHA or VA lender. If a lender wishes to sell a conventional mortgage to GNMA, the lender must be a lender who is approved by the Federal National Mortgage Association. These are just a few of the requirements for lenders who wish to sell to GNMA. If you are interested in all of the requirements, they are listed in detail in the Government National Mortgage Association's *Seller's Guide*.

Tandem programs The programs that are operated under the Special Assistance Function of GNMA are commonly referred to as *tandem programs*. The term *tandem* was originated in 1970 because of several agreements between GNMA and FNMA. Under these agreements, GNMA would agree to issue commitments to purchase mortgages through a special assistance program, then the commitment would be transferred to FNMA, which would actually purchase the mortgage. If the return was below market or the rate established by the FMS auction of FNMA, GNMA would make up the difference. This practice of issuing the commitments and then selling them to FNMA is no longer done, but the term has remained and now refers to the purchase of below-market interest rate loans by GNMA and the selling of these loans to private investors. The ability to make this type of loan and to sell to private investors has a twofold benefit: it aids the housing market, and it reduces the amount of federal monies that must be used to support these types of loans.

In addition to the advantages of the tandem program outlined above, it is a great help to the building industry in that a builder wishing to build either single-family or multifamily units can arrange for the permanent financing of the housing prior to the start of construction, at below market rates. With the permanent financing established, the builder or developer can then arrange for the interim financing to construct the housing.

What are the steps to be followed in applying for a tandem program, or commitment?[2] The steps are as follows:

1. The builder or developer approaches a GNMA-approved seller in order to apply for a commitment from GNMA.

2. The approved GNMA seller approaches GNMA for a commitment.

(If the commitment is issued, it will be for a period of one year, if the structure in question is a single-family dwelling. The commitment can be for a period of thirty-six months for multifamily projects. If the commitment is on a single-family dwelling, the mortgage can be delivered to GNMA at any time during the one-year commitment period. If the lender does not wish to deliver the mortgage to GNMA, the lender will only be charged a commitment fee. This commitment fee at the present time is 1 percent of the loan amount.)

3. GNMA issues the commitment to the mortgage lender.

4. With a firm commitment from GNMA, the lender will then issue its commitment to the builder or developer to furnish the permanent financing for the structure upon completion.

5. The builder or developer will use that commitment from the mortgage lender to arrange for interim, or construction, financing.

6. After the construction is completed, GNMA approved mortgage lender will make the permanent loan to the homebuyer.

After the mortgage lender has closed the permanent loan, the lender has three options:

1. Keep the mortgage as part of the lender's portfolio.

2. Sell the mortgage to a private investor and forfeit the commitment fee paid to GNMA.

3. Sell the mortgage to GNMA under the terms of the commitment, and then GNMA will sell the mortgage to a private investor.

This process is illustrated in Figure 10-11.

Special Assistance Program Announcements Since the program of special assistance has been instituted, some twenty-seven announcements of programs have been instituted by action of the President of the United States or the Secretary of Housing and Urban Development. The first announcement had an effective date of November 1, 1954, and was for disaster housing mortgages. Under this announcement, GNMA would enter into contracts to purchase mortgages that were either insured by FHA or guaranteed by the VA, covering the financing of homes of victims of a major disaster as determined by the President of the United States.

Figure 10-11. Tandem Program Process

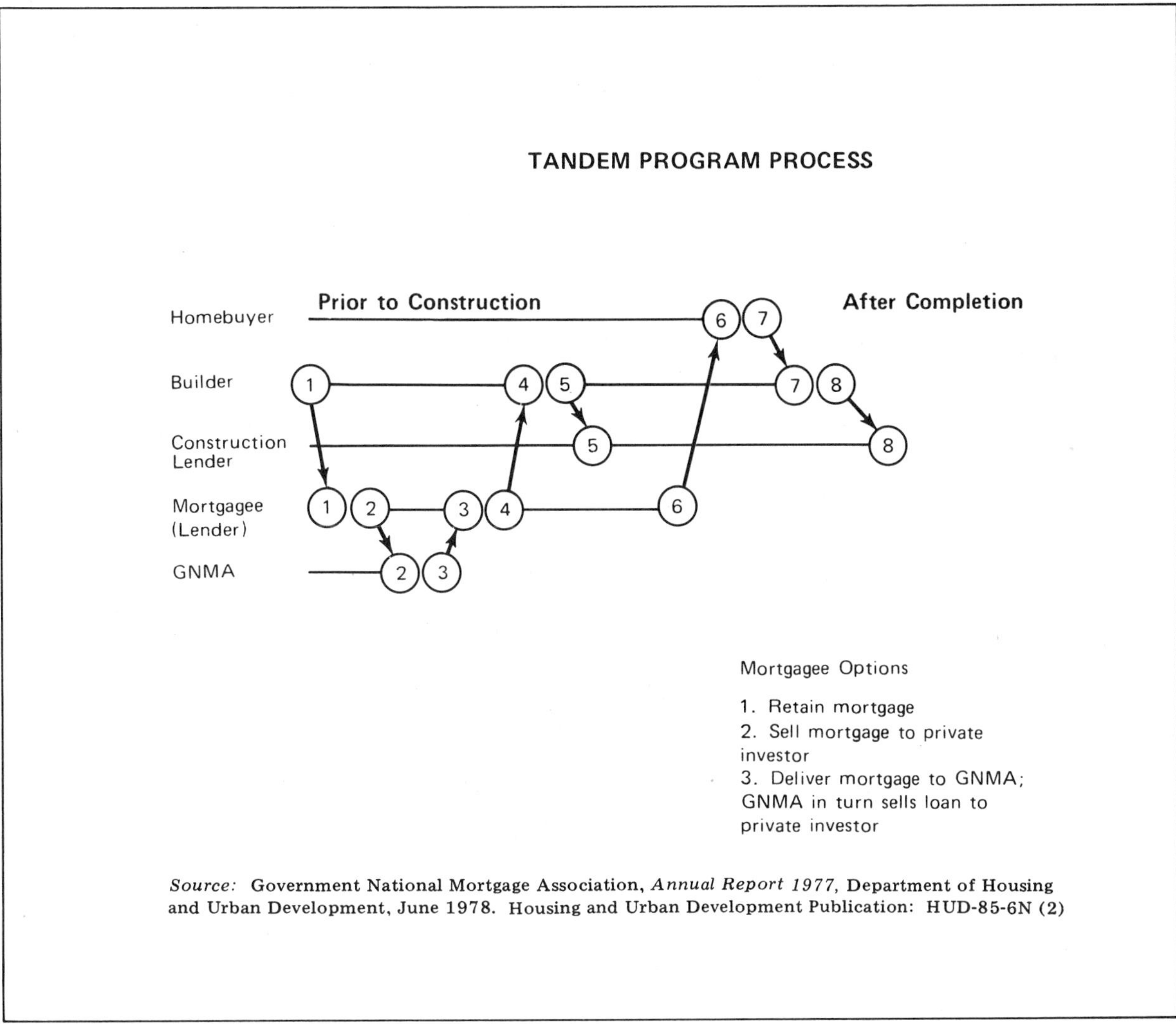

Source: Government National Mortgage Association, *Annual Report 1977*, Department of Housing and Urban Development, June 1978. Housing and Urban Development Publication: HUD-85-6N (2)

The last of the programs announced was the Targeted Tandem Program (numbered Announcement 27) which started in February 1978. It made available below-market interest rate loans for multifamily housing located in cities and urban counties suffering from economic distress. The program was authorized to start on May 27, 1980.

These are just two of the twenty-seven announcements of programs. For further information regarding the other programs available through the SAF of GNMA, contact a GNMA Regional Office.

Mortgage-Backed Securities Program (MBS)

The Mortgage-Backed Securities Program, sometimes called *Pass-Throughs* or *Ginnie Maes*, was authorized by the 1968 amendment of the National Housing Act. The 1968 amendment, in Section 804(b), added subsection (g) to Section 306 of the National Housing Act. The first sentence of the subsection states that

> The Association [GNMA] is authorized, upon such terms and conditions as it may deem appropriate, to guarantee the timely payment of principal of and interest on such certificates or other securities. . . (2) be based on or backed by a trust or pool comprised of mortgages which are insured under the National Housing Act or Title V of the National Housing Act of 1949, or which are insured or guaranteed under the Servicemen's Readjustment Act of 1944 . . . .

The first MBS was issued in February 1970.

Purpose The purpose of the MBS program is to attract investors to invest in the residential mortgage market by the offering of government-backed-and-guaranteed securities. The program has been a great success and, according to GNMA, over $80 billion of MBSs have been issued, thus making the program the third largest supplier of mortgage funds in the United States.

Under this program, the investor or the holder of an MBS is guaranteed the timely payment of principal and interest as per the terms of the MBS. The payment will be made by GNMA whether or not GNMA has received its payment from the originator of the mortgage. Thus, the MBS is one of the safest of all investments, for it is backed by the full faith and credit of the United States of America. In addition to the safety of the MBS, it has other advantages to the investor or purchaser. One such advantage is that the MBS has the highest yield of any federally guaranteed security. Another advantage to the purchaser is that the return on the MBS compares very favorably to the yields of corporate debt issues.

Eligible mortgages and pools As stated earlier, mortgages that may serve as security for the MBS are limited by law. The mortgages that are authorized are mortgages on single-family dwellings either insured by FHA or guaranteed by Veterans Administration, mobile home loans that are either insured by FHA or guaranteed by the VA, and some multifamily project loans insured by FHA.

These mortgages are then packaged into a group of eligible mortgages, called a *pool*. Usually the mortgages in a pool will be of the same type yield. For example, all of the mortgages could be FHA-insured on single-family dwellings—a pool sometimes called a standard FHA pool.

In addition to the standard pool, one additional pool has been authorized—the graduated mortgage pool. This is a pool exclusively comprised of Section 245 FHA graduated payment mortgages.

GNMA has established the minimum size of the pools. For pools of FHA or VA single-family mortgages, the minimum is $1 million. For pools of multifamily project-construction loans or multifamily project loans, the minimum is $500,000. The minimum amount for a pool of mobile home loans is also $500,000.

Types of mortgage-backed securities Presently, three types of mortgage-backed securities are authorized: pass-through, bond, and graduated payment mortgage-backed.

The *pass-through* security is further divided into two types of securities known as the *straight pass-through* and the *modified pass-through*. With the straight pass-through security, the purchaser will receive a proportionate share of the proceeds of the principal and interest as collected, less servicing fees and other costs approved by GNMA. On the other hand the modified pass-through security provides for the payment of the specified principal installment and a fixed rate of interest on the unpaid principal, whether or not these payments are collected from the borrower, and with all prepayments being passed through to the security holder. Both straight pass-through and modified pass-through securities must specify the dates that the payments are to be made to the holder of the security. This date of payment is usually the fifteenth of each month. The minimum amount of the straight and modified pass-through certificate is now $25,000 and may increase in $5,000 increments.

The second type of security authorized to be issued by GNMA is the bond type of security. As the name implies, this is a long-term security and it guarantees the payment of interest on a semiannual basis with principal reduction as per an agreed schedule outlined in the security agreement. This type of MBS has not been issued in large numbers, for the requirements for the mortgage lenders are rather high. GNMA now has the following requirement for any corporation, trust, partnership, or other entity to be able to issue the bond type security: the entity must have at least a net worth of $50 million in assets acceptable to GNMA and have the capacity to assemble acceptable and eligible mortgages to support the minimum pool size. The minimum pool size for the issuance of the bond type security is currently $100 million.

The third security is the graduated payment mortgage-backed security. As of March 29, 1979, GNMA was authorized to guarantee the timely payment of principal and interest on modified pass-through securities that are based on a pool of mortgages with unlevel monthly installments, or those mortgages that are insured under Section 245 of the National Housing Act, provided that the graduated payment mortgages in the pool provide for level monthly installments beginning no later than the sixty-first payment. As with the pass-through and the modified pass-through, the minimum pool is $1 million and the minimum face amount of the securities is $25,000 and can be increased in $5,000 increments.

Eligible issuers of MBSs According to Title 24, Chapter III, of the Code of Federal Regulations, to be eligible to issue securities an issuer must meet the following:

1. Be an approved FHA lender, in good standing
2. Be an approved FNMA seller/servicer in current good standing with FNMA
3. Have adequate experience, management capability, and facilities to issue and service mortgage-backed securities, as determined by GNMA
4. Maintain the minimum acceptable net worth in assets prescribed by GNMA

These are a few of the requirements for lenders. For more information as to the minimum requirements, you should contact the home office of GNMA or request a copy of the *Mortgage-Backed Securities Guide* from

GNMA Services Division
Room 6210
U.S. Department of HUD
Washington, D.C. 20410

Program outline In the previous sections of this chapter we discussed the various aspects of the MBS program, from the history of the program and who can issue MBS, to the types of securities that can be issued. Now let us examine how the program works.

The first step is for the lender to apply to GNMA to become an approved issuer and at the same time apply for a commitment from GNMA for a guaranty of security. Once the approval and the commitment are issued, the mortgage lender starts either to originate the loans required to meet the minimum pool requirement, or if the lender wishes, to acquire mortgages from other lenders in sufficient amounts to make up the required pool. As we learned earlier, the minimum for the standard FHA pool is $1 million.

While the mortgage lender is either originating or acquiring the necessary mortgages, it is also making arrangements with a securities dealer to market the securities when they become available. When the mortgage lender has arranged for the steps above, the process begins (Figure 10-12).

Working through Figure 10-12, one can see that the process is divided into three different stages. In the first stage, the family buys a home and applies for a loan from VA, FHA, or FmHA. Upon approval of the loan, the mortgage lender makes the loan and the homeowners begin the payments.

In the second stage, this mortgage goes into the pool and the mortgage lender sets up the required escrow accounts. The mortgage documents are held in trust by a custodian. Once the pool of mortgages is assembled, the mortgage lender submits all of the required documents to GNMA. GNMA will review all of the documents and effect delivery of the securities within twenty calendar days.

In the third stage, once the review is completed, GNMA will prepare and deliver the securities to the securities dealer as per the mortgage lender's instructions. The securities dealer will sell the securities in the open market to the general public or institutions. When the securities are sold, the GNMA transfer agent is notified and the ownership of the securities is transferred to the purchaser.

Once the securities are sold, the mortgage lender or issuer of the securities is responsible for ensuring that the payment of principal and interest is passed through to the investors, less any fees authorized by GNMA.

Figure 10-12. How the GNMA Mortgage-Backed Securities Program Works

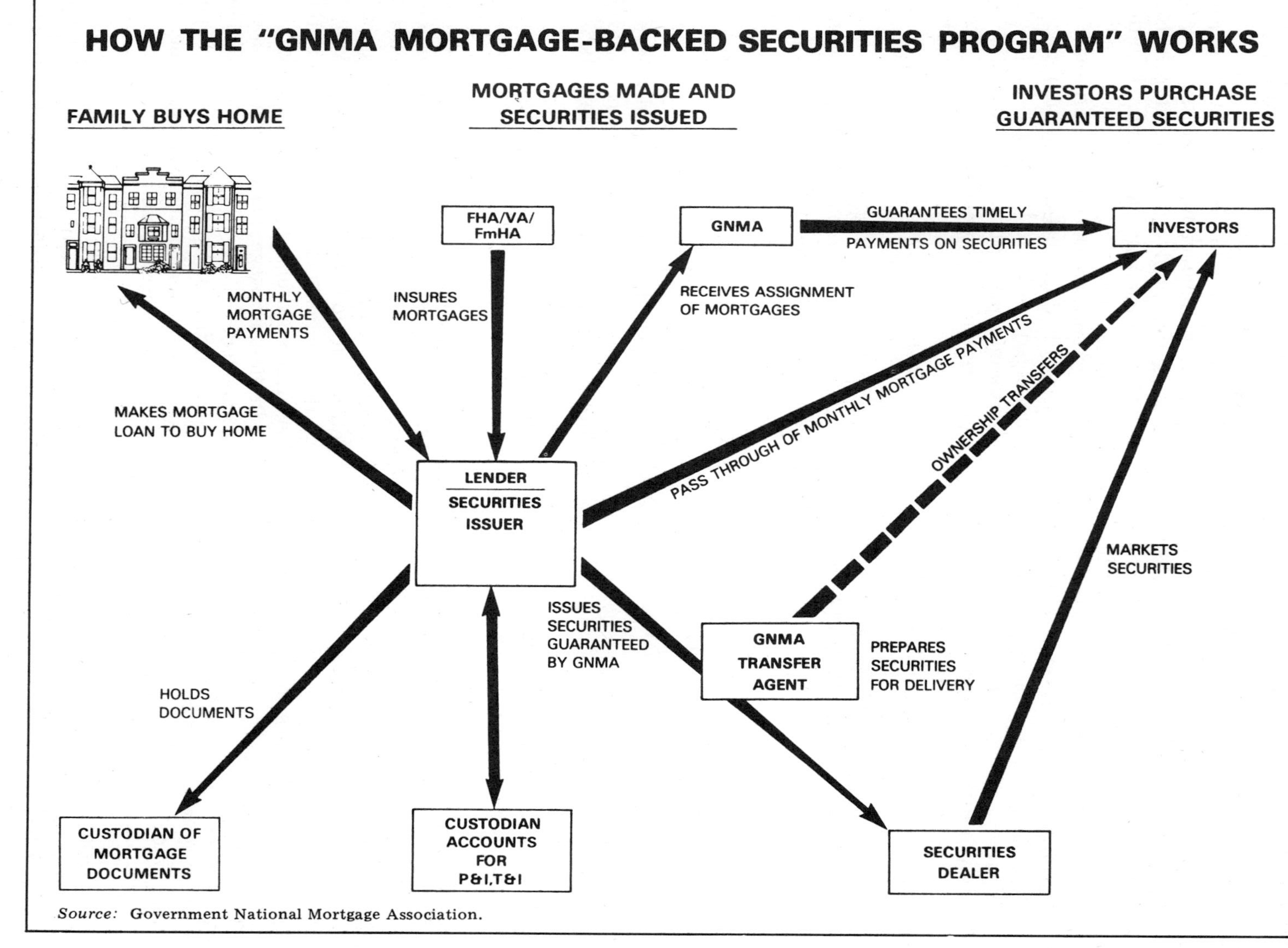

Source: Government National Mortgage Association.

REVIEW QUESTIONS

1. Outline the development of the Government National Mortgage Association.

2. Outline the mortgage purchase program of the Government National Mortgage Association.

3. Explain the operation or the bid pricing system of the Federal Home Loan Mortgage Corporation.

4. Explain the meaning of the term *net yield*.

5. Explain how FHLMC generates funds for the purchase of mortgages.

6. Outline the major mortgage purchase programs of the Federal Home Loan Mortgage Corporation.

7. Explain the mortgage-backed securities program of the Government National Mortgage Association.

8. Name and explain the types of mortgage-backed securities issued by the Government National Mortgage Association.

9. Define the terms *initial adjustment period* and *base index value* as they relate to the FHLMC's adjustable rate mortgage purchase program.

NOTES

[1]U.S., Government National Mortgage Association, *Sellers' Guide*, 1974, Chapter 1, Section 501, p. 19.

[2]U.S., Government National Mortgage Association, *Annual Report 1977*, Department of Housing and Urban Development, June 1978, HUD #85-6-N(2), p. 13.

CHAPTER 11 Qualifying the Property

LEARNING OBJECTIVES

In this chapter we shall examine the various methods used to value property and look at the forms used by the Federal National Mortgage Association/Federal Home Loan Mortgage Corporation, the Federal Housing Administraton, and the Veterans Administration to establish value.

Upon completion of this chapter you should be able to do the following:

- ⋆ **Identify the major professional organizations for certification of appraisers.**
- ⋆ **Explain the three primary methods used to establish the value of real property.**
- ⋆ **Outline the major sections of the appraisal forms used by FNMA/FHLMC, VA, and FHA.**

This lengthy chapter is still only an overview of the complex appraisal process. You will find a more in-depth study in a real estate appraisal course.

PROPERTY APPRAISAL

At the start of our discussion of the appraisal of property, the term *appraisal* must be defined. A simple definition is: an estimate of value of an adequately described piece of real property, as of a specific date, supported by the analysis of relevent data, by a trained professional appraiser, and usually in written form. The term *market value* must also be defined as it will be used throughout this chapter. Market value may be defined as the highest price that a property, when exposed to a competitive and open market for a reasonable time period, would bring to a seller who desires to sell, but is under no duress from an informed buyer who is ready, willing and able to pay for the property. In other words, market value is simply the price at which a seller is willing to sell and a buyer is willing to buy.

Professional Organizations

Our definition of appraisal referred to a trained professional appraiser, a person who has met the training and experience requirements of either of the major professional organizations that certify appraisers.

The first of the organizations is the Society of Real Estate Appraisers (SREA), which originated through the lending institutions. The Society of Real Estate Appraisers presently grants three designations: senior residential appraiser (SRA), senior real property appraiser (SRPA) (for those appraisers who specialize in the appraisal of commercial property), and senior real estate analyst (SREA) (the most prestigious designation given by the SREA). In addition to the training of and setting of standards for the industry, SREA publishes regular sales data for regions of the United States. The sales data books, sometimes referred to as *comp books*,

Figure 11-1. Single-Family Residential Sales Data

SREA MARKET DATA CENTER INC

SINGLE FAMILY RESIDENTIAL SALES DATA

COUNTY HARRIS

MAP CODE / CITY / CENSUS TRACT	PROPERTY ADDRESS	UNIT	$ SALE PRICE	TYPE	CASH DOWN	% 1ST MTG	SALE DATE MO/YR	SALE CLOSED	LOT SIZE OR AREA	LOT ZONE	FLOOD ZONE	SITE INF	OBSOLESCENCE	WATER	SEWER	STYLE	STORIES	FLOOR PLAN	QUALITY	CONDITION	YEAR BUILT	ROOMS	BDRMS	OTHER ROOMS	BATHS FULL	BATHS HALF	SQ. FT. LIVING AREA	% BSMT AREA	BSMT FINISH	A/C	PARKING	POOL	FIREPLACE	EQUIPMENT	REMODELED	OTHER IMP	HEATING	FUEL	TYPE CONSTR	EXT WALLS	TYPE ROOF	FLOORING	AMENITIES	LEASEHOLD	TYPE OWNER	TYPE IMP	
325 -J	24214 ROCKIN SEVEN DR		38,900	F			6-79	N	60X105	R	N		N	P	P	BUN	1	G	E		79	5	3		2		1,361	S		C	A2		1	RDG			A	G	F	X	C	C				S	
	24318 ROCKIN SEVEN DR		38,000	F			6-79	N	60X105	R	N		N	P	P	BUN	1	G	E		79	5	2		2		1,251	S		C	A1		1	RDG			E	E	F	X	C	C				S	
	24319 ROCKIN SEVEN DR		37,900	F			6-79	N	60X105	R	N		N	P	P	BUN	1	G	E		79	5	2		2		1,251	S		C	A1		1	RDG			E	E	F	X	C	C				S	
	24322 ROCKIN SEVEN DR		39,900	F			6-79	N	60X105	R	N		N	P	P	BUN	1	G	E		79	5	3		2		1,407	S		C	A1		1	RDG			E	E	F	X	C	C				S	
	24327 ROCKIN SEVEN DR		39,900	F			8-79	N	60X105	R	N		N	P	P	BUN	1	G	E		79	5	3		2		1,408	S		C	A1		1	RDG			E	E	F	X	C	C				S	
	24407 ROCKIN SEVEN DR		39,900	F			8-79	N	60X105	R	N		N	P	P	BUN	1	G	E		79	5	3		2		1,407	S		C	A1		1	RDG			E	E	F	X	C	C				S	
	24410 ROCKIN SEVEN DR		36,900	F			6-79	N	6,300	R	N		N	P	P	BUN	1	G	E		79	5	2		2		1,251	S		C	A1		1	RDG			E	E	F	X	C	C				S	
	24426 ROCKIN SEVEN DR		38,900	F			6-79	N	6,825	R	N		N	P	P	BUN	1	G	E		79	5	3		2		1,361	S		C	A1		1	RDG			E	E	F	X	C	C				S	
325 -L	2618 KILLDEER LN		50,700	F			7-79	N	60X117	R	N		N	P	P	BUN	1	G	E		79	6	3	DR	2		1,519	S		C	A2		1	RDG			E	E	F	X	C	C				S	
326 -Q	19803 SHADY HILL CR		42,000	C	24%	76%	11-78	Y	17,465	R	N		N	I	S		1	A	A	A	79	7	2	DR+OT	2		1,390	S		C	D2			X			A	E	F	W	C	C				S	
327 -Q	17422 BARKER ST	N	51,300	F			6-79	N	60X105	R	N		N	P	P	BUN	1	G	E		79	8	3	DR	2		1,682	S		C	A2			RDG			E	E	F	X	C	C				S	
327 -Y	16202 BARKLEA		70,600	C		80%	6-79	Y	150X350	R	N			P	P	COL	1	G	G	G	79	8	3	FR+DR+ATOT	2		2,009	S	U	C	G1		1	RDH		L	E	E	B	X	C	C	S			S	
328 -R	17110 LILLIAN LN		72,300	C		80%	7-79	Y	1.00	R	N			P	P	COL	1+	G	G	G	79	7	3	DR+AT+OT	2		2,026	S	U	C	H		1	RDH		L	E	E	B	X	C	C	S			S	
328 -S	14407 CYPRESS CREEK DR		54,400	C			4-79	N	64X105	R	Y		N	P	P	COL	2		A	A	79	6	3	DR+OT	2	1	1,512	S		C	A2			RDG			A	G	B	X	C	C				S	
	14811 CYPRESS MEADOW		70,100	C			4-79	N	65X100	R	N	V	N	P	P	BUN	2	A	A	A		11	4	FR+DR	2	1	2,420			C	D2		1	RDG		D	A	G	F	X	C	C	P		D	S	C
	14714 CYPRESS VALLEY		55,900	C			5-79	N	60X100	R			N	P	P	COL	2	G	A	A	79	6	3	DR	2	1	1,512			C	A2		1	RDG			A	G	C	X	C	C				S	C
	14802 CYPRESS VALLEY		47,900	V			6-79	N	60X100	R	N	W	N	P	P	COL	1	G	G	G		6	3	FR+DR	2		1,416	S		C	A2		1	RDG			A	G	F	X	C	C				S	
328 -T	15026 CYPRESS FALLS DR		58,000	V			7-79	N	58X100	R	N		N	P	P	RNC	1+	G	E	E	78	7	3	FR+DR	2	1	1,544	S		C	A2		1	RDG		L	A	G	F	X	C	C				S	
	14715 CYPRESS MEADOW		46,700	F			7-79	N	6,000	R	N		N		P	BUN	1	G	E		79	6	3	DR	2		1,452	S		C	A2		1	RDG			E	E	F	X	C	C				S	
	14407 CYPRESS SPRING		28,800	F			6-79	N	60X120		N	W	N	C	P	RNC	1		A	A	76	6	3	DR	2		1,530	S		C	D2		1	RDG		Z	A	E	F	X	C	C				S	
	14506 LOVETTA RD		47,900	V			8-79	N	63X120	R	N		N	P	P		1	G	G	G		6	3	DR+OT	2		1,445	S		C	A2		1	RDG		L	A	G	F	X	C	C				S	
328 -U	12930 BOWING OAKS DR		93,900	C			4-79	Y	11,500	R	N	VW	N	P	P	COL	2	A	A	A	79	10	4	FR+DR+BR	2	1	2,734	S		C	D3		1	RDG		PL	A	G	F	X	W	C				S	C
328 -V	12902 BELGRAVE		102,000	C			8-79	N	20,000	R	N	W	N	P	P	CON	1+	G	G	G	79	9	4	FR+DR	3	1	2,918			C	A3		1	RDG		P	A	G	F	X	W	C				S	C
	12818 BOWING OAKS		99,000	C		75%	6-79	Y	15,545	R	N	V	N	P	P	TUD	2	G	G	E	79	10	5	FR+DR+OT	2	1	3,003	S		C	D2		1	RDG		PL	A	E	F	L	W	C	TP			S	
	12866 BOWING OAKS		96,500	C		62%	6-79	Y	14,991	R	N	V	N	P	P	TUD	2	G	G	E	79	9	4	FR+DR+OT	2	1	2,788	S		C	D2		1	RDG		PL	A	E	F	L	W	C	TP			S	
	12907 BOWING OAKS		98,500	C			8-79	N	12,500	R	N	W	N	P	P		2	G	G	G	79	9	4	FR+DR	2	1	2,948			C	D2		1	RDG		P	A	G	F	X	W	C				S	C
	12918 BOWING OAKS		92,900	C			4-79	Y	77X144	R	N	W	N	P	P	COL	1+	A	A	G	79	9	4	FR+DR	2	1	2,662	S		C	D2		1	RDG		PL	A	G	F	X	W	C			D	S	C
	12926 BOWING OAKS		95,000	C		77%	6-79	Y	12,803	R	N	V	N	P	P	TUD	2	G	G	E	79	9	4	FR+DR+OT	2	1	3,017	S		C	D2		1	RDG		PL	A	E	F	L	W	C	TP			S	
	12807 FOREST MEADOW		100,600	C	20%	80%	6-79	Y	12,000		N		N	P	P	COL	2	G	G	G	79	10	4	DN+DR	2	1	2,784	S		C	D2		1	RDG			A	G	F	X	W	C				S	
	14406 LOUETTA RD		47,900	V			6-79	N	63X120	R	N		N	P	P	BUN	1	A	A	E	79	6	3	DR	2		1,447	S		C	A2		1	RDG			A	G	F	X	C	C				S	
328 -W	14923 CYPRESS GREEN		47,900	C			3-79	N	4,777	R	N	V	N	P	P	BUN	1	A	A	G		6	3	DR	2		1,448			C	A2		1	RDG		D	A	G	F	X	C	C	P		D	S	C
	14923 CYPRESS GREEN		48,300	V			8-79	N	45X100	R			N	P	P	BUN	1	A	A	G	79	7	3		2		1,445	S		C	A2		1	RDG			A	G	F	X	C	C				S	
	12802 FOREST MEADOW		106,000	C		52%	4-79	Y	15,950		N		N	P	P	TUD	1+	G	G	G	79	11	4	DN+DR	2	1	2,872	S		C	D2		1	RDG			A	G	F	X	W	C				S	
328 -Z	15139 CAROLS WY		86,900	C	20%	80%	8-79	Y	11,000	R	N	W	N	C	P	MED	1+	G	G	G	79	9	4	FR+DR+AT	2	1	2,407	S		C	A2		1	RDG		L	A	G	F	L	C	C	TP			S	
	12207 CAROLS WAY CR		72,000	C	21%	79%	7-79	Y	70X115	R	N	VW	N	C	P	CON	1	G	G	G	79	7	3	FR+DR+AT	2		1,835	S		C	A2		1	RDG		L	A	G	F	L	C	C	TP			S	
	12210 CAROLS WAY CR		86,500	C		80%	8-79	N	9,900	R	N		N	P	P	TUD	2	A	A	A	79	9	4	FR+DR	2	1	2,205	S		C	D2		1	RDG		LZ	A	E	F	X	W	C	TP			S	
	15210 CAROLS WAY DR		73,300	V			6-79	N	50X122	R	N		N	P	P	CON	1	G	G	E	79	7	3	FR+DR	2		1,943	S		C	A2		1	RDG			A	G	F	X	C	C				S	
	15003 CAROLSWAY		73,900	C	20%	80%	5-79	N	80X120		N	V	N	P	P	TUD	1+	G	G	G	78	9	4	FR+DR	2	1	1,924	S		C	A2		1	RDG			A	G	F	L	W	C	TP			S	
	14903 CYPRESS GREEN DR		64,500	V			8-79	N	9,477	R	N	W	N	P	P	COL	2	G	G	G		10	4	FR+DR	2		2,106	S		C	A2		1	RDG			A	G	F	X	C	C				S	
	15018 OAK BLUFF CT		78,900	C	37%	63%	6-79	Y	11,335	R	N		N	P	P		2	G	G	G		10	4	FR+DR+ATOT	2	1	2,260	S		C	D2		1	RDG		L	A	G	F	X	W	C				S	
	12207 OAK PARK DR		87,900	C		60%	7-79	N	9,481	R		V		P	P	GEO	2	G	G	E	79	8	4	FR+DR	2	1	2,293	S		C	D2		1	RDG		LZ	A	G	F	L	W	C	TP			S	
	12411 OAK PARK DR		81,500	C		80%	6-79	N	70X115	R	N	V	N	P	P	MED	2	A	A	E	79	8	4	FR+DR+OT	2	1	2,175	S		C	D2		1	RDG		LZ	A	G	F	L	W	C	CP			S	
	12411 OAK PARK DR		80,500	C	13%	87%	6-79	N	70X115	R	N	W	N	C	P	TUD	2	G	G	G	79	8	4	FR+DR+AT	2	1	2,150	S		C	D2		1	RDW		Z	A	G	F	L	W	C	TP			S	
	12415 OAK PARK DR		88,400	C	12%	88%	6-79	N	70X115	R	N	W	N	C	P	TUD	1+	G	G	G	79	9	4	FR+DR	2	1	2,198	S		C	D2		1	RDG		Z	A	G	F	L	W	C	TP			S	
	14910 ROSEHILL CT		75,000	C	20%	80%	8-79	N	80X120		N		N	P	P	HRN	2	G	A	G	79	8	4	FR+DR	2		2,467	S		C	D2		1	RDG		D	A	G	F	L	W	C				S	
	12415 ROSEHILL LN		70,500	C	11%	89%	8-79	Y	8,260	R	N	W	N	C	P	TUD	2	G	G	G	79	8	4	FR+DR+ATOT	2	1	2,299	S		C	D2		1	RDG		LZ	A	G	F	L	W	C	CP			S	
329 -L	17522 BONNIE SEAN		54,900	F			7-79	N	60X140	R	N		N	P	P	BUN	1	G	G	G	72	8	4	DN+DR	2		1,780	S		C	A2			RDG		F	E	E	F	X	W	C				S	
	9602 JAN GLEN		52,100	F			9-79	N	65X110	R	N	V	N	P	P	CON	1	A	A	A	73	7	3	FR+DR	2		1,800	S		C	D2		1	RDG		F	A	G	F	X	C	C				S	
329 -Q	16911 BALLYCASTLE		53,900	C		87%	6-79	Y	10,882	R	N	V	N	P	P	RNC	1	A	A	E	79	6	3	FR+DR	2		1,457	S		C	A2		1	RDG			A	G	F	X	C	C				S	
	17322 BARONSHIRE		45,600	V			9-79	N	65X120	R	N		N	P	P	COL	1	A	A	A	77	6	3	FR+DR	2		1,448	S		C	D2		1	RDG			A	E	F	L	C	C				S	
	17114 CAMBERWELL GREEN		58,600	F			7-79	N	65X120	R	N		N	P	P	BUN	1	G	E		79	8	4	DR	2		1,799	S		C	A2		1	RDG			A	G	F	X	C	C				S	
	9519 CHARTER RIDGE		62,500	C			7-79	N	65X115	R	N	V	N	P	P	CON	1	A	A	E	79	6	3	FR+DR	2		1,620	S		C	A2		1	RDG			A	G	F	X	C	C				S	C
	16303 HOLLOW ROCK		62,500	C			8-79	N	8,065	R	N		N	P	P	CON	1	A	A	G	79	6	3	FR+DR	2		1,620	S		C	A2		1	RDG		PF	A	G	F	X	C	C				S	C
	17007 KINGS WALK		55,000	V			7-79	N	65X120	R	N	V	N	P	P	HRN	1+	G	G	E	79	6	3	FR+DR	2	1	1,655	S		C	A2		1	RDG			A	G	F	X	C	C				S	
	9534 MAGNOLIA RIDGE		47,500	C			6-79	N	70X115	R	N	V	N	P	P	BUN	1	A	A	E	79	6	3	FR+DR	2		1,307	S		C	A2			RDG			A	G	F	X	C	C				S	C
	9606 MAGNOLIA RIDGE		54,500	C			6-79	N	66X115	R	N	V	N	P	P	TUD	1	A	A	E	79	6	3	FR+DR	2		1,526	S		C	A2		1	RDG			A	G	F	X	C	C				S	C
	9626 MAGNOLIA RIDGE		56,400	C			7-79	N	62X115	R	N		N	P	P	CON	1+	A	A	G	79	5	3	FR	2		1,489	S		C	A2		1	RDG			A	G	F	X	C	C	TP			S	C
	9510 THISTLE TR		54,500	C			6-79	N	8,057	R	N	V	N	P	P	TUD	1	A	A	E	79	6	3	FR+DR	2		1,526	S		C	A2		1	RDG			A	G	F	X	C	C				S	C
329 -R	9727 BITSAY		50,300	F			9-79	N	60X110	R	N		N	P	P	BUN	1	A	A	A	76	7	3	FR+DR	2		1,538	S		C	A2		1	RDG			A	G	F	X	C	C				S	
	9627 CRAIL		61,900	V			6-79	Y	60X110	R	N	V	N	P	P	BUN	1+	A	A	A	74	8	4	FR+DR	2		2,226	S		C	D2		1	RDG		L	A	G	F	L	W	C				S	
	9630 DORNOCH		73,500	V			8-79	N	60X100	R	N		N	P	P	BUN	1	G	G	G	74	9	5	FR+DR	2	1	2,318	S		C	A2		1	RDG		F	A	G	F	X	W	C				S	
	9710 HALKIRK		54,900	F			7-79	N	60X110	R	N		N	P	P	BUN	1	A	A	A	73	6	3	FR+DR	2		1,883	S		C	A2		1	RDG		L	A	G	F	X	W	C				S	
	9715 HALKIRK		52,900	V			6-79	N	6,600	R	N	V	N	P	P	BUN	1	A	A	A	75	6	3	FR+DR	2		1,517	S		C	A2		1	RDG			A	G	F	X	C	C				S	
	9419 KILRENNY		46,700	A			7-79	N	60X115		N		N	C	P	RNC	1	G	G	G	78	7	3	FR	2		1,556	S		C	A2		1	RDG		F	A	E	F	X	C	C				S	
	9635 KILRENNY		58,500	V			7-79	N	7,130	R	N	V	N	P		BUN	1	A	A	A	77	8	4	FR+DR	2		1,935	S		C	D2		1	RDG		L	A	G	F	X	W	C				S	
	9314 MAGNOLIA RIDGE		45,400	F			8-79	N	66X115	R	N		N	P	P	BUN	1	A	G	E	79	5	3		2		1,359	S		C	A2		1	RDG			A	G	F	X	C	C				S	
	9615 ORANGEVALE		40,600	V			6-79	N	61X110		N		N	P	P	BUN	1	G	E	E	78	5	3		2		1,674	S		C	A2		1	RDG			A	E	F	X	C	C				S	
329 -S	15622 TEN OAKS		105,800	C	20%	80%	7-79	N	11,964	R	N	V	N	P	P	TUD	2	G	G	G	79	10	4	FR+DR+OT	2	1	2,766	S		C	D2		1	RDG		PL	A	G	F	L	W	C	C+			S	
	15415 WINTERHAVEN		76,900	C	61%	39%	12-78	N	22,123	R	N	W	N	P	S	CON	1	G	A	G	78	6	3	FR	2		1,965	S		C	D2		1	RDG			A	G	F	X	C	C				S	
329 -T	16302 CHARTERSTONE DR		43,400	F			6-79	N	1,181	R	N		N	P	P	BUN	1	G	E		79	6	3	DR	2		1,257	S		C	A2		1	RDG			A	G	F	X	C	C				S	
	11818 OAKCROFT		127,000	C	20%	80%	4-79	Y	9,800	R	N	W	N	P	P	TUD	2	A	G	E	79	8	3	DN+DR	3	2	3,052	S		C	D2		1	RDG		Z	A	G	F	X	W	C	C+			S	
329 -U	9810 CHARTER RIDGE		44,700	F			8-79	N	70X121	R	N		N	P	P	BUN	2	G	G	G	79	6	3	DR	2		1,484	S		C	B2		1	RDG			A	G	F	X	C	C	P			S	
	9614 CHARTER RIDGE DR		61,900	F			9-79	N	60X115	R	N		N	P	P	BUN	1+	G	E		79	8	3	DR	2		2,011	S		C	A2		1	RDG			A	G	F	X	C	C				S	
	16307 HOLLOW ROCK DR		54,500	V			8-79	N	63X115	R	N		N	P	P	CON	1+	A	A	A	79	5	3		2		1,490	S		C	A2		1	RDG			A	E	F	X	C	C				S	
	9506 MAGNOLIA RIDGE		54,200	F			8-79	N	61X115	R	N		N	P	P	BUN	1	G	E		79	6	3	DR	2		1,521	S		C	A2		1	RDG			E	E	F	X	C	C				S	
	9806 SUGAR TREE CT		50,100	V			6-79	Y	9,188	R	N	W	N	P	P	COL	2	G	A	G		6	3	FR+DR	2		1,476	S		C	A2		2	RDG			A	G	F	X	C	C				S	
	9403 THISTLE TR		44,900	F			8-79	N	7,741							CON	1	A	A	A	79	6	3		2		1,360	S		C	A2		1	RDG			A	G	F	X	C	C				S	

** THE ABOVE DATA BELIEVED TO BE RELIABLE BUT ACCURACY IS NOT GUARANTEED -- 5-- SOUTH TEXAS 325 -J / 329 -U

Source: SREA Market Data Center, Inc., South Texas Regional Center

list all of the closed transactions that were appraised by SREA members and serve as one of the best sources of information on current sales in a market. An example of one of the pages from an SREA is shown in Figure 11-1.[1]

When these books were originally pubished, they were available only to SREA members, but today they are available to real estate brokers. If you are interested in further information on the sales data books, contact the SREA Market Data Center. The address for the center is:

SREA Market Data Center, Inc.
24 W. St. Joseph St.
Caller Box #23
Arcadia, CA 91006

The second organization that issues designations to appraisers who meet its standards is the American Institute of Real Estate Appraisers (AIREA). This organization is a member group of the National Association of Realtors® and one of the requirements for membership in AIREA is that the person must be a member of the National Association of Realtors®. AIREA issues two designations: member, appraisal institute (MAI), and residential member (RM).

In addition to the issuance of these designations, AIREA is one of the leading publishers of books and articles about the field of appraisal. If you would like more information on AIREA, contact either your local board of Realtors® or the American Institute of Real Estate Appraisers at this address:

American Institute of
Real Estate Appraisers
430 North Michigan Ave.
Chicago, IL 60611

Appraisal Formats

The appraisal may take one of three forms: letter appraisal, narrative appraisal, or report appraisal.

The *letter appraisal*, as the name implies, will be a simple letter stating the value of the property and how the stated value was calculated.

The *narrative appraisal* will usually be in book form. The size of the narrative report will vary with the complexity of the property appraised. Usually this type of appraisal is used for the income type of property. The narrative appraisal report will have several sections. Some of the more common sections are as follows:

1. The introduction will contain a table of contents and a letter of transmittal to the firm that requested the appraisal. The transmittal letter will state the market value of the property to be appraised. If the subject property is a townhouse complex comprised of several different types of units, the transmittal letter will state the market value of each unit as of a specific date. For example:

   As of January 1, 1983, it is our opinion that the present market value of the individual units are as follows:

Unit 101	$51,500
Unit 102	$54,350
Unit 203	$63,500

   It should be noted that the value is expressed at the beginning of the narrative appraisal and all of the additional information is used to support this market value. The reason for this arrangement is that the narrative report can be as few as 10 pages to as many as 100. So with the value stated in the first few pages, a person reviewing the appraisal does not have to read the whole report.

2. The second section of the narrative is the description, analysis, and conclusion. In this section, the appraiser will describe the property to be appraised and the date of the appraisal. Some include a definition of market value.

3. The third section is the market survey. This gives information about the market in which the property is located. This market can be a whole city if the property described will be affected by the complete city, or it could be only a section of a city if the city is large.

4. The fourth section of the report is usually the qualitative study. In this section, the quality of the property is discussed. For example, if the property is a condo project, the report will analyze the common area,

land use, parking facilities, recreational facilities if any, and finally the features of each of the different units in the project.

5. The final major section of the report is the valuation conclusions. In this section, the appraiser will establish the market value of each unit and certify the value as of the date of the report.

6. Some narrative reports will contain an addendum. In this section, the appraiser will furnish a set of photographs of the location of the property, floor plans of the units, a budget for operation of the project, and any other information that will help in the establishment of market value.

A table of contents of a narrative report is shown in Figure 11-2.

The final form an appraisal may take is the *report appraisal*. This is the format that is most commonly used for the appraisal of residential properties, including the two- to four-family dwelling and a unit in a condominium or PUD project. One such form is the standard FNMA Form 1004. There are several other standard forms and they will be discussed in detail later in this chapter.

Basic Principles of Real Property Value

Before we examine the methods of establishing value, we should review some of the basic economic principles that affect the appraisal of property. These economic principles are sometimes referred to as the principles of value. Some of the more important principles are discussed below.

Supply and demand As with any other product or commodity, the one principle that has the greatest effect on the value of property is supply and demand. For example, if there is a high demand for single-family dwellings in a certain area of a city and the builders and the real supply market cannot meet the demand, the prices of the dwellings in the area will escalate at a rapid rate. If there is an oversupply of homes in an area—more homes available than there are buyers—the prices in the area will decline in order to increase demand.

Conformity The principle of conformity is that value is enhanced when the properties in a general area, such as a subdivision, generally have the same styling and the land is used generally for the same purpose. This principle can be illustrated with the following example. If a subdivision is comprised primarily of single-family dwellings in the price range of $60,000 to $80,000 and these homes are located on a standard subdivision lot of 70 × 120 feet, a home that is built in the subdivision which costs $150,000 and sits on a three-fourths of an acre lot is not in conformity, and financing could be a problem.

Substitution This principle of value states that if there are several properties or products available that are substantially the same in quality, the product or property with the lowest price will be in the most demand. For example, let us say that in a subdivision there are two houses available: one is a resale and the other is a new home offered by the builder or developer. They are basically the same house, but the resale home is $1000 less than the one offered by the builder/developer. The resale will be of more interest to the buying public and can be in more demand.

Anticipation This principle of value can be explained in the following manner: items are given value or the value is increased by the anticipation of value or benefit to be received in the future. For example, a house located in an area of a city that in the past has had the highest rate of appreciation for that city will have a greater value, and thus there will be more demand for homes in this area than for homes located in another area of the city, because the prospective buyer will anticipate a greater future value or greater appreciation.

Highest and best use This principle of value to some experts in the field of appraisal is most important in establishing the value of land and/or improvements to the land. The highest and best use of the land at the time of the appraisal is the use that is most likely to produce the greatest return. Stated another way, the highest and best use is the most profitable use of the land. This principle can be illustrated as follows. A one-acre tract of land is located adjacent to a new industrial district and contains a single-family dwelling.

Figure 11-2. Narrative Appraisal Report Table of Contents

TABLE OF CONTENTS

PART 1

INTRODUCTION

PART II

DESCRIPTION, ANALYSIS AND CONCLUSIONS

Figure 11-2. continued

TABLE OF CONTENTS, Continued

Source: Robert L. Stanley and Associates, Appraisers, Houston, Texas.

ROBERT L. STANLEY
& Associates, Appraisers
HOUSTON, TEXAS

In addition to the property being adjacent to the industrial district, across the back boundary there is a railroad spur and across the front of the property there has been built a new divided street leading into the industrial park. From this, it could be stated that the highest and best use of the property has changed from residential to commercial.

Contribution This principle of value can be defined as the amount of value that is added by the addition of an improvement to a property. For example, when a house is added to a lot in a subdivision, the addition of the house is an improvement and the value is greatly increased. It should be noted that all improvements do not increase the value in the same amount as the cost of the improvement. A good example is a swimming pool added to a single-family dwelling. If the home costs $80,000 and the owner builds a $10,000 pool, the property value will not increase in value by $10,000, but it will increase somewhat, depending on many factors.

Change This principle of value states that all things change and that the change is inevitable. Change is constantly happening and cannot usually be reversed. For example, change is occurring in the make-up of the family in the United States, and this change is having an effect on the housing market throughout the nation. This change is inevitable due to outside forces such as the increase in gasoline prices and inflation.

Methods to Determine Property Value

There are three basic methods or approaches to determine the value of real property: the cost method, the market data method, and the income method. We will briefly examine each of the methods, and later in the chapter we will see how the methods are employed in the standard FNMA/FHLMC appraisal reports.

Cost method The cost method of establishing the market value can be described as taking the cost of reproducing or replacing the improvements to the land, adding the value of the land, and subtracting any depreciation.

Depreciation is the loss of value of an asset. In our case it would be the loss of value of the improvements. For the cost method, this loss can include three forms of depreciaton: physical deterioration, functional obsolescence, and economic obsolescence.

Physical deterioration This loss of value is due to the wear and tear of use. This type of deterioration can be either curable or incurable. For example, if a home is in need of a new roof due to age, this would be a curable type of physical deterioration. But if the same house was in need of a foundation due to settling, the cost of the foundation may be prohibitive and the physical deterioration, then, would be incurable.

Functional obsolescence This loss of value can be due to the design of the house, outdated equipment, or the lack of items that are now considered to be normal and expected in today's construction. Once again, functional obsolescence is either curable or incurable. An example of functional obsolescence is a home built along the Gulf Coast without air conditioning. This type of functional obsolescence may be of the curable type if the cost is not prohibitive to add air conditioning and the house can be insulated in sufficient manner to cut the cost of operation of the central air conditioning. Another type of functional obsolescence would be a three-bedroom home with only one bath. This type of obsolescence may be of the incurable type if the house is so designed that the addition of a second bath is impossible.

Economic obsolescence This loss of value is due to occurrences outside the property. For example, an apartment building was built in a quiet, secluded area just outside the city limits of a medium-size city. The city expands its limits to include the apartment building, and the adjacent area to the apartment building is zoned heavy industrial. This would be a factor affecting the value of the apartment building that has nothing to do with the property or the improvements.

The cost method of establishing the market value is primarily used for the appraisal of new or substantially rehabilitated property.

Market data method This method of establishing market value is sometimes referred to as the *sales-comparison method*. In this method recently closed sales of comparable property are compared to the property that is being appraised. The comparable property is often simply called the *comparable*. When comparing properties, several factors are considered, including the following:

1. Proximity of the comparable to the property being appraised.

2. The date of the sale of the comparable. (The closer the date of the sale to the date of the appraisal, the better. If the sale is sometime in the past, the appraiser will adjust the sales price of the comparable.)

3. The design and room count of the comparable compared to that of the property to be appraised.

4. The quality of construction of the comparable compared to that of the property to be appraised.

When comparing the subject property to the comparables, the appraisers will make adjustments, either deducting dollars from the sales prices of the comparable properties where they are superior to the subject property, or adding dollars to the sales prices of the comparable properties where they are inferior.

When the standard appraisal form of FNMA/FHLMC is reviewed later in this chapter, these and other areas of comparison will be shown.

When using the market data approach, the quality of the comparables is of the utmost importance, and most appraisers select them with great care. There are several sources for comparable properties, but the most widely used are those listed in the Society of Real Estate Appraisers sales data books. These books are published either monthly or quarterly and show all closed transactions where an SREA member made the appraisal. A sample page from one of the sales data publications was illustrated in Figure 11-1.

The market data method of determining value is used primarily for properties located in developed areas where there are sufficient and current closed sales to be used as comparables.

Income method The third and final method used to establish the value of property is the income method. This approach is almost exclusively used to establish the value of income-producing properties. It uses the net operating income of the property to establish value.

The net operating income (NOI) is calculated as the gross potential income of the property, less the vacancy rate and credit loss, less operating expenses. The operating expenses are those items that will regularly occur, such as taxes, insurance, utilities, repairs, and maintenance. All expenses and income will be annualized.

The net operating income for a small apartment complex could be figured as follows:

Gross Potential Income	
5 units at $300.00 month	$18,000
Vacancy and Credit Loss	
6% of gross potential income	− 1,080
Gross Possible Income	$16,920
Operating Expenses	
Includes the items listed above and should equal approximately 40% of the gross potential income	− 7,200
Net Operating Income	$ 9,720

This calculation of the net operating income is referred to as a *proforma statement* of the complex. When dealing with income properties, the proforma statement is one of the more important elements used to establish value.

Using the information supplied in the proforma statement of the property, the value of the property can be established by using the NOI. One such method of establishing value is through *capitalization*. By this process, the appraiser can establish value by dividing the NOI by a *capitalization rate* or *cap rate*. This cap rate can change and can be based on several factors. Using our small apartment complex, we can establish the value by dividing the NOI by a cap rate. For example, using a cap rate of 14 percent, what would be the value of the property? We divide the NOI by the 14 percent cap rate.

$$\frac{\$9{,}720}{14\%} = \$69{,}428$$

The value or maximum sales price would be $69,428. Now, let us lower the cap rate to 10 percent and see how this will affect the value of the property.

$$\frac{\$9{,}720}{10\%} = \$97{,}200$$

From this cap rate example, one can see that the lower the cap rate, the higher the value or maximum sales price.

As mentioned above, the cap rate can be figured in several ways and most are very technical, but one may refer to the cap rate as the rate of return an investor is seeking from an investment.

Another method that is often used to calculate the value of a small apartment complex or a duplex, triplex, or fourplex is the *gross rent multiplier (GRM)* method. The GRM is a relationship between the monthly rent and the sales price and can be expressed as:

$$\frac{\text{Sales Price}}{\text{Gross Monthly Rent}} = \text{Gross Rent Multiplier (GRM).}$$

How can this be used to establish value for small income-producing properties?

For example, we are going to purchase a duplex for $85,500 and the monthly rent for both units is $800 per month. The appraiser would then search for properties that are similar to the subject property and calculate the GRM for those sales and apply the calculated GRM to the subject property.

During the search, the appraiser finds that there are several sales that are comparable to the subject and that the average GRM for these sales is 105. He then would apply the GRM to the subject property to establish value:

$$\text{Value} = \text{monthly rent} \times \text{GRM}$$

or

$$= \$800 \times 105 = \$84{,}000$$

From this calculation, we can see that the value is approximately $1500 above the value established by the appraiser.

Now let us calculate the GRM for the subject property using the sales price of $85,500. As was stated earlier, the GRM is calculated by dividing the sales price by the monthly rent, so for our property the calculation would be:

$$\frac{\$85{,}500}{\$800} = 106.87$$

With this information, we can see that the GRM for the property we are interested in is approximately 1.87 above the average for comparable properties in the area.

This is not to say that the property is overpriced or that the rent is too low. The final value would take into consideration many other factors. This example was only intended to show how value could be established using the gross rent multiplier.

Fair Market Value

After all of the methods to establish value are completed, the appraiser will then establish the *fair market value* of the property. This is done by the correlation of the methods that apply to the property being appraised.

For example, if the property is a single-family dwelling located in a subdivision, the only methods that would apply would be the cost approach and the market data approach. Usually the value established by these methods should be close, but if the values are not close, the appraiser must then establish which method will be given emphasis.

STANDARD APPRAISAL REPORTS

Now that we have defined an appraisal, reviewed the standard appraisal formats, and discussed the methods to establish value, let us look at some of the standard forms used in the industry to report the value of property or to request establishing the value of real property with improvements.

We will examine the most common conventional appraisal reports, the standard forms that have been developed by FNMA and/or FHLMC. At the present time, there are three of these forms. The first is the Residential Appraisal Report, FNMA Form 1004/FHLMC Form 70. Page one of this form is shown in Figure 11-3 and page two is illustrated in Figure 11-4. The second form is FNMA Form 1025/FHLMC Form 72, the Appraisal Report—Small Residential Income Property. This form is illustrated in Figures 11-5 and 11-6. The third form developed by FNMA/FHLMC is the Appraisal Report—Individual Condominium or PUD Unit. This form is numbered FNMA Form 1073 and is shown in Figures 11-7 and 11-8.

Figure 11-3. FNMA/FHLMC Residential Appraisal Report, page 1

RESIDENTIAL APPRAISAL REPORT — File No.

To be completed by Lender

Borrower — Census Tract — Map Reference
Property Address
City — County — State — Zip Code
Legal Description
Sale Price $ — Date of Sale — Loan Term — yrs — Property Rights Appraised ☐ Fee ☐ Leasehold ☐ DeMinimis PUD
Actual Real Estate Taxes $ — (yr) Loan charges to be paid by seller $ — Other sales concessions
Lender/Client — Address
Occupant — Appraiser — Instructions to Appraiser

NEIGHBORHOOD

Location ☐ Urban ☐ Suburban ☐ Rural
Built Up ☐ Over 75% ☐ 25% to 75% ☐ Under 25%
Growth Rate ☐ Fully Dev. ☐ Rapid ☐ Steady ☐ Slow
Property Values ☐ Increasing ☐ Stable ☐ Declining
Demand/Supply ☐ Shortage ☐ In Balance ☐ Over Supply
Marketing Time ☐ Under 3 Mos. ☐ 4–6 Mos. ☐ Over 6 Mos.
Present Land Use ___% 1 Family ___% 2–4 Family ___% Apts. ___% Condo ___% Commercial
___% Industrial ___% Vacant ___% ________
Change in Present Land Use ☐ Not Likely ☐ Likely (*) ☐ Taking Place (*)
(*) From ________ To ________
Predominant Occupancy ☐ Owner ☐ Tenant ______% Vacant
Single Family Price Range $ ______ to $ ______ Predominant Value $ ______
Single Family Age ______ yrs to ______ yrs Predominant Age ______ yrs

	Good	Avg.	Fair	Poor
Employment Stability	☐	☐	☐	☐
Convenience to Employment	☐	☐	☐	☐
Convenience to Shopping	☐	☐	☐	☐
Convenience to Schools	☐	☐	☐	☐
Adequacy of Public Transportation	☐	☐	☐	☐
Recreational Facilities	☐	☐	☐	☐
Adequacy of Utilities	☐	☐	☐	☐
Property Compatibility	☐	☐	☐	☐
Protection from Detrimental Conditions	☐	☐	☐	☐
Police and Fire Protection	☐	☐	☐	☐
General Appearance of Properties	☐	☐	☐	☐
Appeal to Market	☐	☐	☐	☐

Note: FHLMC/FNMA do not consider race or the racial composition of the neighborhood to be reliable appraisal factors.
Comments including those factors, favorable or unfavorable, affecting marketability (e.g. public parks, schools, view, noise) ________

SITE

Dimensions ________ = ________ Sq. Ft. or Acres ☐ Corner Lot
Zoning classification ________ Present improvements ☐ do ☐ do not conform to zoning regulations
Highest and best use: ☐ Present use ☐ Other (specify) ________

	Public	Other (Describe)
Elec.	☐	
Gas	☐	
Water	☐	
San. Sewer	☐	
☐ Underground Elect. & Tel.		

OFF SITE IMPROVEMENTS
Street Access: ☐ Public ☐ Private
Surface
Maintenance: ☐ Public ☐ Private
☐ Storm Sewer ☐ Curb/Gutter
☐ Sidewalk ☐ Street Lights

Topo
Size
Shape
View
Drainage
Is the property located in a HUD Identified Special Flood Hazard Area? ☐ No ☐ Yes
Comments (favorable or unfavorable including any apparent adverse easements, encroachments or other adverse conditions) ________

IMPROVEMENTS

☐ Existing ☐ Proposed ☐ Under Constr. — No. Units ____ — Type (det, duplex, semi/det, etc.) — Design (rambler, split level, etc.) — Exterior Walls
Yrs. Age: Actual ____ Effective ____ to ____ — No. Stories ____
Roof Material — Gutters & Downspouts ☐ None — Window (Type): ☐ Storm Sash ☐ Screens ☐ Combination — Insulation ☐ None ☐ Floor ☐ Ceiling ☐ Roof ☐ Walls
☐ Manufactured Housing
Foundation Walls
☐ Slab on Grade ☐ Crawl Space
Comments

BSMT: ____% Basement ☐ Floor Drain — Finished Ceiling
☐ Outside Entrance ☐ Sump Pump — Finished Walls
☐ Concrete Floor ____% Finished — Finished Floor
Evidence of: ☐ Dampness ☐ Termites ☐ Settlement

ROOM LIST

Room List	Foyer	Living	Dining	Kitchen	Den	Family Rm.	Rec. Rm.	Bedrooms	No. Baths	Laundry	Other
Basement											
1st Level											
2nd Level											

Finished area above grade contains a total of ______ rooms ______ bedrooms ______ baths. Gross Living Area ______ sq. ft. Bsmt Area ______ sq. ft.

INTERIOR FINISH & EQUIPMENT

Kitchen Equipment: ☐ Refrigerator ☐ Range/Oven ☐ Disposal ☐ Dishwasher ☐ Fan/Hood ☐ Compactor ☐ Washer ☐ Dryer ☐
HEAT: Type ______ Fuel ______ Cond. ______ AIR COND: ☐ Central ☐ Other ______ ☐ Adequate ☐ Inadequate
Floors ☐ Hardwood ☐ Carpet Over ______ ☐ ______
Walls ☐ Drywall ☐ Plaster ☐ ______
Trim/Finish ☐ Good ☐ Average ☐ Fair ☐ Poor
Bath Floor ☐ Ceramic ☐ ______
Bath Wainscot ☐ Ceramic ☐ ______
Special Features (including energy efficient items) ______
ATTIC: ☐ Yes ☐ No ☐ Stairway ☐ Drop-stair ☐ Scuttle ☐ Floored
Finished (Describe) ______ ☐ Heated
CAR STORAGE: ☐ Garage ☐ Built-in ☐ Attached ☐ Detached ☐ Car Port
No. Cars ______ ☐ Adequate ☐ Inadequate Condition ______

PROPERTY RATING

	Good	Avg.	Fair	Poor
Quality of Construction (Materials & Finish)	☐	☐	☐	☐
Condition of Improvements	☐	☐	☐	☐
Room sizes and layout	☐	☐	☐	☐
Closets and Storage	☐	☐	☐	☐
Insulation—adequacy	☐	☐	☐	☐
Plumbing—adequacy and condition	☐	☐	☐	☐
Electrical—adequacy and condition	☐	☐	☐	☐
Kitchen Cabinets—adequacy and condition	☐	☐	☐	☐
Compatibility to Neighborhood	☐	☐	☐	☐
Overall Livability	☐	☐	☐	☐
Appeal and Marketability	☐	☐	☐	☐

Yrs Est Remaining Economic Life ____ to ____. Explain if less than Loan Term

FIREPLACES, PATIOS, POOL, FENCES, etc. (describe) ______

COMMENTS (including functional or physical inadequacies, repairs needed, modernization, etc.) ______

FHLMC Form 70 Rev. 7/79 — ATTACH DESCRIPTIVE PHOTOGRAPHS OF SUBJECT PROPERTY AND STREET SCENE — FNMA Form 1004 Rev. 7/79

Figure 11-4. FNMA/FHLMC Residential Appraisal Report, Valuation Section

VALUATION SECTION

COST APPROACH

Purpose of Appraisal is to estimate Market Value as defined in Certification & Statement of Limiting Conditions (FHLMC Form 439/FNMA Form 1004B). If submitted for FNMA, the appraiser must attach (1) sketch or map showing location of subject, street names, distance from nearest intersection, and any detrimental conditions and (2) exterior building sketch of improvements showing dimensions.

Measurements	No. Stories	Sq. Ft.
____ x ____	x ____	=
____ x ____	x ____	=
____ x ____	x ____	=
____ x ____	x ____	=
____ x ____	x ____	=
____ x ____	x ____	=

Total Gross Living Area (List in Market Data Analysis below) ____

Comment on functional and economic obsolescence: ____

ESTIMATED REPRODUCTION COST – NEW – OF IMPROVEMENTS:

Dwelling ____ Sq. Ft. @ $ ____ = $ ____

____ Sq. Ft. @ $ ____ = ____

Extras ____ = ____

____ = ____

Special Energy Efficient Items ____ = ____

Porches, Patios, etc. ____ = ____

Garage/Car Port ____ Sq. Ft. @ $ ____ = ____

Site Improvements (driveway, landscaping, etc.) = ____

Total Estimated Cost New . . . . = $ ____

Less Depreciation — Physical $ ____ | Functional $ ____ | Economic $ ____ = $ (____)

Depreciated value of improvements . . . . = $ ____

ESTIMATED LAND VALUE . . . . = $ ____
(If leasehold, show only leasehold value)

INDICATED VALUE BY COST APPROACH . . . $ ____

MARKET DATA ANALYSIS

The undersigned has recited three recent sales of properties most similar and proximate to subject and has considered these in the market analysis. The description includes a dollar adjustment, reflecting market reaction to those items of significant variation between the subject and comparable properties. If a significant item in the comparable property is superior to, or more favorable than, the subject property, a minus (-) adjustment is made, thus reducing the indicated value of subject; if a significant item in the comparable is inferior to, or less favorable than, the subject property, a plus (+) adjustment is made, thus increasing the indicated value of the subject.

ITEM	Subject Property	COMPARABLE NO. 1		COMPARABLE NO. 2		COMPARABLE NO. 3	
Address							
Proximity to Subj.							
Sales Price	$		$		$		$
Price/Living area	$ Ø		$ Ø		$ Ø		$ Ø
Data Source							
Date of Sale and Time Adjustment	DESCRIPTION	DESCRIPTION	+(–)$ Adjustment	DESCRIPTION	+(–)$ Adjustment	DESCRIPTION	+(–)$ Adjustment
Location							
Site/View							
Design and Appeal							
Quality of Const.							
Age							
Condition							
Living Area Room Count and Total Gross Living Area	Total, B-rms, Baths; Sq.Ft.	Total, B-rms, Baths; Sq.Ft.		Total, B-rms, Baths; Sq.Ft.		Total, B-rms, Baths; Sq.Ft.	
Basement & Bsmt. Finished Rooms							
Functional Utility							
Air Conditioning							
Garage/Car Port							
Porches, Patio, Pools, etc.							
Special Energy Efficient Items							
Other (e.g. fireplaces, kitchen equip., remodeling)							
Sales or Financing Concessions							
Net Adj. (Total)		☐ Plus; ☐ Minus	$	☐ Plus; ☐ Minus	$	☐ Plus; ☐ Minus	$
Indicated Value of Subject			$		$		$

Comments on Market Data ____

RECONCILIATION

INDICATED VALUE BY MARKET DATA APPROACH . . . . $ ____

INDICATED VALUE BY INCOME APPROACH (If applicable) Economic Market Rent $ ____ /Mo. x Gross Rent Multiplier ____ = $ ____

This appraisal is made ☐ "as is" ☐ subject to the repairs, alterations, or conditions listed below ☐ completion per plans and specifications.

Comments and Conditions of Appraisal: ____

Final Reconciliation: ____

Construction Warranty ☐ Yes ☐ No Name of Warranty Program ____ Warranty Coverage Expires ____

This appraisal is based upon the above requirements, the certification, contingent and limiting conditions, and Market Value definition that are stated in

☐ FHLMC Form 439 (Rev. 10/78)/FNMA Form 1004B (Rev. 10/78) filed with client ____ 19 ____ ☐ attached.

I ESTIMATE THE MARKET VALUE, AS DEFINED, OF SUBJECT PROPERTY AS OF ____ 19 ____ to be $ ____

Appraiser(s) ____ Review Appraiser (If applicable) ____

☐ Did ☐ Did Not Physically Inspect Property

FHLMC Form 70 Rev. 7/79 REVERSE FNMA Form 1004 Rev. 7/79

Figure 11-5. FNMA/FHLMC Small Residential Income Property Appraisal Report, page 1

APPRAISAL REPORT—SMALL RESIDENTIAL INCOME PROPERTY File No.

To be completed by Lender

Borrower Census Tract Map Reference
Property Address
City County State Zip Code
Legal Description
Sale Price $ Date of Sale Loan Term yrs. Property Rights Appraised: ☐ Fee ☐ Leasehold ☐ Other____
Actual Real Estate Taxes $ (yr) Loan charges to be paid by seller $ Other sales concessions
Lender/Client Address
Occupant Appraiser Instructions to Appraiser

NEIGHBORHOOD

Location . . . . . . ☐ Urban . . . ☐ Suburban . . . ☐ Rural
Built-up . . . . . . ☐ Over 75% . . . ☐ 25% to 75% . . ☐ Under 25%
Present land use . . . ___% Condominiums ___% 1-Family ___% 2-4 Family
___% Apartments ___% Commercial ___% Vacant ___%
Change in present land use . . ☐ Not likely . . ☐ Likely (*) . . ☐ Taking Place(*)
(*) From ______ To ______
Property values . . . ☐ Increasing . . ☐ Stable . . ☐ Declining
Housing demand/supply . . ☐ In balance . . ☐ Shortage . . ☐ Oversupply
Predominant occupancy . . ☐ Owner . . . ☐ Tenant . . . ___% Vacant
Single Family: Price range $ ____ to $ ____ Predominant $ ____
Age ____ yrs. to ____ yrs. Predominant ____ yrs
Typical multifamily bldg. Type ____ No. Stories ____ No. Units ____
Age ____ yrs. Condition ____
Typical rents $____ to $____ ☐ Increasing ☐ Stable ☐ Declining
Est. neighborhood apt. vacancy ___% ☐ Decreasing ☐ Stable ☐ Increasing
Rent controls ☐ No ☐ Yes ☐ Not likely ☐ Likely

OVERALL RATING	Good	Avg.	Fair	Poor
Adequacy of Shopping				
Adequacy of Utilities				
Employment Opportunities . . .				
Police and Fire Protection . . .				
Recreational Facilities				
Property Compatibility				
Protection from Detrimental Conditions				
General Appearance of Properties . .				
Appeal to Market				

	Distance	Access or Convenience
Public Transportation		
Employment Centers		
Shopping Facilities		
Grammar Schools		
Freeway Access		

Note: FHLMC/FNMA do not consider race or the racial composition of the neighborhood to be reliable appraisal factors.
Describe those factors, favorable or unfavorable, affecting marketability (incl. mkt. area population size & financial ability).

SITE

Dimensions ____ = ____ Sq. Ft. or Acres ☐ Corner Lot
Zoning classification ____ Present improvements ☐ do ☐ do not conform to zoning regulations
Highest and best use: ☐ Present use ☐ Other (specify)

	Public	Other (Describe)
Elec.	☐	
Gas	☐	
Water	☐	
San.Sewer	☐	
	☐ Underground Elec. & Tel.	

OFF-SITE IMPROVEMENTS
Street Access: ☐Public ☐ Private
Surface
Maintenance ☐Public ☐Private
☐Storm Sewer ☐ Curb/Gutter
☐Sidewalk ☐ Street Lights

Topo
Size
Shape
View
Drainage
Is the property located in a HUD Identified Special Flood Hazard Area? ☐No ☐Yes

Comments (favorable or unfavorable conditions including any apparent adverse easements or encroachments)

DESCRIPTION OF IMPROVEMENTS

☐ Existing ☐ Proposed ☐ Under Construction Type: ☐ Elevator ☐ Walk-up ☐ Det. ☐ Semi-Det. ☐ Row No. Stories ____
No. Bldgs. ____ No. Units ____ No. Rooms ____ No. Baths ____ Parking Spaces: No. ____ Type ____
Basic Structural System ____ Exterior Walls ____ Roof Covering ____
Foundation Walls ____ Basement ____ % Finished ____ % Describe use ____
Interior Walls ____ Floors ____ Bath Floor and Walls ____
Insulation ____ Adequacy ____ Adequacy of Soundproofing ____
Heating: ☐ Central ☐ Individual Type ____ Fuel ____ Adequacy & Condition ____
Air Conditioning: ☐ Central ☐ Individual Fuel ____ Make ____ Adequacy & Condition ____
Kitchen Cabinets, Drawers and Counter space ☐ Adequate ☐ Inadequate
Total No. Appliances: ____ Range/Oven ____ Fan/Hood ____ Dishwasher
____ Disposal ____ Refrigerator ____ Washer ____ Dryer ____ Compactor
Water Heater(s) (make, capacity, fuel) ____
Plumbing Fixtures (make) ____
Electrical Service (amps per unit) ____
Security Features ____
Special Features (including energy efficient items) ____

OVERALL PROPERTY RATING	Good	Avg.	Fair	Poor
Quality of construction (materials and finish) . . .				
Condition of improvements . . .				
Room sizes and layout . . .				
Closets and storage . . .				
Plumbing—adequacy and condition . . .				
Electrical—adequacy and condition . . .				
Kitchen equipment—adequacy and condition . . .				
Amenities and parking facilities . . .				
Overall livability . . .				
Appeal to market . . .				

Age: Actual ____ yrs., Effective ____ yrs. to ____ yrs. Est. Remaining Economic Life ____ yrs. to ____ yrs. Explain if less than Loan Term
COMMENTS: (including functional or physical inadequacies, repairs needed, modernization, etc.)

COST APPROACH

ESTIMATED REPRODUCTION COST NEW

____ x ____ = ____ sq. ft. x ____ (Stories) = ____ sq. ft. x $____ $____
____ x ____ = ____ sq. ft. x ____ (Stories) = ____ sq. ft. x $____ ____
____ x ____ = ____ sq. ft. x ____ (Stories) = ____ sq. ft. x $____ ____
OTHER IMPROVEMENTS (Including special energy efficient items) ____
SITE IMPROVEMENTS ____
TOTAL ESTIMATED COST NEW OF IMPROVEMENTS . . . . . . $____
LESS DEPRECIATION: Physical $ ____ Functional $ ____ Economic $ ____ . . . . . ( )
DEPRECIATED VALUE OF IMPROVEMENTS . . . . $____
ADD-ESTIMATED LAND VALUE (If leasehold, show only leasehold value – attach calculations) . . . $____
INDICATED VALUE BY THE COST APPROACH ☐ FEE SIMPLE ☐ LEASEHOLD . . . . $____

FHLMC Form 72 7/79
2-12 Units

ATTACH LAYOUT SKETCHES SHOWING UNIT ENTRIES, LOCATION MAP AND DESCRIPTIVE PHOTOGRAPHS OF SUBJECT PROPERTY AND STREET SCENE

FNMA Form 1025 7/79
2-4 Units

Figure 11-6. FNMA/FHLMC Small Residential Income Property Appraisal Report, page 2

***COMPARABLE RENTAL DATA**

ITEM	COMPARABLE No. 1	COMPARABLE No. 2	COMPARABLE No. 3
Address			
Proximity to subject			
Rent survey date			
Description of property and conditions	No. Units___ No. Vac.___ Yr. Blt.: 19___	No. Units___ No. Vac.___ Yr. Blt.: 19___	No. Units___ No. Vac.___ Yr. Blt.: 19___

Individual unit breakdown	Rm.Count Tot BR b	Size Sq. Ft.	Monthly Rent $	¢	Rm	Rm.Count Tot BR b	Size Sq. Ft.	Monthly Rent $	¢	Rm	Rm.Count Tot BR b	Size Sq. Ft.	Monthly Rent $	¢	Rm

	COMPARABLE No. 1	COMPARABLE No. 2	COMPARABLE No. 3
Utilities, furniture and amenities incl. in rent			
Compare comps to subj.			

RENT SCHEDULE

Utilities included in actual rents: ☐ Water ☐ Gas ☐ Heat ☐ Electric ☐ Air Conditioning ☐________

Utilities included in forecasted rents: ☐ Water ☐ Gas ☐ Heat ☐ Electric ☐ Air Conditioning ☐________

No. of Units	Individual Unit Rm Count Tot. BR b	Total Rooms	Sq. Ft. Area Per Unit	No. Units Vacant	ACTUAL RENTS Per Unit Unfurnished	ACTUAL RENTS Per Unit Furnished	ACTUAL RENTS Total Rents	FORECASTED RENTS Per Unit Unfurnished	FORECASTED RENTS Per Unit Furnished	FORECASTED RENTS Per Sq. Ft. or Room		FORECASTED RENTS Total Rents
					$	$	$	$	$		$	$
	TOTAL						$					$

Other Monthly Income (Itemize)____________________ $______

Vacancy: Actual last yr.____% Prev. yr.____% Forecasted: ____% $ ________ Total Gross Monthly Forecasted Rent $______

Discuss rental concessions, forecasted rents: ____________________

MARKET DATA ANALYSIS

ITEM	SUBJECT	COMPARABLE No. 1	COMPARABLE No. 2	COMPARABLE No. 3
Address				
Proximity to subject				
Price	$ ☐ Unf. ☐ F.	$ ☐ Unf. ☐ F.	$ ☐ Unf. ☐ F.	$ ☐ Unf. ☐ F.
Date of sale				
Individual unit breakdown	Yr. Blt.: 19___ No. Vac.:___ No. of Units / Individual Unit Room Count Tot. BR b	Yr. Blt.: 19___ No. Vac.:___ No. of Units / Individual Unit Room Count Tot. BR b	Yr. Blt.: 19___ No. Vac.:___ No. of Units / Individual Unit Room Count Tot. BR b	Yr. Blt.: 19___ No. Vac.:___ No. of Units / Individual Unit Room Count Tot. BR b
Compare to subject, including condition, terms of sale/financing				
Gross Bldg. Area (GBA)	sq. ft.	sq. ft.	sq. ft.	sq. ft.
Gross Monthly Rent	$	$	$	$
Gross Mo. Rent Mult. (1)				
Price Per Unit	$	$	$	$
Price Per Room	$	$	$	$
Price Per S.F. GBA	$ /sq. ft. GBA	$ /sq. ft. GBA	$ /sq. ft. GBA	$ /sq. ft. GBA

(1) Sale Price ÷ Gross Monthly Rent | Value Indication for Subject

Val. Per Unit $______ X ______ Units = $______; Val. Per S.F. G.B.A. $______ X ______ S.F. Bldg. Area = $______

Val. Per Rm $______ X ______ Rms = $______; G.R.M.______ X ______ Total Monthly Rent = $______

Reconciliation:

INDICATED VALUE BY MARKET DATA APPROACH . . . . $______

EXPENSE ANALYSIS

ANNUAL EXPENSE SUMMARY - (If for FNMA - Lender must prepare operating data on sep. form for appraiser to review, comment on & attach to appraisal)

		ACTUAL	FORECAST	CALCULATIONS OR COMMENTS
1. Utilities: ☐ Heat $____ ☐ Electric $____ ☐ Gas $____ ☐ Water & Sewer $____	Total:	$	$	
2. Real Estate Taxes $____ 3. Insurance $____	Total:			
4. Management $____ Salaries $____	Total:			
5. Maint. & Decor.$____ Repairs $____ Reserves $____	Total:			
6. Other ________	Total:			
TOTAL EXPENSES & REPLACEMENT RESERVES		$	$	

This appraisal is made ☐ "as is" ☐ subject to the repairs, alterations, or conditions listed below ☐ completion per plans and specifications.

Comments, Conditions and Final Reconciliation: ____________________

This appraisal is based upon the above requirements, the certification, contingent and limiting conditions, and Market Value definition that are stated in ☐ FHLMC Form 439 (Rev. 10/78)/FNMA Form 1004B (Rev. 10/78) filed with client________ 19____ ☐ attached.

I ESTIMATE THE MARKET VALUE, AS DEFINED, OF SUBJECT PROPERTY AS OF ________ 19____ to be $______

Appraiser(s)________________ Review Appraiser (If applicable) ________________

☐ Did ☐ Did Not Physically Inspect Property

FHLMC Form 72 7/79
2-12 Units

FNMA Form 1025 7/79
2-4 Units

Figure 11-7. FNMA/FHLMC Condominium or PUD Unit Appraisal Report, page 1

APPRAISAL REPORT – INDIVIDUAL ☐CONDOMINIUM OR ☐PUD UNIT File No.

To be completed by Lender

Borrower ______ Census Tract ______ Map Reference ______
Unit No. ______ Address ______ Project Name/Phase No. ______
City ______ County ______ State ______ Zip Code ______
Actual Real Estate Taxes $ ______ (yr.) Sales Price $ ______ Property Rights Appraised ☐ Fee ☐ Leasehold
Loan Charges to be Paid by Seller $ ______ Other Sales Concessions ______
Lender/Client ______ Lender's Address ______
Occupant ______ Appraiser ______ Instructions to Appraiser ______
☐ FNMA 1073A required ☐ FHLMC 465 Addendum A required ☐ FHLMC 465 Addendum B required

NEIGHBORHOOD

Location ☐ Urban ☐ Suburban ☐ Rural
Built Up ☐ Over 75% ☐ 25% to 75% ☐ Under 25%
Growth Rate ☐ Fully Developed ☐ Rapid ☐ Steady ☐ Slow
Property Values ☐ Increasing ☐ Stable ☐ Declining
Demand/Supply ☐ Shortage ☐ In Balance ☐ Oversupply
Marketing Time ☐ Under 3 Mos. ☐ 4–6 Mos. ☐ Over 6 Mos.
Present Land Use ____% 1 Family ____% 2–4 Family ____% Apts. ____% Condo
____% Commercial ____% Industrial ____% Vacant
Change in Present Land Use ☐ Not Likely ☐ Likely* ☐ Taking Place*
*From ______ To ______
Predominant Occupancy ☐ Owner ☐ Tenant ____% Vacant
Condominium: Price Range $ ______ to $ ______ Predominant $ ______
Age ______ yrs. to ____ yrs. Predominant ______ yrs.
Single Family: Price Range $ ______ to $ ______ Predominant $ ______
Age ______ yrs. to ____ yrs. Predominant ______ yrs.
Describe potential for additional Condo/PUD units in nearby area ______

NEIGHBORHOOD RATING	Good	Avg.	Fair	Poor
Adequacy of Shopping	☐	☐	☐	☐
Employment Opportunities	☐	☐	☐	☐
Recreational Facilities	☐	☐	☐	☐
Adequacy of Utilities	☐	☐	☐	☐
Property Compatibility	☐	☐	☐	☐
Protection from Detrimental Cond.	☐	☐	☐	☐
Police and Fire Protection	☐	☐	☐	☐
General Appearance of Properties	☐	☐	☐	☐
Appeal to Market	☐	☐	☐	☐

	Distance	Access or Convenience			
Public Transportation		☐	☐	☐	☐
Employment Centers		☐	☐	☐	☐
Neighborhood Shopping		☐	☐	☐	☐
Grammar Schools		☐	☐	☐	☐
Freeway Access		☐	☐	☐	☐

Note: FHLMC/FNMA do not consider race or the racial composition of the neighborhood to be reliable appraisal factors.
Describe those factors, favorable or unfavorable, affecting marketability (e.g. public parks, schools, noise, view, mkt. area population size & financial ability)

SITE

Lot Dimensions (if PUD) ______ = ______ Sq. Ft. ☐ Corner Lot Project Density When Completed as Planned ______ Units/Acre
Zoning Classification ______ Present Improvements ☐ do ☐ do not conform to zoning regulations.
Highest and Best Use: ☐ Present Use ☐ Other (specify) ______

	Public	Other (describe)
Elec.	☐	______
Gas	☐	______
Water	☐	______
San. Sewer	☐	______
☐ Underground Elec. & Tel.		

OFF-SITE IMPROVEMENTS
Street Access: ☐ Public ☐ Private
Surface: ______
Maintenance: ☐ Public ☐ Private
☐ Storm Sewer ☐ Curb/Gutter
☐ Sidewalk ☐ Street Lights

Project Ingress/Egress (adequacy) ______
Topo ______
Size/Shape ______
View Amenity ______
Drainage/Flood Conditions ______
Is property located in a HUD Identified Special Flood Hazard Area? ☐ No ☐ Yes

COMMENTS (including any easements, encroachments or adverse conditions) ______

PROJECT IMPROVEMENTS

☐ Existing Approx. Year Built 19____ Original Use ______
☐ Condo ☐ PUD ☐ Converted (19____)
TYPE ☐ Proposed ☐ Under Construction
PROJECT ☐ Elevator ☐ Walk-up No. of Stories ______
☐ Row or Town House ☐ Other (specify) ______
☐ Primary Residence ☐ Second Home or Recreational
If Completed: No. Phases ______ No. Units ______ No. Sold ______
If Incomplete: Planned No. Phases ______ No. Units ______ No. Sold ______
Units in Subject Phase: Total ______ Completed ______ Sold ______ Rented ______
Approx. No. Units for Sale: Subject Project ______ Subject Phase ______

PROJECT RATING	Good	Avg.	Fair	Poor
Location	☐	☐	☐	☐
General Appearance	☐	☐	☐	☐
Amenities & Recreational Facilities	☐	☐	☐	☐
Density (units per acre)	☐	☐	☐	☐
Unit Mix	☐	☐	☐	☐
Quality of Constr. (mat'l. & finish)	☐	☐	☐	☐
Condition of Exterior	☐	☐	☐	☐
Condition of Interior	☐	☐	☐	☐
Appeal to Market	☐	☐	☐	☐

Exterior Wall ______ Roof Covering ______ Security Features ______
Elevator: No. ______ Adequacy & Condition ______ Soundproofing: Vertical ______ Horizontal ______
Parking: Total No. Spaces ______ Ratio ______ Spaces/Unit Type ______ No. Spaces for Guest Parking ______
Describe common elements or recreational facilities ______
Are any common elements, rec. facilities or parking leased to Owners Assoc.? ______ If yes, attach addendum describing rental, terms and options.

SUBJECT UNIT

☐ Existing ☐ Proposed ☐ Under Constr. Floor No. ______ Unit Livable Area ______ ⌀ Basement ______ % Finished ______ ⌀
Parking for Unit: No. ______ Type ______ ☐ Assigned ☐ Owned Convenience to Unit ______

Room List	Foyer	Liv	Din	Kit	Bdrm	Bath	Fam	Rec	Lndry	Other
Basement										
1st Level										
2nd Level										

UNIT RATING	Good	Avg.	Fair	Poor
Condition of Improvements	☐	☐	☐	☐
Room Sizes and Layout	☐	☐	☐	☐
Adequacy of Closets and Storage	☐	☐	☐	☐
Kit. Equip., Cabinets & Workspace	☐	☐	☐	☐
Plumbing—Adequacy and Condition	☐	☐	☐	☐
Electrical—Adequacy and Condition	☐	☐	☐	☐
Adequacy of Soundproofing	☐	☐	☐	☐
Adequacy of Insulation	☐	☐	☐	☐
Location within Project or View	☐	☐	☐	☐
Overall Livability	☐	☐	☐	☐
Appeal and Marketability	☐	☐	☐	☐
Est. Effective Age	______ to ______ yrs.			
Est. Remaining Economic Life	______ to ______ yrs.			

Floors ☐ Hardwood ☐ Carpet over ______ ☐ ______
Int. Walls ☐ Drywall ☐ Plaster ☐ ______
Trim/Finish ☐ Good ☐ Average ☐ Fair ☐ Poor
Bath Floor ☐ Ceramic ☐ ______ Wainscot: ☐ Ceramic ☐ ______
Windows (type): ______ ☐ Storm Sash ☐ Screens ☐ Combo
Kitchen Equip: ☐ Refrig. ☐ Range/Oven ☐ Fan/Hood ☐ Washer ☐ Dryer
☐ Intercom ☐ Disposal ☐ Dishwasher ☐ Microwave ☐ Compactor
HEAT: Type ______ Fuel ______ Cond. ______
AIR COND: ☐ Central ☐ Other ______ ☐ Adequate ☐ Inadequate
☐ Earth Sheltered Housing Design ☐ Solar Design/Landscape ☐ Solar Space Heat/Air Cond. ☐ Solar Hot Water
☐ Flue Damper ☐ Elec./Mech. Gas Furn. Ignition ☐ Auto. Setback Thermostat ☐ Dble./Triple Glazed Windows ☐ Caulk/Weatherstrip
INSULATION (state R-Factor if known) ☐ Walls ______ ☐ Ceiling ______ ☐ Floor ______ ☐ Roof/Attic ______ ☐ Water Heater
If rehab proposed, do plans and specs provide for adequate energy conservation? ______ If no, attach description of modification needed.
ENERGY EFFICIENCY APPEARS: ☐ High ☐ Adequate ☐ Low Energy Audit ☐ Yes (attach, if available) ☐ No
COMMENTS (special features, functional or physical inadequacies, modernization or repairs needed, etc.) ______

FHLMC Form 465 9/80 ATTACH DESCRIPTIVE PHOTOGRAPHS OF SUBJECT PROPERTY AND STREET SCENE FNMA Form 1073 9/80

Figure 11-8. FNMA/FHLMC Condominium or PUD Unit Appraisal Report, page 2

BUDGET ANALYSIS

Unit Charge $ ________ /Mo. x 12 = $ ________ /yr. ($ ________ /Sq. Ft./year of livable area). Ground Rent (if any) $ ________ /yr.

Utilities included in unit charge: ☐ None ☐ Heat ☐ Air Cond. ☐ Electricity ☐ Gas ☐ Water ☐ Sewer

Note any fees, other than regular Condo/PUD charges, for use of facilities ________

To properly maintain the project and provide the services anticipated, the budget appears: ☐ High ☐ Adequate ☐ Inadequate

Compared to other competitive projects of similar quality and design subject unit charge appears: ☐ High ☐ Reasonable ☐ Low

Management Group: ☐ Owners Association ☐ Developer ☐ Management Agent (identify) ________

Quality of Management and its enforcement of Rules and Regulations appears: ☐ Superior ☐ Good ☐ Adequate ☐ Inadequate

Special or unusual characteristics in the Condo/PUD Documents or otherwise known to the appraiser, that would affect marketability (if none, so state)

Comments

COST APPROACH

NOTE: FHLMC does not require the cost approach in the appraisal of condominium or PUD units.

Cost Approach (to be used only for detached, semi-detached, and town house units):

Reproduction Cost New ________ Sq. Ft. @ $ ________ per Sq. Ft. = ... $ ________

Less Depreciation: Physical $ ________ Functional $ ________ Economic $ ________ . . . . . (________)

Depreciated Value of Improvements: . . . . ________

Add Land Value (if leasehold, show only leasehold value—attach calculations) . . . . . ________

Pro-rata Share of Value of Amenities . . . . $ ________

Total Indicated Value: ☐ FEE SIMPLE ☐ LEASEHOLD . . . . $ ________

Comments regarding estimate of depreciation and value of land and amenity package ________

MARKET DATA ANALYSIS

The appraiser, whenever possible, should analyze two comparable sales from within the subject project. However, when appraising a unit in a new or newly converted project, at least two comparables shou.d be selected from outside the subject project. In the following analysis, the comparable should always be adjusted to the subject unit and not vice versa. If a significant feature of the comparable is superior to the subject unit, a minus (–) adjustment should be made to the comparable; if such a feature of the comparable is inferior to the subject, a plus (+) adjustment should be made to the comparable.

LIST ONLY THOSE ITEMS THAT REQUIRE ADJUSTMENT

ITEM	Subject Property	COMPARABLE NO. 1		COMPARABLE NO. 2		COMPARABLE NO. 3	
Address-Unit No. Project Name							
Proximity to Subj.							
Sales Price	$		$		$		$
Price/Living Area	$ ⌀		$ ⌀		$ ⌀		$ ⌀
Data Source							
Date of Sale and Time Adjustment	DESCRIPTION	DESCRIPTION	+(–)$ Adjustment	DESCRIPTION	+(–)$ Adjustment	DESCRIPTION	+(–)$ Adjustment
Location							
Site/View							
Design and Appeal							
Quality of Constr.							
Age							
Condition							
Living Area, Room Count and Total	Total | B-rms | Baths	Total | B-rms | Baths		Total | B-rms | Baths		Total | B-rms | Baths	
Gross Living Area	Sq. ft.	Sq. ft.		Sq. ft.		Sq. ft.	
Basement & Bsmt. Finished Rooms							
Functional Utility							
Air Conditioning							
Storage							
Parking Facilities							
Common Elements and Recreation Facilities							
Mo. Assessment							
Leasehold/Fee							
Special Energy Efficient Items							
Other (e.g. fireplaces, kitchen equip., remodeling)							
Sales or Financing Concessions							
Net Adj. (total)		☐Plus ☐Minus	$	☐Plus ☐Minus	$	☐Plus ☐Minus	$
Indicated Value of Subject			$		$		$

Comments on Market Data Analysis ________

INDICATED VALUE BY MARKET DATA APPROACH . . . . $ ________

INDICATED VALUE BY INCOME APPROACH (If applicable) Economic Market Rent $ ________ /Mo. x Gross Rent Multiplier ________ = $ ________

This appraisal is made ☐ "as is". ☐ subject to the repairs, alterations, or conditions listed below. ☐ subject to completion per plans and specifications.

Comments and Conditions of Appraisal ________

Final Reconciliation ________

Construction Warranty ☐ Yes ☐ No Name of Warranty Program ________ Warranty Coverage Expires ________

This appraisal is based upon the above requirements, the certification, contingent and limiting conditions, and Market Value definition that are stated in

☐ FHLMC Form 439 (Rev. 10/78)/FNMA Form 1004B (Rev. 10/78) filed with client ________, 19 ___. ☐ attached

I ESTIMATE THE MARKET VALUE, AS DEFINED, OF SUBJECT PROPERTY AS OF ________, 19 ___ to be $ ________

Appraiser(s) ________ Review Appraiser (if applicable) ________

☐ Did ☐ Did Not Physically Inspect Property

Date Report Signed ________, 19 ___

FHLMC Form 465 9/80 REVERSE FNMA Form 1073 9/80

Since the most widely used of the three forms is the Residential Appraisal Report or Form 1004/Form 70, this form will be covered in detail.

Residential Appraisal Report, FNMA Form 1004/FHLMC Form 70[2]

This form is required on all properties that will serve as security for loans that will be sold to the Federal National Mortgage Association and the Federal Home Loan Mortgage Corporation, and it must be completed according to the guidelines set forth by each. This report is brief and requires the appraiser to be concise in filling it out.

The first page of the report (Figure 11-3) is descriptive in nature, starting with the section that identifies the property and sales information. You will note that in the left margin it explains who is to fill out this section. The lender, then, is asked to supply the name of the borrower and the address of the property, as well as the legal description. The lender is to supply the name of the present owner and the terms of the sale.

The second section of the report is entitled "Neighborhood," and the appraiser is asked to furnish information about the neighborhood, beginning with the location of the property as rural, urban, or suburban. Second, the appraiser is asked to establish the growth rate of the area and the amount of the area that is built up. The appraiser is asked to give information concerning the present land use and to indicate if there will be any change in the present use, along with giving the price range of the homes in the area and the age of the structures in the neighborhood. In the final part of this section, the appraiser must rate, by the use of the grid, twelve factors that may affect the value of the property now or in the future. If the appraiser rates any of the items as either fair or poor, this opinion must be supported by facts in the comment section. For example, the appraiser could rate the convenience to shopping as fair, adding the following explanation: The convenience to shopping is adversely affected by the construction of a major thoroughfare causing the residents to have to travel an additional one mile to reach shopping. The construction will take at least eighteen months to complete.

In the third section of the report, the appraiser is asked to analyze the site of the property with regard to certain aspects that may affect the property value. The items to be reviewed include the following: zoning, if any; if no zoning, how the property standards will be maintained; utilities; off-site improvements; and the highest and best use.

The final section of the first page deals with the improvements to the property. The first part of the section asks that the appraiser review the improvements that are existing, proposed, or under construction and the type of improvements (single-family, duplex, etc.). The appraiser is also asked to describe the roofing material, type of foundation, insulation, and windows used in the house. The appraiser is asked to specify whether the improvement has a basement and if so to give a description. Next, the appraiser will give a room count and square footage of the improvement or house. The information furnished about the interior includes the finish and equipment to be included in the improvement. And finally, the appraiser is asked to rate the property as compared to other similar properties, and once again any rating of fair or poor must be explained. Some lenders view "Appeal and Marketability" as one of the key ratings in this section.

The second page of this report is the Valuation Section, Figure 11-4, where the appraiser will use the three approaches to value to establish the market value of the property. In the first half of this section, the appraiser gives the dimensions of the rooms and calculates the gross living area in the house. In the second or right half of this section, the appraiser is asked to estimate the reproduction costs of the improvements. The appraiser will figure the cost of the dwelling by multiplying the square feet of the dwelling by the cost per square foot to build a comparable dwelling. Then, the value of such items as porches, patios, garages/carports, and driveways is added to the value. If there is any depreciation to be deducted from the total reproduction cost, it is included and itemized and explained on the left side in the comment section. Finally, the value of the land is calculated and added to the depreciated value of the improvements to establish the value by the cost method.

The Market Data Analysis section is provided for the appraiser to compare the subject property to similar properties that have been sold and closed in the general area. You will note that there is space provided for only three of the most comparable sales, but the appraiser may provide as many comparables believed necessary to establish the value of the subject property. The adjustment column should be noted. As mentioned earlier in the chapter, this is where the appraiser will make a dollar adjustment to the comparable to make it more comparable to the subject property. For example, if the comparable was sold three months prior to the appraisal and houses have been appreciating at the rate of $250 per month, he would adjust the sales price of the comparable up by $750. This would be shown as a plus in the adjustment column in the row entitled Date of Sale and Time Adjustment.

If there are any major adjustments or the appraiser has any comments about the Market Data Analysis, they will appear in the comment section. Next, the appraiser will establish the value of the property as calculated by the Market Data Analysis and will show this at the bottom of the section.

The next section of the report is Indicated Value by the Income Approach. This section is used only if the property is to be used as rental property or if any part of the property will be rented to generate income. As we learned earlier in this chapter, to calculate the value by this method, two estimates must be made. One is the monthly rent and the second is the Gross Rent Multiplier (GRM). Once these items have been established, the value can be calculated by multiplying the rent by the GRM.

Following this, the report requires the appraiser to state if the appraisal for existing property is being made "requiring repairs" or in an "as is" condition. If repairs are required, the appraiser will list those to be made. If the property is proposed or under construction, the appraiser will check the block stating the appraisal is being made subject to the completion of the property as per the submitted plans and specifications.

The next part is Final Reconciliation. Here, the appraiser states why more emphasis was given either to the cost approach or the market data approach. In the final statements of the report, the appraiser gives information regarding any warranties on the home, and then the market value of the property is stated as of a certain date. The appraisal is then signed by the appraiser. If there is a requirement for the appraisal to be reviewed, the reviewer will sign the appraisal and will state if the property was physically inspected by the reviewer.

This completes our overview of the standard FNMA/FHLMC appraisal reports. For further study of the three forms, there are sample completed appraisal forms in Appendix L.

Federal Housing Administration and Veterans Administration

Congress, seeing the need for the reduction of forms used by the various federal agencies, mandated that all of the departments and agencies work together to development common forms. One such effort for common forms was between the Department of Housing and Urban Development and the Veterans Administration. The first form developed was a common application for property appraisal and commitment.

This common form was placed in service on July 1, 1981, and according to the VA and FHA instructions, all prior forms were then to be destroyed. The new form is similar to the previous forms used by the VA and FHA, in that the form has an instruction sheet and a list of required exhibits that must be submitted with the application for property appraisal. The instruction sheet, for the most part, applies to both of the agencies; but the exhibits required are not the same. The instruction sheet, therefore, lists the required exhibits for FHA and VA separately.

There is one major difference with the new combined form: when the form is used as a Request for Determination of Reasonable Value (that is, a request for a VA appraisal), it will no longer show the number of square feet of improved living area. FHA-HUD, however, still has the requirement of showing this figure. According to HUD's Mortgagee Letter 81-21, June 2, 1981, any application submitted to FHA-HUD must have this information or the request will be rejected.

As with the previous forms used by FHA-HUD and VA, this is a multipage form and we shall review only those pages that may be of importance to you as a real estate professional or to your client. This review is being done to show the information that will be required to complete this form and to show where you may be able to help provide the necessary data.

The first page of the form is the Application for Property Appraisal and Commitment. This page is illustrated in Figure 11-9. Let us start at the top of the first page and work our way through the more important sections. In the same area as the title of the form, there is one important block if the form is to be used as a HUD application and that block is entitled, "HUD Section of Act." Here the type of mortgage insurance being applied for must be indicated. For example, if the mortgage is to be insured under Section 203(b), this would be placed in the block. Sections 2, 3, and 4 will apply to both FHA and VA. Section 2, Property Address, and section 3, Legal Description, are self-explanatory; but section 4 may require your assisting the lender or originator. According to FHA/VA, title limitations and restrictive covenants may be, but are not limited to, easements, special assessments, mandatory homeowner associations, and so forth. Normally, the originator or lender will have this information, but it may be a good idea at the time of listing a piece of property to secure a copy of a title policy issued on the property, or any other document that may list any limitations to the title, and supply this information to the lender where your client is making application.

The next sections that may require you or your client to provide information are sections 6 through 8. In section 6, the size of the lot must be supplied. It would be advisable to indicate if it is a subdivision lot because some FHA offices will request this information. Section 7 deals with the utilities to the property. If the property is located inside the corporate limits of a city, town, or village, the utilities will normally be public. Only if the property is located outside an incorporated area will additional information possibly be requested. Section 8 is very important. Here the equipment included in the house must be listed, for it will have an affect on the appraised value of the property. Normally, the VA will not include any equipment that is not indicated on the application.

Sections 9-15 deal with improvements to the real property. Sections 9-11 are self-explanatory. Section 12 is one that may be overlooked. For example, section 10 may indicate a detached type of building, but, as with section 9, there is no question whether the structure is a single-family or multifamily unit. Therefore, section 12 is the section that will indicate whether the building is a duplex, triplex, or fourplex.

The following sections starting with section 16 are very important to the real estate professional. If any sections are not completed or are completed with incorrect information, there is a strong possibility that the property will not be appraised. Normally, if the appraiser assigned by HUD or VA cannot readily make contact with the owner or his or her agent to gain access to the property, they will return the application to the person or organization originating the application. Therefore, make sure that the appraiser's access to the property is made as easy as possible. You may want to contact the originator of the application and get the name of the appraiser and arrange to meet him or her at the property in order to answer any questions or to gather any information that may be needed. Some real estate professionals, when meeting the FHA or VA appraiser, will also bring information on recently closed FHA or VA sales in the immediate area of the property. Immediate area is defined by some of the FHA or VA offices as an area of one square mile surrounding the property.

Section 29 will be filled out only if the property is new or proposed construction. Sections 30-37 are self-explanatory. The next large areas are the certifications to be completed and signed by the necessary party or parties.

After this page is completed, the lender will keep the last copy of the form for the files and the following action will be taken:

1. If the application is for FHA mortgage insurance, the lender will call the nearest FHA office and will be given a case number and the name of an appraiser who will make the appraisal. The lender will then forward the seven remaining copies of the form to the appraiser. The appraiser will make the appraisal and return the completed form to FHA within four working days.

2. If the application is for a Certificate of Reasonable Value, the lender will forward the remaining seven pages to the nearest VA Loan Guaranty office, which will assign an appraiser. The assigned appraiser will make the appraisal and return the completed application to the VA.

Figure 11-9. VA Request for Determination of Reasonable Value/HUD Application for Property Appraisal and Commitment

Form Approved
OMB No. 2900-0045

VA REQUEST FOR DETERMINATION OF REASONABLE VALUE (Real Estate)
HUD APPLICATION FOR PROPERTY APPRAISAL AND COMMITMENT

HUD Section of Act | 1. CASE NUMBER

2. PROPERTY ADDRESS *(Include ZIP Code and county)*
3. LEGAL DESCRIPTION
4. TITLE LIMITATIONS AND RESTRICTIVE COVENANTS
1. ☐ CONDOMINIUM 2. ☐ PLANNED UNIT DEVELOPMENT

5. NAME AND ADDRESS OF FIRM OR PERSON MAKING REQUEST/APPLICATION *(Include ZIP Code)*
6. LOT DIMENSIONS:
1. ☐ IRREGULAR: SQ/FT 2. ☐ ACRES:

7. UTILITIES (✓)	ELEC.	GAS	WATER	SAN. SEWER
1. PUBLIC				
2. COMMUNITY				
3. INDIVIDUAL				

8. EQUIP. 1. ☐ RANGE/OVEN 2. ☐ REFRIG. 3. ☐ DISHWASHER 4. ☐ CLOTHES WASHER 5. ☐ DRYER 6. ☐ GARBAGE DISP. 7. ☐ VENT FAN 8. ☐ W/W CARPET 9. ☐

9. BUILDING STATUS: 1. ☐ PROPOSED 2. ☐ SUBSTANTIAL REHABILITATION 3. ☐ UNDER CONSTR. 4. ☐ EXISTING
10. BUILDING TYPE: 1. ☐ DETACHED 2. ☐ SEMI-DETACHED 3. ☐ ROW 4. ☐ APT. UNIT
11. FACTORY FABRICATED? 1. ☐ YES 2. ☐ NO
12. NUMBER OF UNITS
13A. STREET ACCESS: 1. ☐ PRIVATE 2. ☐ PUBLIC
13B. STREET MAINT.: 1. ☐ PRIVATE 2. ☐ PUBLIC

14A. CONSTRUCTION WARRANTY INCLUDED? 1. ☐ YES 2. ☐ NO *(If "Yes," complete Items 14B and C also.)*
14B. NAME OF WARRANTY PROGRAM
14C. EXPIRATION DATE *(Month, day, year)*
15. CONSTR. COMPLETED *(Mo., yr.)*

16. NAME OF OWNER
17. PROPERTY: ☐ OCCUPIED BY OWNER ☐ NEVER OCCUPIED ☐ VACANT ☐ OCCUPIED BY TENANT *(Complete Item 18 also)*
18. RENT *(If applic.)* $ /MONTH

19. NAME OF OCCUPANT
20. TELEPHONE NO.
21. NAME OF BROKER
22. TELEPHONE NO.
23. DATE AND TIME AVAILABLE FOR INSPECTION ☐ AM ☐ PM

24. KEYS AT *(Address)*
25. ORIGINATOR'S IDENT. NO.
26. SPONSOR'S IDENT. NO.
27. INSTITUTION'S CASE NO.

28. PURCHASER'S NAME AND ADDRESS *(Complete mailing address. Include ZIP code.)*

EQUAL OPPORTUNITY IN HOUSING

NOTE – Federal laws and regulations prohibit discrimination because of race, color, religion, sex, or national origin in the sale or rental of residential property. Numerous State statutes and local ordinances also prohibit such discrimination. In addition, section 805 of the Civil Rights Act of 1968 prohibits discriminatory practices in connection with the financing of housing.

If HUD/VA finds there is noncompliance with any antidiscrimination laws or regulations, it may discontinue business with the violator.

29. NEW OR PROPOSED CONSTRUCTION – *Complete Items 29A through 29G for new or proposed construction cases only.*

A. COMPLIANCE INSPECTIONS WILL BE OR WERE MADE BY: ☐ FHA ☐ VA ☐ NONE MADE
B. PLANS *(check one)* ☐ FIRST SUBMISSION ☐ REPEAT CASE *(If checked complete Item 29C.)*
C. PLANS SUBMITTED PREVIOUSLY UNDER CASE NO.:
D. NAME AND ADDRESS OF BUILDER
E. TELEPHONE NO.
F. NAME AND ADDRESS OF WARRANTOR
G. TELEPHONE NO.

30. COMMENTS ON SPECIAL ASSESSMENTS OR HOMEOWNERS ASSOCIATION CHARGES
31. ANNUAL REAL ESTATE TAXES $
32. MINERAL RIGHTS RESERVED? ☐ YES *(Explain)* ☐ NO
33. LEASEHOLD CASES *(Complete if applicable)*
LEASE IS: ☐ 99 YEARS ☐ RENEWABLE ☐ HUD/VA APPROVED
EXPIRES *(Date)*
ANNUAL GROUND RENT $

34. SALE PRICE OF PROPERTY $
35. REFINANCING – AMOUNT OF PROPOSED LOAN $
36. PROPOSED SALE CONTRACT ATTACHED ☐ YES ☐ NO
37. CONTRACT NUMBER PREVIOUSLY APPROVED BY VA THAT WILL BE USED

CERTIFICATIONS FOR SUBMISSIONS TO HUD

In submitting this application for a conditional commitment for mortgage insurance, it is agreed and understood by the parties involved in the transaction, that if, at the time of application for a Firm Commitment, the identity of the seller has changed, the application for a Firm Commitment will be rejected and the application for a Conditional Commitment will be reprocessed upon request by the mortgagee.

It is further agreed and understood that in submitting the request for a Firm Commitment for mortgage insurance, the seller, the purchaser and the broker involved in the transaction shall each certify that the terms of the contract for purchase are true to his or her best knowledge and belief, and that any other agreement entered into by any of these parties in connection with this transaction is attached to the sales agreement.

BUILDER/SELLER'S AGREEMENT: **All Houses:** The undersigned agrees to deliver to the purchaser HUD's statement of appraised value. **Proposed Construction:** The undersigned agrees, upon sale or conveyance of title within one year from date of initial occupancy, to deliver to the purchaser Form HUD-92544, warranting that the house is constructed in substantial conformity with the plans and specifications on which HUD based its value and to furnish HUD a conformed copy with the purchaser's receipt thereon that the original warranty was delivered to him/her. **All Houses:** In consideration of the issuance of the commitment requested by this application, I (we) hereby agree that any deposit or down payment made in connection with the purchase of the property described above, whether received by the undersigned, or an agent of the undersigned, shall upon receipt be deposited in escrow or in trust or in a special account which is not subject to the claims of my creditors and where it will be maintained until it has been disbursed for the benefit of the purchaser or otherwise disposed of in accordance with the terms of the contract of sale.

Signature of: ☐ Mortgagee ☐ Builder ☐ Seller ☐ Other X________ Date ________ 19__

MORTGAGEE'S CERTIFICATE: The undersigned mortgagee certifies that to the best of his/her knowledge, all statements made in this application and the supporting documents are true, correct and complete.

Signature and Title of Mortgage Officer: X________ Date ________ 19__

CERTIFICATIONS FOR SUBMISSIONS TO VA

1. On receipt of "Certificate of Reasonable Value" or advice from the Veterans Administration that a "Certificate of Reasonable Value" will not be issued, we agree to forward to the appraiser the approved fee which we are holding for this purpose.
2. CERTIFICATION REQUIRED ON CONSTRUCTION UNDER FHA SUPERVISION *(Strike out inappropriate phrases in parentheses)*

I hereby certify that plans and specifications and related exhibits, including acceptable FHA Change Orders, if any, supplied to VA in this case, are identical to those (submitted to) (to be submitted to) (approved by) FHA, and that FHA inspections (have been) (will be) made pursuant to FHA approval for mortgage insurance on the basis of proposed construction under Sec.

38. SIGNATURE OF PERSON AUTHORIZING THIS REQUEST
39. TITLE
40. DATE
41. DATE OF ASSIGNMENT
42. NAME OF APPRAISER

WARNING Section 1010 of Title 18, U.S.C. provides: "Whoever for the purpose of . . . influencing such Administration . . . makes, passes, utters or publishes any statement knowing the same to be false . . . shall be fined not more than $5,000 or imprisoned not more than two years or both."

VA FORM 26-1805, AUG 1980
HUD FORM 92800-1
SUPERSEDES VA FORM 26-1805, AUG 1977, AND HUD 92800, JUL 1979, WHICH WILL NOT BE USED.
VA/HUD FILE COPY 1

The next step in the process for either the FHA or VA occurs after the completed appraisal is received. It is reviewed and then the value of the property is approved. Once the appraisal and value is approved, HUD will issue a Conditional Commitment or VA will issue a Certificate of Reasonable Value. This is done by returning copies 2 (Requester's Copy) and 4 (Purchaser's Copy) to the originator or as indicated on the form (see Name and Address of Firm or Person Making Request/Application). Copy 3 will be missing because it is kept by HUD or VA. Copy 4 is shown in Figure 11-10. Pages 2 and 3 are identical.

Normally, the lenders or originators of the application or request will call the applicant to notify him or her of the results and to confirm that the Commitment or Certificate has been received. If possible, you should get a copy of the commitment or certificate and place it in the property file. This will allow you to build your own file of property values in your area.

Now let us review the major sections of the commitment or certificate of reasonable value. The top of the form will indicate whether it is a CRV or a Conditional Commitment. This was done when the first page was completed along with sections 1-13B. The information contained in sections 14-18 of the form are of the utmost importance to the parties to the transaction.

HUD Conditional Commitment Let us review how these sections may be completed if the application is for FHA mortgage insurance. Section 14 will indicate the estimated value of the property, which should equal the sales price of the property. It should be noted that this is only the estimated value of the property and not the maximum loan amount that FHA will insure. The maximum loan amount will be established later. Section 15 will state the estimated remaining economic life of the property. Section 16 will give the expiration date of the conditional commitment. Section 17 is the most important section of the commitment for it will establish the following:

1. Maximum mortgage amount

2. Term of the mortgage

3. If the value is an ''as is'' value

4. Monthly expense estimates will be used by FHA to establish the monthly housing costs for borrower approval

5. Estimated closing costs, which will be used to establish the maximum loan amount (estimated closing costs are usually added to the estimated value of the property to establish the maximum loan amount).

It should be noted that if the sales price of the property exceeds the FHA-estimated value of the property, the purchaser has the right either to proceed with the purchase of the property or to cancel the contract. If the purchaser wishes to proceed with the sale, the purchaser will have to put down additional money.

An authorized agent of HUD will sign the commitment in block 19, indicate the date the commitment was issued in block 20, and, finally, the HUD office issuing the commitment will be shown in block 21.

Accompanying this conditional commitment will be one or more documents outlining the general commitment conditions. These conditions may be an explanation of the maximum mortgage amount and terms, the requirements for issuing a firm commitment, and the statement that all construction, repairs, or alterations proposed shall equal or exceed the FHA minimum property standards.

Either contained in the document mentioned above or in a separate document, FHA-HUD will indicate specific commitment conditions that must be met. These may include required termite control or the execution of a form from a health authority indicating an approval of the water supply and/or that a sewage disposal installation is required.

In addition, these conditions may include required repairs that must be made prior to the funding of the mortgage. These repairs may range from the installation of broken panes of glass to a complete roof.

It must be stressed that all of these specific requirements must be met before HUD-FHA will issue any mortgage insurance on the property in question.

VA Certificate of Reasonable Value Now let us review what sections of pages 2, 3, and 4 will be completed if the application is for a VA Certificate of Reasonable Value. Sections 1-13B will have been completed at the time of

Figure 11-10. VA Request for Determination of Reasonable Value/HUD Application for Property Appraisal and Commitment, Purchaser's Copy (page 4)

☐ VA CERTIFICATE OF REASONABLE VALUE
☐ HUD CONDITIONAL COMMITMENT

HUD Section of Act | 1. CASE NUMBER

2. PROPERTY ADDRESS *(Include ZIP Code and county)*

3. LEGAL DESCRIPTION

4. TITLE LIMITATIONS AND RESTRICTIVE COVENANTS

1. ☐ CONDOMINIUM 2. ☐ PLANNED UNIT DEVELOPMENT

5. NAME AND ADDRESS OF FIRM OR PERSON MAKING REQUEST/APPLICATION *(Include ZIP Code)*

6. LOT DIMENSIONS:

1. ☐ IRREGULAR: SQ/FT 2. ☐ ACRES:

7. UTILITIES (√)	ELEC.	GAS	WATER	SAN. SEWER
1. PUBLIC				
2. COMMUNITY				
3. INDIVIDUAL				

8. EQUIP.
1. ☐ RANGE/OVEN 4. ☐ CLOTHES WASHER 7. ☐ VENT FAN
2. ☐ REFRIG. 5. ☐ DRYER 8. ☐ W/W CARPET
3. ☐ DISH-WASHER 6. ☐ GARBAGE DISP. 9. ☐

9. BUILDING STATUS
1. ☐ PROPOSED 3. ☐ UNDER CONSTR.
2. ☐ SUBSTANTIAL REHABILITATION 4. ☐ EXISTING

10. BUILDING TYPE
1. ☐ DETACHED 3. ☐ ROW
2. ☐ SEMI-DETACHED 4. ☐ APT. UNIT

11. FACTORY FABRICATED?
1. ☐ YES 2. ☐ NO

12. NUMBER OF UNITS

13A. STREET ACCESS
1. ☐ PRIVATE
2. ☐ PUBLIC

13B. STREET MAINT.
1. ☐ PRIVATE
2. ☐ PUBLIC

14. ESTIMATED REASONABLE VALUE OF PROPERTY
$

15. REMAINING ECONOMIC LIFE OF PROPERTY IS ESTIMATED TO BE NOT LESS THAN:
YEARS

16. EXPIRATION DATE

18.
☐ This Certificate of Reasonable Value is valid only if VA Form 26-1843p showing VA General Conditions and the applicable Specific Conditions is attached.

19. ADMINISTRATOR OF VETERANS AFFAIRS, BY *(Signature of authorized agent)*, OR HUD AUTHORIZED AGENT

20. DATE ISSUED

21. VA OR HUD OFFICE

22. PURCHASER'S NAME AND ADDRESS *(Complete mailing address. Include ZIP Code.)*

17. HUD COMMITMENT TERMS	
A. MAXIMUM MORTGAGE AMOUNT	$
B. NO. OF MONTHS	
C. NOTICE OF REJECTION	
D. "AS IS" VALUE	$
E. MONTHLY EXPENSE ESTIMATE	
FIRE INSURANCE	$
TAXES	$
CONDO. COMMUNITY EXPENSE	$
MAINTENANCE AND REPAIRS	$
HEAT AND UTILITIES	$
F. ESTIMATED CLOSING COST	$
G. ☐ EXISTING ☐ PROPOSED	*(See General Condition 3 on attachment.)*
H. IMPROVED LIVING AREA	SQ/FT

I. ☐ This Conditional Commitment is valid only if HUD Form 92800-5a showing HUD General Conditions and the applicable Specific Conditions is attached.

VA FORM 26-1843, AUG 1980 HUD FORM 92800-5

PURCHASER'S COPY 4

the initial application. Once the VA has reviewed the appraisal, the VA will fill out sections 14-16 and 18-21. Section 14 is the most important because it will give the VA's Estimate of Reasonable Value. This reasonable value is also the maximum loan amount for VA. FHA, to get the maximum loan amount, will normally combine the amount in section 14 and the estimated closing cost listed in section 17 I. Sections 15 and 16 are self-explanatory. As noted above, section 17 is not completed. Section 18 is then checked, an official of VA signs in section 19, and places a date in section 20.

If the sales price of the home is more than the amount listed in section 14, the veteran has two options: (1) to cancel the contract and all of the monies paid by the veteran will be returned or (2) to continue with the sale and make a down payment in the amount of the difference.

Home Energy Checklist In addition to the normal appraisal procedures, both VA and HUD now require that any existing home to be appraised must be appraised with regard to deficiencies in thermal protection. In other words, the appraiser will review the property noting any improvements that may be made to increase the energy efficiency of the home and save the prospective homebuyer in heating and cooling expenses.

The agencies have developed a form for this review, The Home Energy Checklist. This form must now accompany all HUD Conditional Commitments and VA Certificates of Reasonable Value. The form is a multipage form and once again we will review only those pages that you or your client will normally see. The first page of the form (Figure 11-11) asks the appraiser to check for potential areas of energy savings. You will notice that these areas range from the simple installation of insulation wrap around the hot water heater to installation of storm windows and storm doors. The appraiser can make any additional suggestions that he or she feels will help the energy efficiency of the home. This form, along with the completed request for Conditional Commitment or Request for a Certificate of Reasonable Value, is returned to the HUD or VA office. Then, HUD or VA will return three pages to the lender. Page 3 of the form is for the lender and page 5 is to be returned, if the request is for a CRV, to the veteran making the request or, if the request is for a HUD commitment, to the person making application. The third copy would go to the other party to the transaction. Page 5 of the form is illustrated in Figure 11-12.

There is a note at the top of this page stating that the amount shown on the Conditional Commitment or CRV in section 14 may be increased if funds were expended for weatherization or energy conservation improvements to the property. When a request for an increase in the valuation is due to the expenditure of funds for energy conservation or weatherization, the increase will be made by one of the following methods:

1. $2,000 or less without a separate value determination.

2. From $2,001 to $3,500 if supported by a value determination made by a HUD-FHA review appraiser or staff appraiser. The value determination is normally made by desk review in house; however, some value determinations may require a field inspection of the property. The review appraiser shall make this inspection.

3. $3,501 or more subject to an inspection made by a HUD-FHA-approved fee appraiser/inspector. The lender will mail all proposals submitted by the homeowner concerning the addition of thermal protection improvements to the Field Office for review. The appraiser/inspector must review the expense involved in adding the thermal improvements and determine what effect the improvements will have on value. This will be done by an on-site inspection. The fee appraiser/inspector will bill the lender for this service but the fee charged cannot exceed those charged for inspections in the geographical area. The lender is responsible for paying the fee appraiser/inspector for this service.[3]

It should be noted that HUD now requires the purchaser to indicate on the application for mortgage insurance that he or she has been given a copy of the Home Energy Checklist and understands the contents of the form.

Request for Reconsideration of Appraisals—HUD If, as a real estate professional, you are working with a seller and have either made an applicaton for, or have had a buyer make an application for, a Conditional Commitment

Figure 11-11. VA Home Energy Checklist, page 1

Form Approved
OMB No. 76-R0743

Veterans Administration

HOME ENERGY CHECKLIST
(Attachment to
VA Form 26-1803, HUD Form 92800-5 and FmHA Form 1922-8)

CASE NUMBER

NOTE TO APPRAISER: The specific areas of the property listed below are those that have been identified as potential sites where home energy can be lost. Examine those areas listed and check each that, if corrected or improved, could result in energy and monetary savings for the homeowner.
IMPORTANT – Press hard. You are making five copies.

AREA(S) FOR POTENTIAL ENERGY SAVINGS *(Check each applicable box)*

☐ 1. THERMOSTATS – Consideration should be given to clock thermostats.

☐ 2. WATER HEATERS – Consideration should be given to an insulation wrap.

☐ 3. HEATING/COOLING SYSTEM – Insulate ducts and pipes in unheated spaces.

☐ 4. ATTIC – Attic and attic door should be insulated to the recommended level.

☐ 5. FLOORS AND FOUNDATION WALLS – Adequate insulation is needed:

☐ A. UNDER FLOORS
☐ B. AROUND BASEMENT
☐ C. CRAWL SPACE
☐ D. FOUNDATION WALLS

☐ 6. WINDOWS AND DOORS – Consideration should be given to installation of:

☐ A. WEATHER-STRIPPING/CAULKING TO PREVENT AIR ESCAPES FROM OPENINGS *(Including pipes/ducts)*
☐ B. ____________ STORM WINDOWS
☐ C. ____________ STORM DOORS
☐ D. DOUBLE OR TRIPLE GLAZED PRIME WINDOWS WITH WEATHER-STRIPPING

ADDITIONAL REMARKS PERTAINING TO ENERGY CONSERVATION

SIGNATURE OF APPRAISER

DATE

VA FORM
SEP 1980 **26-1803a**

VA 1

Figure 11-12. VA Home Energy Checklist, page 5

Form Approved
OMB No. 76-R0743

Veterans Administration

HOME ENERGY CHECKLIST

(Attachment to VA Form 26-1843 and HUD Form 92800-5)

CASE NUMBER

NOTE: The amount of value shown in Item 14 of VA Form 26-1843/HUD Form 92800-5 may be increased by up to one of the following if such increase is expended for weatherization and/or energy conservation improvements to the property: (a) $2000, without a separate value determination; (b) $3500, if supported by a value determination by a designated appraiser; or, (c) more than $3500, subject to appraisal by VA or HUD, as applicable, and subsequent endorsement of the VA Certificate of Reasonable Value or HUD Conditional Commitment.

The specific areas of the property listed below are those that have been identified as potential sites where home energy can be lost. Examine those areas listed and check each that, if corrected or improved, could result in energy and monetary savings for the homeowner.

AREA(S) FOR POTENTIAL ENERGY SAVINGS *(Check each applicable box)*

☐ 1. THERMOSTATS – Consideration should be given to clock thermostats.

☐ 2. WATER HEATERS – Consideration should be given to an insulation wrap.

☐ 3. HEATING/COOLING SYSTEM – Insulate ducts and pipes in unheated spaces.

☐ 4. ATTIC INSULATION – See map below for location of the property and recommended minimum insulation.
CAUTION: Do not forget to consider ventilation.

☐ 5. FLOORS AND FOUNDATION WALLS – Adequate insulation is needed:

☐ A. UNDER FLOORS
☐ B. AROUND BASEMENT
☐ C. CRAWL SPACE
☐ D. FOUNDATION WALLS

☐ 6. WINDOWS AND DOORS – Storm windows are recommended in areas D, E and F for all fuels and for electric heat in areas B and C (see map below). Consideration should be given to installation of:

☐ A. WEATHER-STRIPPING/CAULKING TO PREVENT AIR ESCAPES FROM OPENINGS *(Including pipes/ducts)*
☐ B. ____________ STORM WINDOWS
☐ C. ____________ STORM DOORS
☐ D. DOUBLE OR TRIPLE GLAZED PRIME WINDOWS WITH WEATHER-STRIPPING

RECOMMENDED CEILING INSULATION BY ENERGY TYPE AND DEGREE-DAY ZONE

INSULATION CONVERSION TABLE

R VALUE	EQUIVALENTS	
	BATT OR BLANKET	LOOSE-FILL
19	5½ – 6½ inches	6½ – 8¾ inches
22	6½ inches	7 – 9½ inches
30	9 inches	10 – 11 inches
38	12 inches	13 – 17 inches

The minimum amounts of ceiling insulation that the Department of Energy considers desirable for existing homes are listed below.

The amounts range from R-38 to R-19, according to heating degree-days and type of energy – gas, oil, or electricity – used for heating. Electricity is divided into two categories, resistance heat and the heat pump. The DOE minimums, as shown on the map, are:

Zone A ((0-1000 degree-days) (Includes Hawaii and Puerto Rico)) – All energy types, R-19.
Zone B (1001-2500 degree-days) – Gas, oil and electric heat pump, R-19. Electric resistance heat, R-22.
Zone C (2501-3500 degree-days) – Gas, oil and electric heat pump, R-22. Electric resistance heat, R-30.
Zone D (3501-6000 degree-days) – All energy types, R-30.
Zone E (6001-7000 degree-days) – Gas and oil, R-30. All electric heat, R-38.
Zone F ((7001 or more degree-days) (Includes Alaska)) – All energy types, R-38.

Duct and pipe insulation, and water heater insulation are recommended in all climate zones. Floor insulation is recommended for electric resistance heating in all zones with more than 2500 degree-days and for other energy sources and heat pumps in zones above 3500 degree-days; either R-19 or R-11 is recommended.

VA FORM SEP 1980 **26-1843n** **VETERAN 5**

Figure 11-13. Request for Reconsideration of FHA Appraisal to Houston Insuring Office

REQUEST FOR RECONSIDERATION OF FHA APPRAISAL TO HOUSTON INSURING OFFICE

Note: Comparable sales must be dwellings similar in type, size, and quality of construction, and in the same or comparable neighborhood. Also, these comparables should be RECENT SALES (not appraisals). Submit three (3).

	Subject Property	*Comp. #1*	*Comp. #2*	*Comp. #3*
Case Number (If FHA)				
Address				
Key Map Number				
Lot Size (Front Foot or Dimensions if Irregular)				
Year Built				
Sale Price				
Date of Sale				
Terms of Sale				
House Sq. Ft. (Living Area)				
No. of Stories				
Type of Exterior Walls				
Number of Rooms				
Number of Bedrooms				
Family Room/Den				
Number of Baths				
Patio - Barbeque Swim Pool, etc.				
Type of Heat/Air Cond.				
Type of Floor				
Type of Foundation				
Garage/Carport No. of Cars				
(1) Supplementary Equipment				
(2) Personal Property Included in Sale				
REMARKS				

(1) Built-in Range, Oven, Disposal, etc. (2) Carpets, Drapes, Free-Standing Appliances, etc.

The information herein is from our records or was furnished to us, and to the best of my knowledge is accurate.

(Mortgagee Only: ____________________

Title: ____________________

Date: ____________________

(This form may be reproduced)

FTW/HOU Hdbk. 4150.1 #53 Rev. 7/81

from HUD and the Estimated Value in section 14 of page 2 or 4 (Figure 11-10) is below the sales price thus affecting the maximum mortgage amount, there are procedures to request a reconsideration.

Usually, you will work with the lender or originator of the application to complete a "Request for Reconsideration of FHA Appraisal." A sample of such a form used by the FHA Insuring Office in Houston, Texas is shown in Figure 11-13. All of the FHA Insuring Offices will have a similar form, and the basic information for each of the forms will be the same. You will note that the form calls for recent sales. Some of the offices have established any sale within six months of the application for commitment to be a recent sale. As you will notice, these must be sales and not appraisals. Some of the offices even take this one step further and state that these must be closed sales, not pending sales. If you are gathering information on sales for a request, you should submit only closed sales, even though your nearest insuring office does not state that the sales must be closed sales.

After the request form is completed, the lender or originator of the original application will submit the request to the insuring office. The FHA office will review the request for reasonableness prior to the request going to the appraiser who made the original appraisal. It should be noted that there may be a fee charged for such reconsideration. So, prior to the submission of any request, you should check with the lender or originator. If there will be a fee charged, let your client know the amount of the fee and that they may have to pay it.

Request for Reconsideration of Appraisals—VA According to the Veterans Administration's Appraisal Section in Washington, D.C., there is no written policy for requesting reconsideration of appraisal. It should be noted that some of the Loan Guaranty Offices have instituted a specific program. According to the Appraisal Section, any party to a transaction may request the reconsideration including any real estate agent representing either party to the transaction. The request will have to be made in writing and should include comparable sales data to support the request. Since there is no specific form to be used when making the request, you may wish to use a form similar to the one illustrated in Figure 11-13, but prior to making any request for reconsideration, you should contact the lender making the initial request or the VA Loan Guaranty section that is responsible for your area.

NATIONAL ASSOCIATION OF REVIEW APPRAISERS (NARA)

Reference was made early in this chapter to the major professional organizations that *certify* appraisers. Now there is a national organization to aid and train persons who have the responsibility to *review* appraisals. This organization is the National Association of Review Appraisers, headquartered in St. Paul, Minnesota.

The association sponsors seminars throughout the United States to teach the latest and best methods to persons who review appraisals. In addition to sponsoring seminars, the NARA also publishes an *Appraisal Review Journal* that presents articles of interest to the review appraiser, as well as to the real estate industry. If you would like further information, contact the NARA headquarters at the address below:

National Association of Review Appraisers
National Headquarters
Suite 410, Midwest Federal Building
Saint Paul, MN 55101

REVIEW QUESTIONS

1. Define the term *appraisal.*
2. Define the term *market value*.
3. Name and explain the basic formats of appraisals.
4. Name and explain four principles of real property value.
5. Name and explain the major methods used to determine property value.
6. Define and give examples of the term *functional obsolescence*.
7. Define and give an example of a proforma statement.

8. What are the three basic FNMA and/or FHLMC standard appraisal reports?

9. Explain the major difference between the FNMA/FHLMC appraisal reports and the reports of value used by VA and FHA.

10. What is meant by the abbreviation CRV?

NOTES

[1]SREA Market Data Center, Inc., South Texas Regional Center, Sales Data, July-September 1979, p. 5.

[2]Most of this section is based upon material from National Association of Review Appraisers, *Appraisal Review Journal*, Summer 1979, vol. 2, no. 2, pp. 47-55.

[3]U.S., Department of Housing and Urban Development—Federal Housing Administration, Southeast Texas District, Houston, Texas, *HUD Circular Letter No. 81-9*, December 8, 1981, p. 1.

CHAPTER 12 Borrower Qualification

LEARNING OBJECTIVES

In this chapter we will discuss how the real estate professional qualifies a client in order to best serve that client. After qualifying the client, the professional can select the proper price range of homes and give the client some insight as to the amount of loan he or she will be able to make payments on as per the guidelines set forth by FNMA, FHLMC, VA, and FHA. We will also discuss the application forms used by FNMA, FHLMC, VA, and FHA and the information the client will need to complete the application forms.

When you have completed your study of this chapter, you should be able to do the following:

- ★ **Calculate the maximum loan a client may qualify for based on present income and using the income and long-term debt ratios of FNMA, FHLMC, VA, and FHA.**
- ★ **Define the types of income that may be used to qualify a prospective buyer.**
- ★ **Define the term *net effective income.***
- ★ **Explain the difference between the terms *monthly mortgage payment* and *total housing expenses* and explain how each relates to the qualifying of a prospective purchaser.**
- ★ **Outline the basic method of qualification used by FHA, VA, FNMA, and FHLMC.**

WHY QUALIFY YOUR CLIENT?

Many real estate salespersons wait for the lender to qualify the borrower (after the buyer has selected a home to purchase) and hope that their client will qualify for the loan. The real estate professional in his or her first visit with the client can, however, gather information that will aid the professional in qualifying the prospective buyer. This qualification of the buyer is a help not only to the real estate salesperson, but also to the client. The client will have a better idea of the maximum mortgage amount that he or she can support with his or her present income.

Once the maximum mortgage is established and the client has determined the amount of money available for a down payment, the maximum sales price of a home that the prospective buyer can afford can be calculated. To establish the maximum sales price, the maximum loan amount and the amount of down payment are added together. For example, in your meeting with a prospective client, you learn that the maximum conventional loan your client can afford is $55,450 and he or she has $24,000 for the down payment. The maximum sales price is $79,450. You should explain to the client that the maximum loan amount is based on the current guidelines of the lenders in the area, not just your own guidelines, and for the prospective buyer to afford a home with a higher sales price, he or she must either make a larger down payment or be able to establish the existence of additional income that will meet the lenders' guidelines. Once again, you have informed the buyer as to the maximum affordable house price. If the client wishes to purchase a higher priced house, the client must meet the requirements mentioned.

In addition to knowing the maximum house price prior to the actual showing of any property, the prospective homebuyer, then, will be familiar with the methods the lenders will use to establish whether the buyer can qualify for the mortgage. If you take the time—before you begin showing your prospective homebuyer any properties—to determine the maximum mortgage the buyer can qualify for, you can avoid many headaches for both you and your client. Many times the client will tell you the desired price range without really knowing how much home he or she can actually afford. If this is the case and the real estate salesperson takes the prospective buyer at the buyer's word and starts to show homes without first qualifying the client, there may be surprises for both you and your client. For example, you have as clients a young couple who say they want an $80,000 house. You take them at face value and begin to show them homes in this price range. After looking at several, they find one that fits their needs and they make an offer. Let us assume the offer is accepted. Later, back at the office, you suggest several lenders to whom they may make application for the mortgage of $64,000. At application, however, they state that they only make $20,000 a year and have several long-term debts. This causes them not to qualify for the mortgage at time of application. This not only will cause you to lose a sale, but will make the mortgage lender less anxious to work with you again. The clients will lose faith in your ability and turn to another agent. This is not to say that, with your qualification of the client, you will eliminate the possibilty of rejection of your client by a lender, but it will greatly reduce the number of times your clients are rejected.

INITIAL CLIENT QUALIFICATION

Since one of the factors used by a lender to qualify a prospective buyer for a mortgage is income, we will discuss the significance of the prospective buyer's employment pattern and employment stability as well as the types of income that can be used to establish what the lender refers to as the *stable monthly income.*

Stable Monthly Income

The stable monthly income can be defined as "the borrower's gross monthly income from primary employment base earnings, plus recognizable secondary income."[1] Let us examine the factors that can affect the stable monthly income.

Pattern First, you must establish the employment pattern of your prospective buyer. Has the person been a job hopper, jumping from one type of work or profession to another for no apparent reason? Lenders look for a pattern of full employment and job changes that improve the applicant's and co-applicant's careers.

Stability A second factor that is used to establish the ability of the borrower to repay a mortgage is employment stability—not only the stability of employment in the past, but the potential for future employment. When qualifying your client as to the stability of income, you should establish how long the prospective buyer has been employed in his or her present line of work and how long your client has been at his or her present job. Most conventional lenders have established a minimum of two years in the buyer's present line of work, with no minimum time on the present job. It should be noted that the important factor is the time in the present line of work. Americans have become mobile and, because the availability of jobs has decreased in some areas of the country while increasing in others, people change jobs more frequently now than in the past. For example, let us say that a prospective buyer has for the past several years been a lumber salesperson to the construction industry in New York state and due to the slowdown in construction in that area decided to move to Denver to seek better opportunities. In Denver, the prospective buyer was not able to get a job selling lumber to the construction industry, but was able to get a job selling appliances in a retail store. According to most lenders, the prospective buyer has not changed his or her line of work—sales.

In addition to the length of employment, the type of job or profession is important. For example, a person who is highly skilled as a tool and die maker will always be in demand and will have little worry in finding employment. Today, with advances in computer technology and the ever-expanding use of computers in industry, a person trained in computer science also will not have a problem finding employment. Other people thought to have stable employment are government employees, engineers, and other skilled people employed by large corporations such as American Telephone and Telegraph, Texas Instruments, or one of the major oil companies.

One other factor that was once thought to affect the stability of income was the age of the applicant. Today, with the passage of federal antidiscrimination legislation, the age of the applicant cannot be used as a factor to establish the stability of the applicant's income. For example, in the past a person who was forty-five years old would have had a difficult time securing a thirty-year mortgage, because many lenders would not make loans to a person where the term of the loan would extend past age sixty-five, then the retirement standard. Thus, the forty-five-year-old person could only get a twenty-year loan no matter what his profession.

We will discuss the different employment requirements for FHA, VA, FNMA, and FHLMC later in this chapter.

Types of Income

Now that you have learned how to qualify your client as to the pattern and stability of employment, let us examine the types of income that can be used to establish the stable monthly income.

Salaries This type of income is the easiest for you to establish and for the lender to verify. A prospective homebuyer who is employed by a company or corporation is usually paid a specific amount on a regular basis. The pay period can be weekly, biweekly, monthly, or bimonthly. This type of income is thought to be the most stable. If the prospective homebuyer is married and the spouse is employed, the income from the spouse will also count if the spouse has met the employment pattern and stability requirements of the lender. In the past, many lenders would discount, or in many cases eliminate, the salaried income of a woman if she was capable of having children, no matter what her profession or how long she had been employed. This practice was stopped with the passage of the Equal Credit Opportunity Act, and lenders are no longer allowed to discount income due to sex, age, or marital status.

Overtime This type of income is standard to many jobs and can be counted toward the prospective homebuyer's stable monthly income. It must be proved by the homebuyer that the income has been regular in the past and that the chances are good that it will continue in the future. To establish that the overtime income has existed in the past, the prospective buyer may wish to supply copies of his or her paycheck stubs to the lender showing the overtime hours worked in the past year. To establish whether the overtime will continue, the mortgage lender will, when verifying the income of the applicant, ask the employer to state if there is a possibility of the overtime continuing. The verification forms used by FHA, VA, FNMA, and FHLMC will be reviewed later in the chapter.

Bonus This type of income can also be included in the establishment of the monthly stable income, if the prospective buyer can establish a pattern of payments of the bonus for at least the past two years. This can be done by supplying copies of Internal Revenue Form 1099 if no deductions were withheld from the bonus, or of Internal Revenue Form W-2 if there were deductions made for social security and income taxes. The employer will be asked if there is a possibility that the payment of bonus will continue.

Commissions If the prospective homebuyer is paid by commissions only, or is self-employed, the lenders may require much more information. Usually, the lenders will require either an acceptable profit-and-loss statement and balance sheets for the two years preceding, or complete copies of signed federal income tax forms from the previous two years. If the homebuyer is self-employed and has recently formed a new company, many lenders will require the information outlined above and current financial statements on the business, as well as verification of the employment of the homebuyer for the two previous years. A person on straight commission or royalty income for less than two years will have a difficult time securing a mortgage, in particular if the prospective buyer is a real estate salesperson on a straight commission basis.

Second job Since more and more persons have second jobs, lenders are accepting them more and more as part of the stable monthly income if the prospective homebuyer can establish that the job has existed for at least two years and that the possibilities are good for the job to continue. An example of an acceptable client with a second job would be a police officer who in his or her off-duty hours has served as a security guard in several banks for the past three years. Since this type of second job is in the same field of work and the demand for security in banks is growing, the second job would not only provide extra money, but would be considered by lenders to be stable employment with excellent chances for continuing. Thus, the income would count toward the stable monthly income.

Dividend or interest income This type of income can be counted if it is at least $100 per month and the investment that is providing the income is such that it cannot be sold or cashed in easily. This is true if the dividend or interest income is not the primary source of income. If the dividend or interest income is the primary source of the homebuyer's income, the lenders are going to require the homebuyer to show the source of income. If the income is dividend from stocks, the lender will request either copies of the stocks or a statement from the brokerage firm that is holding the stock as to the actual ownership of the stock and a summary of the stock performance for the past several years. If the income is from interest, once again the lender will ask the source of income. The lender may ask for copies of the certificates of deposit or a statement from the bank or institution holding the CDs as to ownership and the amount of interest paid. In addition to this information, the homebuyer will be asked to supply complete signed copies of his or her tax returns for the past several years.

Rental income Rental income can be counted toward the stable monthly income, but many lenders give this type of income special consideration, reviewing it very closely. On many applications, the lenders provide space for rental income to be included, but require the prospective homebuyer to provide the following information:

1. The gross rental income from the property

2. The amount of the mortgage payment on the property

3. The amount of the taxes on the property

4. A realistic set of operating expenses for the property

When the information is provided, and prior to the lender approving the net operating income as part of the stable monthly income, some lenders will relate the net operating income to the type of property. For example, if the rental property is an efficiency apartment complex near a college and its tenants are college students, the lender may feel that the net operating income may not be constant. As one can see, there are no hard and fast rules as to whether any or all of the income from income producing properties will be used by a lender.

Child support or alimony payments This type of income can be included in the determination of the stable monthly income if the applicant or co-applicant so wishes. Most lenders will review the payment of such monies in regard to the following items:

1. Are the payments made as a result of a court order?

2. What is the length of time the payments have been made?

3. How regularly have the payments been made?

4. What measures are available to demand payments if payments are missed?

5. What are the ages of the children? Are the children all young and are the payments to be made for several years, or are the children near the age of consent?

Welfare assistance This type of income may be counted by the prospective homebuyer if it is to be used as part of the income for repayment of the mortgage. In the past, most lenders discounted or disallowed this type of income as part of the stable monthly income, but this practice was stopped with the passage of the Equal Credit Opportunity Act. These payments, as with any other income, will be verified by the lender as to their amount and frequency.

Retirement income Since the age of the borrower can no longer be used as a criterion for the granting of mortgages, more people are buying homes with the intention of retiring and financing the dwelling based on retirement income and personal savings. So, income from social security and other pensions or trust funds can be used to establish the stable monthly income.

Source of Funds for Down Payment and Closing Costs

After the employment pattern and income of the prospective homebuyer is established, the next major item that should be determined is the source of funds for the down payment and closing. This information is necessary not only to establish the maximum house price, but to provide it for the lender who will ask the prospective homebuyer to supply it. There are two basic sources of the funds: from cash on hand (that is, bank accounts) or from the sale of property.

If the source is either a savings or checking account, the lender will verify with the bank or financial institution the date the account was opened and the average balance for at least the past sixty days. If the balance has seen a dramatic increase in the past sixty days, the lender will ask the prospective homeowner to explain the source of the additional funds. For example, say the balance in the account has been approximately $1000, but at the time of the verification the balance is $10,000. The lender will question the source of the additional funds. If the additional funds are a gift from the parents of an applicant, the lender will require a gift letter from the party giving the money. A form for such a letter is available from the lender or any attorney. If the additional funds are from a bequest from a will, a copy of the will and a letter from the administrator of the estate may be required.

If the additional cash is due to the sale of property and is so stated at the time of the application or in the initial meeting, the prospective homebuyer will be required to provide the lender with a copy of the earnest money contract, if the transaction has not closed. If the transaction is closed, or upon closing, the prospective homebuyer must provide the lender with a copy of the closing statement, showing the proceeds to the seller and signed by all parties to the transaction. Some lenders will require a copy of the seller's proceeds check and a copy of the deposit slip.

These are only a few of the types of situations that may arise in determining the amount and source of the down payment and closing costs.

Emotional Needs for Housing

In addition to the prospective income and cash on hand, there are emotional needs for housing. As a real estate professional, you should have an insight to some of the more important needs.

Desire for Homeownership During the initial qualification of your client, you need to establish the underlying desire for homeownership. There can be many reasons, including the following:

1. *Nesting*. This is important to the young who either have or are expecting a child.

2. *Economic*. To beat inflation or to use the home as a tax shelter.

3. *Retirement*. An older couple who has owned a large home is now looking for housing that meets the needs of an older couple and can serve as a home for their later years.

No matter what the emotional need of the prospective buyers, many lenders look to see the underlying desire for homeownership.

Desire to pay This emotional aspect is closely related to the income of the prospective homebuyer. Many of your prospects may be marginal in their ability to pay by mathematical analysis of their income. These prospective homebuyers, though, may have the desire to pay and are willing to make sacrifices in order to buy the home they want. This desire to pay can be shown by the past payment record of a previous mortgage. On the other hand, a person who has previously owned a home and has adequate income to meet the financial requirements of a mortgage may have a payment record which has not demonstrated the desire to pay, for example, payments may have been regularly late. Thus, in some cases the prospect with the desire to make payments will be given favorable consideration by lenders.

Liabilities

In addition to the income and emotional reason for buying, the next item that needs to be discussed with prospective homebuyers is their debts and/or obligations. These debts and/or obligations can be divided into two types: long-term and short-term. Most investors are interested in only the long-term debts, for they can have a major effect on a borrower's ability to repay the mortgage. Guidelines used by FHA, FNMA, and FHLMC to determine what constitutes a long-term debt will be discussed later.

What are some of the typical debts that prospective homebuyers may have? We will describe some below.

Installment debts This type of debt can be payments made on a regular basis to department stores for a revolving charge account or a contract on appliances. It can also be payments made on bank credit where there is a continuous balance. Most families have a car loan or a bank loan that may be counted as a long-term debt.

Loans other than bank loans Many people are members of credit unions and have loans from the credit union that are used for many purposes. For example, they may be used to purchase stocks and sometimes to purchase recreational lots or acreage.

Co-maker or endorser of a note In some cases a member of a family will have been a co-signer on a note or loan for one of the older children or a friend. This will have to be shown on the loan application of the homebuyer.

Child support or alimony This type of court-enforced obligation of the prospective homebuyer can be the most major of the payments made apart from the mortgage payment. It should also be pointed out that with the changing divorce laws throughout the United States, in addition to the father being required to make child support payments, some women have been ordered to make child support payments to the father if he has been given custody of the children.

These are just a few examples of debts and obligations that may affect the ability of the prospective homebuyer to qualify for a mortgage.

INCOME AND DEBT ANALYSIS

In the past, many real estate professionals have used the formula for the amount of loan a person or family can qualify for as approximately 2.5 times the annual salary. No reference was made to the amount of debts that the person or family had, or how much of the income was used to satisfy those obligations. Today, there are no hard and fast rules used by all conventional lenders to establish ratios of housing cost to income and long-term debts to income. The ratios used by VA and FHA are used by all lenders for underwriting loans either insured by FHA or guaranteed by VA. If your client is going to apply for either a loan insured by FHA or guaranteed by VA, you should be able to show your client the method for income and debt analysis and be able to determine the approximate loan amount he or she will be able to repay, based on the information he or she supplied.

Conventional Guidelines

Many conventional lenders have adopted the income-to-payment and long-term-debt-to-income ratios of FNMA/FHLMC for the underwriting of their loans. These guidelines are as follows:

Income-to-payment ratio The maximum amount a person or family may spend for the monthly payment on housing is 25 to 27 percent of the total gross stable monthly income. The monthly payment will include the following: payments for principal and interest, the amount needed to pay for private mortgage insurance if required, an escrow amount collected monthly to cover the taxes and insurance on the property, and sufficient funds to pay any other fees that may affect title to the property. Such additional fees could be homeowners association fees or special assessments levied by a taxing authority for streets or curbs and gutters.

Many lenders will allow a higher monthly payment ratio if it can be shown that the borrower and the coborrower can devote more of his or her income to the cost of housing or the property is constructed to be energy efficient. According to the *Seller's Guide—Conventional Mortgages*, issued by the Federal Home Loan Mortgage Corporation, higher monthly payment ratios may be appropriate if the following conditions are met:

> (i) energy efficient property which reduces energy costs;
> (ii) demonstrated ability of Borrower to devote a greater portion of income to basic needs, such as housing;
> (iii) demonstrated ability of Borrower to maintain a good credit history, accumulate savings and maintain a debt-free position;
> (iv) a larger down payment on the purchase of the property;
> (v) Borrower's potential for increased earnings based on education, job training or time employed or practiced in his/her profession; and
> (vi) Borrower's net worth being substantial enough to evidence ability to repay the mortgage regardless of income.[2]

Long-term debt-to-income ratio According to the ratios in effect in 1982, the maximum amount of an applicant's income that could be spent for the payment of long-term debts was from 33⅓ percent to 36 percent. According to FNMA/FHLMC, a long-term debt is any debt which extends beyond ten months and must include the amount of the house payment as outlined above. The long-term debt must include any child support or alimony payments.

In reviewing these ratios, you will notice that there is a range used for both the payment-to-income ratio and the long-term debt-to-income ratio. The ratio used will be determined by the loan-to-value ratio.

For example, for a loan with an LTV ratio of 90.1 to 95 percent, the maximum ratios are as follows:

1. House-payment-to-income ratio may not exceed 25 percent

2. Long-term debt-to-income ratio may not exceed 33⅓ percent

If the loan-to-value ratio is 80.1 to 90 percent, the following ratios are used:

1. House-payment-to-income ratio may not exceed 27 percent

2. Long-term debt-to-income ratio may not exceed 35 percent

Now, let us work through a sample client qualification for a conventional mortgage. The information in Figure 12-1 is the basic information on our prospective homebuyers. Let us calculate whether they can qualify for the 90 percent loan at 11½ percent interest in the amount of $63,000.

First, knowing that Mr. Palmer's overtime has been continual for the past twelve months and is very likely to continue for the next year, we will establish the gross stable income for the Palmer family.

Mr. Palmer:	
Weekly wages (40 hrs @ $13.50/hr)	$540.00
Overtime (10 hrs @ $20.25/hr)	$202.50
Total Weekly Wages	$742.50
Monthly Wages ($742.50 × 4)	$2,970.00
Mrs. Palmer:	
Monthly Wages	$300.00

For this example we will use 4 times Mr. Palmer's salary instead of 4.3, which is normally used in this calculation. (A person who can qualify using 4 weeks per month should have no trouble qualifying for the actual 4.3 weeks per month.) Adding Mr. and Mrs. Palmer's salaries, we find that their gross stable monthly income is $3270.

What would the Palmers' monthly payment be if they borrowed $63,000 at 11½ percent for thirty years? Since the loan-to-value ratio is 90 percent, we must remember to include private mortgage insurance (PMI).

Principal and interest	$624.33
Estimated taxes ($950/yr)	$79.17
Homeowner's insurance ($300/yr)	$25.00
PMI	$14.00
Other fees or assessments	-0-
Total Monthly Payment	$742.50

As mentioned previously, the monthly housing payment may not exceed 27 percent of the gross stable monthly income. We must

Figure 12-1. Loan information for the Palmer family

Client: Mr. and Mrs. J.C. Palmer

Dependents: 2 children, aged 10 and 14

Employment:

Mr. Palmer
employer—ABC Oil Field Equipment Co. (National)
job and years on job—Machinist 10 years experience
salary—$13.50/hr, average work week 50 hrs. overtime is 1.5 times after 40 hrs.

Mrs. Palmer
employer—XYZ Department Store (part-time)
job and years on job—Salesperson 2.5 years
salary—$300.00 per month

Obligations:

	Balance	*Payment*
Master Card	$500.00	$50.00/month
ABC Credit Union (auto)	$3,000.00	$120.00/month
Sears	$200.00	$50.00/month
Furniture Payment	$500.00	$100.00/month

Cash on Hand:

Checking	$1,500.00
Savings	$7,000.00

Real Estate:

Presently, the Palmers have a contract on their present home that will net them an additional $11,000 after closing costs and the sales commission are paid.

Loan Information:

Purchase Price of the House	$70,000
Amount of Down Payment (10%)	7,000
Loan Amount	$63,000

Interest Rate	11½%
Term	30 years

Estimated Closing Costs and Prepaids: (including 2 point discount) $3,000

then figure what percentage the $742.50 monthly payment is of the Palmers' gross stable monthly income:

$$\frac{\text{Monthly Payment}}{\text{Gross Stable Monthly Income}}$$

$$\text{or } \frac{742.50}{3270.00} = 22.7\%$$

The Palmers' housing expenses, then, are below the maximum percentage allowed, and so far they will qualify for the mortgage.

There is one other ratio that we must calculate in order to see if the Palmers' can qualify for the mortgage. This is the ratio of the long-term debts to the family income.

Remembering that FNMA/FHLMC and many conventional lenders count any debt that will take ten monthly payments or more as a long-term debt, the Palmers' long-term debts are:

Housing costs	$742.50
Master Card	$50.00
Credit union	$120.00
Total long-term debt	$912.50

The ratio of long-term debts to total gross stable monthly income is found by dividing the debt by the income. In the Palmers' case, it would be:

$$\frac{912.50}{3270.00} = 27.9\%$$

Since the maximum that the lender would allow is a maximum of 35 percent and the Palmers are below the maximum, they should be able to qualify for the mortgage.

It must be noted that not only are these ratios used to qualify the prospective homebuyer by the lender. The credit of the prospect must also be investigated, as well as his or her payment record of the previous mortgage. This type of investigation can only be done by the lender and you as a real estate professional can only ask prospects if they have had any problems with securing credit in the past. If they have, you may suggest that they contact the credit reporting agency in the area and try to work out any problems that might exist.

The only other question that needs to be answered is whether the Palmers will have the necessary cash for the down payment and closing costs.

Money available:	
Checking account	$1,500.00
Savings account	$7,000.00
Proceeds from sale of real estate	$11,000.00
	$19,500.00

Money needed:	
Down payment	$7,000.00
Closing cost, prepaids, and loan discount points	$3,000.00
	$10,000.00

It is obvious that the Palmers have the necessary cash to close the transaction, and from this initial qualification meeting it is obvious that the Palmers are excellent prospects for the conventional mortgage.

Federal Housing Administration Guidelines

When qualifying a prospective buyer, FHA also uses a ratio of income to housing expense and income to long-term debts. However, FHA's method of qualifying the prospective homebuyer is very different from the conventional method outlined in the previous section. FHA does not use an income multiplier as many people in the real estate profession believe.

First of all, FHA uses a different monthly income base than the conventional guidelines. This base is called *net effective income* and is figured in a different manner. The same types of income can be counted and FHA uses the two-year time frame as outlined previously, but that is where the similarity ends. The net effective income can be defined as the total gross income of the prospective homebuyer less federal withholding taxes. Using this definition, let us now apply this to the Palmer family.

The deductions from the salaries of Mr. and Mrs. Palmer can be either calculated by using the Internal Revenue tables payroll deductions or taken from their pay stubs. Remember that Mr. Palmer's total weekly wage was $742.50. We would now consult the tax table for a worker who is paid weekly with four dependents. Let us assume the tax is $185.63. The net effective income for Mr. Palmer is:

Total wages	$742.50
Tax deduction	−$185.63
Net Effective Income	$556.87

To get the monthly net effective income for Mr. Palmer, the weekly net effective income will be multiplied by 4 (for 4 weeks in a month):

$$\$556.87 \times 4 = \$2227.48$$

Now, we must calculate the net effective income for Mrs. Palmer. Mrs. Palmer's salary is $300.00 per month. When we consult the tax table this time we will use the table for an employee who is paid monthly. Let us assume that for a married person with four deductions, the tax is $60.00. The net effective income for Mrs. Palmer would be:

Monthly wages	$300.00
Tax deduction	− $60.00
Net Effective Income	$240.00

Adding the two together, we have the total net effective income for the family:

Mr. Palmer, net effective income	$2227.48
Mrs. Palmer, net effective income	$240.00
Total Net Effective Income	$2467.48

From this example we can see that FHA gives us a lower starting income to use for our ratios, but the percentages used by FHA are higher.

After we have calculated the net effective income, we now must establish the monthly housing expenses. This is also figured in a manner different from the conventional method. In addition to the money needed for the principal and interest, FHA includes the following:

1. Mortgage insurance (FHA Mortgage Insurance)
2. Hazard insurance or homeowners insurance
3. Taxes
4. Maintenance
5. Heat and utilities

Taking these items into consideration, let us now calculate the monthly housing expenses for the Palmers:

Principal and interest	$624.33
Mortgage insurance (0.5% per month)	$19.85
Hazard or homeowners insurance	$25.00
Taxes	$79.17
Total Mortgage Payment	$748.35

To the total mortgage payment, FHA adds an amount for maintenance of the property and for heat and utilities. These figures can be secured from the nearest FHA office or they can be estimated. If the estimated maintenance is $30 per month and the estimated utilities are $70 per month, then the total estimated amount for maintenance and utilities would be $100 per month. The total monthly housing expenses, then, would be:

Total mortgage payment	$748.35
Total maintenance and utilities	$100.00
Total Monthly Housing Expenses	$848.35

Next, you will need to figure the ratio of net effective income to the total monthly housing expenses, which may not exceed 35 percent.

$$\frac{\text{Total Monthly Housing Expense}}{\text{Net Effective Income}}$$

$$\text{or } \frac{848.35}{2467.48} = 34.4\%$$

The next ratio to be figured is the ratio of the net effective income to the long-term debts of the Palmers. As with the monthly housing expenses, FHA figures the long-term debts in a manner different from the conventional method. First, the FHA defines a long-term debt as any debt that has a term of twelve or more months, instead of ten or more. These debts include those outlined in the conventional section. FHA also includes any charge that recurs regularly. These charges include social security, life insurance, union dues, automobile insurance that is not paid in one lump sum, and the total monthly housing expense. With the above criteria in mind, let us calculate the long-term debts of the Palmers:

ABC Credit Union (25 months)	$120.00/month
Social security	$244.00/month
Life insurance	$21.00/month
Total Monthly Housing Expense	$848.35
Total Long-term Debts	$1233.35

With the long-term debts calculated, we can determine the ratio of the long-term debts to the net effective income of the Palmers:

$$\frac{\text{Long-term Debts}}{\text{Net Effective Income}} \text{ or } \frac{1233.35}{2467.48} = 49.98\%$$

Many FHA regional offices state that the long-term debts, including the monthly housing expenses, may not equal more than 50 percent of the net effective income. Thus, the Palmers squeeze under the requirement, since their long-term debts equal 49.98 percent of their net effective income.

The Veterans Administration

The Veterans Administration uses a method similar to that of FHA to see if the applicant qualifies for the mortgage. One major difference is that the VA uses six months of payments as the rule to establish if a debt is a long-term debt, instead of FHA's twelve months. The VA will count any debt that is less than six months in duration if the payment is of such an amount that it can cause severe impact on the family's ability to make the mortgage payment. For example, a debt of $500 which is to be paid back in five months would have to be counted as a long-term debt. If you are working with a client who has any monthly payment of $100 or more, even if for less than six months, that debt should be included in your estimate of his or her long-term debts.

A second major difference is that the VA does not use ratios as used in the conventional and FHA guidelines. Instead, VA uses the amount of money remaining after all of the appropriate monies are deducted from the total gross income of the family. This amount is referred to as the *balance for family support*. The VA feels that the income for the support of the family is a significant factor in determining whether the veteran has the ability to repay the loan. It should be noted that the VA uses no single factor in qualifying a veteran for a GI loan, but looks at many factors. The VA considers each case individually. You as the real estate professional, in qualifying your client for a VA loan, should use the following rough guideline to calculate the balance for family support.

After deducting the appropriate expenses, long-term debts, and monthly housing costs, the veteran should have at least a remaining amount equal to the following:

1. $250 per adult and teenager per month
2. $160 per child per month
3. $400 for a single adult

It should be stressed that this is only a guideline and it will vary among different family sizes, different cities, and even among different areas within a city. For a more accurate estimate for your area, contact a VA-approved lender in your area.

With the above guidelines in mind, let us now qualify the Palmers for a VA loan in the amount of $63,000 at 11½ percent interest for thirty years with no money down. Remember that Mr. and Mrs. Palmer have a ten- and a fourteen-year-old child. The following is the amount needed for family support:

Two adults @ $250/month	$500
One teenager @ $250/month	$250
One child @ $160/month	$160
Balance Required for Family Support	$910

Once again, it should be stressed that this is the minimum and it will be influenced by many factors, but it will serve as a guideline. The appropriate deductions are shown in Figure 12-2. Since the amount required for family support for the Palmers is $910.00, we can see that with $1643.25 the Palmers have sufficient funds left for the support of the family after all of the deductions are made. Once again, the actual qualification of the family is not based only on one factor, for the VA reviews many items. If you would like more information either contact a VA-approved lender, the VA office nearest you, or request DVB Circular 26-80-11, "Credit Standards," from

The Department of Veteran Benefits
Veterans Administration
Washington, D.C. 20420

This circular outlines the loan analysis procedures of the VA and will give you in-depth information on the underwriting of VA mortgages.

SUMMARY

We have outlined the underwriting guidelines of FNMA/FHLMC, FHA, and VA in this chapter. Since these are so important to you and your clients, the following is a summary of the guidelines.

Conventional (FNMA/FHLMC)

According to FNMA/FHLMC, the house payment may not exceed 25 to 27 percent of the stable gross monthly income of the prospective home-buying family or individual; the long-term debts of the prospective family or individual, including the house payment, may not exceed 33⅓ to 36 percent of the gross stable monthly income. FNMA/FHLMC defines a long-term debt as one that will require ten or more monthly payments to pay.

Federal Housing Administration

According to some of the FHA regional offices, the total monthly housing expense may not exceed 35 percent of the net effective income of the homebuyer; the long-term debts, including total monthly housing expense, may not exceed 50 percent of the net effective

Figure 12-2. VA Loan Qualifying

Gross Income per month:			
Mr. Palmer	$2,970.00		
Mrs. Palmer	$300.00		$3,270.00
Less Income Tax:			
Mr. Palmer	$ 185.63		
Mrs. Palmer	$ 60.00	$ 245.63	
Less Retirement:			
This is to be used if the family income is not subject to social security taxes, such as employees of the State of Texas		0	
Less Social Security:			
Mr. Palmer	$ 237.60		
Mrs. Palmer	$ 24.00	$ 261.60	
Less Debts:			
(over 6 months or any payment) $100 or more a month)			
Master Card	$ 50.00		
Automobile	$ 120.00		
Furniture	$ 100.00	$ 270.00	
Less Child Support		0	
Less Child Care:		0	
Less Insurance:	$ 21.00	$ 21.00	
Less Commuting Costs:		0	
Less Housing Costs:			
Principal and Interest	$ 624.33		
Taxes	$ 79.17		
Insurance	$ 25.00		
Maintenance	$ 30.00		
Utilities	$ 70.00	$ 828.50	
Amount of Deductions		$1,626.73	−$1,626.73
Amount Remaining for Family Support (Amount Required for Family Support = $910.00)			$1,643.27

income of the homebuyer. FHA defines a long-term debt as a debt that will require twelve or more monthly payments to repay.

Veterans Administration

VA's guidelines differ from FHA's in that VA uses the concept of "balance for family support." In other words, after all of the expenses are deducted from the gross monthly income of the prospective homebuyer, there must be sufficient funds left over to support the family. A good guideline to use is $250 per adult or teenager and $160 per child.

In Appendix M, there are some examples of worksheets that may be used to qualify your clients. Worksheets are also available through the National Association of Realtors®.

REVIEW QUESTIONS

1. Name and define three types of income that may be used to qualify a prospective homebuyer.
2. Define the term *net effective income.*
3. Define the term *gross stable monthly income*
4. Explain the ratios of 25-27 percent and 33⅓-36 percent.
5. Give the maximum percentage of the net effective income that may go to monthly housing expense and long-term debts.

6. Explain the difference between the terms *monthly mortgage payment* and *total housing expense*.

7. Define the term *long-term debts* according to FNMA/FHLMC, VA, and FHA.

8. Give your reason for prequalifying the prospective homebuyer.

NOTES

[1] *Underwriting Guidelines, Home Mortgages,* Federal Home Loan Mortgage Corporation, July 1979, p. 12.

[2] Federal Home Loan Mortgage Corporation, "Conventional Mortgages," Seller's Guide, Part 3, Section 4, p. 142.

CHAPTER 13 Loan Processing and Underwriting

LEARNING OBJECTIVES

In this chapter we will discuss how loans are processed and, in general, how they are underwritten. In addition, we will review the application forms of FNMA/FHLMC, FHA, and VA, as well as the information or items on the application forms that will be verified by the lender.

Upon completion of this chapter you should be able to do the following:

- ★ **Define the term *underwriting*.**
- ★ **List the steps in the processing and underwriting of a real estate loan.**
- ★ **Recognize the application forms used by FNMA/FHLMC, FHA, and VA.**
- ★ **Counsel a client on the information that will be needed by the lender to complete an application form.**

LOAN APPLICATION

All loan processing and underwriting begins with an application. The application may be in several forms, but we will review only those forms used by FNMA/FHLMC, FHA, and VA.

Usually the application is only completed after a face-to-face interview with an employee or agent of the lender, at which time the terms of the mortgage are discussed. The interest rate, term, loan-to-value ratio, and loan amount are established and agreed upon. Once these items have been established, the lender will proceed with the filling out of the loan application.

The loan application may take several forms, but there is basic information which is common to all applications:

1. Identification of the borrower and coborrower
2. Complete legal description of the property to be used as security for the mortgage
3. Exact amount of the loan the applicant is seeking
4. Term and interest rate of the loan
5. Purpose of the mortgage
6. Information regarding the finances and employment of the borrower and coborrower:

a. *Employment.* They must supply their employment history for a period of at least two years. This information will include the name and address of the employer, job title, dates of employment, and their salaries at the time of leaving the employment if either the borrower or coborrower have had more than one employer.

b. *Bank accounts.* The lenders will need information on all bank accounts of the borrower and coborrower. This information will include the account numbers, name and address of the institution, and balance at the time of application.

c. *Financial obligations.* The lender will also want information regarding all financial obligations of the borrower and coborrower. This will include all loans and long-term obligations as previously discussed in the chapter on qualifying the borrower.

d. *Other property.* If the borrower or coborrower owns any additional properties, the lender will need information regarding any loans against the property. If the property is held for investment purposes or if the property is rental property, the lender will ask for information regarding the monthly rental and expenses.

e. *Additional information.* The lender at the time of application may ask for any other information that will be necessary to make a lending decision.

It should be noted that the lender is also limited to the type of information that it can ask and use to make the lending decision. These limitations were placed on the mortgage lender by the passage of the Equal Credit Opportunity Act of 1975.

Equal Credit Opportunity Act (ECOA)

The Equal Credit Opportunity Act (ECOA) became law on October 25, 1975. It has been amended several times since its original passage, but the intent of the law remains the same. It was enacted to prohibit in a credit transaction any discrimination based on sex, marital status, age, race, color, country of national origin, or the receipt of income from public assistance programs. This law has a direct effect on the real estate industry in that it applies to anyone who regularly participates in the decision of whether to grant or extend credit. Thus, most mortgage lenders are covered by the provisions of ECOA.

One of the amendments to the act in 1978 had a major impact on the real estate industry and, in particular, the real estate professional who recommends a mortgage lender to a client. According to the change, if a salesperson recommends a lender to a client, and the client later feels that the lender has discriminated against him or her, the salesperson can in some cases also be accused of discrimination, due to the actions of the lender.

ECOA outlines the questions and information that may be included on the application form, and Section 202.5 of ECOA outlines the information that is prohibited on an application form. ECOA also makes the following prohibitions:

1. The lender may not seek information regarding the birth control practices or childbearing capacities of the borrower or coborrower.

2. The lender may not discount or exclude from consideration any income because of the source of the income.

3. The lender cannot refuse an applicant credit because the applicant cannot secure health, life, or accident insurance due to the age of the borrower or coborrower.

4. The lender cannot ask if the borrower or coborrower is divorced or widowed (but the lender can ask if the borrower or coborrower is married, unmarried, or separated).

5. The lender may not request information concerning the spouse or former spouse of the applicant, unless that person will be contractually liable for the repayment of the loan.

ECOA requires the lender to notify the borrower and coborrower as to the action taken by the lender within the following limits:

1. Thirty days after receiving a completed application and/or

2. Thirty days after the lender has taken adverse action on an application

Adverse action is the denial of credit by a lender. Notice of adverse action must give the reason for the denial of credit and the name and address of the federal agency that oversees compliance with ECOA by the credit-granting organization. An example of such a letter is shown in Figure 13-1. This is the format that is prescribed by FNMA for use by an approved seller/servicer.

Real Estate Settlement Procedures Act (RESPA)

In addition to the Equal Credit Opportunity Act, there is additional federal legislation that has an effect on the application procedure for a real estate mortgage. It is the Real Estate Settlement Procedures Act, sometimes referred to as RESPA. This act was passed in 1974 and later amended in 1976.

RESPA covers most residential mortgages used to finance the purchase of one- to four-family properties. The statute is not designed to set the fees for the settlement services, but is designed to help the prospective buyer better understand the settlement procedure and to require lenders and settlement agencies to conform to certain practices.

In regard to the application for a residential mortgage, RESPA requires the lender at the time of application or within three days to mail to the applicant and co-applicant a copy of an information booklet prescribed by the Department of Housing and Urban Development. The table of contents of such a booklet is illustrated in Figure 13-2.

The lender is required to supply the applicant and co-applicant with a ''good faith estimate of settlement costs'' at the time of application or within three days by mail. A common format for this estimate is shown in Figure 13-3.

In addition to these provisions, RESPA has provisions that will affect the closing of the transaction. These will be discussed in the next chapter.

Standard Application Forms

In the following section we will examine some of the standard loan application forms. Since most lenders require a face-to-face interview with the prospective homebuyer, the application is usually filled in at the time of this interview.

Federal National Mortgage Association/ Federal Home Loan Mortgage Corporation Application The form that will be reviewed in this section is FNMA Form 1003/FHLMC Form 65, revised August 1978. In addition to establishing the secondary market, FNMA/FHLMC has a responsibility to establish industry standards. FNMA/FHLMC has, for example, set standardized forms. One such form is the application form shown in Figure 13-4. Because this form meets the requirements of ECOA, many conventional lenders have adopted it.

The importance of the application cannot be overstated, for the information supplied on this form will determine whether the loan is approved or rejected. Many times the loan has been rejected by an investor if the originator of the mortgage has not properly filled out the application or has omitted some supporting data. This supporting data will be discussed later in this chapter. Now let us review the main section of the application.

The first section of the application has to do with the type of mortgage being applied for: conventional, VA, or FHA. The interest rate and the term of the mortgage as well as the monthly payments are calculated, and finally the escrow or impounds are indicated.

In the next section of the application, ''Subject Property,'' the property is identified by both a street address and a legal description. Next, the lender will need to know the purpose of the loan, whether it is to purchase, to construct, or to refinance existing financing. If the purpose is either to construct or to refinance, additional information is requested. The final portion of this section asks in whose names the title to the property will be held and in what manner the title will be held: fee simple, fee conditional, joint tenancy, and so forth. Therefore, you will need to tell the prospective homebuyer how the title can be held and help him or her

Figure 13-1. Notice of Adverse Action

FNMA CONVENTIONAL HOME MORTGAGE SELLING
APPENDIX A CONTRACT SUPPLEMENT FORM 1011

Consumer Disclosure Letter
(Equal Credit Opportunity Act/Fair Credit Reporting Act)

____
(Date)

APPLICANT(S): ____
(Type Full Name) (City) (State)

DESCRIPTION OF REQUESTED CREDIT: ______________________________

____

Dear (Name of Applicant):

This is to advise you that your recent application for an extension of credit has been submitted to Federal National Mortgage Association for their evaluation.

☐ 1. In compliance with Regulation "B" (Equal Credit Opportunity Act), you are advised that the application is being held pending further review or receipt of additional information. This notice of the status of your application is required to be given to you by the Federal Equal Credit Opportunity Act. We will notify you of the decision on your application as soon as possible.

☐ 2. In compliance with Regulation "B" (Equal Credit Opportunity Act), you are advised that the application has been declined. The decision to deny your application was based on the following reasons:

CREDIT
- ☐ No credit file
- ☐ Insufficient credit references
- ☐ Insufficient credit file
- ☐ Unable to verify credit references
- ☐ Garnishment, attachment, foreclosure, repossession or suit
- ☐ Insufficient income for total obligations
- ☐ Unacceptable payment record on previous mortgage
- ☐ Delinquent credit obligations
- ☐ Bankruptcy
- ☐ Information from a consumer reporting agency
- ☐ Lack of cash reserves

EMPLOYMENT STATUS
- ☐ Unable to verify employment
- ☐ Length of employment
- ☐ Insufficient stability of income

(SEE NEXT PAGE)

FNMA Form 1011
Rev. 7/77

Figure 13-1. continued

FNMA CONVENTIONAL HOME MORTGAGE SELLING

APPENDIX A CONTRACT SUPPLEMENT FORM 1011

INCOME
- ☐ Insufficient income for mortgage payments
- ☐ Unable to verify income

RESIDENCY
- ☐ Secondary residence

PROPERTY
- ☐ Unacceptable property
- ☐ Insufficient data-property
- ☐ Unacceptable appraisal
- ☐ Unacceptable leasehold estate

OTHER
- ☐ Insufficient funds to close the loan
- ☐ Credit application incomplete
- ☐ We do not grant credit to any applicant on the terms and conditions you request

3. DISCLOSURE OF USE OF INFORMATION OBTAINED FROM AN OUTSIDE SOURCE

☐ Disclosure inapplicable

☐ In compliance with Fair Credit Reporting Act, Section 615, your application was declined either wholly or partly because of:

☐ Information obtained in a report from a consumer reporting agency:

(Full Name at Credit Bureau) (Address & Telephone Number)

This information is obtained as a routine matter in connection with a mortgage application. Any questions you may have concerning this information should be addressed to the consumer reporting agency shown above, rather than to us.

☐ Information obtained from an outside source other than a consumer reporting agency. You have the right to make a written request of us for disclosure of the nature of this information. However, to be honored, such written request must be received by us within 60 days from the date you received this notice.

4. The Federal Equal Credit Opportunity Act prohibits creditors from discriminating against credit applicants on the basis of race, color, religion, national origin, sex, marital status, age (provided that the applicant has the capacity to enter into a binding contract); because all or part of the applicant's income derives from any public assistance program; or because the applicant has in good faith exercised any right under the Consumer Credit Protection Act. The Federal agency that administers compliance with this law concerning Federal National Mortgage Association is the Federal Trade Commission, Equal Credit Opportunity, Washington, D.C. 20580.

(SEE NEXT PAGE)

FNMA Form 1011
Rev. 7/77

Figure 13-1. continued

FNMA CONVENTIONAL HOME MORTGAGE SELLING

APPENDIX A — CONTRACT SUPPLEMENT — FORM 1011

5. Should you have any additional information which might assist us in evaluating your creditworthiness, please let us know. Thank you for applying.

This notification is given by us on behalf of Federal National Mortgage Association.

Notice ☐ delivered or ☐ mailed on ____________________

____

By: ____________________

____
(Address)

(City) (State) (Telephone)

FNMA Form 1011
Rev. 7/77

Figure 13-2. Table of Contents to Settlement Costs, A HUD Guide

TABLE OF CONTENTS

Figure 13-3. Good Faith Estimates

"GOOD FAITH ESTIMATES"
(Required by RESPA)

This list gives an estimate of most of the charges, based on the contract and/or general experience, that you will have to pay at the settlement of the loan. The figures shown, as estimated, are subject to change. The numbers listed on the left hand column of the estimated settlement charges correspond to the lines of the Uniform Settlement Statement (HUD-1), which will be used in the closing of your loan. The figures shown are based on the sales price and proposed mortgage amount as reflected by your loan application. For further explanation of the charges, consult your special information booklet.

ESTIMATED SETTLEMENT CHARGES

801	Loan Origination Fee (_____%)	________
803	Appraisal Fee	________
804	Credit Report	________
805	Lender's Inspection Fee	________
806	Mortgage Insurance Application Fee	________
901	Interest (*See Below)	________
902	Mortgage Insurance Premium	________
1105	Document Preparation	________
1108	Title Insurance	________
1201	Recording Fees	________
1301	Survey	________
	Total	$________

*This interest calculation represents the greatest amount of interest you could be required to pay at settlement. The actual amount will be determined by which day of the month your settlement is conducted. To determine the amount you will have to pay, multiply the number of days remaining in the month in which you settle, times $________, which is the daily interest charge for your loan.

The Lender requires that ____________, Attorneys be used for mortgage loan document preparation. The name, address and telephone number of such firm is ____________ ____________, and the services to be rendered by such firm will be document preparation for the mortgage loan closing. The above estimate of Lender for the document preparation is based upon the charge furnished by ____________, Attorneys. The firm of ____________ ____________, Attorneys has a business relationship with Lender.

(   ) Check if applicable
The contract between you and the seller indicates to us that you will be required to pay a fixed amount of $________ for all charges imposed at settlement for the settlement services listed above. You are exempt from settlement disclosure under Section 3500.8(d)(2) of HUD Regulation X.

(   ) Check if applicable
The contract between you and the seller indicates to us that you will be required to pay no settlement charges. You are exempt from settlement disclosure under Section 3500.8(d)(1) of HUD Regulation X.

Source: Mercantile Mortgage Corporation of Texas, 2714 Louisiana, Houston, Texas 77006

arrive at a decision, or advise them of the lender's requirements as to how the title will be held.

The next sections have to do with the borrower and coborrower. Normally, a lender will not allow the borrower to give the information for the coborrower or vice versa. Both parties, therefore, must be present at the time of application. What information is required seems self-explanatory, but there are some important items that should be reviewed. The first is the applicant's present address. If either the borrower or coborrower has resided at his present address for less than two years, the lender will request the prior address to establish residency for the past two years. If the borrower or coborrower has rented, the lender will need the name and address of the landlord or rental agent to verify the residency and payment record of the borrower or coborrower. If the borrower or coborrower has owned or was purchasing a home and was making mortgage payments, he will have to supply the name and address of the mortgage lender as well as his account number, for the lender will verify the mortgage and payment record of the borrower and/or coborrower. The borrower and/or the

Figure 13-4. FNMA/FHLMC Residential Loan Application, page 1

RESIDENTIAL LOAN APPLICATION

MORTGAGE APPLIED FOR: ☐ Conventional ☐ FHA ☐ VA ☐ ______ | Amount $ | Interest Rate % | No. of Months | Monthly Payment Principal & Interest $ | Escrow/Impounds (to be collected monthly) ☐ Taxes ☐ Hazard Ins. ☐ Mtg. Ins. ☐ ______

Prepayment Option

SUBJECT PROPERTY

Property Street Address | City | County | State | Zip | No. Units

Legal Description (Attach description if necessary) | Year Built

Purpose of Loan: ☐ Purchase ☐ Construction-Permanent ☐ Construction ☐ Refinance ☐ Other (Explain)

Complete this line if Construction-Permanent or Construction Loan | Lot Value Data | Year Acquired | Original Cost $ | Present Value (a) $ | Cost of Imps. (b) $ | Total (a + b) $ | ENTER TOTAL AS PURCHASE PRICE IN DETAILS OF PURCHASE.

Complete this line if a Refinance Loan | Year Acquired | Original Cost $ | Amt. Existing Liens $ | Purpose of Refinance | Describe Improvements [ ] made [ ] to be made | Cost: $

Title Will Be Held In What Name(s) | Manner In Which Title Will Be Held

Source of Down Payment and Settlement Charges

This application is designed to be completed by the borrower(s) with the lender's assistance. The Co-Borrower Section and all other Co-Borrower questions must be completed and the appropriate box(es) checked if ☐ another person will be jointly obligated with the Borrower on the loan, or ☐ the Borrower is relying on income from alimony, child support or separate maintenance or on the income or assets of another person as a basis for repayment of the loan, or ☐ the Borrower is married and resides, or the property is located, in a community property state.

BORROWER	CO-BORROWER
Name / Age / School Yrs	Name / Age / School Yrs
Present Address No. Years ☐ Own ☐ Rent	Present Address No. Years ☐ Own ☐ Rent
Street	Street
City/State/Zip	City/State/Zip
Former address if less than 2 years at present address	Former address if less than 2 years at present address
Street	Street
City/State/Zip	City/State/Zip
Years at former address ☐ Own ☐ Rent	Years at former address ☐ Own ☐ Rent
Marital Status ☐ Married ☐ Separated ☐ Unmarried (incl. single, divorced, widowed) — Dependents other than listed by Co-Borrower: No / Ages	Marital Status ☐ Married ☐ Separated ☐ Unmarried (incl. single, divorced, widowed) — Dependents other than listed by Borrower: No / Ages
Name and Address of Employer / Years employed in this line of work or profession? ____ years / Years on this job ____ / ☐ Self Employed*	Name and Address of Employer / Years employed in this line of work or profession? ____ years / Years on this job ____ / ☐ Self Employed*
Position/Title / Type of Business	Position/Title / Type of Business
Social Security Number*** / Home Phone / Business Phone	Social Security Number*** / Home Phone / Business Phone

GROSS MONTHLY INCOME

Item	Borrower	Co-Borrower	Total
Base Empl. Income	$	$	$
Overtime			
Bonuses			
Commissions			
Dividends/Interest			
Net Rental Income			
Other† (Before completing, see notice under Describe Other Income below.)			
Total	$	$	$

MONTHLY HOUSING EXPENSE**

	PRESENT	PROPOSED
Rent	$	
First Mortgage (P&I)		$
Other Financing (P&I)		
Hazard Insurance		
Real Estate Taxes		
Mortgage Insurance		
Homeowner Assn. Dues		
Other		
Total Monthly Pmt.	$	$
Utilities		
Total	$	$

DETAILS OF PURCHASE

Do Not Complete If Refinance

a. Purchase Price	$
b. Total Closing Costs (Est.)	
c. Prepaid Escrows (Est.)	
d. Total (a + b + c)	$
e. Amount This Mortgage	( )
f. Other Financing	( )
g. Other Equity	( )
h. Amount of Cash Deposit	( )
i. Closing Costs Paid by Seller	( )
j. Cash Reqd. For Closing (Est.)	$

DESCRIBE OTHER INCOME

B-Borrower C-Co-Borrower | NOTICE: † Alimony, child support, or separate maintenance income need not be revealed if the Borrower or Co-Borrower does not choose to have it considered as a basis for repaying this loan. | Monthly Amount $

IF EMPLOYED IN CURRENT POSITION FOR LESS THAN TWO YEARS COMPLETE THE FOLLOWING

B/C	Previous Employer/School	City/State	Type of Business	Position/Title	Dates From/To	Monthly Income
						$

THESE QUESTIONS APPLY TO BOTH BORROWER AND CO-BORROWER

If a "yes" answer is given to a question in this column, explain on an attached sheet.	Borrower Yes or No	Co-Borrower Yes or No
Have you any outstanding judgments? In the last 7 years, have you been declared bankrupt?		
Have you had property foreclosed upon or given title or deed in lieu thereof?		
Are you a co-maker or endorser on a note?		
Are you a party in a law suit?		
Are you obligated to pay alimony, child support, or separate maintenance?		
Is any part of the down payment borrowed?		

If applicable, explain Other Financing or Other Equity (provide addendum if more space is needed).

*FHLMC/FNMA require business credit report, signed Federal Income Tax returns for last two years, and, if available, audited Profit and Loss Statements plus balance sheet for same period.

**All Present Monthly Housing Expenses of Borrower and Co-Borrower should be listed on a combined basis.

***Neither FHLMC nor FNMA requires this information.

FHLMC 65 Rev. 8/78 FNMA 1003 Rev. 8/78

coborrower will also need to furnish the names and addresses of employers for the past two years. These addresses should be accurate, for the lender will wish to verify the employment. If the address is incorrect, it can slow the processing of the application.

The next section of the application is divided into three sections: Gross Monthly Income, Monthly Housing Expenses, and Details of the Purchase. This section is self-explanatory and the information required is not difficult to furnish.

In the next section of the application, the borrower or coborrower describes other income, if any. Once again, sufficient information must be supplied to allow the lender to verify the income.

In the section entitled "If Employed in the Current Position For Less Than Two Years," the borrower and coborrower are given additional room to establish a two-year work record; the information must be sufficient to allow the lender to verify the employment.

The final section of the first page is composed of several questions. If any question is answered "yes" by either the borrower or coborrower, the answer must be explained in depth.

The second page of the application (Figure 13-5) is devoted primarily to the financial and credit history of the borrower and coborrower. The first section is divided into two parts, the first being the assets and the second being the liabilities of the borrower or coborrower. The information that is requested needs no in-depth explanation here. It should be noted, however, that complete information for the installment debts is once again required; the lender verifying the credit of the borrower or coborrower will need this information for the credit-checking agency.

At the end of the liability and assets section is a place for the borrower and coborrower to list all of the real estate they own. You will note that, after the address of the property, the borrower or coborrower must state whether the property is sold, whether a sale is pending, or whether the property is being held for rental purposes. If the property is sold, the lender will require a copy of a closing statement. If the sale is pending, the lender may request a copy of the earnest money contract and will not close the loan until a copy of the closing statement is furnished, if the sale proceeds are to be used as part of the down payment or for closing costs.

The next major section of the application is for previous credit references. Here you will list any loans or charge accounts which have been paid in full to any credit-granting organization.

Immediately below the previous credit section is an agreement that the borrower and coborrower must sign. The borrower and coborrower at this time must declare their intent either to occupy or not to occupy the property. By signing the statement, the borrower and coborrower acknowledge that they can be punished by the federal government if they knowingly make any false statement.

Some of the information that is needed to determine if a lender is discriminating due to color, race, or sex is contained in a section entitled "Information for Government Monitoring Purposes." Since this information is not used in the processing or approval of a loan, the borrower and coborrower are not required to furnish the requested information, but they must initial the section stating that they do not wish to furnish the information. A sample of the information that will be requested is shown in Figure 13-6.

Federal Housing Administration/Veterans Administration This is the second of the major common forms that has been developed by FHA, VA, and the Farmers Home Administration. This application, HUD form 92900, will be used for any application for a HUD-FHA commitment for mortgage, VA, or FmHA loan guaranty after July 31, 1982. Any application submitted on any other form will be rejected.

First, let's review how the common form will be used by HUD-FHA and the information that will be required. Since this is a multipurpose form, it is an eight-page carbon form and contains pages for use by all three agencies. HUD-FHA only uses pages 1, 4-7, and 8. The real estate professional will only be interested in pages 1 (the application page) and 4 (the Certificate of Commitment for a HUD-insured mortgage).

Page 1 is the actual application and is shown in Figure 13-7. The first step is to indicate in the first line that this is an application of HUD-FHA mortgage insurance. The next block that will be filled out at the time of application is Block 3, the name and address of the borrower and/or coborrower. This information must be complete and must

Figure 13-5. FNMA/FHLMC Residential Loan Application, page 2

This Statement and any applicable supporting schedules may be completed jointly by both married and unmarried co-borrowers if their assets and liabilities are sufficiently joined so that the Statement can be meaningfully and fairly presented on a combined basis; otherwise separate Statements and Schedules are required (FHLMC 65A/FNMA 1003A). If the co-borrower section was completed about a spouse, this statement and supporting schedules must be completed about that spouse also. ☐ Completed Jointly ☐ Not Completed Jointly

STATEMENT OF ASSETS AND LIABILITIES

ASSETS		LIABILITIES AND PLEDGED ASSETS			
Indicate by (*) those liabilities or pledged assets which will be satisfied upon sale of real estate owned or upon refinancing of subject property					
Description	Cash or Market Value	Creditors' Name, Address and Account Number	Acct. Name If Not Borrower's	Mo. Pmt. and Mos. left to pay	Unpaid Balance
Cash Deposit Toward Purchase Held By	$	Installment Debts (include "revolving" charge accts)		$ Pmt./Mos.	$
				/	
Checking and Savings Accounts (Show Names of Institutions/Acct. Nos.)				/	
				/	
				/	
Stocks and Bonds (No./Description)				/	
				/	
Life Insurance Net Cash Value Face Amount ($)				/	
SUBTOTAL LIQUID ASSETS	$	Other Debts Including Stock Pledges			
Real Estate Owned (Enter Market Value from Schedule of Real Estate Owned)				/	
Vested Interest in Retirement Fund		Real Estate Loans		╳	
Net Worth of Business Owned (ATTACH FINANCIAL STATEMENT)				╳	
Automobiles (Make and Year)		Automobile Loans		/	
Furniture and Personal Property		Alimony, Child Support and Separate Maintenance Payments Owed To		/	╳
Other Assets (Itemize)					
		TOTAL MONTHLY PAYMENTS		$	╳
TOTAL ASSETS	A $	NET WORTH (A minus B) $		TOTAL LIABILITIES	B $

SCHEDULE OF REAL ESTATE OWNED (If Additional Properties Owned Attach Separate Schedule)

Address of Property (Indicate S if Sold, PS if Pending Sale or R if Rental being held for income)	⇩	Type of Property	Present Market Value	Amount of Mortgages & Liens	Gross Rental Income	Mortgage Payments	Taxes, Ins. Maintenance and Misc.	Net Rental Income
			$	$	$	$	$	$
		TOTALS →	$	$	$	$	$	$

LIST PREVIOUS CREDIT REFERENCES

⇩ B–Borrower C–Co-Borrower	Creditor's Name and Address	Account Number	Purpose	Highest Balance	Date Paid
				$	

List any additional names under which credit has previously been received ______

AGREEMENT: The undersigned applies for the loan indicated in this application to be secured by a first mortgage or deed of trust on the property described herein, and represents that the property will not be used for any illegal or restricted purpose, and that all statements made in this application are true and are made for the purpose of obtaining the loan. Verification may be obtained from any source named in this application. The original or a copy of this application will be retained by the lender, even if the loan is not granted. The undersigned ☐ intend or ☐ do not intend to occupy the property as their primary residence.

I/we fully understand that it is a federal crime punishable by fine or imprisonment, or both, to knowingly make any false statements concerning any of the above facts as applicable under the provisions of Title 18, United States Code, Section 1014.

______ Borrower's Signature Date ______ ______ Co-Borrower's Signature Date ______

INFORMATION FOR GOVERNMENT MONITORING PURPOSES

Instructions: Lenders must insert in this space, or on an attached addendum, a provision for furnishing the monitoring information required or requested under present Federal and/or present state law or regulation. For most lenders, the inserts provided in FHLMC Form 65-B/FNMA Form 1003-B can be used.

FOR LENDER'S USE ONLY

(FNMA REQUIREMENT ONLY) This application was taken by ☐ face to face interview ☐ by mail ☐ by telephone

______ (Interviewer) ______ Name of Employer of Interviewer

FHLMC 65 Rev. 8/78 **REVERSE** FNMA 1003 Rev. 8/78

Figure 13-6. FNMA Conventional Home Mortgage Selling Contract Supplement

FNMA CONVENTIONAL HOME MORTGAGE SELLING
APPENDIX A CONTRACT SUPPLEMENT FORM 1003B

INFORMATION FOR GOVERNMENT MONITORING PURPOSES - INSERTS

The following are "camera-ready" versions of language which may be inserted to complete the "Information for Government Monitoring Purposes" section of the Residential Loan Application Form (FHLMC Form 65/FNMA 1003). The language in the first insert has been approved by both Federal Deposit Insurance Corporation and Federal Home Loan Bank Board.

Before printing an insert, it should be reviewed to assure conformity with state law. In particular, all lenders, who may be subject to a state fair housing or equal opportunity law which has monitoring requirements, should determine whether the applicable disclosure statement is in compliance with the legal requirements of that state.

INSERT FOR FHLBB OR FDIC REGULATED LENDERS

The following information is requested by the Federal Government if this loan is related to a dwelling, in order to monitor the lender's compliance with equal credit opportunity and fair housing laws. You are not required to furnish this information, but are encouraged to do so. The law provides that a lender may neither discriminate on the basis of this information, nor on whether you choose to furnish it. However, if you choose not to furnish it, under Federal regulations this lender is required to note race and sex on the basis of visual observation or surname. If you do not wish to furnish the above information, please initial below

BORROWER: I do not wish to furnish this information (initials)______	**CO-BORROWER:** I do not wish to furnish this information (initials)______
RACE/ NATIONAL ORIGIN ☐ American Indian, Alaskan Native ☐ Asian, Pacific Islander ☐ Black ☐ Hispanic ☐ White ☐ Other (specify) ______ **SEX:** ☐ Female ☐ Male	**RACE/ NATIONAL ORIGIN** ☐ American Indian, Alaskan Native ☐ Asian, Pacific Islander ☐ Black ☐ Hispanic ☐ White ☐ Other (specify) ______ **SEX** ☐ Female ☐ Male

INSERT FOR LENDERS SUBJECT ONLY TO FEDERAL RESERVE SYSTEM REGULATION B

If this loan is for purchase or construction of a home, the following information is requested by the Federal Government to monitor this lender's compliance with Equal Credit Opportunity and Fair Housing Laws. The law provides that a lender may neither discriminate on the basis of this information nor on whether or not it is furnished. Furnishing this information is optional. If you do not wish to furnish the following information, please initial below.

BORROWER: I do not wish to furnish this information (initials) ______	**CO-BORROWER:** I do not wish to furnish this information (initials) ______
RACE/ NATIONAL ORIGIN ☐ American Indian, Alaskan Native ☐ Asian, Pacific Islander ☐ Black ☐ Hispanic ☐ White ☐ Other (specify) ______ **SEX** ☐ Female ☐ Male	**RACE/ NATIONAL ORIGIN** ☐ American Indian, Alaskan Native ☐ Asian, Pacific Islander ☐ Black ☐ Hispanic ☐ White ☐ Other (specify) ______ **SEX** ☐ Female ☐ Male

Note: This form will be amended in the event that the Comptroller of the Currency or the National Credit Union Administration issue regulations which are not accommodated by the insert "FOR LENDERS SUBJECT TO FEDERAL RESERVE SYSTEM REGULATION B." Until such time, lenders regulated by these agencies should continue to use the Regulation B insert. Before printing any insert, it should be reviewed to assure compliance with any applicable state legal requirements.

FHLMC 65B 8/78 FNMA 1003B 8/78

include the proper zip code. Blocks 4A, 4B, and 4C are not completed by the borrower. The lender supplies this information.

Blocks 5A through 5C and 6A through 6C are requirements of federal civil rights law. The lender must advise the applicants of this fact and that the information will not affect any lending decision of the lender or the issuance of mortgage insurance by HUD-FHA. If the lender and/or originator of the mortgage advises the applicant of the purpose for securing this information and the applicant refuses, the lender will then ask the applicant to initial the appropriate block. This will indicate to HUD-FHA that the information was not given by a decision of the applicant.

Block 7 is very important and must be complete and correct. The reason for including the property address, the name of the subdivision, the lot and block number, and the zip code is to make sure the application covers the correct property.

Blocks 8A through 8C deal with the terms of the loan which will be insured by HUD-FHA. You will need to see that the loan amount and the interest rate are correct. The final block, 8C, states the term of the mortgage, normally thirty years unless the loan is a Growing Equity Mortgage or the borrower is making application for mortgage insurance that allows for an extended term.

Blocks 8D and 8E will only be filled out if the borrower/coborrower is to pay discount points, which is allowed in some instances, but normally is not allowed. This completes our review of the top portion of the form that will apply to HUD-FHA.

The next portion of the form, Section I—Purpose, Amount, Terms of and Security for proposed loan, deals with the property and the repayment of the mortgage. Block 9A, Purpose of Loan, will tell HUD-FHA how the proceeds are to be used. There are eight specific uses shown and the applicants will need to select the proper purpose. Applicants indicate in Block 9B whether they will be an occupant or landlord. If the property used as security is a duplex, triplex or fourplex and the borrower/coborrower will be living in one of the units, they will need to mark both landlord and occupant boxes.

Blocks 11 through 13 are self-explanatory.

Block 14, Estimated Taxes, Insurance and Assessments, items A through F, will be completed by the lender. The information that will be used for this block will be from fact sheets supplied by the nearest HUD-FHA office.

In Block 15, the lender will complete the information required to establish the monthly payment. One item that must be added is the mortgage insurance premium. (Since it is a common form, it was omitted.) All of the amounts are then totaled.

In Block 16 of Section II, Personal and Financial Status of Applicant, HUD-FHA is establishing who will be obligated on the mortgage in addition to the borrower. Also, HUD-FHA wants to establish if the property is located in a state that has a community property law. Block D is checked if the borrower will rely on child support and/or alimony or separate maintenance from a spouse or former spouse for repayment of the loan. If so, HUD-FHA will require information on the spouse or former spouse. This source of funds to repay the mortgage can be true for either a male or female. As a good real estate salesperson, you should see if this type of income will be used for repayment of the loan and have the applicants gather the required information.

Blocks 17A through 17D and 18A through 18C are self-explanatory.

If the borrower/coborrower are presently making mortgage payments, HUD-FHA wants to know the amount of their total monthly housing expense, which is entered in block 20A. This should include principal and interest, insurance, utilities and any other fees that may affect the title to the property. If the applicants are renters, HUD-FHA would like information regarding the monthly rent. Whether the monthly housing expense includes money for utilities is indicated in block 20B. Your clients should have all of this information at the time of application. If they do not, it could slow down processing the application.

In block 21 the applicant will need to list all assets that will show his or her financial strength. Each category in block 21 is explained below:

A. Cash—This should include all cash accounts in banks, credit unions, money market funds (if there is check writing capabilities). According to HUD-FHA, significant amounts of cash on hand should be supported by an explanation as

Figure 13-7. HUD Form 92900, page 1

Form Approved OMB No. 2900-0144

☐ VA Application for Home Loan Guaranty | ☐ USDA-FmHA Application for FmHA Guaranteed Loan | ☐ HUD/FHA Application for Commitment for Insurance under the National Housing Act

1. AGENCY CASE NUMBER | 2A. LENDER'S CASE NUMBER | 2B. SECTION OF THE ACT *(HUD Only)*

3. NAME AND PRESENT ADDRESS OF BORROWER *(Include ZIP Code)*

4A. NAME AND ADDRESS OF LENDER *(Include ZIP Code)*

4B. ORIGINATORS' I.D. *(HUD Only)* | 4C. SPONSOR'S I.D. *(HUD Only)*

5A. BORROWER: *If you do not wish to complete Items 5B or 5C, please initial in the space to the right.* | INITIALS

5B. RACE/NATIONAL ORIGIN: 1 ☐ WHITE, NOT HISPANIC; 2 ☐ BLACK, NOT HISPANIC; 3 ☐ AMERICAN INDIAN OR ALASKAN NATIVE; 4 ☐ ASIAN OR PACIFIC ISLANDER; 5 ☐ HISPANIC

5C. SEX: 1 ☐ MALE; 2 ☐ FEMALE

6A. SPOUSE OR OTHER BORROWER: *If you do not wish to complete Items 6B or 6C, please initial in space to the right.* | INITIALS

6B. RACE/NATIONAL ORIGIN: 1 ☐ WHITE, NOT HISPANIC; 2 ☐ BLACK, NOT HISPANIC; 3 ☐ AMERICAN INDIAN OR ALASKAN NATIVE; 4 ☐ ASIAN OR PACIFIC ISLANDER; 5 ☐ HISPANIC

6C. SEX: 1 ☐ MALE; 2 ☐ FEMALE

7. PROPERTY ADDRESS INCLUDING NAME OF SUBDIVISION, LOT AND BLOCK NO., AND ZIP CODE

8A. LOAN AMOUNT	8B. INT. RATE	8C. PROPOSED MATURITY
$	%	YRS. MOS.
DISCOUNT: *(Only if borrower to pay)*	8D. PERCENT %	8E. AMOUNT $

VA ONLY: Veteran and lender hereby apply to the Administrator of Veterans Affairs for Guaranty of the loan described here under Section 1810, Chapter 37, Title 38, United States Code to the full extent permitted by the veteran's entitlement and severally agree that the Regulations promulgated pursuant to Chapter 37, and in effect on the date of the loan shall govern the rights, duties, and liabilities of the parties.
HUD/FHA ONLY: Mortgagee's application for mortgagor approval and commitment for mortgage insurance under the National Housing Act.

SECTION I - PURPOSE, AMOUNT, TERMS OF AND SECURITY FOR PROPOSED LOAN

9A. PURPOSE OF LOAN – TO: 1 ☐ PURCHASE EXISTING HOUSE PREVIOUSLY OCCUPIED; 2 ☐ FINANCE IMPROVEMENTS TO EXISTING PROPERTY; 3 ☐ REFINANCE; 4 ☐ PURCHASE NEW CONDO. UNIT; 5 ☐ PURCHASE EXISTING CONDO. UNIT; 6 ☐ PURCHASE EXISTING HOME NOT PREVIOUSLY OCCUPIED; 7 ☐ CONSTRUCT A HOME - PROCEEDS TO BE PAID OUT DURING CONSTRUCTION; 8 ☐ HUD ONLY – FINANCE COOP-PURCHASE

9B. HUD ONLY – BORROWER WILL BE: 1 ☐ OCCUPANT; 2 ☐ LANDLORD; 3 ☐ BUILDER; 4 ☐ OPERATIVE BUILDER; 5 ☐ ESCROW COMMITMENT

10. VA ONLY – TITLE WILL BE VESTED IN: ☐ VETERAN; ☐ VETERAN AND SPOUSE; ☐ OTHER *(Specify)*

11. LIEN: ☐ FIRST MORTGAGE; ☐ OTHER *(Specify)*

12. ESTATE WILL BE: ☐ FEE SIMPLE; ☐ LEASEHOLD *(Show expiration date)*

13. IS THERE A MANDATORY HOMEOWNERS ASSOC.? ☐ YES ☐ NO *(If "Yes," complete Item 14F.)*

14. ESTIMATED TAXES, INSURANCE AND ASSESSMENTS		15. ESTIMATED MONTHLY PAYMENT	
A. ANNUAL TAXES	$	A. PRINCIPAL AND INTEREST	$
B. AMOUNT OF HAZARD INSURANCE ON SECURITY		B. TAXES AND INSURANCE DEPOSITS	
C. ANNUAL HAZARD INSURANCE PREMIUM		C. OTHER	
D. ANNUAL SPECIAL ASSESSMENT PAYMENT			
E. UNPAID SPECIAL ASSESSMENT BALANCE			
F. ANNUAL MAINTENANCE ASSESSMENT		TOTAL	$

SECTION II - PERSONAL AND FINANCIAL STATUS OF APPLICANT

16. PLEASE CHECK APPROPRIATE BOX(ES). IF ONE OR MORE ARE CHECKED, ITEMS 18B, 21, 22 AND 23 MUST INCLUDE INFORMATION CONCERNING BORROWER'S SPOUSE *(or former spouse if box "D" is checked)*. IF NO BOXES ARE CHECKED, NO INFORMATION CONCERNING THE SPOUSE NEED BE FURNISHED IN ITEMS 18B, 21, 22 AND 23.

A. ☐ THE SPOUSE WILL BE JOINTLY OBLIGATED WITH THE BORROWER ON THE LOAN
B. ☐ THE BORROWER IS RELYING ON THE SPOUSE'S INCOME AS A BASIS FOR REPAYMENT OF THE LOAN.
C. ☐ THE BORROWER IS MARRIED AND THE PROPERTY TO SECURE THE LOAN IS LOCATED IN A COMMUNITY PROPERTY STATE.
D. ☐ THE BORROWER IS RELYING ON ALIMONY, CHILD SUPPORT, OR SEPARATE MAINTENANCE PAYMENTS FROM A SPOUSE OR FORMER SPOUSE AS A BASIS FOR REPAYMENT OF THE LOAN.

17A. MARITAL STATUS OF BORROWER	17B. MARITAL STATUS OF COBORROWER OTHER THAN SPOUSE	17C. MONTHLY CHILD SUPPORT OBLIGATION	17D. MONTHLY ALIMONY OBLIGATION	18A. AGE OF BORROWER	18B. AGE OF SPOUSE OR COBORROWER	18C. AGE(S) OF DEPENDENT(S)
1 ☐ MARRIED 2 ☐ SEPARATED 3 ☐ UNMARRIED	1 ☐ MARRIED 2 ☐ SEPARATED 3 ☐ UNMARRIED	$	$			

19. NAME AND ADDRESS OF NEAREST LIVING RELATIVE *(Include telephone number, if available).* | 20A. CURRENT MONTHLY HOUSING EXPENSE $ | 20B. UTILITIES INCLUDED? ☐ YES ☐ NO

21. ASSETS		22. LIABILITIES *(Itemize all debts)*		
		NAME OF CREDITOR	MO. PAYMENT	BALANCE
A. CASH *(Including deposit on purchase)*	$			
B. SAVINGS BONDS - OTHER SECURITIES			$	$
C. REAL ESTATE OWNED				
D. AUTO				
E. FURNITURE AND HOUSEHOLD GOODS				
F. OTHER *(Use separate sheet, if necessary)*		JOB-RELATED EXPENSE *(Specify)*		
G. TOTAL	$	TOTAL	$	$

23. INCOME AND OCCUPATIONAL STATUS				
ITEM	BORROWER		SPOUSE OR COBORROWER	
A. OCCUPATION				
B. NAME OF EMPLOYER				
C. NUMBER OF YEARS EMPLOYED				
D. GROSS PAY	MONTHLY $	HOURLY $	MONTHLY $	HOURLY $
E. OTHER INCOME *(Disclosure of child support, alimony and separate maintenance income is optional.)*	MONTHLY $		MONTHLY $	

NOTE – If land acquired by separate transaction, complete Items 25A and 25B.

25A. DATE ACQUIRED | 25B. UNPAID BALANCE $

24. ESTIMATED TOTAL COST	
ITEM	AMOUNT
A. PURCHASE EXISTING HOME	$
B. ALTERATIONS, IMPROVEMENTS, REPAIRS	
C. CONSTRUCTION	
D. LAND *(If acquired separately)*	
E. PURCHASE OF CONDOMINIUM UNIT	
F. REFINANCE	
G. PREPAID ITEMS	
H. ESTIMATED CLOSING COSTS	
I. DISCOUNT *(Only if borrower permitted to pay)*	
J. TOTAL COSTS *(Add Items 24A through 24I)*	
K. LESS CASH FROM BORROWER	
L. LESS OTHER CREDITS	
M. AMOUNT OF LOAN	$

VA FORM 26-1802a, JAN 1982 HUD FORM 92900.1 | SUPERSEDES VA FORM 26-1802a, APR 1979, WHICH WILL NOT BE USED. HUD FORM 92900, JUL 1980, MAY BE USED FOR HUD PURPOSES. | VA/HUD COPY 1

to the source of such funds which could be the sale of a house, stocks or other items or by death of a relative.

B. Savings Bonds-Other Securities—If savings bonds are to be shown as an asset, the face value should be used unless a schedule of value was given at the time of purchase, in which case the actual value should be used. As for "other securities," HUD-FHA states that these are any assets that are readily converted to cash.

C. Real Estate Owned—This section is self-explanatory.

D. Auto—If an auto is listed as an asset, the amount listed should be based on the replacement value of the vehicle.

E. Furniture and Household Goods—If furniture and household goods are listed as an asset, the amount listed should be equal to the value of household goods listed in the homeowner's insurance policy, unless the goods are itemized and individually appraised.

F. Other—In this category the applicant should list any other item that has cash value and is not listed in section B. This would include jewelry, artwork, or any item for which the value can be established.

The borrower/coborrower lists in block 22 any liabilities or debts, including any real estate loans even though the property is to be sold. The borrower/coborrower also lists all retail accounts, including the name and address and the approximate balance and monthly payments. The borrower/coborrower will also list all bank loans or any other type of long-term debt that may adversely affect his or her credit status. One other important section is Job-Related Expense. Here, the borrower/coborrower should list any costs of child care, union dues, significant commuting costs, group hospitalization, or life insurance deducted from his or her check. These are not all of the job-related expenses, but only some examples. You will need to determine if your client has any of these expenses or any others.

In block 23 the borrower, spouse or coborrower will have to supply employment and salary information for the past two years to indicate income and occupational status. It should be noted that only the primary employment should be listed on the application; any part-time, overtime, and secondary income must be listed separately and attached to the application.

The lender will determine the estimated total cost of the acquisition of the property and put it into block 24. This total cost will include all closing costs and prepaid items. From the total cost, the lender then deducts the amount of the down payment of the borrower/coborrower, which will give the amount of the loan. The amount in box 24M should be the same as the amount in box 8A of the application.

The next major section of the application is on the back of page 1, shown in Figure 13-8. The part of this page that applies to a HUD-FHA-insured loan is Section V—Borrowers Certification. This must be signed by both the borrower, and if there is one, the coborrower.

Question 1 of 31A asks if the borrower/coborrower owns or has sold any real estate in the past twelve months. If the answer is "yes," HUD-FHA wants information about the sales price and the original mortgage amount. HUD-FHA also wants to know if it was insured by HUD-FHA and, if so, the name and address of the lender. The remaining two questions are self-explanatory.

The next part that applies to a HUD-FHA insured loan, 31B, reminds the borrower/coborower of his or her responsibility for repayment of the loan. This section also states that if the property is sold in any other manner than the mortgage having been paid in full, the original borrower/coborrower is still liable for the repayment of the mortgage. However, if HUD-FHA feels the buyer is acceptable, then HUD-FHA will release the original borrower/coborrower from the liability for repayment. The borrower is asked to certify that he or she has read and understands the section of the borrower/coborrower liability for repayment of the loan.

Statement 3 under 31B deals with the valuation and sales price. If the sales price is more than the value set by HUD-FHA, the borrower must attest to paying more than the

Figure 13-8. HUD Form 92900, page 2

SECTION III - LENDER'S CERTIFICATION *(Must be signed by lender)*

The undersigned lender makes the following certifications to induce the Veterans Administration to issue a certificate of commitment to guarantee the subject loan under Title 38, U.S. Code, or to induce the Department of Housing and Urban Development - Federal Housing Commissioner to issue a firm commitment for mortgage insurance under the National Housing Act.

26A. The information furnished in Section I is true, accurate and complete.
26B. The information contained in Section II was obtained directly from the borrower by a full-time employee of the undersigned lender or its duly authorized agent and is true to the best of the lender's knowledge and belief.
26C. The credit report submitted on the subject borrower *(and spouse, if any)* was ordered by the undersigned lender or its duly authorized agent directly from the credit bureau which prepared the report and was received directly from said credit bureau.
26D. The verification of employment and verification of deposits were requested and received by the lender or its duly authorized agent without passing through the hands of any third persons and are true to the best of the lender's knowledge and belief.
26E. This application was signed by the borrower after Sections I, II and V were completed.
26F. This proposed loan to the named borrower meets the income and credit requirements of the governing law in the judgment of the undersigned.
26G through 26I - TO BE COMPLETED OR APPLICABLE FOR VA LOANS ONLY.
26G. The names and functions of any duly authorized agents who developed on behalf of the lender any of the information or supporting credit data submitted are as follows:

	NAME	ADDRESS	FUNCTION *(e.g., obtained information in Sec. II; ordered credit report, verification of employment, verif. of deposits, etc.)*
(1)			
(2)			
(3)			

☐ *(Check box if all information and supporting credit data were obtained directly by the lender.)*
26H. The undersigned lender understands and agrees that it is responsible for the acts of agents identified in item 26G as to the functions with which they are identified.
26I. The proposed loan conforms otherwise with the applicable provisions of Title 38, U.S. Code, and of the regulations concerning guaranty or insurance of loans to veterans.

27. Date	28. Name of Lender	29. Telephone Number *(Include Area Code)*	30. Signature and Title of Officer of Lender

SECTION IV - NOTICE TO BORROWERS

PRIVACY ACT INFORMATION - The information requested in this form is authorized by 38 U.S.C. 1810 *(if VA)* and 12 U.S.C. 1701 et seq., *(if HUD/FHA)* and will be used in determining whether you qualify as a mortgagor. Any disclosure of information outside VA or HUD/FHA will only be made as permitted by law. Disclosure of this information is voluntary but no loan may be approved unless a completed application is received.
NOTICE TO BORROWERS - This is notice to you as required by the Right to Financial Privacy Act of 1978 that the VA or HUD/FHA has a right of access to financial records held by financial institutions in connection with the consideration or administration of assistance to you. Financial records involving your transaction will be available to VA and HUD/FHA without further notice or authorization but will not be disclosed or released to another Government Agency or Department without your consent except as required or permitted by law.

SECTION V - BORROWERS CERTIFICATION *(Must be signed by Borrower(s))*

31A. COMPLETE FOR HUD/FHA INSURED MORTGAGE ONLY.
(1) Do you own or have you sold, within the past 12 months, other real estate? ☐ Yes ☐ No   Is it to be sold? ☐ Yes ☐ No   HUD/FHA Mortgage? ☐ Yes ☐ No   Sales Price $________   Original Mortgage Amount $________

Address: ________   Lender: ________

(2) Have you ever been obligated on a home loan, home improvement loan or a mobile home loan which resulted in foreclosure, transfer of title in lieu of foreclosure or judgment? ☐ Yes ☐ No. If "Yes" give details including date, property address, name and address of lender, FHA or VA Case Number, if any, and reasons for the action.

(3) If dwelling to be covered by this mortgage is to be rented, is it a part of, adjacent or contiguous to any project, subdivision, or group rental properties involving eight or more dwelling units in which you have any financial interest? ☐ Yes ☐ No ☐ Not to be rented. If "Yes" give details. Do you own four or more dwelling units with mortgages insured under any title of the National Housing Act? ☐ Yes ☐ No. If "Yes" submit form HUD-92561.

31B. APPLICABLE FOR BOTH VA AND HUD. As a home loan borrower, you will be legally obligated to make the mortgage payments called for by your mortgage loan contract. The fact that you dispose of your property after the loan has been made WILL NOT RELIEVE YOU OF LIABILITY FOR MAKING THESE PAYMENTS. PAYMENT OF THE LOAN IN FULL IS ORDINARILY THE WAY LIABILITY ON A MORTGAGE NOTE IS ENDED.
Some home buyers have the mistaken impression that if they sell their homes when they move to another locality, or dispose of it for any other reasons, they are no longer liable for the mortgage payments and that liability for these payments is solely that of the new owners. Even though the new owners may agree in writing to assume liability for your mortgage payments, this assumption agreement will not relieve you from liability to the holder of the note which you signed when you obtained the loan to buy the property. Also, unless you are able to sell the property to a buyer who is acceptable to the VA or to HUD/FHA and who will assume the payment of your obligation to the lender, you will not be relieved from liability to repay any claim which the VA or HUD/FHA may be required to pay your lender on account of default in your loan payments. The amount of any such claim payment will be a debt owed by you to the Federal Government. This debt will be the object of established collection procedures.
I, THE UNDERSIGNED BORROWER(S) CERTIFY THAT:
(1) I have read and understand the foregoing concerning my liability on the loan.
(2) VA Only *(check applicable box)* ☐ Purchase or Construction Loan. I now actually occupy the above-described property as my home or intend to move into and occupy said property as my home within a reasonable period of time. ☐ Home Improvement or Refinancing Loan. I own and personally occupy as my home the property described in Item 7 of the Application.
(3) Check applicable box *(not applicable for Home Improvement or Refinancing Loan)*, I have been informed that $ is ☐ the reasonable value of the property as determined by the VA, ☐ the statement of appraised value as determined by HUD/FHA. IF THE CONTRACT PRICE OR COST EXCEEDS THE VA REASONABLE VALUE OR HUD/FHA STATEMENT OF APPRAISED VALUE, COMPLETE EITHER ITEM (a) or (b), WHICHEVER IS APPLICABLE.
(a) ☐ I was aware of this valuation when I signed my contract and I have paid or will pay in cash from my own resources at or prior to loan closing a sum equal to the difference between the contract purchase price or cost and the VA or HUD/FHA established value. I do not and will not have outstanding after loan closing any unpaid contractual obligation on account of such cash payment;
(b) ☐ I was not aware of this valuation when I signed my contract but have elected to complete the transaction at the contract purchase price or cost. I have paid or will pay in cash from my own resources at or prior to loan closing a sum equal to the difference between contract purchase price or cost and the VA or HUD/FHA established value. I do not and will not have outstanding after loan closing any unpaid contractual obligation on account of such cash payment.
(4) Neither I, nor anyone authorized to act for me, will refuse to sell or rent, after the making of a bona fide offer, or refuse to negotiate for the sale or rental of, or otherwise make unavailable or deny the dwelling or property covered by this loan to any person because of race, color, religion, sex or national origin. I recognize that any restrictive covenant on this property relating to race, color, religion, sex or national origin is illegal and void and civil action for preventive relief may be brought by the Attorney General of the United States in any appropriate U.S. District Court against any person responsible for the violation of the applicable law.
(5) The Borrower certifies that all information in this application is given for the purpose of obtaining a loan to be insured under the National Housing Act, or guaranteed by the Veterans Administration and the information in Section II is true and complete to the best of his/her knowledge and belief. Verification may be obtained from any source named herein.
HUD ONLY
(6) For properties constructed prior to 1950 - I have received the brochure "Watchout for Lead Paint Poisoning" ☐ ☐ NA
(7) ☐ I have read and understand the contents of the Home Energy Checklist attached to HUD-92800-4.

READ CERTIFICATIONS CAREFULLY - DO NOT SIGN UNLESS APPLICATION IS FULLY COMPLETED.	32. DATE	33. SIGNATURE OF BORROWER(S) *(Before signing, review accuracy of application and certifications.)*

Federal statutes provide severe penalties for any fraud, intentional misrepresentation, or criminal connivance or conspiracy purposed to influence the issuance of any guaranty or insurance by the VA or USDA-FmHA Administrator or the HUD/FHA Commissioner.

established value and must agree that the difference will be paid in cash.

Next, the borrower/coborrower is asked to certify that renting or selling the property covered by an insured loan will not be denied due to race, creed, religion, sex, or national origin. The final statement is that the borrower/coborrower has made these statements in order to receive a home mortgage insured by the National Housing Act or VA and that the statements are true and complete to the best of his or her knowledge.

After the application is completed, the lender will give page 6 of the form to the borrower (Figure 13-9). The lender will then verify all of the information. Upon receipt of the completed verifications—if the lender feels that the borrower/coborrower and the property meet HUD-FHA requirements—the application along with all of the necessary supporting documents will be sent to HUD-FHA for approval. The lender will retain page 8 of the form. After HUD-FHA has reviewed all of the information and approves the application, the mortgage credit section of the HUD-FHA office will send the lender a Certificate of Commitment (Figure 13-10).

You will notice that sections 1 through 6E are identical to those on page 1 of the form. Since this is a multipage carboned form, these sections were filled out at the time the original application was completed.

Just below the first section is the statement where HUD-FHA accepts the note and the mortgage/deed of trust described in the first section, or will accept the note and mortgage/deed of trust as modified. The modifications, if any, are described just below the statement in the box entitled "Modified and Accepted as Follows."

Another key section of this certificate is the box entitled, "Estimate of Value and Closing Costs." The estimate of value should equal the sales price of the property. Also, the lender will usually supply a copy of the certificate of commitment to the borrower/coborrower.

The VA will use pages 1-3, 6, and 8. Page 1 (Figure 13-7) will be filled out similarly for the VA as it was for HUD-FHA. We will, therefore, only review the differences. First, in the top section of the form, the box indicating that the application is for Home Loan Guaranty will be marked instead of the one indicating mortgage insurance or FmHA-guaranteed loan. The next difference occurs when box 2B is left blank with boxes 1 and 2A completed. Except for boxes 4B and 4C, boxes 3 through 8E are completed as per the discussion above.

Most of Section I—Purpose, Amount, Terms of and Security for Proposed Loan will be completed in the same manner as outlined for HUD-FHA. The one difference is that box 10 instead of box 9B will be completed. In Section II, HUD-FHA did not require completing box 19. VA does require this information and will not process the application if this information is missing.

Page 2 of the application (Figure 13-8) has information that is to be filled out if the mortgage is to be guaranteed by the VA. HUD-FHA did not require the lender to complete Section III, but VA does require the lender to make the certifications. This is not signed by the borrower/coborrower.

In Section V, Borrowers Certification, the veteran does not complete 31A, but does make the required certifications in 31B; then the borrower/coborrower signs in box 33. You will notice the statement just before box 32 tells the borrower/coborrower to read the certifications carefully and not to sign the applications unless the application is completely filled out.

After the application is completed, the lender will give page 6 to the borrower/coborrower and will retain page 8. The remainder of the application, less pages 4 and 5, is then sent along with all of the necessary supporting data to the VA for approval. Upon approval of VA, a completed page 2 (Figure 13-11) will be returned to the lender. Once again we see that the top portion of the Certificate of Commitment was completed at the time the application was completed. The only additional information added by the VA is under the heading, "For VA Use Only." Here, the VA will show the percent of guaranty. This is calculated by dividing $27,500 by the loan amount. For example, the veteran is purchasing a home with a CRV of $84,000. With no money down, the guaranty would be $27,500 divided by $84,000 or 32.7 percent guaranty. Once again the lender will normally give a copy of the certificate of commitment to the borrower/coborrower. It is a good policy, though, to remind the borrower/coborrower to get a copy of this commitment.

Figure 13-9. HUD Form 92900, page 6

Form Approved
OMB No. 2900-0144

VA Application for Home Loan Guaranty	USDA-FmHA Application for FmHA Guaranteed Loan	HUD/FHA Application for Commitment for Insurance under the National Housing Act	1. AGENCY CASE NUMBER	2A. LENDER'S CASE NUMBER	2B. SECTION OF THE ACT (HUD Only)

3. NAME AND PRESENT ADDRESS OF BORROWER *(Include ZIP Code)*

4A. NAME AND ADDRESS OF LENDER *(Include ZIP Code)*

4B. ORIGINATORS' I.D. *(HUD Only)* | 4C. SPONSOR'S I.D. *(HUD Only)*

5A. BORROWER: *If you do not wish to complete Items 5B or 5C, please initial in the space to the right.* | INITIALS

5B. RACE/NATIONAL ORIGIN: 1 WHITE, NOT HISPANIC; 2 BLACK, NOT HISPANIC; 3 AMERICAN INDIAN OR ALASKAN NATIVE; 4 ASIAN OR PACIFIC ISLANDER; 5 HISPANIC

5C. SEX: 1 MALE; 2 FEMALE

6A. SPOUSE OR OTHER BORROWER: *If you do not wish to complete Items 6B or 6C, please initial in space to the right.* | INITIALS

6B. RACE/NATIONAL ORIGIN: 1 WHITE, NOT HISPANIC; 2 BLACK, NOT HISPANIC; 3 AMERICAN INDIAN OR ALASKAN NATIVE; 4 ASIAN OR PACIFIC ISLANDER; 5 HISPANIC

6C. SEX: 1 MALE; 2 FEMALE

7. PROPERTY ADDRESS INCLUDING NAME OF SUBDIVISION, LOT AND BLOCK NO., AND ZIP CODE

8A. LOAN AMOUNT	8B. INT. RATE	8C. PROPOSED MATURITY
$	%	YRS. MOS.
DISCOUNT: *(Only if borrower to pay)*	8D. PERCENT %	8E. AMOUNT $

VA ONLY: Veteran and lender hereby apply to the Administrator of Veterans Affairs for Guaranty of the loan described here under Section 1810, Chapter 37, Title 38, United States Code to the full extent permitted by the veteran's entitlement and severally agree that the Regulations promulgated pursuant to Chapter 37, and in effect on the date of the loan shall govern the rights, duties, and liabilities of the parties.
HUD/FHA ONLY: Mortgagee's application for mortgagor approval and commitment for mortgage insurance under the National Housing Act.

SECTION I - PURPOSE, AMOUNT, TERMS OF AND SECURITY FOR PROPOSED LOAN

9A. PURPOSE OF LOAN – TO: 1 PURCHASE EXISTING HOUSE PREVIOUSLY OCCUPIED; 2 FINANCE IMPROVEMENTS TO EXISTING PROPERTY; 3 REFINANCE; 4 PURCHASE NEW CONDO. UNIT; 5 PURCHASE EXISTING CONDO. UNIT; 6 PURCHASE EXISTING HOME NOT PREVIOUSLY OCCUPIED; 7 CONSTRUCT A HOME - PROCEEDS TO BE PAID OUT DURING CONSTRUCTION; 8 HUD ONLY – FINANCE COOP-PURCHASE

9B. HUD ONLY – BORROWER WILL BE: 1 OCCUPANT; 2 LANDLORD; 3 BUILDER; 4 OPERATIVE BUILDER; 5 ESCROW COMMITMENT

10. VA ONLY – TITLE WILL BE VESTED IN: VETERAN; VETERAN AND SPOUSE; OTHER *(Specify)*

11. LIEN: FIRST MORTGAGE; OTHER *(Specify)*

12. ESTATE WILL BE: FEE SIMPLE; LEASEHOLD *(Show expiration date)*

13. IS THERE A MANDATORY HOMEOWNERS ASSOC.? YES NO *(If "Yes," complete Item 14F.)*

14. ESTIMATED TAXES, INSURANCE AND ASSESSMENTS		15. ESTIMATED MONTHLY PAYMENT	
A. ANNUAL TAXES	$	A. PRINCIPAL AND INTEREST	$
B. AMOUNT OF HAZARD INSURANCE ON SECURITY		B. TAXES AND INSURANCE DEPOSITS	
C. ANNUAL HAZARD INSURANCE PREMIUM		C. OTHER	
D. ANNUAL SPECIAL ASSESSMENT PAYMENT			
E. UNPAID SPECIAL ASSESSMENT BALANCE			
F. ANNUAL MAINTENANCE ASSESSMENT		TOTAL	$

SECTION II - PERSONAL AND FINANCIAL STATUS OF APPLICANT

16. PLEASE CHECK APPROPRIATE BOX(ES). IF ONE OR MORE ARE CHECKED, ITEMS 18B, 21, 22 AND 23 MUST INCLUDE INFORMATION CONCERNING BORROWER'S SPOUSE *(or former spouse if box "D" is checked)*. IF NO BOXES ARE CHECKED, NO INFORMATION CONCERNING THE SPOUSE NEED BE FURNISHED IN ITEMS 18B, 21, 22 AND 23.

A. THE SPOUSE WILL BE JOINTLY OBLIGATED WITH THE BORROWER ON THE LOAN
B. THE BORROWER IS RELYING ON THE SPOUSE'S INCOME AS A BASIS FOR REPAYMENT OF THE LOAN.
C. THE BORROWER IS MARRIED AND THE PROPERTY TO SECURE THE LOAN IS LOCATED IN A COMMUNITY PROPERTY STATE.
D. THE BORROWER IS RELYING ON ALIMONY, CHILD SUPPORT, OR SEPARATE MAINTENANCE PAYMENTS FROM A SPOUSE OR FORMER SPOUSE AS A BASIS FOR REPAYMENT OF THE LOAN.

17A. MARITAL STATUS OF BORROWER	17B. MARITAL STATUS OF COBORROWER OTHER THAN SPOUSE	17C. MONTHLY CHILD SUPPORT OBLIGATION	17D. MONTHLY ALIMONY OBLIGATION	18A. AGE OF BORROWER	18B. AGE OF SPOUSE OR COBORROWER	18C. AGE(S) OF DEPENDENT(S)
1 MARRIED 3 UNMARRIED 2 SEPARATED	1 MARRIED 3 UNMARRIED 2 SEPARATED	$	$			

19. NAME AND ADDRESS OF NEAREST LIVING RELATIVE *(Include telephone number, if available).* | 20A. CURRENT MONTHLY HOUSING EXPENSE $ | 20B. UTILITIES INCLUDED? YES NO

21. ASSETS		22. LIABILITIES *(Itemize all debts)*		
A. CASH *(Including deposit on purchase)*	$	NAME OF CREDITOR	MO. PAYMENT	BALANCE
B. SAVINGS BONDS - OTHER SECURITIES			$	$
C. REAL ESTATE OWNED				
D. AUTO				
E. FURNITURE AND HOUSEHOLD GOODS				
F. OTHER *(Use separate sheet, if necessary)*		JOB-RELATED EXPENSE *(Specify)*		
G. TOTAL	$	TOTAL	$	$

23. INCOME AND OCCUPATIONAL STATUS

ITEM	BORROWER		SPOUSE OR COBORROWER	
A. OCCUPATION				
B. NAME OF EMPLOYER				
C. NUMBER OF YEARS EMPLOYED				
D. GROSS PAY	MONTHLY $	HOURLY $	MONTHLY $	HOURLY $
E. OTHER INCOME *(Disclosure of child support, alimony and separate maintenance income is optional.)*	MONTHLY $		MONTHLY $	

NOTE – If land acquired by separate transaction, complete Items 25A and 25B.

25A. DATE ACQUIRED | 25B. UNPAID BALANCE $

24. ESTIMATED TOTAL COST

ITEM	AMOUNT
A. PURCHASE EXISTING HOME	$
B. ALTERATIONS, IMPROVEMENTS, REPAIRS	
C. CONSTRUCTION	
D. LAND *(If acquired separately)*	
E. PURCHASE OF CONDOMINIUM UNIT	
F. REFINANCE	
G. PREPAID ITEMS	
H. ESTIMATED CLOSING COSTS	
I. DISCOUNT *(Only if borrower permitted to pay)*	
J. TOTAL COSTS *(Add Items 24A through 24I)*	
K. LESS CASH FROM BORROWER	
L. LESS OTHER CREDITS	
M. AMOUNT OF LOAN	$

VA FORM 26-1802a, JAN 1982
HUD FORM 92900.6

SUPERSEDES VA FORM 26-1802a, APR 1979, WHICH WILL NOT BE USED. HUD FORM 92900, JUL 1980, MAY BE USED FOR HUD PURPOSES.

DELIVER TO BORROWER - COPY 6

Figure 13-10. HUD Certificate of Commitment sent to lender

CERTIFICATE OF COMMITMENT
(FOR HUD INSURED MORTGAGE)

1. AGENCY CASE NUMBER | 2A. LENDER'S CASE NUMBER | 2B. SECTION OF THE ACT *(HUD Only)*

3. NAME AND PRESENT ADDRESS OF BORROWER *(Include ZIP Code)*

4A. NAME AND ADDRESS OF LENDER *(Include ZIP Code)*

4B. ORIGINATOR'S I.D. | 4C. SPONSOR'S I.D.

5. PROPERTY ADDRESS INCLUDING NAME OF SUBDIVISION, LOT AND BLOCK NO., AND ZIP CODE

6A. LOAN AMOUNT	6B. INT. RATE	6C. PROPOSED MATURITY
$	%	YRS. MOS.
DISCOUNT: *(Only if borrower to pay)*	6D. PERCENT %	6E. AMOUNT $

☐ ACCEPTED: A note and mortgage described above or as modified below will be insured under the National Housing Act provided one of the mortgagors will be an owner-occupant and all conditions appearing in any outstanding commitment issued under the above case number and those set forth below are fulfilled.

IMPROVED FLOOR AREA = square feet.

☐ MODIFIED AND ACCEPTED AS FOLLOWS	Mortgage Amount	Interest Rate	No. of Months	Monthly Payment
	$	%		$

ESTIMATE OF VALUE AND CLOSING COSTS

VALUE OF PROPERTY $________

Closing Costs $________

ADDITIONAL CONDITIONS

☐ 2544 - Builders warranty required. ☐ Owner-occupancy NOT required. *(Delete (b) - Mtgrs. Cert.)*
☐ The property is to be insured under Section 221(d)(2); a code compliance inspection is required.

This is to certify, in compliance with the Right to Financial Privacy Act of 1978, that, in connection with any subsequent request for access to financial records for the purpose of considering or administering assistance to this applicant, the Department of Housing and Urban Development is in compliance with the applicable provisions of said Act.

DATE OF THIS COMMITMENT:

________, 19 ____

THIS COMMITMENT EXPIRES:

________, 19
(Expiration Date)

____
(Authorized Agent for the Federal Housing Commissioner)

____
(Field Office)

INSTRUCTIONS TO MORTGAGEE - Forward to the HUD Field Office; (1) this commitment signed by the mortgagee and mortgagor; (2) a copy of the note or other credit instrument; (3) a copy of the mortgage or other security instrument; (4) a copy of the settlement statement, *(Form HUD-1)* signed by the mortgagee which itemizes all charges and fees collected by the mortgagee from the mortgagor and seller; and (5) HUD/FHA Mortgage Insurance Certificate completed with case number, Section of the National Housing Act, mortgage amount, property address, mortgagors' names and mortgagee's name and address. Attach Form HUD-92900 Supplement.

HUD 92900.4, JAN 1982 | LENDER COPY 4

VERIFICATION FORMS

As with the application forms, various lenders have forms to verify employment, income, deposits, mortgage loan payments, rental history, and credit. In this discussion we will examine those forms approved or authorized by FNMA/FHLMC, FHA, and VA.

Verification of Employment and Income

FNMA Form 1005, "Request for Verification of Employment," is illustrated in Figure 13-12. The form is divided into three sections. The first section is to be completed by the lender. This section is usually completed at the time of application and is signed by the applicant. Normally the lender will have the applicant sign several of the forms, just in case the original form that is sent to the employer is lost. The second section of the form is to be completed by the present employer. The employer states that the applicant or co-applicant is still in his employment. You will notice that Part II of Figure 13-12 is divided into two parts: employment record and pay data. As mentioned in Chapter 12, line 13 of the employment section inquires about the existence of overtime and/or bonuses, and, if they are paid, what the likelihood is of their continuance in the future. Part III of the form, "Verification of

Figure 13-11. VA Certificate of Commitment sent to lender

CERTIFICATE OF COMMITMENT (FOR VA LOAN GUARANTY)	1. AGENCY CASE NUMBER	2A. LENDER'S CASE NUMBER	2B. SECTION OF THE ACT *(HUD Only)*
3. NAME AND PRESENT ADDRESS OF BORROWER *(Include ZIP Code)*			
4. NAME AND ADDRESS OF LENDER *(Include ZIP Code)*			

5. PROPERTY ADDRESS INCLUDING NAME OF SUBDIVISION, LOT AND BLOCK NO., AND ZIP CODE	6A. LOAN AMOUNT $	6B. INT. RATE %	6C. PROPOSED MATURITY YRS. MOS.
	DISCOUNT: *(Only if borrower to pay)*	6D. PERCENT %	6E. AMOUNT $

FOR VA USE ONLY *(To be completed by VA and returned to lender.)*

PERCENT OF GUARANTY %	☐ CERTIFICATION OF ACTIVE DUTY STATUS AS OF DATE OF NOTE REQUIRED *(Applicable if checked)*

TERMS OF COMMITMENT

The documents submitted in connection with the loan described above on this certificate have been examined and the loan has been determined to be eligible under Chapter 37, Title 38, U.S.C., and the regulations effective thereunder.

Upon receipt of a duly executed "Certificate of Loan Disbursement"* showing full compliance with the applicable regulations, the Administrator will issue: A Loan Guaranty Certificate as indicated above on this Certificate; subject to any adjustment necessary under Section 36:4303(g) of the Regulations upon ascertainment of the exact principal amount of the loan, or upon submission of the loan disbursement report under Section 36:4305 thereof.

In the case of a joint loan as defined in Section 36:4307 of the Regulations the portion of such loan eligible for guaranty shall be as provided therein.

This Certificate of Commitment will expire and will be invalid 6 months from the date hereof, unless the loan described herein is closed prior to such expiration date.

*If the loan described above on this Certificate is made by the lending institution named herein this certificate need not be returned to the VA. Otherwise this certificate or a copy of the agreement assigning this certificate must accompany the Certificate of Loan Disbursement.

ADMINISTRATOR OF VETERANS AFFAIRS, BY *(Authorized Agent)*	ISSUING OFFICE	DATE

VA FORM JAN 1982 **26-1866a** LENDER COPY 2

Previous Employment," is to be filled out by the employer only if the person signing the request is no longer an employee. This form will be forwarded directly to the employer and upon its completion the employer will return the completed form directly to the lender. Do not ask the lender if you can hand carry the verification to help speed up approval; the statement at the bottom specifies that the form must be transmitted directly to the lender without passing through the hands of the applicant or any other party.

The second employment verification form to be reviewed is the one used by both FHA and VA, illustrated in Figure 13-13. This form is divided into four sections and requests basically the same information as the FNMA form. There is one major difference and that is item 3, where FHA and VA require the lender to certify that the verification was sent directly to the employer and has not passed through the hands of any other party. As with the FNMA form, the FHA/VA form part I is completed at the time of application and signed by the applicant.

Verification of Bank Accounts and Loans

FNMA Form 1006, entitled "Request for Verification of Deposit," is shown in Figure 13-14. This form is divided into two sections. The first section is completed by the lender

Figure 13-12. FNMA Request for Verification of Employment

FNMA

Federal National Mortgage Association

REQUEST FOR VERIFICATION OF EMPLOYMENT

INSTRUCTIONS: LENDER- Complete items 1 thru 7. Have applicant complete item 8. Forward directly to employer named in item 1.
EMPLOYER-Please complete either Part II or Part III as applicable. Sign and return directly to lender named in item 2.

PART I REQUEST

1. TO *(Name and address of employer)*	2. FROM *(Name and address of lender)*

3. SIGNATURE OF LENDER	4. TITLE	5. DATE	6. LENDER'S NUMBER *(optional)*

I have applied for a mortgage loan and stated that I am now or was formerly employed by you. My signature below authorizes verification of this information.

7. NAME AND ADDRESS OF APPLICANT *(Include employee or badge number)*	8. SIGNATURE OF APPLICANT

PART II - VERIFICATION OF PRESENT EMPLOYMENT

EMPLOYMENT DATA

9. APPLICANT'S DATE OF EMPLOYMENT

10. PRESENT POSITION

11. PROBABILITY OF CONTINUED EMPLOYMENT

13. IF OVERTIME OR BONUS IS APPLICABLE, IS ITS CONTINUANCE LIKELY?

OVERTIME ☐ YES ☐ NO
BONUS ☐ YES ☐ NO

PAY DATA

12A. BASE PAY ☐ ANNUAL ☐ MONTHLY ☐ WEEKLY ☐ HOURLY ☐ OTHER *(specify)*

12B. EARNINGS

TYPE	YEAR TO DATE	PAST YEAR
BASE PAY	$	$
OVERTIME	$	$
COMMISSIONS	$	$
BONUS	$	$

12C. FOR MILITARY PERSONNEL ONLY

PAY GRADE

TYPE	MONTHLY AMOUNT
BASE PAY	$
RATIONS	$
FLIGHT OR HAZARD	$
CLOTHING	$
QUARTERS	$
PRO PAY	$
OVER SEAS OR COMBAT	$

14. REMARKS *(if paid hourly, please indicate average hours worked each week during current and past year)*

PART III - VERIFICATION OF PREVIOUS EMPLOYMENT

15. DATES OF EMPLOYMENT	16. SALARY/WAGE AT TERMINATION PER (Year) (Month) (Week) BASE ______ OVERTIME ______ COMMISSIONS ______ BONUS ______

17. REASON FOR LEAVING	18. POSITION HELD

The above information is provided in strict confidence in response to your request.

19. SIGNATURE OF EMPLOYER	20. TITLE	21. DATE

The information on this form is Confidential. It is to be transmitted directly to the lender, without passing through the hands of the applicant or any other party.

PREVIOUS EDITIONS MAY BE USED UNTIL OCT. 1, 1977

FNMA Form 1005
Feb. 77

Figure 13-13. FHA/VA Request for Verification of Employment

Form Approved
OMB No. 2502-0059

PRIVACY ACT NOTICE: This information is to be used by the agency collecting it in determining whether you qualify as a prospective mortgagor or borrower under its program. It will not be disclosed outside the agency without your consent except to your employer(s) for verification of employment and as required and permitted by law. You do not have to give us this information, but if you do not your application for approval as a prospective mortgagor or borrower may be delayed or rejected. The information requested in this form is authorized by Title 38, U.S.C., Chapter 37 *(if VA)*; by 12 U.S.C., Section 1701 et seq. *(if HUD/FHA)*; by 42 U.S.C., Section 1452b *(if HUD/CPD)*; and Title 42, U.S.C., 1471 et seq., or 7 U.S.C., 1921 et seq. *(if U.S.D.A., FmHA)*.

VETERANS ADMINISTRATION,
U.S.D.A., FARMERS HOME ADMINISTRATION, AND
U.S. DEPARTMENT OF HOUSING AND URBAN DEVELOPMENT -
(Community Planning and Development, and
Housing - Federal Housing Commissioner)

REQUEST FOR VERIFICATION OF EMPLOYMENT

INSTRUCTIONS

LENDER OR LOCAL PROCESSING AGENCY (LPA): Complete Items 1 through 7. Have the applicant complete Item 8. Forward the completed form directly to the employer named in Item 1. EMPLOYER: Complete either Parts II and IV or Parts III and IV. Return form directly to the Lender or Local Processing Agency named in Item 2 of Part I.

PART I - REQUEST

1. TO: *(Name and Address of Employer)*

2. FROM: *(Name and Address of Lender or Local Processing Agency)*

3. *I certify that this verification has been sent directly to the employer and has not passed through the hands of the applicant or any other interested party.*

(Signature of Lender, Official of LPA, or FmHA Loan Packager)

4. TITLE OF LENDER, OFFICIAL OF LPA, OR FmHA LOAN PACKAGER

5. DATE

6. HUD/FHA/CPD, VA, OR FmHA NO.

7. NAME AND ADDRESS OF APPLICANT

I have applied for a mortgage loan or a rehabilitation loan and stated that I am/was employed by you. My signature in the block below authorizes verification of my employment information.

8. EMPLOYEE'S IDENTIFICATION

SIGNATURE OF APPLICANT

PART II - VERIFICATION OF PRESENT EMPLOYMENT

EMPLOYMENT DATA

9. APPLICANT'S DATE OF EMPLOYMENT

10. PRESENT POSITION

11. PROBABILITY OF CONTINUED EMPLOYMENT

13. IF OVERTIME OR BONUS IS APPLICABLE, IS ITS CONTINUANCE LIKELY?

OVERTIME ☐ Yes ☐ No
BONUS ☐ Yes ☐ No

PAY DATA

12A. BASE PAY *(Current)*

$______ ☐ Annual $______ ☐ Hourly
$______ ☐ Monthly $______ ☐ Weekly
$______ ☐ Other *(Specify)*

12B. EARNINGS

Type	Year to Date	Past Year
BASE PAY	$	$
OVERTIME	$	$
COMMISSIONS	$	$
BONUS	$	$

FOR MILITARY PERSONNEL ONLY

Type	Monthly Amount
BASE PAY	$
RATIONS	$
FLIGHT OR HAZARD	$
CLOTHING	$
QUARTERS	$
PRO PAY	$
OVERSEAS OR COMBAT	$

14. REMARKS *(If paid hourly, please indicate average hours worked each week during current and past year)*

PART III - VERIFICATION OF PREVIOUS EMPLOYMENT

15. DATES OF EMPLOYMENT

16. SALARY/WAGE AT TERMINATION PER ☐ YEAR ☐ MONTH ☐ WEEK

BASE PAY	OVERTIME	COMMISSIONS	BONUS
$	$	$	$

17. REASONS FOR LEAVING

18. POSITION HELD

PART IV - CERTIFICATION

Federal statutes provide severe penalties for any fraud, intentional misrepresentation, or criminal connivance or conspiracy purposed to influence the issuance of any guaranty or insurance by the VA Administrator, the U.S.D.A., FmHA Administrator, the HUD/FHA Commissioner, or the HUD/CPD Assistant Secretary.

19. SIGNATURE

20. TITLE OF EMPLOYER

21. DATE

Previous Editions May be Used until Supply is Exhausted

HUD-6233/92004-g; VA 26-8497; FmHA-410-5 (12-80)

RETURN DIRECTLY TO LENDER OR LOCAL PROCESSING AGENCY

from information supplied by the applicant and is signed by the applicant, authorizing the financial institution to release the information to the lender. The second section of the form is to be completed by the financial institution. The financial institution is asked to give information about the deposit accounts and outstanding loans of the applicant. In the section dealing with deposit accounts, the financial institution is asked to give the current balance and also the average balance for the previous two months There is reason for such a request. For example, if the present balance in the account is $10,000 and the average balance for the previous two months has been only $3000, the lender will ask the applicant to explain the reason for the radical increase. The applicant can do this by writing a source of funds letter. A sample of such a letter will be given later, in Figure 13-18. In item 12a, the institution is asked to give any additional information that may aid the lender in determining the credit worthiness of the applicant. This should include information about loans which have been paid in full.

The FHA/VA form entitled "Request for Verification of Deposit," Figure 13-15, requests similar information as the FNMA form, but once again the form is somewhat different. As with the employment verification form, the lender is once again required to certify that the verification was sent directly to the bank and that the form did not pass through the hands of the applicant or any other interested party. One major difference in the verification part of the form is that FHA/VA does not ask about the average balance for the past two months. They only ask if the account has been opened for less than two months. The actual date of the opening is to be given in Part II, item 11B.

Mortgage Verification and/or Rental Verification

If the applicant has made mortgage payments, the lender will wish to verify the mortgage as to the type of mortgage, the original date and amount of the mortgage, and the payment record of the applicant. If the applicant and/or co-applicant have rented previously, the lender will verify with the landlord, rental agent, or manager of the property the dates of the rental period and the manner of payment of the applicant or co-applicant. An example of a mortgage verification letter is shown in Figure 13-16 and a sample rental verification letter is shown in Figure 13-17.

Credit Verification

The credit of an applicant is verified by the lender by ordering a credit report from the local credit-reporting agency. The report will give the applicant's payment history on accounts or loans held by members of the credit-reporting agency. By federal law, the applicant and co-applicant are not allowed to view their credit reports furnished to the mortgage lender. It should also be noted that if the lender rejects the application and it, along with all of the supporting data, is transferred to another mortgage lender, the credit report may not be transferred and a new report will have to be ordered from the credit-reporting agency. If the applicant or co-applicant wishes to inquire into his or her credit, he must go personally to the credit reporting agency and request to view the information contained in his file. The applicant or co-applicant will not be allowed to view the actual file, but will be able to see an abstract of the information in the file. The cost of these reports is usually paid by the applicant or co-applicant.

Source of Funds Letter

As mentioned earlier in the section on bank account verification, if the balance in a checking or savings account has had a marked increase in the past two months, the lender may request that the applicant or co-applicant furnish information as to the source of funds for the increase. If the source of funds is the sale of property, the applicant and co-applicant must supply a letter stating the source and furnish a copy of the settlement statement covering the transfer of the property. An example of such a letter is shown in Figure 13-18.

If the additional funds were derived from a gift, then the lender may ask the applicant or co-applicant to furnish a letter stating that the money deposited was a gift and the giver does not expect the funds to be repayed. A form for such a letter is shown in Figure 13-19.

Figure 13-14. FNMA Request for Verification of Deposit

FNMA

Federal National Mortgage Association

REQUEST FOR VERIFICATION OF DEPOSIT

INSTRUCTIONS: LENDER - *Complete Items 1 thru 8. Have applicant(s) complete Item 9. Forward directly to depository named in Item 1.*

DEPOSITORY - *Please complete Items 10 thru 15 and return DIRECTLY to lender named in Item 2.*

PART I - REQUEST

1. TO *(Name and address of depository)*	2. FROM *(Name and address of lender)*

3. SIGNATURE OF LENDER	4. TITLE	5. DATE	6. LENDER'S NUMBER *(Optional)*

7. INFORMATION TO BE VERIFIED

TYPE OF ACCOUNT	ACCOUNT IN NAME OF	ACCOUNT NUMBER	BALANCE
			$
			$
			$
			$

TO DEPOSITORY: *I have applied for a mortgage loan and stated in my financial statement that the balance on deposit with you is as shown above. You are authorized to verify this information and to supply the lender identified above with the information requested in Items 10 thru 12. Your response is solely a matter of courtesy for which no responsibility is attached to your institution or any of your officers.*

8. NAME AND ADDRESS OF APPLICANT(s)	9. SIGNATURE OF APPLICANT(s)

TO BE COMPLETED BY DEPOSITORY

PART II - VERIFICATION OF DEPOSITORY

10. DEPOSIT ACCOUNTS OF APPLICANT(s)

TYPE OF ACCOUNT	ACCOUNT NUMBER	CURRENT BALANCE	AVERAGE BALANCE FOR PREVIOUS TWO MONTHS	DATE OPENED
		$	$	
		$	$	
		$	$	
		$	$	

11. LOANS OUTSTANDING TO APPLICANT(s)

LOAN NUMBER	DATE OF LOAN	ORIGINAL AMOUNT	CURRENT BALANCE	INSTALLMENTS *(Monthly/Quarterly)*	SECURED BY	NUMBER OF LATE PAYMENTS
		$	$	$ per		
		$	$	$ per		
		$	$	$ per		

12. ADDITIONAL INFORMATION WHICH MAY BE OF ASSISTANCE IN DETERMINATION OF CREDIT WORTHINESS *(Please include information on loans paid-in-full as in Item 11 above)*

Subject to the requirements of the Fair Credit Reporting Act, the information provided in Items 10 thru 12 is furnished to you in strict confidence in response to your request. The accuracy of such information is not guaranteed.

13. SIGNATURE OF DEPOSITORY	14. TITLE	15. DATE

This form is to be transmitted directly to the lender and is not to be transmitted through the applicant or any other party.

FNMA Form 1006
Rev. Dec. 75

★ ★ ★ ★ THIS FORM MUST BE REPRODUCED BY LENDER ★ ★ ★ ★

Figure 13-15. FHA/VA Request for Verification of Deposit

Form Approved
OMB No. 63R-1062

VETERANS ADMINISTRATION AND U.S. DEPARTMENT OF HOUSING AND URBAN DEVELOPMENT
HUD COMMUNITY PLANNING AND DEVELOPMENT
HUD HOUSING - FEDERAL HOUSING COMMISSIONER

REQUEST FOR VERIFICATION OF DEPOSIT

PRIVACY ACT NOTICE STATEMENT - This information is to be used by the agency collecting it in determining whether you qualify as a prospective mortgagor for mortgage insurance or guaranty or as a borrower for a rehabilitation loan under the agency's program. It will not be disclosed outside the agency without your consent except to financial institutions for verification of your deposits and as required and permitted by law. You do not have to give us this information, but, if you do not, your application for approval as a prospective mortgagor for mortgage insurance or guaranty or as a borrower for a rehabilitation loan may be delayed or rejected. This information request is authorized by Title 38, U.S.C., Chapter 37 *(if VA)*; by 12 U.S.C., Section 1701 et seq., *(if HUD/FHA)*; and by 42 U.S.C., Section 1452b *(if HUD/CPD)*.

INSTRUCTIONS

LENDER OR LOCAL PROCESSING AGENCY: Complete Items 1 through 8. Have applicant(s) complete Item 9. Forward directly to the Depository named in Item 1. DEPOSITORY: Please complete Items 10 through 15 and return DIRECTLY to Lender or Local Processing Agency named in Item 2.

PART I - REQUEST

1. TO *(Name and Address of Depository)*	2. FROM *(Name and Address of Lender or Local Processing Agency)*

I certify that this verification has been sent directly to the bank or depository and has not passed through the hands of the applicant or any other party.

3. Signature of Lender or Official of Local Processing Agency	4. Title	5. Date	6. Lender's Number *(Optional)*

7. INFORMATION TO BE VERIFIED:

Type of Account and/or Loan	Account/Loan in Name of	Account/Loan Number	Balance
			$
			$
			$
			$

TO DEPOSITORY: I have applied for mortgage insurance or guaranty or for a rehabilitation loan and stated that the balance on deposit and/or outstanding loans with you are as shown above. You are authorized to verify this information and to supply the lender or the local processing agency identified above with the information requested in Items 10 through 12. Your response is solely a matter of courtesy for which no responsibility is attached to your institution or any of your officers.

8. NAME AND ADDRESS OF APPLICANT(S)	9. SIGNATURE OF APPLICANT(S)

TO BE COMPLETED BY DEPOSITORY

PART II - VERIFICATION OF DEPOSITORY

10. DEPOSIT ACCOUNTS OF APPLICANT(S)

Type of Account	Account Number	Current Balance	Average Balance for Previous Two Months	Date Opened
		$	$	
		$	$	
		$	$	
		$	$	

11. LOANS OUTSTANDING TO APPLICANT(S)

Loan Number	Date of Loan	Original Amount	Current Balance	Installments *(Monthly/Quarterly)*	Secured by	Number of Late Payments within Last 12 Months
		$	$	$ per		
		$	$	$ per		
		$	$	$ per		

12. ADDITIONAL INFORMATION WHICH MAY BE OF ASSISTANCE IN DETERMINATION OF CREDIT WORTHINESS: *Please include information on loans paid-in-full as in Item 11 above)*

13. Signature of Depository Official	14. Title	15. Date

The confidentiality of the information you have furnished will be preserved except where disclosure of this information is required by applicable law. The completed form is to be transmitted directly to the lender or local processing agency and is not to be transmitted through the applicant or any other party.

Replaces Form FHA-2004-F, which is Obsolete

VA 26-8497a/HUD-92004-F-6234 (7-80)

Figure 13-16. Mortgage Verification Form

MORTGAGE VERIFICATION

APPLICANT ____________________ ADDRESS ____________________
CO-APPLICANT ____________________ ADDRESS ____________________
LOAN NUMBER ____________________ DATE ____________________

Since the previous/present mortgagor has applied for a new loan through this company, the current status of the mortgage on the subject property is required. We will appreciate your answering the questions listed below. Please return this letter in the enclosed self-addressed envelope provided.

As per your request, the following information is furnished in strict confidence and is not to be construed as a pay-off figure.

Approved:
Applicant ____________________ Co-applicant ____________________

Yours very truly
Loan Processor

1. Original Mortgagor ____________________ Date of Mortgage ____________________
2. Original Amount and Term: $ ____________________ Years ____________________
3. Type of Mortgage: Conv __________ VA __________ FHA __________
4. Present Unpaid Balance: $ __________ ; Payment Experience:
   Prompt ______ Slow ______ Unsatisfactory ______

   If the above loan is an FHA or VA loan now owned by persons other than above, please give the following information:

5. Date of Assumption ____________________ Name of Assumptor ____________________
6. Payment experience of the assumptor ____________________
7. Status of Loan ____________________

Date ____________________ ____________________
Mortgagee

____
Signature and Title

Source: Mercantile Mortgage Corporation of Texas, Houston, Texas

Figure 13-17. Rental Verification Form

RENTAL VERIFICATION

APPLICANT ____________________ ADDRESS ____________________
CO-APPLICANT ____________________ ADDRESS ____________________

The above mentioned persons have applied for a new mortgage through this mortgage company, and have indicated that they have been a renter/leaser from your organization.

We would appreciate your answering the questions listed below and returning the same to us in the self-addressed envelope provided. Your prompt consideration to this matter will be greatly appreciated.

Approved:
APPLICANT ____________________ CO-APPLICANT ____________________
DATE __________ DATE __________

As per your request, the following information is furnished:

1. How long has the applicant/co-applicant been renting __________, leasing __________?
2. Amount of monthly rent $__________ Does this rent or lease payment include utilities?
   Yes ______ No ______
3. Manner of payment:
   Prompt ______ Slow ______ Unsatisfactory ______

Date ____________________ ____________________
Manager/Landlord

Source: Mercantile Mortgage Corporation of Texas, Houston, Texas

Figure 13-18. Source of Funds Letter

EXAMPLE

SOURCE OF FUNDS LETTER

Date

XYZ Mortgage Company
123 Main Street
Houston, Texas 77001

Gentlemen:

This is to certify that the $11,500.00 that I have deposited to our account at the First State Bank of Bellaire, Bellaire, Texas, was recently deposited. This money was realized from the sale of my home located at 3456 Limping Lane, La Grange, Texas. This sale was closed on February 15, 1982 at American Title, La Grange, Texas. A copy of the closing statement is attached.

Sincerely,

Applicant________________________ Co-applicant________________________

Source: Mortgage Bankers Association of America, Washington, D.C.

Figure 13-19. Gift Letter and Receipt Acknowledgement

EXAMPLE

GIFT LETTER

To Whom it may concern:

I, __________________________, do hereby certify that I have made a gift of $___________________ to my (relationship) ______, to be used for the purchase of the property located at _________________________.

I hereby further certify there is no repayment expected or implied on this gift either in the form of cash or services in the future from ____ (applicant) ______ or ____ (co-applicant) ____.

Date___________________ ______________________________
Donor

RECEIPT ACKNOWLEDGEMENT

We or I ___________________________, __________________________ hereby certify that we or I have received a gift in the amount of $_____ ____________ from _________________________ my (relationship) ____ and that it is to be applied toward the purchase of the property located at ____.

Date___________________ ______________________________
Applicant

____
Co-applicant

Source: Mortgage Bankers Association of America, Washington, D.C.

LOAN PACKAGING OR COLLATION

After the loan application is completed and the supporting documents that will accompany the application are received, the mortgage lender will then start to gather the information required for underwriting. This collection of information is sometimes referred to as *loan packaging*. The loan package required by lenders will vary, but in the following section we will review some of the standard items that can make up a loan package.

Conventional Loan Packaging

Since many conventional lenders have their own requirements, any of the following items may be included in the conventional loan package.

1. Submission letter (This is a cover letter outlining the items enclosed in the loan package. Usually, the letter will outline the terms and loan-to-value ratio of the mortgage. If the mortgage is one to be purchased by FNMA, they require a form entitled Transmittal Summary, in place of the submission letter.)
2. Loan application
3. Standard factual credit report (This credit report should be current. Many lenders require the report to be less than ninety days old and provided by an approved credit-reporting agency. Many lenders, including FNMA/FHLMC, FHA, and VA, have a list of approved credit-reporting agencies. It should be noted that if the credit report is from an agency that is not approved by the lender, the loan package may be rejected or the lender will order a credit report from the approved agency. In either case, processing or approval time will be increased.)
4. Verification of deposits
5. Verification of employment
6. If the applicant is self-employed, the following information will be supplied in lieu of the verification of employment:
    a. Business credit report
    b. Signed federal income tax returns for the past two years
    c. If available, an audited profit-and-loss statement and balance sheets for the past two years
7. Verification of previous mortgage and payment record or rental verification with payment record
8. Property appraisal on the lender's approved form
9. Floor plan and plot sketch
10. Photographs of the property. (Many lenders require several pictures of the property showing the front, back, and a view looking both ways from the front.)
11. A copy of the earnest money contract
12. If PMI is required by the lender, a copy of the PMI commitment

Federal Housing Administration Loan Packaging

An FHA loan package may include the following items:

1. Loan application, page 1 of FHA Form 2900
2. The conditional commitment, FHA Form 2800, page 5
3. A copy of the earnest money contract
4. A credit report from an FHA-approved credit reporting agency less than ninety days old
5. Verification of employment
6. Verification of deposits
7. Other documents that may be included:
    a. Source of funds letter
    b. Gift letter

c. If the applicant is self-employed, a business credit report, signed federal income tax returns for the past two years and, if available, profit-and-loss statement and balance sheets for the current period of operation

d. A letter from the mortgage company or lender explaining or giving support to the application for mortgage insurance

Veterans Administration Loan Packaging

A VA loan package may include the following items:

1. Transmittal letter, outlining the loan and the documents that are included in the package (In some areas, the VA guaranty section requires that the documents be in a specific order.)

2. Certificate of Eligibility

3. Loan application, VA Form 26-1802a

4. Copy of the earnest money contract

5. Credit report from an approved credit-reporting agency

6. Verification of employment

7. Verification of deposits

8. A copy of the Certificate of Reasonable Value, VA Form 26-1843

9. Borrower's statement of liability, VA Form 26-8106 (This is a statement signed by the veteran stating that if the VA approves the application for home loan guaranty, the veteran is obligated to repay the mortgage.)

Once the loan package is completed, the next step is for the package to be forwarded to the lender for underwriting, or if the originating mortgage company or financial institution has the ability or authority, the loan package will be approved or underwritten by the originator.

LOAN UNDERWRITING OR APPROVAL

Loan underwriting is the analysis or evaluation of the risk involved with a loan and matching the risk to the proper return.

Areas of Concern

Many lenders now use the concept that the property is the primary concern in the underwriting process. The reason for this was the introduction of the long-term self-amortizing mortgage. Many lenders use the theory, "If the borrower defaults, will we be able to sell the property for a sufficient amount to recapture the amount of the mortgage?" But it should be noted that the borrower is still of concern to the lender. This analysis of the risk is sometimes referred to as the analysis of the "Four Cs": Character, Capacity, Capital, and Collateral. One can see that the majority of the Four Cs relates to the applicant and the final C relates to the property. Let us examine the Four Cs.

Character This is an analysis of the applicant and co-applicant's trustworthiness, their reputations, and most of all, their demonstration to meet their financial obligations. The lender uses the credit report and the verification of payment record on the previous mortgage or payment of rent as a good indicator of a person's sense of obligation. If the person is self-employed, the lender will review the payment record of the applicant or co-applicant in relation to the financial obligation of the business. Lenders will see will see if the applicant or co-applicant will pay himself or herself first and let the obligation of the company go without payment.

Capacity This is the analysis of the earning ability of the applicant or co-applicant. In this analysis, the lender will look not only at the present earning ability, but will try to evaluate the future capability of the applicants. The lender will take into consideration the training, educational experiences, and need for the skills possessed by the applicants. For example, if the applicant is a master plumber, the lender is somewhat assured that the applicant's skills will be in demand in the future.

Capital This analysis looks at the cash and assets of the applicant and co-applicant, in particular to see if the assets of the applicant and co-applicant exceed the liabilities. In addition, some lenders take into consideration the type of assets owned and, if the applicant and co-applicant need to sell any of these assets, how quickly can they be converted to cash.

Collateral The last of the Four Cs is the property that will be used to secure the mortgage. As stated earlier in this section, many lenders place more emphasis on this aspect of underwriting. Here the underwriter will review the property as to location, neighborhood, supply and demand in the area, construction, and marketability in case of foreclosure. The underwriter will take into consideration the purchase price of the property in relationship to the average sale price for other properties in the area. If the applicant is marginal, but is buying the property several thousand dollars below the average sale price in the area, the lender may look favorably upon the application and approve the loan.

How Loans Are Underwritten

Because loan underwriting has been discussed in an earlier chapter, this will be a brief review.

Mortgage companies Usually these types of lenders do not have the ability to approve or underwrite mortgages. They usually process the mortgage and after the packaging of the mortgage, review the information. If they feel the application meets the underwriting requirements of the investor, the package will be sent to the investor for approval. It should be noted that through the Delegated Underwriter Program some mortgage companies have the ability to give in-house approval on mortgages that will be sold to FNMA, as explained in Chapter 9. If the mortgage is to be either insured by FHA or guaranteed by VA, once again the lenders will process the application, and if the mortgage company feels the application meets the underwriting guidelines of FHA or VA, the package will be forwarded to the nearest insuring office of FHA or the loan guaranty section of the nearest VA office. Some of the underwriting guidelines of FNMA/FHLMC, FHA, and VA have been discussed in Chapter 12.

Regulated lenders These types of lenders are those that are regulated by an agency of either the federal government or a state government. These lenders in some cases have the ability to give in-house approval on loans insured by FHA or guaranteed by VA. If the institution (such as a savings and loan association) has this ability, then after the loan application is completed, after all of the supporting documents are received, and after the S and L feels that the mortgage meets the underwriting requirements of either FHA or VA, the institution may approve the application and FHA or VA must either issue the insurance or the guaranty on the mortgage. Usually the institution is more strict than FHA or VA. If the mortgage is borderline, it will normally be forwarded to FHA or VA for approval. In regard to conventional mortgages, if the institution is lending its own funds, it will approve or disapprove the loan upon the packaging of the materials and the submitting of the loan package to the loan committee. This committee usually meets once a week to review all of the completed and packaged loans and to approve or disapprove them. If the mortgage is to be sold to FNMA, the mortgage may be approved in-house if the institution has a delegated underwriter or the mortgage can be forwarded to the nearest FNMA office for prior approval. Once again, all mortgages that are sold to FNMA will have to be approved by the loan committee.

REVIEW QUESTIONS

1. Define the term *underwriting.*
2. Explain the first step in loan processing.
3. Outline the information that a lender may wish to verify.
4. Outline the major sections of the FNMA, FHA, and VA loan applications.
5. Outline the provisions of the Real Estate Settlement Procedures Act regarding the taking of loan applications.
6. Outline some of the information a lender may not ask at time of loan application.

CHAPTER 14 Loan Closing

LEARNING OBJECTIVES

In this chapter we will examine the process of concluding the real estate transaction. This process is sometimes referred to as the *closing* or *loan closing*.

Upon completion of this chapter, you should be able to do the following:

- ★ **Outline the requirements of the Real Estate Settlement Procedures Act in regard to loan closing.**
- ★ **Outline the procedures in closing after the approval of the property and the borrower.**
- ★ **Describe the basic closing requirements of the mortgage lender.**
- ★ **List some of the basic closing costs.**

DEFINITION

Loan closing can be defined as the conclusion of the real estate transaction. This conclusion can include any of the following: the delivery of a deed, the transfer of title to real property through a tax free exchange, or the signing of a note and mortgage/deed of trust by the purchaser/borrower.

Our discussion of the closing process will only reflect actions taken if the purchase of the property is to be financed by someone other than the purchaser—normally a mortgage lender.

OVERVIEW OF THE CLOSING PROCESS

All parties to the transaction—buyer, seller, buyer's agent, seller's agent, and the person who will conduct the closing—usually meet and exchange the necessary documents to insure the speedy and legal transfer of the title of the subject property. The agent for the buyer or seller can either be the real estate broker who represented the party in the negotiation of the earnest money contract or an attorney. In some states the transfer agency or escrow agent is a title company. Usually, the title company that conducts the closing will issue the title policy on the property. In most cases, the title company will not charge a fee to conduct the closing. The title company that handles the closing will also have been the escrow agent listed in the earnest money contract.

The final step in the closing after all of the documents have been signed by all of the parties is the *funding* of the transaction. In funding, the buyer delivers to the seller the money or additional money that will equal the price for the property agreed upon in the earnest money contract. The money can be in the form of a cashier's check from the buyer (if the buyer has sufficient funds to pay cash for the property) or in the form of a check from the mortgage lender to whom the buyer made application and was approved. If this latter method is the case, the buyer will have additional documents to execute and to have acknowledged. Some of these additional documents will be reviewed later in this chapter.

In regard to the actual funding of the transaction, there are two basic methods: table funding and funding at a later date.

Table Funding

Table funding is the receiving of funds at the time of closing, or "at the table," by all parties to the transaction who are to receive funds. This means that the closing agent will have all of the checks prepared for the title insurance, the inspections, the attorneys who have drawn the papers, and most important, the real estate firms involved in the transaction. For table funding to occur, all of the documents in the transaction, all of the instructions supplied by either the mortgage lender or the taxing authorities, and any other documents and items that could affect the title to the property must be in order.

Funding at a Later Date

Funding at a later date refers to a transaction that will not be funded until a specific date or after some specific actions have been taken. Usually the reason for funding at a later date is that the mortgage lender wishes to review the completed closing package or wants to review all of the documents involved in the transaction. This can take as little as twenty-four hours from the time the completed loan package is delivered to the mortgage lender or as long as months, but the lender usually will fund the mortgage in forty-eight hours after the package is received, if all of the documents are in order. We will review later in the chapter the mortgage lender's instructions and mortgage package.

REAL ESTATE SETTLEMENT PROCEDURES ACT (RESPA)

As mentioned in the last chapter, the Real Estate Settlement Procedures Act (RESPA) was passed to standardize the settlement or closing of real estate transactions, and in that chapter we saw how the law affects the application procedure.

It should be noted at this time that after the initial passage of RESPA, there was a great deal of opposition to the act not only from the lenders, but from the closing agents and homebuyers. After lengthy hearings, Regulation X of the act was revised and the revisions became law in 1976. The revised RESPA has nine basic requirements.

1-2. The first two of the requirements were discussed in the previous chapter. They require the lender to provide the applicant with the Good Faith Estimate of Costs and the HUD booklet on settlement costs.

The remainder of the provisions cover the actual closing of the transaction:

3. *Uniform Settlement Statement*. RESPA requires the use of the Uniform Settlement Statement, otherwise known as either HUD Form 1 or the closing statement. This statement will be reviewed later in this section.

4. *Selection of the title company*. RESPA makes it illegal for the seller to condition the sale of the property upon the buyer's selection of the title company. This means that the seller cannot force the buyer to use a specific title company.

5. *Kickbacks*. RESPA prohibits anyone involved in the transaction from receiving or giving a fee, kickback, or anything of value for the promise of future business. It also makes the acceptance or offer of a fee illegal when no service has been rendered. It should be noted that this requirement does not prohibit a person who actually provides a service in the transaction from collecting a fee or payment for services. It does prohibit, for example, a title or mortgage company from making an agreement with a real estate agent or firm, so that for every closing or applicant the agent or firm sends, the agent or firm will receive something of value.

6. *Escrows*. RESPA prohibits the lender from collecting excessive amounts to be placed in escrow accounts. The act

allows the lender to collect sufficient amounts to make necessary payments plus two months of escrow deposits. Thus, at the time of closing the mortgage lender usually requires the collection of three months of escrow payments for taxes, insurance (homeowners), PMI premiums, and any other fee or assessment that will affect the title to the property. The lender will collect the first year's insurance premium, for a total of fifteen months.

7. *Preparation of the uniform settlement statement and truth-in-lending statement.* The lender is prohibited from charging a fee for the preparation of these two statements. It should be noted that only the lender is prohibited from charging a fee for the preparation of the statements.

8. *Loans to fiduciaries.* Institutions insured by either FDIC or FSLIC must require that the borrower disclose the identity of the person or company that is receiving the beneficial interest in a loan made to a fiduciary. *Fiduciary* is the holding by a person or organization of something in trust. Thus, if you are purchasing a piece of property from a person or organization that is holding the property in trust, the institution will require the person or organization holding the property to identify the person or persons that will ultimately benefit from the proceeds of the mortgage.

9. *Preview of settlement statement.* The final provision of RESPA allows the borrower or his or her agent to view the Uniform Settlement Statement one business day prior to the closing and see the amount which the borrower may be required to pay at the time of closing. This reviewing of the Uniform Settlement Statement is a good idea not only for the borrower, but also for the real estate agent who represents the borrower. This will allow the borrower to have either sufficient cash or a cashier's check to pay the required amount. If the agent reviews the Uniform Settlement Statement prior to closing, he or she can see if the client is paying the proper items and amounts outlined in the earnest money contract. Thus, there will be no surprises at the time of closing.

Uniform Settlement Statement

As was mentioned in the previous section, RESPA requires the use of a Uniform Settlement Statement in the settlement or closing of the sale of any one- to four-family residential property, sale of a lot with a mobile home, or sale of a lot on which a home can or is planned to be built. The Uniform Settlement Statement, or HUD Form 1, is illustrated in Figures 14-1 and 14-2.

Let us review some of the major sections of the form. The first section of the form, items A through I, are self-explanatory, identifying the parties to the closing or settlement and the type of mortgage involved in the transaction. Item J summarizes the borrower's portion of the transaction, whereas item K summarizes the seller's portion of the transaction.

The second page of the statement is a detailed outline of the money to be paid at the time of the closing and who is to pay each of the charges. You will notice that the page is divided into seven sections, starting with a section showing the real estate commission and to whom the commission is to be paid. The second section sets forth the items that are to be paid in conjunction with the origination and processing of the mortgage. Not all of these fees will be paid to the lender. For example, the appraisal fee will usually be paid to an appraiser, and the cost of the credit report will be paid to the local credit bureau. The next section is entitled "Items Required by the Lender to be Paid in Advance," which is self-explanatory. The fourth section, "Reserves Deposited with Lender," shows a breakdown of prepaids collected. The next section, "Title Charges," has to do with the closing title search, document preparation, issuance of the title insurance, and other fees involved with the actual closing of the transaction. When the documents are filed—like all documents relating to the transfer of real property—the charges for such recording will be indicated in section six. If tax stamps are not used in your state, there will be no charge on line 1202 or 1203, but there may still be a charge for tax certificates. The tax certificates, from the taxing authorities that

Figure 14-1. HUD Uniform Settlement Statement, page 1

Form Approved
OMB No. 63-R1501

A. U.S. DEPARTMENT OF HOUSING AND URBAN DEVELOPMENT SETTLEMENT STATEMENT	B. TYPE OF LOAN: 1. ☐ FHA 2. ☐ FMHA 3. ☐ CONV. UNINS. 4. ☐ VA 5. ☐ CONV. INS. 6. FILE NUMBER 7. LOAN NUMBER 8. MORTG. INS. CASE NO.

C. NOTE: This form is furnished to give you a statement of actual settlement costs. Amounts paid to and by the settlement agent are shown. Items marked "(p.o.c.)" were paid outside the closing; they are shown here for informational purposes and are not included in the totals.

D. NAME OF BORROWER	E. NAME OF SELLER	F. NAME OF LENDER
G. PROPERTY LOCATION	H. SETTLEMENT AGENT PLACE OF SETTLEMENT	I. SETTLEMENT DATE:

J. SUMMARY OF BORROWER'S TRANSACTION			K. SUMMARY OF SELLER'S TRANSACTION		
100. **GROSS AMOUNT DUE FROM BORROWER:**			400. **GROSS AMOUNT DUE TO SELLER:**		
101. Contract sales price			401. Contract sales price		
102. Personal property			402. Personal property		
103. Settlement charges to borrower *(line 1400)*			403.		
104.			404.		
105.			405.		
Adjustments for items paid by seller in advance:			Adjustments for items paid by seller in advance:		
106. City/town taxes	to		406. City/town taxes	to	
107. County taxes	to		407. County taxes	to	
108. Assessments	to		408. Assessments	to	
109. Maintenance	to		409. Maintenance	to	
110. School/Taxes	to		410. Commitment Fee	to	
111.	to		411.	to	
112.	to		412.	to	
			420. **GROSS AMOUNT DUE TO SELLER:**		
120. **GROSS AMOUNT DUE FROM BORROWER:**			500. **REDUCTIONS IN AMOUNT DUE TO SELLER:**		
200. **AMOUNTS PAID BY OR IN BEHALF OF BORROWER:**			501. Excess deposit (see instructions)		
201. Deposit or earnest money			502. Settlement charges to seller *(line 1400)*		
202. Principal amount of new loan(s)			503. Existing loan(s) taken subject to		
203. Existing loan(s) taken subject to			504. Payoff of first mortgage loan		
204. Commitment Fee			505. Payoff of second mortgage loan		
205.			506.		
206			507.		
207.			508.		
208.			509.		
209.					
Adjustments for items unpaid by seller:			Adjustments for items unpaid by seller:		
210. City/town taxes	to		510. City/town taxes	to	
211. County taxes	to		511. County Taxes	to	
212. Assessments	to		512. Assessments	to	
213. School/Taxes	to		513. Maintenance	to	
214.	to		514. School/Taxes	to	
215.	to		515.	to	
216.	to		516.	to	
217.	to		517.	to	
218.	to		518.	to	
219.	to		519.	to	
220. **TOTAL PAID BY/FOR BORROWER:**			520. **TOTAL REDUCTION AMOUNT DUE SELLER:**		
300. **CASH AT SETTLEMENT FROM/TO BORROWER:**			600. **CASH AT SETTLEMENT TO/FROM SELLER:**		
301. Gross amount due from borrower *(line 120)*			601. Gross amount due to seller *(line 420)*		
302. Less amounts paid by/for borrower *(line 220)*		( )	602. Less total reductions in amount due seller *(line 520)*		( )
303. CASH (☐ FROM) (☐ TO) BORROWER:			603. **CASH (☐ TO) (☐ FROM) SELLER**		

HUD-1 (Rev. 5-76)

Figure 14-2. HUD Uniform Settlement Statement, page 2

PAGE 2 OF
Form Approved OMB No. 63-R1501

L. SETTLEMENT CHARGES	PAID FROM BORROWER'S FUNDS AT SETTLEMENT	PAID FROM SELLER'S FUNDS AT SETTLEMENT
700. **TOTAL SALES/BROKER'S COMMISSION Based on price $ @ %=**		
Division of commission *(line 700)* as follows:		
701. $ to		
702. $ to		
703. Commission paid at settlement		
704.		
800. **ITEMS PAYABLE IN CONNECTION WITH LOAN.**		
801. Loan Origination fee %		
802. Loan Discount %		
803. Appraisal Fee to		
804. Credit Report to		
805. Lender's inspection fee		
806. Mortgage Insurance application fee to		
807. Assumption Fee		
808. Commitment Fee		
809. FNMA Processing Fee		
810. Pictures		
811.		
900. **ITEMS REQUIRED BY LENDER TO BE PAID IN ADVANCE.**		
901. Interest from to @ $ /day		
902. Mortgage insurance premium for mo. to		
903. Hazard insurance premium for yrs. to		
904. Flood Insurance yrs. to		
905.		
1000. **RESERVES DEPOSITED WITH LENDER**		
1001. Hazard insurance mo. @ $ per mo.		
1002. Mortgage insurance mo. @ $ per mo.		
1003. City property taxes mo. @ $ per mo.		
1004. County property taxes mo. @ $ per mo.		
1005. Annual assessments (Maint.) mo. @ $ per mo.		
1006. School Property Taxes mo. @ $ per mo.		
1007. Water Dist. Prop. Tax mo. @ $ per mo.		
1008. Flood Insurance mo. @ $ per mo.		
1100. **TITLE CHARGES:**		
1101. Settlement or closing fee to		
1102. Abstract or title search to		
1103. Title examination to		
1104. Title insurance binder to		
1105. Document preparation to		
1106. Notary fees to		
1107. Attorney's fees to to		
(includes above items No.:		
1108. Title insurance to		
(includes above items No.:		
1109. Lender's coverage $		
1110. Owner's coverage $		
1111. Escrow Fee		
1112. Restrictions		
1113. Messenger Service		
1200. **GOVERNMENT RECORDING AND TRANSFER CHARGES**		
1201. Recording fees: Deed $ Mortgage $ Releases $		
1202. City/county tax/stamps: Deed $ Mortgage $		
1203. State tax/stamps: Deed $ Mortgage $		
1204. Tax Certificates		
1205.		
1300. **ADDITIONAL SETTLEMENT CHARGES**		
1301. Survey to		
1302. Pest inspection to		
1303.		
1304.		
1305.		
1400. **TOTAL SETTLEMENT CHARGES** *(entered on lines 103, Section J and 502, Section K)*		

SELLER'S AND/OR PURCHASER'S STATEMENT

Seller's and Purchaser's signature hereon acknowledges his/their approval of tax prorations, and signifies their understanding that prorations were based on figures for preceding year, or estimates for current year, and in event of any change for current year, all necessary adjustments must be made between Seller and Purchaser direct; likewise any DEFICIT in delinquent taxes will be reimbursed to Title Company by the Seller.

We approve the foregoing settlement statement, in its entirety, authorize payments in accordance therewith and acknowledge receipt of a copy thereof.

Signature________________ ________________

Seller Purchaser

Escrow Officer

HUD-1 (Rev. 5-76)

have jurisdiction over the subject property, state that the taxes are current. These certificates, for example, may be issued by the city, county, and school district. The last section has space for other settlement charges, which can include those listed, as well as other types of inspections and repairs.

TRUTH-IN-LENDING LAW

The Truth-in-Lending law, passed by the U.S. Congress in 1968, became effective July 1969. It requires that a Truth-in-Lending Statement be given to a borrower providing certain information about the mortgage or loan. The information may include, but is not limited to, the annual percentage rate (APR), the finance charge, the dollar amount the credit will cost the borrower, the number of payments, and late charges and how they will be calculated.

Then, in March 1980, the Congress passed the Depository Institutions Deregulation and Monetary Control Act (Public Law 96-221), which contained Title VI and is entitled the Truth-in-Lending Simplification and Reform Act. The purpose of this act was to make sweeping revisions to the truth-in-lending law. Even though the effective date of the act was not until October 1, 1982, the act required the Federal Reserve to adopt a final rule to implement the act no later than April 1, 1981.

The act made major changes to many areas covered by the original law. One of the types of transactions affected was the real estate transaction. Some of the major changes affecting real estate transactions are as follows:

1. The sale of rental property not to be owner occupied is excluded and no Truth-in-Lending Statement is required

2. The term *refinancing* was redefined to include any and only those loan or mortgage agreements that pay off existing debt with the execution of a new mortgage or loan

3. Any points paid by the seller when calculating the finance charges are excluded from the calculation of finance charges, but any points paid by the buyer are still included

As with the previous rules, the extension of agriculture credit is exempt. Agricultural credit includes credit for the purpose of purchasing real property without or with improvements, including a home, if the property is to be used primarily for agriculture purposes.

In addition to these changes, the rules adopted by the Federal Reserve also contained suggested formats for several loan disclosure forms. Some of these relate to real estate transactions and are illustrated in Figures 14-3, 14-4, 14-5, and 14-6.

In addition to the suggested forms, the Federal Reserve has proposed several clauses to be used with the Variable Rate and the Demand Feature Model Disclosures. The Federal Reserve has also published suggested clauses for use with mortgages that include an assumption provision and/or a clause stating that the APR does not include any required deposit. These suggested clauses are illustrated in Figure 14-7.

The Truth-in-Lending Statement does not have to be given at the time of the application or within three days of the application, as do the Good Faith Estimate and the HUD Settlement Booklet. The statement is usually furnished to the borrower at the time of closing. If a borrower wishes to know the actual interest that he or she will pay, it is a good idea for the borrower to request this information at the time of application.

In this discussion of truth-in-lending, we have referred to the *annual percentage rate* (APR). This rate can be different from the interest rate quoted by the lender as the rate of the mortgage for which the borrower is making application. The reason for the difference is that the APR includes not only the face rate of the mortgage, but also all fees and/or discount points paid by the buyer.

The agencies that have responsibility for the enforcement of truth-in-lending (Regulation Z) are listed in Figure 14-8.

This completes our examination of the major federal legislation that has an effect on the closing of the real estate transaction.

SETTING THE CLOSING

How is the date of the closing determined? The date is established by two factors: (1) the negotiation of the earnest money contract and

Figure 14-3. Loan Model Form

ANNUAL PERCENTAGE RATE The cost of your credit as a yearly rate.	FINANCE CHARGE The dollar amount the credit will cost you.	Amount Financed The amount of credit provided to you or on your behalf.	Total of Payments The amount you will have paid after you have made all payments as scheduled.
%	$	$	$

You have the right to receive at this time an itemization of the Amount Financed.
☐ I want an itemization. ☐ I do not want an itemization.

Your payment schedule will be:

Number of Payments	Amount of Payments	When Payments Are Due

Insurance
Credit life insurance and credit disability insurance are not required to obtain credit, and will not be provided unless you sign and agree to pay the additional cost.

Type	Premium	Signature
Credit Life		I want credit life insurance. ____________ Signature
Credit Disability		I want credit disability insurance. ____________ Signature
Credit Life and Disability		I want credit life and disability insurance. ____________ Signature

You may obtain property insurance from anyone you want that is acceptable to (creditor). If you get the insurance from (creditor), you will pay $____________.

Security: You are giving a security interest in:
☐ the goods or property being purchased.
☐ (brief description of other property).

Filing fees $ ____________ **Non-filing insurance $** ____________

Late Charge: If a payment is late, you will be charged $__________/__________% of the payment.

Prepayment: If you pay off early, you
☐ may ☐ will not have to pay a penalty.
☐ may ☐ will not be entitled to a refund of part of the finance charge.

See your contract documents for any additional information about nonpayment, default, any required repayment in full before the scheduled date, and prepayment refunds and penalties.

e means an estimate

Source: U.S., Federal Reserve System, *Final Rule; Truth-in-Lending; Revised Regulation Z, Appendix H*, April 1, 1981, p. 66.

Figure 14-4. Mortgage with Demand Feature

Mortgage Savings and Loan Assoc.
Date: April 15, 1981

Glenn Jones
700 Oak Drive
Little Creek, USA

ANNUAL PERCENTAGE RATE The cost of your credit as a yearly rate.	FINANCE CHARGE The dollar amount the credit will cost you.	Amount Financed The amount of credit provided to you or on your behalf.	Total of Payments The amount you will have paid after you have made all payments as scheduled.
14.85%	$156,551.54	$44,605.66	$201,157.20

Your payment schedule will be:

Number of Payments	Amount of Payments	When Payments Are Due
360	$558.77	Monthly beginning 6/1/81

This obligation has a demand feature.

You may obtain property insurance from anyone you want that is acceptable to Mortgage Savings and Loan Assoc. If you get the insurance from Mortgage Savings and Loan Assoc. you will pay $ 150 – 1 year

Security: You are giving a security interest in:
☒ the goods or property being purchased.
☐ ______________________

Late Charge: If a payment is late, you will be charged $ N/A / 5 % of the payment.

Prepayment: If you pay off early, you may have to pay a penalty.

Assumption: Someone buying your house may, subject to conditions, be allowed to assume the remainder of the mortgage on the original terms.

See your contract documents for any additional information about nonpayment, default, any required repayment in full before the scheduled date, and prepayment refunds and penalties.

e means an estimate

Source: U.S., Federal Reserve System, *Final Rule; Truth-in-Lending; Revised Regulation Z*, April 1, 1981, p. 74.

Figure 14-5. Variable-Rate Mortgage

State Savings and Loan Assoc.

Anne Jones
600 Pine Lane
Little Creek, USA

Account number: 210802-47

ANNUAL PERCENTAGE RATE The cost of your credit as a yearly rate.	FINANCE CHARGE The dollar amount the credit will cost you.	Amount Financed The amount of credit provided to you or on your behalf.	Total of Payments The amount you will have paid after you have made all payments as scheduled.
15.07 %	$157,155.20	$ 44,002—	$ 201,157.20

Your payment schedule will be:

Number of Payments	Amount of Payments	When Payments Are Due
360	$558.77	Monthly beginning 6-1-81

Variable Rate:
The annual percentage rate may increase during the term of this transaction if the prime rate of State Savings and Loan Assoc. increases. The rate may not increase more often than once a year, and may not increase by more than 1% annually. The interest rate will not increase above 19.75 %. Any increase will take the form of higher payment amounts. If the interest rate increases by 1 % in one year, your regular payment would increase to $ 594.51

Security: You are giving a security interest in the property being purchased.

Late Charge: If a payment is late, you will be charged 5% of the payment.

Prepayment: If you pay off early, you ☒ may ☐ will not have to pay a penalty.

Assumption: Someone buying your house may, subject to conditions, be allowed to assume the remainder of the mortgage on the original terms.

See your contract documents for any additional information about nonpayment, default, any required repayment in full before the scheduled date, and prepayment refunds and penalties.

---

e means an estimate

Source: U.S., Federal Reserve System, *Final Rule; Truth-in-Lending, Revised Regulation Z; Appendix H*, April 1, 1981, p. 75.

Figure 14-6. Graduated-Payment Mortgage

Convenient Savings and Loan

Account number: 4862-88

Michael Jones
500 Walnut Court, Little Creek USA

ANNUAL PERCENTAGE RATE The cost of your credit as a yearly rate.	FINANCE CHARGE The dollar amount the credit will cost you.	Amount Financed The amount of credit provided to you or on your behalf.	Total of Payments The amount you will have paid after you have made all payments as scheduled.
15.37%	$177,970.44	$43,777	$221,548.44

Your payment schedule will be:

Number of Payments	Amount of Payments	When Payments Are Due
12	$446.62	monthly beginning 6/1/81
12	$479.67	" " 6/1/82
12	$515.11	" " 6/1/83
12	$553.13	" " 6/1/84
12	$593.91	" " 6/1/85
300	varying from $637.68 to $627.37	" " 6/1/86

Security: You are giving a security interest in the property being purchased.

Late Charge: If a payment is late, you will be charged 5% of the payment.

Prepayment: If you pay off early, you
☒ may ☐ will not have to pay a penalty.
☒ may ☐ will not be entitled to a refund of part of the finance charge.

Assumption: Someone buying your home cannot assume the remainder of the mortgage on the original terms.

See your contract documents for any additional information about nonpayment, default, any required repayment in full before the scheduled date, and prepayment refunds and penalties.

e means an estimate

Source: U.S., Federal Reserve System, Final Rule; Truth-in-Lending, Revised Regulation Z; Appendix H, April 1, 1981, p. 76.

Figure 14-7. Model Clauses

H-4—Variable Rate Model Clauses

The annual percentage rate may increase during the term of this transaction if:
(the prime interest rate of (creditor) increases.)
(the balance in your deposit account falls below $ ________.)
(you terminate your employment with (employer) .)

(The interest rate will not increase above ______%.)
(The maximum interest rate increase at one time will be ______%.)
(The rate will not increase more than once every (time period) .)

Any increase will take the form of:
(higher payment amounts.)
(more payments of the same amount.)
(a larger amount due at maturity.)

Example based on the specific transaction
(If the interest rate increases by ______ % in (time period),
(your regular payments will increase to $ ________.)
(you will have to make ____ additional payments.)
(your final payment will increase to $ ________.))

Example based on a typical transaction
(If your loan were for $ ________ at ______% for (term) and the rate increased to % in (time period),
(your regular payments would increase by $ ________.)
(you would have to make ____ additional payments.)
(your final payment would increase by $ ________.))

H-5—Demand Feature Model Clauses

This obligation (is payable on demand.)
(has a demand feature.)
(All disclosures are based on an assumed maturity of one year.)

H-6—Assumption Policy Model Clause

Assumption: Someone buying your house (may, subject to conditions, be allowed to) (cannot) assume the remainder of the mortgage on the original terms.

H-7—Required Deposit Model Clause

The annual percentage rate does not take into account your required deposit.

Source: U.S., Federal Reserve System, Final Rule; Truth-in-Lending, Revised Regulation Z; Appendix H, April 1, 1981, p. 68.

Figure 14-8. Federal Enforcement Agencies

The following list indicates which federal agency enforces Regulation Z for particular classes of businesses. Any questions concerning compliance by a particular business should be directed to the appropriate enforcement agency.

National Banks

Office of Customer and Community Programs
Comptroller of the Currency
Washington, D.C. 20219

State Member Banks

Federal Reserve Bank serving the district in which the State member bank is located.

Nonmember Insured Banks

Federal Deposit Insurance Corporation Regional Director for the region in which the nonmember insured bank is located.

Savings Institutions Insured by the FSLIC and Members of the FHLBB System (Except for Savings Banks Insured by FDIC)

The Federal Home Loan Bank Board Supervisory Agent in the district in which the institution is located.

Federal Credit Unions

Regional office of the National Credit Union Administration serving the area in which the federal credit union is located.

Creditors Subject to Civil Aeronautics Board

Director, Bureau of Consumer Protection
Civil Aeronautics Board
1825 Connecticut Avenue, N.W.
Washington, D.C. 20428

Creditors Subject to Packers and Stockyards Act

Nearest Packers and Stockyards Administration area supervisor.

Federal Land Banks, Federal Land Bank Associations, Federal Intermediate Credit Banks and Production Credit Associations

Farm Credit Administration
490 L'Enfant Plaza, S.W.
Washington, D.C. 20578

Retail, Department Stores, Consumer Finance Companies, All Other Creditors, and All Nonbank Credit Card Issuers (Creditors operating on a local or regional basis should use the address of the FTC Regional Office in which they operate.)

Division of Credit Practices
Bureau of Consumer Protection
Federal Trade Commission
Washington, D.C. 20580

Source: U.S., Federal Reserve System, *Final Rule; Truth-in-Lending, Revised Regulation Z; Appendix I,* April 1, 1981, p. 77.

(2) loan approval. With regard to negotiation of the earnest money contract, many contain a statement that closing will occur on or before the specified date in the contract. The loan approval factor is noted in many contract forms in that the closing portion of the contracts contain the following wording: ". . . if necessary to complete loan requirements, the Closing Date shall be extended daily up to 15 days." It is important, then, for real estate professionals to be familiar with the time necessary for loans to be processed in their area of operation in order to schedule a realistic number of days from the time the earnest money contract is effective until the scheduled day of closing. This time frame will vary with the area of the state as well as with the type of mortgage and the complexity of the application and information to be verified.

MORTGAGE LENDERS CLOSING PROCEDURES

After approval of both the property and the borrower is received by the mortgage lender or the mortgage company from the loan committee and/or the investor, the application and all of the supporting documents are transferred to the closing department of the mortgage lender or mortgage company. The closing department then initiates actions that will prepare the mortgage for closing through the closing agent. The following are usually some of the major actions taken, but not necessarily in the order listed.

Mortgagee's Information Letter (MIL)

The mortgage lender or mortgage company will order the mortgagee's information letter (MIL). This is sometimes referred to as the title report. It is completely different from the mortgage information letter sent by the listing broker to the mortgage company requesting information regarding the present mortgage on a property being listed. In some states the mortgagee's information letter is called the *binder to insure.*

The mortgagee's information letter is usually issued by the title company that will issue the title policy on the property that is serving as security for the mortgage. The form of the MIL is prescribed by a state board of insurance and usually contains three sections. We will discuss the more important information contained in each section.

Section A This section of the MIL gives information on the type of lien to be insured, identifies the property to be insured, and identifies the person or persons in whom the fee simple title to the property will be vested. The information is usually shown as follows:

> You are advised that in such policy:
>
> a. The lien to be insured will be described as follows: *Papers to be drawn securing a valid first lien on form and manner acceptable to the company (the title insuring company).*
>
> b. The property covered by such lien will be described as follows: *The legal description of the property will be inserted as either one of lot and block type or metes and bounds.*
>
> c. The fee simple title to such property will be shown vested in: *The names of the persons responsible for the repayment of the mortgage will be inserted.*

Section B This section of the mortgagee's information letter contains information on the exceptions that will not be covered by the title policy and contains the following information:

> Schedule "B" of such policy will contain the following exceptions:
>
> 1. All restrictive covenants affecting the above described property but the Company guarantees that any such restrictive covenants have not been violated so as to affect, and that a future violation thereof will not affect the validity or priority of the mortgage hereby insured.
>
> 2. Any discrepancies, conflicts, or shortages in area or boundary lines, or any encroachments or any overlapping of improvements which a correct survey would show. (May be deleted if Manual provisions concerning survey are complied with.)
>
> 3. Taxes for the year 19 ____ and subsequent years, not yet due and payable.
>
> 4. Usury or claims of usury.
>
> 5. Any right of recission contained in any CONSUMER CREDIT PROTECTION, TRUTH-IN-LENDING LAW.
>
> 6. (Insert here all other specific exceptions as to liens, easements, outstanding mineral and royalty interest, etc., which will be shown as exception in the Mortgagee's Policy.)

Under this last portion of Section B will be listed such items as:

1. Public Utility easements including above ground, surface, and underground
2. Building Set Back requirements
3. Storm sewer easements

Section C The final section of the MIL is Section C, where we find all other matters that will affect the title and any other requirements that must be met prior to the issuance of a title policy. The information contained in this section is as follows:

> Matters affecting title to the hereinabove described property and other requirements and conditions which must be disposed of to our satisfaction at or prior to the date of the issuance of the above mentioned policy.
>
> 1. Execution, delivery, and recording of proper and valid instrument or instruments vesting title in borrower and creating lien described above under Section A.
>
> 2. Any defect, lien, encumbrance, or other matter affecting the title to the subject property or the lien to be insured, which may be filed or may arise subsequent to the date hereof.
>
> 3. Determination by us of owner's acceptance of any new construction or repairs, and payment of labor and material bills.
>
> 4. Payment to or for the account of the mortgagors of the full proceeds of the loan.
>
> 5. Payment to the undersigned company of its premium for title insurance and other proper charges incurred in connection with processing this matter.
>
> 6. Satisfactory evidence that restrictions or restrictive covenants have not been violated.

7. (Here show outstanding liens or other matters which must be disposed of at or before disbursement.)

Paragraph 7 of Section C may contain some of the following liens and further requirements:

1. That a General Warranty Deed be recorded in favor of the purchaser

2. That a Deed of Trust be recorded in favor of the lender

3. That a release of a Mechanics and Materialman's lien, if one is on record against the property, be filed

4. That all assessments against the property by a municipal utility district (MUD) are current

5. That a release of lien, if the property is presently financed by a first lien mortgage, be filed

These are only a few of the other requirements that must be met before the issuance of the title policy. Many of the MIL under this section have the following statement:

FOR YOUR INFORMATION
This is to certify that we have checked the records against your borrower, __________, and find the following Federal Tax Lien: (Here the title company will insert either the words None of Record or the information covering any such liens.)

All tax liens against the borrower must be cleared prior to the funding of the mortgage. Usually, the liens are not against the borrower, but against persons with the same name. The borrower must file an affidavit to that effect. It can take several days or weeks to clear the records.

Survey

The mortgage lender or mortgage company will, after the approval, also request a survey of the property in question. The survey that is usually ordered by the mortgage lender or the mortgage company is not a true survey but a drawing or copy of the plat of the property and usually carries the following certification:

I certify that the above is an accurate plat of the property of (the name of the present owner is inserted), known as, (the street address is inserted), the correct map of which is recorded in (the recording information is inserted), as inspected under my supervision. There were no encroachments at the time of this inspection. This plat is not to be used for construction purposes.

(Signed by licensed surveyor)
Name of Surveyor
State Registration Number

In addition to the above certification, the following note is usually included on the plat:

NOTE: This is a plat to be used for loan purposes and is not a boundary or staked survey.

This survey will show all improvements to the property including buildings, driveways, and sidewalks. The plat will also show all of the recorded easements and building lines. This is the type of survey that is usually used in conjunction with loans on residential property located inside recorded subdivisions. If the property is not located inside a city subdivision or the property involves more than a normal subdivision lot, the mortgage lender or the title company may require an "on-the-ground staked boundary survey with full field notes." This is a true survey where the surveyor sends a crew to the property and the property and all improvements are physically located.

Document Preparation

After the MIL and survey are received, the closing department will request the attorney firm that represents the mortgage lender or mortgage company to "draw" or prepare the following documents:

1. The note on the lender's prescribed form. If the mortgage is to be sold to FNMA or FHLMC, the standard note for FNMA/FHLMC will be completed. If the mortgage is to be either insured by FHA or guaranteed by VA, the attorney will use the authorized Note.

2. In addition to the note, the attorneys will draw the accompanying mortgage/deed of trust, using the lender's approved form.

One additional document that will be prepared for, or by, the closing department is the Truth-in-Lending Statement.

After all of the documents are prepared along with all of the necessary forms, the mortgage lender prepares the closing package, and this along with specific instructions is sent to the title company for the closing.

CLOSING INSTRUCTIONS

The most important document in the closing package to the agent of the title company closing the transaction is the closing instructions. These are the instructions given to the closing agent by the mortgage lender or the mortgage company listing the things that are to be done or checked by the closing agent. The closing instructions will be different for conventional mortgages, for FHA-insured mortgages, and for VA-guaranteed mortgages. A sample of closing instructions for a conventional mortgage is illustrated in Figures 14-9 and 14-10.

The instructions are divided into six sections. The first section, which is not numbered, deals with the funding of the mortgage, whether it is to be table funded or funded at a later date. The instructions on page 1 give the closing agent instructions on closing the loan and tell how the title policy is to be issued. The last instructions on page 1 deal with the hazard insurance policy. The instructions mandate a minimum rating for the company issuing the policy and state that certain types of policies are not acceptable to the lender. Also the instructions state that the policy may be furnished by an agent of the purchaser's choice.

Page 2 of the instructions (Figure 14-10) begins with an outline of the charges that the borrower will pay. The final portion of page 2 gives instructions as to what the closer is to furnish to the mortgage lender or mortgage company.

CLOSING COSTS

We will now examine some of the more common closing costs or fees that are connected with the application for, the processing of, and the closing of the mortgage.

Application fee This fee is collected at the time of the application. The amount of the fee will vary with the type of mortgage applied for. The application fees for a mortgage insured by FHA or guaranteed by VA are set by the agency involved. If the application is for a conventional mortgage, there is no standard fee, and therefore the real estate professional should have information on the fees charged by the conventional lenders in the area. The application fee usually covers those items that the mortgage lender or the mortgage company will have to pay during the processing of the application. These items include, but are not limited to (1) the credit report fee, and (2) the cost of the appraisal. The application fee for a conventional mortgage application can range from $90 to $200, with the average at $120. The application fee set by FHA and VA in late 1980 was $115.

Origination fee This is the fee that the lender will charge for the taking of the application and the processing of the loan application. Once again this fee for an FHA-insured loan and a VA-guaranteed mortgage is set by the agency. It is now 1 percent of the mortgage amount. For conventional mortgages, the fee can vary with the lender, but once again averages 1 percent of the loan amount. This fee has remained rather constant at 1 percent. Since the amount of the mortgage has been increasing as the cost of housing has increased, the amount of money generated has also increased, and many lenders feel that the fee has almost kept up with the cost of application and processing.

Attorney's fee This is a fee charged by the attorney involved with the transaction. If the mortgage is a simple conventional FNMA/FHLMC mortgage, there is only one attorney involved, the attorney for the mortgage lender. The fee charged will vary with each lender. Therefore, it is a good practice to be familiar with the fees charged by the lenders in your area.

Loan discounts These are the points charged by the investor who will buy the mortgage. If the mortgage is a conventional one, either the buyer or seller can pay the points, but if the mortgage is insured by FHA or guaranteed by VA, only the seller is allowed to pay the

Figure 14-9. Conventional Mortgage Closing Instructions, part 1

Closing Instructions: Conventional Loan

MERCANTILE MORTGAGE CORPORATION (713) 522-8903

Date of Instructions: ________ Closing Date: ________ Closer: ________
Title Company: ________ Mortgagor: ________
GF #: ________
Loan Amount: $ ________ Address: ________
Maturity: ________ months
Interest Rate: ________ %
P & I Payments: $ ________ Appraised Lot Size: ________
(If less than this, contact us before proceeding with closing)

The following instructions are to be observed and followed implicitly by you in closing the above referenced loan. Should you not be able to meet the requirements set forth below, contact us before proceeding with the closing of the loan.

( ) Mercantile Mortgage Corporation will fund this loan upon receiving the instruments later referred to in these instructions, in form and content acceptable to us.

( ) A Check in the amount of $ ________ is attached, and is to be disbursed by you at closing, if all conditions of closing and our written instructions are followed correctly. Please note: Items marked with an asterisk (*) apply only to our requirements as applied to disbursement at closing, and are not applicable if this loan is not "table funded".

( )

I. In closing this loan, please observe the following:

(a) If the loan is not closed completely by buyer and seller within seven days from date of instructions, do not proceed with closing without permission from Mercantile Mortgage Corporation.

(*) A funding number must be obtained prior to disbursement of proceeds by calling Mercantile Mortgage Corporation. When funding number is issued and loan is closed, the documents referred to in Section V must be in the office of Mercantile Mortgage Corporation within 24 hours. The funding number is ________ , obtained from ________ at MERCANTILE MORTGAGE CORPORATION on ________.

(b) The closing must be in accordance with the enclosed earnest money contract as to sales price and downpayment.

(c) In examining the title and survey, if you find any easements more than twelve feet wide, any violation of restrictions, encroachments, or any exceptions of an unusual nature, e.g., a pipeline easement, advise us immediately and secure our approval before proceeding.

(d) All papers in connection with this loan are to be drawn by an attorney approved by Mercantile Mortgage Corporation.

(e) All documents must be signed as the names appear on the note and deed of trust, and all documents must be signed in the same manner.

(f) If the property is located in a water district, we must be forwarded a copy of the required affidavit.

(g) Any erasures, riders, gummed supplements or strikeovers on papers to be signed must be initialed by all parties.

(h)

II. Please issue your mortgagee's title policy observing the following:

(a) Policy must insure the deed of trust as a first lien, and the name of the insured must be: MERCANTILE MORTGAGE CORPORATION, Houston, Texas.

(b) Policy must not contain any exceptions to areas, boundaries, and encroachments, and must set out restrictions as "none of record" EXCEPT (list exceptions in usual manner), etc. The survey exception must be deleted and initialed.

(c) We will allow an exception to restrictive covenants provided they are not violated to date, and that future violation(s) will not affect the validity of the insured deed of trust. This loan is not to be closed if the restrictions contain a right of reversion.

(d) There is to be no secondary financing in connection with this loan, nor any outstanding liens, judgments, taxes or assessments.

(e) The policy must describe this new lien completely and accurately, reciting the county clerk's filing or recording dates for this deed of trust, and it must be dated even with, or after, the recited filing date.

(f) The policy must not contain any exceptions except those shown on your Mortgagee's Information Letter from which our closing preparations have been made.

(g) All taxes must be guaranteed prior to the current year. If this loan is closed after September 30, taxes must be guaranteed through the current year. The tax exception must show "taxes not yet due and payable".

(h) All easement exceptions must give size, location, purpose and recording, and must agree with the survey.

(i) All Maintenance charges must be subordinated to all valid purchase money liens. A 60-day letter is not acceptable. Next due date must be given.

(j)

III. Please examine the hazard insurance policy, observing the following:

1. Policy may be furnished by Agent of purchaser's choice.
2. The name(s) of the mortgagor(s) and legal description of the security property must be identical to those in the loan instruments; the street address must agree with the survey.
3. The insuring company must have a "BEST" rating of at least A + AA.
4. Reciprocal or assessment hazard insurance companies are not acceptable.

Source: Mercantile Mortgage Corporation of Texas, Houston, Texas

Figure 14-10. Conventional Mortgage Closing Instructions, part 2

III. (Continued)

5. The amount of the fire and extended coverage and PLF # 148 must be in the minumum amount of the loan as set out above, with loss payable clause to: MERCANTILE MORTGAGE CORPORATION AND/OR ASSIGNS, P. O. Box 40281, Houston, Texas 77040.
6. The invoice or receipt must be marked "PAID" and bear the statement, "This policy will not be cancelled for one year for non-payment of premium" and must be signed by the issuing agent.
7.

IV. Please make the following collections from the appropriate parties:

NOTE TO CLOSER: PURCHASER MUST PAY PREPAID ITEMS.
PURCHASER MUST NOT PAY MORE THAN ______ POINTS. SEE ATTACHMENT FOR ALLOWABLE CLOSING COSTS.

Title Co. use	No.	Item	Amount
( )	1.	______% Origination fee from buyer/seller	$ ______
( )	2.	______% Loan Discount from buyer/seller	______
( )	3.	Private mortgage insurance examination fee	______
( )	4.	Credit Report	______
( )	5.	Photographs	______
( )	6.	Completion Photographs	______
( )	7.	Appraisal fee	______
( )	8.	Amortization schedule	______
( )	9.	Inspection fee	______
( )	10.	Two months' hazard insurance for deposit to escrow	______
( )	11.	Two months' flood insurance for deposit to escrow	______
( )	12.	Taxes from November 1 to date of 1st payment	______
( )	13.	Maintenance fee charges from December 1 to date of first payment	______
( )	14.	Preliminary interest from date of disbursement check to a date 30 days prior to first installment date	______
( )	15.	Attorney's fee for legal papers per invoice	______
( )	16.	Long distance calls	______
( )	17.	Processing fee	______
( )	18.	Warehouse fee	______
( )	19.	FNMA underwriting fee	______
( )	20.	Tax service fee—Seller	______
		TOTAL FEES DUE FOR IMPOUNDS AND LENDER CHARGES	$ ______
( )	21.	First year's hazard insurance premium	______
( )	22.	First year's flood insurance premium	______
( )	23.	PMI INS premium	______
( )	24.		______
		TOTAL FEES AND CHARGES	$ ______

( ) WE REQUIRE FLOOD INSURANCE COVERAGE IN THE AMOUNT OF $ ______________.

V. When you have completed Sections I through IV and have filed the deed of trust of record, please forward the following to MERCANTILE MORTGAGE CORPORATION for disbursement:

( ) 1. Copy of mortgagee's title policy.
( ) 2. Original and two certified copies of note.
( ) 3. Two certified copies of deed of trust with filing receipt.
( ) 4. Two Certified copy of warranty deed.
( ) 5. Tax information sheet, signed by closer, showing all taxing authorities, their mailing address(es), tax account number(s) and amount of last taxes paid.
( ) 6. Oringial hazard insurance policy with receipted invoice (see instructions above) and copy of premium note if applicable.
( ) 7. Statement of cost of loan, in triplicate, which has been executed by purchaser and wife, exactly as name appears on note, properly acknowledged by closer.
( ) 8. Two certified copies of both the buyer's and seller's closing statement, executed by the closer.
( ) 9. Affidavit (our form) executed in duplicate by the purchasers.
( ) 10. Original and one copy of the PMI payment authorization form, if applicable.
( ) 11. FNMA form 1009, properly executed by purchasers and/or vendors.
( ) 12. Two copies of the survey, properly certified by a registered engineer. Be sure survey information agrees exactly with legal papers. It must reflect the borrower's name, property address, current date, house and lot dimensions, directional arrows, and distance to nearest intersection. Easements shown on survey must agree with those shown on mortgagee's title policy. Check lot, block, name of addition, and map references, making sure they agree with legal papers.
( ) 13.

( ) ( ) (*) FINAL INSPECTION OF SECURITY IF REQUIRED ON THIS LOAN. DO NOT FUND UNLESS NOTIFIED BY MERCANTILE MORTGAGE CORPORATION THAT INSPECTION IS IN FILE.

If disbursement check is not attached for funding at closing, disbursement will be made only after we have had an opportunity to check the entire file and after repairs and requirements have been complied with. Disbursement is subject to compliance with any requirements called for by the MERCANTILE MORTGAGE'S INVESTOR. If this loan is not closed and all requirements fully complied with within 7 days, any commitment by MERCANTILE MORTGAGE CORPORATION to close this loan is void.

MERCANTILE MORTGAGE CORPORATION

Source: Mercantile Mortgage Corporation of Texas, Houston, Texas

points. It should also be noted that FNMA has restricted the number of points a buyer can pay to three, and if more than three are paid, FNMA will start to discount the amount of the mortgage.

Copy cost of deed restrictions This is the cost to the title company for the copy of the deed restriction covering the subject property. These restrictions can be very important if the property is located in a planned unit development, condominium, subdivision, or area without zoning. These restrictions will outline what the owner may do with the property in regard to any addition to the property, fencing of the property, and many other aspects of land use and improvements.

Survey The cost of required surveying varies from area to area within a state and can be paid by either the buyer or seller.

Real estate commission This is of vital importance to the real estate salesperson. As we learned earlier, this is the first item of page 2 of the Uniform Settlement Statement. The commission is usually paid by the seller and is agreed upon at the time the property is listed by the owner.

Cost of amortization schedule This cost is usually paid for by the buyer and it pays for the preparation of a schedule of payments showing the breakdown of the amount of each payment that will be credited to principal reduction and the payment of interest. It should be furnished to a buyer for federal income tax purposes. The schedule is normally prepared by the lender or mortgage company.

Recording fees These fees are self-explanatory and are listed on the second page of the Uniform Settlement Statement. They cover the recording of the required documents to transfer title to the property and to secure the first lien mortgage.

Private mortgage insurance This is the cost of the PMI coverage required by the conventional lender and is usually paid by the buyer, since it is insurance on the mortgage that was applied for by the buyer.

Interest charges Since most mortgages are not closed on the last day of the month, the lender will require that the borrower pay interest at the time of closing for the period between the time of closing and the first of the next month. Since only interest is charged on the mortgage after the money is used, the lender will collect the money outlined and no other payment is due until the first of the following month. For example, a closing was held on the seventeenth of the month. The mortgage amount was $70,000, the interest rate was 12 percent, and the month had thirty days. The lender will figure the amount of interest charged each day and multiply that rate times the mortgage to get the amount of interest to be collected each day. Since the mortgage was closed on the seventeenth, interest will be collected beginning on the eighteenth through the last day of the month, or thirteen days. To calculate the interest, the mortgage amount is multiplied by the interest rate ($70,000 × 12% = $8400). The $8400 represents the interest that would be paid in a year. Then to get the amount of interest paid in one month, the $8400 is divided by twelve months, or $8400/12 = $700. To get the daily amount of interest, the $700 is divided by the days in the month; in this example, thirty: $700/30 = $23.33 per day. The total amount of interest to be collected, therefore, would be the daily interest rate times the number of days from closing to the first day of the next month, or $23.33 × 13 = $303.29.

This completes our discussion of some of the major charges and fees that can or will be collected in connection with the loan application, processing, and closing. Additional charges or fees could include:

Inspections

Insurance (homeowners)

Pre-paids of insurance, taxes, and any other fee or assessment that may affect the title to the property

Mortgage insurance premium, if the mortgage is insured by FHA

DISBURSEMENT OF FUNDS

As mentioned earlier, the final step in loan closing is the funding to all parties involved in the transaction. This is done by the closing agent, usually in the form of a cashier's check.

REVIEW QUESTIONS

1. List two of the provisions of the Real Estate Settlement Procedures Act that affect the closing of the real estate transaction.

2. Name and explain some of the procedures or actions taken by the mortgage lender or mortgage company after the approval of the property and purchaser.

3. List and explain five basic closing costs related to the closing of a real estate first lien mortgage.

4. Briefly outline the process of closing the real estate transaction.

5. List some of the basic information contained in the Truth-in-Lending Statement.

6. Explain the difference between the Mortgagee's Information Letter and the MIL that is completed by the listing broker and sent to the mortgage lender or mortgage company.

7. What are the major sections of the Mortgagee's Information Letter?

8. What is meant by the term *closing instructions*?

CHAPTER 15 Community Reinvestment

LEARNING OBJECTIVES

In this chapter we will briefly review the Community Reinvestment Act (CRA), the Home Mortgage Disclosure Act, and the provisions of these acts that could affect you as a real estate professional.

Upon completion of this chapter you should be able to do the following:

- ★ **Outline the history of the Community Reinvestment Act (CRA).**
- ★ **Identify the institutions that are covered by the CRA.**
- ★ **List some of the major requirements of the CRA as they apply to the affected institutions.**
- ★ **Name and explain some of the major programs that can apply to an institution's compliance to the CRA.**
- ★ **Outline the requirements of the Home Mortgage Disclosure Act.**

BACKGROUND

The concept of community reinvestment was contained in Title VIII of the Housing and Community Development Act of 1977. This section was entitled the "Community Reinvestment Act of 1977." Section 802 of the act outlines Congress' intent in regard to community reinvestment and meeting the needs of the communities served by a financial institution. The Community Reinvestment Act expanded the responsibility of the financial institutions to meet not only the deposit needs of the community they serve, but also the credit needs of the community. The act also required the appropriate federal financial supervisory agency to use its authority when examining a financial institution, to encourage the institution to meet the credit needs of the community.

Section 804 of the Community Reinvestment Act allows the federal financial supervisory agency, in connection with the regular examination of the institution, to assess the institution's record of meeting the credit needs of the entire community served by the institution, including the needs of low- and moderate-income families.

At this time, let us define the federal financial supervisory agencies as they pertain to the Community Reinvestment Act. According to Section 803 of the act, the term *federal financial supervisory agency* refers to:

1. The Comptroller of the Currency
2. The Board of Governors of the Federal Reserve System
3. The Federal Deposit Insurance Corporation
4. The Federal Home Loan Bank Board and the Federal Savings and Loan Insurance Corporation

From this list of federal supervisory agencies, one can see that the majority of the financial institutions in the United States—including national banks, state banks that are insured by FDIC or are members of the Federal Reserve System, and savings and loan associations insured by FSLIC—are covered by the Community Reinvestment Act.

The Community Reinvestment Act has been implemented by the major financial supervisory agencies by the issuance of federal regulations.

PURPOSE[1]

The purpose of the act and the regulations issued by the supervisory agencies is to encourage the financial institutions to meet the credit needs of their communities, including low- and moderate-income families. The act and the regulations also guide the financial institutions as to how the supervisory agencies will assess an institution's record in meeting those credit needs. The programs offered to meet these needs should be consistent with safe and sound operation of the institutions.

SIGNIFICANCE TO THE REAL ESTATE INDUSTRY

The major significance of CRA to the real estate industry is that the act requires the federally supervised financial institutions to meet the credit needs of the community they serve. These credit needs are not just consumer loans or home-repair loans, but loans for the financing of housing and redevelopment of the community, particularly in predominantly low- to moderate-income areas. Thus, the act can serve the agent working in any city that has a need for the expansion of housing and facilities for families with low to moderate income.

REQUIREMENTS OF THE ACT AND FEDERAL REGULATIONS

The Community Reinvestment Act and the associated regulations contain many provisions, but the following are the four basic requirements that all institutions covered by the regulations must meet:

1. Define the area or community served
2. List the types of credit offered
3. Post a public notice stating that the institution is reviewed by a federal supervisory agency
4. Prepare a Community Reinvestment Act statement and give notice that the statement is available for public inspection.

Community Reinvestment Act Statement

Requirement 4, above, is that the lender must prepare a Community Reinvestment Act statement. This statement can be of great assistance to the real estate professional, for it will give insight into the financial institution's activities to aid the housing and community needs of low- to moderate-income families and the whole community that the institution serves. Now let us look at some of the major portions of the CRA statement.

First, the CRA statement must contain these items:

1. The institution must define its community by specific boundaries and illustrate it by a map. The institution must also describe the method it used to determine its community.
2. The institution is required to state the types of credit it is making available to the persons in its community.
3. The institution must maintain a file containing the comments from the general public about the performance of the institution in meeting or not meeting the credit needs of the community.
4. The CRA statement should contain a copy of the public notice posted in the lobby of the institution. The information and language of this notice is prescribed by a federal regulation. The required notice for those institutions under the jurisdiction of the Federal Home Loan Bank Board is shown in Figure 15-1.

Figure 15-1. Community Reinvestment Act Notice

The Federal Community Reinvestment Act (CRA) requires the Federal Home Loan Bank Board to evaluate our performance in helping to meet the credit needs of this community, and to take this evaluation into account when deciding on certain applications submitted by us. Your involvement is encouraged.

You may obtain our current CRA statement for this community in this office. [Current CRA statements for other communities served by us are available at our home office, located at ______________ ______________.]

You may send signed, written comments about our CRA statement(s) or our performance in helping to meet community credit needs to (title and address of institution official) and to (title of officer), Federal Home Loan Bank of ______________ (address). Your letter, together with any response by us, may be made public.

You may look at a file of all signed, written comments received by us within the past 2 years, any responses we have made to the comments, and all CRA statements in effect during the past 2 years at our office located at (address). [You also may look at the file about this community at (name and address of designated office).]

You may ask to look at any comments received by the Federal Home Loan Bank of ______________ ______________.

You also may request from the Federal Home Loan Bank of ______________ an announcement of applications covered by the CRA filed with the Federal Home Loan Bank Board.

Source: *Code of Federal Regulations*, Title 12—Banks and Banking: Section 563e.6, Public Notice, p. 752.

In addition to the required information contained in the CRA statement, the institution *may* include, and is encouraged by the supervisory agencies to include, the following information:

> (1) A description of how its current efforts, including special credit-related programs, help to meet community credit needs;
>
> (2) A periodic report regarding its record of helping to meet community credit needs; and
>
> (3) A description of its efforts to ascertain the credit needs of its community, including efforts to communicate with members of its community regarding credit services.[2]

Now that we have reviewed the major provisions of the act and the related federal regulations, let us look at the methods that an institution may use to designate or define its community. The federal regulations set forth three methods that may be used by the institutions:

1. *Existing boundaries*,[3] such as the boundaries of a standard metropolitan statistical area or counties in which the institution is located or has branch offices. A smaller institution may designate an area inside the larger metropolitan area as its community.
2. *Effective lending territory*. This method is defined as "that local area or areas around each office or group of offices where it makes a substantial portion of its loans and all other areas equidistant from its offices as those areas."[4]
3. The third method of establishing the community is described in the regulations as follows: "An institution may use other reasonable delineated local area that meets the purposes of the Community Reinvestment Act (CRA) and does not exclude low- and moderate-income neighborhoods."[5]

Of the three methods, the most meaningful to the real estate professional is the effective lending territory method, the plotting of a sampling of the actual loans that have been made by the institution in the area. This method will best define the actual area of operation and specialization of the institution.

The second type of information in the CRA statement that will be of importance to the real estate professional is the information regarding the type of credit extended by the institution. The regulations require the institution to list the specific types of credit granted in certain categories. The categories that are listed in the regulations are as follows:

1. Residential loans for one- to four-family residences
2. Residential loans for five or more dwelling units
3. Loans for housing rehabilitation

4. Loans for home improvement
5. Loans for financing small businesses
6. Community development loans
7. Commercial loans
8. Consumer loans

From this list, the real estate professional can pair the proper institution to the proper type of loan. For example, if you are working with a client who specializes in the purchase of properties that need rehabilitation, you would look for an institution that makes rehabilitation loans and serves the community in which the property is located.

These are the two main areas of the CRA statement that will be of help to the real estate professional. Being familiar with the CRA statements of the institutions in your community will be a service to your clients, for you will be better able to counsel them about the financing available through federally supervised financial institutions.

ASSESSING THE PERFORMANCE OF THE INSTITUTION

As mentioned earlier, the Community Reinvestment Act gives the supervisory agency that examines the institution the authority to assess the institution's performance in helping to meet the credit needs of its entire community, including the low- and moderate-income neighborhoods.

The supervisory agencies will review the institution's CRA statement and any signed written comments retained by the institution regarding their credit-granting activities. The supervisory agency, in addition to reviewing the above information, will review many areas of the institution's operation in order to assess the institution's performance. Some of those items reviewed are as follows:

How the institution ascertained the credit needs of the entire community

The geographic distribution of the credit extended and denied

The institution's participation, including investments, in local community development and redevelopment programs and projects

The institution's origination of residential loans, housing rehabilitation loans, and home improvement loans, or the purchase of these types of mortgages made in the institution's community

The institution's participation in government-insured, -guaranteed, or -subsidized loan programs for housing, small businesses, or small farms in the institution's community

Because the above items are reviewed by the federal supervisory agencies, financial institutions are more prone to make these types of mortgages, thus making it easier to get financing in low- to moderate-income neighborhoods.

One example of a financial institution being willing to participate in such loan programs was a rehabilitation loans program in low- to moderate-income areas of Houston. The program was passed by the Houston city council and was signed as an ordinance in February 1979. Entitled Rehabilitation Loan Agreement, the program was an agreement between the city of Houston and a group of financial institutions for a two-year pilot project to establish the feasibility of a program of rehabilitation loans in which the city of Houston would guarantee the repayment of any loan made under the provisions of the program. The financial institutions taking part in the agreement would make available a total of $1 million at all times during the program for making rehabilitation loans.

Under this program, both owner and non-owner occupied property was eligible and the properties were to be located in areas that had a great deal of substandard property and were inside the Houston city limits.

The amount, term, and interest rate on these loans were as follows:

Owner-occupied property

Type A: A single-unit residential structure occupied by the owner

Loan Amount:	$12,000
Interest Rate:	3%
Loan Period:	15 years

Type B: A residential dwelling structure containing two to four units, one of which is occupied by the owner

Loan Amount: The lesser of $5000 per unit or $20,000
Interest Rate: 3%
Loan Period 15 years

Investor-owned property

Type A: One or more unattached single-unit dwelling structures, none of which is occupied by the owner

Loan Amount: The lesser of $12,000 per unit or $50,000
Interest Rate: 6%
Loan Period: 15 years

Type B: A dwelling containing two or more attached units, none of which are occupied by the owner

Loan Amount: The lesser of $5000 per unit or $50,000
Interest Rate: 6%
Loan Period: 15 years

Type C: A dwelling structure containing five or more attached units whether or not one is occupied by the owner

Loan Amount: The lesser of $5000 per unit or $50,000
Interest Rate: 6%
Loan Period: 15 years

In addition to the immediate effects on the financial institutions not meeting obligations under the Community Reinvestment Act, it may have an effect on the institution if it should wish to expand. The community reinvestment regulations governing the institutions also state than an institution's performance shall be taken into account if it makes application for insurance under FDIC or FSLIC for addition of a savings and loan association branch office, for relocation of a main office or branch, for merger or consolidation, or for acquisition of assets or assumption of liabilities of another institution. In other words, the involvement of a financial institution in community reinvestment is quite important.

The importance of community development can be further shown in that the Federal Home Loan Bank Board now requires any federally chartered savings and loan association that invests more than 2 percent of its assets in a service corporation to also make an investment in the community. The regulation requires that if the savings and loan invests 2.5 percent of its assets in the service corporation, it must invest at least 0.5 percent of its total assets in community, inner-city, or community development investments. If the association invests as much as is authorized by the regulation (3 percent of its assets) in a service corporation, it must invest a sum equal to 1 percent of its assets in investments that serve primarily community, inner-city, or community development purposes.

> The Federal Home Loan Bank Board believes investments that would qualify as primarily related to "community, inner-city, and community development purposes" would be substantially directed at programs for development, preservation, and revitalization of low- and moderate-income areas, both urban and rural.[6]

Thus, the savings and loan institutions are again required to invest in the community and to help the low- to moderate-income areas of the community.

> In determining if an investment qualifies as primarily related to "community, inner-city, and community development purposes," the board would consider:
>
> 1. Whether the investment demonstrates substantial involvement in innovative loans which contribute to the development, preservation, or revitalization of either urban or rural communities; or
>
> 2. Whether the investment meets community development and housing needs and priorities, principally for low- and moderate-income areas, or contributes to the elimination of slums or blight; or
>
> 3. Whether the investment demonstrates commitment to participate in government- or privately-sponsored programs aimed at community development, preservation, or revitalization; or
>
> 4. Whether the investment involves a local partnership aimed at assisting existing residents in neighborhoods experiencing reinvestments.[7]

QUALIFYING GOVERNMENTAL PROGRAMS

The following governmental programs can help financial institutions meet the requirements of the Community Reinvestment Act:

1. Urban Development Action Grants
2. Urban Homesteading
3. Community Development Block Grants
4. Neighborhood Reinvestment Corporations; Title VI
5. Section 203(b) One- to Four-Family Mortgage Insurance (HUD)
6. Section 245, Graduated Payment Mortgage (HUD)
7. Section 221(d)(3) and (4) Multifamily Rental Housing for Low- and Moderate-Income Families (HUD)
8. Section 235 Revised (HUD)
9. Section 312 Housing Rehabilitation Loans (HUD)
10. Section 8 Housing Assistance Payments Programs (HUD)
11. Title I Home Improvement Loan Insurance (HUD)
12. Section 502, Single-Family Rural Housing Loans Guaranteed by Farmers Home Administration
13. Section 7(a), Direct, Immediate Participation and Guaranteed Loans (SBA)
14. Section 502, Local Development Companies Loan Program (SBA)
15. Veterans Administration Single-Family Guarantee (VA).

Although this is not a complete list, if any of the listed governmental programs are implemented by a financial institution, they will aid the institution in meeting the requirements of the Community Reinvestment Act. Some of these programs will be of more use to the real estate professional in rural areas than in urban ones.

HOME MORTGAGE DISCLOSURE ACT

Another important piece of legislation that has affected the financial institutions in the field of community reinvestment is the Home Mortgage Disclosure Act (HMDA), which requires that financial institutions located in standard metropolitan statistical areas (SMSAs) disclose information about home mortgages and home improvement loans they make.

The HMDA was amended by the Housing and Community Development Act of 1980, which requires the compilation and disclosure of loan data by calendar year rather than by fiscal year. All of the data must now be reported by census tract and county rather than census tract and zip code. The amendment further requires that a standard disclosure format be used and that a central repository be established in each SMSA in the United States.

The act requires any depository institution with assets in excess of $10 million to make the required disclosures. State-chartered institutions are exempt from the provisions of the HMDA.

Some of the major provisions of the act are:

1. *Compilation of loan data.* Each institution shall compile data on loans by the number and dollar amount of home purchase and home improvement loans that the institution both originates and purchases each calendar year beginning with 1981.
2. *Disclosure format.* The institution will use the prescribed format shown in Figures 15-2, and 15-3.
3. *Reporting area.* All loan data reported by the institution will be by SMSA, with the SMSA further divided into census tracts. This means that each loan will be shown by the broad area of the SMSA and then as to the particular census tract inside the SMSA where the property is located.
4. *Types of loans.* The regulations require the institution to report loans by the following types:

Figure 15-2. Mortgage Loan Disclosure Statement, page 1

FRB HMDA-1
OMB No. 7100-0090
Approval expires September 1984

MORTGAGE LOAN DISCLOSURE STATEMENT

Report for loans made in 19 ____

This report is required by law (12 U.S.C. 2801-2811 and 12 CFR 203).

Depository Institution

Name ________________

Address ________________

Enforcement Agency for this Institution

Name ________________

Address ________________

Census tract series used: ____ 1970 series ____ 1980 series

SMSA (location of property) ________________

PART A—ORIGINATIONS

SECTION 1—LOANS ON PROPERTY LOCATED WITHIN THOSE SMSAs IN WHICH INSTITUTION HAS HOME OR BRANCH OFFICES

CENSUS TRACT (in numerical sequence) where property located or COUNTY (name) where property located	Loans on 1 - to - 4 family dwellings						Loans on Multi-family Dwellings for 5 or more families (home purchases and home improvement)		Addendum Item: Non-occupant Loans on 1 - to - 4 family dwellings	
	Home Purchase Loans				Home Improvement Loans		D		E	
	FHA, FmHA, and VA A		Other ("Conventional") B		C					
	No. of Loans	Principal Amount (Thousands)	No. of Loans	Principal Amount (Thousands)	No. of Loans	Principal Amount (Thousands)	No. of Loans	Principal Amount (Thousands)	No. of Loans	Principal Amount (Thousands)
SMSA TOTAL										

SECTION 2—LOANS ON ALL PROPERTY LOCATED ELSEWHERE

(shaded)									(shaded)	(shaded)

Source: "Rules and Regulations," *Federal Register*, January 7, 1982, vol. 47, no. 4, p. 753.

Figure 15-3. ***Mortgage Loan Disclosure Statement, page 2***

PART B—PURCHASES

SECTION 1—DATA FOR PROPERTY LOCATED WITHIN THOSE SMSAs IN WHICH INSTITUTION HAS HOME OR BRANCH OFFICES

CENSUS TRACT (in numerical sequence) where property located or COUNTY (name) where property located	Loans on 1 - to - 4 family dwellings						Loans on Multi-family Dwellings for 5 or more families (home purchases and home improvement)		Addendum Item: Non-occupant Loans on 1 - to - 4 family dwellings	
	Home Purchase Loans				Home Improvement Loans					
	FHA, FmHA, and VA A		Other ("Conventional") B		C		D		E	
	No. of Loans	Principal Amount (Thousands)	No. of Loans	Principal Amount (Thousands)	No. of Loans	Principal Amount (Thousands)	No. of Loans	Principal Amount (Thousands)	No. of Loans	Principal Amount (Thousands)
SMSA TOTAL										

SECTION 2—LOANS ON ALL PROPERTY LOCATED ELSEWHERE

Source: "Rules and Regulations," *Federal Register*, January 7, 1982, vol. 47, no. 4, p. 754.

a. FHA, VA, and FmHA loans on one- to four-family dwellings

b. Other home mortgages (conventional) on one- to four-family dwellings

c. Home improvement loans on one- to four-family dwellings

d. Total purchase and home improvement loans on dwellings with four or more families

e. Loans made to either purchase or improve properties that were not to be used as the primary residence of the borrower

In addition to the provisions outlined above, the act requires that the institution make the information available to the general public. Thus, the institutions are required to have a copy of the Disclosure Statement available at their home offices as well as at least one branch office located in each of the SMSAs in which the institution has shown activity in the previous twelve-month period. To gain access to an institution's statement, one must make a request to the institution in person at any office of the institution during normal office hours. If a person requests a copy of the statement and if the institution has copying capabilities, the institution may charge a reasonable price for the copying service.

This law is another effort of the U.S. Congress to see that the financial institutions meet the total credit needs of all segments of the communities they serve. It also makes available to the public information indicating whether the institution is truly meeting the needs of its community. As a real estate professional, this information required by the HMDA can help you find the institutions that may assist you in financing properties in low- to moderate-income areas.

SUMMARY

Community reinvestment is a concept designed to help large cities throughout the United States, particularly cities with declining areas in the inner city and elsewhere. The program will have the greatest effect on cities with a population of 200,000 or more. Community reinvestment can be of great assistance to the real estate professional who is working in the inner city or the transitional areas of a city. Even if you are not working in these areas, you should become familiar with the efforts of the financial institutions in your area to meet the requirements of the Community Reinvestment Act.

REVIEW QUESTIONS

1. Outline the history of the Community Reinvestment Act.

2. Identify the financial institutions covered by the CRA.

3. Name and explain some of the major requirements placed on the financial institutions by the CRA.

4. Give the major purpose of the Community Reinvestment Act.

5. Explain how the Community Reinvestment Act statement of a financial institution can aid the real estate professional.

6. Name and explain the three methods used by a financial institution to define its community.

7. List some of the guidelines used by the supervisory agencies to judge the performance of financial institutions.

8. Examine the Community Reinvestment Act statements of several financial institutions in your area and assess in your opinion how well the institutions are meeting the credit needs of their community.

NOTES

[1]Most of this section is based upon material from the *Code of Federal Regulations*, Title 12, Parts 25.2, 228.2, 344.2 and 563e.2, January 1, 1980, pp. 276, 757, 294 and 750.

[2]*Code of Federal Regulations*, Title 12, Part 284.4(c)(1), (2), and (3), January 1, 1980, p. 758.

[3]*Code of Federal Regulations*, Title 12, Part 563e.3(b)(1), January 1, 1980, p. 750.

[4]*Code of Federal Regulations*, Title 12, Part 563e.3(b)(2), January 1, 1980, p. 750.

[5]*Code of Federal Regulations*, Title 12, Part 563e.3(b)(3), January 1, 1980, pp. 750-51.

[6]Federal Home Loan Bank Board, *Draft of Code of Federal Regulations*, Title 12, Part 545, undated, p. 2.

[7]Federal Home Loan Bank Board, *Draft of Code of Federal Regulations*, Title 12, Part 545, undated, pp.2-3.

CHAPTER 16 Creative Financing Methods

LEARNING OBJECTIVES

In this final chapter we will examine some of the creative methods that may be used to finance the residential real estate transaction. Upon completion of this chapter, you should be able to do the following:

- ★ **Define *wraparound mortgage*.**
- ★ **Name the three types of wraparound mortgages.**
- ★ **Explain owner financing.**
- ★ **Explain the Federal National Mortgage Association's Home Seller Loan Program.**

DEFINITION

Creative financing can be defined as the financing of the real estate transaction using methods that are not normally available through the traditional sources of mortgage financing.

However, since the real estate market has been plagued by high interest rates and rapid inflation of the price of housing, the use of creative financing has become rather commonplace, and some creative methods have now actually become common. Some of these methods were discussed in Chapter 3.

The following creative financing methods are by no means the only ones available, but they are some of the more commonly used.

WRAPAROUND MORTGAGE

As discussed in Chapter 2, a *wraparound mortgage* is the structuring of secondary financing to include an existing mortgage on real property. This structuring is done in a way that virtually makes the wraparound mortgage a first lien mortgage. Because of the structuring of the wraparound mortgage, it is sometimes called the all-inclusive mortgage. If the wraparound mortgage is executed using a deed of trust, it is sometimes referred to as an all-inclusive deed of trust mortgage.

There are three types of wraparound mortgages.

Additional fund wrap This is the most common wraparound mortgage. It is used when the existing financing has a below-market interest rate or the existing mortgage includes a restrictive or no prepayment provision. The additional fund wrap combines the mortgage balance with the additional funds that are to be advanced. We will give an example of this type of wrap later in the chapter.

Simultaneous wrap This type of wrap can be used to reduce the loan-to-value ratio of a first lien mortgage. For example, the purchaser of an office building can only secure an 80 percent mortgage, but would like to reduce this ratio. Thus, the purchaser arranges for a wrap mortgage that is equal to 10 percent of the value. This reduces the purchaser's equity position to only 10 percent. The wrap is negotiated simultaneously with the first lien mortgage.

Extended-term wrap This type of wrap is used only to extend the term of existing financing. The only reason for the extension is to improve the cash flow on a piece of income-producing property.

Residential Use of a Wrap

The wraparound mortgage has been used for years in the financing of commercial properties. Now it is a possible method of financing the sale of residential properties. With the advent of the higher interest rates in late 1979, the wrap has become a popular alternative means of financing, but its use has been somewhat limited by the implementation of the *call* or *due-on-sale clause* in many conventional mortgages. Since neither the FHA-insured mortgage nor the VA-guaranteed mortgage has such a provision, the wraparound mortgage is a logical method for financing a transaction involving an existing FHA or VA mortgage.

With this in mind, the Mortgage Guaranty Insurance Corporation has devised a mortgage that combines the advantages of the wraparound mortgage and the safety of an insured conventional mortgage. They call this mortgage "the Magic-Wrap."

The Federal Home Loan Bank Board has realized the importance of the wraparound mortgage as a possible method of fostering homeownership for the first-time homebuyer. The Depository Institutions Deregulation and Monetary Control Act of 1980 (Section 501) states that any federally related mortgage loan, secured by a first lien on residential real property, made after March 31, 1980, is exempt from state usury ceilings. The FHLBB, under this act, has proposed regulations that would permit some lenders to issue wraparound mortgages that would not be subject to the restraint of state usury laws, provided that certain conditions are met.

The FHLBB believes that the wraparound would provide a money-saving alternative to the prospective homebuyer and has taken the position that the wraparound meets the first lien requirement of the 1980 Deregulation Act if (1) The wraparound lender agrees to continue to pay the monthly payments on the existing mortgage on the home to be purchased at the original interest rate of the existing mortgage; and (2) the wraparound lender agrees to make any additional payments needed to meet the purchase price of the home to be purchased.

This agreement means that the term of the original mortgage will continue to be met, the seller will be paid for the sale of the property, and the homebuyer is able to purchase and take advantage of a below-market interest charged by the wraparound lender. Note that if the wraparound lender will not make the wraparound mortgage at a below-market interest rate, the advantage of the wraparound mortgage may be lost.

If approved, the proposed FHLBB regulations would require that the wraparound lenders meet the following criteria to ensure that they can protect their investments and satisfy their commitment to the borrowers:

1. The wraparound lender shall at all times have sufficient funds available to satisfy all prior liens on the security property

2. The borrower will reimburse the lender for sums advanced in order to secure or protect the wraparound lender's investment. For example, if private mortgage insurance is required, the borrower would have to pay the premiums.

Note that the FHLBB has limited these regulations to the financing of residential properties.

A Wraparound Mortgage Example

Let us assume that a family wishes to buy a home with a purchase price of $125,000 and an existing mortgage of $80,000 with an interest rate of 9.5 percent. The seller is requiring a down payment of 10 percent, or $12,500.

If the buyer had to execute a new mortgage for the balance of $112,500 at, say, an interest rate of 14 percent, the monthly principal and interest payment would be $1333.

Let us assume that the seller would allow the purchaser to execute a wrap-around mortgage with a lender that would agree to continue to pay the monthly payments on the original $80,000 at 9.5 percent. Thus, the amount of the wraparound mortgage would be $80,000 plus the remainder of the seller's equity of $32,500, or a total of $112,500. Let us also assume that the wraparound lender would charge 11.5 percent interest. The principal and interest payments to the borrower would be reduced to approximately $1114 per month.

With the use of the wraparound mortgage, all parties gain advantages. The seller is able to sell his house, the purchaser is able to buy the house with a reduced payment, and the lender is able to make a return on not only the amount advanced, but also on the original mortgage amount. How is this so? First, the wraparound lender is paying an interest rate of 9.5 percent on the original financing, but since it is included in the wraparound, the lender is collecting 11.5 percent, thus making a spread of 2 percent. The wrap lender is collecting a full 11.5 percent on the $32,500 loaned the purchaser to pay the seller's equity in full.

BLENDED YIELD MORTGAGE

The blended yield mortgage (BYM), sometimes called a consolidated mortgage or blended mortgage, can be defined as a first lien mortgage secured by real property that combines an existing first lien mortgage and any type of secondary financing that may be used to achieve a sale of real property. In other words, the BYM is used when a sale of real property would normally involve a second or wraparound mortgage. The normal operation of a BYM is that the lender holding the first lien on the property will allow the property to be sold and will take an average of the interest rate on the existing mortgage and the present yield on secondary financing or first lien mortgage in the market and will refinance the purchase of the property at an interest rate below the prevailing market rate. A good example of the blended yield mortgage or blended mortgage is the FNMA Resale/Refinance Program. This program is discussed in detail in Chapter 9.

The blended mortgage has advantages for both lenders and borrowers. The most obvious to lenders is that they are able to get low-yielding mortgages out of their portfolios. This type of mortgage slows the use of the wraparound mortgage or the second mortgage, which retains the low-yield mortgage.

The primary advantage to the borrower/co-borrower is that he or she may purchase the property of his or her choice at a below-market interest rate. This rate may cost the borrower/coborrower less per month than making a combined monthly payment on an existing first and a new second mortgage. An example of such a situation is shown in Figure 9-4 in Chapter 9.

It should be noted that this may be a possible method of selling a piece of real property if the existing first lien is held by a lender who was not affected by the U.S. Supreme Court decision of June 28, 1982. This decision upheld the 1976 Federal Home Loan Bank Board regulation preempting state laws that unlimited or prohibited federally chartered thrifts from implementing the due-on-sale clause in a mortgage/deed of trust.

BALLOON MORTGAGE

A *balloon mortgage* is usually used for the financing of raw land or income-producing properties. The purpose of the balloon mortgage is to allow low monthly payments with a large payment due at the term of the mortgage. For example, a person wishes to purchase a parcel of vacant land with the hopes of selling the property in, say, three years. The cost of the property is $50,000 and the purchaser would like to be able to pay as little as possible monthly. So the seller agrees to a balloon mortgage with the following terms:

1. The purchaser is to make a down payment of 10 percent, or $5000

2. The note will be executed with monthly payments based on an amortization schedule as if the mortgage was to be paid

out in twenty years, but the remaining principal is due and payable at the end of five years or upon sale of the property

Thus, the purchaser is able to pay a lesser amount per month while he is trying to sell the property, with one large, or balloon, payment due at the term of the mortgage or at the sale of the property.

The balloon mortgage also can allow the purchaser of property to pay interest only for a specific term (for example, three years) at the end of which the full principal amount of the mortgage is due.

Federally chartered thrifts were allowed to make the balloon mortgage, but due to the changing real estate market and the high interest rates, the FHLBB saw a need to liberalize this rule. After publishing the rule for public comment on July 14, 1981, and receiving comments, the Board issued its Final Rule revising the authority of Federal thrifts to make the balloon mortgage, effective October 21, 1981.

This revision made sweeping changes in the authority. Before this change, the thrifts could only make balloon loans for a maximum term of five years and with a maximum loan-to-value ratio of 60 percent. This would require the borrower to make a down payment of 40 percent. The revision now allows a maximum term of forty years and allows a loan-to-value ratio of up to 95 percent.

The revision also allows the thrifts to adjust the interest rate on the balloon mortgage. The rule regarding the adjustment of the interest rate is the same as that of the AML reviewed in Chapter 15.

The revised rule does contain a disclosure requirement. According to the revised rule, the application and the loan contract is to contain a disclosure notice. The form and content of this notice is shown in Figure 16-1. The other required notice is at the time of a rate or payment change. The rule states that this notice must be given at least 45 days, but not more than 90 days, prior to the maturity of the balloon mortgage. The notice must contain the following:

1. The maturity date
2. The amount due at maturity
3. Whether, and under what conditions, the mortgage will be refinanced

The board feels that this revised rule gives the federal thrifts the flexibility to structure the balloon mortgage to make it attractive to the prospective homebuyer. The FHLBB feels that the balloon mortgage will offer borrowers the advantage of a fixed-rate mortgage without being tied to a long-term mortgage that has a high interest rate.

The balloon mortgage may provide an excellent vehicle for a client who is being transferred into your area and knows that he or she will be there for a limited period, say up to four years. The balloon will allow this person the advantages of a short-term fixed rate mortgage with all of the monies paid to the lender being tax deductible. This type of mortgage is, however, not suitable for the person who is purchasing a home in which he or she plans to spend many years.

PARTICIPATION MORTGAGE

In this type of financing, the lender will participate in the property, in either the appreciation of the property upon its sale, or in the revenue generated by the property.

Until recently, the participation mortgage was limited to income-producing properties. With the advent of the shared appreciation mortgage, however, lenders are now sharing in the appreciation, or profit, from the sale of residential property. The other type of participation by the lender is limited to the income-producing property. Here, the lender will make a mortgage financing, for example, an office building and in return the borrower must give the lender a share of the income derived from the property. For example, a lender may agree to make a 75 percent mortgage at an interest rate of 11.5 percent for twenty years. The lender will receive 15 percent of the net income before federal taxes and depreciation. Let us say the building has a net income of $20,000 before taxes and depreciation. The lender would not only receive the interest income from the mortgage, but would receive $3000 of the net income of the building.

EQUITY PARTICIPATION MORTGAGE

As mentioned in the previous section, the participation mortgage was limited to the financing of commercial real estate trans-

Figure 16-1. Balloon Disclosure

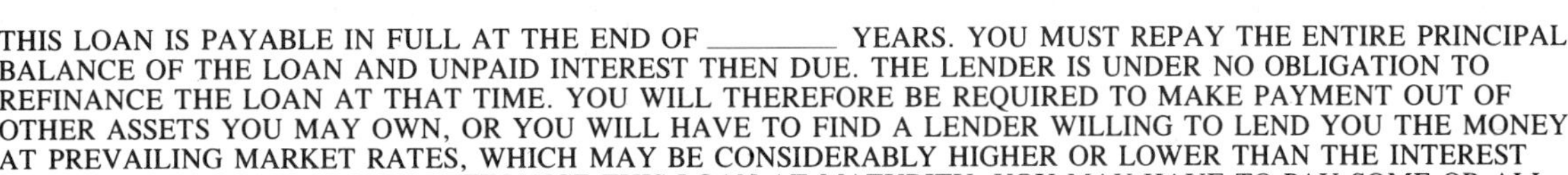
To be Included in Loan Application and Loan Contract:

THIS LOAN IS PAYABLE IN FULL AT THE END OF ________ YEARS. YOU MUST REPAY THE ENTIRE PRINCIPAL BALANCE OF THE LOAN AND UNPAID INTEREST THEN DUE. THE LENDER IS UNDER NO OBLIGATION TO REFINANCE THE LOAN AT THAT TIME. YOU WILL THEREFORE BE REQUIRED TO MAKE PAYMENT OUT OF OTHER ASSETS YOU MAY OWN, OR YOU WILL HAVE TO FIND A LENDER WILLING TO LEND YOU THE MONEY AT PREVAILING MARKET RATES, WHICH MAY BE CONSIDERABLY HIGHER OR LOWER THAN THE INTEREST RATE ON THIS LOAN. IF YOU REFINANCE THIS LOAN AT MATURITY, YOU MAY HAVE TO PAY SOME OR ALL CLOSING COSTS NORMALLY ASSOCIATED WITH A NEW LOAN, EVEN IF YOU OBTAIN REFINANCING FROM THE SAME LENDER.

Source: "Rules and Regulations," *Federal Register*, October 23, 1981, vol. 26, no. 205, p. 51896.

actions. However, with the continuing high interest rates in the early 1980s, the participation mortgage became an alternative way to finance residential real estate. These mortgages were called by many titles, one of the most common being equity participation mortgage (EPM). This type of residential creative financing involves the borrower/co-borrower who will occupy the property and an investor who will not occupy the property. It should be noted that the investor may or may not be the institution making the first lien loan.

The EPM is designed for a builder, developer, or seller of single-family dwellings who knows of individuals or businesses interested in getting the tax advantages of investing in nonowner-occupied one- to four-family dwellings. Once the builder, seller, or developer finds a person or persons who would like to purchase a dwelling but does not have the necessary income or down payment to qualify for the mortgage on his or her own, the seller contacts one of the parties that would like to invest in one of these dwellings. Then the owner/occupant and the investor split the down payment and all of the costs of ownership. The percentage paid by the two parties is set by the EPM documents. If it is a 50/50 split, the borrower will put up half of the down payment, pay half of the closing costs and pay half of the monthly payment. Normally, the investor has no right to occupy the property, but shares half of all tax benefits derived from the payment of interest on the mortgage and can also take depreciation on his or her half of the dwelling since he or she does not occupy the unit.

The borrower also can claim a tax deduction for his portion of the interest paid. The occupant of the unit will also pay a rental fee to the investor/nonowner occupant.

The term of an EPM ranges from three to five years and the procedure followed at the end of the EPM term is outlined in the original loan documents. Normally there are three options available at the end of the term: (1) the owner/occupant can pay off the remaining principal balance by refinancing or from the sale of other assets; (2) the EPM may be renegotiated and run for another specific number of years; or (3) the home can be sold and the profits distributed as per the original loan documents. For the occupant, the third method is obviously the least desirable; the first is the best option in most cases.

As one can see, the EPM is a very involved type of mortgage that can have many pitfalls for both the investor and the owner/occupant. Before working with any builder, seller, or developer using the EPM you should have all of the documents reviewed by an attorney or have your client, prior to signing any EPM documents, take the documents to an attorney.

OWNER FINANCING

This is a method of financing the real estate transaction in which the seller actually finances the purchase of the property. It can be used when the property is free of all existing debt. The importance of this type of financing has been shown by some real estate commissions' promulgation of a standard contract for an all-cash sale or owner-financed sale of property. Realizing the importance of this method of financing, the Federal National Mortgage Association has created a mortgage purchase program that will allow the homeowner who finances the sale of his or her property by taking back a first lien mortgage to sell this mortgage to FNMA.

Home Seller Loan Program (FNMA)

Under FNMA's program, a home seller could contract with an FNMA-approved lender to perform the services associated with the origination and processing of the loan and collection of the monthly payments.

The mortgage will be underwritten using the standard FNMA Note and Mortgage/Deed of Trust. This will allow the seller wishing to finance the purchase of a home to use the services of a professional lender and have the ability to convert the first-lien mortgage to cash at any time during the term of the mortgage.

When the seller is ready to convert the mortgage to cash, he or she will contact the lender, who will in turn arrange with FNMA to purchase the mortgage. The purchase price of the mortgage would be based on the current mortgage rates. For example, the seller would negotiate with the buyer a first-lien mortgage with an interest rate of 12.5 percent face rate. Then, two years later, the seller wishes to be cashed out of the mortgage and arranges with the FNMA-approved lender to sell the mortgage to FNMA. If the current mortgage market rate was 12.5 percent, the seller would be able to sell the mortgage at par or for the full amount, less some fees. But if the mortgage market rate was more than 12.5 percent, the seller would have to pay discount points in order to bring the yield of the mortgage to the current mortgage market rate. This is one of the major drawbacks to the program. However, it does give the seller an opportunity to finance the sale of his or her home with liquidity.

SECOND MORTGAGES

Second mortgages have been used extensively to aid in the financing of real estate by assumption. Either the seller or a financial institution can execute a second mortgage for a portion of the down payment.

As the name implies, the mortgage executed is an inferior mortgage to the first-lien mortgage held by the original lender, as was mentioned earlier in this text. For example, a person wishes to purchase a piece of property by assuming the existing mortgage. (Not all existing conventional mortgages may be assumed without prior approval of the lender.) The purchase price of the property is $80,000, the balance on the existing mortgage is $50,000 with an interest rate of 9.5 percent, and the lender will require the interest rate to increase to 10.5 percent. The seller's equity in the property is $30,000, or the difference between the purchase price and the remaining principal balance of the existing mortgage. The purchaser agrees to the sales price, but only wishes to give the seller $20,000 in cash and to arrange for a second mortgage in the amount of $10,000.

At this point the seller has a choice. Does the seller wish to make the second to the purchaser or to have the purchaser go to a financial institution that specializes in second mortgages? If the seller selects to originate or carry the second, the purchaser would then make the payments directly to the seller. Thus, the seller would get $20,000 in cash, as well as principal reduction and interest on the $10,000 second mortgage.

LAND LEASING

A new method that has been used to finance the real estate transaction is *land leasing*, which is to separate the land from the home, thus making the cost of the house less. Under this method, the house, if financed using some type of first-lien mortgage, and the land is placed on a ninety-nine-year lease to the party or parties that purchase the home. It has been proposed that the ground lease be an escalating type lease that will allow for the initial lease payments to be at a lower amount for a specific number of years, say three years.

For example, if a person wished to purchase a home costing $84,500 including the land, financing 90 percent of the purchase price over thirty years at 12 percent interest, the payment for principal and interest would be $782.04. If the land was separated from the house, the payment could be lowered. For this example, let us say the land is valued at $18,000. The actual value of the house would then be $66,500. The principal and interest payment on 90 percent, or a mortgage of approximately $59,900 at 12 percent, would be $616.37, or $165.67 a month less. For our purposes, let us say that the cost of the land lease would be approximately $100 per month for the first three years. The buyer's total monthly payment then would be $716.27. The lease payment would escalate by an amount agreed upon between the parties to the lease. At the end of the first three-year period, the income of the purchaser should have increased to a level that equals or exceeds the increase in the lease payments.

REVIEW QUESTIONS

1. Define *wraparound mortgage*.
2. Name and explain the types of wraparound mortgages.
3. Explain how owner financing may be used.
4. Explain the Federal National Mortgage Association Home Seller Loan Program.
5. Explain how a balloon mortgage can be used to finance a residential transaction.
6. What is meant by the term *second mortgage?*
7. Contact lenders or developers in your area to see what additional types of creative financing they have developed.

APPENDIX A HUD Area Offices and FHA Service Offices

Alabama
Birmingham 35233
Daniel Bldg.
15 South 20th St.

Alaska
Anchorage 99501
334 West 5th Ave.

Arizona
Phoenix 85003
Arizona Bank Bldg.
18th Floor
101 North First Ave.

Arkansas
Little Rock 72201
Room 1490
One Union National Plaza

California
Los Angeles 90057
2500 Wilshire Blvd.

Sacramento 95809
545 Downtown Plaza
Suite 250
P.O. Box 1978

San Diego 92112
Federal Office Bldg.
880 Front St.

San Francisco 94111
1 Embarcadero Ctr.
Suite 1600

Santa Ana 92701
34 Civic Ctr.
Plaza, Room 164

Colorado
Denver 80202
Executive Towers
1405 Curtis St.

Connecticut
Hartford 06103
One Financial Plaza

District of Columbia
Washington, D.C. 20009
Universal North Bldg.
1875 Connecticut Ave., N.W.

Florida
Coral Gables 33134
3001 Ponce de Leon Blvd.

Jacksonville 32204
Peninsular Plaza
661 Riverside Ave.

Tampa 33602
Federal Bldg.
700 Twiggs St.
P.O. Box 2097

Georgia
Atlanta 30303
Richard B. Russell Federal Bldg.
75 Spring St., SW

Hawaii
Honolulu 96850
Prince Jonah Kuhio Kalanianaole
Federal Bldg.
300 Ala Moana Blvd.
Suite 3318

Idaho
Boise 83705
419 North Curtis Rd.
P.O. Box 32

Indiana
Indianapolis 46207
151 North Delaware St.

Iowa
Des Moines 50309
Room 259
Federal Bldg.
210 Walnut St.

Kansas
Kansas City 64106
Professional Bldg.
1103 Grand Ave.

Kentucky
Louisville 40201
539 River City Mall

Louisiana
New Orleans 70113
Plaza Tower
1001 Howard Ave.

Shreveport 71120
New Federal Bldg.
500 Fannin, 6th Floor

Maryland
Baltimore 21201
Two Hopkins Plaza
Mercantile Bank and
Trust Bldg.

Massachusetts
Boston 02114
Bulfinch Bldg.
15 New Chardon St.

Michigan
Detroit 48226
Patrick V. McNamara
Federal Bldg.
477 Michigan Ave.

Grand Rapids 49505
Northbrook Bldg. Number 11
2922 Fuller Ave. NE

Minnesota
Minneapolis-St. Paul 55435
6400 France Ave.
Minneapolis, Minnesota

Mississippi
Jackson 39201
Federal Bldg., Suite 1016
100 W. Capitol St.

Missouri
St. Louis 63101
210 North 12th St.

Montana
Helena 59601
Federal Office Bldg.
Drawer 10095
301 S. Park, Rm. 340

Nebraska
Omaha 68106
Univac Bldg.
7100 West Ctr. Rd.

Nevada
Reno 89505
1050 Bible Way
P.O. Box 4700

New Hampshire
Manchester 03103
Norris Cotton
Federal Bldg.
275 Chestnut St.

New Jersey
Camden 08103
The Parkdale Bldg.
519 Federal St.

Newark 07102
Gateway Bldg. No. 1
Raymond Plaza

New Mexico
Albuquerque 87110
625 Truman St. NE

New York
Albany 12207
Leo W. O'Brien
Federal Bldg.
North Pearl St. & Clinton Ave.

Buffalo 14202
Suite 800
Statler Bldg.
107 Delaware Ave.

New York 10028
26 Federal Plaza

North Carolina
Greensboro 27401
415 N. Edgewood St.

Ohio
Cincinnati 45202
Federal Office Bldg.
Room 9009
550 Main St.

Cleveland 44114
777 Rockwell

Columbus 43215
New Federal Bldg.
200 North High St.

Oklahoma
Oklahoma City 73102
200 N.W. 5th St.

Tulsa 74127
Robert S. Kerr Bldg.
440 South Houston Ave.

Oregon
Portland 97204
520 Southwest 6th Ave.

Pennsylvania
Philadelphia 19106
Curtis Bldg.
625 Walnut St.

Pittsburgh 15219
Fort Pitt Commons
445 Fort Pitt Blvd.

Puerto Rico
San Juan 00917
Federal Office Bldg.
Room 428
Carlos Chardon Ave.
Hato Rey, Puerto Rico
Mailing Address:
G Post Office Box 3869
San Juan, Puerto Rico 00936

Rhode Island
Providence 02903
330 John O. Pastore Federal Bldg.
& U.S. Post Office

South Carolina
Columbia 29201
Strom Thurmond Bldg.
1835-45 Assembly St.

Tennessee
Knoxville 37919
One Northshore Bldg.
1111 Northshore Drive

Memphis 38103
28th Floor
100 North Main St.

Nashville 37203
U.S. Courthouse
Federal Building Annex
801 Broadway

Texas
Dallas 75201
2001 Bryon Tower, 4th Floor

Fort Worth 76102
Room 13A01 Federal Bldg.
819 Taylor St.

Houston 77046
Two Greenway Plaza East
Suite 200

Lubbock 79408
Courthouse & Federal Office Bldg.
1205 Texas Ave.
P.O. Box 1647

San Antonio 78285
Washington Square
800 Dolorosa
P.O. Box 9163

Utah
Salt Lake City 84147
125 South State St.
P.O. Box 11009

Virginia
Richmond 23219
701 East Franklin St.

Washington
Seattle 98101
Arcade Plaza Bldg.
1321 Second Ave.

Spokane 99201
West 920 Riverside Ave.

West Virginia
Charleston 25301
Kanawha Valley Bldg.
Capitol & Lee Sts.

Wisconsin
Milwaukee 53203
744 North 4th St.

Source: U.S., Department of Housing and Urban Development, *Departmental Programs*, August 1980, pp. 93-95.

APPENDIX B Section 203(b) One- to Four-Family Mortgage Limits

For any market area (county or part of a county) not listed in Appendix below, the following maximum mortgage limits shall apply: $67,500 for a one-family unit; $76,000 for a two-family unit; $92,000 for a three-family unit; and $107,000 for a four-family unit.

Market area designation and local jurisdictions	Section 203(b) mortgage limits			
	1-family	2-family	3-family	4-family
Region I				
HUD Field Office: Hartford Area Office				
Bridgeport, CT SMSA:				
Fairfield County (part)	$70,500	$79,500	$96,500	$112,000
Bridgeport City				
Shelton City				
Easton Town				
Fairfield Town				
Monroe Town				
Stratford Town				
Trumbull Town				
New Haven County (part)				
Derby City				
Milford City				
Bristol, CT SMSA:				
Hartford County (part)	71,000	80,000	97,000	113,000
Bristol City				
Burlington Town				
Litchfield County				
Plymouth Town				
Danbury, CT SMSA:				
Fairfield County (part)	80,000	90,000	109,000	127,000
Danbury City				
Bethel Town				
Brookfield Town				
New Fairfield Town				
Newtown Town				
Redding Town				
Litchfield County (part)				
New Milford Town				

Market area designation and local jurisdictions	Section 203(b) mortgage limits			
	1-family	2-family	3-family	4-family
Hartford, CT SMSA:				
Hartford County (part)	68,000	77,000	93,000	108,000
Hartford City				
Avon Town				
Bloomfield Town				
Canton Town				
East Granby Town				
East Hartford Town				
East Windsor Town				
Enfield Town				
Farmington Town				
Glastonbury Town				
Granby Town				
Manchester Town				
Marlborough Town				
Newington Town				
Rocky Hill Town				
Simsbury Town				
South Windsor Town				
Suffield Town				
West Hartford Town				
Wethersfield Town				
Windsor Town				
Windsor Locks Town				
Litchfield County (part)				
New Hartford Town				
Middlesex County (part)				
Cromwell Town				
East Hampton Town				
Portland Town				
New London County				
Colchester Town				
Tolland County (part)				
Andover Town				
Bolton Town				
Columbia Town				
Coventry Town				
Ellington Town				
Hebron Town				
Stafford Town				
Tolland Town				
Vernon Town				
Willington Town				
Norwalk, CT SMSA:				
Fairfield County (part)	90,000	101,300	122,650	142,650
Norwalk City				
Weston Town				
Westport Town				
Wilton Town				
Stamford, CT SMSA:				
Fairfield County (part)	90,000	101,300	122,650	142,650
Stamford City				
Darien Town				
Greenwich Town				
New Canaan Town				

REGION II

HUD Field Office: New York Area Office

Market area designation and local jurisdictions	1-family	2-family	3-family	4-family
New York and Nassau-Suffolk, NY SMSAS (combined):				
Bronx County	$72,000	$81,000	$98,500	$114,500
Kings County				
Nassau County				
New York County				
Putnam County				
Queens County				
Richmond County				
Rockland County				
Suffolk County				
Westchester County				

HUD Field Office: Newark Area Office

Market area designation and local jurisdictions	1-family	2-family	3-family	4-family
State of New Jersey—northern metro areas:				
Bergen County	$83,500	$94,000	$113,500	$132,000
Essex County				
Hudson County				
Middlesex County				
Monmouth County				
Morris County				
Passaic County				
Somerest County				
Union County				

HUD Field Office: Camden Service Office

Market area designation and local jurisdictions	1-family	2-family	3-family	4-family
Atlantic City, NJ SMSA: Atlantic County	$89,000	$100,000	$121,000	$141,000
Trenton, NJ SMSA: Mercer County	68,500	77,000	93,500	108,000

Market area designation and local jurisdictions	Section 203(b) mortgage limits			
	1-family	2-family	3-family	4-family
Region III				
HUD Field Office: Washington, DC Area Office				
Washington, DC-MD-VA SMSA: District of Columbia; Montgomery County, MD; Prince Georges County, MD; Alexandria City, VA; Fairfax City, VA; Fairfax County, VA; Falls Church City, VA; Manassas City, VA; Manassas Park City, VA; Arlington County, VA; Loudoun County, VA; Prince William County, VA	$89,500	$100,500	$122,000	$141,500
HUD Field Office: Baltimore Area Office				
Washington, DC-MD-VA SMSA: Charles County	$89,500	$100,500	$122,000	$141,500
Baltimore, MD SMSA (part): Howard County; Anne Arundel County	78,500	88,000	107,000	124,000
HUD Field Office: Richmond Area Office				
Newport News-Hampton and Norfolk-VA Beach-Portsmouth, VA SMSA (combined): Chesapeake City; Hampton City; Newport News City; Norfolk City; Poquoson City; Portsmouth City; Suffolk City; Virginia Beach City; Williamsburg City; Gloucester County; James City County; York County	$76,500	$86,000	$104,500	$120,500
Region IV				
HUD Field Office: Greensboro Area Office				
Newport News-Hampton and Norfolk-VA Beach-Portsmouth, VA SMSA: Currituck County	$76,500	$86,000	$104,500	$120,500
HUD Field Office: Columbia Area Office				
Charleston-North Charleston, SC SMSA: Berkeley County; Charleston County; Dorchester County	$80,500	$90,500	$110,000	$127,500
HUD Field Office: Atlanta Area Office				
Atlanta, GA SMSA: Butts County; Cherokee County; Clayton County; Cobb County; De Kalb County; Douglas County; Fayette County; Forsyth County; Fulton County; Gwinnett County; Henry County; Newton County; Paulding County; Rockdale County; Walton County	$78,500	$88,500	$107,000	$124,500
HUD Field Office: Birmingham Area Office				
Mobile, AL SMSA: Baldwin County; Mobile County	$75,000	$84,000	$102,500	$118,000
Montgomery, AL SMSA: Autauga County; Elmore County; Montgomery County	75,000	84,000	102,500	118,000
HUD Field Office: Memphis Service Office				
Memphis, TN-AR-MS SMSA: Shelby County; Tipton County	$75,000	$84,000	$102,500	$118,000

Market area designation and local jurisdictions	Section 203(b) mortgage limits			
	1-family	2-family	3-family	4-family
HUD Field Office: Jackson Area Office				
Memphis, TN-AR-MS SMSA: De Soto County	$75,000	$84,000	$102,500	$118,000
HUD Field Office: Coral Gables Service Office				
Ft. Lauderdale-Hollywood, FL SMSA: Broward County	$72,500	$81,500	$98,500	$115,000
Miami, FL SMSA: Dade County	71,500	80,500	97,500	113,500
West Palm Beach-Boca Raton, FL SMSA: Palm Beach County	73,500	82,500	100,000	115,500
REGION V				
HUD Field Office: Minneapolis-St. Paul Area Office				
Minneapolis-St. Paul, MN SMSA:				
Anoka County	$74,000	$83,000	$101,000	$117,500
Carver County				
Chisago County				
Dakota County				
Hennepin County				
Ramsey County				
Scott County				
Washington County				
Wright County				
St. Cloud, MN SMSA:				
Benton County	68,500	77,000	93,500	108,500
Sherburne County				
Stearns County				
HUD Field Office: Milwaukee Area Office				
Minneapolis-St. Paul, MN SMSA: St. Croix County	$74,000	$83,000	$101,000	$117,500
Milwaukee, WI SMSA:				
Milwaukee County	73,500	83,000	100,500	116,500
Ozaukee County				
Washington County				
Waukesha County				
HUD Field Office: Chicago Area Office				
Chicago, IL SMSA:				
Cook County	$82,000	$92,000	$111,500	$129,500
DuPage County				
Kane County				
Lake County				
McHenry County				
Will County				
HUD Field Office: Detroit Area Office				
Detroit, MI SMSA:				
Lapeer County	$69,500	$83,500	$101,500	$118,000
Livingston County				
Macomb County				
Oakland County				
St. Clair County				
Wayne County				
HUD Field Office: Columbus Area Office				
Cleveland, OH SMSA:				
Cuyahoga County	$70,500	$79,000	$96,000	$111,500
Geauga County				
Lake County				
Medina County				
REGION VI				
HUD Field Office: Dallas Area Office				
Dallas-Ft. Worth, TX SMSA:				
Collin County	$85,000	$95,500	$115,500	$134,500
Dallas County				
Denton County				
Ellis County				
Kaufman County				
Rockwall County				
Sherman-Denison, TX SMSA: Grayson County	78,000	88,000	106,500	124,000
HUD Field Office: Fort Worth Service Office				
Dallas-Ft. Worth, TX SMSA:				
Hood County	$85,000	$95,500	$115,500	$134,500
Johnson County				
Parker County				
Tarrant County				
Wise County				

Market area designation and local jurisdictions	Section 203(b) mortgage limits			
	1-family	2-family	3-family	4-family
HUD Field Office: Houston Service Office				
Houston, TX SMSA:				
Brazoria County	$69,500	$78,000	$95,000	$110,500
Ft. Bend County				
Harris County				
Liberty County				
Montgomery County				
Waller County				
HUD Field Office: Lubbock Service Office				
Amarillo, TX SMSA:				
Potter County	$66,500	$77,000	$93,500	$108,500
Randall County				
Lubbock, TX SMSA: Lubbock County	70,000	78,500	95,500	110,500
Midland, TX SMSA: Midland County	70,000	78,500	95,500	110,500
HUD Field Office: San Antonio Area Office				
Austin and San Antonio, TX SMSAS (combined):				
Bexar County	$69,500	$78,500	$95,500	$110,000
Comal County				
Guadalupe County				
Hays County				
Travis County				
Williamson County				
Corpus Christi, TX SMSA:				
Nueces County	70,000	78,500	95,500	110,500
San Patricio County				
HUD Field Office: Little Rock Area Office				
Memphis, TN-AR-MS SMSA: Crittenden County	$75,000	$84,000	$102,500	$118,000
HUD Field Office: Oklahoma City Area Office				
Oklahoma City, OK SMSA:				
Canadian County	$68,000	$76,500	$93,000	$108,000
Cleveland County				
McClain County				
Oklahoma County				
Pottawatomie County				
HUD Field Office: New Orleans Area Office				
Baton Rouge and New Orleans, LA SMSAS (combined):				
Ascension Parish	$76,000	$85,500	$103,500	$120,500
East Baton Rouge Parish				
Jefferson Parish				
Livingston Parish				
Orleans Parish				
St. Bernard Parish				
St. Tammany Parish				
West Baton Rouge Parish				
HUD Field Office: Albuquerque Service Office				
Albuquerque, NM SMSA:				
Bernalillo County	$76,500	$86,000	$104,000	$121,000
Sandoval County				
HUD Field Office: Tulsa Service Office				
Tulsa, OK SMSA:				
Creek County	$71,500	$80,500	$97,500	$113,500
Mayes County				
Osage County				
Rogers County				
Tulsa County				
Wagoner County				
REGION VIII				
HUD Field Office: Denver Regional/Area Office				
Denver-Boulder, CO SMSA:				
Adams County	$76,000	$85,500	$103,500	$120,500
Arapahoe County				
Boulder County				
Denver County				
Douglas County				
Gilpin County				
Jefferson County				
Greeley, CO SMSA: Weld County	70,500	79,500	96,500	111,500
Colorado statewide non-SMSA areas	70,500	79,500	96,500	111,500

Market area designation and local jurisdictions	Section 203(b) mortgage limits			
	1-family	2-family	3-family	4-family
HUD Field Office: Helena Service Office				
State of Montana, SMSA and non-SMSA areas	$75,500	$84,000	$102,500	$118,000
Region IX				
HUD Field Office: Los Angeles Area Office				
Los Angeles area, office metro and nonmetro areas: Los Angeles County, San Luis Obispo County, Santa Barbara County, Ventura County	$90,000	$101,300	$122,600	$142,600
HUD Field Office: San Francisco Area Office				
San Francisco area office metro and nonmetro areas: Alameda County, Contra Costa County, Del Norte County, Humboldt County, Lake County, Marin County, Mendocino County, Monterey County, Napa County, San Benito County, San Francisco County, San Mateo County, Santa Clara County, Santa Cruz County, Solano County, Sonoma County	$90,000	$101,300	$122,600	$142,600
HUD Field Office: Fresno Service Office				
Fresno service office metro and nonmetro areas: Fresno County, Kern County, Kings County, Madera County, Mariposa County, Merced County, Stanislaus County, Tulare County	$71,500	$80,500	$98,000	$113,000
HUD Field Office: Sacramento Service Office				
Sacramento service office metro and nonmetro areas: Alpine County, Amador County, Butte County, Calaveras County, Colusa County, El Dorado County, Glenn County, Lassen County, Modoc County, Nevada County, Placer County, Plumas County, Sacramento County, San Joaquin County, Shasta County, Sierra County, Siskiyou County, Sutter County, Tehama County, Trinity County, Tuolumne County, Yolo County, Yuba County	$84,000	$95,000	$115,000	$133,500
HUD Field Office: San Diego Service Office				
San Diego service office metro and nonmetro areas: Imperial County, San Diego County	$90,000	$101,300	$122,600	$142,600
HUD Field Office: Santa Ana Service Office				
Santa Ana service office metro areas: Orange County, Riverside County, San Bernardino County	$90,000	$101,300	$122,600	$142,600
Santa Ana service office nonmetro areas: Inyo County, Mono County	71,500	80,500	98,000	113,000

Market area designation and local jurisdictions	Section 203(b) mortgage limits			
	1-family	2-family	3-family	4-family
HUD Field Office: Las Vegas Service Office				
Las Vegas, NV SMSA: Clark County	$90,000	$101,300	$122,600	$142,600
State of Nevada—nonmetro areas:				
Lincoln County	75,000	84,000	102,500	118,000
Nye County (part)				
HUD Field Office: Reno Service Office				
Reno, NV SMSA: Washoe County	$89,500	$101,000	$122,000	$142,000
State of Nevada—nonmetro areas:				
Carson City County	75,000	84,000	102,500	118,000
Churchill County				
Douglas County				
Elko County				
Esmeralda County				
Eureka County				
Humboldt County				
Lander County				
Lyon County				
Mineral County				
Nye County (part)				
Pershing County				
Storey County				
White Pine County				
HUD Field Office: Phoenix Service Office				
Phoenix, AZ SMSA: Maricopa County	$81,000	$91,500	$111,500	$128,500
HUD Field Office: Tucson Service Office				
Tucson, AZ SMSA: Pima County	$68,500	$77,000	$94,000	$108,000
HUD Field Office: Honolulu Area Office				
State of Hawaii metro and nonmetro areas	$135,000	$151,950	$183,975	$213,975
REGION X				
HUD Field Office: Seattle Area Office				
Richland-Kennewick and Yakima, WA SMSAS (combined): Yakima County	$72,000	$81,500	$99,000	$114,000
Seattle-Everett, WA SMSA:				
King County	72,000	81,500	99,000	114,000
Snohomish County				
Tacoma, WA SMSA: Pierce County	71,000	80,000	97,500	112,500
HUD Field Office: Spokane Service Office				
Richland-Kennewick and Yakima, WA SMSAS (combined):				
Benton County	$72,000	$81,500	$99,000	$114,000
Franklin County				
Spokane, WA SMSA: Spokane County	72,000	81,500	99,000	114,000
HUD Field Office: Boise Service Office				
Boise City, ID SMSA: Ada County	$75,000	$84,000	$102,500	$118,000

Source: "Rules and Regulations," *Federal Register*, January 7, 1982, vol. 47, no. 4, pp. 917-24.

APPENDIX C Outstanding Loan Balance Factors—Section 245, Plan III

PLAN III GRADUATED PAYMENT MORTGAGE (SECTION 245)
WITH INCREASING PAYMENTS FOR 5 YEARS AT 7.50 PERCENT EACH YEAR

OUTSTANDING PRINCIPAL BALANCE FACTORS
(PER THOUSAND DOLLARS OF ORIGINAL LOAN PROCEEDS)

FOR 30 YEAR MORTGAGES WITH ANNUAL CONTRACT INTEREST RATES OF

INSTALL- MENT NUMBER	7.75	8.00	8.25	8.50	8.75	9.00	9.25	9.50	9.75	10.00
1	1001.0866	1001.1566	1001.2250	1001.2919	1001.3572	1001.4212	1001.4837	1001.5448	1001.6046	1001.6630
2	1002.1803	1002.3209	1002.4584	1002.5929	1002.7244	1002.8530	1002.9788	1003.1018	1003.2221	1003.3398
3	1003.2810	1003.4929	1003.7003	1003.9031	1004.1015	1004.2956	1004.4855	1004.6712	1004.8529	1005.0306
4	1004.3888	1004.6728	1004.9507	1005.2226	1005.4887	1005.7490	1006.0037	1006.2530	1006.4969	1006.7355
5	1005.5038	1005.8606	1006.2097	1006.5515	1006.8859	1007.2133	1007.5337	1007.8473	1008.1542	1008.4546
6	1006.6260	1007.0562	1007.4774	1007.8897	1008.2934	1008.6886	1009.0754	1009.4542	1009.8250	1010.1881
7	1007.7554	1008.2599	1008.7538	1009.2375	1009.7111	1010.1749	1010.6291	1011.0738	1011.5094	1011.9360
8	1008.8922	1009.4715	1010.0390	1010.5948	1011.1392	1011.6724	1012.1947	1012.7063	1013.2075	1013.6984
9	1010.0362	1010.6912	1011.3330	1011.9617	1012.5776	1013.1811	1013.7724	1014.3517	1014.9193	1015.4755
10	1011.1877	1011.9191	1012.6359	1013.3383	1014.0266	1014.7011	1015.3622	1016.0101	1016.6451	1017.2675
11	1012.3466	1013.1551	1013.9477	1014.7246	1015.4861	1016.2326	1016.9643	1017.6817	1018.3849	1019.0743
12	1013.5130	1014.3994	1015.2686	1016.1208	1016.9563	1017.7755	1018.5788	1019.3664	1020.1388	1020.8963
13	1014.2840	1015.2388	1016.1748	1017.0924	1017.9921	1018.8741	1019.7368	1020.5867	1021.4180	1022.2331
14	1015.0600	1016.0837	1017.0872	1018.0710	1019.0354	1019.9809	1020.9078	1021.8165	1022.7075	1023.5811
15	1015.8410	1016.9342	1018.0059	1019.0565	1020.0864	1021.0960	1022.0858	1023.0562	1024.0075	1024.9403
16	1016.6271	1017.7905	1018.9310	1020.0490	1021.1450	1022.2195	1023.2729	1024.3056	1025.3181	1026.3108
17	1017.4183	1018.6524	1019.8623	1021.0485	1022.2114	1023.3514	1024.4691	1025.5649	1026.6393	1027.6928
18	1018.2145	1019.5201	1020.8001	1022.0551	1023.2855	1024.4918	1025.6746	1026.8342	1027.9713	1029.0863
19	1019.0159	1020.3936	1021.7444	1023.0688	1024.3675	1025.6408	1026.8893	1028.1136	1029.3141	1030.4914
20	1019.8225	1021.2728	1022.6951	1024.0897	1025.4573	1026.7984	1028.1134	1029.4031	1030.6678	1031.9082
21	1020.6343	1022.1580	1023.6523	1025.1179	1026.5551	1027.9646	1029.3470	1030.7027	1032.0325	1033.3368
22	1021.4513	1023.0491	1024.6162	1026.1533	1027.6609	1029.1396	1030.5900	1032.0127	1033.4083	1034.7773
23	1022.2736	1023.9460	1025.5867	1027.1960	1028.7747	1030.3234	1031.8427	1033.3330	1034.7952	1036.2298
24	1023.1012	1024.8490	1026.5638	1028.2462	1029.8967	1031.5161	1033.1049	1034.6638	1036.1935	1037.6944
25	1023.5011	1025.3138	1027.0921	1028.8368	1030.5484	1032.2276	1033.8751	1035.4914	1037.0773	1038.6334
26	1023.9035	1025.7816	1027.6241	1029.4316	1031.2049	1032.9445	1034.6512	1036.3256	1037.9684	1039.5803
27	1024.3086	1026.2526	1028.1597	1030.0307	1031.8661	1033.6668	1035.4333	1037.1663	1038.8667	1040.5350
28	1024.7162	1026.7267	1028.6990	1030.6339	1032.5322	1034.3944	1036.2214	1038.0138	1039.7723	1041.4977
29	1025.1265	1027.2039	1029.2420	1031.2415	1033.2031	1035.1275	1037.0156	1038.8679	1040.6853	1042.4685
30	1025.5395	1027.6844	1029.7887	1031.8534	1033.8789	1035.8662	1037.8159	1039.7288	1041.6056	1043.4473
31	1025.9551	1028.1680	1030.3392	1032.4695	1034.5596	1036.6103	1038.6223	1040.5965	1042.5335	1044.4342
32	1026.3734	1028.6549	1030.8935	1033.0901	1035.2453	1037.3600	1039.4350	1041.4710	1043.4689	1045.4294
33	1026.7944	1029.1450	1031.4516	1033.7150	1035.9360	1038.1154	1040.2540	1042.3525	1044.4119	1046.4329
34	1027.2181	1029.6384	1032.0136	1034.3444	1036.6318	1038.8764	1041.0792	1043.2410	1045.3625	1047.4447
35	1027.6445	1030.1350	1032.5793	1034.9783	1037.3326	1039.6432	1041.9109	1044.1365	1046.3209	1048.4650
36	1028.0738	1030.6350	1033.1490	1035.6166	1038.0385	1040.4157	1042.7489	1045.0391	1047.2871	1049.4938
37	1028.0402	1030.6608	1033.2329	1035.7575	1038.2352	1040.6671	1043.0539	1045.3965	1047.6960	1049.9530
38	1028.0063	1030.6867	1033.3174	1035.8994	1038.4334	1040.9204	1043.3612	1045.7569	1048.1082	1050.4161
39	1027.9723	1030.7128	1033.4025	1036.0422	1038.6330	1041.1756	1043.6709	1046.1200	1048.5237	1050.8830
40	1027.9381	1030.7390	1033.4881	1036.1861	1038.8340	1041.4327	1043.9830	1046.4860	1048.9426	1051.3538
41	1027.9036	1030.7655	1033.5744	1036.3311	1039.0366	1041.6917	1044.2975	1046.8550	1049.3650	1051.8285
42	1027.8689	1030.7921	1033.6612	1036.4770	1039.2405	1041.9527	1044.6145	1047.2268	1049.7907	1052.3072
43	1027.8340	1030.8189	1033.7486	1036.6240	1039.4460	1042.2157	1044.9339	1047.6016	1050.2199	1052.7899
44	1027.7988	1030.8459	1033.8366	1036.7720	1039.6530	1042.4806	1045.2557	1047.9794	1050.6526	1053.2765
45	1027.7635	1030.8730	1033.9253	1036.9211	1039.8615	1042.7475	1045.5800	1048.3601	1051.0889	1053.7673
46	1027.7279	1030.9004	1034.0145	1037.0712	1040.0715	1043.0164	1045.9068	1048.7439	1051.5286	1054.2621
47	1027.6920	1030.9279	1034.1044	1037.2224	1040.2831	1043.2873	1046.2362	1049.1307	1051.9720	1054.7611
48	1027.6560	1030.9556	1034.1948	1037.3747	1040.4962	1043.5603	1046.5680	1049.5206	1052.4189	1055.2642

NOTE: DUE TO THE ROUNDING INVOLVED IN COMPUTING ACTUAL PAYMENTS, ACTUAL OUTSTANDING BALANCES WILL TEND TO BE LOWER THAN THOSE COMPUTED USING THE ABOVE FACTORS.

THE HIGHEST OUTSTANDING BALANCE AND FACTORS ARE UNDERLINED.

PLAN III GRADUATED PAYMENT MORTGAGE (SECTION 245)
WITH INCREASING PAYMENTS FOR 5 YEARS AT 7.50 PERCENT EACH YEAR

OUTSTANDING PRINCIPAL BALANCE FACTORS
(PER THOUSAND DOLLARS OF ORIGINAL LOAN PROCEEDS)

INSTALL-MENT NUMBER	FOR 30 YEAR MORTGAGES WITH ANNUAL CONTRACT INTEREST RATES OF									
	7.75	8.00	8.25	8.50	8.75	9.00	9.25	9.50	9.75	10.00
49	1027.1192	1030.4701	1033.7595	1036.9884	1040.1579	1043.2689	1046.3225	1049.3198	1052.2620	1055.1500
50	1026.5789	1029.9813	1033.3212	1036.5994	1039.8171	1042.9753	1046.0751	1049.1175	1052.1037	1055.0349
51	1026.0352	1029.4893	1032.8798	1036.2077	1039.4739	1042.6795	1045.8258	1048.9136	1051.9442	1054.9188
52	1025.4879	1028.9941	1032.4355	1035.8131	1039.1281	1042.3816	1045.5745	1048.7081	1051.7834	1054.8017
53	1024.9372	1028.4955	1031.9880	1035.4158	1038.7799	1042.0813	1045.3213	1048.5009	1051.6213	1054.6837
54	1024.3828	1027.9936	1031.5375	1035.0157	1038.4291	1041.7789	1045.0662	1048.2921	1051.4579	1054.5647
55	1023.8249	1027.4883	1031.0839	1034.6127	1038.0757	1041.4741	1044.8091	1048.0817	1051.2931	1054.4446
56	1023.2634	1026.9797	1030.6272	1034.2069	1037.7198	1041.1671	1044.5500	1047.8695	1051.1270	1054.3236
57	1022.6982	1026.4677	1030.1673	1033.7982	1037.3613	1040.8578	1044.2869	1047.6557	1050.9596	1054.2016
58	1022.1294	1025.9523	1029.7043	1033.3866	1037.0001	1040.5461	1044.0258	1047.4402	1050.7908	1054.0786
59	1021.5569	1025.4334	1029.2381	1032.9721	1036.6364	1040.2322	1043.7607	1047.2230	1050.6206	1053.9545
60	1020.9807	1024.9111	1028.7687	1032.5546	1036.2699	1039.9158	1043.4935	1047.0041	1050.4490	1053.8294
61	1019.8628	1023.8334	1027.7302	1031.5541	1035.3064	1038.9883	1042.6008	1046.1453	1049.6230	1053.0352
62	1018.7377	1022.7485	1026.6845	1030.5466	1034.3359	1038.0537	1041.7012	1045.2796	1048.7902	1052.2343
63	1017.6052	1021.6564	1025.6316	1029.5319	1033.3583	1037.1122	1040.7947	1044.4071	1047.9507	1051.4268
64	1016.4655	1020.5570	1024.5715	1028.5100	1032.3736	1036.1636	1039.8812	1043.5277	1047.1043	1050.6125
65	1015.3184	1019.4503	1023.5041	1027.4808	1031.3817	1035.2079	1038.9607	1042.6413	1046.2511	1049.7915
66	1014.1639	1018.3362	1022.4294	1026.4444	1030.3826	1034.2450	1038.0330	1041.7479	1045.3910	1048.9636
67	1013.0020	1017.2147	1021.3472	1025.4006	1029.3761	1033.2749	1037.0983	1040.8474	1044.5238	1048.1288
68	1011.8325	1016.0857	1020.2577	1024.3495	1028.3624	1032.2975	1036.1563	1039.9398	1043.6496	1047.2870
69	1010.6555	1014.9492	1019.1606	1023.2909	1027.3412	1031.3128	1035.2070	1039.0251	1042.7683	1046.4383
70	1009.4709	1013.8051	1018.0560	1022.2248	1026.3126	1030.3208	1034.2504	1038.1030	1041.8799	1045.5824
71	1008.2786	1012.6534	1016.9438	1021.1511	1025.2765	1029.3212	1033.2865	1037.1737	1040.9842	1044.7194
72	1007.0787	1011.4940	1015.8240	1020.0699	1024.2329	1028.3142	1032.3151	1036.2370	1040.0813	1043.8493
73	1005.8710	1010.3268	1014.6964	1018.9810	1023.1816	1027.2996	1031.3363	1035.2929	1039.1710	1042.9719
74	1004.6555	1009.1519	1013.5611	1017.8843	1022.1227	1026.2774	1030.3499	1034.3414	1038.2533	1042.0871
75	1003.4321	1007.9691	1012.4181	1016.7800	1021.0560	1025.2476	1029.3559	1033.3823	1037.3282	1041.1951
76	1002.2008	1006.7785	1011.2671	1015.6677	1019.9816	1024.2100	1028.3542	1032.4156	1036.3955	1040.2955
77	1000.9616	1005.5799	1010.1082	1014.5476	1018.8994	1023.1646	1027.3448	1031.4412	1035.4553	1039.3885
78	999.7144	1004.3734	1008.9414	1013.4196	1017.8092	1022.1114	1026.3276	1030.4591	1034.5074	1038.4739
79	998.4591	1003.1588	1007.7665	1012.2836	1016.7111	1021.0503	1025.3026	1029.4693	1033.5519	1037.5517
80	997.1958	1001.9361	1006.5836	1011.1395	1015.6050	1019.9813	1024.2697	1028.4716	1032.5885	1036.6218
81	995.9242	1000.7052	1005.3925	1009.9873	1014.4908	1018.9042	1023.2288	1027.4661	1031.6174	1035.6842
82	994.6445	999.4661	1004.1933	1008.8270	1013.3685	1017.8190	1022.1799	1026.4525	1030.6383	1034.7387
83	993.3565	998.2188	1002.9858	1007.6585	1012.2380	1016.7257	1021.1229	1025.4310	1029.6513	1033.7854
84	992.0601	996.9632	1001.7700	1006.4816	1011.0993	1015.6243	1020.0578	1024.4013	1028.6563	1032.8241
85	990.7554	995.6992	1000.5458	1005.2965	1009.9523	1014.5145	1018.9845	1023.3635	1027.6532	1031.8548
86	989.4423	994.4267	999.3133	1004.1029	1008.7969	1013.3964	1017.9028	1022.3175	1026.6419	1030.8775
87	988.1207	993.1458	998.0722	1002.9009	1007.6331	1012.2700	1016.8129	1021.2632	1025.6224	1029.8919
88	986.7905	991.8564	996.8226	1001.6904	1006.4608	1011.1351	1015.7145	1020.2006	1024.5946	1028.8982
89	985.4518	990.5583	995.5644	1000.4713	1005.2799	1009.9916	1014.6077	1019.1295	1023.5585	1027.8962
90	984.1044	989.2516	994.2976	999.2435	1004.0905	1008.8396	1013.4924	1018.0500	1022.5140	1026.8859
91	982.7483	987.9362	993.0221	998.0071	1002.8923	1007.6790	1012.3684	1016.9619	1021.4610	1025.8671
92	981.3835	986.6120	991.7378	996.7619	1001.6855	1006.5096	1011.2358	1015.8652	1020.3994	1024.8398
93	980.0098	985.2790	990.4447	995.5079	1000.4698	1005.3315	1010.0944	1014.7599	1019.3292	1023.8040
94	978.6273	983.9371	989.1426	994.2450	999.2452	1004.1446	1008.9443	1013.6457	1018.2503	1022.7595
95	977.2358	982.5862	987.8317	992.9732	998.0118	1002.9487	1007.7853	1012.5228	1017.1627	1021.7064
96	975.8354	981.2264	986.5117	991.6923	996.7693	1001.7439	1006.6173	1011.3910	1016.0662	1020.6445

NOTE: DUE TO THE ROUNDING INVOLVED IN COMPUTING ACTUAL PAYMENTS, ACTUAL OUTSTANDING BALANCES WILL TEND TO BE LOWER THAN THOSE COMPUTED USING THE ABOVE FACTORS.

THE HIGHEST OUTSTANDING BALANCE AND FACTORS ARE UNDERLINED.

PLAN III GRADUATED PAYMENT MORTGAGE (SECTION 245)
WITH INCREASING PAYMENTS FOR 5 YEARS AT 7.50 PERCENT EACH YEAR

OUTSTANDING PRINCIPAL BALANCE FACTORS
(PER THOUSAND DOLLARS OF ORIGINAL LOAN PROCEEDS)

INSTALL-MENT NUMBER	FOR 30 YEAR MORTGAGES WITH ANNUAL CONTRACT INTEREST RATES OF									
	7.75	8.00	8.25	8.50	8.75	9.00	9.25	9.50	9.75	10.00
97	974.4259	979.8574	985.1826	990.4024	995.5178	1000.5301	1005.4404	1010.2502	1014.9608	1019.5737
98	973.0073	978.4794	983.8444	989.1033	994.2572	999.3071	1004.2544	1009.1003	1013.8464	1018.4940
99	971.5795	977.0922	982.4970	987.7951	992.9873	998.0750	1003.0592	1007.9414	1012.7229	1017.4053
100	970.1425	975.6957	981.1404	986.4775	991.7082	996.8336	1001.8548	1006.7733	1011.5904	1016.3075
101	968.6963	974.2899	979.7744	985.1507	990.4198	995.5829	1000.6412	1005.5959	1010.4486	1015.2005
102	967.2407	972.8747	978.3990	983.8144	989.1220	994.3228	999.4182	1004.4093	1009.2975	1014.0844
103	965.7757	971.4501	977.0142	982.4687	987.8147	993.0533	998.1857	1003.2132	1008.1371	1012.9589
104	964.3012	970.0160	975.6198	981.1134	986.4979	991.7743	996.9438	1002.0077	1006.9673	1011.8241
105	962.8172	968.5724	974.2159	979.7486	985.1715	990.4857	995.6923	1000.7926	1005.7880	1010.6798
106	961.3237	967.1191	972.8023	978.3741	983.8354	989.1874	994.4311	999.5679	1004.5990	1009.5260
107	959.8205	965.6561	971.3790	976.9898	982.4896	987.8793	993.1602	998.3335	1003.4005	1008.3626
108	958.3075	964.1834	969.9459	975.5957	981.1339	986.5615	991.8796	997.0893	1002.1922	1007.1894
109	956.7849	962.7009	968.5029	974.1918	979.7684	985.2338	990.5890	995.8353	1000.9740	1006.0065
110	955.2523	961.2084	967.0500	972.7779	978.3929	983.8961	989.2865	994.5714	999.7460	1004.8137
111	953.7099	959.7061	965.5872	971.3540	977.0074	982.5484	987.9780	993.2974	998.5080	1003.6110
112	952.1575	958.1937	964.1143	969.9200	975.6118	981.1906	986.6574	992.0134	997.2599	1002.3983
113	950.5951	956.6712	962.6312	968.4759	974.2060	979.8226	985.3266	990.7192	996.0017	1001.1755
114	949.0226	955.1386	961.1380	967.0215	972.7900	978.4443	983.9855	989.4147	994.7333	999.9424
115	947.4400	953.5957	959.6345	965.5568	971.3636	977.0557	982.6341	988.1000	993.4545	998.6991
116	945.8471	952.0426	958.1206	964.0818	969.9268	975.6567	981.2723	986.7748	992.1654	997.4455
117	944.2439	950.4791	956.5964	962.5963	968.4796	974.2472	979.9000	985.4391	990.8658	996.1814
118	942.6304	948.9052	955.0617	961.1003	967.0218	972.8271	978.5171	984.0929	989.5557	994.9067
119	941.0065	947.3208	953.5164	959.5937	965.5534	971.3963	977.1235	982.7360	988.2349	993.6215
120	939.3720	945.7259	951.9605	958.0764	964.0742	969.9549	975.7192	981.3683	986.9033	992.3255
121	937.7270	944.1203	950.3939	956.5483	962.5843	968.5026	974.3041	979.9898	985.5610	991.0187
122	936.0714	942.5040	948.8165	955.0095	961.0835	967.0394	972.8781	978.6005	984.2077	989.7010
123	934.4051	940.8769	947.2283	953.4597	959.5718	965.5653	971.4410	977.2001	982.8434	988.3724
124	932.7281	939.2390	945.6292	951.8990	958.0491	964.0801	969.99[illegible]0	975.7886	981.4681	987.0327
125	931.0402	937.5902	944.0190	950.3272	956.5152	962.5838	968.5337	974.3659	980.0816	985.6818
126	929.3414	935.9303	942.3978	948.7443	954.9702	961.0762	967.0632	972.9320	978.6838	984.3197
127	927.6316	934.2594	940.7655	947.1501	953.4139	959.5573	965.5813	971.4868	977.2747	982.9462
128	925.9108	932.5774	939.1219	945.5447	951.8462	958.0271	964.0881	970.0301	975.8541	981.5612
129	924.1789	930.8842	937.4671	943.9279	950.2671	956.4854	962.5833	968.5618	974.4219	980.1647
130	922.4358	929.1796	935.8008	942.2996	948.6765	954.9321	961.0669	967.0820	972.9782	978.7566
131	920.6814	927.4637	934.1231	940.6599	947.0743	953.3671	959.5389	965.5904	971.5227	977.3368
132	918.9157	925.7364	932.4339	939.0085	945.4605	951.7904	957.9990	964.0870	970.0554	975.9051
133	917.1386	923.9975	930.7330	937.3454	943.8348	950.2019	956.4473	962.5717	968.5761	974.4615
134	915.3501	922.2471	929.0205	935.6705	942.1973	948.6015	954.8836	961.0445	967.0849	973.0058
135	913.5499	920.4850	927.2962	933.9837	940.5479	946.9891	953.3079	959.5051	965.5815	971.5381
136	911.7382	918.7111	925.5600	932.2850	938.8864	945.3646	951.7200	957.9535	964.0659	970.0581
137	909.9147	916.9254	923.8119	930.5743	937.2128	943.7279	950.1199	956.3897	962.5380	968.5657
138	908.0795	915.1278	922.0518	928.8515	935.5271	942.0789	948.5075	954.8135	960.9977	967.0609
139	906.2324	913.3182	920.2796	927.1164	933.8290	940.4175	946.8826	953.2248	959.4448	965.5436
140	904.3734	911.4966	918.4952	925.3691	932.1185	938.7437	945.2452	951.6235	957.8794	964.0137
141	902.5024	909.6628	916.6985	923.6094	930.3956	937.0574	943.5952	950.0095	956.3012	962.4710
142	900.6193	907.8168	914.8895	921.8372	928.6601	935.3584	941.9324	948.3828	954.7102	960.9154
143	898.7240	905.9585	913.0680	920.0525	926.9119	933.6466	940.2569	946.7432	953.1063	959.3469
144	896.8165	904.0878	911.2340	918.2551	925.1511	931.9220	938.5684	945.0906	951.4893	957.7653

NOTE: DUE TO THE ROUNDING INVOLVED IN COMPUTING ACTUAL PAYMENTS, ACTUAL OUTSTANDING BALANCES WILL TEND TO BE LOWER THAN THOSE COMPUTED USING THE ABOVE FACTORS.

THE HIGHEST OUTSTANDING BALANCE AND FACTORS ARE UNDERLINED.

PLAN III GRADUATED PAYMENT MORTGAGE (SECTION 245)
WITH INCREASING PAYMENTS FOR 5 YEARS AT 7.50 PERCENT EACH YEAR

OUTSTANDING PRINCIPAL BALANCE FACTORS
(PER THOUSAND DOLLARS OF ORIGINAL LOAN PROCEEDS)

INSTALL- MENT NUMBER	FOR 30 YEAR MORTGAGES WITH ANNUAL CONTRACT INTEREST RATES OF									
	10.25	10.50	10.75	11.00	11.25	11.50	11.75	12.00	12.25	12.50
1	1001.7201	1001.7760	1001.8306	1001.8840	1001.9363	1001.9874	1002.0374	1002.0862	1002.1341	1002.1809
2	1003.4549	1003.5675	1003.6776	1003.7853	1003.8907	1003.9938	1004.0947	1004.1934	1004.2900	1004.3845
3	1005.2045	1005.3747	1005.5411	1005.7040	1005.8634	1006.0194	1006.1721	1006.3215	1006.4678	1006.6110
4	1006.9691	1007.1977	1007.4214	1007.6403	1007.8547	1008.0645	1008.2699	1008.4710	1008.6679	1008.8608
5	1008.7487	1009.0366	1009.3185	1009.5944	1009.8646	1010.1291	1010.3882	1010.6420	1010.8905	1011.1340
6	1010.5436	1010.8917	1011.2325	1011.5664	1011.8933	1012.2136	1012.5273	1012.8346	1013.1358	1013.4308
7	1012.3537	1012.7629	1013.1638	1013.5564	1013.9411	1014.3180	1014.6873	1015.0492	1015.4039	1015.7516
8	1014.1794	1014.6506	1015.1123	1015.5647	1016.0080	1016.4426	1016.8685	1017.2860	1017.6953	1018.0966
9	1016.0206	1016.5547	1017.0783	1017.5914	1018.0944	1018.5875	1019.0710	1019.5451	1020.0100	1020.4660
10	1017.8775	1018.4756	1019.0618	1019.6367	1020.2003	1020.7530	1021.2951	1021.8268	1022.3483	1022.8601
11	1019.7503	1020.4132	1021.0632	1021.7007	1022.3259	1022.9393	1023.5409	1024.1313	1024.7106	1025.2791
12	1021.6392	1022.3678	1023.0825	1023.7836	1024.4715	1025.1465	1025.8088	1026.4588	1027.0969	1027.7233
13	1023.0325	1023.8164	1024.5853	1025.3395	1026.0793	1026.8051	1027.5173	1028.2161	1028.9020	1029.5753
14	1024.4377	1025.2777	1026.1016	1026.9096	1027.7021	1028.4797	1029.2425	1029.9910	1030.7256	1031.4465
15	1025.8549	1026.7518	1027.6314	1028.4941	1029.3402	1030.1703	1030.9846	1031.7837	1032.5678	1033.3373
16	1027.2843	1028.2388	1029.1750	1030.0931	1030.9936	1031.8771	1032.7438	1033.5942	1034.4287	1035.2478
17	1028.7258	1029.7388	1030.7323	1031.7068	1032.6626	1033.6002	1034.5202	1035.4229	1036.3087	1037.1781
18	1030.1797	1031.2520	1032.3037	1033.3352	1034.3471	1035.3399	1036.3140	1037.2698	1038.2079	1039.1286
19	1031.6460	1032.7783	1033.8891	1034.9786	1036.0475	1037.0962	1038.1253	1039.1352	1040.1264	1041.0994
20	1033.1248	1034.3181	1035.4887	1036.6371	1037.7638	1038.8694	1039.9544	1041.0193	1042.0646	1043.0907
21	1034.6162	1035.8713	1037.1026	1038.3107	1039.4962	1040.6596	1041.8014	1042.9222	1044.0225	1045.1028
22	1036.1204	1037.4381	1038.7310	1039.9997	1041.2449	1042.4669	1043.6665	1044.8441	1046.0004	1047.1358
23	1037.6374	1039.0186	1040.3740	1041.7042	1043.0099	1044.2916	1045.5498	1046.7853	1047.9985	1049.1900
24	1039.1674	1040.6129	1042.0317	1043.4243	1044.7915	1046.1337	1047.4516	1048.7459	1050.0170	1051.2656
25	1040.1604	1041.6589	1043.1296	1044.5730	1045.9900	1047.3811	1048.7468	1050.0880	1051.4051	1052.6988
26	1041.1620	1042.7141	1044.2373	1045.7323	1047.1998	1048.6404	1050.0547	1051.4435	1052.8074	1054.1470
27	1042.1720	1043.7784	1045.3549	1046.9022	1048.4209	1049.9118	1051.3755	1052.8127	1054.2240	1055.6102
28	1043.1908	1044.8521	1046.4826	1048.0828	1049.6534	1051.1953	1052.7091	1054.1955	1055.6551	1057.0886
29	1044.2182	1045.9352	1047.6203	1049.2742	1050.8976	1052.4912	1054.0558	1055.5921	1057.1007	1058.5825
30	1045.2544	1047.0278	1048.7683	1050.4765	1052.1533	1053.7995	1055.4157	1057.0027	1058.5612	1060.0919
31	1046.2994	1048.1299	1049.9265	1051.6899	1053.4209	1055.1203	1056.7889	1058.4274	1060.0365	1061.6171
32	1047.3534	1049.2417	1051.0951	1052.9144	1054.7003	1056.4538	1058.1755	1059.8663	1061.5269	1063.1581
33	1048.4164	1050.3632	1052.2742	1054.1501	1055.9918	1057.8000	1059.5757	1061.3196	1063.0325	1064.7152
34	1049.4885	1051.4945	1053.4638	1055.3971	1057.2953	1059.1592	1060.9897	1062.7875	1064.5535	1066.2885
35	1050.5697	1052.6357	1054.6641	1056.6556	1058.6110	1060.5314	1062.4174	1064.2701	1066.0900	1067.8782
36	1051.6601	1053.7869	1055.8751	1057.9256	1059.9391	1061.9167	1063.8592	1065.7674	1067.6422	1069.4845
37	1052.1687	1054.3438	1056.4792	1058.5760	1060.6350	1062.6570	1064.6430	1066.5939	1068.5105	1070.3936
38	1052.6815	1054.9055	1057.0888	1059.2324	1061.3373	1063.4043	1065.4345	1067.4286	1069.3876	1071.3123
39	1053.1988	1055.4721	1057.7038	1059.8948	1062.0462	1064.1589	1066.2337	1068.2716	1070.2736	1072.2405
40	1053.7205	1056.0436	1058.3243	1060.5633	1062.7618	1064.9206	1067.0407	1069.1231	1071.1687	1073.1784
41	1054.2466	1056.6202	1058.9503	1061.2379	1063.4841	1065.6896	1067.8557	1069.9831	1072.0729	1074.1260
42	1054.7772	1057.2018	1059.5820	1061.9187	1064.2131	1066.4661	1068.6786	1070.8517	1072.9864	1075.0836
43	1055.3124	1057.7885	1060.2193	1062.6058	1064.9490	1067.2499	1069.5096	1071.7290	1073.9092	1076.0511
44	1055.8521	1058.3803	1060.8623	1063.2991	1065.6918	1068.0413	1070.3487	1072.6151	1074.8414	1077.0287
45	1056.3964	1058.9774	1061.5111	1063.9988	1066.4415	1068.8402	1071.1960	1073.5100	1075.7831	1078.0164
46	1056.9454	1059.5796	1062.1657	1064.7050	1067.1983	1069.6468	1072.0517	1074.4139	1076.7344	1079.0145
47	1057.4991	1060.1871	1062.8262	1065.4175	1067.9622	1070.4612	1072.9157	1075.3268	1077.6955	1080.0229
48	<u>1058.0575</u>	<u>1060.7999</u>	1063.4926	1066.1367	1068.7332	1071.2833	1073.7882	1076.2488	1078.6664	1081.0419

NOTE: DUE TO THE ROUNDING INVOLVED IN COMPUTING ACTUAL PAYMENTS, ACTUAL OUTSTANDING BALANCES WILL TEND TO BE LOWER THAN THOSE COMPUTED USING THE ABOVE FACTORS.

THE HIGHEST OUTSTANDING BALANCE FACTORS ARE UNDERLINED.

PLAN III GRADUATED PAYMENT MORTGAGE (SECTION 245)
WITH INCREASING PAYMENTS FOR 5 YEARS AT 7.50 PERCENT EACH YEAR

OUTSTANDING PRINCIPAL BALANCE FACTORS
(PER THOUSAND DOLLARS OF ORIGINAL LOAN PROCEEDS)

INSTALL-MENT NUMBER	FOR 30 YEAR MORTGAGES WITH ANNUAL CONTRACT INTEREST RATES OF									
	10.25	10.50	10.75	11.00	11.25	11.50	11.75	12.00	12.25	12.50
49	1057.9851	1060.7683	1063.5009	1066.1838	1068.8184	1071.4056	1073.9467	1076.4427	1078.8948	1081.3041
50	1057.9121	1060.7364	1063.5092	1066.2314	1068.9043	1071.5291	1074.1068	1076.6386	1079.1256	1081.5690
51	1057.8384	1060.7043	1063.5176	1066.2795	1068.9911	1071.6537	1074.2684	1076.8364	1079.3588	1081.8368
52	1057.7641	1060.6718	1063.5261	1066.3279	1069.0787	1071.7796	1074.4317	1077.0362	1079.5943	1082.1073
53	1057.6892	1060.6391	1063.5346	1066.3769	1069.1671	1071.9066	1074.5965	1077.2380	1079.8323	1082.3806
54	1057.6137	1060.6061	1063.5432	1066.4262	1069.2564	1072.0349	1074.7629	1077.4418	1080.0727	1082.6567
55	1057.5375	1060.5728	1063.5519	1066.4761	1069.3465	1072.1643	1074.9310	1077.6476	1080.3155	1082.9358
56	1057.4606	1060.539[illegible]	1063.5607	1066.5263	1069.4374	1072.2951	1075.1007	1077.8555	1080.5608	1083.2177
57	1057.3831	1060.505	1063.5696	1066.5771	1069.5292	1072.4271	1075.2721	1078.0655	1080.8086	1083.5026
58	1057.3050	1060.471[illegible]	1063.5785	1066.6283	1069.6218	1072.5603	1075.4452	1078.2776	1081.0589	1083.7905
59	1057.2261	1060.4367	1063.5875	1066.6800	1069.7153	1072.6948	1075.6199	1078.4918	1081.3118	1084.0813
60	1057.1466	1060.4019	1063.5966	1066.7321	1069.8097	1072.8307	1075.7964	1078.7082	1081.5673	1084.3752
61	1056.3832	1059.6683	1062.8919	1066.0553	1069.1599	1072.2070	1075.1979	1078.1340	1081.0167	1083.8472
62	1055.6132	1058.9283	1062.1809	1065.3723	1068.5040	1071.5773	1074.5935	1077.5541	1080.4604	1083.3138
63	1054.8367	1058.1818	1061.4634	1064.6830	1067.8420	1070.9416	1073.9833	1076.9685	1079.8985	1082.7748
64	1054.0535	1057.4288	1060.7396	1063.9875	1067.1737	1070.2998	1073.3670	1076.3769	1079.3308	1082.2302
65	1053.2637	1056.6691	1060.0093	1063.2855	1066.4992	1069.6518	1072.7448	1075.7795	1078.7574	1081.6799
66	1052.4671	1055.9029	1059.2724	1062.5771	1065.8184	1068.9977	1072.1164	1075.1761	1078.1781	1081.1238
67	1051.6637	1055.1299	1058.5289	1061.8622	1065.1312	1068.3372	1071.4819	1074.5666	1077.5928	1080.5620
68	1050.8534	1054.3502	1057.7788	1061.1408	1064.4375	1067.6705	1070.8412	1073.9511	1077.0016	1079.9943
69	1050.0362	1053.5636	1057.0220	1060.4127	1063.7373	1066.9973	1070.1942	1073.3294	1076.4044	1079.4207
70	1049.2120	1052.7702	1056.2583	1059.6780	1063.0306	1066.3177	1069.5408	1072.7014	1075.8011	1078.8412
71	1048.3808	1051.9698	1055.4879	1058.9365	1062.3173	1065.6316	1068.8811	1072.0672	1075.1916	1078.2556
72	1047.5425	1051.1624	1054.7105	1058.1882	1061.5972	1064.9389	1068.2149	1071.4267	1074.5759	1077.6639
73	1046.6970	1050.3480	1053.9261	1057.4331	1060.8704	1064.2396	1067.5422	1070.7798	1073.9538	1077.0660
74	1045.8443	1049.5264	1053.1348	1056.6711	1060.1368	1063.5336	1066.8629	1070.1263	1073.3255	1076.4619
75	1044.9844	1048.6976	1052.3363	1055.9020	1059.3963	1062.8208	1066.1769	1069.4664	1072.6907	1075.8515
76	1044.1170	1047.8616	1051.5307	1055.1260	1058.6489	1062.1012	1065.4843	1068.7998	1072.0495	1075.2348
77	1043.2423	1047.0183	1050.7179	1054.3428	1057.8945	1061.3746	1064.7848	1068.1266	1071.4017	1074.6116
78	1042.3601	1046.1676	1049.8978	1053.5524	1057.1330	1060.6411	1064.0785	1067.4467	1070.7473	1073.9820
79	1041.4704	1045.3094	1049.0703	1052.7548	1056.3643	1059.9006	1063.3653	1066.7599	1070.0862	1073.3457
80	1040.5730	1044.4437	1048.2355	1051.9499	1055.5885	1059.1530	1062.6451	1066.0663	1069.4184	1072.7029
81	1039.6680	1043.5705	1047.3931	1051.1375	1054.8054	1058.3983	1061.9178	1065.3658	1068.7437	1072.0534
82	1038.7553	1042.6896	1046.5432	1050.3178	1054.0149	1057.6362	1061.1834	1064.6582	1068.0622	1071.3970
83	1037.8348	1041.8010	1045.6857	1049.4905	1053.2170	1056.8669	1060.4419	1063.9436	1067.3737	1070.7339
84	1036.9064	1040.9047	1044.8206	1048.6557	1052.4117	1056.0903	1059.6931	1063.2218	1066.6782	1070.0639
85	1035.9701	1040.0005	1043.9476	1047.8132	1051.5988	1055.3061	1058.9369	1062.4928	1065.9755	1069.3868
86	1035.0257	1039.0883	1043.0669	1046.9629	1050.7783	1054.5145	1058.1733	1061.7565	1065.2657	1068.7027
87	1034.0734	1038.1682	1042.1782	1046.1049	1049.9500	1053.7153	1057.4023	1061.0129	1064.5487	1068.0115
88	1033.1128	1037.2401	1041.2816	1045.2390	1049.1141	1052.9084	1056.6237	1060.2618	1063.8243	1067.3131
89	1032.1441	1036.3038	1040.3770	1044.3652	1048.2702	1052.0938	1055.8375	1059.5032	1063.0926	1066.6074
90	1031.1671	1035.3594	1039.4642	1043.4834	1047.4185	1051.2713	1055.0436	1058.7370	1062.3533	1065.8944
91	1030.1818	1034.4066	1038.5433	1042.5935	1046.5588	1050.4410	1054.2419	1057.9631	1061.6066	1065.1739
92	1029.1880	1033.4456	1037.6141	1041.6954	1045.6910	1049.6028	1053.4323	1057.1816	1060.8522	1064.4460
93	1028.1858	1032.4761	1036.6767	1040.7891	1044.8151	1048.7565	1052.6149	1056.3922	1060.0901	1063.7104
94	1027.1750	1031.4982	1035.7308	1039.8745	1043.9310	1047.9021	1051.7894	1055.5949	1059.3202	1062.9672
95	1026.1555	1030.5116	1034.7764	1038.9515	1043.0386	1047.0395	1050.9559	1054.7896	1058.5425	1062.2162
96	1025.1274	1029.5165	1033.8135	1038.0200	1042.1378	1046.1686	1050.1142	1053.9763	1057.7568	1061.4575

NOTE: DUE TO THE ROUNDING INVOLVED IN COMPUTING ACTUAL PAYMENTS, ACTUAL OUTSTANDING BALANCES WILL TEND TO BE LOWER THAN THOSE COMPUTED USING THE ABOVE FACTORS.

THE HIGHEST OUTSTANDING BALANCE FACTORS ARE UNDERLINED.

PLAN III GRADUATED PAYMENT MORTGAGE (SECTION 245)
WITH INCREASING PAYMENTS FOR 5 YEARS AT 7.50 PERCENT EACH YEAR

OUTSTANDING PRINCIPAL BALANCE FACTORS
(PER THOUSAND DOLLARS OF ORIGINAL LOAN PROCEEDS)

INSTALL- MENT NUMBER	FOR 30 YEAR MORTGAGES WITH ANNUAL CONTRACT INTEREST RATES OF									
	10.25	10.50	10.75	11.00	11.25	11.50	11.75	12.00	12.25	12.50
97	1024.0904	1028.5126	1032.8419	1037.0800	1041.2286	1045.2894	1049.2642	1053.1548	1056.9631	1060.6908
98	1023.0446	1027.5000	1031.8617	1036.1314	1040.3108	1044.4017	1048.4059	1052.3252	1056.1613	1059.9161
99	1021.9899	1026.4785	1030.8727	1035.1741	1039.3845	1043.5056	1047.5392	1051.4872	1055.3513	1059.1334
100	1020.9262	1025.4481	1029.8748	1034.2080	1038.4495	1042.6009	1046.6641	1050.6409	1054.5331	1058.3425
101	1019.8534	1024.4086	1028.8680	1033.2331	1037.5057	1041.6875	1045.7803	1049.7861	1053.7064	1057.5434
102	1018.7714	1023.3601	1027.8521	1032.2492	1036.5530	1040.7653	1044.8880	1048.9227	1052.8714	1056.7359
103	1017.6802	1022.3024	1026.8272	1031.2563	1035.5914	1039.8343	1043.9868	1048.0507	1052.0278	1055.9200
104	1016.5796	1021.2354	1025.7931	1030.2543	1034.6208	1038.8944	1043.0769	1047.1700	1051.1757	1055.0957
105	1015.4697	1020.1591	1024.7497	1029.2431	1033.6411	1037.9455	1042.1580	1046.2805	1050.3148	1054.2627
106	1014.3502	1019.0733	1023.6969	1028.2227	1032.6523	1036.9875	1041.2302	1045.3821	1049.4451	1053.4211
107	1013.2213	1017.9781	1022.6348	1027.1929	1031.6541	1036.0203	1040.2932	1044.4747	1048.5666	1052.5707
108	1012.0826	1016.8733	1021.5631	1026.1536	1030.6466	1035.0438	1039.3471	1043.5582	1047.6791	1051.7115
109	1010.9343	1015.7588	1020.4818	1025.1048	1029.6297	1034.0580	1038.3917	1042.6326	1046.7825	1050.8433
110	1009.7761	1014.6346	1019.3908	1024.0464	1028.6032	1033.0628	1037.4270	1041.6977	1045.8768	1049.9660
111	1008.6080	1013.5005	1018.2901	1022.9784	1027.5671	1032.0579	1036.4528	1040.7535	1044.9618	1049.0796
112	1007.4300	1012.3565	1017.1795	1021.9005	1026.5212	1031.0435	1035.4691	1039.7998	1044.0375	1048.1840
113	1006.2419	1011.2025	1016.0589	1020.8127	1025.4656	1030.0194	1034.4757	1038.8366	1043.1037	1047.2791
114	1005.0437	1010.0384	1014.9283	1019.7150	1024.4001	1028.9854	1033.4727	1037.8637	1042.1604	1046.3647
115	1003.8352	1008.8642	1013.7876	1018.6072	1023.3246	1027.9415	1032.4597	1036.8811	1041.2075	1045.4408
116	1002.6164	1007.6796	1012.6367	1017.4892	1022.2390	1026.8876	1031.4369	1035.8887	1040.2449	1044.5073
117	1001.3872	1006.4847	1011.4754	1016.3610	1021.1432	1025.8236	1030.4041	1034.8864	1039.2724	1043.5640
118	1000.1475	1005.2793	1010.3038	1015.2225	1020.0372	1024.7495	1029.3611	1033.8741	1038.2900	1042.6110
119	998.8971	1004.0634	1009.1216	1014.0735	1018.9207	1023.6650	1028.3080	1032.8516	1037.2976	1041.6480
120	997.6362	1002.8368	1007.9289	1012.9140	1017.7939	1022.5701	1027.2445	1031.8189	1036.2951	1040.6749
121	996.3644	1001.5995	1006.7255	1011.7439	1016.6564	1021.4647	1026.1706	1030.7759	1035.2823	1039.6918
122	995.0818	1000.3514	1005.5113	1010.5630	1015.5083	1020.3488	1025.0862	1029.7224	1034.2592	1038.6984
123	993.7882	999.0923	1004.2862	1009.3713	1014.3494	1019.2221	1023.9912	1028.6584	1033.2256	1037.6946
124	992.4836	997.8223	1003.0501	1008.1687	1013.1797	1018.0847	1022.8855	1027.5838	1032.1815	1036.6804
125	991.1678	996.5411	1001.8030	1006.9551	1011.9990	1016.9364	1021.7689	1026.4984	1031.1267	1035.6556
126	989.8408	995.2487	1000.5447	1005.7303	1010.8072	1015.7770	1020.6414	1025.4022	1030.0611	1034.6202
127	988.5025	993.9450	999.2751	1004.4944	1009.6043	1014.6065	1019.5029	1024.2950	1028.9847	1033.5739
128	987.1527	992.6299	997.9942	1003.2470	1008.3901	1013.4249	1018.3532	1023.1767	1027.8973	1032.5168
129	985.7914	991.3033	996.7018	1001.9883	1007.1644	1012.2319	1017.1922	1022.0473	1026.7988	1031.4486
130	984.4185	989.9651	995.3978	1000.7180	1005.9274	1011.0274	1016.0199	1020.9065	1025.6891	1030.3694
131	983.0338	988.6151	994.0821	999.4361	1004.6787	1009.8115	1014.8361	1019.7544	1024.5680	1029.2789
132	981.6374	987.2534	992.7546	998.1424	1003.4183	1008.5838	1013.6407	1018.5907	1023.4355	1028.1770
133	980.2289	985.8798	991.4152	996.8368	1002.1460	1007.3444	1012.4336	1017.4154	1022.2915	1027.0636
134	978.8085	984.4941	990.0639	995.5193	1000.8619	1006.0932	1011.2147	1016.2283	1021.1357	1025.9387
135	977.3759	983.0963	988.7004	994.1897	999.5657	1004.8299	1009.9839	1015.0294	1019.9682	1024.8020
136	975.9311	981.6863	987.3247	992.8480	998.2574	1003.5545	1008.7410	1013.8185	1018.7887	1023.6535
137	974.4740	980.2639	985.9367	991.4939	996.9368	1002.2669	1007.4859	1012.5955	1017.5972	1022.4930
138	973.0044	978.8291	984.5363	990.1274	995.6038	1000.9670	1006.2186	1011.3602	1016.3936	1021.3205
139	971.5222	977.3817	983.1233	988.7484	994.2583	999.6546	1004.9388	1010.1126	1015.1776	1020.1357
140	970.0274	975.9217	981.6977	987.3567	992.9002	998.3296	1003.6465	1008.8525	1013.9493	1018.9386
141	968.5198	974.4489	980.2593	985.9523	991.5294	996.9920	1002.3416	1007.5798	1012.7084	1017.7290
142	966.9994	972.9632	978.8080	984.5350	990.1457	995.6415	1001.0238	1006.2944	1011.4548	1016.5068
143	965.4659	971.4645	977.3437	983.1048	988.7491	994.2781	999.6932	1004.9961	1010.1884	1015.2719
144	963.9194	969.9527	975.8663	981.6614	987.3393	992.9016	998.3495	1003.6849	1008.9092	1014.0241

NOTE: DUE TO THE ROUNDING INVOLVED IN COMPUTING ACTUAL PAYMENTS, ACTUAL OUTSTANDING BALANCES WILL TEND TO BE LOWER THAN THOSE COMPUTED USING THE ABOVE FACTORS.

THE HIGHEST OUTSTANDING BALANCE FACTORS ARE UNDERLINED.

PLAN III GRADUATED PAYMENT MORTGAGE (SECTION 245)
WITH INCREASING PAYMENTS FOR 5 YEARS AT 7.50 PERCENT EACH YEAR

OUTSTANDING PRINCIPAL BALANCE FACTORS
(PER THOUSAND DOLLARS OF ORIGINAL LOAN PROCEEDS)

INSTALL-MENT NUMBER	FOR 30 YEAR MORTGAGES WITH ANNUAL CONTRACT INTEREST RATES OF									
	12.75	13.00	13.25	13.50	13.75	14.00	14.25	14.50	14.75	15.00
1	1002.2267	1002.2715	1002.3154	1002.3583	1002.4003	1002.4415	1002.4817	1002.5212	1002.5598	1002.5977
2	1004.4770	1004.5676	1004.6563	1004.7431	1004.8281	1004.9114	1004.9930	1005.0728	1005.1511	1005.2278
3	1006.7513	1006.8886	1007.0230	1007.1548	1007.2838	1007.4102	1007.5340	1007.6553	1007.7743	1007.8908
4	1009.0497	1009.2347	1009.4159	1009.5935	1009.7675	1009.9381	1010.1052	1010.2690	1010.4297	1010.5871
5	1011.3725	1011.6062	1011.8353	1012.0597	1012.2798	1012.4955	1012.7069	1012.9143	1013.1177	1013.3172
6	1013.7200	1014.0035	1014.2813	1014.5537	1014.8208	1015.0827	1015.3396	1015.5915	1015.8387	1016.0813
7	1016.0925	1016.4267	1016.7544	1017.0757	1017.3909	1017.7001	1018.0035	1018.3011	1018.5933	1018.8800
8	1018.4901	1018.8761	1019.2547	1019.6261	1019.9905	1020.3481	1020.6990	1021.0435	1021.3816	1021.7136
9	1020.9133	1021.3521	1021.7827	1022.2052	1022.6199	1023.0269	1023.4266	1023.8189	1024.2043	1024.5827
10	1023.3622	1023.8549	1024.3385	1024.8133	1025.2794	1025.7370	1026.1865	1026.6279	1027.0616	1027.4877
11	1025.8371	1026.3848	1026.9226	1027.4507	1027.9693	1028.4788	1028.9792	1029.4709	1029.9541	1030.4290
12	1028.3383	1028.9422	1029.5353	1030.1178	1030.6901	1031.2525	1031.8051	1032.3482	1032.8821	1033.4070
13	1030.2362	1030.8851	1031.5223	1032.1481	1032.7628	1033.3666	1033.9600	1034.5431	1035.1162	1035.6796
14	1032.1542	1032.8490	1033.5312	1034.2011	1034.8591	1035.5055	1036.1405	1036.7645	1037.3778	1037.9806
15	1034.0927	1034.8342	1035.5623	1036.2773	1036.9795	1037.6693	1038.3469	1039.0128	1039.6672	1040.3103
16	1036.0517	1036.8410	1037.6159	1038.3768	1039.1242	1039.8583	1040.5796	1041.2882	1041.9847	1042.6692
17	1038.0316	1038.8694	1039.6921	1040.5000	1041.2935	1042.0729	1042.8387	1043.5912	1044.3307	1045.0576
18	1040.0325	1040.9199	1041.7913	1042.6470	1043.4876	1044.3133	1045.1246	1045.9219	1046.7055	1047.4758
19	1042.0546	1042.9925	1043.9136	1044.8182	1045.7068	1046.5799	1047.4377	1048.2808	1049.1095	1049.9242
20	1044.0983	1045.0876	1046.0593	1047.0138	1047.9515	1048.8729	1049.7783	1050.6683	1051.5431	1052.4033
21	1046.1636	1047.2054	1048.2288	1049.2341	1050.2219	1051.1926	1052.1467	1053.0845	1054.0066	1054.9133
22	1048.2509	1049.3462	1050.4222	1051.4794	1052.5183	1053.5394	1054.5432	1055.5300	1056.5004	1057.4547
23	1050.3604	1051.5101	1052.6398	1053.7500	1054.8411	1055.9136	1056.9681	1058.0050	1059.0248	1060.0279
24	1052.4923	1053.6975	1054.8819	1056.0461	1057.1904	1058.3155	1059.4219	1060.5099	1061.5803	1062.6333
25	1053.9697	1055.2183	1056.4453	1057.6511	1058.8364	1060.0016	1061.1474	1062.2742	1063.3825	1064.4728
26	1055.4628	1056.7556	1058.0258	1059.2742	1060.5012	1061.7074	1062.8935	1064.0598	1065.2069	1066.3353
27	1056.9718	1058.3095	1059.6239	1060.9155	1062.1851	1063.4332	1064.6602	1065.8669	1067.0537	1068.2211
28	1058.4968	1059.8802	1061.2395	1062.5754	1063.8883	1065.1790	1066.4480	1067.6959	1068.9232	1070.1305
29	1060.0380	1061.4680	1062.8730	1064.2538	1065.6110	1066.9452	1068.2570	1069.5469	1070.8157	1072.0638
30	1061.5956	1063.0729	1064.5246	1065.9512	1067.3535	1068.7320	1070.0874	1071.4204	1072.7314	1074.0212
31	1063.1698	1064.6953	1066.1944	1067.6677	1069.1159	1070.5397	1071.9396	1073.3165	1074.6708	1076.0031
32	1064.7606	1066.3352	1067.8826	1069.4035	1070.8985	1072.3684	1073.8138	1075.2355	1076.6339	1078.0097
33	1066.3684	1067.9929	1069.5895	1071.1588	1072.7015	1074.2185	1075.7103	1077.1776	1078.6212	1080.0415
34	1067.9933	1069.6686	1071.3152	1072.9338	1074.5252	1076.0902	1077.6293	1079.1433	1080.6329	1082.0986
35	1069.6354	1071.3624	1073.0599	1074.7288	1076.3698	1077.9837	1079.5710	1081.1327	1082.6693	1084.1815
36	1071.2950	1073.0745	1074.8239	1076.5440	1078.2356	1079.8992	1081.5359	1083.1461	1084.7307	1086.2904
37	1072.2443	1074.0631	1075.8511	1077.6090	1079.3376	1081.0376	1082.7099	1084.3551	1085.9740	1087.5674
38	1073.2036	1075.0625	1076.8896	1078.6860	1080.4522	1082.1893	1083.8979	1085.5787	1087.2326	1088.8603
39	1074.1732	1076.0727	1077.9396	1079.7750	1081.5797	1083.3544	1085.0999	1086.8171	1088.5067	1090.1695
40	1075.1531	1077.0938	1079.0012	1080.8764	1082.7200	1084.5331	1086.3163	1088.0705	1089.7964	1091.4949
41	1076.1434	1078.1259	1080.0745	1081.9901	1083.8734	1085.7255	1087.5471	1089.3390	1091.1020	1092.8370
42	1077.1442	1079.1693	1081.1597	1083.1163	1085.0401	1086.9318	1088.7925	1090.6228	1092.4237	1094.1958
43	1078.1557	1080.2239	1082.2568	1084.2552	1086.2201	1088.1523	1090.0527	1091.9221	1093.7615	1095.5716
44	1079.1779	1081.2900	1083.3661	1085.4069	1087.4136	1089.3869	1091.3278	1093.2372	1095.1158	1096.9647
45	1080.2109	1082.3677	1084.4876	1086.5716	1088.6208	1090.6360	1092.6181	1094.5681	1096.4868	1098.3751
46	1081.2550	1083.4570	1085.6214	1087.7494	1089.8418	1091.8996	1093.9238	1095.9151	1097.8746	1099.8031
47	1082.3101	1084.5581	1086.7678	1088.9404	1091.0768	1093.1780	1095.2449	1097.2784	1099.2795	1101.2491
48	1083.3764	1085.6711	1087.9269	1090.1449	1092.3260	1094.4713	1096.5817	1098.6582	1100.7017	1102.7130

PLAN III GRADUATED PAYMENT MORTGAGE (SECTION 245)
WITH INCREASING PAYMENTS FOR 5 YEARS AT 7.50 PERCENT EACH YEAR

OUTSTANDING PRINCIPAL BALANCE FACTORS
(PER THOUSAND DOLLARS OF ORIGINAL LOAN PROCEEDS)

INSTALL-MENT NUMBER	FOR 30 YEAR MORTGAGES WITH ANNUAL CONTRACT INTEREST RATES OF									
	12.75	13.00	13.25	13.50	13.75	14.00	14.25	14.50	14.75	15.00
49	1083.6716	1085.9985	1088.2857	1090.5344	1092.7455	1094.9201	1097.0592	1099.1637	1101.2345	1103.2727
50	1083.9699	1086.3294	1088.6485	1090.9283	1093.1699	1095.3742	1097.5424	1099.6753	1101.7740	1103.8393
51	1084.2714	1086.6639	1089.0153	1091.3266	1093.5991	1095.8336	1098.0313	1100.1931	1102.3201	1104.4131
52	1084.5761	1087.0020	1089.3861	1091.7294	1094.0332	1096.2984	1098.5260	1100.7172	1102.8728	1104.9940
53	1084.8840	1087.3438	1089.7610	1092.1368	1094.4723	1096.7685	1099.0266	1101.2475	1103.4324	1105.5822
54	1085.1952	1087.6893	1090.1401	1092.5487	1094.9164	1097.2442	1099.5331	1101.7843	1103.9989	1106.1777
55	1085.5097	1088.0385	1090.5233	1092.9653	1095.3656	1097.7254	1100.0457	1102.3276	1104.5723	1106.7807
56	1085.8276	1088.3915	1090.9108	1093.3865	1095.8200	1098.2122	1100.5643	1102.8775	1105.1527	1107.3912
57	1086.1488	1088.7484	1091.3025	1093.8125	1096.2795	1098.7047	1101.0891	1103.4340	1105.7403	1108.0093
58	1086.4734	1089.1091	1091.6986	1094.2433	1096.7443	1099.2029	1101.6201	1103.9972	1106.3352	1108.6352
59	1086.8015	1089.4737	1092.0991	1094.6789	1097.2145	1099.7070	1102.1575	1104.5672	1106.9373	1109.2688
60	1087.1331	1089.8422	1092.5039	1095.1195	1097.6900	1100.2169	1102.7012	1105.1441	1107.5468	1109.9105
61	1086.6270	1089.3572	1092.0393	1094.6744	1097.2638	1099.8088	1102.3105	1104.7702	1107.1891	1109.5683
62	1086.1155	1088.8670	1091.5694	1094.2242	1096.8326	1099.3959	1101.9152	1104.3919	1106.8270	1109.2218
63	1085.5986	1088.3714	1091.0944	1093.7691	1096.3966	1098.9782	1101.5152	1104.0089	1106.4604	1108.8710
64	1085.0762	1087.8705	1090.6142	1093.3088	1095.9555	1098.5556	1101.1105	1103.6213	1106.0894	1108.5158
65	1084.5483	1087.3641	1090.1287	1092.8433	1095.5093	1098.1281	1100.7009	1103.2291	1105.7137	1108.1562
66	1084.0148	1086.8523	1089.6377	1092.3726	1095.0581	1097.6956	1100.2865	1102.8321	1105.3335	1107.7921
67	1083.4755	1086.3349	1089.1414	1091.8966	1094.6017	1097.2581	1099.8672	1102.4303	1104.9486	1107.4234
68	1082.9306	1085.8119	1088.6396	1091.4152	1094.1400	1096.8155	1099.4429	1102.0236	1104.5589	1107.0501
69	1082.3799	1085.2832	1088.1322	1090.9284	1093.6731	1096.3677	1099.0135	1101.6120	1104.1645	1106.6722
70	1081.8233	1084.7488	1087.6193	1090.4361	1093.2008	1095.9146	1098.5791	1101.1955	1103.7652	1106.2895
71	1081.2608	1084.2086	1087.1007	1089.9383	1092.7231	1095.4563	1098.1395	1100.7739	1103.3610	1105.9020
72	1080.6923	1083.6626	1086.5763	1089.4349	1092.2399	1094.9927	1097.6946	1100.3472	1102.9518	1105.5097
73	1080.1178	1083.1107	1086.0462	1088.9259	1091.7512	1094.5236	1097.2445	1099.9154	1102.5376	1105.1125
74	1079.5371	1082.5527	1085.5102	1088.4111	1091.2569	1094.0491	1096.7891	1099.4784	1102.1183	1104.7104
75	1078.9504	1081.9888	1084.9683	1087.8905	1090.7569	1093.5690	1096.3282	1099.0360	1101.6939	1104.3032
76	1078.3573	1081.4187	1084.4204	1087.3641	1090.2512	1093.0833	1095.8619	1098.5884	1101.2642	1103.8909
77	1077.7580	1080.8424	1083.8665	1086.8317	1089.7397	1092.5920	1095.3900	1098.1353	1100.8293	1103.4735
78	1077.1523	1080.2599	1083.3064	1086.2934	1089.2223	1092.0949	1094.9125	1097.6767	1100.3890	1103.0508
79	1076.5402	1079.6711	1082.7402	1085.7490	1088.6991	1091.5920	1094.4294	1097.2126	1099.9433	1102.6229
80	1075.9215	1079.0759	1082.1677	1085.1984	1088.1698	1091.0833	1093.9405	1096.7429	1099.4921	1102.1896
81	1075.2963	1078.4743	1081.5889	1084.6417	1087.6344	1090.5686	1093.4458	1096.2675	1099.0354	1101.7509
82	1074.6645	1077.8661	1081.0037	1084.0787	1087.0929	1090.0479	1092.9452	1095.7864	1098.5731	1101.3067
83	1074.0259	1077.2514	1080.4120	1083.5094	1086.5453	1089.5211	1092.4387	1095.2995	1098.1050	1100.8569
84	1073.3806	1076.6300	1079.8138	1082.9337	1085.9913	1088.9882	1091.9262	1094.8067	1097.6313	1100.4016
85	1072.7284	1076.0019	1079.2090	1082.3515	1085.4310	1088.4491	1091.4076	1094.3079	1097.1517	1099.9405
86	1072.0692	1075.3669	1078.5975	1081.7627	1084.8643	1087.9037	1090.8828	1093.8031	1096.6662	1099.4737
87	1071.4031	1074.7251	1077.9793	1081.1674	1084.2910	1087.3519	1090.3518	1093.2922	1096.1747	1099.0011
88	1070.7299	1074.0763	1077.3542	1080.5653	1083.7112	1086.7937	1089.8145	1092.7751	1095.6772	1098.5225
89	1070.0495	1073.4205	1076.7223	1079.9565	1083.1248	1086.2290	1089.2708	1092.2518	1095.1736	1098.0380
90	1069.3619	1072.7576	1076.0833	1079.3408	1082.5316	1085.6577	1088.7206	1091.7221	1094.6638	1097.5474
91	1068.6670	1072.0875	1075.4373	1078.7181	1081.9317	1085.0797	1088.1640	1091.1861	1094.1477	1097.0506
92	1067.9647	1071.4102	1074.7842	1078.0885	1081.3249	1084.4950	1087.6007	1090.6435	1093.6253	1096.5477
93	1067.2550	1070.7255	1074.1239	1077.4518	1080.7111	1083.9035	1087.0307	1090.0945	1093.0965	1096.0385
94	1066.5377	1070.0334	1073.4562	1076.8079	1080.0903	1083.3050	1086.4539	1089.5387	1092.5612	1095.5229
95	1065.8128	1069.3338	1072.7812	1076.1568	1079.4623	1082.6996	1085.8703	1088.9763	1092.0193	1095.0008
96	1065.0801	1068.6267	1072.0988	1075.4984	1078.8272	1082.0871	1085.2798	1088.4071	1091.4707	1094.4723

NOTE: DUE TO THE ROUNDING INVOLVED IN COMPUTING ACTUAL PAYMENTS, ACTUAL OUTSTANDING BALANCES WILL TEND TO BE LOWER THAN COMPUTED USING THE ABOVE FACTORS.

THE HIGHEST OUTSTANDING BALANCE FACTORS ARE UNDERLINED.

PLAN III GRADUATED PAYMENT MORTGAGE (SECTION 245)
WITH INCREASING PAYMENTS FOR 5 YEARS AT 7.50 PERCENT EACH YEAR

OUTSTANDING PRINCIPAL BALANCE FACTORS
(PER THOUSAND DOLLARS OF ORIGINAL LOAN PROCEEDS)

INSTALL-MENT	FOR 30 YEAR MORTGAGES WITH ANNUAL CONTRACT INTEREST RATES OF									
NUMBER	12.75	13.00	13.25	13.50	13.75	14.00	14.25	14.50	14.75	15.00
97	1064.3398	1067.9118	1071.4088	1074.8325	1078.1848	1081.4675	1084.6823	1087.8310	1090.9154	1093.9371
98	1063.5915	1067.1892	1070.7112	1074.1592	1077.5351	1080.8406	1084.0776	1087.2479	1090.3532	1093.3953
99	1062.8353	1066.4588	1070.0059	1073.4783	1076.8779	1080.2064	1083.4658	1086.6578	1089.7842	1092.8466
100	1062.0710	1065.7205	1069.2928	1072.7897	1076.2131	1079.5649	1082.8467	1086.0606	1089.2081	1092.2911
101	1061.2987	1064.9742	1068.5718	1072.0934	1075.5408	1078.9158	1082.2203	1085.4561	1088.6250	1091.7287
102	1060.5181	1064.2198	1067.8429	1071.3892	1074.8607	1078.2592	1081.5864	1084.8443	1088.0347	1091.1592
103	1059.7292	1063.4572	1067.1059	1070.6772	1074.1729	1077.5949	1080.9451	1084.2252	1087.4371	1090.5826
104	1058.9320	1062.6864	1066.3608	1069.9571	1073.4771	1076.9228	1080.2960	1083.5986	1086.8322	1089.9989
105	1058.1262	1061.9072	1065.6074	1069.2289	1072.7734	1076.2430	1079.6393	1082.9643	1086.2199	1089.4078
106	1057.3120	1061.1195	1064.8458	1068.4925	1072.0617	1075.5552	1078.9748	1082.3225	1085.6000	1088.8093
107	1056.4890	1060.3234	1064.0757	1067.7478	1071.3418	1074.8593	1078.3024	1081.6729	1084.9726	1088.2033
108	1055.6573	1059.5186	1063.2971	1066.9948	1070.6136	1074.1554	1077.6220	1081.0154	1084.3374	1087.5898
109	1054.8168	1058.7051	1062.5099	1066.2333	1069.8771	1073.4432	1076.9335	1080.3500	1083.6944	1086.9686
110	1053.9674	1057.8828	1061.7141	1065.4632	1069.1321	1072.7227	1076.2369	1079.6765	1083.0435	1086.3396
111	1053.1089	1057.0515	1060.9094	1064.6845	1068.3786	1071.9938	1075.5319	1078.9949	1082.3846	1085.7028
112	1052.2413	1056.2113	1060.0959	1063.8970	1067.6165	1071.2564	1074.8186	1078.3051	1081.7176	1085.0580
113	1051.3645	1055.3620	1059.2734	1063.1006	1066.8457	1070.5104	1074.0969	1077.6069	1081.0424	1084.4052
114	1050.4784	1054.5034	1058.4417	1062.2953	1066.0660	1069.7558	1073.3665	1076.9003	1080.3589	1083.7442
115	1049.5828	1053.6356	1057.6010	1061.4809	1065.2774	1068.9923	1072.6275	1076.1851	1079.6670	1083.0749
116	1048.6778	1052.7583	1056.7509	1060.6574	1064.4797	1068.2198	1071.8798	1075.4613	1078.9665	1082.3973
117	1047.7631	1051.8716	1055.8914	1059.8245	1063.6729	1067.4384	1071.1231	1074.7288	1078.2575	1081.7112
118	1046.8387	1050.9753	1055.0225	1058.9824	1062.8569	1066.6479	1070.3574	1073.9874	1077.5398	1081.0165
119	1045.9045	1050.0692	1054.1439	1058.1307	1062.0315	1065.8481	1069.5827	1073.2371	1076.8132	1080.3131
120	1044.9604	1049.1533	1053.2557	1057.2695	1061.1966	1065.0391	1068.7988	1072.4777	1076.0778	1079.6009
121	1044.0062	1048.2275	1052.3577	1056.3986	1060.3522	1064.2205	1068.0055	1071.7091	1075.3332	1078.8799
122	1043.0419	1047.2917	1051.4497	1055.5178	1059.4981	1063.3924	1067.2028	1070.9312	1074.5796	1078.1498
123	1042.0673	1046.3457	1050.5317	1054.6272	1058.6342	1062.5547	1066.3906	1070.1440	1073.8166	1077.4106
124	1041.0824	1045.3895	1049.6036	1053.7266	1057.7605	1061.7072	1065.5688	1069.3472	1073.0443	1076.6622
125	1040.0871	1044.4229	1048.6652	1052.8158	1056.8767	1060.8498	1064.7372	1068.5408	1072.2625	1075.9044
126	1039.0811	1043.4459	1047.7165	1051.8948	1055.9827	1059.9824	1063.8957	1067.7246	1071.4711	1075.1371
127	1038.0645	1042.4583	1046.7573	1050.9634	1055.0786	1059.1049	1063.0442	1066.8986	1070.6699	1074.3603
128	1037.0370	1041.4599	1045.7874	1050.0215	1054.1641	1058.2171	1062.1826	1066.0626	1069.8589	1073.5737
129	1035.9987	1040.4508	1044.8069	1049.0690	1053.2391	1057.3190	1061.3108	1065.2165	1069.0380	1072.7773
130	1034.9493	1039.4307	1043.8156	1048.1059	1052.3035	1056.4104	1060.4286	1064.3602	1068.2069	1071.9709
131	1033.8888	1038.3996	1042.8133	1047.1319	1051.3572	1055.4912	1059.5360	1063.4935	1067.3657	1071.1545
132	1032.8169	1037.3573	1041.8000	1046.1469	1050.4000	1054.5613	1058.6328	1062.6163	1066.5140	1070.3278
133	1031.7338	1036.3037	1040.7754	1045.1508	1049.4319	1053.6205	1057.7188	1061.7286	1065.6520	1069.4909
134	1030.6390	1035.2387	1039.7396	1044.1436	1048.4527	1052.6688	1056.7940	1060.8301	1064.7793	1068.6434
135	1029.5327	1034.1622	1038.6923	1043.1250	1047.4622	1051.7059	1055.8581	1059.9208	1063.8959	1067.7854
136	1028.4146	1033.0740	1037.6334	1042.0949	1046.4604	1050.7319	1054.9112	1059.0005	1063.0016	1066.9166
137	1027.2847	1031.9740	1036.5629	1041.0533	1045.4472	1049.7464	1053.9531	1058.0691	1062.0964	1066.0370
138	1026.1427	1030.8621	1035.4805	1039.9999	1044.4223	1048.7495	1052.9835	1057.1264	1061.1800	1065.1464
139	1024.9886	1029.7381	1034.3862	1038.9347	1043.3857	1047.7409	1052.0025	1056.1723	1060.2524	1064.2447
140	1023.8222	1028.6020	1033.2798	1037.8576	1042.3372	1046.7206	1051.0098	1055.2067	1059.3133	1063.3317
141	1022.6434	1027.4536	1032.1612	1036.7682	1041.2766	1045.6883	1050.0053	1054.2294	1058.3627	1062.4072
142	1021.4522	1026.2927	1031.0302	1035.6667	1040.2040	1044.6440	1048.9888	1053.2403	1057.4005	1061.4713
143	1020.2482	1025.1192	1029.8868	1034.5527	1039.1190	1043.5876	1047.9603	1052.2393	1056.4264	1060.5236
144	1019.0315	1023.9331	1028.7307	1033.4262	1038.0216	1042.5188	1046.9196	1051.2261	1055.4403	1059.5640

PLAN III GRADUATED PAYMENT MORTGAGE (SECTION 245)
WITH INCREASING PAYMENTS FOR 5 YEARS AT 7.50 PERCENT EACH YEAR

OUTSTANDING PRINCIPAL BALANCE FACTORS
(PER THOUSAND DOLLARS OF ORIGINAL LOAN PROCEEDS)

INSTALL-MENT NUMBER	FOR 30 YEAR MORTGAGES WITH ANNUAL CONTRACT INTEREST RATES OF									
	15.25	15.50	15.75	16.00	16.25	16.50	16.75	17.00	17.25	17.50
1	1002.6347	1002.6711	1002.7067	1002.7415	1002.7757	1002.8092	1002.8421	1002.8743	1002.9058	1002.9368
2	1005.3030	1005.3766	1005.4488	1005.5196	1005.5890	1005.6570	1005.7238	1005.7892	1005.8534	1005.9164
3	1008.0051	1008.1171	1008.2270	1008.3347	1008.4404	1008.5440	1008.6457	1008.7455	1008.8434	1008.9395
4	1010.7416	1010.8931	1011.0416	1011.1874	1011.3304	1011.4707	1011.6085	1011.7436	1011.8763	1012.0066
5	1013.5128	1013.7048	1013.8932	1014.0781	1014.2595	1014.4377	1014.6125	1014.7843	1014.9529	1015.1185
6	1016.3193	1016.5529	1016.7822	1017.0073	1017.2283	1017.4454	1017.6586	1017.8680	1018.0737	1018.2758
7	1019.1614	1019.4378	1019.7091	1019.9756	1020.2373	1020.4945	1020.7471	1020.9953	1021.2393	1021.4791
8	1022.0397	1022.3599	1022.6745	1022.9835	1023.2871	1023.5855	1023.8787	1024.1670	1024.4504	1024.7291
9	1024.9545	1025.3198	1025.6787	1026.0314	1026.3782	1026.7190	1027.0541	1027.3836	1027.7077	1028.0265
10	1027.9064	1028.3179	1028.7224	1029.1201	1029.5111	1029.8956	1030.2738	1030.6458	1031.0119	1031.3720
11	1030.8958	1031.3547	1031.8060	1032.2498	1032.6864	1033.1159	1033.5384	1033.9542	1034.3635	1034.7663
12	1033.9232	1034.4308	1034.9301	1035.4214	1035.9047	1036.3804	1036.8486	1037.3095	1037.7633	1038.2101
13	1036.2335	1036.7782	1037.3139	1037.8408	1038.3592	1038.8693	1039.3713	1039.8654	1040.3518	1040.8307
14	1038.5732	1039.1559	1039.7289	1040.2925	1040.8469	1041.3924	1041.9292	1042.4575	1042.9775	1043.4894
15	1040.9426	1041.5643	1042.1756	1042.7769	1043.3683	1043.9502	1044.5228	1045.0863	1045.6409	1046.1869
16	1043.3421	1044.0038	1044.6544	1045.2944	1045.9238	1046.5432	1047.1526	1047.7523	1048.3426	1048.9238
17	1045.7722	1046.4748	1047.1658	1047.8454	1048.5140	1049.1718	1049.8191	1050.4561	1051.0832	1051.7006
18	1048.2331	1048.9778	1049.7101	1050.4305	1051.1392	1051.8365	1052.5228	1053.1982	1053.8632	1054.5178
19	1050.7253	1051.5130	1052.2878	1053.0500	1053.8000	1054.5379	1055.2642	1055.9792	1056.6831	1057.3762
20	1053.2491	1054.0810	1054.8994	1055.7045	1056.4968	1057.2765	1058.0440	1058.7996	1059.5435	1060.2762
21	1055.8051	1056.6822	1057.5452	1058.3944	1059.2301	1060.0527	1060.8625	1061.6599	1062.4451	1063.2185
22	1058.3935	1059.3170	1060.2258	1061.1201	1062.0004	1062.8671	1063.7204	1064.5607	1065.3884	1066.2038
23	1061.0148	1061.9858	1062.9415	1063.8822	1064.8083	1065.7201	1066.6181	1067.5026	1068.3740	1069.2325
24	1063.6694	1064.6891	1065.6929	1066.6811	1067.6541	1068.6124	1069.5563	1070.4863	1071.4025	1072.3055
25	1065.5456	1066.6013	1067.6404	1068.6634	1069.6706	1070.6624	1071.6393	1072.6017	1073.5499	1074.4842
26	1067.4456	1068.5382	1069.6135	1070.6720	1071.7143	1072.7406	1073.7514	1074.7471	1075.7281	1076.6947
27	1069.3698	1070.5000	1071.6125	1072.7075	1073.7856	1074.8473	1075.8929	1076.9229	1077.9376	1078.9375
28	1071.3184	1072.4873	1073.6377	1074.7701	1075.8851	1076.9830	1078.0643	1079.1295	1080.1789	1081.2130
29	1073.2917	1074.5001	1075.6895	1076.8602	1078.0129	1079.1481	1080.2660	1081.3673	1082.4524	1083.5216
30	1075.2902	1076.5390	1077.7682	1078.9782	1080.1696	1081.3429	1082.4985	1083.6369	1084.7586	1085.8639
31	1077.3141	1078.6042	1079.8742	1081.1244	1082.3555	1083.5679	1084.7621	1085.9386	1087.0979	1088.2404
32	1079.3636	1080.6961	1082.0078	1083.2993	1084.5710	1085.8235	1087.0573	1088.2730	1089.4709	1090.6516
33	1081.4393	1082.8151	1084.1695	1085.5031	1086.8165	1088.1101	1089.3846	1090.6404	1091.8780	1093.0979
34	1083.5413	1084.9613	1086.3595	1087.7363	1089.0924	1090.4282	1091.7443	1093.0413	1094.3197	1095.5798
35	1085.6700	1087.1354	1088.5783	1089.9993	1091.3991	1092.7781	1094.1370	1095.4763	1096.7964	1098.0980
36	1087.8257	1089.3374	1090.8262	1092.2925	1093.7370	1095.1604	1096.5631	1097.9457	1099.3088	1100.6529
37	1089.1358	1090.6800	1092.2006	1093.6982	1095.1735	1096.6271	1098.0596	1099.4714	1100.8633	1102.2356
38	1090.4625	1092.0398	1093.5930	1095.1227	1096.6295	1098.1140	1099.5769	1101.0188	1102.4401	1103.8414
39	1091.8061	1093.4173	1095.0037	1096.5662	1098.1052	1099.6214	1101.1155	1102.5880	1104.0395	1105.4706
40	1093.1667	1094.8125	1096.4330	1098.0289	1099.6008	1101.1495	1102.6755	1104.1795	1105.6620	1107.1236
41	1094.5447	1096.2257	1097.8810	1099.5111	1101.1167	1102.6986	1104.2573	1105.7935	1107.3077	1108.8007
42	1095.9401	1097.6572	1099.3480	1101.0131	1102.6532	1104.2690	1105.8612	1107.4303	1108.9772	1110.5022
43	1097.3533	1099.1072	1100.8343	1102.5351	1104.2104	1105.8610	1107.4874	1109.0904	1110.6706	1112.2286
44	1098.7844	1100.5760	1102.3400	1104.0774	1105.7887	1107.4748	1109.1364	1110.7740	1112.3884	1113.9801
45	1100.2338	1102.0637	1103.8656	1105.6402	1107.3884	1109.1109	1110.8083	1112.4814	1114.1308	1115.7572
46	1101.7015	1103.5706	1105.4111	1107.2239	1109.0098	1110.7695	1112.5037	1114.2131	1115.8983	1117.5602
47	1103.1879	1105.0969	1106.9769	1108.8288	1110.6531	1112.4508	1114.2226	1115.9692	1117.6913	1119.3895
48	1104.6932	1106.6430	1108.5633	1110.4550	1112.3187	1114.1553	1115.9656	1117.7502	1119.5100	1121.2455

PLAN III GRADUATED PAYMENT MORTGAGE (SECTION 245)
WITH INCREASING PAYMENTS FOR 5 YEARS AT 7.50 PERCENT EACH YEAR

OUTSTANDING PRINCIPAL BALANCE FACTORS
(PER THOUSAND DOLLARS OF ORIGINAL LOAN PROCEEDS)

FOR 30 YEAR MORTGAGES WITH ANNUAL CONTRACT INTEREST RATES OF

INSTALL-MENT NUMBER	15.25	15.50	15.75	16.00	16.25	16.50	16.75	17.00	17.25	17.50
49	1105.2790	1107.2545	1109.1998	1111.1160	1113.0037	1114.8639	1116.6972	1118.5044	1120.2862	1122.0433
50	1105.8723	1107.8738	1109.8447	1111.7858	1113.6981	1115.5822	1117.4390	1119.2692	1121.0736	1122.8529
51	1106.4732	1108.5012	1110.4980	1112.4646	1114.4018	1116.3103	1118.1911	1120.0448	1121.8723	1123.6742
52	1107.0816	1109.1366	1111.1599	1113.1525	1115.1150	1117.0485	1118.9537	1120.8314	1122.6825	1124.5075
53	1107.6978	1109.7803	1111.8305	1113.8495	1115.8379	1117.7968	1119.7270	1121.6292	1123.5043	1125.3530
54	1108.3218	1110.4323	1112.5099	1114.5558	1116.5706	1118.5555	1120.5111	1122.4383	1124.3379	1126.2108
55	1108.9538	1111.0927	1113.1982	1115.2715	1117.3133	1119.3245	1121.3061	1123.2588	1125.1836	1127.0811
56	1109.5938	1111.7616	1113.8956	1115.9967	1118.0659	1120.1041	1122.1122	1124.0910	1126.0414	1127.9641
57	1110.2419	1112.4392	1114.6021	1116.7316	1118.8288	1120.8945	1122.9296	1124.9350	1126.9115	1128.8600
58	1110.8983	1113.1255	1115.3179	1117.4764	1119.6020	1121.6957	1123.7583	1125.7909	1127.7941	1129.7689
59	1111.5629	1113.8207	1116.0430	1118.2310	1120.3857	1122.5079	1124.5987	1126.6589	1128.6894	1130.6911
60	1112.2361	1114.5248	1116.7777	1118.9957	1121.1800	1123.3313	1125.4508	1127.5392	1129.5976	1131.6268
61	1111.9088	1114.2119	1116.4785	1118.7098	1120.9067	1123.0702	1125.2013	1127.3010	1129.3701	1131.4095
62	1111.5774	1113.8949	1116.1754	1118.4200	1120.6297	1122.8055	1124.9484	1127.0594	1129.1393	1131.1891
63	1111.2417	1113.5738	1115.8683	1118.1264	1120.3490	1122.5371	1124.6919	1126.8143	1128.9052	1130.9655
64	1110.9018	1113.2486	1115.5572	1117.8288	1120.0644	1122.2651	1124.4319	1126.5658	1128.6677	1130.7386
65	1110.5576	1112.9192	1115.2420	1117.5273	1119.7760	1121.9893	1124.1682	1126.3138	1128.4268	1130.5085
66	1110.2090	1112.5855	1114.9227	1117.2217	1119.4837	1121.7098	1123.9009	1126.0581	1128.1825	1130.2749
67	1109.8560	1112.2475	1114.5992	1116.9121	1119.1875	1121.4264	1123.6298	1125.7989	1127.9346	1130.0380
68	1109.4984	1111.9051	1114.2714	1116.5984	1118.8872	1121.1391	1123.3550	1125.5360	1127.6832	1129.7976
69	1109.1364	1111.5583	1113.9393	1116.2804	1118.5829	1120.8478	1123.0763	1125.2694	1127.4282	1129.5537
70	1108.7697	1111.2071	1113.6029	1115.9583	1118.2744	1120.5525	1122.7937	1124.9990	1127.1695	1129.3062
71	1108.3984	1110.8513	1113.2620	1115.6318	1117.9618	1120.2532	1122.5072	1124.7247	1126.9071	1129.0551
72	1108.0223	1110.4909	1112.9167	1115.3010	1117.6449	1119.9498	1122.2166	1124.4466	1126.6409	1128.8004
73	1107.6415	1110.1259	1112.5668	1114.9657	1117.3238	1119.6422	1121.9220	1124.1646	1126.3708	1128.5419
74	1107.2558	1109.7561	1112.2124	1114.6260	1116.9983	1119.3303	1121.6233	1123.8785	1126.0969	1128.2797
75	1106.8653	1109.3816	1111.8533	1114.2818	1116.6684	1119.0142	1121.3205	1123.5884	1125.8191	1128.0137
76	1106.4698	1109.0022	1111.4895	1113.9330	1116.3340	1118.6937	1121.0134	1123.2942	1125.5373	1127.7438
77	1106.0692	1108.6179	1111.1209	1113.5795	1115.9951	1118.3688	1120.7020	1122.9958	1125.2514	1127.4699
78	1105.6636	1108.2287	1110.7475	1113.2214	1115.6516	1118.0395	1120.3863	1122.6932	1124.9614	1127.1920
79	1105.2528	1107.8344	1110.3692	1112.8584	1115.3035	1117.7056	1120.0661	1122.3863	1124.6672	1126.9101
80	1104.8367	1107.4350	1109.9859	1112.4906	1114.9506	1117.3671	1119.7415	1122.0750	1124.3688	1126.6241
81	1104.4154	1107.0305	1109.5975	1112.1179	1114.5930	1117.0240	1119.4124	1121.7594	1124.0662	1126.3339
82	1103.9888	1106.6208	1109.2041	1111.7402	1114.2305	1116.6762	1119.0787	1121.4392	1123.7591	1126.0395
83	1103.5567	1106.2057	1108.8055	1111.3575	1113.8631	1116.3236	1118.7403	1121.1146	1123.4477	1125.7408
84	1103.1191	1105.7853	1108.4017	1110.9697	1113.4907	1115.9661	1118.3972	1120.7853	1123.1318	1125.4377
85	1102.6760	1105.3595	1107.9926	1110.5767	1113.1133	1115.6037	1118.0493	1120.4514	1122.8113	1125.1303
86	1102.2272	1104.9282	1107.5781	1110.1785	1112.7308	1115.2363	1117.6965	1120.1127	1122.4862	1124.8183
87	1101.7727	1104.4913	1107.1582	1109.7750	1112.3431	1114.8639	1117.3389	1119.7693	1122.1565	1124.5018
88	1101.3125	1104.0487	1106.7328	1109.3661	1111.9501	1114.4864	1116.9762	1119.4210	1121.8220	1124.1806
89	1100.8464	1103.6005	1106.3017	1108.9517	1111.5519	1114.1036	1116.6085	1119.0677	1121.4827	1123.8548
90	1100.3744	1103.1464	1105.8651	1108.5318	1111.1482	1113.7156	1116.2356	1118.7094	1121.1385	1123.5242
91	1099.8964	1102.6865	1105.4227	1108.1063	1110.7391	1113.3223	1115.8575	1118.3461	1120.7894	1123.1888
92	1099.4123	1102.2207	1104.9744	1107.6752	1110.3244	1112.9236	1115.4742	1117.9776	1120.4353	1122.8486
93	1098.9220	1101.7488	1104.5204	1107.2383	1109.9041	1112.5194	1115.0855	1117.6039	1120.0761	1122.5033
94	1098.4256	1101.2708	1104.0603	1106.7956	1109.4781	1112.1096	1114.6914	1117.2249	1119.7117	1122.1530
95	1097.9228	1100.7867	1103.5942	1106.3469	1109.0464	1111.6942	1114.2917	1116.8405	1119.3420	1121.7976
96	1097.4136	1100.2963	1103.1220	1105.8923	1108.6088	1111.2730	1113.8865	1116.4507	1118.9671	1121.4371

PLAN III GRADUATED PAYMENT MORTGAGE (SECTION 245)
WITH INCREASING PAYMENTS FOR 5 YEARS AT 7.50 PERCENT EACH YEAR

OUTSTANDING PRINCIPAL BALANCE FACTORS
(PER THOUSAND DOLLARS OF ORIGINAL LOAN PROCEEDS)

INSTALL-MENT NUMBER	FOR 30 YEAR MORTGAGES WITH ANNUAL CONTRACT INTEREST RATES OF									
	15.25	15.50	15.75	16.00	16.25	16.50	16.75	17.00	17.25	17.50
97	1096.8980	1099.7996	1102.6436	1105.4316	1108.1653	1110.8461	1113.4757	1116.0554	1118.5868	1121.0712
98	1096.3758	1099.2964	1102.1589	1104.9648	1107.7158	1110.4133	1113.0591	1115.6545	1118.2010	1120.7001
99	1095.8469	1098.7868	1101.6678	1104.4918	1107.2602	1109.9746	1112.6367	1115.2478	1117.8096	1120.3235
100	1095.3114	1098.2705	1101.1703	1104.0124	1106.7984	1109.5298	1112.2084	1114.8355	1117.4127	1119.9414
101	1094.7690	1097.7477	1100.6663	1103.5267	1106.3303	1109.0789	1111.7741	1114.4172	1117.0100	1119.5538
102	1094.2198	1097.2180	1100.1557	1103.0344	1105.8560	1108.6219	1111.3337	1113.9931	1116.6015	1119.1605
103	1093.6635	1096.6815	1099.6383	1102.5357	1105.3752	1108.1585	1110.8872	1113.5630	1116.1872	1118.7614
104	1093.1002	1096.1381	1099.1142	1102.0302	1104.8879	1107.6888	1110.4345	1113.1267	1115.7669	1118.3566
105	1092.5298	1095.5877	1098.5832	1101.5181	1104.3940	1107.2126	1109.9755	1112.6843	1115.3406	1117.9458
106	1091.9521	1095.0301	1098.0452	1100.9991	1103.8934	1106.7298	1109.5100	1112.2356	1114.9081	1117.5291
107	1091.3670	1094.4654	1097.5002	1100.4731	1103.3860	1106.2404	1109.0381	1111.7805	1114.4694	1117.1063
108	1090.7745	1093.8933	1096.9480	1099.9402	1102.8717	1105.7443	1108.5595	1111.3190	1114.0244	1116.6773
109	1090.1745	1093.3139	1096.3885	1099.4002	1102.3505	1105.2414	1108.0743	1110.8510	1113.5731	1116.2420
110	1089.5669	1092.7270	1095.8217	1098.8529	1101.8223	1104.7315	1107.5823	1110.3763	1113.1152	1115.8005
111	1088.9515	1092.1325	1095.2475	1098.2984	1101.2869	1104.2147	1107.0835	1109.8950	1112.6507	1115.3524
112	1088.3283	1091.5303	1094.6657	1097.7364	1100.7442	1103.6907	1106.5777	1109.4068	1112.1796	1114.8979
113	1087.6972	1090.9203	1094.0763	1097.1670	1100.1942	1103.1595	1106.0648	1108.9116	1111.7017	1114.4367
114	1087.0581	1090.3025	1093.4792	1096.5900	1099.6367	1102.6210	1105.5447	1108.4095	1111.2169	1113.9687
115	1086.4109	1089.6767	1092.8742	1096.0053	1099.0717	1102.0752	1105.0174	1107.9002	1110.7252	1113.4940
116	1085.7554	1089.0428	1092.2613	1095.4128	1098.4990	1101.5218	1104.4828	1107.3838	1110.2264	1113.0123
117	1085.0916	1088.4007	1091.6404	1094.8124	1097.9186	1100.9608	1103.9407	1106.8600	1109.7204	1112.5236
118	1084.4194	1087.7503	1091.0113	1094.2040	1097.3303	1100.3921	1103.3910	1106.3288	1109.2072	1112.0278
119	1083.7386	1087.0915	1090.3739	1093.5875	1096.7341	1099.8155	1102.8336	1105.7900	1108.6865	1111.5248
120	1083.0491	1086.4243	1089.7282	1092.9627	1096.1298	1099.2311	1102.2685	1105.2437	1108.1584	1111.0144
121	1082.3510	1085.7484	1089.0740	1092.3296	1095.5173	1098.6386	1101.6955	1104.6896	1107.6227	1110.4966
122	1081.6439	1085.0637	1088.4112	1091.6881	1094.8965	1098.0380	1101.1144	1104.1276	1107.0793	1109.9712
123	1080.9278	1084.3702	1087.7397	1091.0381	1094.2672	1097.4291	1100.5253	1103.5577	1106.5281	1109.4381
124	1080.2027	1083.6678	1087.0594	1090.3793	1093.6295	1096.8118	1099.9279	1102.9797	1105.9690	1108.8973
125	1079.4683	1082.9563	1086.3701	1089.7118	1092.9832	1096.1860	1099.3222	1102.3936	1105.4018	1108.3486
126	1078.7246	1082.2356	1085.6719	1089.0354	1092.3280	1095.5517	1098.7081	1101.7991	1104.8265	1107.7919
127	1077.9715	1081.5056	1084.9644	1088.3500	1091.6641	1094.9086	1098.0854	1101.1962	1104.2428	1107.2271
128	1077.2088	1080.7661	1084.2477	1087.6554	1090.9911	1094.2567	1097.4539	1100.5847	1103.6509	1106.6540
129	1076.4363	1080.0171	1083.5216	1086.9515	1090.3090	1093.5958	1096.8137	1099.9646	1103.0504	1106.0726
130	1075.6541	1079.2585	1082.7859	1086.2383	1089.6177	1092.9258	1096.1645	1099.3358	1102.4412	1105.4827
131	1074.8619	1078.4900	1082.0406	1085.5156	1088.9170	1092.2466	1095.5063	1098.6980	1101.8233	1104.8842
132	1074.0597	1077.7116	1081.2855	1084.7832	1088.2068	1091.5581	1094.8389	1098.0511	1101.1966	1104.2770
133	1073.2473	1076.9232	1080.5204	1084.0411	1087.4870	1090.8601	1094.1622	1097.3951	1100.5608	1103.6609
134	1072.4245	1076.1245	1079.7454	1083.2891	1086.7575	1090.1525	1093.4760	1096.7298	1099.9159	1103.0359
135	1071.5913	1075.3156	1078.9602	1082.5270	1086.0180	1089.4351	1092.7802	1096.0551	1099.2617	1102.4017
136	1070.7475	1074.4962	1078.1646	1081.7548	1085.2686	1088.7080	1092.0748	1095.3708	1098.5981	1101.7582
137	1069.8930	1073.6662	1077.3587	1080.9723	1084.5090	1087.9708	1091.3594	1094.6769	1097.9249	1101.1054
138	1069.0276	1072.8255	1076.5421	1080.1793	1083.7392	1087.2235	1090.6341	1093.9731	1097.2421	1100.4401
139	1068.1512	1071.9739	1075.7148	1079.3758	1082.9589	1086.4659	1089.8987	1093.2593	1096.5495	1099.7711
140	1067.2637	1071.1114	1074.8767	1078.5616	1082.1680	1085.6978	1089.1530	1092.5354	1095.8469	1099.0893
141	1066.3649	1070.2377	1074.0276	1077.7365	1081.3664	1084.9193	1088.3969	1091.8013	1095.1342	1098.3976
142	1065.4547	1069.3527	1073.1673	1076.9004	1080.5540	1084.1300	1087.6303	1091.0568	1094.4113	1097.6957
143	1064.5329	1068.4563	1072.2957	1076.0532	1079.7306	1083.3299	1086.8529	1090.3017	1093.6780	1096.9837
144	1063.5994	1067.5483	1071.4127	1075.1946	1078.8960	1082.5187	1086.0647	1089.5359	1092.9341	1096.2612

Source: U.S., Department of Housing and Urban Development, The Graduated Payment Mortgage Program—A HUD Handbook, 4240.2 Rev.

APPENDIX D Factors for Calculating Monthly Payments—Section 245, Plan III

Plan III Graduated Payment Mortgage (Section 245)
With Increasing Payments for 5 Years at 7.50 Percent Each Year

Factors for computing monthly installment to principal and interest (per thousand dollars of original loan proceeds)

For 30-year mortgages with annual contract interest rates of

Year	7.75	8.00	8.25	8.50	8.75	9.00	9.25	9.50	9.75	10.00
1	5.3717	5.5101	5.6500	5.7915	5.9344	6.0788	6.2246	6.3719	6.5204	6.6704
2	5.7746	5.9233	6.0738	6.2258	6.3795	6.5347	6.6915	6.8498	7.0095	7.1706
3	6.2077	6.3676	6.5293	6.6928	6.8580	7.0248	7.1934	7.3635	7.5352	7.7084
4	6.6732	6.8452	7.0190	7.1947	7.3723	7.5517	7.7329	7.9158	8.1003	8.2866
5	7.1737	7.3585	7.5454	7.7343	7.9252	8.1181	8.3128	8.5094	8.7079	8.9081
Remaining payments	7.7118	7.9104	8.1113	8.3144	8.5196	8.7269	8.9363	9.1476	9.3609	9.5762

Year	10.25	10.50	10.75	11.00	11.25	11.50	11.75	12.00	12.25	12.50
1	6.8216	6.9740	7.1277	7.2826	7.4387	7.5960	7.7543	7.9138	8.0743	8.2358
2	7.3332	7.4971	7.6623	7.8288	7.9966	8.1657	8.3359	8.5073	8.6798	8.8535
3	7.8832	8.0594	8.2370	8.4160	8.5964	8.7781	8.9611	9.1453	9.3308	9.5175
4	8.4744	8.6638	8.8548	9.0472	9.2411	9.4364	9.6332	9.8312	10.0306	10.2313
5	9.1100	9.3136	9.5189	9.7257	9.9342	10.1442	10.3556	10.5686	10.7829	10.9986
Remaining payments	9.7932	10.0121	10.2328	10.4552	10.6793	10.9050	11.1323	11.3612	11.5916	11.8235

Note: Because of rounding, utilization of these factors can result in small differences in the actual outstanding balances and mortgage insurance premiums.

Year	12.75	13.00	13.25	13.50	13.75	14.00	14.25	14.50	14.75	15.00
1	8.3983	8.5618	8.7263	8.8917	9.0580	9.2252	9.3933	9.5621	9.7318	9.9023
2	9.0282	9.2040	9.3808	9.5586	9.7374	9.9171	10.0978	10.2793	10.4617	10.6450
3	9.7053	9.8943	10.0843	10.2755	10.4677	10.6609	10.8551	11.0502	11.2464	11.4434
4	10.4332	10.6363	10.8407	11.0461	11.2528	11.4604	11.6692	11.8790	12.0898	12.3016
5	11.2157	11.4341	11.6537	11.8746	12.0967	12.3200	12.5444	12.7699	12.9966	13.2243
Remaining payments	12.0569	12.2916	12.5277	12.7652	13.0040	13.2440	13.4852	13.7277	13.9713	14.2161

Year	15.25	15.50	15.75	16.00	16.25	16.50	16.75	17.00	17.25	17.50
1	10.0736	10.2456	10.4183	10.5918	10.7660	10.9408	11.1163	11.2924	11.4692	11.6465
2	10.8291	11.0140	11.1997	11.3862	11.5734	11.7613	11.9500	12.1393	12.3294	12.5200
3	11.6413	11.8401	12.0397	12.2402	12.4414	12.6435	12.8463	13.0498	13.2541	13.4590
4	12.5144	12.7281	12.9427	13.1582	13.3745	13.5917	13.8097	14.0285	14.2481	14.4685
5	13.4530	13.6827	13.9134	14.1450	14.3776	14.6111	14.8454	15.0807	15.3167	15.5536
Remaining payments	14.4619	14.7089	14.9569	15.2059	15.4559	15.7069	15.9589	16.2117	16.4655	16.7201

Source: U.S., Department of Housing and Urban Development, *The Graduated Payment Mortgage Program—A HUD Handbook*, 4240.2 Rev.

APPENDIX E Factors for Calculating Monthly Mortgage Insurance Premiums—Section 245, Plan III

PLAN III GRADUATED PAYMENT MORTGAGE (SECTION 245)
WITH INCREASING PAYMENTS FOR 5 YEARS AT 7.50 PERCENT EACH YEAR

FACTORS FOR COMPUTING MONTHLY MORTGAGE INSURANCE PREMIUMS
(PER THOUSAND DOLLARS OF ORIGINAL LOAN PROCEEDS)

PREMIUM	FOR 30 YEAR MORTGAGES WITH ANNUAL CONTRACT INTEREST RATES OF									
YEAR	7.75	8.00	8.25	8.50	8.75	9.00	9.25	9.50	9.75	10.00
1	.4192	.4194	.4195	.4197	.4199	.4200	.4202	.4203	.4204	.4206
2	.4241	.4246	.4252	.4257	.4262	.4267	.4271	.4276	.4281	.4285
3	.4272	.4281	.4290	.4298	.4307	.4315	.4323	.4331	.4338	.4346
4	.4283	.4295	.4307	.4318	.4330	.4341	.4352	.4363	.4373	.4384
5	.4269	.4284	.4299	.4313	.4327	.4341	.4355	.4368	.4381	.4394
6	.4228	.4245	.4262	.4279	.4295	.4311	.4327	.4342	.4357	.4372
7	.4168	.4187	.4206	.4225	.4243	.4261	.4278	.4295	.4312	.4329
8	.4103	.4124	.4145	.4166	.4186	.4206	.4225	.4244	.4262	.4281
9	.4033	.4056	.4079	.4102	.4124	.4145	.4167	.4187	.4208	.4227
10	.3957	.3983	.4008	.4032	.4056	.4079	.4102	.4125	.4147	.4169
11	.3876	.3903	.3930	.3956	.3982	.4007	.4032	.4057	.4080	.4104
12	.3787	.3816	.3845	.3874	.3901	.3928	.3955	.3981	.4007	.4032
13	.3692	.3723	.3754	.3784	.3813	.3842	.3871	.3899	.3926	.3953
14	.3589	.3622	.3654	.3686	.3717	.3748	.3778	.3808	.3837	.3866
15	.3477	.3512	.3546	.3579	.3612	.3645	.3676	.3708	.3739	.3769
16	.3357	.3393	.3428	.3463	.3498	.3532	.3565	.3598	.3630	.3662
17	.3227	.3264	.3301	.3337	.3373	.3408	.3443	.3477	.3511	.3545
18	.3087	.3125	.3162	.3200	.3237	.3273	.3309	.3345	.3380	.3414
19	.2935	.2974	.3012	.3050	.3088	.3125	.3162	.3199	.3235	.3270
20	.2771	.2810	.2849	.2888	.2926	.2964	.3001	.3038	.3075	.3112
21	.2594	.2633	.2672	.2710	.2749	.2787	.2825	.2862	.2899	.2936
22	.2403	.2441	.2480	.2518	.2556	.2593	.2631	.2668	.2705	.2742
23	.2196	.2234	.2271	.2308	.2345	.2382	.2419	.2455	.2492	.2528
24	.1973	.2009	.2044	.2080	.2115	.2151	.2186	.2221	.2256	.2291
25	.1732	.1765	.1798	.1831	.1864	.1898	.1931	.1964	.1997	.2030
26	.1471	.1501	.1531	.1561	.1591	.1621	.1651	.1681	.1711	.1741
27	.1190	.1215	.1241	.1266	.1292	.1318	.1344	.1370	.1396	.1422
28	.0886	.0906	.0926	.0946	.0966	.0987	.1007	.1028	.1048	.1069
29	.0558	.0571	.0584	.0597	.0611	.0625	.0638	.0652	.0666	.0680
30	.0203	.0208	.0213	.0218	.0223	.0228	.0234	.0239	.0244	.0250

PLAN III GRADUATED PAYMENT MORTGAGE (SECTION 245)
WITH INCREASING PAYMENTS FOR 5 YEARS AT 7.50 PERCENT EACH YEAR

MONTHLY MORTGAGE INSURANCE PREMIUM FACTORS
(PER THOUSAND DOLLARS OF ORIGINAL LOAN PROCEEDS)

PREMIUM	FOR 30 YEAR MORTGAGES WITH ANNUAL CONTRACT INTEREST RATES OF									
YEAR	10.25	10.50	10.75	11.00	11.25	11.50	11.75	12.00	12.25	12.50
1	.4207	.4209	.4210	.4211	.4212	.4214	.4215	.4216	.4217	.4218
2	.4290	.4294	.4298	.4303	.4307	.4311	.4315	.4319	.4322	.4326
3	.4353	.4361	.4368	.4375	.4382	.4388	.4395	.4402	.4408	.4414
4	.4394	.4404	.4414	.4423	.4433	.4442	.4451	.4460	.4469	.4478
5	.4407	.4419	.4431	.4443	.4455	.4467	.4478	.4489	.4500	.4511
6	.4387	.4401	.4415	.4429	.4442	.4455	.4468	.4481	.4493	.4506
7	.4345	.4361	.4376	.4391	.4406	.4421	.4435	.4449	.4463	.4476
8	.4298	.4316	.4333	.4349	.4366	.4382	.4397	.4413	.4428	.4443
9	.4247	.4266	.4285	.4303	.4321	.4338	.4355	.4372	.4388	.4405
10	.4190	.4211	.4231	.4251	.4270	.4289	.4308	.4326	.4344	.4362
11	.4127	.4149	.4171	.4193	.4214	.4235	.4255	.4275	.4294	.4313
12	.4057	.4081	.4105	.4128	.4151	.4173	.4195	.4216	.4237	.4258
13	.3980	.4005	.4031	.4056	.4080	.4104	.4128	.4151	.4173	.4195
14	.3894	.3921	.3949	.3975	.4001	.4027	.4052	.4077	.4101	.4124
15	.3799	.3828	.3857	.3885	.3913	.3940	.3967	.3993	.4019	.4044
16	.3694	.3725	.3755	.3785	.3814	.3843	.3872	.3899	.3927	.3954
17	.3577	.3610	.3642	.3673	.3704	.3734	.3764	.3794	.3822	.3851
18	.3448	.3482	.3515	.3548	.3580	.3612	.3644	.3674	.3705	.3735
19	.3306	.3340	.3375	.3409	.3442	.3475	.3508	.3540	.3572	.3603
20	.3148	.3183	.3218	.3253	.3288	.3322	.3355	.3389	.3421	.3454
21	.2972	.3009	.3044	.3080	.3115	.3150	.3184	.3218	.3252	.3285
22	.2779	.2815	.2851	.2886	.2922	.2957	.2991	.3026	.3060	.3093
23	.2564	.2600	.2635	.2670	.2705	.2740	.2775	.2809	.2843	.2877
24	.2326	.2361	.2395	.2429	.2464	.2498	.2531	.2565	.2598	.2631
25	.2063	.2095	.2128	.2161	.2193	.2225	.2258	.2290	.2322	.2354
26	.1771	.1801	.1831	.1861	.1891	.1920	.1950	.1980	.2010	.2039
27	.1448	.1474	.1500	.1526	.1552	.1578	.1605	.1631	.1657	.1683
28	.1090	.1111	.1132	.1153	.1174	.1195	.1216	.1237	.1258	.1279
29	.0694	.0708	.0722	.0736	.0750	.0765	.0779	.0794	.0808	.0823
30	.0255	.0260	.0266	.0271	.0277	.0283	.0288	.0294	.0300	.0305

PLAN III GRADUATED PAYMENT MORTGAGE (SECTION 245)
WITH INCREASING PAYMENTS FOR 5 YEARS AT 7.50 PERCENT EACH YEAR

MONTHLY MORTGAGE INSURANCE PREMIUM FACTORS
(PER THOUSAND DOLLARS OF ORIGINAL LOAN PROCEEDS)

PREMIUM	FOR 30 YEAR MORTGAGES WITH ANNUAL CONTRACT INTEREST RATES OF									
YEAR	12.75	13.00	13.25	13.50	13.75	14.00	14.25	14.50	14.75	15.00
1	.4220	.4221	.4222	.4223	.4224	.4225	.4226	.4227	.4228	.4229
2	.4330	.4333	.4337	.4340	.4344	.4347	.4351	.4354	.4357	.4360
3	.4420	.4427	.4433	.4438	.4444	.4450	.4455	.4461	.4466	.4472
4	.4486	.4495	.4503	.4511	.4519	.4527	.4534	.4542	.4549	.4557
5	.4521	.4531	.4542	.4552	.4561	.4571	.4580	.4590	.4599	.4608
6	.4518	.4529	.4541	.4552	.4564	.4575	.4585	.4596	.4606	.4616
7	.4489	.4502	.4515	.4527	.4539	.4551	.4563	.4574	.4586	.4597
8	.4457	.4471	.4485	.4498	.4512	.4525	.4537	.4550	.4562	.4574
9	.4420	.4436	.4451	.4465	.4480	.4494	.4508	.4521	.4535	.4548
10	.4379	.4395	.4412	.4428	.4443	.4459	.4474	.4488	.4503	.4517
11	.4331	.4349	.4367	.4385	.4402	.4418	.4434	.4450	.4466	.4481
12	.4278	.4297	.4316	.4335	.4354	.4372	.4389	.4406	.4423	.4440
13	.4217	.4238	.4259	.4279	.4299	.4318	.4337	.4356	.4374	.4392
14	.4148	.4170	.4193	.4214	.4236	.4257	.4277	.4297	.4317	.4336
15	.4069	.4093	.4117	.4141	.4163	.4186	.4208	.4229	.4250	.4271
16	.3980	.4006	.4031	.4056	.4081	.4105	.4128	.4151	.4174	.4196
17	.3879	.3906	.3933	.3960	.3986	.4011	.4036	.4061	.4085	.4109
18	.3764	.3793	.3821	.3849	.3877	.3904	.3930	.3957	.3982	.4007
19	.3634	.3664	.3694	.3723	.3752	.3780	.3808	.3836	.3863	.3890
20	.3486	.3517	.3548	.3579	.3609	.3639	.3668	.3697	.3725	.3753
21	.3318	.3350	.3382	.3414	.3445	.3476	.3506	.3536	.3566	.3595
22	.3127	.3160	.3192	.3225	.3257	.3288	.3320	.3350	.3381	.3411
23	.2910	.2943	.2976	.3009	.3041	.3073	.3105	.3136	.3167	.3198
24	.2664	.2697	.2730	.2762	.2794	.2826	.2857	.2888	.2919	.2950
25	.2385	.2417	.2448	.2479	.2510	.2541	.2572	.2602	.2632	.2662
26	.2069	.2098	.2127	.2156	.2185	.2214	.2243	.2272	.2300	.2329
27	.1709	.1735	.1761	.1787	.1813	.1839	.1864	.1890	.1916	.1941
28	.1301	.1322	.1343	.1364	.1385	.1407	.1428	.1449	.1470	.1491
29	.0837	.0852	.0866	.0881	.0896	.0910	.0925	.0940	.0955	.0969
30	.0311	.0317	.0323	.0328	.0334	.0340	.0346	.0352	.0358	.0364

PLAN III GRADUATED PAYMENT MORTGAGE (SECTION 245)
WITH INCREASING PAYMENTS FOR 5 YEARS AT 7.50 PERCENT EACH YEAR

MONTHLY MORTGAGE INSURANCE PREMIUM FACTORS
(PER THOUSAND DOLLARS OF ORIGINAL LOAN PROCEEDS)

PREMIUM		FOR 30 YEAR MORTGAGES WITH ANNUAL CONTRACT INTEREST RATES OF								
YEAR	15.25	15.50	15.75	16.00	16.25	16.50	16.75	17.00	17.25	17.50
1	.4230	.4231	.4231	.4232	.4233	.4234	.4235	.4236	.4237	.4237
2	.4363	.4366	.4369	.4372	.4375	.4378	.4381	.4384	.4386	.4389
3	.4477	.4482	.4487	.4492	.4497	.4502	.4507	.4511	.4516	.4520
4	.4564	.4571	.4578	.4585	.4592	.4598	.4605	.4611	.4618	.4624
5	.4617	.4626	.4634	.4643	.4651	.4659	.4667	.4675	.4683	.4691
6	.4626	.4636	.4646	.4656	.4665	.4674	.4683	.4692	.4701	.4710
7	.4608	.4618	.4629	.4639	.4649	.4659	.4669	.4678	.4688	.4697
8	.4586	.4597	.4609	.4620	.4630	.4641	.4652	.4662	.4672	.4682
9	.4560	.4573	.4585	.4597	.4609	.4620	.4631	.4642	.4653	.4664
10	.4531	.4544	.4557	.4570	.4583	.4595	.4607	.4619	.4631	.4642
11	.4496	.4511	.4525	.4539	.4553	.4566	.4579	.4592	.4604	.4617
12	.4456	.4472	.4487	.4502	.4517	.4531	.4546	.4559	.4573	.4586
13	.4409	.4426	.4443	.4459	.4475	.4491	.4506	.4521	.4536	.4550
14	.4355	.4373	.4391	.4409	.4426	.4443	.4459	.4476	.4491	.4507
15	.4291	.4311	.4331	.4350	.4368	.4386	.4404	.4422	.4439	.4456
16	.4218	.4239	.4260	.4280	.4300	.4320	.4339	.4358	.4377	.4395
17	.4132	.4155	.4177	.4199	.4221	.4242	.4262	.4283	.4303	.4322
18	.4032	.4056	.4080	.4104	.4127	.4149	.4172	.4193	.4215	.4236
19	.3916	.3942	.3967	.3992	.4017	.4041	.4065	.4088	.4111	.4133
20	.3781	.3808	.3835	.3861	.3887	.3913	.3938	.3963	.3987	.4011
21	.3624	.3652	.3680	.3708	.3735	.3762	.3789	.3815	.3840	.3866
22	.3441	.3470	.3499	.3528	.3556	.3584	.3612	.3639	.3666	.3693
23	.3228	.3258	.3288	.3317	.3346	.3375	.3404	.3432	.3459	.3487
24	.2980	.3011	.3040	.3070	.3099	.3129	.3157	.3186	.3214	.3242
25	.2692	.2722	.2751	.2780	.2809	.2838	.2867	.2895	.2923	.2951
26	.2357	.2385	.2413	.2441	.2468	.2496	.2523	.2550	.2577	.2604
27	.1967	.1992	.2017	.2043	.2068	.2093	.2118	.2143	.2167	.2192
28	.1513	.1534	.1555	.1576	.1597	.1618	.1639	.1660	.1681	.1702
29	.0984	.0999	.1014	.1029	.1044	.1059	.1073	.1088	.1103	.1118
30	.0370	.0375	.0381	.0387	.0393	.0399	.0405	.0412	.0418	.0424

Source: U.S., Department of Housing and Urban Development, The Graduated Payment Mortgage Program—A HUD Handbook, 4240.2 Rev.

APPENDIX F Growing Equity Mortgage

with increasing payments for 10 years and monthly mortgage insurance premium factors for 30-year mortgages at 2.00 and 3.00 percent each year

Section 203(B) Growing Equity Mortgage
With Increasing Payments for 10 Years at 2.00 Percent Each Year

Monthly Installment Per Thousand Dollars of Original Loan Proceeds

For 30-Year mortgages with annual contract interest rates of

Year	7.75	8.00	8.25	8.50	8.75	9.00	9.25	9.50	9.75	10.00
1	7.164122	7.337646	7.512666	7.689135	7.867004	8.046226	8.226754	8.408542	8.591544	8.77571
2	7.307405	7.484399	7.662919	7.842918	8.024344	8.207151	8.391289	8.576713	8.763375	8.95123
3	7.453553	7.634087	7.816178	7.999776	8.184831	8.371294	8.559115	8.748247	8.938643	9.13025
4	7.602624	7.786768	7.972501	8.159771	8.348528	8.538720	8.730297	8.923212	9.117415	9.31286
5	7.754677	7.942504	8.131951	8.322967	8.515498	8.709494	8.904903	9.101676	9.299764	9.49911
6	7.909770	8.101354	8.294590	8.489426	8.685808	8.883684	9.083001	9.283710	9.485759	9.68909
7	8.067965	8.263381	8.460482	8.659215	8.859524	9.061358	9.264661	9.469384	9.675474	9.88288
8	8.229325	8.428648	8.629692	8.832399	9.036715	9.242585	9.449955	9.658772	9.868984	10.08053
9	8.393911	8.597221	8.802286	9.009047	9.217449	9.427436	9.638954	9.851947	10.066363	10.28215
10	8.561790	8.769166	8.978331	9.189228	9.401798	9.615985	9.831733	10.048986	10.267691	10.48779
Remaining payments										
	8.733025	8.944549	9.157898	9.373012	9.589834	9.808305	10.028368	10.249966	10.473044	10.69754
Term in months										
	251	249	246	244	242	240	237	235	233	231

Year	10.25	10.50	10.75	11.00	11.25	11.50	11.75	12.00	12.25	12.50
1	8.961013	9.147393	9.334814	9.523234	9.712614	9.902914	10.094097	10.286126	10.478964	10.672578
2	9.140233	9.330341	9.521510	9.713699	9.906866	10.100973	10.295979	10.491848	10.688544	10.886029
3	9.323038	9.516948	9.711940	9.907973	10.105003	10.302992	10.501899	10.701685	10.902314	11.103750
4	9.509499	9.707287	9.906179	10.106132	10.307104	10.509052	10.711937	10.915719	11.120361	11.325825
5	9.699689	9.901432	10.104302	10.308255	10.513246	10.719233	10.926176	11.134034	11.342768	11.552341
6	9.893682	10.099461	10.306389	10.514420	10.723511	10.933618	11.144699	11.356714	11.569623	11.783388
7	10.091556	10.301450	10.512516	10.724708	10.937981	11.152290	11.367593	11.583849	11.801016	12.019056
8	10.293387	10.507479	10.722767	10.939202	11.156740	11.375336	11.594945	11.815525	12.037036	12.259437
9	10.499255	10.717629	10.937222	11.157986	11.379875	11.602842	11.826844	12.051836	12.277777	12.504626
10	10.709240	10.931981	11.155966	11.381146	11.607473	11.834899	12.063381	12.292873	12.523332	12.754718
Remaining payments										
	10.923425	11.150621	11.379086	11.608769	11.839622	12.071597	12.304648	12.538730	12.773799	13.009813
Term in months										
	229	227	224	222	220	218	216	214	212	210

Year	12.75	13.00	13.25	13.50	13.75	14.00	14.25	14.50	14.75	15.00
1	10.866932	11.061995	11.257735	11.454122	11.651125	11.848718	12.046871	12.245559	12.444757	12.644440
2	11.084271	11.283235	11.482890	11.683204	11.884148	12.085692	12.287808	12.490470	12.693652	12.897329
3	11.305956	11.508900	11.712548	11.916868	12.121831	12.327406	12.533565	12.740280	12.947525	13.155276
4	11.532075	11.739078	11.946799	12.155206	12.364267	12.573954	12.784236	12.995085	13.206476	13.418381
5	11.762717	11.973859	12.185735	12.398310	12.611553	12.825433	13.039921	13.254987	13.470605	13.686749
6	11.997971	12.213337	12.429449	12.646276	12.863784	13.081942	13.300719	13.520087	13.740017	13.960484
7	12.237931	12.457603	12.678038	12.899201	13.121059	13.343580	13.566733	13.790489	14.014818	14.239693
8	12.482689	12.706755	12.931599	13.157186	13.383481	13.610452	13.838068	14.066298	14.295114	14.524487
9	12.732343	12.960890	13.190231	13.420329	13.651150	13.882661	14.114829	14.347624	14.581016	14.814977
10	12.986990	13.220108	13.454036	13.688736	13.924173	14.160314	14.397126	14.634577	14.872637	15.111277
Remaining payments										
	13.246730	13.484510	13.723116	13.962511	14.202657	14.443521	14.685068	14.927268	15.170090	15.413502
Term in months										
	208	206	204	202	200	198	196	194	193	191

Source: U.S., Department of Housing and Urban Development, Memorandum from the Office of the Assistant Secretary for Housing—Federal Housing Commissioner, June 4, 1982, Appendix B.

Year	15.25	15.50	15.75	16.00	16.25	16.50	16.75	17.00	17.25	17.50
1	12.844585	13.045169	13.246171	13.447570	13.649346	13.851481	14.053956	14.256753	14.459858	14.663252
2	13.101477	13.306073	13.511094	13.716521	13.922333	14.128510	14.335035	14.541889	14.749055	14.956517
3	13.363506	13.572194	13.781316	13.990852	14.200780	14.411081	14.621735	14.832726	15.044036	15.255648
4	13.630776	13.843638	14.056943	14.270669	14.484795	14.699302	14.914170	15.129381	15.344917	15.560761
5	13.903392	14.120511	14.338082	14.556082	14.774491	14.993288	15.212454	15.431968	15.651815	15.871976
6	14.181460	14.402921	14.624843	14.847204	15.069981	15.293154	15.516703	15.740608	15.964851	16.189415
7	14.465089	14.690979	14.917340	15.144148	15.371381	15.599017	15.827037	16.055420	16.284148	16.513204
8	14.754391	14.984799	15.215687	15.447031	15.678808	15.910998	16.143577	16.376528	16.609831	16.843468
9	15.049479	15.284495	15.520001	15.755972	15.992385	16.229217	16.466449	16.704059	16.942028	17.180337
10	15.350468	15.590185	15.830401	16.071091	16.312232	16.553802	16.795778	17.038140	17.280868	71.523944
Remaining payments										
	15.657477	15.901988	16.147009	16.392513	16.638477	16.884878	17.131694	17.378903	17.626486	17.874423
Term in months										
	189	187	186	184	182	181	179	178	176	175

Source: U.S., Department of Housing and Urban Development, Memorandum from the Office of the Assistant Secretary for Housing—Federal Housing Commissioner, June 15, 1982.

Section 203(B) Growing Equity Mortgage
With Increasing Payments for 10 Years at 3.00 Percent Each Year

Monthly Installment per Thousand Dollars of Original Loan Proceeds

	For 30-year mortgages with annual contract interest rates of									
Year	7.75	8.00	8.25	8.50	8.75	9.00	9.25	9.50	9.75	10.00
1	7.164122	7.337646	7.512666	7.689135	7.867004	8.046226	8.226754	8.408542	8.591544	8.775716
2	7.379046	7.557775	7.738046	7.919809	8.103014	8.287613	8.473557	8.660798	8.849290	9.038987
3	7.600418	7.784508	7.970187	8.157403	8.346105	8.536241	8.727764	8.920622	9.114769	9.310157
4	7.828430	8.018044	8.209293	8.402125	8.596488	8.792329	8.989596	9.188241	9.388212	9.589461
5	8.063283	8.258585	8.455572	8.654189	8.854382	9.056098	9.259284	9.463888	9.669859	9.877145
6	8.305181	8.056342	8.709239	8.913815	9.120014	9.327781	9.537063	9.747805	9.959954	10.173460
7	8.554337	8.761533	8.970516	9.181229	9.393614	9.607615	9.823175	10.040239	10.258753	10.478663
8	8.810967	9.024379	9.239632	9.456666	9.675423	9.895843	10.117870	10.341446	10.566516	10.793023
9	9.075296	9.295110	9.516821	9.740366	9.965685	10.192719	10.421406	10.651690	10.883511	11.116814
10	9.347555	9.573963	9.802325	10.032577	10.264656	10.498500	10.734048	10.971240	11.210016	11.450319
Remaining payments										
	9.627982	9.861182	10.096395	10.333554	10.572596	10.813455	11.056070	11.300377	11.546317	11.793828
Term in Months										
	221	219	217	215	212	210	208	206	204	202

Year	10.25	10.50	10.75	11.00	11.25	11.50	11.75	12.00	12.25	12.50
1	8.961013	9.147393	9.334814	9.523234	9.712614	9.902914	10.094097	10.286126	10.478964	10.672578
2	9.229843	9.421815	9.614858	9.808931	10.003992	10.200002	10.396920	10.594710	10.793333	10.992755
3	9.506739	9.704469	9.903304	10.103199	10.304112	10.506002	10.708828	10.912551	11.117133	11.322538
4	9.791941	9.995603	10.200403	10.406295	10.613235	10.821182	11.030093	11.239928	11.450647	11.662214
5	10.085699	10.295471	10.506415	10.718484	10.931632	11.145817	11.360995	11.577125	11.794167	12.012080
6	10.388270	10.604335	10.821607	11.040038	11.259581	11.480192	11.701825	11.924439	12.147992	12.372443
7	10.699918	10.922466	11.146256	11.371239	11.597369	11.824598	12.052880	12.282172	12.512431	12.743616
8	11.020916	11.250140	11.480643	11.712377	11.945290	12.179336	12.414467	12.650638	12.887804	13.125924
9	11.351543	11.587644	11.825063	12.063748	12.303649	12.544716	12.786901	13.030157	13.274438	13.519702
10	11.692089	11.935273	12.179815	12.425660	12.672758	12.921057	13.170508	13.421061	13.672672	13.925293
Remaining payments	12.042852	12.293331	12.545209	12.798430	13.052941	13.308689	13.565623	13.823693	14.082852	14.343052
Term in months	200	198	196	194	192	190	188	186	185	183

Year	12.75	13.00	13.25	13.50	13.75	14.00	14.25	14.50	14.75	15.00
1	10.866932	11.061995	11.257735	11.454122	11.651125	11.848718	12.046871	12.245559	12.444757	12.644440
2	11.192940	11.393855	11.595467	11.797745	12.000659	12.204179	12.408277	12.612926	12.818100	13.023773
3	11.528728	11.735671	11.943331	12.151678	12.360679	12.570304	12.780525	12.991314	13.202643	13.414487
4	11.874590	12.087741	12.301631	12.516228	12.731499	12.947414	13.163941	13.381053	13.598722	13.816921
5	12.230828	12.450373	12.670680	12.891715	13.113444	13.335836	13.558859	13.782485	14.006684	14.231429
6	12.597753	12.823884	13.050801	13.278466	13.506848	13.735911	13.965625	14.195959	14.426884	14.658372
7	12.975685	13.208601	13.442325	13.676820	13.912053	14.147988	14.384594	14.621838	14.859691	15.098123
8	13.364956	13.604859	13.845594	14.087125	14.329415	14.572428	14.816132	15.060493	15.305482	15.551067
9	13.765904	14.013005	14.260962	14.509739	14.759297	15.009601	15.260616	15.512308	15.764646	16.017599
10	14.178882	14.433395	14.688791	14.945031	15.202076	15.459889	15.718434	15.977677	16.237585	16.498127
Remaining payments	14.604248	14.866397	15.129455	15.393382	15.658138	15.923686	16.189987	16.457008	16.724713	16.993070
Term in months	181	179	177	176	174	173	171	169	168	166

Source: U.S., Department of Housing and Urban Development, Memorandum from the Office of the Assistant Secretary for Housing—Federal Housing Commissioner, June 4, 1982, Appendix B.

Year	15.25	15.50	15.75	16.00	16.25	16.50	16.75	17.00	17.25	17.50
1	12.844585	13.045169	13.246171	13.447570	13.649346	13.851481	14.053956	14.256753	14.459858	14.663252
2	13.229923	13.436524	13.643556	13.850997	14.058827	14.267025	14.475574	14.684456	14.893653	15.103150
3	13.626820	13.839620	14.052863	14.266527	14.480591	14.695036	14.909842	15.124990	15.340463	15.556244
4	14.035625	14.254809	14.474449	14.694523	14.915009	15.135887	15.357137	15.578739	15.800677	16.022932
5	14.456694	14.682453	14.908682	15.135358	15.362459	15.589964	15.817851	16.046102	16.274697	16.503620
6	14.890394	15.122926	15.355943	15.589419	15.823333	16.057663	16.292386	16.527485	16.762938	16.998728
7	15.337106	15.576614	15.816621	16.057102	16.298033	16.539392	16.781158	17.023309	17.265826	17.508690
8	15.797219	16.043913	16.291120	16.538815	16.786974	17.035574	17.284593	17.534008	17.783801	18.033951
9	16.271136	16.525230	16.779853	17.034979	17.290583	17.546642	17.803131	18.060029	18.317315	18.574969
10	16.759270	17.020987	17.283249	17.546029	17.809301	18.073041	18.337224	18.601830	18.866834	19.132218
Remaining payments	17.262048	17.531617	17.801746	18.072410	18.343580	18.615232	18.887341	19.159884	19.432839	19.706185
Term in months	165	163	162	160	159	158	156	155	154	152

Source: U.S., Department of Housing and Urban Development, Memorandum from the Office of the Assistant Secretary for Housing—Federal Housing Commissioner, June 15, 1982.

Section 203(B) Growing Equity Mortgage
With Increasing Payments for 10 Years at 2.00 Percent Each Year

Monthly Mortgage Insurance Premium Factors
per Thousand Dollars of Original Loan Proceeds

Premium Year	For 30-year mortgages with annual contract interest rates of									
	7.75	8.00	8.25	8.50	8.75	9.00	9.25	9.50	9.75	10.00
1	.4150	.4151	.4152	.4152	.4153	.4154	.4154	.4155	.4156	.4156
2	.4109	.4111	.4114	.4116	.4118	.4120	.4122	.4124	.4126	.4128
3	.4057	.4061	.4065	.4068	.4072	.4075	.4079	.4082	.4084	.4087
4	.3993	.3998	.4003	.4008	.4013	.4017	.4022	.4026	.4029	.4033
5	.3916	.3923	.3929	.3935	.3940	.3945	.3950	.3955	.3959	.3963
6	.3825	.3832	.3839	.3846	.3852	.3857	.3863	.3868	.3872	.3876
7	.3719	.3726	.3734	.3740	.3746	.3752	.3757	.3762	.3766	.3770
8	.3596	.3603	.3610	.3617	.3622	.3628	.3632	.3636	.3640	.3643
9	.3454	.3461	.3467	.3473	.3478	.3482	.3485	.3488	.3490	.3492
10	.3293	.3298	.3303	.3307	.3310	.3313	.3314	.3315	.3315	.3315
11	.3110	.3113	.3116	.3117	.3118	.3118	.3117	.3115	.3112	.3108
12	.2907	.2908	.2907	.2906	.2903	.2899	.2894	.2888	.2881	.2873
13	.2688	.2685	.2681	.2675	.2668	.2660	.2650	.2639	.2627	.2614
14	.2451	.2444	.2435	.2424	.2412	.2398	.2383	.2366	.2347	.2327
15	.2196	.2183	.2168	.2151	.2133	.2112	.2090	.2065	.2039	.2011
16	.1919	.1900	.1878	.1854	.1828	.1799	.1768	.1735	.1699	.1661
17	.1621	.1593	.1563	.1530	.1495	.1457	.1416	.1372	.1325	.1275
18	.1299	.1262	.1222	.1178	.1132	.1082	.1029	.0973	.0912	.0849
19	.0951	.0902	.0851	.0795	.0736	.0672	.0605	.0534	.0458	.0377
20	.0574	.0513	.0448	.0378	.0304	.0224	.0151	.0091	.0046	.0015
21	.0170	.0110	.0062	.0027	.0006					

Premium Year	10.25	10.50	10.75	11.00	11.25	11.50	11.75	12.00	12.25	12.50
1	.4157	.4157	.4158	.4158	.4159	.4159	.4160	.4160	.4160	.4161
2	.4130	.4131	.4133	.4134	.4135	.4137	.4138	.4139	.4140	.4141
3	.4090	.4092	.4095	.4097	.4099	.4101	.4103	.4105	.4106	.4108
4	.4036	.4039	.4042	.4045	.4048	.4050	.4052	.4055	.4056	.4058
5	.3967	.3971	.3974	.3977	.3980	.3982	.3985	.3987	.3989	.3990
6	.3880	.3884	.3887	.3890	.3893	.3895	.3897	.3899	.3900	.3901
7	.3774	.3777	.3780	.3782	.3784	.3786	.3787	.3788	.3782	.3788
8	.3646	.3648	.3649	.3651	.3651	.3651	.3651	.3650	.3649	.3648
9	.3493	.3493	.3493	.3492	.3491	.3489	.3487	.3483	.3480	.3476
10	.3311	.3313	.3308	.3304	.3300	.3295	.3289	.3283	.3275	.3267
11	.3103	.3097	.3090	.3083	.3074	.3065	.3055	.3043	.3031	.3019
12	.2864	.2853	.2842	.2829	.2815	.2800	.2784	.2767	.2749	.2729
13	.2599	.2582	.2565	.2546	.2525	.2503	.2480	.2455	.2429	.2401
14	.2305	.2282	.2257	.2230	.2201	.2170	.2138	.2104	.2068	.2030
15	.1981	.1948	.1914	.1877	.1838	.1797	.1754	.1708	.1660	.1610
16	.1621	.1578	.1532	.1484	.1432	.1379	.1322	.1262	.1200	.1134
17	.1222	.1166	.1107	.1045	.0979	.0909	.0836	.0760	.0679	.0595
18	.0781	.0710	.0634	.0555	.0471	.0383	.0291	.0204	.0131	.0074
19	.0293	.0207	.0134	.0076	.0034	.0008				
20	.0001									

Premium Year	12.75	13.00	13.25	13.50	13.75	14.00	14.25	14.50	14.75	15.00
1	.4161	.4161	.4162	.4162	.4162	.4162	.4163	.4163	.4163	.4163
2	.4142	.4143	.4144	.4145	.4146	.4146	.4147	.4148	.4148	.4149
3	.4109	.4111	.4112	.4113	.4114	.4115	.4116	.4117	.4118	.4119
4	.4060	.4062	.4063	.4064	.4065	.4066	.4067	.4068	.4069	.4069
5	.3992	.3993	.3995	.3996	.3996	.3997	.3998	.3998	.3998	.3998

Premium Year	12.75	13.00	13.25	13.50	13.75	14.00	14.25	14.50	14.75	15.00
6	.3902	.3903	.3904	.3904	.3904	.3904	.3903	.3903	.3902	.3901
7	.3788	.3788	.3787	.3786	.3784	.3783	.3781	.3779	.3776	.3773
8	.3646	.3643	.3640	.3637	.3634	.3630	.3625	.3621	.3615	.3610
9	.3471	.3466	.3460	.3453	.3447	.3439	.3431	.3423	.3414	.3405
10	.3259	.3250	.3240	.3229	.3218	.3206	.3193	.3180	.3166	.3152
11	.3005	.2990	.2974	.2958	.2941	.2923	.2904	.2884	.2863	.2841
12	.2709	.2687	.2664	.2640	.2615	.2589	.2561	.2533	.2503	.2472
13	.2372	.2342	.2310	.2276	.2241	.2205	.2167	.2127	.2086	.2044
14	.1991	.1949	.1906	.1860	.1813	.1764	.1712	.1659	.1604	.1546
15	.1557	.1502	.1445	.1385	.1322	.1257	.1189	.1118	.1045	.0969
16	.1066	.0994	.0919	.0841	.0759	.0674	.0586	.0494	.0398	.0302
17	.0507	.0415	.0319	.0229	.0153	.0092	.0046	.0015	.0001	
18	.0032	.0007								

Source: U.S., Department of Housing and Urban Development, Memorandum from the Office of the Assistant Secretary for Housing—Federal Housing Commissioner, June 4, 1982.

Premium Year	15.25	15.50	15.75	16.00	16.25	16.50	16.75	17.00	17.25	17.50
1	.4163	.4164	.4164	.4164	.4164	.4164	.4164	.4165	.4165	.4165
2	.4149	.4150	.4150	.4151	.4151	.4152	.4152	.4152	.4153	.4153
3	.4119	.4120	.4120	.4121	.4121	.4122	.4122	.4122	.4123	.4123
4	.4070	.4070	.4071	.4071	.4071	.4071	.4071	.4071	.4071	.4071
5	.3998	.3998	.3998	.3997	.3997	.3996	.3995	.3994	.3993	.3992
6	.3900	.3898	.3897	.3895	.3893	.3891	.3889	.3887	.3884	.3882
7	.3770	.3767	.3764	.3760	.3756	.3752	.3747	.3743	.3738	.3733
8	.3604	.3598	.3592	.3585	.3578	.3570	.3563	.3555	.3546	.3538
9	.3395	.3385	.3375	.3364	.3352	.3340	.3328	.3315	.3301	.3288
10	.3136	.3121	.3104	.3087	.3070	.3051	.3032	.3013	.2993	.2972
11	.2819	.2795	.2771	.2746	.2720	.2693	.2666	.2637	.2608	.2577
12	.2440	.2407	.2372	.2337	.2300	.2262	.2223	.2182	.2140	.2097
13	.1999	.1953	.1906	.1857	.1806	.1754	.1699	.1644	.1586	.1526
14	.1486	.1425	.1360	.1294	.1226	.1155	.1081	.1006	.0928	.0847
15	.0890	.0808	.0723	.0635	.0544	.0449	.0353	.0267	.0193	.0130
16	.0217	.0146	.0089	.0046	.0016	.0002				

Source: U.S., Department of Housing and Urban Development, Memorandum from the Office of the Assistant Secretary for Housing—Federal Housing Commissioner, June 15, 1982.

Section 203(B) Growing Equity Mortgage
With Increasing Payments for 10 Years at 3.00 Percent Each Year

Monthly Mortgage Insurance Premium Factors
per Thousand Dollars of Original Loan Proceeds

Premium	For 30-year mortgages with annual contract interest rates of									
Year	7.75	8.00	8.25	8.50	8.75	9.00	9.25	9.50	9.75	10.00
1	.4150	.4151	.4152	.4152	.4153	.4154	.4154	.4155	.4156	.4156
2	.4107	.4110	.4112	.4114	.4116	.4118	.4120	.4122	.4124	.4126
3	.4050	.4053	.4057	.4061	.4064	.4067	.4070	.4073	.4076	.4078
4	.3976	.3981	.3985	.3990	.3994	.3998	.4001	.4005	.4008	.4011
5	.3884	.3889	.3895	.3899	.3904	.3908	.3912	.3916	.3919	.3922
6	.3772	.3778	.3783	.3788	.3793	.3797	.3800	.3804	.3806	.3809
7	.3639	.3644	.3649	.3653	.3657	.3660	.3663	.3665	.3667	.3668
8	.3482	.3486	.3489	.3492	.3494	.3496	.3497	.3497	.3497	.3496
9	.3299	.3301	.3302	.3303	.3302	.3301	.3299	.3297	.3293	.3289
10	.3087	.3086	.3084	.3081	.3077	.3072	.3067	.3060	.3052	.3044
11	.2844	.2839	.2832	.2825	.2816	.2806	.2795	.2783	.2770	.2775
12	.2574	.2563	.2551	.2537	.2522	.2506	.2488	.2469	.2448	.2426
13	.2282	.2264	.2245	.2224	.2202	.2177	.2151	.2124	.2094	.2063
14	.1966	.1941	.1913	.1884	.1852	.1818	.1782	.1744	.1704	.1661
15	.1625	.1590	.1553	.1513	.1470	.1425	.1377	.1327	.1274	.1218
16	.1257	.1211	.1161	.1109	.1054	.0995	.0933	.0868	.0800	.0728
17	.0859	.0800	.0737	.0670	.0599	.0525	.0447	.0364	.0277	.0195
18	.0429	.0354	.0275	.0195	.0127	.0073	.0033	.0008		
19	.0044	.0015	.0001							

Premium Year	10.25	10.50	10.75	11.00	11.25	11.50	11.75	12.00	12.25	12.50
1	.4157	.4157	.4158	.4158	.4159	.4159	.4160	.4160	.4160	.4161
2	.4127	.4129	.4130	.4132	.4133	.4134	.4135	.4137	.4138	.4139
3	.4081	.4083	.4085	.4087	.4089	.4091	.4092	.4094	.4095	.4097
4	.4014	.4017	.4019	.4021	.4023	.4025	.4027	.4029	.4030	.4031
5	.3925	.3928	.3930	.3932	.3934	.3935	.3937	.3938	.3938	.3939
6	.3811	.3813	.3814	.3816	.3816	.3817	.3817	.3817	.3817	.3816
7	.3669	.3669	.3669	.3669	.3668	.3666	.3665	.3662	.3660	.3657
8	.3495	.3493	.3490	.3487	.3483	.3479	.3474	.3469	.3463	.3457
9	.3285	.3279	.3273	.3266	.3258	.3250	.3241	.3232	.3221	.3210
10	.3035	.3024	.3013	.3001	.2988	.2974	.2959	.2944	.2927	.2910
11	.2739	.2723	.2705	.2686	.2666	.2644	.2622	.2598	.2573	.2548
12	.2403	.2378	.2351	.2323	.2294	.2263	.2231	.2197	.2162	.2125
13	.2029	.1994	.1958	.1919	.1878	.1836	.1792	.1745	.1697	.1647
14	.1616	.1569	.1520	.1468	.1414	.1357	.1298	.1236	.1172	.1105
15	.1159	.1097	.1032	.0965	.0894	.0820	.0743	.0663	.0579	.0492
16	.0652	.0573	.0490	.0403	.0312	.0226	.0153	.0094	.0048	.0018
17	.0126	.0072	.0032	.0008						

Premium Year	12.75	13.00	13.25	13.50	13.75	14.00	14.25	14.50	14.75	15.00
1	.4161	.4161	.4162	.4162	.4162	.4162	.4163	.4163	.4163	.4163
2	.4140	.4140	.4141	.4142	.4143	.4143	.4144	.4145	.4145	.4146
3	.4098	.4099	.4100	.4101	.4102	.4103	.4103	.4104	.4105	.4105
4	.4032	.4033	.4034	.4035	.4035	.4036	.4036	.4036	.4037	.4037
5	.3939	.3940	.3940	.3940	.3939	.3939	.3938	.3937	.3936	.3935
6	.3815	.3814	.3812	.3810	.3808	.3806	.3804	.3801	.3798	.3795
7	.3654	.3650	.3646	.3642	.3637	.3632	.3627	.3621	.3615	.3609
8	.3450	.3443	.3436	.3428	.3419	.3410	.3400	.3391	.3380	.3369
9	.3199	.3187	.3174	.3160	.3146	.3131	.3116	.3100	.3084	.3067
10	.2892	.2873	.2853	.2832	.2810	.2788	.2765	.2741	.2716	.2690

Premium Year	12.75	13.00	13.25	13.50	13.75	14.00	14.25	14.50	14.75	15.00
11	.2521	.2493	.2463	.2433	.2401	.2369	.2335	.2300	.2264	.2226
12	.2087	.2047	.2006	.1963	.1919	.1873	.1826	.1777	.1726	.1674
13	.1595	.1541	.1484	.1426	.1366	.1303	.1239	.1172	.1103	.1032
14	.1036	.0964	.0889	.0812	.0732	.0649	.0563	.0474	.0382	.2096
15	.0402	.0309	.0227	.0157	.0100	.0054	.0023	.0005		
16	.0002									

Source: U.S., Department of Housing and Urban Development, Memorandum from the Office of the Assistant Secretary for Housing—Federal Housing Commissioner, June 4, 1982.

Premium Year	15.25	15.50	15.75	16.00	16.25	16.50	16.75	17.00	17.25	17.50
1	.4163	.4164	.4164	.4164	.4164	.4164	.4164	.4165	.4165	.4165
2	.4146	.4147	.4147	.4148	.4148	.4148	.4149	.4149	.4149	.4149
3	.4106	.4106	.4106	.4107	.4107	.4107	.4107	.4107	.4107	.4107
4	.4037	.4036	.4036	.4036	.4035	.4035	.4034	.4033	.4033	.4032
5	.3934	.3933	.3931	.3929	.3927	.3926	.3923	.3921	.3919	.3917
6	.3792	.3788	.3784	.3780	.3776	.3772	.3768	.3763	.3758	.3753
7	.3603	.3596	.3589	.3581	.3574	.3566	.3558	.3549	.3540	.3532
8	.3358	.3347	.3335	.3322	.3309	.3296	.3283	.3269	.3254	.3240
9	.3049	.3031	.3012	.2992	.2972	.2952	.2931	.2909	.2887	.2864
10	.2663	.2636	.2608	.2579	.2549	.2518	.2486	.2454	.2421	.2387
11	.2188	.2148	.2107	.2066	.2022	.1978	.1933	.1886	.1838	.1789
12	.1620	.1564	.1507	.1448	.1388	.1326	.1262	.1196	.1129	.1060
13	.0959	.0883	.0805	.0725	.0642	.0557	.0470	.0383	.0304	.0234
14	.0221	.0156	.0103	.0060	.0029	.0009				

Source: U.S., Department of Housing and Urban Development, Memorandum from the Office of the Assistant Secretary for Housing—Federal Housing Commissioner, June 15, 1982.

APPENDIX G Section 234(c) Maximum Mortgage Amounts

For any market area (county or part of a county) not listed in Appendix below, the maximum mortgage limit for a one-family condominium unit insured under section 234(c) shall be: $67,500.

Market area designation and local jurisdictions	Section 234(c) mortgage limit
REGION I.—HUD Field Office: Hartford Area Office	
Bridgeport, CT SMSA	$70,500
Fairfield County (part)	
Bridgeport City	
Shelton City	
Easton Town	
Fairfield Town	
Monroe Town	
Stratford Town	
Trumbull Town	
New Haven County (part)	
Derby City	
Milford City	
Bristol, CT SMSA	71,000
Hartford County (part)	
Bristol City	
Burlington Town	
Litchfield County	
Plymouth Town	
Danbury, CT SMSA	74,900
Fairfield County (part)	
Danbury City	
Bethel Town	
Brookfield Town	
New Fairfield Town	
Newtown Town	
Redding Town	
Litchfield County (part)	
New Milford Town	
Hartford, CT SMSA	68,000
Hartford County (part)	
Hartford City; Manchester Town	
Avon Town; Marlborough Town	
Bloomfield Town; Newington Town	
Canton Town; Rocky Hill Town	
East Granby Town; Simsbury Town	
East Hartford Town; South Windsor Town	
East Windsor Town; Suffield Town	
Enfield Town; West Hartford Town	
Farmington Town; Wethersfield Town	
Glastonbury Town; Windsor Town	
Granby Town; Windsor Locks Town	
Litchfield County (part)	
New Hartford Town	
Middlesex County (part)	
Cromwell Town	
East Hampton Town	
Portland Town	
New London County	
Colchester Town	
Tolland County (part)	
Andover Town; Hebron Town	
Bolton Town; Stafford Town	
Columbia Town; Tolland Town	
Coventry Town; Vernon Town	
Ellington Town; Willington Town	
Norwalk, CT SMSA	74,900
Fairfield County (part)	
Norwalk City	
Weston Town	
Westport Town	
Wilton Town	
Stamford, CT SMSA	74,900
Fairfield County (part)	
Stamford City	
Darien Town	
Greenwich Town	
New Canaan Town	
REGION II.—HUD Field Office: New York Area Office	
New York and Nassau-Suffolk, NY SMSAS (combined)	72,000
Bronx County; Queens County	
Kings County; Richmond County	
Nassau County; Rockland County	
New York County; Suffolk County	
Putnam County; Westchester County	
HUD Field Office: Newark Area Office	
State of New Jersey—northern metro areas	74,900
Bergen County; Morris County	
Essex County; Passaic County	
Hudson County; Somerset County	
Middlesex County; Union County	
Monmouth County	
HUD Field Office: Camden Service Office	
Atlantic City, NJ SMSA, Atlantic County	74,900
Trenton, NJ SMSA, Mercer County	68,500
REGION III.—HUD FIELD OFFICE: WASHINGTON, DC AREA OFFICE	
Washington, DC-MD-VA SMSA	74,900
District of Columbia	
Montgomery County, MD	
Prince Georges County, MD	
Alexandria City, VA	
Fairfax City, VA	
Fairfax County, VA	
Falls Church City, VA	
Manassas City, VA	
Manassas Park City, VA	
Arlington County, VA	
Loudoun County, Va	
Prince William County, VA	

Market area designation and local jurisdictions	Section 234(c) mortgage limit
Washington, DC–MD–VA SMSA, Charles County, MD	74,900
Baltimore, MD SMSA (part)	74,900
Howard County	
Anne Arundel County	
HUD Field Office: Richmond Area Office	
Newport News-Hampton and Norfolk-VA Beach-Portsmouth, VA SMSA (combined)	74,900
Chesapeake City; Suffolk City; Hampton City; Virginia Beach City; Newport News City; Williamsburg City; Norfolk City; Gloucester County; Poquoson City; James City County; Portsmouth City; York County	
REGION IV.—HUD Field Office: Greensboro Area Office	
Newport News-Hampton and Norfolk-VA Beach-Portsmouth, VA SMSA, Currituck County	74,900
HUD Field Office: Columbia Area Office	
Charleston-North Charleston, SC SMSA	74,900
Berkeley County; Charleston County; Dorchester County	
HUD Field Office: Atlanta Area Office	
Atlanta, GA SMSA	74,900
Butts County; Fulton County; Cherokee County; Gwinnett County; Clayton County; Henry County; Cobb County; Newton County; De Kalb County; Paulding County; Douglas County; Rockdale County; Fayette County; Walton County; Forsyth County	
HUD Field Office: Birmingham Area Office	
Mobile, AL SMSA	74,900
Baldwin County; Mobile County	
Montgomery, AL SMSA	74,900
Autauga County; Elmore County; Montgomery County	
HUD Field Office: Memphis Service Office	
Memphis, TN–AR–MS SMSA	74,900
Shelby County; Tipton County	
HUD Field Office: Jackson Area Office	
Memphis, TN–AR–MS SMSA, DeSoto County	74,900
HUD Field Office: Coral Gables Service Office	
Miami, FL SMSA, Dade County	71,500
West Palm Beach-Boca Raton, FL SMSA, Palm Beach County	73,500
REGION V.—HUD Field Office: Minneapolis-St. Paul Area Office	
Minneapolis-St. Paul, MN SMSA	74,000
Anoka County; Ramsey County; Carver County; Scott County; Chisago County; Washington County; Dakota County; Wright County; Hennepin County	
St. Cloud, MN SMSA	68,500
Benton County; Sherburne County; Stearns County	
HUD Field Office: Milwaukee Area Office	
Minneapolis-St. Paul, MN SMSA, St. Croix County	74,000
Milwaukee, WI SMSA	73,500
Milwaukee County; Washington County; Ozaukee County; Waukesha County	

Market area designation and local jurisdictions	Section 234(c) mortgage limit
HUD Field Office: Detroit Area Office	
Detroit, MI SMSA	69,500
Lapeer County; Oakland County; Livingston County; St. Clair County; Macomb County; Wayne County	
HUD Field Office: Columbus Area Office	
Cleveland, OH SMSA	70,500
Cuyahoga County; Geauga County; Lake County; Medina County	
REGION VI.—HUD Field Office: Dallas Area Office	
Dallas-Ft. Worth, TX SMSA	74,900
Collin County; Ellis County; Dallas Count; Kaufman County; Denton County; Rockwall County	
Sherman-Denison, TX SMSA, Grayson County	74,900
HUD Field Office: Forth Worth Service Office	
Dallas-Ft. Worth, TX SMSA	74,900
Hood County; Johnson County; Parker County; Tarrant County; Wise County	
HUD Field Office: Houston Service Office	
Houston, TX SMSA	69,500
Brazoria County; Liberty County; Ft. Bend County; Montgomery County; Harris County; Waller County	
HUD Field Office: Lubbock Service Office	
Amarillo, TX SMSA	68,500
Potter County; Randall County	
Lubbock, TX SMSA, Lubbock County	70,000
Midland, TX SMSA, Midland County	70,000
HUD Field Office: San Antonio Area Office	
Austin and San Antonio, TX SMSAS (combined)	69,500
Bexar County; Hays County; Comal County; Travis County; Guadalupe County; Williamson County	
Corpus Christi, TX SMSA	70,000
Nueces County; San Patricio County	
HUD Field Office: Little Rock Area Office	
Memphis, TN–AR–MS SMSA, Crittenden County	74,900
HUD Field Office: Oklahoma City Area Office	
Oklahoma City, OK SMSA	68,000
Canadian County; Cleveland County; McClain County; Oklahoma County; Pottawatomie County	
HUD Field Office: New Orleans Area Office	
Baton Rouge and New Orleans, LA SMSAS (combined)	74,900
Ascension Parish; East Baton Rouge Parish; Jefferson Parish; Livingston Parish; Orleans Parish; St. Bernard Parish; St. Tammany Parish; West Baton Rouge Parish	

Market area designation and local jurisdictions	Section 234(c) mortgage limit
HUD Field Office: Albuquerque Service Office	
Alburque, NM SMSA	74,900
Bernalillo County	
Sandoval County	
HUD Field Office: Tulsa Service Office	
Tulsa, OK SMSA	71,500
Creek County	
Mayes County	
Osage County	
Rogers County	
Tulsa County	
Wagoner County	
REGION VIII.—HUD Field Office: Denver Regional/Area Office	
Denver-Boulder, CO SMSA	70,500
Adams County	
Arapahoe County	
Boulder County	
Denver County	
Douglas County	
Gilpin County	
Jefferson County	
Greeley, CO SMSA, Weld County	70,500
Colorado Statewide non-SMSA areas	70,500
HUD Field Office: Helena Service Office	
State of Montana, SMSA and non-SMSA areas	74,900
REGION IX.—HUD Field Office: Los Angeles Area Office	
Los Angeles area office metro and non-metro areas	74,900
Los Angeles County	
San Luis Obispo County	
Santa Barbara County	
Ventura County	
HUD Field Office: San Francisco Area Office	
San Francisco area office metro and non-metro areas	$74,900
Alameda County; Contra Costa County; Del Norte County; Humboldt County; Lake County; Marin County; Mendocin County; Monterey County; Napa County; San Benito County; San Francisco County; San Mateo County; Santa Clara County; Santa Cruz County; Solano County; Sonoma County	
HUD Field Office: Fresno Service Office	
Fresno service office metro and non-metro areas	$71,500
Fresno County	
Kern County	
Kings County	
Madera County	
Mariposa County	
Merced County	
Stanislaus County	
Tulare County	
HUD Field Office: Sacramento Service Office	
Sacramento service office metro and non-metro areas	$74,900
Alpine County; Amador County; Butte County; Calaveras County; Colusa County; El Dorado County; Glenn County; Lassen County; Modoc County; Nevada County; Placer County; Plumas County; Sacramento County; San Joaquin County; Shasta County; Sierra County; Siskiyou County; Sutter County; Tehama County; Trinity County; Tuolumne County; Yolo County; Yuba County	

Market area designation and local jurisdictions	Section 234(c) mortgage limit
HUD Field Office: San Diego Service Office	
San Diego service office metro and non-metro areas	$74,900
Imperial County	
San Diego County	
HUD Field Office: Santa Ana Service Office	
Santa Ana service office metro areas	$74,900
Orange County	
Riverside County	
San Bernardino County	
Santa Ana service office metro and non-metro areas	$71,500
Inyo County	
Mono County	
HUD Field Office: Las Vegas Service Office	
Las Vegas, NV SMSA, Clark County	$74,900
State of Nevada—non-metro areas	$74,900
Lincoln County	
Nye County (part)	
HUD Field Office: Reno Service Office	
Reno, NV SMSA, Washoe County	$74,900
State of Nevada—non-metro areas	$74,900
Carson City County; Churchill County; Douglas County; Elko County; Esmeralda County; Eureka County; Humboldt County; Lander County; Lyon County; Mineral County; Nye County (part); Pershing County; Storey County; White Pine County	
HUD Field Office: Phoenix Service Office	
Phoenix, AZ SMSA, Maricopa County	$74,900
HUD Field Office: Tucson Service Office	
Tucson, AZ SMSA, Pima County	$68,500
HUD Field Office: Honolulu Area Office	
State of Hawaii metro and non-metro areas	$101,250
REGION X.—HUD Field Office: Seattle Area Office	
Richland-Kennewick and Yakima, WA SMSAS (combined), Yakima County	$72,000
Seattle-Everett, WA SMSA	$72,000
King County	
Snohomish County	
Tacoma, WA SMSA, Pierce County	$71,000
HUD Field Office: Spokane Service Office	
Richland-Kennewick and Yakima, WA SMSAS (combined)	$72,000
Benton County	
Franklin County	
Spokane, WA SMSA, Spokane County	$72,000
HUD Field Office: Boise Service Office	
Boise City, ID SMSA, Ada County	$74,900

(Secs. 203(b)(2), 211, 234(c), National Housing Act (12 U.S.C. 1703(b)(2), 1709, 1715y(c))

Issued at Washington, D.C., December 30, 1981.

Philip D. Winn,
Assistant Secretary for Housing—Federal Housing Commissioner.

[FR Doc. 82–286 Filed 1–6–82; 8:45 am]
BILLING CODE 4210–01–M

Source: "Rules and Regulations," *Federal Register*, January 7, 1982, vol. 47, no. 4, pp. 924-26.

APPENDIX H Programs of HUD

Section	*Nature of Program (Selected)*	*Eligibility*	*Information Source*
202	Long-term direct loans to eligible, private nonprofit sponsors finance rental or cooperative housing facilities for elderly or handicapped persons. The current interest rate is based on the average rate paid on federal obligations during the preceding fiscal year. (Until the program was revised in 1974, the statutory rate was 3 percent.) Participation in the Section 8 rental housing program is required for a minimum of 20 percent of the Section 202 units.	Private, nonprofit sponsors may qualify for loans. Households of one or more persons, the head of which is at least 62 years old or is handicapped, are eligible to live in the structures.	HUD area offices or local lenders.
203 (i)	By insuring commercial lenders against loss, HUD encourages them to invest capital in the home mortgage market. HUD insures loans made by private financial institutions for up to 97 percent of the property value and for terms of up to 30 years. The loans may finance homes in rural areas (except farm homes). Less rigid construction standards are permitted in rural areas.	Any person able to make the cash investment and the mortgage payments.	HUD area offices or local HUD-approved lenders.
207	HUD insures mortgages made by private lending institutions to finance the construction or rehabilitation of multifamily rental housing by private or public developers. The project must contain at least eight dwelling units. Housing financed under this program, whether in urban or suburban areas, should be able to accommodate families (with or without children) at reasonable rents.	Investors, builders, developers, and others who meet HUD requirements may apply for funds to an FHA-approved lending institution after conferring with their local office. The housing project must be located in an area approved by HUD for rental housing and in which market conditions show a need for such housing.	HUD area offices.

Section	*Nature of Program (Selected)*	*Eligibility*	*Information Source*
213	HUD insures mortgages made by private lending institutions on cooperative housing projects for five or more dwelling units to be occupied by members of nonprofit cooperative ownership housing corporations. These loans may finance: new construction, rehabilitation, acquisition, improvement or repair of a project already owned, and resale of individual memberships; construction of projects composed of individual family dwellings to be bought by individual members with separate insured mortgages; and construction or rehabilitation of projects that the owners intend to sell to nonprofit cooperatives.	Nonprofit corporations or trusts organized to construct homes for members of the corporation or beneficiaries of the trust; and qualified sponsors who intend to sell the project to a nonprofit corporation or trust.	HUD area offices or local lenders.
221(d) (3) and (4)	To help finance construction or substantial rehabilitation of multifamily (5 or more units) rental or cooperative housing for low- and moderate-income or displaced families, HUD conducts two related programs. Projects in both cases may consist of detached, semi-detached, row, walk-up, or elevator structures. The insured mortgage amounts are controlled by statutory dollar limits per unit which are intended to assure moderate construction costs. Units financed under both programs may qualify for assistance under Section 8 if occupied by eligible low-income families. Currently, the principal differences between the programs are two: HUD may insure 100 percent of total project cost under Section 221(d)(3) for nonprofit and cooperative mortgagors but only 90 percent under Section 221(d)(4) irrespective of the type of mortgagor; and statutory unit limit mortgage amounts are less for Section 221(d)(3) than for Section 221(d)(4).	Section 221(d)(3) mortgages may be obtained by: public agencies, nonprofit, limited-dividend or cooperative organizations; private builders or investors who sell completed projects to such organizations. Section 221(d)(4) mortgages are limited to profit-motivated sponsors. Tenant occupancy is not restricted by income limits, except in the case of tenants receiving subsidies.	HUD area offices.
223(f)	HUD insures mortgages to purchase or refinance existing multifamily projects originally financed with or without Federal mortgage insurance. HUD may insure mortgages on existing multifamily projects under this program that do not require substantial rehabilitation. Project must contain eight or more units, and must be at least three years old.	Investors, builders developers, and others who meet HUD requirements.	HUD area offices or local lenders.
231	To assure a supply of rental housing suited to the needs of the elderly or handicapped, HUD insures mortgages to build or rehabilitate multifamily projects consisting of eight or more units.	Investors, builders, developers, public bodies, and nonprofit sponsors may qualify for mortgage insurance. Persons at least 62 years old are eligible to rent such units.	HUD area offices or local lenders.

Section	*Nature of Program (Selected)*	*Eligibility*	*Information Source*
232	HUD insures mortgages to finance construction or renovation of facilities to accommodate 20 or more patients requiring skilled nursing care and related medical services, or those in need of minimum but continuous care provided by licensed or trained personnel. Nursing home and intermediate care services may be combined in the same facility covered by an insured mortgage or may be separate facilities. Major equipment needed to operate the facility may be included in the mortgage.	Investors, builders, developers, and private nonprofit corporations or associations, which are licensed or regulated by the State to accommodate convalescents and persons requiring skilled nursing care or intermediate care, may qualify for mortgage insurance. Patients requiring skilled nursing or intermediate care are eligible to live in these facilities.	HUD area offices or local lenders.
234(c)	HUD insures mortgages made by private lending institutions for the purchase of individual family units in multifamily housing projects. Sponsors may also obtain FHA-insured mortgages to finance the construction or rehabilitation of housing projects which they intend to sell as individual condominium units under Section 234(d). A project must contain at least four dwelling units; they may be in detached, semi-detached, row, walkup, or elevator structures. A condominium is defined as joint ownership of common areas and facilities by the separate owners of single dwelling units in the project.	Any qualified profit-motivated or nonprofit sponsor may apply for a blanket mortgage covering the project after conferring with his local FHA insuring office; any credit-worthy person may apply for a mortgage on individual units in a project.	HUD area offices.
244	HUD insures 80 percent of the losses on mortgages made by State housing finance agencies to finance multifamily projects. This guarantee makes it easier for the State agencies to obtain credit in the private market through the issuance of State bonds. The remaining 20 percent of the risk is borne by the agencies themselves and, indirectly, by investors in the bonds.	State housing finance agencies.	See administering office.

Source: From *Programs of HUD,* U.S. Department of Housing and Urban Development, HUD-214-4-PA(3), November, 1978.

APPENDIX I Veterans Administration Offices

Loan Guaranty Service
Regional Office Address List

NOTE: Loan Guaranty consolidated with Philadelphia.

ALABAMA
VA Regional Office
Aronov Building
474 South Court Street
Montgomery, AL 36104

ALASKA
VA Regional Office
235 East 8th Avenue
Anchorage, AK 99501

ARIZONA
VA Regional Office
3225 North Central Avenue
Phoenix, AZ 85012

ARKANSAS
VA Regional Office
1200 West 3d Street
Little Rock, AR 72201

CALIFORNIA
VA Regional Office
Federal Building
11000 Wilshire Boulevard
West Los Angeles, CA 90024

VA Regional Office
211 Main Street
San Francisco, CA 94105

COLORADO
VA Regional Office
Denver Federal Center, Building 20
Denver, CO 80225

CONNECTICUT
VA Regional Office
450 Main Street
Hartford, CT 06103

DELAWARE
VA Medical and Regional Office Center
1601 Kirkwood Highway
Wilmington, DE 19805

DISTRICT OF COLUMBIA
VA Regional Office
941 North Capitol Street, NE
Washington, D.C. 20421

FLORIDA
VA Regional Office
P.O. Box 1437
144 First Avenue, South
St. Petersburg, FL 33731

GEORGIA
VA Regional Office
730 Peachtree Street, NE
Atlanta, GA 30308

HAWAII
VA Regional Office
P.O. Box 50188
PJKK Federal Building
300 Ala Moana Boulevard
Honolulu, HI 96813

IDAHO
VA Regional Office
Federal Building and U.S. Courthouse
550 West Fort Street
Box 044
Boise, ID 83724

ILLINOIS
VA Regional Office
536 S. Clark Street
P.O. Box 8136
Chicago, IL 60680

INDIANA
VA Regional Office
575 North Pennsylvania Street
Indianapolis, IN 46204

IOWA
VA Regional Office
210 Walnut Street
Des Moines, IA 50309

KANSAS
VA Medical and Regional Office Center
901 George Washington Boulevard
Wichita, KS 67211

KENTUCKY
VA Regional Office
600 Federal Place
Louisville, KY 40202

LOUISIANA
VA Regional Office
701 Loyola Avenue
New Orleans, LA 70113

MAINE
VA Medical and Regional Office Center
Togus, ME 04330

MARYLAND
VA Regional Office
Federal Building
31 Hopkins Plaza
Baltimore, MD 21201

NOTE: Montgomery and Prince Georges counties are under the jurisdiction of VARO Washington, D.C.

MASSACHUSETTS
VA Regional Office
John F. Kennedy Building
Government Center
Boston, MA 02203

MICHIGAN
VA Regional Office
Federal Building
477 Michigan Avenue
Detroit, MI 48226

MINNESOTA
VA Regional Office and
Insurance Center
Federal Building
Fort Snelling
St. Paul, MN 55111

MISSISSIPPI
VA Regional Office
100 W. Capitol St.
Jackson, MS 39201

MISSOURI
VA Regional Office
Federal Building, Room 4705
1520 Market Street
St. Louis, MO 63103

MONTANA
VA Medical and Regional Office Center
Fort Harrison, MT 59636

NEBRASKA
VA Regional Office
Federal Building
100 Centennial Mall North
Lincoln, NE 68508

NEVADA
VA Regional Office
245 East Liberty Street
Reno, NV 89520

Note: Loan Guaranty consolidated with San Francisco. Loan Guaranty activities for Clark and Lincoln counties, Nevada consolidated with Los Angeles.

NEW HAMPSHIRE
VA Regional Office
Norris Cotton Federal Building
275 Chestnut Street
Manchester, NH 03103

NEW JERSEY
VA Regional Office
20 Washington Place
Newark, NJ 07102

NEW MEXICO
VA Regional Office
Dennis Chavez Federal
Building, U.S. Courthouse
500 Gold Avenue, SW
Albuquerque, NM 87102

NEW YORK
VA Regional Office
Federal Building
111 West Huron Street
Buffalo, NY 14202

VA Regional Office
252 Seventh Avenue at 24th St.
New York, NY 10001

NORTH CAROLINA
VA Regional Office
Federal Building
251 North Main Street
Winston-Salem, NC 27102

NORTH DAKOTA
VA Medical and Regional Office Center
655 First Avenue North
Fargo, ND 58102

NOTE: Loan Guaranty consolidated with St. Paul.

OHIO
VA Regional Office
Anthony J. Celebrezze Federal Bldg.
1240 East Ninth Street
Cleveland, OH 44199

OKLAHOMA
VA Regional Office
125 S. Main Street
Muskogee, OK 74401

OREGON
VA Regional Office
1220 S.W. 3rd Avenue
Portland, OR 97204

PENNSYLVANIA
VA Regional Office and Insurance Center
P.O. Box 8079
5000 Wissahickon Avenue
Philadelphia, PA 19101

VA Regional Office
1000 Liberty Avenue
Pittsburgh, PA 15222

PUERTO RICO
VA Medical and Regional Office Center
Federico Degetau Fed. Bldg. & Courthouse
Carlos E. Chardon Ave.
Hato Rey, PR 00918

RHODE ISLAND
VA Regional Office
321 South Main Street
Providence, RI 02903

NOTE: Loan Guaranty consolidated with Boston.

SOUTH CAROLINA
VA Regional Office
1801 Assembly Street
Columbia, SC 29201

SOUTH DAKOTA
VA Medical and Regional Office Center
Courthouse Plaza Building
300 N. Dakota Avenue
Sioux Falls, SD 57101

NOTE: Loan Guaranty consolidated with St. Paul.

TENNESSEE
VA Regional Office
110 Ninth Avenue, South
Nashville, TN 37203

TEXAS
VA Regional Office
2515 Murworth Drive
Houston, TX 77054

VA Regional Office
1400 North Valley Mills Drive
Waco, TX 76799

UTAH
VA Regional Office
125 South State Street
Salt Lake City, UT 84138

VERMONT
VA Medical and Regional Office Center
White River Junction, VT 05001

WEST VIRGINIA
VA Regional Office
640 4th Avenue
Huntington, WV 25701

NOTE: Brooke, Hancock, Marshall, and Ohio counties are under the jurisdiction of the VARO Pittsburgh, PA.

WISCONSIN
VA Regional Office
342 North Water Street
Milwaukee, WI 53202

WYOMING
VA Medical and Regional Office Center
2360 East Pershing Boulevard
Cheyenne, WY 82001

NOTE: Loan Guaranty consolidated with Denver.

VIRGINIA
VA Regional Office
210 Franklin Road, SW
Roanoke, VA 24011

NOTE: Arlington, Fairfax, Loudoun, Prince William, Spotsylvania, and Stafford counties and the cities of Alexandria, Fairfax, Falls Church, and Fredericksburg, are under the jurisdiction of VARO Washington, D.C.

WASHINGTON
VA Regional Office
915 Second Avenue
Seattle, WA 98174

NOTE: Clark, Klickitat, and Skamania counties are under the jurisdiction of VARO Portland, Oregon.

Source: Veterans Administration, *Guaranteed and Direct Loans for Veterans—1981*, pp. 22-25.

APPENDIX J Farmers Home Administration Loan Programs

Type of Loan	Purpose of Loan	Who May Apply	Where to Apply
Operating	Operating loans to family farms for land improvement, equipment, labor, and development resources necessary to successful farming, including the development of recreational enterprises to be operated as part of farms.	Operators of not larger than family farms.	Local Farmers Home Administration Office.
Farm Ownership	To develop and buy family farms	Farmers and ranchers who are or will become operators of not larger than family farms.	Same
Conservation	Soil and water conservation loans to develop, conserve and make better use of their soil and water resources.	Individual farm operators and owners.	Same
Water and Waste Disposal Programs	Loans and grants for the construction of rural community water and waste disposal systems.	Public bodies and non-profit organizations.	Same
Other Community Facilities	Insured loans for construction of rural community facilities other than water and waste disposal systems.	Same	Same
Irrigation	Loans to develop irrigation systems, drain farmland, and carry out soil conservation measures.	Groups of farmers and ranchers.	Same

Type of Loan	Purpose of Loan	Who May Apply	Where to Apply
Grazing Areas	Loans to develop grazing areas for mutual use.	Same	Same
Rural Housing	To construct and repair needed homes and essential farm buildings, purchase previously occupied homes or buy sites on which to build homes.	Farmers and other rural residents in open country and rural communities of not more than 20,000.	Same
Rural Rental Housing	Loans to provide rental housing for the rural elderly and for younger rural residents of low and moderate income.	Individuals, profit corporations, private nonprofit corporations, public bodies.	Same
Cooperative Housing	Loans to develop cooperative housing for the rural elderly and younger rural residents of low and moderate income.	Consumer cooperatives, housing cooperatives and nonprofit corporations that can legally operate as housing cooperatives.	Same
Housing for Labor	Loans to finance housing facilities for domestic farm labor.	Individual farmers, groups of farmers, and public or private nonprofit organizations.	Same
Labor Housing Grants	Grants to help finance housing facilities for domestic farm labor.	Public bodies or broadly-based nonprofit organizations.	Same
Disaster	Emergency loans in designated areas where natural disasters such as floods and droughts have brought about a temporary need for credit not available from other sources.	Farmers	Same
Economic Emergency	Loans to farmers in economic distress due to general lack of commercial credit resources or adverse economic factors such as high production costs and low prices for farm goods.	Same	Same
Watershed	Watershed loans to help finance projects that protect and develop land and water resources in small watersheds.	Local organizations.	Same
Business and Industry	Guarantee of loans by private lenders to business and industries in rural areas and towns of up to 50,000 population to create or preserve employment for rural people.	Business concerns.	Same
Industrial Development Grants	Preparation of improvement of industrial site areas in rural countryside and rural towns of not more than 10,000.	Local public bodies.	Same

Source: Handbook for Small Business, 4th ed., 1979, Select Committee on Small Business—United States Senate, p. 19.

APPENDIX K Federal Home Loan Mortgage Corporation

American Mortgage Insurance Company
5401 Six Forks Road
P.O. Box 27387
Raleigh, NC 27611

AMI Mortgage Insurance Company
P.O. Box 50005
San Jose, CA 95150

Commercial Credit Mortgage Insurance Company
300 St. Paul Place-BCH09B
Baltimore, MD 21202

Commonwealth Mortgage Assurance Company
1512 Walnut Street
Philadelphia, PA 19102

Foremost Guaranty Corporation
P.O. Box 7062
Madison, WI 53707

General Electric Mortgage Insurance Corporation
P.O. Box 41910
11353 Reed Hartman Highway
Cincinnati, OH 45241

General Electric Mortgage Insurance Corporation of Florida
P.O. Box 30006
Tampa, FL 33630

Home Guaranty Insurance Corporation
180 East Belt Boulevard
Richmond, VA 23224

Integon Mortgage Guaranty Corporation
P.O. Box 3199
Winston-Salem, NC 27102

Investors Mortgage Insurance Company
225 Franklin Street
Boston, MA 02102

Liberty Mortgage Insurance Corporation
P.O. Box 7066
Madison, WI 53707

Mortgage Guaranty Insurance Corporation
MGIC Plaza
250 East Kilbourn Avenue
Milwaukee, WI 53202

PAMICO Mortgage Insurance Company
1750 Walton Road
Blue Bell, PA 19422

PMI Mortgage Insurance Co.
601 Montgomery Street
San Francisco, CA 94111

Republic Mortgage Insurance Company
P.O. Box 2514
Winston-Salem, NC 27102

Also known as RMIC Insurance Company for mortgages on properties located in Texas only.

Ticor Mortgage Insurance Company
6300 Wilshire Boulevard
Los Angeles, CA 90048

United Guaranty Residential Insurance Company
P.O. Box 21367
Greensboro, NC 27420

Verex Assurance, Inc.
P.O. Box 7066
Madison, WI 53707

Source: U.S., Federal Home Loan Mortgage Corporation, *Sellers' Guide: Conventional Mortgages*, Exhibit V, p. 237.

APPENDIX L Samples of Completed Appraisal Forms

RLS **ROBERT L. STANLEY** and Associates

RESIDENTIAL APPRAISAL REPORT

File No.

To be completed by Lender

Borrower John Smith | Census Tract 000 | Map Reference XYZ

Property Address 702 Banning Ct.

City Houston | County Harris | State Texas | Zip Code

Legal Description Lot 100, Block 4, Darrington Place, Section 6, Harris County, Texas

Sale Price $ N/A | Date of Sale | Loan Term yrs | Property Rights Appraised [X] Fee [ ] Leasehold [ ] DeMinimis PUD

Actual Real Estate Taxes $ (yr) | Loan charges to be paid by seller $ | Other sales concessions

Lender/Client ABC Mortgage Company | Address 6500 Smith Street, Houston, Texas

Occupant Vacant | Appraiser R.L. Stanley & Assoc. | Instructions to Appraiser Estimate market value as of date of Inspection.

NEIGHBORHOOD

Location	[ ] Urban	[X] Suburban	[ ] Rural
Built Up	[ ] Over 75%	[X] 25% to 75%	[ ] Under 25%
Growth Rate [ ] Fully Dev.	[X] Rapid	[ ] Steady	[ ] Slow
Property Values	[X] Increasing	[ ] Stable	[ ] Declining
Demand/Supply	[ ] Shortage	[X] In Balance	[ ] Over Supply
Marketing Time	[X] Under 3 Mos.	[ ] 4–6 Mos.	[ ] Over 6 Mos.

Present Land Use *50 % 1 Family 0 % 2–4 Family 0 % Apts 0 % Condo 5 % Commercial 0 % Industrial 40 % Vacant 5 % School

Change in Present Land Use [ ] Not Likely [ ] Likely (*) [X] Taking Place (*)

(*) From Vacant To SFD

Predominant Occupancy [X] Owner [ ] Tenant ___ % Vacant

Single Family Price Range $ 100,000 to $ 150,000 Predominant Value $ 130,000

Single Family Age New yrs to 4 yrs Predominant Age 1 yrs

	Good	Avg.	Fair	Poor
Employment Stability **	[ ]	[X]	[ ]	[ ]
Convenience to Employment	[ ]	[X]	[ ]	[ ]
Convenience to Shopping	[ ]	[X]	[ ]	[ ]
Convenience to Schools	[ ]	[X]	[ ]	[ ]
Adequacy of Public Transportation	[ ]	[ ]	[X]	[ ]
Recreational Facilities	[ ]	[X]	[ ]	[ ]
Adequacy of Utilities	[ ]	[X]	[ ]	[ ]
Property Compatibility	[ ]	[X]	[ ]	[ ]
Protection from Detrimental Conditions	[ ]	[X]	[ ]	[ ]
Police and Fire Protection	[ ]	[X]	[ ]	[ ]
General Appearance of Properties	[ ]	[X]	[ ]	[ ]
Appeal to Market	[ ]	[X]	[ ]	[ ]

Note: FHLMC/FNMA do not consider race or the racial composition of the neighborhood to be reliable appraisal factors.

Comments including those factors, favorable or unfavorable, affecting marketability (e.g. public parks, schools, view, noise) No public transportation is available; however, this is typical of the area and has no effect on the subject's marketability. Good location with excellent access to I-10, shopping, schools, and employment centers along I-10. Subject neighborhood is approximately 24 miles west of downtown Houston. * Immediate neighborhood is 100% deed restricted to Single Family Dwellings.
** "Average" rating compares subject to competing neighborhoods and homes.

SITE

Dimensions 73.72 x 117.0 x 86.86 x 123.5 = 9635+ Sq. Ft. [X] Corner Lot

Zoning classification Deed - Single Family Dwelling | Present improvements [X] do [ ] do not conform to zoning regulations

Highest and best use: [X] Present use [ ] Other (specify)

	Public	Other (Describe)
Elec.	[X]	
Gas	[X]	
Water	[X]	
San. Sewer	[X]	
	[X] Underground Elect. & Tel.	

OFF SITE IMPROVEMENTS: Street Access: [X] Public [ ] Private | Surface Concrete | Maintenance: [X] Public [ ] Private | [X] Storm Sewer [X] Curb/Gutter | [ ] Sidewalk [X] Street Lights

Topo Generally level, slopes to street for drainage
Size Comparable to others in area
Shape Rectangular
View Good view site, typical of area
Drainage Appears to be adequate

Is the property located in a HUD Identified Special Flood Hazard Area? [X] No [ ] Yes

Comments (favorable or unfavorable including any apparent adverse easements, encroachments or other adverse conditions) Standard utility easement located at rear of property with no effect on the subject's marketability, use, enjoyment, and/or stated value. Subject is located 2 blocks north of Carmel Independent School District High School with no adverse effect on the subject's marketability.

IMPROVEMENTS

[X] Existing [ ] Proposed [ ] Under Constr. | No. Units 1 | Type (det, duplex, semi/det, etc.) Detached | Design (rambler, split level, etc.) French | Exterior Walls Brick Veneer

Yrs. Age: Actual New Effective New to New | No. Stories 2

Roof Material Wood Shingle | Gutters & Downspouts [X] None — Adequate roof overhang | Window (Type) Aluminum [ ] Storm Sash [ ] Screens [X] Combination | Insulation [ ] None [ ] Floor [X] Ceiling [ ] Roof [X] Walls

[ ] Manufactured Housing

Foundation Walls Concrete

[X] Slab on Grade [ ] Crawl Space

BSMT.: 0 % Basement | [ ] Outside Entrance | [ ] Concrete Floor | ___ % Finished | Evidence of: [ ] Dampness [ ] Termites [ ] Settlement | [ ] Floor Drain | [ ] Sump Pump | Finished Ceiling | Finished Walls | Finished Floor

Comments New construction with no evidence of settlement at time of inspection.

ROOM LIST

Room List	Foyer	Living	Dining	Kitchen	Den	Family Rm.	Rec. Rm.	Bedrooms	No. Baths	Laundry	Other
Basement											
1st Level	1	Study	1	1		1		1	1½	1	Breakfast area
2nd Level							1	3	2		

Finished area above grade contains a total of 10 rooms 4 bedrooms 3½ baths. Gross Living Area 3301 sq. ft. Bsmt Area 0 sq. ft.

INTERIOR FINISH & EQUIPMENT

Kitchen Equipment: [ ] Refrigerator [X] Range/Oven [X] Disposal [X] Dishwasher [X] Fan/Hood [ ] Compactor [ ] Washer [ ] Dryer [X] Microwave

HEAT: Type GFWA Fuel N.G. Cond. Good | AIR COND: [X] Central [ ] Other | [X] Adequate [ ] Inadequate

Floors [ ] Hardwood [X] Carpet Over Conc. [x] Vinyl

Walls [X] Drywall [ ] Plaster [X] Panel, wallpaper

Trim/Finish [X] Good [ ] Average [ ] Fair [ ] Poor

Bath Floor [ ] Ceramic [X] Carpet

Bath Wainscot [ ] Ceramic [X] Marble

Special Features (including energy efficient items) Intercom, crown moldings, marble entry floor, block panel & dec. beam ceiling in family room, wet bar

ATTIC: [X] Yes [ ] No [ ] Stairway [X] Drop-stair [ ] Scuttle [ ] Floored [ ] Heated

Finished (Describe) Unfinished

CAR STORAGE: [X] Garage [ ] Built in [ ] Attached [X] Detached [ ] Car Port

No. Cars 2 [X] Adequate [ ] Inadequate Condition Good

PROPERTY RATING

	Good	Avg.	Fair	Poor
Quality of Construction (Materials & Finish)	[X]	[ ]	[ ]	[ ]
Condition of Improvements	[ ]	[X]	[ ]	[ ]
Room sizes and layout	[ ]	[X]	[ ]	[ ]
Closets and Storage	[ ]	[X]	[ ]	[ ]
Insulation—adequacy	[ ]	[X]	[ ]	[ ]
Plumbing—adequacy and condition	[ ]	[X]	[ ]	[ ]
Electrical—adequacy and condition	[ ]	[X]	[ ]	[ ]
Kitchen Cabinets—adequacy and condition	[ ]	[X]	[ ]	[ ]
Compatibility to Neighborhood	[ ]	[X]	[ ]	[ ]
Overall Livability	[ ]	[X]	[ ]	[ ]
Appeal and Marketability	[ ]	[X]	[ ]	[ ]

Yrs Est Remaining Economic Life 50 to 55 **Explain if less than Loan Term**

FIREPLACES, PATIOS, POOL, FENCES, etc. (describe) Deluxe 8' fireplace, 195□ open patio, 65□ covered walk, 6' wood fence at rear of lot. Subject has extra landscaping at builder cost of $2,000.00

COMMENTS (including functional or physical inadequacies, repairs needed, modernization, etc.) None required to meet minimum property standards; however, some paint and trim work remain to be completed by the builder and is covered by builder warranty. Appraisal made subject to completion of builder's final items in good workmanlike manner.

FHLMC Form 70 Rev. 7/79 | ATTACH DESCRIPTIVE PHOTOGRAPHS OF SUBJECT PROPERTY AND STREET SCENE | FNMA Form 1004 Rev. 7/79

Source: Robert L. Stanley and Associates, Appraisers; Houston, Texas.

VALUATION SECTION

Purpose of Appraisal is to estimate Market Value as defined in Certification & Statement of Limiting Conditions (FHLMC Form 439/FNMA Form 1004B). If submitted for FNMA, the appraiser must attach (1) sketch or map showing location of subject, street names, distance from nearest intersection, and any detrimental conditions and (2) exterior building sketch of improvements showing dimensions.

COST APPROACH

Measurements		No. Stories	Sq. Ft.
33.5 x	50.0 x	1st Floor	= 1,675.0
33.5 x	50.0 x	2nd Floor	= 1,675.0

Total Gross Living Area (List in Market Data Analysis below) 3350+

Comment on functional and economic obsolescence: None observed.

ESTIMATED REPRODUCTION COST – NEW – OF IMPROVEMENTS:

Dwelling 3350 Sq. Ft. @ $ 35.50	=	$ 118,925
Sq. Ft. @ $	=	
Extras 65ɸ covered walk	=	400
6' wood fence	=	1,600
Special Energy Efficient Items	=	
Porches, Patios, etc. 195ɸ patio	=	275
Garage/~~Car Port~~ 471 Sq. Ft. @ $ 8.00	=	3,768
Site Improvements (driveway, landscaping, etc.)	=	4,000
Total Estimated Cost New	=	$ 128,968
Less Depreciation: Physical $ -0- Functional $ -0- Economic $ -0-	=	$ (-0-)
Depreciated value of improvements	=	$ 128,968
ESTIMATED LAND VALUE (If leasehold, show only leasehold value)	=	$ 30,000
INDICATED VALUE BY COST APPROACH		$ 158,968

MARKET DATA ANALYSIS

The undersigned has recited three recent sales of properties most similar and proximate to subject and has considered these in the market analysis. The description includes a dollar adjustment, reflecting market reaction to those items of significant variation between the subject and comparable properties. If a significant item in the comparable property is superior to, or more favorable than, the subject property, a minus (-) adjustment is made, thus reducing the indicated value of subject; if a significant item in the comparable is inferior to, or less favorable than, the subject property, a plus (+) adjustment is made, thus increasing the indicated value of the subject.

ITEM	Subject Property	COMPARABLE NO. 1		COMPARABLE NO. 2		COMPARABLE NO. 3	
Address	702 Banning Ct.	1103 Castle		20638 River Court		20743 Banning Drive	
Proximity to Subj.		4 blocks south		1 block north		1 block southwest	
Sales Price	$ N/A		$ 146,900		$ 155,000		$ 152,000
Price/Living area	$ N/A ɸ		$ 48.16 ɸ		$ 47.69 ɸ		$ 44.06 ɸ
Data Source	Inspection	Agent		Agent		Agent	
Date of Sale and Time Adjustment	DESCRIPTION 8/80	DESCRIPTION 6/80	+(–)$ Adjustment +2900	DESCRIPTION 7/80	+(–)$ Adjustment +1550	DESCRIPTION 6/80	+(–)$ Adjustment +3000
Location	Good	Equal		Equal		Equal	
Site/View	9635+ Inside	Superior Corn.	-2000	Similar Inside		Similar Inside	
Design and Appeal	Good	Equal		Equal		Equal	
Quality of Const.	Excellent	Equal		Equal		Equal	
Age	1980	1980		1980		1980	
Condition	Good	Equal		Equal		Equal	
Living Area Room Count and Total	Total 10 / B-rms 4 / Baths 3½	Total 9 / B-rms 4 / Baths 2½	+1000	Total 10 / B-rms 4 / Baths 3½		Total 10 / B-rms 4 / Baths 3½	
Gross Living Area	3350 Sq.Ft.	3050 Sq.Ft.	+7500	3250 Sq.Ft.	+2500	3450 Sq.Ft.	-2500
Basement & Bsmt. Finished Rooms							
Functional Utility	Good	Equal		Equal		Equal	
Air Conditioning	Central A/C	Equal		Equal		Equal	
Garage/Car Port	D 2	Equal		Equal		Equal	
Porches, Patio, Pools, etc.	Patio Extra Landscape	Patio Inferior	+2000	Patio Inferior	+2000	Patio Inferior	+2000
Special Energy Efficient Items							
Other (e.g. fireplaces, kitchen equip., remodeling)	RO, VH, GD, DW, MW CH FP	Equal		Equal		Equal	
Sales or Financing Concessions	Conventional	20% Down Conventional		20% Down Conventional		30% Down Conventional	+1500
Net Adj. (Total)		[X] Plus; [ ] Minus	$ 11,400	[X] Plus; [ ] Minus	$ 6,050	[X] Plus; [ ] Minus	$ 4,000
Indicated Value of Subject			$ 158,300		$ 161,050		$ 156,000

Comments on Market Data All comparable sales were given weighted consideration in value analysis and indicated values support final value conclusion within 1.9% range. Adjustment of 1% per month for time is supported by additional data maintained in appraiser's office.

INDICATED VALUE BY MARKET DATA APPROACH . . . $ 158,000

INDICATED VALUE BY INCOME APPROACH (If applicable) Economic Market Rent $ ______ /Mo. x Gross Rent Multiplier ______ = $ N/A

This appraisal is made [ ] "as is" [ ] subject to the repairs, alterations, or conditions listed below [X] completion per plans and specifications.

Comments and Conditions of Appraisal: Income Approach is not considered applicable in the appraisal of single family dwellings since they are not typically purchased for their income producing capabilities. Appraisal made subject to completion of final paint and trim items by builder - Estimated cost - $1,000.00.

Final Reconciliation: Market and Cost Approaches both given weighted consideration in the appraisal of new construction such as the subject property and are supportive of the final value conclusion.

Construction Warranty [X] Yes [ ] No Name of Warranty Program GHBA Warranty Coverage Expires 1 year

This appraisal is based upon the above requirements, the certification, contingent and limiting conditions, and Market Value definition that are stated in

[ ] FHLMC Form 439 (Rev. 10/78)/FNMA Form 1004B (Rev. 10/78) filed with client ______ 19 ____ [ ] attached.

I ESTIMATE THE MARKET VALUE, AS DEFINED, OF SUBJECT PROPERTY AS OF August 12, 19 80 to be $ 158,000.00

Appraiser(s) Robert L. Stanley, Jr., SRA, ASA

Review Appraiser (If applicable) [X] Did [ ] Did Not Physically Inspect Property

FHLMC Form 70 Rev. 7/79 REVERSE FNMA Form 1004 Rev. 7/79

Source: Robert L. Stanley and Associates, Appraisers; Houston, Texas.

APPRAISAL REPORT—INDIVIDUAL [X] CONDOMINIUM OR [ ] PUD UNIT File No.

To be compld by Lender

Borrower/Client John A. Doe Census Tract 000 Map Reference XYZ
Unit No. 1106 W Address 1550 West Street Project Name The Hamilton
City Houston County Harris State Texas Zip Code
Legal Description Unit 1106 W. The Hamilton Property Rights Appraised [X] Fee [ ] Leasehold
Actual Real Estate Taxes $ (yr) Loan charges to be paid by seller $ Other sales concessions
Lender ABC Mortgage Company Lender's Address 6500 Smith St., Houston, Texas
Occupant Appraiser Instructions to Appraiser Estimate market value as of date of inspection.
1073A Required [ ]

NEIGHBORHOOD

Location [ ] Urban [X] Suburban [ ] Rural
Built Up [X] Over 75% [ ] 25% to 75% [ ] Under 25%
Growth Rate [ ] Fully Developed [X] Rapid [ ] Steady [ ] Slow
Property Values [X] Increasing [ ] Stable [ ] Declining
Demand/Supply [ ] Shortage [X] In Balance [ ] Over Supply
Marketing Time [X] Under 3 Mos. [ ] 4-6 Mos. [ ] Over 6 Mos.
Present Land Use 10% 1 Family 0% 2-4 Family 30% Apts. 20% Condo 30% Commercial 0% Industrial 10% Vacant
Change in Present Land Use [ ] Not Likely [X] Likely (*) [ ] Taking Place (*)
(*) From Vacant To Comm/MFD
Predominant Occupancy [ ] Owner [X] Tenant 5 % Vacant
Single Family Price Range $55,000 to $ 65,000 Predominant Value $ 60,000
Single Family Age 15 yrs to 20 yrs Predominant Age 15 yrs.
Describe potential for additional Condo/PUD units in nearby area Average potential for const. of new condo/PUDs or conversions.

NEIGHBORHOOD RATING	Good	Avg.	Fair	Poor
Employment Stability	[ ]	[X]	[ ]	[ ]
Recreational Facilities	[ ]	[X]	[ ]	[ ]
Adequacy of Utilities	[ ]	[X]	[ ]	[ ]
Property Compatibility	[ ]	[X]	[ ]	[ ]
Protection from Detrimental Cond.	[ ]	[X]	[ ]	[ ]
Police and Fire Protection	[ ]	[X]	[ ]	[ ]
General Appearance of Properties	[ ]	[X]	[ ]	[ ]
Appeal to Market	[ ]	[X]	[ ]	[ ]

	Distance	Access or Convenience			
Public Transportation	1 blk	[X]	[ ]	[ ]	[ ]
Employment Centers	6 blks	[X]	[ ]	[ ]	[ ]
Neighborhood Shopping	1 blk	[X]	[ ]	[ ]	[ ]
Schools	1 mi.	[ ]	[X]	[ ]	[ ]
Freeway Access	5 blks	[X]	[ ]	[ ]	[ ]

Describe type of buyers most attracted to this area Single and married, middle to upper middle income class. Mixture of white collar, skilled blue collar and young professionals.
Comments inclding factors affecting marketability (e.g. public parks, schools, view, noise) Excellent proximity to schools, churches, shopping, recreational and employment facilities. Few SFDs in immediate neighborhood.
Note: FNMA does not consider the racial composition of the neighborhood to be a relevant factor and it must not be considered in the appraisal.

PROJECT SITE

Area 4.41 sq. ft. or acres. Completed project density (or when completed as planned) 51.7 units/acre
Zoning classification Deed - Condo Present improvements [X] do [ ] do not conform to zoning regulations
Highest and best use: [X] Present use [ ] Other (specify)

	Public	Other (Describe)
Elec.	[X]	
Gas	[X]	
Water	[X]	
San. Sewer	[X]	
	[ ] Underground Elect. & Tel.	

OFF SITE IMPROVEMENTS
Street Access: [X] Public [ ] Private
Surface Concrete
Maintenance: [X] Public [ ] Private
[X] Storm Sewer [X] Curb/Gutter
[X] Sidewalk [X] Street Lights

Ingress and Egress (Adequacy) Good
Topography Level - wooded
View Amenity Good view site, highrise building
Drainage and Flood Conditions Appears to be adequate
Is property located in a HUD identified Special Flood Hazard Area? [X] No [ ] Yes
COMMENTS (Including any easements, encroachments or adverse conditions) Standard utility easement located at rear of property with no effect on the subject's marketability, use, enjoyment, and/or stated value.

PROJECT IMPROVEMENTS

[X] Existing Approx. Year Built 19 64
[ ] Built as Condo/PUD [X] Converted (19 79)
TYPE [ ] Proposed [ ] Under Construction
PROJECT [X] Elevator [ ] Walk-up No. of Stories
[ ] Row or Townhouse [ ] Other (specify)
[X] Primary Residence [ ] 2nd home or recreational 6 in subject
Approx. No. units for sale in subject project 32 in both phases; bldg.
If project completed: No. phases 2 No. bldgs. 2 No. units 228
Units in Subject Phase: Total 114 Completed 114 Sold 108 Rented 0
Exterior Walls Brick Veneer Roof Covering B.U. Tar & Gravel
Security Features Controlled access, lobby w/cameras, 24 hr. security guard.
Elevator(s): Number 4 Automatic Yes Adequacy and Condition Good Availability of Off-Site Parking Good
Parking: Total No. spaces 360+ Ratio 1.58 spaces/unit Type Cov/Uncov. No. spaces for guest parking Adeq. open parking
Describe other Common Elements or Recreational Facilities 2 club areas, 2 pools, 2 tennis courts, 2 laundry rooms, landscaped walkways
Are any of the common elements, recreational facilities, or parking leased? No If yes, attach addendum describing rental, terms and options

PROJECT RATING	Good	Avg.	Fair	Poor
Location	[ ]	[X]	[ ]	[ ]
General Appearance	[ ]	[X]	[ ]	[ ]
Density (Units per Acre)	[ ]	[X]	[ ]	[ ]
Unit Mix	[ ]	[X]	[ ]	[ ]
Quality of Construction (Material & Finish)	[ ]	[X]	[ ]	[ ]
Condition of Exterior	[X]	[ ]	[ ]	[ ]
Condition of Interior	[X]	[ ]	[ ]	[ ]
Amenities and Recreational Facilities	[ ]	[X]	[ ]	[ ]
Appeal to Market	[ ]	[X]	[ ]	[ ]

SUBJECT UNIT

Unit Location: Type Building High-rise Floor No. 11 Unit livable area 675 sq. ft.

Room List	Foyer	Living	Dining	Kitchen	Bedrooms	Baths	Family Rm	Rec. Rm.	Laundry	Balcony	Other
Basement											
1st Level		AREA		1	1	1					
2nd Level											

Kitchen Equipment: [ ] Refrigerator [X] Range/Oven [X] Disposal [X] Dishwasher [X] Fan/Hood [ ] Compactor [ ] Washer [ ] Dryer [ ]
HEAT: Type Wall Fuel Elect. Cond. Good AIR COND.: [X] Central [ ] Other [X] Adequate [ ] Inadequate
Parking for unit: No. 1 Type Uncovered [X] Assigned [ ] Owned Convenience to unit Average

Floors [ ] Hardwood [X] Carpet Over Conc [X] VA
Interior Walls [X] Drywall [ ] Plaster [X] Wallpaper
Trim/Finish [ ] Good [X] Average [ ] Fair [ ] Poor
Bath Floor [X] Ceramic [X] Carpet over tile
Bath Wainscot [X] Ceramic [ ]
Insulation [ ] None [X] Floor [X] Ceiling [ ] Roof [X] Walls
Ins. Material Batt Est. Adequacy Average
Soundproofing: Vertical Batt Horizontal Concrete
Est. Adequacy of Soundproofing Average to Good
Window (Type): Alum. [ ] Storm Sash [ ] Screens [X] Combination
0 % Basement [ ] Concrete Floor % Finished (describe)

UNIT RATING	Good	Avg.	Fair	Poor
Location within project or view	[X]	[ ]	[ ]	[ ]
Room sizes and layout	[ ]	[X]	[ ]	[ ]
Adequacy of closets and storage	[ ]	[X]	[ ]	[ ]
Kitchen equipment, cabinets & workspace	[ ]	[X]	[ ]	[ ]
Qual. of Const. (Material & Finish)	[ ]	[X]	[ ]	[ ]
Condition of Improvements	[ ]	[X]	[ ]	[ ]
Plumbing—adequacy and condition	[ ]	[X]	[ ]	[ ]
Electrical—adequacy and condition	[ ]	[X]	[ ]	[ ]
Overall livability	[ ]	[X]	[ ]	[ ]
Appeal and Marketability	[ ]	[X]	[ ]	[ ]

Est. Effective Age, Approx. 5 to 10 yrs. Est. Remaining Economic Life, Approx. 40 to 45 yrs.

COMMENTS: (Special features, functional or physical inadequacies, modernization or repairs needed, etc.) Well designed, functional, floor plan. Subject is currently being renovated to include new carpet, wallpaper, and new kitchen appliances.

THIS FORM MUST BE REPRODUCEDBY SELLER/SERVICERS 1 of 2 FNMA FORM 1073 Feb. 78

Source: Robert L. Stanley and Associates, Appraisers, Houston, Texas.

COST APPROACH

Cost Approach (to be used only for detached, semi-detached, and town house units):

Unit area & reproduction cost new: ________ sq. ft. @ $ ________ per sq. ft. = $ N/A

less depreciation attributed to all causes: .... ________

Depreciated value of improvements: .... ________

Add: Land value and value of all amenities attributable to unit .... ________

Total indicated value: .... $ N/A

Comments regarding estimate of depreciation and value of land and amenity package: The Cost Approach is not considered applicable in the appraisal of single condo units such as the subject property.

BUDGET ANALYSIS

Unit Charge $ 70.00 /Mo. x 12 = $ 840 /yr. ($ 1.24 /Sq. Ft./year of livable area). Ground Rent (if any) $ N/A /yr.

Project operating expense and replacement budget:

To properly maintain the project and provide the services anticipated, the budget appears: ☐ High ☒ Adequate ☐ Inadequate

Compared to other competitive projects of similar quality and design subject unti charge appears: ☐ High ☒ Reasonable ☐ Low

Management Group: ☐ Owners Association ☐ Management Agent (Identify) ☐ Developer ☐ Other ACME Management

Quality of Management and its enforcement of Rules and Regulations appears: ☐ Superior ☒ Good ☐ Adequate ☐ Inadequate

Comment Typical management policies for this type project.

Sepcial or unusual characteristics in the Condo/PUD Documents or otherwise known to the appraiser, that would affect marketability (if none, so state)
None noted upon examination of appropriate documents.

MARKET DATA ANALYSIS

The appraiser, whenever possible, should analyze two comparable sales from within the subject project. However, when appraising a unit in a new or newly converted project, at least two comparables should be selected from outside the subject project. The appraiser should remember that, in the following analysis, the comparable should always be adjusted to the subject unit and not vice versa. If a significant feature of the comparable is superior to the subject unit, a minus (—) adjustment should be made to the comparable; if such a feature of the comparable is inferior to the subject, a plus (+) adjustment should be made to the comparable.

LIST ONLY THOSE ITEMS THAT REQUIRE ADJUSTMENT

ITEM	Subject Property	COMPARABLE NO. 1		COMPARABLE NO. 2		COMPARABLE NO. 3	
Address-unit no. Project name	1550 West Unit 1106 W.	Unit 1502 W		Unit 1202 W		Unit 1606 W	
Proximity to Subj.		Same project		Same project		Same project	
Sales Price	$ 44,000		$46,000		$44,500		$45,750
Price/Living area	$ 65.19 ☐		$68.15 ☐		$65.93 ☐		$67.78 ☐
Data Source	Inspection	Sales Office		Sales Office		Sales Office	
	DESCRIPTION	DESCRIPTION	+(—)$ Adjustment	DESCRIPTION	+(—)$ Adjustment	DESCRIPTION	+(—)$ Adjustment
Date of Sale and Time Adjustment	9/80	7/80	+900	4/80	+2200	6/80	+1400
Location	Good	Equal		Equal		Equal	
Site/View	Good 11th Fl.	Good 15th Fl.	-2000	12th Floor	- 500	16th Floor	-2500
Design and Appeal	Good	Equal		Equal		Equal	
Quality of Const.	Good	Equal		Equal		Equal	
Age	1964	Equal		Equal		Equal	
Condition	Good	Equal		Equal		Equal	
Living Area, Room Count and Total Gross Living Area	Total 3, B-rms 1, Baths 1; 675 Sq.ft.	Total 3, B-rms 1, Baths 1; 675 Sq.ft.		Total 3, B-rms 1, Baths 1; 675 Sq.ft.		Total 3, B-rms 1, Baths 1; 675 Sq.ft.	
Basement & Bsmt. Finished Rooms	None	Equal		Equal		Equal	
Functional Utility	Good	Equal		Equal		Equal	
Air Conditioning	Wall	Equal		Equal		Equal	
Storage	None	Equal		Equal		Equal	
Parking facilities	1 uncov.	Equal		Equal		Equal	
Common elements and Rec. facilities	Pool, tennis courts, laundry	Equal		Equal		Equal	
Mo. Assessment	70.00	Equal		Equal		Equal	
Leasehold/Fee Simple	Fee	Equal		Equal		Equal	
Terms of Sale or Financing	Conventional	VA		Conventional		Cash	+1000
Net Adj. (Total)		☐ Plus; ☒ Minus	$ 1100	☒ Plus; ☐ Minus	$ 1700	☐ Plus; ☒ Minus	$ 100
Indicated Value of Subject			$ 44,900		$46,200		$ 45,650

Comments on Market Data Comparable #2 given greater weight in value conclusion due to more comparagle location within project and terms of sale. Market Data indicates adjustment of $500 per floor due to view amenities. Cash Sale #3 discounted by seller.

[illegible] .... $ 46,000.00

[illegible] (If applicable) Economic Market Rent $ ________ /Mo. x Gross Rent Multiplier $ N/A

This appraisal is made ☒ "as is" ☐ subject to the repairs, alterations, or conditions listed below

Comments and Conditions of Appraisal: Income Approach is not considered applicable in the appraisal of single family dwellings since they are not typically purchased for their income producing capabilities. Seller's costs are typical of today's market and have no effect on the appraisal value.

Final Reconciliation: Market Approach is considered the only applicable approach in the appraisal of single condominium units such as the subject property.

This appraisal is based upon the above requirements, the certification, contingent and limiting conditions, and Market Value definition that are stated in FNMA Form 1004B filed with client ________ 19 ____ ☐ attached

I ESTIMATE THE MARKET VALUE, AS DEFINED, OF SUBJECT PROPERTY AS OF September 10, 1980 to be $ 46,000.00

Appraiser(s) Robert L. Stanley, Jr., SRA, ASA

Review Appraiser (if applicable) ________ ☒ Did ☐ Did Not Physically Inspect Property

2 of 2

FNMA FORM 1073 Feb. 78

Source: Robert L. Stanley and Associates, Appraisers, Houston, Texas.

APPENDIX M Worksheets for Borrower Qualifications

CONVENTIONAL LOAN QUALIFYING

Gross Monthly Income		*Proposed Monthly Payment*	
Borrowers Income	$______	Principal & Interest	$______
Co-Borrower Income	$______	Private Mort. Insurance	$______
Overtime	$______	Taxes	$______
Part-time	$______	Homeowners Insurance	$______
Other	$______	Home Owners Assoc.	$______
Total Income	$______	Total First Mortgage Pymt . . .	$______

Total Mortgage Pymt $______ divided by total Income $______ equals ______% (cannot exceed 25%).

Obligations (Debts Lasting over 10 months)

Balance		*Owed To*	*Purpose*
$______	@mo. ______	______	______
$______	@mo. ______	______	______
$______	@mo. ______	______	______
$______	@mo. ______	______	______
$______	@mo. ______	______	______
$______	@mo. ______	______	______

Total Obligations $______ + Total Mortgage Payment $______ = Total Fixed Payment $______ Divided by Gross Income $______ = ______ % (cannot exceed $33^1/_3$%)

Move-In Costs		*Source: Down Payment and Closing Costs*	
Sales Price	$______	Banks	$______
Loan Amount	$______	Savings	$______
Required Down Pymt	$______	Net from sale of Real Est . . .	$______
Closing and Prepaids	$______	Other (List)	$______
Other	$______		
Total Move-In	$______	Total Available	$______

The Total Available should equal or exceed the Total Move-In Costs.

U.S. DEPARTMENT OF HOUSING AND URBAN DEVELOPMENT
HOUSING – FEDERAL HOUSING COMMISSIONER

MORTGAGE CREDIT ANALYSIS WORKSHEET

CASE NUMBER

SECTION I – LOAN DATA

1. NAME OF BORROWER AND CO-BORROWER	2. AMOUNT OF MORTGAGE	3. CASH DOWN PAYMENT ON PURCHASE PRICE
	$	$

SECTION II – BORROWER'S/CO-BORROWER'S PERSONAL AND FINANCIAL STATUS

4. BORROWER'S AGE	5. OCCUPATION OF BORROWER	6. NO. OF YRS. AT PRESENT ADDRESS	7. ASSETS AVAILABLE FOR CLOSING	8. CURRENT MONTHLY RENTAL OR OTHER HOUSING EXPENSE
▲				▲

9. IS CO-BORROWER EMPLOYED?	10. CO-BORROWER'S AGE	11. OCCUPATION OF CO-BORROWER	12. NO. OF YEARS AT PRESENT EMPLOYMENT	13. OTHER DEPENDENTS
	▲		B– C–	▲ (a) Ages ____ (b) Number ____

SECTION III – ESTIMATED MONTHLY SHELTER EXPENSES *(This Property)*

14. TERM OF LOAN *(Months)*

15. FUTURE MONTHLY PAYMENTS

(a) Principal and Interest	$
(b) FHA Mortgage Insurance Premium	$
(c) Ground Rent *(Leasehold ONLY)*	$
(d) TOTAL DEBT SERVICE *(A + B + C)* ▲	$
(e) Hazard Insurance	$
(f) Taxes, Special Assessments ▲	$
(g) TOTAL MTG. PAYMENT *(D + E + F)* ▲	$
(h) Maintenance and Common Expense ▲	$
(i) Heat and Utilities	$
(j) TOTAL HSG. EXPENSE *(G + H + I)* ▲	$
(k) Other Recurring Charges *(explain)*	$
(l) TOTAL FIXED PAYMENT *(j + K)* ▲	$

16. **SETTLEMENT REQUIREMENTS**

(a) Existing Debt *(Refinancing ONLY)*	$
(b) Sale Price *(Realty ONLY)* ▲	$
(c) Repairs and Improvements	$
(d) Closing Costs ▲	$
(e) TOTAL ACQUISITION COST *(A + B + C + D)* ▲	$
(f) Mortgage Amount	$
(g) Borrower(s)' Required Investment *(E minus F)*	$
(h) Prepayable Expenses ▲	$
(i) Non-Realty and Other Items	$
(j) TOTAL REQUIREMENTS *(G + H + I)* ▲	$
(k) Amount paid ☐ cash ☐ other *(explain)*	$
(l) Amt. to be paid ☐ cash ☐ other *(explain)* ▲	$
(m) TOTAL ASSETS AVAILABLE FOR CLOSING ▲	$

SECTION IV – MONTHLY EFFECTIVE INCOME

17. Borrower's Base Pay ▲	$
18. Other Earnings *(explain)*	$
19. Co-Borrower's Base Pay ▲	$
20. Other Earnings *(explain)*	$
21. Income, Real Estate	$
22. TOTAL MONTHLY EFFECTIVE INCOME ▲	$
23. Less Federal Tax	$
24. NET EFFECTIVE INCOME ▲	$

SECTION V – DEBTS AND OBLIGATIONS

ITEM	✓	Monthly Payment	Unpaid Balance
25. State and Local Income Taxes		$	$
26. Social Security/Retirement			
27. Child Care Expense/Support			
28. Operating Exp., Other R.E.			
29.			
30.			
31.			
32.			
33. TOTAL		$	$ ▲

SECTION VI – BORROWER RATING

34. Borrower Rating	
35. Credit Characteristics	
36. Adequacy of Eff. Income	
37. Stability of Eff. Income	
38. Adequacy of Available Assets	

39. FINAL
☐ Approve Application
☐ Reject Application

SECTION VII-RATIOS

40. Loan to Value Ratio ____ %
▲
41. Total Payment to Rental Value ____ %
▲
42. Debt Service to Rental Income ____ %

43. ☐ Ratio of Net Effective Income to
Total Housing Expense ____ %
Total Fixed Payment ____ %

44. REMARKS *(Use reverse, if necessary)*   *First Time Home Buyer?* ☐ Yes ☐ No

45. SIGNATURE OF EXAMINER	46. DATE

FORWARD TO MANAGEMENT SYSTEMS WITH HUD-92800-8   HUD-92900-WS 5-81

VA LOAN QUALIFYING

LOAN ANALYSIS

LOAN NUMBER

SECTION A–LOAN DATA

1. NAME OF BORROWER	2. AMOUNT OF LOAN	3. CASH DOWN PAYMENT ON PURCHASE PRICE
	$	$

SECTION B–BORROWER'S PERSONAL AND FINANCIAL STATUS

4. APPLICANT'S AGE	5. OCCUPATION OF APPLICANT	6. NUMBER OF YEARS AT PRESENT EMPLOYMENT	7. LIQUID ASSETS *(Cash, savings, bonds, etc.)*	8. CURRENT MONTHLY RENTAL OR OTHER HOUSING EXPENSE
			$	$

9. IS SPOUSE EMPLOYED?	10. SPOUSE'S AGE	11. OCCUPATION OF SPOUSE	12. NUMBER OF YEARS AT PRESENT EMPLOYMENT	13. AGE OF OTHER DEPENDENTS
☐ YES ☐ NO				

SECTION C – ESTIMATED MONTHLY SHELTER EXPENSES *(This Property)*

SECTION D – DEBTS AND OBLIGATIONS *(Itemize and indicate by (√) which debts considered in Section E, Line 41)*

	ITEMS	AMOUNT		ITEMS	(√)	MO. PAYMENT	UNPAID BAL.
14.	TERM OF LOAN: YEARS		23.			$	$
15.	MORTGAGE PAYMENT *(Principal and Interest)*@ ________ %	$	24.				
16.	REALTY TAXES		25.				
17.	HAZARD INSURANCE		26.				
18.	SPECIAL ASSESSMENTS		27.				
19.	MAINTENANCE		28.				
20.	UTILITIES *(Including heat)*		29.				
21.	OTHER *(HOA, Condo fees, etc.)*		30.	JOB RELATED EXPENSE			
22.	TOTAL	$	31.	TOTAL		$	$

SECTION E – MONTHLY INCOME AND DEDUCTIONS

	ITEMS		SPOUSE	BORROWER	TOTAL
32.	GROSS SALARY OR EARNINGS FROM EMPLOYMENT		$	$	$
33.	DEDUCTIONS	FEDERAL INCOME TAX			
34.		STATE INCOME TAX			
35.		RETIREMENT OR SOCIAL SECURITY			
36.		OTHER *(Specify)*			
37.		TOTAL DEDUCTIONS	$	$	$
38.	NET TAKE-HOME PAY				
39.	PENSION, COMPENSATION OR OTHER NET INCOME *(Specify)*				
40.	TOTAL *(Sum of lines 38 and 39)*		$	$	$
41.	LESS THOSE OBLIGATIONS LISTED IN SECTION D WHICH SHOULD BE DEDUCTED FROM INCOME				
42.	TOTAL NET EFFECTIVE INCOME				$
43.	LESS ESTIMATED MONTHLY SHELTER EXPENSE *(Line 22)*				
44.	BALANCE AVAILABLE FOR FAMILY SUPPORT				$

45. PAST CREDIT RECORD	46. DOES LOAN MEET VA CREDIT STANDARDS? *(Give reasons for decision under "Remarks," if necessary, e.g., borderline case)*
☐ SATISFACTORY ☐ UNSATISFACTORY	☐ YES ☐ NO

47. REMARKS *(Use reverse, if necessary)*

SECTION F – DISPOSITION OF APPLICATION

☐ Recommend that the application be approved since it meets all requirements of Chapter 37, Title 38, U.S. Code and applicable VA Regulations and directives.

☐ Recommend that the application be disapproved for the reasons stated under "Remarks" above.

48. DATE	49. SIGNATURE OF EXAMINER	
50. FINAL ACTION ☐ APPROVE APPLICATION ☐ REJECT APPLICATION	51. DATE	52. SIGNATURE AND TITLE OF APPROVING OFFICIAL

VA FORM OCT 1976 **26-6393**   EXISTING STOCK OF VA FORM 26-6393, AUG 1975, WILL BE USED.

GLOSSARY

A

Abstract of title. A short version of the history of title to a piece of property, tracing the ownership or title. It covers the period from the origin of the parcel of land or property to the present day. This history is based on the information filed or recorded in the county clerk's records in the county in which the property is located.

Acceleration clause. A provision or covenant in a written mortgage, deed of trust, note, bond, or conditional sales contract which states that, in the event of default, due to nonpayment or if other terms of the written agreement are not met, the remaining unpaid principal balance is due and payable at once.

Accretion. An addition to the land, usually through natural causes such as wind or water flow.

Acknowledgment. A declaration made by a person to a notary public or other public official authorized to take such a statement, that the document was executed by him or her and that the execution was a free and voluntary act.

Appreciation. An increase in the value of real or personal property.

Alternative mortgage. Sometimes referred to as an AMI, a mortgage in which one of the four basic characteristics of the mortgage changes over the life of the mortgage, such as the interest rate, amount of the principal, repayment term, or amount of the payment.

Amortization. The reduction of a financial obligation by regularly scheduled payments.

Appraisal. An estimate of value of an adequately described piece of real property, as of a specific date, supported by the analysis of relevant data by a trained professional, and usually in written form.

Assessed valuation (assessed value). For real estate purposes, the estimate of a property's value strictly for the purpose of taxation. Usually determined by a governmental unit, i.e., county government or municipal utility district (MUD).

Assessment. The valuation and listing of property by a taxing authority for the purpose of apporting or establishing the tax upon the property.

Assignee. The person or corporation to whom an interest in real property has been assigned or transferred.

Assignment of mortgage. The documented transfer of ownership of a mortgage from one lender to another lender or party.

Assignor. The person or corporation who assigns or transfers an interest in property, mortgage, or rents.

Assumption of mortgage. The transfer of title to property whereby the purchaser assumes the primary liability for the repayment of an existing mortgage on said property. The original purchaser, unless released in writing, remains also liable for the original mortgage if the purchaser for some reason defaults and is unable to repay the debt in full.

Attachment. Property seized by court order pending the outcome of a lender's or creditor's suit.

B

Balloon mortgage. A type of mortgage where the periodic payments of principal and interest are not sufficient to fully repay the loan by the end of the term of the mortgage. The balance of the loan mortgage is due and payable at a specific time, usually at the end of the term.

Balloon payment. The payment that is due sometime in the future that will be sufficient to pay back the unpaid principal amount of a balloon mortgage.

Basis point. One one-hundredth of one percent of interest.

Bill of sale. A written instrument whereby a person or corporation transfers title to personal property to another person or corporation.

Blanket. The coverage of one or more pieces of property by one instrument such as a blanket insurance policy. Sometimes this is referred to as a master policy.

Blanket mortgage. A single mortgage that covers more than one piece of real property.

Blended yield mortgage. First-lien mortgage secured by real property that combines the yield on an existing mortgage and the yield on any type of secondary financing used to achieve a sale of real property.

Buy-down mortgage. A fixed-rate, fixed-term mortgage where the effective interest rate to the borrower is lowered by the use of an escrow account, sometimes referred to as a 3-2-1 mortgage.

BYM. An acronym for blended yield mortgage.

Break-even point. The point at which the property's income from rentals and any other source equals operating expenses and debt service.

Broker (real estate). Any person, corporation, association, firm, or partnership who for a fee will sell or exchange real property on the behalf of a seller and who holds a valid license to sell or exchange property. The broker will represent the seller and will be paid by the seller upon closing and funding of the transaction.

C

Call clause or provision. A provision in a note, mortgage, or deed of trust giving the lender the right to declare the remaining unpaid balance due and payable on a specified date or upon a special event, such as the death of a comaker on a note.

Capitalization. A method to establish the value of an income producing property, based on the income stream of the property.

Cash flow. The net income or spendable cash generated by an income-producing property after deducting all expenses and debt service from the gross income generated by the property.

Cash flow after taxes. The amount of cash remaining after all taxes have been paid.

Certificate of commitment. A form issued by the Veterans Administration upon approval of a mortgage application for the VA's loan guarantee (VA form 26-1866a, p.3).

Certificate of eligibility. A certificate issued by the VA that establishes a veteran's eligibility for and the amount of guarantee available to the veteran.

Certificate of occupancy. A written statement from a governmental agency stating that a structure, either new or substantially rehabilitated, is fit for occupancy.

Certificate of reasonable value (CRV). VA Form 26-1843. When completed, it establishes the value and maximum loan amount the VA will guarantee for a specific property.

Certificate of title. A document prepared by either a title company or an attorney stating that the person or corporation selling a piece of property has clear, marketable, and insurable title to said property.

Chain of title. A history of all documents pertaining to the transfer of title to a specific piece of property, beginning with the earliest and ending with the latest transfer.

Chattel. An item of personal property.

Chattel mortgage. Any type of debt instrument that applies to any item of personal property.

Clear title. A title to a piece of real property with no defects, sometimes referred to as encumbrances or clouds.

Closed period. A period of time in a note, mortgage, or any other debt instrument when the debt may not be prepaid.

Closing. The consummation of a transaction.

Closing costs. Sometimes referred to as settlement costs, these are the monies paid by either the buyer or seller at the time of closing of the transaction. These may include but are not limited to origination fee, title insurance, discount points, attorney's fees, and prepaid items.

Closing instructions. A list of instructions issued by the mortgage company or lender to a settlement agent listing all of the instructions to be followed in closing a particular mortgage.

Cloud on title. Any claim or encumbrance revealed by a title search that may affect the title to a piece of real property.

Commercial paper. Unsecured corporate debt issued for a period of 1 to 12 months by corporations to meet short-term money needs.

Commitment. A written agreement between a lender and a borrower that mortgage money will be available at some time in the future when all of the terms of the commitment are met. This can also be an agreement between a corporation in the secondary market (such as FNMA) who agrees to purchase mortgages that meet the underwriting guidelines of the corporation, and a mortgage lender.

Commitment fee. A fee paid by the borrower to the lender for a commitment either to loan money or to purchase mortgages.

Common areas. Those areas in a condominium or planned unit development that are held by the homeowners association for the benefit and use of all of the tenants and/or home or unit owners (for example, swimming pools, tennis courts, and parking areas).

Community property. Any type of property either personal or real that by law belongs equally to both husband and wife when acquired by either using joint funds.

Condemnation. The process by which private property is taken by a governmental agency or body for public use.

Conditional commitment (FHA). A promise from the agency to insure to the lender the repayment of a mortgage, meeting FHA insurance requirements.

Condominium. A multi-unit project of either offices or family units where the family or individual holds title to the unit occupied and a pro rata share ownership in all of the common areas.

Constant, mortgage. The percent of the original unpaid principal balance of a mortgage that is repaid annually. This is expressed as a percentage, for example, 11.25 percent. Thus for an original balance of $75,000, $8437.50 would be repaid each year.

Construction loan. A short-term loan for specifically constructing houses or commercial property. Sometimes this is referred to as interim financing.

Contiguous. Adjoining.

Contingent interest. An interest charge that is assessed by a lender making a mortgage equal to a specific percentage of the property's net appreciation.

Contract for deed. A written sales agreement whereby the seller agrees to deliver to the buyer a deed to the property only after all of the required payments have been made.

Conventional loan. Any loan secured by real property that is neither insured nor guaranteed by a government agency.

Conveyance. Any written instrument that is evidence of the transfer of title to some interest in real property from one individual or corporation to another individual or corporation. This can be in the form of a deed, mortgage, or lease.

Cooperative (co-op). A multifamily building or group of buildings in which the owners buy shares in the corporation that holds title to the property. The shares of stock allow the persons purchasing the stock to occupy units in the building. The cost of operation of the cooperative is prorated by the number of shares a person owns in the corporation.

Correspondent. In lending terms, this means a person or company that represents or services mortgage loans for the person or company that actually owns the mortgages.

Covenant. An agreement between the borrower and the lender as set forth in a mortgage or deed of trust. Sometimes these are referred to as uniform and nonuniform covenants as in the FNMA/FHLMC Mortgage/Deed of Trust.

D

DD-214. A form issued by one of the armed forces of the United States that establishes a veteran's time of service and is sometimes a requirement for the issuance of a Certificate of Eligibility.

Debenture. An unsecured debt obligation.

Debt coverage ratio. The ratio of the net effective income of a property to the debt service. For example, if the annual debt service on a property is $12,000 and the net effective income is $24,000, the debt coverage ratio is 2.

Debt service. The amount of money paid annually to repay the principal and the interest on a debt.

Deed. A written instrument that transfers the ownership of land from one individual or corporation to another. This is usually a general warranty deed but may take the form of a special warranty deed or a sheriff's deed.

Deed of trust. This is the written instrument that is used in place of a mortgage. The title to the property is transferred, in trust, to a third party. When the debt is paid in full, the trustee transfers the title to the borrower. In the case of default by the borrower, the trustee, at the lender's request, will institute foreclosure proceedings.

Default. Failure to live up to the terms of an obligation or debt.

Delinquent. The status of an obligation or debt if a payment is not received by the due date.

Depreciation. The loss of value of improvements to real property. This can be from age, physical deterioration, functional obsolescence, or economic obsolescence.

Devise. A gift of real property by a will.

Devisee. The person or persons who receive the property from a will.

Disclosure statement. A statement required by Regulation Z (Truth-in-Lending Law) from the lender to the borrower.

Discount. The amount at which an investor will purchase a mortgage. This amount is usually less than the face amount of the mortgage and is expressed as a percentage.

Discount point. See *Point*.

E

Earnest money. A sum of money given usually by the buyer to bind the sale, or to show good faith in the completion of the transaction.

ECOA. An abbreviation for the Equal Credit Opportunity Act, a federal law that requires all lenders to make credit available without regard to sex, race, color, religion, national origin, age, marital status, or receipt of public assistance.

Effective rate. See *Yield*.

EPM. An acronym for equity participation mortgage.

Equity participation mortgage. A first-lien mortgage involving an owner/occupant and an investor who share the cost of ownership, equity, and tax benefits.

Equity. In real estate, the difference between the fair market value and the indebtedness against the property.

Equity participation. The participation or sharing of the ownership in a piece of property by the lender.

Escalator clause. Sometimes referred to as escalation, this is a clause in a mortgage that allows the lender to increase the interest rate. In terms of leases, this clause allows the property owner or his agent to increase or decrease the rent as required by operating costs.

Exception. Sometimes referred to as an encumbrance. In a title policy this is an item not covered by the policy. In legal descriptions it refers to any property or piece of property to be excluded.

F

Fair market value. See *Market value*.

Farmers Home Administration (FmHA). An arm of the Department of Agriculture whose primary purpose is to furnish mortgage money to the rural areas of the United States.

Fed. An abbreviation for the Federal Reserve Board.

FHA. An abbreviation for the Federal Housing Administration, a division of the Department of Housing and Urban Development. FHA's main purpose is to issue mortgage insurance on mortgages made by private lenders.

FHA mortgage. A mortgage made by a private lender according to the underwriting guidelines of FHA, who then will issue insurance to protect the lender from default by the borrower.

FNMA. An abbreviation for the Federal National Mortgage Association. Its purpose is to raise money in the capital markets and issue commitments to purchase mortgages from approved lenders.

FHLMC. An abbreviation for the Federal Home Loan Mortgage Corporation, sometimes referred to as "The Mortgage Corporation."

Fee simple. Sometimes referred to as fee simple absolute; the most comprehensive method of owning property, whereby the owner may dispose of the real property by trade, sale, or will as the owner chooses.

Foreclosure. A legal process instituted by the lender through a mortgage or deed of trust to terminate the borrower's interest in a property after the default of the borrower.

Free market system auction. Sometimes abbreviated FMS, a biweekly auction of mortgage purchase commitments held by the Federal National Mortgage Association.

G

GEM. An acronym for the growing equity mortgage.

GI-guaranteed loan. A loan where part of the repayment is guaranteed by the Veterans Administration.

GNMA. An abbreviation for the Government National Mortgage Association, created by the division of FNMA by the Congress in 1968.

Graduated payment adjustable mortgage. A hybrid mortgage that combines the rate adjustment features of the renegotiable rate mortgage (RRM) with the graduated payment feature of the graduated payment mortgage (GPM).

Graduated payment adjustable mortgage loan. A hybrid mortgage that combines the rate adjustment feature of the adjustable mortgage loan (AML) with the graduated payment feature of the graduated payment mortgage (GPM).

Graduated payment mortgage. A mortgage where the initial monthly payments start at a level below a standard mortgage and an increase or are graduated at a specific rate at specific time intervals.

Grantee. A buyer.

Grantor. A seller.

Gross income. The total amount of income produced by a property from all sources (for example, rents, parking, and fees).

Gross rent multiplier (GRM). The relationship of the monthly rent of a property to the sales price. It may be expressed as: sales price/gross monthly rent = GRM.

Gross stable monthly income. The total monthly income of an applicant without deductions.

Growing equity mortgage. A fixed rate first lien mortgage in which the monthly payments increase at a specified rate per year for a specific number of years. All increases are credited to principal reduction.

Guaranteed loan. A loan that is guaranteed by an agency of either the federal or a state government (for example, FHA, FmHA, or a State Agriculture Department).

H

Homeowners association. An organization of homeowners in a particular subdivision, planned unit development, or condominium development or project formed for the specific purpose of maintaining common areas and providing other services for the residents of the area.

Homestead. Land and the improvements thereon which the owner has declared as his or her homestead; protected by the laws of some states from forced sale by certain creditors of the owner or owners.

HUD. The Department of Housing and Urban Development created by the passage of the Urban Development Act of 1965.

I

Improvements. As related to real estate, the additions to raw land that increase the value of the land, such as the addition of a house to a lot.

Income property. Real property that is developed for the specific purpose of producing income for the owner.

In-house approval. The ability of a lender to approve a loan application without having to submit it to an investor or lender for approval.

Institutional lender. A lender that makes real estate mortgages or any other type of mortgage and holds the mortgage in its own portfolio.

Interest rate. The sum, expressed as a percentage, that is charged for the use of loaned funds.

Interest. A term that is sometimes substituted for interest rate. Also means a share of the ownership in a property.

Investor. The person supplying the funds to make mortgages and for whom the mortgage banker or financial institution services the mortgage.

J

Joint note. A note or mortgage that is signed by two or more people who are equally liable for the repayment of the note or mortgage.

Joint tenancy. Title to real property held equally by two parties, with right of survivorship.

Junior mortgage. A mortgage that is inferior to a prior mortgage.

L

Late charge. An additional fee charged by the lender to the borrower if the payment is not paid on time.

Lessee. Renter or tenant.

Lessor. Landlord or owner.

Level payment mortgage. A type of mortgage where the monthly payment remains constant for the life of the mortgage.

Leverage. The ability to borrow a larger amount of money than the borrower has invested in the property.

Lien. A claim or encumbrance by a creditor against a piece of property used as security for a debt.

Loan closing. See *Closing*.

Loan origination. The solicitation of mortgage loans by a lender or their agent. This process sometimes includes the taking of the loan application.

Loan processing. The gathering of the information that will enable the lender or the lender's agent either to approve or disapprove the loan, based on the applicant and the property.

Loan submission. The delivery of a completed loan package to a potential lender for approval.

Loan-to-value ratio. The relationship of the amount of loan to the value of the property. Usually expressed as a percentage, such as 95 percent.

M

Market value. The price at which a seller is willing to sell and a buyer is willing to pay.

Maturity. In reference to mortgages or any type of debt, the date in the debt that the last payment is due.

Mechanic's lien. Sometimes referred to as a material and mechanic's lien (M & ML). A statutory claim against the property of others in favor of persons who have either provided materials or done work on improvements to real property.

Mortgage. A written document pledging property as security for a debt or the fulfillment of an obligation. Upon the repayment of the debt or fulfillment of the obligation, the mortgage is void.

Mortgage banker. A company, individual, or corporation that originates mortgages and then sells the mortgages to an investor and services the mortgages for the investor.

Mortgage broker. A company, individual, or corporation that is paid a fee to bring together those needing loanable funds with those that have loanable funds.

Mortgagee. The borrower of money.

Mortgage insurance premium. A fee paid to FHA for the mortgage insurance issued by FHA.

Mortgage portfolio. The mortgages held by a lender or an investor; or the mortgages serviced by a mortgage banker.

Mortgagor. The lender of money.

N

NCUA. An acronym for National Credit Union Administration.

Negative cash flow. In reference to income-producing properties, occurs when the total annual cash outlay is more than the cash received from the property.

Net appreciated value. The value established in regard to the shared appreciation mortgage.

Net effective income. The income base used by FHA. It is the gross stable monthly income less federal income tax withholding.

Net income. In reference to income-producing properties, it is the gross income of the property less operating expenses and a factor for vacancy and credit loss.

Net operating income (NOI). See *Net income*.

Net profit. The cash remaining after all expenses and taxes are paid.

Note. A written document creating a debt.

Notice of default. A legal notice filed by the trustee in a deed of trust that the property is to be sold at a trustee's sale.

O

Offeree. One receiving an offer.

Offeror. One making an offer.

Open end mortgage. A mortgage that has no due date and that allows the lender to advance additional funds without rewriting the mortgage.

Operating expenses. The costs of doing business.

Origination fee. A charge collected by a company or lender to cover the cost of processing and taking a mortgage application. Usually expressed as a percentage of the mortgage amount.

P

Package mortgage. A mortgage including not only the real estate, but some of the appliances and other items that are part of the structure.

Packing and shipping. The grouping of mortgages that meet a particular investor's guidelines. The group or package is then shipped to the investor.

Participation loan. A mortgage with more than one lender. This type of mortgage is primarily used to finance large commercial projects.

Permanent investor. A lender that provides long-term financing.

Personal property. Usually any item that is not considered real property or a fixture to real property.

PITI. An abbreviation for principal, interest, taxes, and insurance charges which are collected monthly as the mortgage payment.

Plat. A map of a subdivision or PUD, usually recorded in the county clerk's office.

Point. Usually expressed as a percentage of the loan amount. Thus, one point equals one percent of the loan amount.

Prepaid items. An advance payment of taxes, hazard insurance, and mortgage insurance, if the mortgage is insured by FHA or a private mortgage insurance company. This payment is collected at the time of closing and is held in escrow by the lender or the servicing agent for the lender.

Prepayment penalty. A fee collected by the lender as per the loan agreement for the repayment of a mortgage prior to the maturity date.

Prepayment privilege. The right of the borrower to prepay the loan or mortgage prior to the maturity date.

Price level adjusted mortgage. Sometimes abbreviated PLAM, this is a mortgage in which the interest rate as well as the principal amount is adjusted periodically.

Principal balance. In pertaining to mortgages, the remaining balance of the mortgage less any interest or fees.
Private mortgage insurance. Mortgage default insurance issued in the name of the lender by an approved private mortgage insurance company.
Processing. See *Loan processing*.
Pro forma statement. The projected income and expenses of an income-producing property, usually for a period of one year.
PUD. An abbreviation for planned unit development, a large area that has a comprehensive land development plan and usually contains roads, homes, and common areas. The most common PUDs are large townhouse developments.
Purchase money mortgage. A mortgage that is executed by the purchaser of the property as part of the sales price, naming the seller as mortgagor.

Q

Quitclaim deed. A written instrument that conveys whatever rights the grantor may presently have in the subject piece of property.

R

Rate. Another term for interest rate.
Real estate. Real property and all improvements.
Realtor®. A licensee, either a broker or salesperson, who is a member of a local real estate board that is affiliated with the National Association of Realtors®.
Recordation. The act of filing a legal document in the office of the county clerk.
Redemption. The acquiring of property taken by court or sold at auction by the original owner.
Redemption period. The period of time the owner may repurchase property by paying all judgments and fees against the property.
Refinance. The paying off of one indebtedness on a piece of property, using the proceeds from another mortgage or loan on the same property as security.
Release of lien. Upon payment of a debt in full, the written instrument that is filed to release the property from the lien.
Renegotiable rate mortgage. Sometimes referred to as a rollover mortgage, this is a series of short-term loans issued for a term of three to five years each, secured by a long-term mortgage.
RESPA. The Real Estate Settlement Procedures Act, a federal law that sets standards for the settlement or closing of the real estate transaction.
Restrictions. Legal limitations contained in the deed regarding the use of the real property.

S

Secondary financing. A second mortgage on a piece of real property.
Secondary mortgage market. An unorganized market in which mortgages are bought and sold.
Second mortgage. See *Junior mortgage*.
Seller-servicer. The name given by FNMA to an approved lender.
Separate property. Property of a married person that was acquired prior to marriage or by gift or as a result of a bequest.
Settlement costs. See *Closing costs*.
Shared appreciation mortgage. A mortgage on residential real estate in which the lender agrees to share in the property's appreciation and in return offers the borrower a below-market interest rate.
Sheriff's deed. A deed to property given by a sheriff when property is purchased at a court-ordered sale for back taxes.
Situs. Location.
Spot loan. A single loan on a single house. Sometimes the term is used to refer to mortgages solicited from a real estate firm.
Subordination. The act of making one debt inferior to another when both debts are on the same property.
Sweat equity. A term used by FHA for value added to property by the efforts of the homebuyer. It refers to the sweat and toil of the homebuyer.
Syndication. A group of people organized for the specific purpose of purchasing "in total or an interest in" real estate.

T

Take-out loan. A commitment of permanent financing upon completion of the structure. It is called a take-out because it takes the interim lender out of the structure.
Term. The period or length of a mortgage or lease.
Title. Written evidence to one's right to, or ownership in, a specific piece of property.

Title defects. See *Exception*.
Trust deed. See *Deed of trust*.
Trustee. The third party to a deed of trust to whom the title to the property is transferred in trust.

U

Underwriting. The evaluation or analysis of the risk involved with a loan and matching the risk to the proper return.
Unsecured loan. A loan made by an individual, firm, or corporation that is not secured by property, personal or real.
Usury. Charging an interest rate more than is allowed by law.

V

VA. Veterans Administration, a federal agency created by the Servicemen's Readjustment Act of 1944. The purpose of the VA is to administer the veterans benefit programs.
Variable rate mortgage. A mortgage with the characteristic of an interest rate that may vary at a specific time, as little as one month, based on a specific index.
VA loan. See *GI-guaranteed loan*.
Vendee. Purchaser.
Vendor. Seller.
Veterans entitlement. In mortgage lending, the amount of VA loan guarantee that is available to a veteran.

W

Warehousing. In reference to mortgage bankers, the borrowing of funds for a short term in order to fund a mortgage or loan prior to the lender or investor actually purchasing the mortgage or loan.
Warranty deed. See *Deed*.
Wrap or wraparound mortgage. A mortgage used to finance real property which will include an existing first lien mortgage.

Y

Yield. As it applies to mortgage financing, the return or annual income generated by a mortgage. Usually expressed as a percentage.

INDEX